THE HISTORY OF
THE BRITISH COAL INDUSTRY

VOLUME 4

1913–1946: THE POLITICAL ECONOMY OF DECLINE

THE HISTORY OF
THE BRITISH COAL
INDUSTRY

VOLUME 4

1913–1946: The Political Economy of Decline

BY

BARRY SUPPLE

CLARENDON PRESS · OXFORD
1987

Oxford University Press, Walton Street, Oxford OX2 6DP
Oxford New York Toronto
Delhi Bombay Calcutta Madras Karachi
Petaling Jaya Singapore Hong Kong Tokyo
Nairobi Dar es Salaam Cape Town
Melbourne Auckland
and associated companies in
Beirut Berlin Ibadan Nicosia

Oxford is a trade mark of Oxford University Press

Published in the United States
by Oxford University Press, New York

British Library Cataloguing in Publication Data
The history of the British coal industry.
Vol. 4: 1913-1946: the political
economy of decline.
1. Coal Mines and mining–Great Britain
–History
I. Supple, Barry
338.2´724´0941   HD9551.5
ISBN 0-19-828294-X

Library of Congress Cataloging in Publication Data
(Revised for vol. 4)
The History of the British coal industry.
Includes bibliographies and indexes.
Contents: –v. 2. 1700-1830, the Industrial
Revolution / by Michael W. Flinn with the assistance
of David S. Stoker–v. 3. 1830-1913, Victorian
pre-eminence / by Roy Church, with the assistance of
Alan Hall and John Kanesfky–v. 4. 1913-1946, the
political economy of decline / by Barry Supple.
1. Coal trade–Great Britain–History. 2. Coal
mines and mining–Great Britain–History. I. Flinn,
Michael W. (Michael Walter), 1917-
HD9551.5.H57   1984   338.2´724´0941   83-4194
ISBN 0-19-828294-X

Set by Joshua Associates Ltd
Printed in Great Britain
by Biddles Ltd.,
Guildford and King's Lynn

Preface

It is perhaps only when the author of a monograph such as this comes to one of the last tasks of all—writing a Preface—that a full appreciation of the immodest enormity of the original ambition is brought forcibly home. The coalmining industry is quite unusually distinctive, of the greatest significance in British economic and social history, and extraordinarily complex and diverse. A sole author and a single lifetime would be inadequate to encompass even its twentieth-century history.

It would at least be reassuring to think that the time which has elapsed since I was asked to contribute this volume to the series so generously sponsored by the National Coal Board (now British Coal) has been an accurate measure of the effort I have been able to devote to it. Alas, the passing of so many years is an index more of other preoccupations and my own scholarly and organizational deficiencies, than of intensity of effort alone. Yet even if these years had been devoted exclusively to the history of the coal industry between its apotheosis in 1913 and its half-humiliating nationalization in 1946, that could hardly have done justice to its manifold characteristics and developments—or to the lives and efforts of the millions of people who were concerned with it over those decades.

Many different sorts of books might be written about the industry in the twentieth century. I chose to concentrate on its political economy, the clash of contemporary argument, and the evolution of institutions. This was not because I concluded that a close economic analysis of its performance and technology, or a comparative study of the sociology of its various communities, or an appreciation of its work processes and industrial relations were unimportant. (I have tried to take account of such considerations where relevant.) Rather, it seemed to me that the theme which best united the history of the industry for its last thirty or so years under private enterprise, and which indeed still characterizes it, was the extent to which it became a *political* issue. Obviously, there is a good deal of oversimplification involved in such a view, just as there is in the treatment of coalmining as a single industry rather than an alliance (sometimes a very loose and disjointed alliance) of different industries. And I am guilty in both respects. I certainly regret that the choice of one

perspective and the exigencies of time and space have prevented me from pursuing deeper analyses and more varied evidence. But the picture I offer of the industry is one which is consistent with the terms and approaches familiar to those who worked in it, and to those who struggled to accommodate it to the body politic over a long generation. It is also one which relates its evolution to the larger story of Britain's modern industrial history.

If the completion of such a study reminds one of the gap between ambition and achievement, it also brings home the limited extent to which a historian working on such a topic can be self-sufficient. Given the nature of the coalmining industry, I have been peculiarly dependent on the help and goodwill of others—and quite exceptionally fortunate in the friends and colleagues who have supported my efforts, and in the aid and advice which have been available from so many directions. Not all those who have been associated with this study will agree with my interpretations. But in arriving at them I have been constantly aware of how much I owe to the unstinting support and help of so many people of such diverse views on such a controversial topic.

I must acknowledge, first, the very great help of British Coal and its members. This was not simply a matter of the corporation having given an indispensable lead at the very outset, crucial as that was. It was also embodied in consistently tolerant encouragement and generous underwriting. Of course, economic and business historians are now growing accustomed to enlightened attitudes towards their activities on the part of those responsible for the management of complex enterprises. Even so, the full cooperation and wholehearted support (not to speak of the exemplary patience) of British Coal throughout this project has been a vital element in it. Joined as these attitudes were to a most generous willingness to fund heavy research costs over a period of years, they reflect a quite exceptional altruism and objectivity. No historian could have asked for a more generous (or less intrusive) sponsor. At the same time, no historian could have asked for a more congenial, understanding, and objective group of people to work with. I am particularly grateful to the Secretary, David Brandrick, for his calm and unstinting advice and guidance, and to the members of the Central Secretariat whose administrative assistance was so essential to the project and to me personally: Anne Parsonage, Martin Povey, and John Kanefsky. It is also fitting that I should emphasize how much the entire series owes to Lord Ezra, whose initiative, when Chairman of the NCB, was largely responsible for the five-volume History; and to my good friend and colleague, Peter Mathias, whose role as general editor and adviser was both indispensable and fulfilled with invariable charm and perception.

In terms of detailed research and writing, my greatest debt is to those who helped directly and continuously with the gathering of material and the sorting and presentation of information. My research assistants, Stephanie Tailby and Nick Tiratsoo, each worked for about two years on the project. Many of their tasks were tedious; all were carried out with splendid enthusiasm, enterprise, and efficiency. Only they, who gathered so much material, can fully appreciate my regret at being able to include only such a small proportion of such a huge labour. Yet this book embodies more than the fruits of their archival research. It also reflects the invaluable stimulus of their scholarly efforts and learned companionship. I remain profoundly grateful to them as colleagues as well as assistants. Sonia Supple was less continuously involved in the research, but her efforts and encouragement (not merely in libraries and archives, but at all stages of the work) were more prolonged and equally indispensable to its completion. Her sensitivity to contemporary sources was matched only by the tolerance which, as an exploited non-professional, she displayed towards the foibles of an author and the demands of such an extensive project.

I am also very much in the debt of those many scholars who were unstinting in their willingness to share with me the results of their own research, and who therefore not merely facilitated but made possible much of what follows. I wish to thank in particular Bill Ashworth, Roy Church, Michael Distenfass, Ben Fine, David Greasley, John Goldthorpe, Edwin Greene, Kenneth Morgan, Quentin Outram, Martha Prevezer, David Rossiter, Gustav Schmidt, Jay Winter, Clemens Wurm, and Ina-Maria Zweiniger.

In spite of my earlier expectations, this was not a study where oral history could play a large role. There were, however, a few people who had been concerned with the coal industry during the period, whom it was both possible and very productive to interview. In this respect I am most grateful to Sir Andrew Bryan, Harry Collins, the late Lord Fulton, and the late Lord Shinwell. I am also most grateful to those managers and officials who guided my faltering steps around their collieries, thus giving me a very brief, but indispensable, experience of the unique world of deep mining.

As this last expression of gratitude implies, the nature of the coal industry naturally meant that the process of research was also a process of geographic discovery. Not all of it was at the coalface. And among the pleasures of working on an industry as close-knit and human as coalmining was to meet and receive help from those who guard its archives as well as those who still work within it. In a similar vein, I was able to make use of material directly or indirectly relating to the industry, but now retained in public or private archives. I therefore thank the librarians and archivists in the Bodleian Library, the Brotherton Library of Leeds University, the Cambridge University Library, Glasgow University Archives, Leeds City Archives Department, the London School of Economics and Political Science, Newcastle University Library, Nuffield College Library, Sheffield Central Library, University of Sussex, British Coal, the Department of Energy, the House of Lords Record Office, the Public Record Office, the Scottish Record Office, the National Library of Wales, the Derbyshire Record Office, the Durham County Record Office, the Lancashire County Record Office, the Leicestershire Record Office, the Northumberland County Record Office, the Nottinghamshire Record Office, the Bank of England, the British Steel Corporation (East Midlands Regional Records Centre), the Trades Union Congress, the Labour Party, and the National Union of Miners. In addition, Viscount Bridgeman and George Lane-Fox were exceptionally kind and helpful in granting me liberal access to private diaries in their possession, and I thank them most warmly.

The Steel–Maitland Papers in the Scottish Record Office were used with the kind permission of Mrs R. M. Stafford of Sauchieburn, Stirling. I am most grateful for this, and for permission to make use of closed files in the Public Records Office and Department of Energy, the Runciman Papers (University of Newcastle), and the records of the Securities Management Trust (Bank of England Archives).

Finally, since not even the wonders of modern word processing and the personal computer can yet make academic authors technically independent, I am glad to acknowledge the patience, skill, and goodwill with which Sylvia Sylvester, Pat Stone, and Caroline Howard produced so many typescripts so efficiently, and with which Maggie Oakley, Jinny Crum-Jones, and Eva Wong, all of the Cambridge University Computer Laboratory, helped me with such patience through the obscure underworld of computing and text-editing.

I dedicate this book to my wife, whose constant support and encouragement have made it possible, and to the memory of my

father, whose hard life and admirable loyalties find so many poignant
echoes in this story.

BARRY SUPPLE

St Catharine's College, Cambridge
December 1986

Contents

Illustrations

Tables

Figures

References to Sources

Manuscript sources. The collections used are listed in the Bibliography. Footnote references to the papers or diary of an individual generally refer to the individual by name (e.g. 'Runciman Papers', 'Lane-Fox Diary'), fuller details being provided in the list of abbreviations. There are, however, two principal exceptions to this rule: the Lloyd George Papers (in the House of Lords Record Office) and the Steel–Maitland Papers (in the Scottish Record Office), which are referred to by their call numbers (beginning 'F' and 'GD' respectively). Other (non-personal) collections are referred to by abbreviations which are more fully described in the following list. This applies to material in the Public Record Office, for which references are to an abbreviation of their class (e.g. 'POWE' to 'CAB'). In the case of the records of the various district coalowners' associations, these are indicated by the appropriate abbreviation, as listed below (e.g. 'MSWCOA' identifies the records of the Monmouthshire and South Wales Coal Owners' Association in the National Library of Wales). However, unless there is a possibility of confusion with more than one category of the relevant collection, such references to coalowners' records omit catalogue numbers and rely on the date of the entry alone. This is because the material in such cases is derived from the chronological records of the relevant central body.

Books, published reports, articles, and theses. Published and typescript materials used are comprehensively listed in the Bibliography. Footnote references normally refer solely to the author's name and date of publication. However, in the case of a small number of frequently cited publications (for example, the *Colliery Guardian* ('*CG*') or the *Colliery Year Book and Coal Trades Directory* ('*CYB*') or the *Annual Reports of the Mining Association of Great Britain*, ('*MAGB*', followed by year)) an abbreviation is used—and explained in the list of abbreviations. In the case of frequently published journals (e.g., *The Economist* or the *Colliery Guardian*) volume numbers are omitted, reference being made to the date of publication alone, followed by the appropriate page numbers.

Parliamentary papers and official publications. Titles are normally given in full, except for frequently cited publications, which are referred to by an abbreviation (more fully explained in the list of abbreviations). Examples are the *Reports* and *Evidence* of such Royal Commissions as the Sankey and Samuel Inquiries or that on safety in mines, the *Annual Reports of the Secretary for Mines* ('*ARSM*', followed by the year), or the *Report of the Technical Advisory Committee on Coal Mining* ('*Reid Report*'). As with unofficial journals, volume numbers are omitted in references to the *House of Commons Debates*, which are referred to simply by the use of an abbreviation ('*Hansard*'—there are no references to the House of Lords Debates), followed by the date and column number. Normally, the annual volume of the *Parliamentary Papers* as well as the appropriate Command number is given. In the case of the various commissions of inquiry which figured so prominently in the history of coalmining, arabic numerals without prefix stand for the relevant page numbers; but where specific questions in the volumes of evidence are being cited, the numerals are preceded with 'Q' or 'QQ' to indicate the number(s) of the question(s), rather than the page(s).

Weights and Currencies

For simplicity of presentation, and to prevent confusion between text and quotations from contemporary sources, the weight of coal and amounts of money have been left in their original form—i.e. imperial tons (one ton = 1.016 metric tonnes) and pre-decimal pounds, shillings, and pence (2.4*d.* = 1p and 1*s.* = 5p). The only exception to this occurs in Table 10.2, where simplicity of presentation on a comparative basis argued in favour of translation into decimal units of shillings.

Abbreviations in Text and Notes

ARSM	Mines Department, *Annual Report of the Secretary for Mines*
Asquith Papers	in Bodleian Library, Oxford
Baldwin Papers	in Cambridge University Library
BT	Records of the Board of Trade, Public Record Office
Buckmaster Proceedings	*Minutes of Proceedings of a Court of Inquiry* re *the Wages Position in the Coalmining Industry* (Ministry of Labour, 1924)
Buckmaster Report	*Industrial Courts Act. Report by a Court of Inquiry Concerning the Wages Position in the Coal Mining Industry* (Cmd. 2129. 1924; *Parliamentary Papers 1924* XI)
CAB	Records of the Cabinet, Public Record Office
CG	*Colliery Guardian and Journal of the Coal and Iron Trades*
CMOC	Coal Mining Organisation Committee
CMOC	*Report of the Departmental Committee Appointed to Inquire into the Conditions Prevailing in the Coal Mining Industry Due to the War: First Report* (Cmd. 7939. 1915; *Parliamentary Papers 1914-16* XXVII); *Evidence and Index* (Cmd. 8009. 1915; *Parliamentary Papers 1914-16* XXVIII); *Second General Report* (Cmd. 8147. 1915; *Parliamentary Papers 1914-16* XXVIII); *Third General Report* (Cmd. 8345. 1916; *Parliamentary Papers 1916* VI)
CMRC	Coal Mines Reorganisation Commission
COAL	Records of the National Coal Board, Public Record Office
CYB	*Colliery Year Book and Coal Trades Directory*
Dalton Diary	*The Second World War Diary of Hugh Dalton, 1940-1945*, edited by Ben Pimlott (1986)
Dalton Papers	Papers of Hugh Dalton in London School of Economics
DCOA	Records of the Durham Coal Owners' Association, Durham County Record Office
DCRPC	*Report of the Departmental Committee Appointed by the Board of Trade to Inquire into the Causes of the Present Rise in the Retail Price of Coal for Domestic Use. Report*

	(Cmd. 7866. 1915; *Parliamentary Papers 1914-16 XXIX*); *Minutes of Evidence and Appendices* (Cmd. 7923. 1915; *Parliamentary Papers 1914-16* XXIX)
DSIR	Records of the Department of Scientific and Industrial Research, Public Record Office
FO	Records of Foreign Office, General Correspondence, Public Record Office
FS	Records of the Registrar of Friendly Societies, Public Record Office
Gainford Papers	in Nuffield College, Oxford
Hansard	Hansard, *Parliamentary Debates, House of Commons*, Fifth Series
HLG	Records of Ministry of Housing and Local Government, Public Record Office
HLRO	House of Lords Record Office
ICTR	*Iron and Coal Trades Review*
JMK	*The Collected Writings of John Maynard Keynes* (1971–), edited by Donald Moggridge
Joint Sub-Committee, 1925	Mining Association of Great Britain. Miners' Federation of Great Britain, *Minutes of Proceedings of a Joint Sub-Committee appointed to investigate the Economic Position of the Coal Industry* (3 volumes, 18 March to 23 June 1925; British Coal Library, Hobart House)
Jones, *Whitehall Diary*	Thomas Jones, *Whitehall Diary*, edited by Keith Middlemas (1971)
LAB	Records of Ministry of Labour, Public Record Office
Lane-Fox Diary	Diary of G. R. Lane-Fox, MP, in Bramham Park, Wetherby, west Yorkshire
LCMA	Records of the Lanarkshire Coal Masters' Association, Glasgow University Archives
LCOA	Records of the Leicestershire Coal Owners' Association, Leicestershire Office
List of Mines	Mines Department, *List of Mines in Great Britain and the Isle of Man*
Macmillan	*Industrial Courts Act, 1919. Report by a Court of Inquiry concerning the Coal Mining Dispute, 1925* (Cmd. 2478. 1925; *Parliamentary Papers, 1924-5* XIII
MAGB	*Annual Report of the Mining Association of Great Britain*
MFGB	*Annual Reports of the Miners' (subsequently Mineworkers') Federation of Great Britain*
MH	Records of the Ministry of Health, Public Records Office
Milner Papers	in Bodleian Library, Oxford

Mitchell, *Abstract*   B. R. Mitchell, *Abstract of British Historical Statistics* (Cambridge, 1962)

MSWCOA   Records of the Monmouthshire & South Wales Coal Owners' Association, National Library of Wales

MUN   Records of the Ministry of Munitions, Public Record Office

NRO   Northumberland Record Office

POWE   Records of the Ministry of Fuel and Power, Public Record Office

PP   *Parliamentary Papers*

PREM   Prime Ministers' records, Public Record Office

RCSM Evidence   *Minutes of Evidence of the Royal Commission on Safety in Coal Mines* (Mines Department, 1936–8)

RCSM Report   *Report of the Royal Commission on Safety in Coal Mines* (Cmd. 5890. 1938; *Parliamentary Papers 1938-39* XIII)

RDR   Records in Labour Party Archives

Reid Report   *Report of the Technical Advisory Committee on Coal Mining, March 14, 1945* (Cmd. 6610. 1945; *Parliamentary Papers 1944-45* IV)

Runciman Papers   in University of Newcastle upon Tyne Library

Samuel Appendices   Mines Department, *Report of the Royal Commission on the Coal Industry (1925)*, Vol. III, *Appendices and Index* (1926)

Samuel Evidence   Mines Department, *Report of the Royal Commission on the Coal Industry (1925)*, Vol. II, *Minutes of Evidence* (1926)

Samuel Report   *Report of the Royal Commission on the Coal Industry (1925)*, Vol. I, *Report, Annexes* (Cmd. 2600. 1926; *Parliamentary Papers 1926* XIV)

Sankey Evidence, I   Minutes of Evidence from *Coal Industry Commission. 1919 Reports and Evidence on the First Stage of the Inquiry* (Cmd. 359. 1919; *Parliamentary Papers 1919* XI)

Sankey Evidence, II   Minutes of Evidence from *Coal Industry Commission. Volume II. Reports and Minutes of Evidence on the Second Stage of the Inquiry* (Cmd. 360. 1919; *Parliamentary Papers 1919* XII)

Sankey Report, I   *Coal Industry Commission Act. 1919 Interim Reports* (Cmd. 84–6. 1919; *Parliamentary Papers 1919* XI), also in *Coal Industry Commission. 1919 Reports and Evidence on the First Stage of the Inquiry* (Cmd. 359. 1919; *Parliamentary Papers 1919* XI)

Sankey Report, II   Reports from *Coal Industry Commission. Volume II.*

	Reports and Minutes of Evidence on the Second Stage of the Inquiry (Cmd. 360. 1919; *Parliamentary Papers 1919* XII). Also in Cmd. 210. 1919; *Parliamentary Papers 1919* XI
SCOA	Records of the Scottish Coal Owners' Association, University of Glasgow Archives
SDCOA	Records of the South Derbyshire Coal Owners' Association, Derbyshire Record Office
SMT	Records of the Securities Management Trust, Archives of the Bank of England
SRO	Scottish Record Office, Edinburgh
SYCOA	Records of South Yorkshire Coal Owners' Association, Sheffield City Library
TIME	*Transactions of the Institution of Mining Engineers*
WSC	Martin Gilbert, *Winston S. Churchill*, Vol. V, Companion Part I (1979)
WYCOA	Records of the West Yorkshire Coal Owners' Association, Brotherton Library, University of Leeds

PART A

INTRODUCTION

CHAPTER 1

From Pre-eminence to Adversity
The Coal Industry, 1913–1946

> Everything being now relative, there is no longer absolute depend-
> ence to be placed on God, Free Trade, Marriage, Consols, Coal or
> Caste.
>
> John Galsworthy, *A Modern Comedy* (1929).

The principal themes of this book derive from the economic, social, and
political *travails* of an industry in decline. That decline dominated the
working and social lives of those involved in coalmining. It also posed
severe problems of understanding and political action for the rest of
society. And it reflected, albeit in an extreme form, the problems of
Britain's nineteenth-century staple industries as they were obliged to
come to terms with the economic world of the twentieth century. As far
as coal was concerned, this meant adapting to the growth of competition and a deceleration of demand. It is, of course, true that although
stagnation and dislocation coloured its public image, they were not the
only motifs of the coalmining after 1913: new fields were developed,
technical improvements took place, living standards and profits did not
fall either continuously or decisively. There were important changes in
the *pattern*, as well as the overall performance, of the industry. Nevertheless, once the effects (themselves disruptive) of the First World War
had subsided, the industry was above all confronted with an inescapable
problem of excess capacity.

In essence, the coal industry created by the long Victorian and
Edwardian boom was simply too large for its markets after the First
World War. Nothing could have reversed the decline in output and
(even more) employment, although greater resilience in organization,
attitudes, and techniques would no doubt have reduced its pace and
absorbed some of its stresses. The fact remains that the character of the
industry and its actual history in the decades after 1913 focused attention and events very sharply on the quasi-political as well as economic
issues which are normally associated with chronically excess capacity:

1. Map of the British coalfields in the early 1940s

structural strains, industrial-relations strife, disputes over wages and profits, threats to social stability, and controversial pressures to secure institutional reform, state intervention, or cooperative industrial control. Consequently, it is these themes which receive most attention in the following pages. Detailed economic and technical analysis would no doubt be relevant to an explanation of the depth and pattern of the industry's economic crisis; but its *existence* and most of its intensity present few analytical problems, while their implications and even more their historical *consequences*, are questions more for political economy than economics.

Central to this study, therefore, is the view that the extreme stagnation of demand for British coal was not primarily caused (even though it was obviously exacerbated) by the industry's own failings. By the same token, the issues which have figured so prominently in the academic discussion of the economic history of coalmining—the caution or enterprise of its businessmen and managers, the neglect or absence of economies of scale, the economic effects of its highly fragmented structure, the shortage of investment funds, the pace of mechanization, the commercially inhibiting influence of uncooperative workers or bad industrial relations—seem pertinent less to an explanation of secular trends in output and employment (although those trends would obviously have been different had the industry's response to adversity been different) than to the remuneration of the factors of production and the pain or ease with which the industry adjusted to a new situation. Given the fall in demand, the evolution of coalmining for much of the twentieth century has been organized around institutions and relationships, politics and social pressures. To a very large extent it has been a history of accommodation or resistance, of the threat of crisis and search for bulwarks against collapse.

The pursuit of this history is made the more demanding because coalmining was simultaneously the most visible and the least familiar of all Britain's principal industries. Its visibility, of course, derived from its sheer size (in 1913 coal miners accounted for about 10 per cent of the country's male labour force) and its impact on the political as well as economic life of the country. Yet the strangeness and variety of its work and social routines meant that its experiences were not always fully grasped, because they were neither shared by outsiders nor uniform in their incidence and implications. Indeed, even those involved in the industry tended to be familiar with only limited aspects of what was in effect a *variety* of industries, each with its own structures, products, markets, working methods, and language. The nature of such an activity, and the emotions it harboured, were not readily appreciated by other contemporaries and remain relatively inaccessible to the historian. Writing about it is therefore more an exercise in imperfect discovery and partial comprehension than the application of familiar descriptive categories to easily grasped events and relationships.

i. The contours of achievement and decline

The position of the British coalmining industry on the eve of the First World War represented a peak of economic achievement. In spite of anxieties about industrial relations, commercial competitiveness, and labour productivity, coal occupied a supreme position in the British economy. In the course of the late nineteenth century it had come into its own as an overwhelmingly predominant source of heat, light, and power in the expanding world economy as well as in Britain—which was in many respects the centre of that economy. Coal, or its direct derivatives, fuelled the locomotives and steamships which had come to dominate transport; smelted the ores which supplied the metals which were ubiquitously used in manufacturing; raised the steam power for the machinery and pumps of modern industry; generated the gas and electricity which, in developed lands, increasingly provided essential heat, light, and power; and were (in the relative absence of petroleum) still the basis of much of the chemical industry. In 1913 in the world as a whole coal and lignite accounted for some 75 per cent of all energy; in Britain the figure (for coal, coke, and manufactured fuels) was not less than 94.5 per cent, while gas and electricity (both produced with coal) accounted for almost a further 5 per cent.[1]

Given Britain's superabundant coal resources, their proximity to inexpensive transport, and the country's early experience of industrialization, coalmining had grown into a huge industry and the overseas sale of coal to other developing economies was a vital aspect of it. Thus, in 1913 the industry employed over 1.1 million men and boys, and produced 287 million tons of fuel—a level of output which was never again to be achieved. Admittedly, coal production in the United States had overtaken Britain's in 1900 (by 1913 the United States produced almost 80 per cent more coal than Britain), and German output was increasing very rapidly in the prewar years. Nevertheless, the British

[1] International Labour Office 1938, I, 32, 36. It was estimated that firewood accounted for 17.6% of the world's energy.

coal industry was still a dominant international force: its annual production was equivalent to some 23 per cent of the world's total supply; and it shipped abroad as direct exports and as foreign 'bunkers' (fuel for shipping engaged in overseas trade) about 97 million tons of coal, coke, and manufactured fuel. This represented one-third of its entire output. Indeed, Britain's overseas shipments, which were virtually 10 per cent of the rest of the world's needs, accounted for no less than 55 per cent of all the coal traded internationally.

In 1913, then, Britain's still impressive production of goods and services, its relative prosperity, and its economic place in the world were indisputably based on its coal supplies. Admittedly, the security of that basis had from time to time been questioned by those who feared the exhaustion of low-cost reserves, or doubted the wisdom of relying on the export of a vital and unprocessed raw material to potential industrial rivals. Perhaps more pertinently there was anxiety about the apparent slowness of technical or structural change in coalmining, its labour-intensity, and the apparently turgid progress of labour productivity (output per man-year fell by more than 10 per cent in 1900–13, while Germany's rose slightly and America's increased quite dramatically).[1] Yet from·the standpoint of the Edwardian economy there was little obvious indication that these anxieties were sufficiently well grounded to warrant any drastic action. The Royal Commission on Coal Resources (1901–5) had confirmed the existence of abundant long-run reserves, sufficient for centuries of industrial activity;[2] the real price of coal (i.e. the price relative to other goods) was high, and returns to factors of production good; and even though output per manshift had declined (in part owing to the reduction of underground working hours through the Eight Hours Act of 1908), the absolute level of Britain's labour productivity, and its labour and total costs, still compared well with continental countries', while recent estimates of hourly productivity suggest stability rather than retrogression.[3]

Altogether, then, the British coalmining industry had proved itself fairly sensitive to changing markets as the pre-1914 commercial world

[1] Church 1986, 774.

[2] The Commission estimated that there were some 101,000 million tons of unworked coal lying in seams of one foot or more in thickness and less than 4,000 feet deep. About 80% of this coal was in seams of 2 feet or more. However, it pointed out that 'whether a particular seam is workable or not depends not so much on its thickness as upon its quality, the nature of the roof and floor, its geographical position, the cost of working and the selling price'. *Final Report of the Royal Commission on Coal Resources* (*PP* 1905 XVI), 2–4.

[3] Church 1986, 768.

Table 1.1. *Employment, output, prices, and overseas shipments in British coalmining, 1913-1946*

Year	Employment[a] 000	Output m. tons	Average selling value per ton at pit[b] s. d.	Total selling value at the pit[c] £ m.	Exports[d] m. tons	Foreign bunkers m. tons
1903–12 (av.)	957.8	254.1	8 5	102.6	59.7	18.5
1913	1,127.9	287.4	10 2	145.5	76.7	21.0
1914 (31 July)	1,133.0					
(31 Dec.)	981.3	265.7	10 0	132.6	61.8	18.5
1915	953.6	253.2	12 6	157.8	45.7	13.6
1916	998.1	256.4	15 7	200.0	41.2	13.0
1917	1,021.3	248.5	16 9	207.8	37.8	10.2
1918	1,008.9	227.7	20 11	238.2	34.2	8.8
1919	1,191.3	229.8	27 4	314.1	38.2	12.0
1920	1,248.2	229.5	34 7	396.9	28.8	13.9
1921	1,144.3	163.3	26 2	213.7	26.3	11.0
1922	1,162.8	249.6	17 8	220.0	67.9	18.3
1923	1,220.4	276.0	18 10	259.7	84.6	18.2
1924	1,230.2	267.1	18 10	251.7	65.6	17.7
1925	1,117.8	243.2	16 4	199.0	54.1	16.4
1926 (Mar.)	1,128.2	126.3	19 7	123.4	21.8	7.7
(Dec.)	955.1					
1927	1,005.0	251.2	14 7	183.5	54.3	16.8
1928	921.3	237.5	12 10	152.5	53.6	16.7

1929	939.4	257.9	13	5	173.2	64.4	16.4
1930	914.3	243.9	13	7	165.7	58.3	15.6
1931	851.6	219.5	13	6	147.7	45.9	14.6
1932	803.6	208.7	13	3	138.4	41.9	14.2
1933	773.6	207.1	13	0	134.6	42.1	13.5
1934	772.8	220.7	12	11	142.1	42.4	13.5
1935	754.3	222.2	13	0	144.5	41.9	12.5
1936	751.7	228.4	14	0	160.1	37.3	12.0
1937	776.1	240.4	15	2	182.7	43.5	11.7
1938	781.7	227.0	17	4	188.8	38.2	10.5
1939	766.3	231.3	17	11	197.5	36.9	9.6
1940	749.2	224.3	20	5	218.9	19.6	7.0
1941	697.6	206.3	24	1	236.2	5.1	4.3
1942	709.3	204.9e	26	4	253.8	4.3	3.5
1943	707.8	198.9e	28	11	264.7	4.8	3.2
1944	710.2	192.7e	33	3	306.4	5.7	2.4
1945	708.9	182.8e	38	2	326.3	5.5	3.1
1946	696.7	190.0e	39	5	n/a^f	4.5	4.7

a 'Numbers employed' (1903–38) or 'numbers on books' (1938–47). As from the beginning of 1922 (1) the figures relating to the number of wage-earners employed and output of coal refer to Great Britain, while those for the previous years include Ireland, (2) the figures relating to the number of wage-earners on colliery books no longer include clerks and salaried persons, who in 1922 numbered on the average about 24,000 and in 1946 about 21,000, inclusive in each case of clerks and salaried persons employed at headquarter offices.

b Average proceeds, from 1938.

c Excluding opencast coal.

d Coal, coke, and manufactured fuel (1903–38) or coal alone (1939–46). From 1 Apr. 1923, coal sent to Eire is included as an export and not as home consumption.

e Including coal from opencast operations amounting to 1.3 m. tons in 1942, 4.4 m. tons in 1943, 8.6 m. tons in 1944, 8.1 m. tons in 1945, 8.8 m. tons in 1946, and 10.2 m. tons in 1947.

f = not available.

Sources: ARSM 1938; ARSM 1924; ARSM 1926; CYB 1948; Ministry of Fuel and Power. Statistical Digest for the Years 1946 & 1947 (Cmd. 7548. 1948), 3.

understood those changes, well adapted to its geological circumstances and resource endowments, and commercially buoyant.[1] Profits were reasonable, employment had risen enormously, and wages were relatively high. Prosperity—at least in the context of the early twentieth century—appeared stable. 'The horns of plenty', wrote the principal trade journal, the *Colliery Guardian*, in its review of 1913, 'have distributed their blessings more widely and with less intermittence than is sometimes the case in a year of prosperous trading'.[2]

In spite of all this, however, in the generation after 1913 the coal industry experienced a disastrous retreat from this position of international dominance, as output, exports, and employment all fell. The world of 1913 melted away. The decline is summarized in Table 1.1 and represented in Fig. 1.1—which also shows the punishing volatility of prices and values during and immediately after the First World War. Measured in terms of isolated years, the fall in the production of deep-mined coal between 1913 and 1946 was quite dramatic: from 287.4 million to 181.2 million tons—a reduction of more than one-third. During the Second World War, there was some compensation in terms of the emergence of opencast mining, which produced almost 9 million tons in 1946. In addition, since the data on deep-mined output are based on single years (including the record achievement of 1913), they slightly exaggerate the long-run trend in production. Taking averages of adjacent years, the decline was from 269.5 million tons in 1909–1913 to 194 million tons (188 million tons deep-mined) in 1942–46. Yet this fall of about 27 per cent (30 per cent in deep-mined output) was hardly a reassuring record, and since labour productivity was also growing, employment in coalmining fell even faster—from over 1.1 million in 1913 to 697,000 in 1946. Coalmining, which on the eve of the First World War had appeared so strong and substantial, came out of the Second World War a vulnerable, smaller, and enfeebled industry.

Within this trend in output, of course, there were shorter-run fluctuations—a fall during the First World War to just over 229 million tons; a brief postwar recovery to 267 million tons in 1924; further decline in the late 1920s and early 1930s (output in 1932 was some 209 million tons); a mild recovery during the late 1930s; and further decline (albeit for different reasons) in the war years of the 1940s.[3]

---

[1] Church 1986, 778–9.

[2] *CG* 2 Jan. 1914, 31.

[3] In addition, this history ends on the eve of another phase of postwar growth in production: by 1952–5 annual output averaged over 210 million tons.

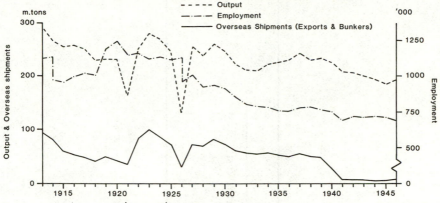

Fig. 1.1. Output, employment, and overseas shipments in British coalmining, 1913–1946

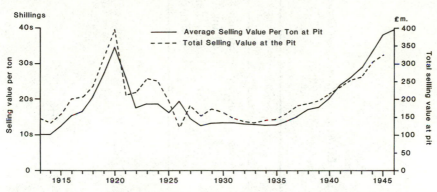

Fig. 1.2. Total value of output and average selling value per ton of British coal, 1913–1946

At the root of this stagnation lay the growth of much keener competition in overseas markets, drastic changes in the pattern of demand for coal, and a sharp reduction in the growth of aggregate consumption. These developments will be considered in more detail in later chapters.[1] Here, it is only necessary to indicate their salient manifestations.

The extraordinary pre-eminence of British coal exports in 1913 has already been noted, and overseas sales (but not the shipment of foreign bunkers) in that year are summarized in Table 1.2. Over half of all exports went to the Baltic (including Russia) and north and west Europe—markets which maintained much of the industry in eastern

[1] Below, ch. 5 and 7.

Table 1.2. *Export of coal from Great Britain, 1913*
(m. tons)

To:	From: East Scotland	North-East	Humber	British Channel (including S. Wales)	North-West	West Scotland	Total	%
Baltic Sea (including Russia and Scandinavia)	4.08	5.92	4.31	0.93	0.13	0.41	15.89	21.7
North Sea (including Germany, Low Countries, Belgium, France)	3.34	10.05	3.45	8.20	0.07	0.53	25.95	35.3
Western Mediterranean (including Spain, Italy, N. Africa)	0.36	4.71	0.42	9.40	0.25	0.79	15.93	21.7

Eastern Mediterranean (including Austro-Hungary, Balkans, Egypt, Turkey)	0.27	1.53	0.36	3.17	0.14	0.15	5.63	7.7
West Africa and Atlantic	negl.	0.42	negl.	1.32	negl.	negl.	1.77	2.4
East Africa	—	negl.	negl.	0.12	negl.	negl.	0.20	0.3
Arabia, Indian Ocean, Asia	—	0.03	0.02	0.72	negl.	negl.	0.80	1.1
North & Central America	negl.	negl.	negl.	0.07	negl.	negl.	0.17	0.2
South America and other regions (including Falklands, Greenland, Iceland)	0.20	0.33	0.3	5.90	0.11	0.20	7.07	9.6
TOTAL	8.25	23.02	8.88	29.88	0.25	2.18	73.40	100.0

Source: ARSM 1924, 122–3.

Scotland and the North-East, and significant parts of the Yorkshire field, as well as accounting for between one-quarter and one-third of sales from South Wales (principally to western Europe). They were markets which were to be particularly disrupted by war and the growth of continental competition. The Mediterranean took about a quarter of Britain's coal exports, and of this over one-half came from South Wales. South America was the other big customer for British coal, which was sold in every continent and (with the obvious exception of the United States) was inextricably related to the world economy as a whole.[1]

All this was altered by the trends of the interwar period. Indeed, the most critical change in the British coal industry in the period was the collapse of exports and overseas bunkers—a reflection of the stagnation of world demand and the rise of competition, even before the scarcities of the 1940s enforced a comprehensive redirection of sales to the domestic market. From a position of trading pre-eminence, coalmining had shrunk to much more modest proportions in 1938 (selling only just over 20 per cent of a reduced output and accounting for less than 38 per cent of the world trade in coal, as against 55 per cent in 1913).[2] By the mid-1940s it had become insignificant on the world scene.

Long-run trends in the market for coal are placed in a broader context in Table 1.3, which shows the principal uses for British consumption in benchmark years between 1913 and 1946. (The figures of consumption do not coincide with those of deep-mined output, since they include opencast coal and coal taken from stocks.)

The dramatic decline in exports has already been mentioned. At home, the demand for coal also fell (albeit to a lesser extent), as economies in its use combined with the rise of alternative fuels to outweigh the influence of the long-run growth of the economy on consumption. On the other hand, the diffused character of its use in 1946 as well as 1913 is a reminder of its continued ubiquity and economic significance. More than this, considering the statistics of decline in domestic sales, it might be argued that they embodied only a marginal change. Nevertheless, in the context of growth elsewhere in the economy and the reduction in the industry's manpower needs, it compounded the diminution in the

---

[1] In 1913, the following countries imported more than 3 million tons of British coal: France (12.8 m.), Austro-Hungary (9.7 m.), Germany (9.0 m.), Russia (6.0 m.), Sweden (4.6 m.), Argentina (3.7 m.), Egypt (3.2 m.), Denmark (3.0 m.) (*ARSM* 1028, 118-19).

[2] *ARSM* 1938, 10. However, a more modern source implies an even greater fall—to 29% of world trade. See below, Table 7.2, citing Darmstadter 1971.

Table 1.3. *Output, exports, and domestic consumption of British coal, 1913–1946*

	1913		1924		1938		1946	
	m. tons	%	m. tons	%	m. tons	%	m. tons	%
A. GENERAL								
Output: deep-mined	287.4		267.1		227.0		181.2	
opencast	—		—		—		9.0	
Overseas shipments[a]	97.7		83.3		48.7		9.2	
Domestic consumption[b]	183.8		180.4		175.1		183.5	
B. DOMESTIC CONSUMPTION								
Iron works (blast furnaces)	21.2	11.5	14.2	7.9	11.6	6.6	20.1[d]	11.0
Other iron & steel	10.2	5.5	10.3	5.7	7.2	4.0	9.6	5.2
Collieries	18.0	9.8	16.6	9.2	11.9	6.8	10.3	5.6
Gas works	16.7	9.1	16.7	9.2	18.2	10.4	22.7	12.4
Electricity works	4.9	2.7	7.7	4.3	14.9	8.5	26.2	14.3
Railways	13.2	7.2	13.5	7.5	12.5	7.1	15.1	8.2
Coastwise bunkers	1.9	1.0	1.3	0.7	1.2	0.7	1.0	0.5
Domestic[c]	40.0	21.8	40.0	22.2	} 97.7	55.9	36.1	19.7
General manufacturing and all other	57.7	31.4	60.1	33.3			47.2	23.1
TOTAL	183.8	100.0	180.4	100.0	175.1	100.0	183.5	100.0

[a] Coal, coke, manufactured fuel.
[b] Before adjustment of stocks.
[c] Including miners' coal allowances.
[d] 'Coke ovens'.

Sources: 1913, 1924, and 1938: *ARSM* 1929, 126; 1938, 184. Ministry of Fuel and Power. *Statistical Digest for the Years 1946 and 1947* (Cmd. 7548. 1948), 85.

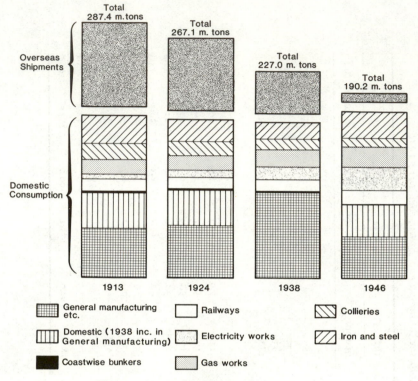

Fig. 1.3. Uses of British coal, 1913–1946

economic importance and the 'presence' of the industry. That development was also more directly reflected in the changing pattern of domestic demand for coal itself, as the huge increase in the importance of the electricity industry (and to a smaller extent that of gasworks) testified to the growing use of intermediate sources of energy—and symbolized the hitherto inconceivable threat that coal might one day be dethroned.

ii. Coal and coalfields

The coalmining industry which had grown so rapidly in the decades before the Great War consisted of a variety of products serving a variety of markets and was subject to a changing pattern of demand and prices. More than this, the economics of production, and the modes of work and organization in the different districts (and mines within each district), were heavily influenced by physical and geological considerations: the types, depth and thickness of coal, its faulting, inclination and the state of roofs and floors, the gassiness and wetness of its seams. Coal-mining districts, colliery undertakings, individual mines, and even seams within a mine, therefore varied in their industrial structures and techniques, their systems of working and the tasks of labour, their levels of efficiency and profitability.

Coalmining was, in effect, *several* industries; and a good deal of the political perturbation which characterized its history was associated with intermittent attempts to deal with wages, prices, organization, or marketing as if it was a single industry. In generalizing about coalmining it will rarely be possible to avoid such simplification; but it will be constantly necessary to bear in mind the great variety of conditions and structures in coalmining, and the resulting 'fatal danger of averages'.[1]

This variety began, of course, with the character of the mineral itself. For, while all coal burned, its varying chemical and physical qualities meant that it was by no means all equally useful for all heat-generating or by-product purposes. In this respect the most important variables were the carbon content of the coal, the presence of volatile matter (i.e. matter other than moisture, 'fixed carbon', and the ash left after exposure to severe heat), which was broadly inverse to the amount of carbon, and the tendency to 'caking' (i.e. to form coalesced lumps when exposed to heat). These, and allied characteristics, partly set out in Table 1.4, determined the presence or absence of fumes or smoke during the combustion of coal, its free-burning or calorific quality, its tendency to leave residues, its effectiveness for the stoking of boilers in ships or locomotives, its appropriateness for the production of gas or different types of coke, and its effectiveness as a source of by-products. As a result, different coals had distinctively different economic uses—although evolving technology altered the utility of individual coals for particular uses, and the boundaries were in any case not inflexible: as was exemplified during wartime, it was possible, if costly, to burn 'inappropriate' types of coal for particular purposes.

Coal was generally 'ranked' in descending order of carbon (and ascending order of volatile content), as is exemplified in Table 1.4. Anthracite was the highest ranking coal, with a very high proportion of carbon. It also contained only a tiny amount of moisture and had very little tendency to smoke or give off noxious fumes. It was therefore very suitable for use in closed and domestic stoves and in the drying of fruit or the processing of food. Next in ranking, and sharing some of

[1] *CG* 2 July 1915, 24.

Table 1.4. *Examples of British coals, illustrating changes of rank*

| | Ultimate Analysis (dry ash-free basis) | | | | | Proximate Analysis | | | | (Dry ash-free basis) | Calorific Value (dry ash-free basis) |
| | (Air-dried basis) | | | | | | | |
	Carbon	Hydrogen	Oxygen	Nitrogen	Sulphur	Moisture	Volatile matter	Fixed carbon	Ash	Volatile matter	B.Th.U. per lb.
Wood	49.8	6.2	43.4	0.3	0.3	16.7	71.8	10.9	0.6	86.8	8,400
Peat (Devon)	61.8	6.0	30.1	1.6	0.5	13.4	58.1	26.5	2.0	68.6	9,900
Lignite (Devon)	66.8	5.6	24.0	1.3	2.3	16.0	46.2	31.8	6.0	59.2	11,500
Leicestershire non-caking coal	78.6	5.2	11.7	1.6	2.8	13.1	36.3	45.5	5.1	44.4	13,990
Yorkshire weakly caking coal	82.6	5.2	9.2	1.8	1.2	4.1	35.2	57.4	3.3	38.0	14,510
Yorkshire medium-caking coal	84.8	5.2	7.6	1.7	0.7	2.7	33.4	61.3	2.6	35.3	15,090
Durham coking coal	88.5	5.0	4.1	1.6	0.8	0.9	28.5	66.8	3.8	29.9	15,630
South Wales caking steam coal	90.5	4.8	2.3	1.5	0.9	0.3	17.7	77.3	4.7	18.6	15,710
South Wales dry steam coal	92.5	3.9	1.4	1.5	0.7	0.9	10.8	84.7	3.6	11.3	15,610
South Wales anthracite	93.5	3.5	1.0	1.2	0.8	1.9	7.5	87.6	3.0	7.9	15,590

Source: P. C. Pope (ed.), *Coal: Production, Distribution, Utilisation* (1949), p. 21.

anthracite's properties, came dry steam coals, with little or no tendency to caking,[1] which burned well with little smoke (and were therefore also much favoured for use in steamships and railway locomotives).

Below these, coals which still had a fairly high rank and a moderate amount of volatile matter (20–30 per cent) made high-quality metal-lurgical coke, while lower ranked coals, with a greater proportion of volatiles, were most suitable for the production of coal- and producer-gas, for domestic use and, in the case of 'steam coals', for general purpose steam-raising in industry. ('Coking steam coals' could be blended effectively to make coke as well as raise steam.) Coals with a low ash content were in demand for domestic and general industrial use. Cutting across some of these categories, the actual size of the pieces of coal (which depended on how it was extracted and subsequently treated as well as on its natural conditions) could be large or small—with a premium on large coals for household use and locomotives; and on small coals for industrial steam-raising.

Finally, it must be remembered that while certain types of coal (and therefore market potential) were obviously more concentrated in some districts and collieries than in others, individual districts might contain a very wide variety of coals. It was perfectly possible for individual mines, and even individual seams, to contain more than one type. Within the resulting bewildering variety, South Wales dominated the supply of anthracite, dry steam, and coking steam coal, while sharing with Durham the lead in prime (metallurgical) coking fuel; Scotland was an important producer of general steam-raising and some coking coal and anthracite; Durham, in addition to its wide range of coking coal, was a vital producer of gas-making coal, and together with Northumberland was an important source of general utility coal; and Yorkshire and the Midland fields were well represented among producers of coking (other than prime coking), gas-making, general utility and steam-raising, and more especially domestic coals.[2]

The different coalfields of Britain each exemplified great variety with respect to the location, depth, quality, composition, and market of its

---

[1] As Table 1.4 indicates, some steam coals had a significant tendency to caking.

[2] Roughly speaking, high-rank steam and coking coal (varying from medium to strongly caking) was primarily produced in South Wales, northern Lancashire, and west Durham; low-rank, weakly caking coal used for general industrial and domestic purposes was principally mined in the south and east Midlands and in Scotland; and much of the Yorkshire field concentrated on the production of middle- to low-rank coking, gas, and general purpose coal. For discussion of rankings and uses of coal, see Pope 1949; Manchester Joint Research Council 1960, 45 ff.

coals. Nevertheless, there was a degree of consistency within districts, and the economic characteristics, and performance, of individual fields did indeed vary on average. It is, therefore, possible to distinguish the principal districts, no matter how roughly, by their product range and markets, working methods and costs, wage and profit levels, economic interests and outlook. And these considerations will be implicit in the detailed appraisal of the industry's history with which this book is concerned.

At a general level, the relative importance of the different coalfields is best assessed in terms of production. And the position in this respect in 1913, and the change over the next three decades, is summarized in Table 1.5 and Fig. 1.4. Considered solely in terms of relative shares of total output, the two principal changes were a violent decline in the importance of the South Wales field (from some 20 to just under 12 per cent of Britain's output) and the growth to national dominance of South Yorkshire and the East Midlands.

In 1913 the two dominant British coalfields were South Wales (primarily Monmouthshire and east Glamorganshire) and north-east England (Northumberland and Durham). Both areas were heavily dependent on export markets, and together they accounted for some 40 per cent of total British coal output. (By 1946 Yorkshire and the East Midlands were to account for the same proportion.) Although South Wales and the North-East did not retain their original lead, and in many respects—technical, organizational, labour relations—offered strong contrasts to each other, they were to shape the national consciousness of coalmining in the early twentieth century.

The South Wales industry, based on a field of some 1,000 square miles, was perhaps the most spectacular example of the boom in coal-mining in the late nineteenth and very early twentieth centuries. This was principally because of the pace and scale of its growth in the principality: between the early 1880s and 1907–13 production in South Wales grew by about 120 per cent, until it accounted for virtually 20 per cent of all British output, and was rivalled only by the North-East.[1] But the reputation of South Wales as a coalfield was determined not merely by its rate of growth. It was also attributable to the intensity of mining operations, the tensions between labour and capital, and the general configuration of the industry, clustered as it was in narrow and deeply etched valleys which gave birth to tightly knit and distinctive communities.

[1] Church 1986, 3, 10.

Table 1.5. *Output of deep-mined coal and employment by mining district, Great Britain, 1913-1946*

A. PRODUCTION

District	1913		1924		1938		1946	
	m. tons	%	m. tons	%	m. tons	%	m. tons	%
South Wales	56.8	19.8	51.1	19.1	35.3	15.5	21.0	11.6
Scotland	42.5	14.8	36.2	13.5	30.3	13.3	22.7	12.5
Northern	58.7	20.4	52.5	19.7	46.3	20.4	34.6	19.1
North-West	28.1	9.8	23.2	8.7	17.0	7.5	12.9	7.1
Yorkshire	43.7	15.2	46.6	17.4	43.4	18.5	36.3	20.0
East Midlands	33.7	11.7	34.2	12.8	32.2	14.2	34.5	19.0
West Midlands	20.8	7.3	20.3	7.6	19.7	8.7	16.6	9.2
Great Britain	287.4	100.0	267.1	100.0	227.0	100.0	181.2	100.0

B. EMPLOYMENT

District	1913		1924		1938		1946	
	000	%	000	%	000	%	000	%
South Wales	232.8	21.1	250.0	23.3	136.0	19.4	107.6	15.5
Scotland	139.4	12.6	141.8	13.2	90.0	12.8	79.1	11.4
Northern	236.8	21.4	241.7	22.5	167.8	23.9	150.3	21.6
North-West	123.5	11.2	124.7	11.6	68.0	9.7	58.1	8.3
Yorkshire	160.4	14.5	195.3	18.2	144.7	20.6	133.3	19.1
(S. Yorkshire)	(96.6)	(8.7)	(122.6)	(11.4)	(100.2)	(14.3)	(93.2)	13.4
East Midlands	100.7	9.1	125.5	11.7	92.1	13.1	85.5	12.3
West Midlands	94.0	8.5	107.6	10.0	76.9	11.0	69.4	10.0
Great Britain	1,104.4		1.213.7		790.9		696.7	

Northern: Durham, Northumberland, and Cumberland (Durham accounted for about 67–71% of the Northern field, Northumberland for about 25–30%, and Cumberland for about 3–4%.
North-West: Lancashire & Cheshire and North Wales (Lancashire & Cheshire accounted for about 80% of the district's output).
East Midlands: Leicestershire, South Derbyshire, North Derbyshire, and Nottinghamshire (Nottinghamshire increased its share of the district's output from 37 to 45%, while North Derbyshire's share fell from 50 to 39%; Leicestershire accounted for the bulk of the remainder).
West Midlands: North Staffordshire, South Staffordshire, Cannock Chase, Shropshire, Warwickshire.

Sources: calculated from *ARSM*, various years; MFP, *Statistical Digest for the Years 1946 and 1947* (Cmd. 7548, 1948) and *Supplement to Cmd. 7548–Regional and District Coal Production Figures* (Ministry of Fuel and Power, 1948).

At its western extremity the South Wales field produced an abundance of very good anthracite in small mines working disturbed and difficult strata. But its most important natural advantage lay in its reserves of the world's best and most abundant steam coal, especially for

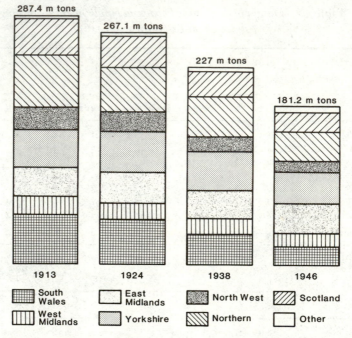

Fig. 1.4. Production of deep-mined coal by district, 1913–1946

high-performance steamships (the output of a limited number of col-lieries met the Navy's stringent criteria, and those mines were placed on the 'Admiralty List'). In addition, the South Wales field produced a wide range of gas and coking coal, and general industrial fuel. The district was also exceptional in terms of its reliance on exports: in 1913 over 60 per cent of its output of 56.8 million tons was shipped overseas—29.9 mil-lion tons as cargo exports and 5 million tons as foreign bunkers. Corre-spondingly, South Wales dominated the nation's coal trade. It was responsible for 41 per cent of the coal (38 per cent of the coal, coke, and bunkers) shipped from all British ports.[1] Finally, the bituminous (non-anthracite) Welsh field was characterized by very large mines and throughout the district the coal seams were dry, fiery, and gassy. The social geography of the coal-producing valleys, the increasing impersonality of corporate coalmining, the scale and concentration of mining operations, and the heat, discomfort, and dangers of working conditions helped explain the specific and uncommon industrial relations and economic circumstances of the South Wales coalfield.

[1] Jevons 1915, 113.

Although not quite as specialized as South Wales, the slightly larger coalfield of Northumberland and Durham was also oriented to the export trade (which in 1913 took about 23 million tons of its output of 56.3 million tons). This export orientation, and the competitiveness of markets, was reputed to have made miners as well as owners[1] more cost-conscious than in other fields, and to have created a distinctive context for wage-bargaining. Durham (where coal seams were abundant, level, and uniform in thickness) was significantly more important than Northumberland, accounting for an output of 41.5 million as against 14.8 million tons in 1913. In west Durham, where outcrops had facilitated mining for very many years, high-quality metallurgical coking coal was produced for the local iron industry; while further north and east, and ultimately far under the sea, deeper seams yielded a variety of steam, house, coking, and gas coals. In addition to supplying manufacturing and domestic consumers therefore, there was a profitable trade (mostly carried on by coastal shipments) between Durham and the gasworks of the heavily populated South-East.

Scottish coal production, which averaged over 40 million tons (some 15 per cent of national output) in the years before the War, was generally referred to as if it was based on a single geological and economic district, stretching from sea to sea across the central 'waist' of the country. Certainly, within the usual variety, the Scottish mines of 1913 tended to be characterized by similar geological formations (in particular relatively difficult workings subject to flooding and very frequently thin seams, albeit lying at shallow depths), by relatively small size, and by a dependence on exports. On the other hand, Scottish coal was actually produced in more or less distinct fields, the three most important of which being those in Lanarkshire, Fife, and Ayrshire. Of these, the Lanarkshire or central field was the largest in 1913, accounting for just over half Scotland's output. But by 1913 some of its most accessible coal was exhausted and economic difficulties were beginning to loom. Fife, with more economically abundant reserves and having experienced particularly rapid growth since the 1870s, accounted for 24 per cent of Scottish production and exported over half of its output of 10 million tons.[2] The two slightly lesser fields of Lothian and

[1] The term 'owners' (or coalowners) in the coal industry was applied to the active owners and senior managers of coalmining enterprises. The owners of the actual coal before it was mined were known as 'royalty owners' or occasionally 'mineral owners'.

[2] The figures are for Fife and the tiny associated field of Clackmannan. For the Scottish industry, see Long 1978, 12–13.

Ayrshire produced some 21 per cent of Scotland's coal in 1913. By 1946 their share had risen to 32 per cent, that of Fife to 28 per cent, and Lanarkshire's had fallen to 39 per cent.

Although South Wales and Durham, and to a lesser extent Scotland, dominated the public perception of the coalmining industry for much of the first half of the twentieth century, its real abundance and potential buoyancy, as has already been remarked, were to be found in the coal deposits stretching from Yorkshire down to Nottinghamshire and north Derbyshire. These were originally part of a huge primeval coalfield which had been separated by the upthrust of the Pennines and by folding and faulting of the Earth's strata until more or less separate fields had been formed in Lancashire and Cheshire and North Wales; Yorkshire, Nottinghamshire, and North Derbyshire; South Derbyshire and Leicestershire; and North Staffordshire, South Staffordshire, Warwickshire, and Shropshire. In 1913 Yorkshire alone produced over 15 per cent of Britain's output (a proportion which exceeded Scotland's) and had grown particularly rapidly—virtually doubling between 1890 and 1913. Within the county, however, there were, in effect, two districts. The older exposed coalfield of West Yorkshire, which largely supplied household and general industrial consumers, produced only just over one-third of the county's output. In South Yorkshire, on the other hand, where a greater proportion of coking and gas coal was produced, the concealed coal measures were being rapidly (and very profitably) exploited by deep, large-scale, capital-intensive mines.[1] Indeed, the South Yorkshire seams stretched more or less continuously southwards into Nottinghamshire (where the most spectacular mining developments of the 1920s were to occur)[1] and North Derbyshire, to form the richest coal district in the twentieth century.

Together, even by 1913, production in the South Yorkshire and East Midlands fields exceeded that of South Wales. Including the still rich mines of the West Midlands (Warwickshire, Staffordshire, Shropshire), which accounted for some 7 per cent of the national total, the central areas of England produced about one-third of Britain's output—and a much greater proportion of its domestic consumption. The only other coalfield of any significance in 1913 was that of Lancashire and Cheshire (almost 9 per cent of national production). There, the costs and difficulties of faulted seams were to some extent compensated for by the proximity of local industrial markets, and the relative absence of competition.[2]

[1] Below, ch. 5, sect. ii.
[2] The other British fields in the early years of the century (Cumberland, North Wales, the

As we have already seen, the various coalfields participated to differing extents in the decline of the industry after 1913. The most extreme victim was undoubtedly South Wales, which was heavily dependent on export sales and on specific varieties of coal (as well as being peculiarly susceptible to low productivity). Between 1913 and 1946 its output fell by some 60 per cent. Other export districts—notably Scotland and the North-East—managed to restrain the speed of the fall in their output (by finding alternative markets and by operating in overseas areas where demand was not so restrained) and so experienced only a modest reduction in their share of national production. Similarly, Lancashire coalmines, which initially suffered from obsolescence and the collapse of the local cotton industry, managed to stabilize their share of output from the early 1930s.

Finally, of the major districts, Yorkshire and the Midlands did significantly better than the national average. Their performance reflected two advantages. On the one hand, fields such as Warwickshire, North Staffordshire, and South Staffordshire and Cannock Chase (which in any case had relatively productive seams) combined the production of general purpose coals suitable for home manufacturing industry and varied household use, with high-quality fuel for domestic hearths (in the case of South Staffordshire and Cannock Chase) and good 'caking' coal suitable for gas-making and coke ovens (in the case of Warwickshire). On the other hand, and much more important, the East Midlands and South Yorkshire were relatively new fields with enormous potential. In the late nineteenth and early twentieth centuries they attracted large-scale investment to sink deep, modern pits. These new collieries were able to exploit rich seams of highly marketable coal. The outcome was that even during the long period of stagnation for the industry as a whole, these districts became more and more important.

As has already been seen, the figures for the county of Yorkshire are slightly misleading, since they include the old collieries of West Yorkshire, whose output declined from 16 million tons (37 per cent of the county total) in 1913 to 10.6 million tons (29 per cent) in 1946. South Yorkshire, by contrast, more or less maintained or even increased its output for most of the period, only falling slightly below the 1913 level

Forest of Dean, and Bristol and Somerset) were unimportant—in total producing only about 3% of the nation's coal. Kent was a later, and never a particularly important, coalfield, never producing as much as 1% of the nation's output before nationalization. For more detailed discussion of the various coalfields at different stages of their twentieth-century history, see below, ch. 5, sect. ii and ch. 7, sect. i.

in 1946. As a result, its share of British deep-mined production rose sharply from about 9 to 14 per cent. In the East Midlands, which was to prove the mainstay of the coal industry in the middle and later years of the century, Nottinghamshire did spectacularly well: its output rose from 12.4 to 15.3 million tons at a time when the industry as a whole shrank by more than 30 per cent.

By the eve of nationalization, therefore, the decline of national production (especially for export) and the advantages and vigorous exploitation of relatively new fields, had given a new shape to the British coalmining industry. In some respects, perhaps, the change was not quite as uniformly drastic as it might have been: Scotland and the North-East had managed to hold on to a significant part of their share of output, declining at only a marginally faster rate than the industry as a whole; and the Lancashire & Cheshire field had arrested its decline during the 1930s, although in proportionate terms it suffered quite badly over the long run. Nevertheless, the fact remains that the traditional sites of the industry came under the greatest pressure and ceased to dominate coalmining (and the social picture of coalmining) in the ways that they had done in the nineteenth and early twentieth centuries. The centre of gravity of the industry moved towards central Britain. Increasingly, production and profitability were concentrated in the Midlands and South Yorkshire. It was true that as late as 1946 they still did not quite account for 50 per cent of national output. But that was where the industry could be most successful, and that was where its future economic heart lay. In any case, for much of the first half of the century it was this transition which dominated the commercial, institutional, and political history of coalmining. Its economic and social costs had been enormous, and their memory and effects would endure.

iii. Techniques and structures

The long-run history of coalmining after 1913 was, of course, much more than a matter of trends in output and demand. Behind the former, and helping to explain the latter, were the technical and structural characteristics of the industry which affected its vitality in the face of adversity.[1] These will be considered in some detail at the appropriate

---

[1] For detailed descriptions of working methods and systems in coalmining, see Church 1986, ch. 4; Bulman & Redmayne; Griffin 1971; *Digest of Evidence Given before the Royal Commission on Coal Resources (1901-1905)*, I, *passim*. For the nature of underground work, see ch. 10, sect. i.

points in the following pages, but it is also necessary to provide an introductory overview of mining methods and organization as they appeared on the eve of the First World War and as they changed, or failed to change, in the next third of a century.

Coalmining was primarily an underground occupation: the great majority of mineworkers (about 80 per cent) worked below the surface,[1] while a large number of surface workers were older men who had begun their working lives down the pit. The enormous variety of methods used to cut or 'get' coal at the coalface was shaped by geology and economics, industrial relations and local history, tradition and technology. Within the variety, however, there were two broad systems of work organization. These were the pillar and stall and the longwall methods, versions of which are illustrated in Figs. 1.5–1.8. (It must be emphasized, however, that each had its own variants, and that versions of the two systems could coexist within the same mine and even occasionally within the same seam in a mine.)

In pillar and stall (the variants of which had different regional names such as 'room and pillar' or 'stoop and room'), roadway tunnels were driven into a large panel of the coal seam in a criss-cross or grid-like pattern enabling coal to be extracted along the lines of the roads while the solid, rectangular pillars of coal which were left supported the roof.[2] Initially, only a small proportion of the coal was cut in this way, in order to leave massive and secure pillars. At the completion of this stage in one part of the panel, all or some of the pillars themselves would be worked and in part of the resulting void ('goaf' or 'gob') packs would be built to preserve roadways from subsidence.

Pillar and stall methods of working had been dominant in the nineteenth century, but in the twentieth century were to be superseded by longwall working, which was more suitable for deep mines, for thinner seams, and for mechanized cutting and conveying. Longwall working, as its name implies, involved cutting the coal in panels along continuous swathes, which could be hundreds of yards long. However, the face might also be stepped into fairly short lengths and in any case, until major mechanization, it was customary for small teams of miners to work in sections (also called 'stalls') of a few tens of yards. Until the

[1] *ARSM*, various years. This figure applies to the principal coalmining districts other than South Wales & Monmouthshire, where the figure was 84%. Census returns, by contrast, indicate that the proportion underground was about 87 or 88% for most areas outside South Wales, and between 91 and 93% in that district.

[2] This sort of work was carried out within large 'districts' or 'panels', divided from each other by barriers of the coal seam.

Working place

Coal left permanently for support

Coal to be worked

Goaf–usually packed with waste

Boundary of area being worked

Key to Figs 1.5–8

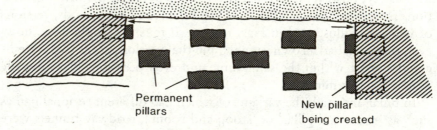

Permanent
pillars

New pillar
being created

Fig. 1.5. Pillar and stall

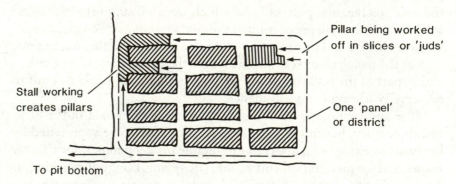

Pillar being worked
off in slices or 'juds'

Stall working
creates pillars

One 'panel'
or district

To pit bottom

Fig. 1.6. Modified pillar and stall or bord and pillar

Second World War 'longwall advancing', in which work proceeded outwards from the shaft, was very much more important than 'longwall retreating', in which roadways were driven out to the boundaries of the coal seams before cutting commenced.[1]

By 1913 longwall working was already very prominent in Yorkshire,

[1] For a discussion of longwall advancing and retreating and their respective advantages, see below, ch. 9, sect. ii.

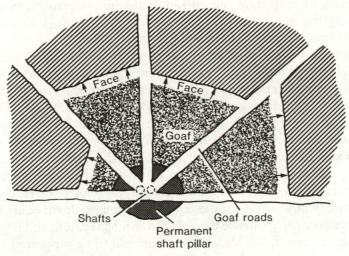

Fig. 1.7. Longwall advancing

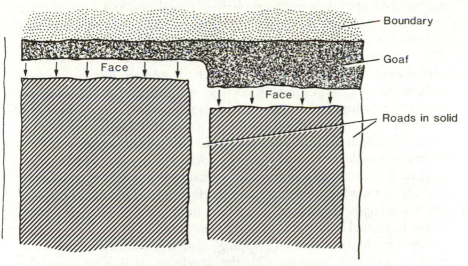

Fig. 1.8. Longwall retreating

Lancashire, and much of the East Midlands. Pillar and stall predomin-
ated in eastern Scotland, and both systems coexisted, in varying degrees,
in South Wales, central Scotland, and the North-East. However, longwall was inexorably extended as deeper and thinner seams were worked,
and as its organizational and technological advantages (particularly its
productive potential for the application of machines to the cutting and

conveying of coal) were recognized or became relevant to new conditions. By the late 1930s about 75 per cent, and by 1948 almost 90 per
cent, of coal was produced by longwall methods.[1]

Whatever the system used, until cutter-loader machines were introduced in the middle years of this century, the coal had first to be
undercut by hewers, who used a hand-pick or machine to extract a
narrow but deep horizontal slice of earth or coal from the base of the
seams, to a depth of about three feet. Undercutting by hand was a
relatively skilled and very arduous task, the hewers having to work in
cramped conditions and in most uncomfortable postures. After undercutting, the coal would be brought down by explosives or wedges or
pneumatic picks. (In some mines, notably in South Wales, the seams
were sufficiently friable for the coal to be brought down easily without
much undercutting—hence the delay in mechanization, and hence, too,
the dangers from falls.) Meanwhile, roofs had to be supported, temporarily by props and chocks, and then by stone packs, while at some point
the props would be withdrawn and the roof allowed to subside. Roof-
support and prop-drawing were obviously vital jobs and were in some
areas the responsibilities of specialists and in others the responsibilities
of hewers and their assistants. When the coal had been brought down,
'fillers' or (depending on local practice) the hewers themselves loaded it,
with shovels and forks, or even literally by hand, into tubs or (increasingly as the century progressed) on to face conveyors. (If the seam was
too narrow to bring tubs to the workings the coal was dragged or 'cast'
along the face to the nearest roadway.) Once in tubs (face conveyors
frequently disgorged into tubs, since main haulage conveyors were only
gradually installed), the coal would be taken by, or with a combination
of, human effort, ponies, or mechanized haulage (powered by stationary
engine), to the shaft bottom, where the tubs would be placed in cages
and wound up to the surface by steam or (more rarely) electrical power.

Much manual work of a more or less continuous nature was also
involved in the construction ('ripping') and safe maintenance of roadways or 'gates' to keep up with the development of new areas, the
advance of cutting, and the needs of haulage and ventilation. At the face
itself mining involved a good deal of supervisory work (mostly by
deputies or 'firemen'),[2] while throughout the mine continuity of
production depended not only on hewers, fillers, 'putters' (responsible
for the haulage of tubs), and 'stonemen' (who drove new roadways),

[1] *Digest of Evidence Given before the Royal Commission on Coal Resources (1901-1905)*, I, 192–
220; *Reid Report*, 42; National Coal Board, *Annual Report*, 1948, 15.
[2] Below, ch. 10, sect. i.

and their various assistants, but on mechanics, fitters, electricians, general labourers, pony minders, and many others.

In the opening years of the twentieth century, therefore, coalmining was an extremely labour-intensive process, involving a huge amount of arduous effort by various specialists. It also required the careful balancing of two principal types of operations—hewing coal and then hauling it along the face and underground tunnels and up a mine shaft—each of which might prove a constraint or bottleneck on overall production. What changes took place after 1913?

It is not easy to present a clear picture of the course of technical and organizational change in an industry like coalmining. Much of it was concealed in varied and locally distinctive developments within a myriad of individual firms. But if we make use of the rather general measures which were the focus of much contemporary anxiety, such as the proportion of coal produced with the help of mechanical cutters and conveyors, the record suggests a reasonable, if not considerable, achievement. From negligible proportions before the First World War the amount of coal mechanically cut rose to 61 per cent, and the amount conveyed along the face to 58 per cent, by 1939. Following the wartime programmes, these figures had risen, by 1946, to some 75 and 70 per cent respectively.[1]

Yet this achievement (apart from lagging behind some of Britain's principal competitors) was by no means always matched by commensurate increases in labour productivity (output per manshift at the face). Nor was there a consistent relationship from district to district between the growth of mechanization and changes in labour productivity. From the 1920s the export districts in particular had a very bad record in terms of output per manshift.[2] But in any case, taking the country as a whole,

---

[1] For a more detailed consideration of the process of mechanization, see below, ch. 9, sect. ii.

[2] For this and other aspects of the course of change in mechanization, organization, and productivity, see *Reid Report*, ch. II and III. The following figures of mechanization at the face (ibid., II) summarize the position of the export districts:

District	% cut (machine)		% conveyed (machine)		% increase in OMS
	1927	1939	1928	1939	1927/8-39
S. Wales	7	16	26	48	+4.32
Scotland	56	25	80	59	−0.39
Durham	18	6	43	27	+0.97
North'land	42	13	92	45	+6.07
Gt. Brit.	23	12	61	58	+16.29

the latter did not increase as fast as mechanization, and from the mid-1930s more or less stagnated. Even with the help of underground reorganization which extended the system of longwall production and true machine mining, the twentieth-century record of British labour productivity was disappointing. In the 25 years after the outbreak of the First World War output per manshift (for all workers in mines) rose by merely 13 per cent; that for Belgium, Germany, Poland, and the United States rose by between 36 and 60 per cent; in the Netherlands it more than doubled.[1]

Little of this can be explained by the natural difficulties of British coal seams. Geology was not always favourable to good productivity, and in most districts conditions deteriorated as time passed. But there is no reason to believe that the deterioration proceeded faster than organizational and technical devices improved. Most of the explanation for relatively poor performance must lie somewhere in the range of factors which were increasingly brought into the reckoning in the early 1940s: shortage of investment funds and fragmentation of ownership, poor underground layout and production systems, inadequate training, short-term attitudes among owners and conservatism among managers, poor industrial relations, and lack of worker–manager cooperation in full-scale mechanization.[2]

In this context, therefore, the bare statistics of mechanization are misleading. It is true that vital improvements in the hewing operation ultimately depended on the introduction of longwall systems and mechanization—hence the contemporary anxiety concerning the apparently slow speed at which the latter was applied to British mining. In the long run, however, although much public attention was concentrated on coal *cutting*, the fact was that its haulage underground and to the surface, the integrated adjustment of *all* underground operations, and the efficient access to remoter or more difficult seams were at least equally important and were to prove the more sensitive aspects of the technical weakness of mining. Indeed, by the 1940s the crucial deficiency of British coalmining came increasingly to be identified as inefficient haulage and the lack of adequate integration and modern layout of underground operations.[3] In practice, the moderately impressive extention of cutting and conveying at the face in the 1920s and 1930s could have little effect as long as the pace of technical and organizational

[1] *Reid Report*, Appendix I.
[2] These issues were summarized by the Reid Committee. See ibid., 37–8, and below, 616–19.
[3] Below, ch. 13, sect. iii–v.

change throughout the productive network of individual coalmines remained slow.

The reasons for these disappointments, and the extent to which they can be counted as a culpable 'failure' by those engaged in the industry, will form the subject-matter of later parts of this study. But it is important to mention at the outset a feature of the industry which was widely assumed to be an endemic cause of its inability to adjust rapidly to new circumstances. This related to its commercial and productive structure.

The overriding characteristic of the coalmining industry's organization in 1913 was its fragmentation, and this was to remain the case until it was taken into public ownership after the Second World War. In round figures, there were some 1,400 firms and 2,600 mines on the eve of the First World War.[1] Such statistics undoubtedly exaggerate the individualistic nature of business structures in coal. Quite apart from the possibilities of coordination inherent in the local coalowners' associations (united by a national federation), the production of some *types* of coal was fairly well concentrated, many pits and firms were tiny private enterprises and statistically insignificant, and within individual districts many firms were interconnected by shared business interests and by interlocking shareholdings and directorships.[2] Nevertheless, the coalowners' associations existed not so much to subsume their business interests as to strengthen their lobbying and industrial-relations power; and even after small-scale enterprises and close business links have been taken into account, coalmining remained one of the most highly fragmented of the staple industries, with output dispersed among a large number of substantial as well as medium-sized and small firms. No one undertaking or small group of undertakings was able to dominate the general markets for coal.

In 1913, for example, less than 50 per cent of the industry's labour force was employed in the largest firms (each with 3,000 or more miners)—and there were, in any case, no less than 94 such firms, owning 600 mines. Further, as much as one-third of all miners were employed by the 211 middling firms which employed between 1,000 and 1,999 men.[3]

---

[1] The industrial and business structure of the coal industry is considered in more detail below, ch. 9, sect. i.   [2] Below, ch. 9, sect. i.

[3] The 211 firms owned 563 mines. The 36 largest firms (each employing at least 5,000 men) accounted for no more than 25% of the industry's manpower. Actual units of production were also dispersed: the 70 largest pits (each employing more than 1,999 men) accounted for only 17% of the industry's labour force; and over 650 mines employed between 500 and 1,999 men, and accounted for 60% of the miners in the industry. For further data on the size distribution of colliery enterprises (and mines) see below, ch. 9, sect. i and Table 9.4.

There was, of course, regional variety in the degree of structural dispersion, but even in the districts where production was relatively more
concentrated, the results were insignificant compared with other heavy
industries. (In South Wales, for example, the 11 largest colliery firms—
out of the 80 which employed more than 500 men—still accounted for
less than 40 per cent of the district's manpower.)[1] As will be seen in
Chapter 9, this corporate structure was slow to change. By 1938,
although larger firms had become more important, there was still
relatively little concentration: by 1938 the industrial share (of total manpower) of those undertakings employing over 3,000 men had risen
slightly, from 46.5 per cent to 52.9 per cent; but they were still very
numerous (66 as against 94 undertakings). And one-third of all miners
were employed in pits owned by almost 150 firms with between 1,000
and 2,999 men. The industry remained highly fragmented throughout its
history under a regime of private enterprise.

There were two noteworthy implications of this pattern of enterprise.
First, the pattern of ownership and control was extremely varied. There
were, of course, important examples of large-scale, relatively impersonal
joint-stock companies, especially in South Yorkshire and the East
Midlands and in South Wales, and where coalmining was conjoined
with the production of iron and steel. Yet private companies, partnerships, and family enterprises, some of them surprisingly large, remained
the most common forms of enterprise in the coal industry. Matching the
individualism and insularity of *business* behaviour in the industry, the
organization of capital and control in colliery undertakings—where
dynasties and access to private funds were at least as important as joint-
stock companies and conventional share capital—remained an outstanding example of resistance to 'modern' corporate and administrative
forms.

The second implication of the industry's fragmented character was,
of course, that the business, and therefore the business strategy, of coalmining were unusually competitive and individualistic. In spite of
intermittent attempts to abate competition (by novel marketing devices
or consultation between owners), price movements, sales, and the
pattern of output remained largely determined by market forces, and
were correspondingly unstable in the precarious years after 1913. By the
same token, and of increasing importance, it proved extremely difficult
to secure coordinated economic policies on the part of the multifarious
independent business interests which comprised coalmining produc-

[1] For data on individual districts, see below, ch. 9, sect. i.

tion.[1] To many observers it seemed that the very structure of coalmining enterprise rendered it incapable of mustering the resources or confidence or cooperation which would have been necessary to reorganize production and reform the industry. In the event, this proved the most long-lasting ground for controversy about the industry's performance and about public policy towards it; and by the 1940s it had come to dominate all other considerations.[2] In effect, once given the gross deterioration of the market for coal, the problems of coalmining seemed to be inherent in the organization of the industry, in the inhibitions of the sectional interests within it, and in the resulting deterioration in the relationships between them, rather than in any peculiar psychological failings of its businessmen and their employees.

iv. The political economy of coal

The prolonged deterioration in the commercial climate of the coal industry after 1913 was not accompanied by a commensurately far-reaching change in its inherited structures. As a result the history of coalmining in the period was largely shaped by industrial relations and attitudes, by unsuccessful attempts at the structural reform of production, and by frustrated measures designed to introduce coordinated decision-making or new forms of social control into its operations. The politics of coal were to prove more important than its economics.

Inextricably related to these politics was the position of the mining labour force. The nature of miners' work—the effort involved, the distinctiveness of manual tasks and underground organization—naturally had a pervasive and rather special effect on relationships within the industry, on the social cohesiveness of the men involved, and on their perception of the rest of society—not merely of their employers and managers, but also of workers in other industries and society at large. By the same token, mining communities bore a special character, and could not be dissociated from the colliery organizations which they served. In coalmining more than in virtually any other industry, distinctiveness of the human element and its social implications influenced the course of economic change and political events. These considerations will be discussed in some detail in Chapter 10. Here, however, it is necessary to

---

[1] For a more detailed discussion of the evolving structure and character of ownership and control, see below, ch. 9. The situation up to 1913 is analysed in Church 1986, 133–46 and ch. 5.

[2] Below, ch. 13, sect. ii–v.

describe some of the salient features of the *economic* position of miners and the wage system by which they were paid.

The labour-intensive character of coalmining operations was, of course, reflected in its cost structures. In 1913, for example, the average cost of production per ton of British coal (including royalty payments of 5½d. to mineral owners) was 8s. 7½d. Of this, wages accounted for 6s. 4d. This proportion—75 per cent or even more—was generally characteristic of the industry until the early 1920s, when the economic vicissitudes of the industry led to pressure on wages which reduced their share of production costs to about 66 per cent.[1]

Implicit in these figures is another important characteristic of the economics of coalmining in the early twentieth century: compared to much of modern industry, capital embodied in reproducible plant, machinery, and equipment was relatively unimportant; 'investment' consisted not so much of the acquisition or construction of buildings and machines, as of the constant use of direct labour power to extend and maintain underground workings. And since, in any case, the pool of labour power used for such a purpose in an existing mine was also frequently and indistinguishably used for current production, the very concepts of 'capital' and 'investment' in coalmining operations is ambiguous, not to say dubious.[2]

The complexity of mining work was also amply reflected in a complexity of wage systems, which comprised the networks within which much of the industry's internal politics was played out.[3] In some districts and for some purposes a subcontracting or 'butty' system survived. In these cases the subcontractor was paid a piece rate for a specific task, and he paid his own 'employees'. More generally, individual hewers worked on piece rates, although they frequently employed their own assistants at day rates or for a share of their income, and occasionally groups of miners collectively employed helpers. However, the simplest conceptual distinction was between day-rate, or 'datal', and piece-rate work. Day rates tended to be paid to miners whose work was irregular or unskilled or routine, or was dependent on the flow of production or the occurrence of problems completely outside their control (this applied to many men working on main haulage or employed as general labourers or undertaking mechanics' or electricians' tasks). Piece rates, on the other hand, were paid where

[1] Below, ch. 5, sect. iv.   [2] Below, ch. 9, sect. ii.
[3] Types and methods of wage payments in coalmining are described in Rowe 1923 and Jevons 1915. Also see below, 435.

intensity of effort was necessary to maintain production, continuous supervision was impossible, and incentives were judged to be necessary. Hewing, face-haulage, prop-setting, and road-making could all fall into this category.

Given the nature of coalmining—and in particular the extraordinary variety of conditions between and within mines—the complexity of payment systems did not stop with the variety of workmen. A myriad of allowances and possible deductions, together with the fact that piece-rate workers would often be engaged on a variety of tasks (hewing, filling, prop-setting, etc.) each with its own piece rate, made the settlement of pay a peculiarly complicated and delicate task. More than this, the determination of an appropriate or agreed rate would vary with the immediate conditions of work. And these, in turn, would be determined by geological circumstances at particular workplaces within a mine, its age and depth, the stage of development of a seam, unexpected changes in the underground environment or the characteristics of the coal, etc. Thus it was that tables of piece rates, or 'price lists' as they were known, were subject to constant local change and renegotiation.

But even this description gives too simplistic a view of the situation. In practice, the benchmark for wages was normally derived from a fixed point in the past, so that on the eve of the First World War 'basis wages' were derived from 'standards' of (for example) 1879 in the case of South Wales and the North-East, and 1888 in the case of Scotland and the Yorkshire and Midlands fields. Standard wages were therefore the rates paid at each pit in a particular district for a specific task at a given date. By the same token, however, *new* price lists and 'basis' rates would have to be settled when new conditions arose or new mines were sunk or new seams or faces were opened up.

Yet this was only the beginning of the story: *actual* wage rates by the early twentieth century depended on percentage *additions* to basis rates, such additions being determined by alterations in the economic circumstances of the industry, and the respective power of the owners and miners in the course of negotiations (which were normally conducted on a district basis). Wage levels were therefore expressed in terms of percentages above 'standard' or 'basis wages'. Finally, *earnings*, as distinct from wage rates, would be affected not simply by the regularity of available work or the constant alteration of the 'standard', but (in the case of pieceworkers) by the variable intensity of individual effort and the ease or difficulty of particular work-places, and (in the case of dayworkers) by the level of pay set at each pit.[1] The horrifying complexity of wage systems in coalmining was a perpetual mystery to outsiders: 'What a method of regulating wages for a great industry!' exclaimed the Chairman of one government inquiry after pondering the requisite algebraic formulae. 'It is an astonishing thing', he mused, 'that you could have managed to pay wages so regularly and get men to understand what they were receiving.'[2]

Wage adjustments during the First World War introduced a change in these arrangements (in particular, miners' pay was supplemented by uniform national increases), but the general system was reinstated in 1921 and lasted, with relatively little change until the Second World War.[3] At all periods, however, the systems and principles by which wages (and hours) were determined were, together with industrial structure, at the heart of the political economy of coal.

By 1913 wage bargaining was the responsibility of district conciliation boards, with equal representations of owners and miners, and independent chairmen (whose authority was strictly circumscribed). Normally, there were limits on the extent to which wage rates might be altered at any one time, and board chairmen could not make independent 'awards' (they were frequently limited to deciding between the rival claims of owners and miners).

The conciliation board system had evolved from the late nineteenth century as an alternative to cruder forms of negotiation or to the quasi-automatic determination of wages by movements in the price of coal ('sliding-scale' agreements). In spite of this, and of the miners' understandable preference in favour of wages determining prices, rather than prices determining wages, conciliation board discussions were often dominated by reference to the price, and therefore the presumed profitability, of coal. This was especially so in the export districts, where the dependence of output, employment, and returns on uncontrollable competition was more obvious. Indeed, in Northumberland the conciliation board agreement of 1912 still provided for the operation of a sliding scale (with deleterious results for miners' pay in the early years of the Great War and even in the early spring of 1917)[4] and in Scotland the

---

[1] Normally, standard *district* rates did not exist, since the basis of piece and day rates varied according to local circumstances in each pit. However, there *was* a notional 'county average' (expressed in terms of shift earnings) which was used as a criterion to consider claims to increase or reduce wage levels in Northumberland and Durham. An analogous, but somewhat less specific figure existed in Scotland in the shape of a 'common' or 'field price'.

[2] *Buckmaster Proceedings*, 72.   [3] Below, ch. 12, sect. iv.

[4] Below, ch. 2, sect. iv; ch. 3, sect. iii.

agreement also took specific account of changes in the price of the product.

There was a sense, however, in which such specific arrangements were irrelevant to the issues which, although not always on the surface of affairs in 1913, were to be the most disturbing and troublesome in future years. We have already noted the relatively optimistic, even complacent, attitude towards the business of coalmining in 1913. The fact remained that the industry had only recently had to rely on the government to resolve a serious wage dispute. The minimum wage legislation of 1912 (which designated local conciliation boards as the machinery to establish district minima), like the Eight Hours Act of 1908, was an index of the special political sensitivity of the industry—and of the potential for cohesive power which existed among the miners.[1] With a trade-union membership (by no means exclusively in the Miners' Federation of Great Britain) already in excess of 75 per cent,[2] and with the ability, if only from time to time, to secure unity of economic and political action between its federated district units, the union was well placed to apply pressure to industrial affairs. This had been well exemplified in 1908 and 1912, and at its annual conference of 1913 the MFGB decided that all conciliation board agreements should be terminated simultaneously in April 1915. At that time the union would press for new, coordinated wage standards, overriding the economic differences between districts. The decision carried with it the possibility of a renewed *national* crisis of industrial relations.

Of course, the owners were also far from powerless as an economic, social, and political pressure group. Moreover, they, too, had strengthened the federal organization (the Mining Association of Great Britain) which linked the various districts. Admittedly, the local associations, each facing its own economic and commercial environment, were naturally reluctant to give the MAGB any explicit authority over wage determination or business affairs. Nevertheless, the owners' national association, like the MFGB, was inevitably to become a nodal point of political controversy and economic confrontation.[3]

Even within the industry, therefore, the events of the two decades or so before the First World War can be seen as a period of converging tensions. Moreover, these actual and potential stresses were not confined to 'internal' industrial relations. Perhaps even more

[1] Church 1986, 736 ff., 784–8.
[2] Below, ch. 3, sect. iii.
[3] For the MAGB, see below, ch. 4, sect. v; ch. 9, sect. iv.

significantly, they had begun to transform relationships with the state.[1] For the size, importance, and vulnerability of coalmining easily overcame any ideological prejudices concerning government intervention in industrial affairs.

Yet if the prospective clash of outlook and action between the principal interest groups within coalmining is one reason for not taking the optimism of 1913 at its face value, the economic future was another. Beneath the superficial calm—even complacency—of the last year of peace, coalmining was vulnerable to drastic changes in markets or novel pressures on resources and organization. In the event, the achievements up to 1913, and the structural characteristics of the industry at that date, were to prove inadequate in the face of the economic and political stresses which were introduced by the Great War and further transformed by its aftermath. Over the long run, the structure and profitability of coalmining were altogether too dependent on the continuance of rising demand from heavy industry and a booming international trade in coal. And even in the short run, as we shall see in the next two chapters, some of its frailties were exposed by the peculiar circumstances of a prospective shortage of coal in wartime conditions. Paradoxically, scarcity began a process which glut was to complete. The Great War proved to be a watershed in terms of the internal politics as well as the economics of the industry. After 1913 the evolution of coalmining largely reflected the impaired ability of a great industry to deal with the erosion of the prolonged boom which had brought it to what had proved to be only a temporary pre-eminence.

[1] Church 1986, 787-9.

PART B

THE GREAT WAR AND POLITICAL CRISIS, 1914–1921

CHAPTER 2

The Industry at War, 1914–1916

The First World War was also the first war in which the military outcome was shaped not simply by national wealth but by the ability to mobilize the generality of the nation's resources: manpower and overseas investments, engineering and shipbuilding industries, food supplies and coal reserves. In the case of the last of these, its strategic significance was obvious to the most casual observer. Coal, in Lloyd George's phrase, was 'everything for us', the country's life and blood, its 'international coinage'.[1] Coal accounted for virtually all Europe's fuel supplies, and Britain's mining industry was crucial for the effectiveness of the Navy, the war potential of the Allies, the home transport system, the morale of the civilian population, the output of the munitions industries, and the supply of TNT and a wide range of strategic products.

The history of the coal industry in wartime is largely the history of an evolving national policy, rooted in the tensions which characterized the industry's adaptation to abnormal market forces and opportunities. The economic and social performance of the industry (summarized in Table 2.1) was shaped less by any organizational or technical changes than by the effects of the chronology and needs of the conflict on its manpower, costs, and prices, and by the interaction between national necessities and private and sectional opportunities. Many of the new policies and structures were, of course, concerned with a possible shortage of output, and were therefore directed towards the sustaining of production. But until 1918, although production sagged, the diminution of the industry's output never posed a really substantial threat to the war effort. The sheer abundance of Britain's prewar output and its huge exports provided effective buffers against the threat of serious and widespread shortages. As a result, there was never really any very great pressure to amend the organization or technology of the industry—a point of considerable contrast with the experience of the Second World War.[2]

[1] Speech to coal-industry conference, 29 July 1915, reprinted in Lloyd George 1915, 178–9.
[2] Below, ch. 11, sect. vi; ch. 12, sect. ii.

Table 2.1. *Output, sales, employment and wages in British coalmining 1913–1918*

	(i) Tonnage raised	(ii) Exports and bunkers	(iii) Average selling value at pit (per ton)		(iv) Profit and Royalties	(v) Profits[a] (per ton)		(vi) Costs per ton Wages		(vi) Total[b]		(vii) Persons employed	(viii) Output per employee	(ix) Wages Per person per year	(x) As % of 1909–13
	m. tons	m. tons	s.	d.	£ m.	s.	d.	s.	d.	s.	d.	000	tons	£	
1909–13	269.6	88.3	8	$8\frac{3}{4}$		0	$11\frac{1}{2}$	5	$5\frac{3}{4}$	7	$9\frac{1}{4}$	1,048	215	—	100.0
1913	287.4	98.3	10	$1\frac{1}{2}$	28.0	1	6	6	4	8	$7\frac{1}{2}$	1,106	260	82	108.5
1914	265.7	81.0	9	$11\frac{3}{4}$	21.5	1	2	6	$2\frac{3}{4}$	8	$9\frac{3}{4}$	1,037	253	79	106.5
1915	253.2	60.0	12	$5\frac{1}{2}$	27.4	1	$8\frac{1}{4}$	7	$9\frac{1}{2}$	10	$9\frac{1}{4}$	936	271	105	127.2
1916	256.4	55.0	15	$7\frac{1}{4}$	43.8	2	$11\frac{1}{4}$	9	9	12	8	981	261	127	145.3
1917	248.5	48.7	16	$8\frac{3}{4}$	33.7	2	$2\frac{3}{4}$	10	$5\frac{1}{4}$	14	6	1,002	248	129	174.4
1918	227.7	43.4	22	$4\frac{1}{4}$	35.5	2	$2\frac{1}{4}$	13	$3\frac{1}{2}$	18	$1\frac{3}{4}$	991	230	159	206.0

[a] Excluding royalties.
[b] Including royalties.

Sources:

(i), (iii), (iv), and (vi): *CYB* 1932, 598.

(ii): POWE 26/14.

(v) and (ix): R. A. S. Redmayne, *The British Coal-Mining Industry During the War* (1923), 284.

(vii), (viii), and (x): *CYB* 1931, 631.

For the same reason, it is possible to examine the industry's experience in 1914–18 primarily in terms of the responses of capital and labour to the violent changes in monetary values brought about by the War, and of the evolution of government policy and responsibilities which resulted. Essentially, the War was the beginning of that prolonged experience of industrial politics which was to shape the history of coal-mining for another two generations.

The wartime history of the coal industry can be divided into two phases. During the first of these, *laissez-faire* slowly gave way to *ad hoc* government intervention, which culminated in the state's assumption of control of the South Wales coalfield in December 1916, and of all the nation's coalmines some three months later. During the second period, the industry's history reflected the consequences of that control and the evolving responses of interest groups to the approximation to 'total war'. These two phases form the subject-matter of this and the next chapter, respectively.

Of course, no institutional change is new in every respect. Although the First World War 'nationalized' the question of coal output and finances, the industry's hours, wages, industrial relations, and working conditions had been matters of public concern and official intervention well before the outbreak of hostilities. After August 1914 that intervention assumed a new urgency and significance because the War introduced new pressures—strategic shortages, the disruption of established patterns of demand, the loss of a high proportion of the industry's skilled manpower. The state could not ignore the determinants of output and distribution, labour supply and productivity, prices and profits. Above all, the political economy of the coal industry in wartime was determined by problems of demand and supply on the one hand, and labour performance and reward on the other. The first two sections of this chapter discuss the shortages of coal in 1914–16 and the growth of intervention in the coal trade at home and abroad which resulted from those shortages. The later sections consider the problems of production, manpower, and industrial supply which lay at the root of the industry's wartime difficulties.

i. Demand and supply: the erosion of *laissez-faire*

The variety of Britain's coalfields—the fact that they produced different types of product, catered to different markets, and were served by different transport systems—meant that the initial upheaval of war was not uniformly experienced throughout the country's mining areas. Thus, those districts which supplied the domestic and civilian market were little affected in the first few months, except in so far as the temporary dislocation of economic relationships or fears about a possible depression produced a momentary fall in sales.

This happened in some parts of South Wales, where pits supplying manufacturing industry went on to a three-day week for a few months—although other Welsh pits, which produced high-quality steam coal, were pressed by the Admiralty to increase output and even to work on Sundays.[1] But the most severe disruption occurred in Scotland and Northumberland, which had previously carried on an extensive export trade to northern and central Europe. Indeed, the loss of German and Austro-Hungarian markets, the invasion of Belgium, and the effective closing of the Baltic (and therefore the Russian market) reduced the export demand for British coal by some 18 million tons, or about 25 per cent of the 1913 level. Northumberland in particular, which had exported 80 per cent of its output, much of it to Russia, Germany, and Belgium, had an inauspicious start to the War: sales and prices tumbled, and dragged down wage rates (by about three per cent in August–October 1914) through the operation of sliding-scale agreements. Depression and short-time working reduced earnings even more and the county's mines lost a large number of men to the army or to more regular, better paid, and more attractive work in the munitions factories of nearby Elswick.[2]

In this respect, then, important parts of the coal industry suffered from the initial commercial disruptions which misled many contemporaries about the economic consequences of modern warfare. And it was significant that the Miners' Federation of Great Britain played a prominent and occasionally dominating part in the formation and leadership of the War Emergency Workers' National Committee, which was formed in August 1914 to press for policies to 'arrest existing distress, and prevent as far as possible further distress, and unemployment in the future'. But such fears were groundless. The economic problem in general as well as within the coal industry was one of shortage not surplus. Hence, although miners had been active as donors

---

[1] *CMOC* Q 3189; below, 57.

[2] *CMOC*, I, 10; *CMOC* QQ 60, 4334; *ARSM* 1923, Table 30 and *ARSM* 1931, Table 29; *CG* 1 Jan. 1915, 28. The sales of Northumberland coal revived in early 1915 with the growth of French demand. West Yorkshire, which had exported something over 25% of its output to north-west Europe, also experienced a temporary war-induced depression in late 1914: *CMOC* QQ 3710 ff.

and recipients of relief funds (30 Northumberland pits were getting £1,000 weekly in October 1914), by early 1915 they were embarrassed by the accumulation of money when so little relief was needed.[1]

The apprehensions about coal in the autumn of 1914 were misplaced in large part because the War was to be fought over some of the principal coalfields of continental Europe: Silesia and Galicia in the East; the Liège, Charleroi, and Mons basins in Belgium; the Nord and Pas-de-Calais in France. By the early months of 1915 Germany's exports had dried up; France had lost half her mines and was effectively dependent on British coal; neutral nations were desperate for supplies; and even the domestic economy had begun to experience shortages.[2] More than this, the War generated newly intense needs—not merely for the domestic war effort but also for Britain's international role as a belligerent. In South Wales, for example, where the Navy had purchased about 1.5 million tons for the predominantly coal-fired Fleet before the War, such demands were running at an annual rate of 15 million tons (almost 25 per cent of the district's output) by the spring of 1915, and were to be buoyed up by the Admiralty's role as purchasing agent for the War Office's expeditionary force, the allied navies, the French, Italian, and Egyptian state railways, and the United States armed services in Europe from 1917.[3]

In spite of the example of the Admiralty, however, it is important to emphasize that the problems of coal supply which began to loom in the first spring of the War were primarily posed not by a dramatic increase in total demand above the existing capacity of the industry, but by a shift in the pattern of demand and a marginal decline in output. Indeed, had the industry been able to continue producing at the level of 1913, and distributing its product with equal efficiency, essential wartime needs would have been met with relative ease. As Table 2.1 indicates, over the war years as a whole, annual output fell by about 12 per cent until the crisis year of 1918, when it declined by a further 10 per cent. The nature of the transition from peace to war, however, is better illustrated by a comparison of the twelve-month periods ending July 1914 and 1915, when total output fell from 281.1 to 250.4 million tons and exports (including foreign bunkers) from 97.3 to 61.4 million tons. Put another

---

[1] Harrison 1971, 225; *MFGB* 1914, Executive Committee, 27 and 28 Oct. 1914; *CG* 19 Feb. 1915, 389.

[2] *CG* 1 Jan. 1915, 28; POWE 16/176.

[3] *CG* 19 Feb. 1915, 390; *Sankey Evidence* I, QQ 17ff., 1845, 1824ff., 1882, 3288ff.; POWE 16/176.

way, the decline in direct sales to foreigners 'freed' some 36 million tons, but the output of British pits fell by almost 31 million tons and the Services' demand grew by significantly more than the difference.

The decline in coal production to what appeared to be a potentially dangerously low level was to be a principal preoccupation of the industry and the government for most of the rest of the War. But its proximate cause was never in doubt: a very large proportion of the work-force in an industry which was notoriously labour-intensive had joined the army. By 27 February 1915 some 18 per cent of the miners of August 1914 had left the industry, although new recruitment to the pits reduced this figure to a net loss of 13.5 per cent. In the first year of the War roughly 250,000 miners had enlisted, representing over one-fifth of the original work-force. And this drain of manpower was the more serious in that those who flocked into the Army under the influence of patriotism, youthful adventurousness, temporary unemployment, or aversion to industrial conditions, were obviously drawn from the youngest, physically fittest, and most productive of the mining community: about 40 per cent of all miners aged between 19 and 38 enlisted in the first seven months of the War. Even when they were replaced (the net loss in the first year was 16 per cent), it was on the whole by less fit and less productive workers.[1]

The harmful consequences of this loss of manpower were mitigated by organizational adjustments: the work-force was concentrated in more productive work-places and seams, miners were persuaded to work on conventional holidays and rest days, exploratory work was curtailed. As a result, although there was an accumulation of arrears of repair and development work, the output of coal fell by less than the number of miners (roughly 11 per cent as against 16 per cent in the first year of the War).[2] Yet the fact remained that the general situation with regard to coal supplies did deteriorate during the winter of 1914–15: supplies could not meet needs. The problem was not solely a matter of manpower shortages and deficient output; it also reflected the disruption of transport systems. Shortages of coastal shipping (the Admiralty commandeered 80 per cent of the colliers normally used to ship coal between the North-East and the South) and the threat of sea warfare

---

[1] CMOC I, 6–8; II, 309. Northumberland and Fife, the coal-producing counties most affected by economic dislocation in 1914, had the highest levels of miners' enlistment—about 24% by Feb. 1915, compared with less than 15% in the Midlands fields, which supplied the more stable domestic market.

[2] CMOC Evidence, passim; CMOC I, 9; II, 309–10. Also see Report of the Departmental Committee on the Coal Trade after the War in PP 1918 XIII, 6–7; CG 12 May 1916, 903.

impeded trade and pushed up freight rates. As a result, the specialist coal from Durham and Northumberland, normally shipped by sea to the gas, electrical, and industrial undertakings of London and the South-East, crowded on to the railways and sharply reduced the capacity available to transport Midlands coal to domestic consumers. Very soon, the railways became severely congested (it took up to six weeks for coal wagons to make the round trip between Yorkshire and London) and the potential wastefulness of the uncoordinated private ownership and management of wagons became obvious.[1]

Given this situation, it was not surprising that the first serious wartime crisis of coal supply affected London consumers rather than the armed services or the munitions industries. The price of coal in the South-East rose sharply from late 1914, and by mid-February 1915 'Best Derbyshire' coal was more than 40 per cent above the level of June 1914. This increase in costs was most sensitively felt by relatively poor consumers, for whom poverty and the lack of storage facilities meant a dependence on the purchase of coal in small amounts at premium prices from 'trolleymen'. More than this, they used coal for cooking as well as heating, and therefore bought the best and most expensive fuel 'because the poor man's fire has to serve all purposes'.[2]

The rise in coal prices was part of a more general inflation (the cost of living rose 20 per cent in the first five months of the War), and political pressure ultimately obliged a reluctant government to take some action—although not before inept parliamentary performances by the President of the Board of Trade and the Prime Minister (whose brief underestimated the increase in the price of coal by 50 per cent) had provoked even their supporters.[3] In the country at large the War Emergency Workers' National Committee (with the miners' union President, Robert Smillie, in the chair) held a series of meetings demanding government control of the price and distribution of coal; and the Miners' Federation of Great Britain began to press for a 20 per cent wage increase to compensate for higher living costs and to protest at the 'shamefully high prices' of coal.[4] Meanwhile, industrialists and, even more critically, gas and electricity undertakings (which had statutory obligations to provide energy, but no guarantee of their

[1] DCRPC passim; CG 19 Feb. 1915, 390; 29 Jan. 1915, 233; and 26 Feb. 1915, 47.
[2] DCRPC 3, 11.
[3] There were Commons Debates on 'the rise in the price of the necessities of life' on 11 and 17 Feb. 1915. Also see CG 19 Feb. 1915, 389.
[4] CG 26 Feb. 1915, 446; 19 Mar. 1915, 611–12.

principal raw material) were also beginning to complain about the rising cost of fuel. There were even demands for the suspension of the Eight Hours Act of 1908, or at least for state intervention in the transport of coal and restrictions on the recruitment of miners into the Army and on exports.[1]

All these pressures finally elicited an official response at the end of February 1915. On 23 February the Home Secretary, Reginald McKenna, appointed a departmental committee on coalmining organization, and two days later the President of the Board of Trade, Walter Runciman, appointed another on the retail price of coal. As their terms of reference and membership indicate, these two bodies—the hesitant beginnings of state control—had different, if related, purposes.

The Coal Mining Organisation Committee was, in effect, an industrial advisory body.[2] It consisted of six men from the industry (with equal representation of the Mining Association and the Miners' Federation) under the chairmanship of the Chief Inspector of Mines, Sir Richard Redmayne. It was charged with examining the

conditions prevailing in the coal mining industry with a view to promoting such organisation of work and such cooperation between employers and workmen as having regard to the large number of miners who are enlisting for naval or military service, will secure the necessary production of coal during the war.

In the event, the CMOC was entirely dependent on the voluntary cooperation of those engaged in the industry. This was exemplified by the fact that the union successfully refused to participate until the government had formally acknowledged that the Committee was precluded from considering the Eight Hours Act and had deleted from the original terms of reference any reference to the need to facilitate enlistment (which the MFGB interpreted as a slur on the miners and a device to encourage further recruitment).[3]

The Board of Trade's Committee, on the other hand, had a more

---

[1] *CG* 29 Jan. 1915, 233; 5 Mar. 1915, 495. The owners did not believe that the miners would work longer hours even if the Act were suspended, and the miners were furiously opposed to the proposal: *MAGB* 1915, 30–1; *MFGB* 1915, Executive Committee, 2 Feb. 1915.

[2] The Committee's various Reports and Minutes of Evidence are in *PP* 1914–16 XXVIII and 1916 VI. They were published as Cd. 7939, 8009, 8147, and 8345.

[3] *CG* 26 Feb. 1915, 445; *MFGB* 1915, Executive Committee and Special Conference, 25 Feb. 1915; *Hansard* 1 Mar. 1915, col. 551.

traditional political function.[1] It was appointed to 'inquire into the causes of the present rise in the retail price of coal sold for domestic use, especially to the poorer classes of consumers in London and other centres'; and its non-industrial membership reflected its prime concern with general policy and civilian morale. (It was, indeed, condemned by the *Colliery Guardian* on the grounds that not one of its members 'has the remotest knowledge of the coal trade in its practical aspects'.)[2] In the event, however, the retail price committee, while confirming general criticisms of the inadequacies of transport arrangements and the possibility of collusion among coal merchants, was obliged to consider a much wider range of problems than London's household fuel supplies. Even so, its actual proposals were relatively innocuous. (It assumed that prices could not be fixed, and advocated the restriction of exports to neutral countries and the improvement of transport and storage systems.)[3]

Hurried and imperfect as its work may have been, however, the Committee contributed to an important change in the political presuppositions, for it raised questions of control and the national interest which were to be of the utmost general significance in wartime economic policy. For example, it argued that 'only by measures taking account of the coal industry as a whole can relief be brought to the domestic consumer'; that the conduct of a great industry like coal-mining 'cannot be safely left in a time of crisis to the working of an unregulated system of supply and demand'; and that if high prices continued the government would be justified 'in considering a scheme for assuming control of the output of the collieries of the United Kingdom.'

In the spring of 1915, however, the starting-point for any coal policy had to be on the side of production. As a result, the Coal Mining Organisation Committee emerged as the crucial body—a standing committee to which were referred the report of the committee on retail prices, the question of price controls, the organization of industrial conferences, and the attempts to reduce absenteeism and increase labour productivity. The CMOC's own initial inquiries soon confirmed that the core of the industry's problems lay with the shortage of manpower and the loss of miners to the armed services.

[1] The Report and minutes of evidence of the committee are in *PP* 1914-16 XXIX. They were published in 1915 as Cd. 7866 and 7923.
[2] *CG* 9 Apr. 1915, 762.
[3] See the severe criticisms in *CG* 9 Apr. 1915, 761-2.

On the other hand, the Committee's composition meant that it had to avoid proposals which might seem sensitive or provocative as far as the miners' union was concerned (these included the length of the working day underground, the lowering of the age at which boys could work below ground, the use of women in surface jobs, or the possible links between absenteeism and drink). As a result of its assumption that 'the cordial cooperation of workmen and employers' was a prerequisite of any effective policy, the Committee's discussion of specific remedies was hedged and conditional: absenteeism was to be left to exhortations by union representatives; any reduction in the number of holidays or traditional stop days was a matter not for official action, but for formal discussion 'through the proper and recognized channels of negotiation'; there was no scope for an increase in daily hours of work; owners were urged to cooperate with the MFGB in its opposition to non-unionists. Even on the question of organization—the ostensible reason for the Committee's appointment—the report was not particularly elaborate: there was some scope for time-saving in haulage and attention might be paid to the concentration of work, although witnesses had been pessimistic about such efforts, especially if they depended on the movement of miners between districts.[1]

Although the Coal Mining Organisation Committee thus appeared to place more emphasis on exhortations to harmony than on determined administrative action, it could be said to be eminently realistic. There was no immediate crisis of supply and the coal industry was not (nor, indeed, ever would be) one which could be administered in opposition to the wishes of the labour force. Even when, later in the War, the problems of coal supply were aggravated and government control introduced, not much more could be done about production (as distinct from the regulation of prices, transport, exports, and finance) than had been envisaged by the CMOC in the innocent spring of 1915.

ii. The control of marketing

Although the importance of production was widely appreciated, the shortages and high prices of coal in 1915 were in the first instance inter-

[1] In addition to the CMOC's reports, see the Minutes of Evidence, QQ 717–18, 1194, 1198, 2317–18, 3357, 3362, 3453, 5597, 5868. For other confirmations of the inutility of an increase in hours and of the miners' tendency to 'cling with extraordinary tenacity' to their communities and even to their familiar coal seams, see Runciman to the Cabinet Committee on War Policy, 19 Aug. 1915 (Asquith Papers, 119/110) and CG 13 Aug. 1915, 327 ('Robbing the Pits'). Cf. the similar experiences of the Ministry of Fuel and Power in the Second World War: below, 547–8.

preted as the result of the characteristics of the coal trade. Government intervention and structural changes were therefore confined to the control of exports, trading margins, the allocation of supplies to British consumers, and the limitation of price margins. And since these were areas of economic activity where the Board of Trade had prime responsibility, the traditional responsibility of the Home Office for the industry (rooted in its prewar control of safety standards, and logically extended to the affairs of the Coal Mining Organisation Committee) was now rivalled by another department of state. More than this, the growing importance of the economic significance of coalmining, and of state intervention in its commercial aspects, gave the Board of Trade a role which could only grow. By the postwar years, it was to become the department with overriding responsibility for the industry.

Shortages of coal in Britain could obviously be alleviated by a reduction in exports. Yet it would have been quite unrealistic to envisage a complete prohibition on overseas sales. Indeed, such sales were as much a part of the war effort as the direct provision of fuel for armaments manufacture. On the one hand, the military strength of both of France and Italy (the latter declared war on Austria and Hungary in May 1915) were dependent on British supplies.[1] On the other, exports to neutral countries not merely kept freight rates low for essential imports, but also helped generate the purchasing (and the political bargaining) power needed to acquire food and raw materials for Britain's own war effort.[2] Nevertheless, the insistent problem of allocation as between home and overseas markets could not be left to market mechanisms, and the need to limit, yet manage, exports could have only one outcome.

On 5 May 1915 the unrestricted export of coal, other than to British possessions and allied countries, was prohibited except under licence. And in August, control was extended to allied customers.[3] By that time licensing was the more important in that the introduction of price control over home sales created a huge differential between home and export prices—before the end of the War there was a fourfold difference—which would soon have denuded the British market of fuel had not the government restrained overseas sales.[4] Licenses were issued by a

[1] France had purchased half her prewar imports of 20 million tons from Belgium and Germany. These supplies, and much of her own productive capacity, were now denied to her. French import needs were estimated at 26 million tons in 1916; POWE 16/176.

[2] CMOC QQ 3385, 3389, 6118, 6203.

[3] See POWE 16/176, which describes the regulation of distribution and prices until the autumn of 1916.

[4] Redmayne 1923, 263. For price control, see below, 54-5.

coal export advisory committee, which was linked to the Coal Mining Organisation Committee through the Chairmanship of Sir Richard Redmayne.

The Committee appeared to have the desired effect: private exports and domestic prices were reduced.[1] But state intervention in the maritime coal trade could not stop there. Early in 1916 France and Italy began to complain about high freight rates and coal prices. As a result, the Board of Trade successfully urged British shippers and coalowners to coordinate their activities and limit their charges and prices. By May 1916 a more or less complete system for the regulation of exports had been brought into existence. War needs meant that such regulation had to achieve more than a mere curtailment of sales. Exports were bound to decline as priorities changed. (Exports and foreign bunkers amounted to 12.4 million tons in the first three months of 1917, compared with 23.4 million in the first three months of 1914.) But the realization that there was such a thing as 'coal power'—not merely to enable the War to be fought in a direct fashion, but also to maintain Britain's hold over neutral States—obliged the government to pay considerable attention to the needs of overseas markets for the rest of the War.[2]

The domestic coal trade was made the object of a similar, even more extreme intervention, which stemmed from the political anxieties about the price of coal in February 1915.[3] On 22 April the President of the Board of Trade, Walter Runciman, warned leading coalowners of the unrest among consumers (especially those in London, 'who had considerable influence on the sentiments and feelings of the House of Commons') and appealed for 'some reassuring statements' about prices.[4] But, although the owners expressed a wish to cooperate, Runciman was soon driven to the conclusion that a more drastic policy was necessary, and in June he consulted the Coal Mining Organisation Committee on the desirability of controlling the price of coal.

After the CMOC report (submitted on 8 July 1915), price-control legislation was introduced. The pithead price of coal for British consumption, other than for Admiralty sales, was not to be more than 4s. per ton higher than the price for the same type of coal sold in similar amounts at a corresponding date in the year ended 30 June 1914.

[1] Exports in Jan.–June 1914, 1915, and 1916 were 36.4, 23.6, and 20.1 million tons (POWE 16/176). For the beneficial effects on domestic supplies and prices, see CG 6 Aug. 1915, 284 and Runciman Papers, WR 147 (15 Sept. 1915).

[2] CAB 37/49/25 (10 June 1916).

[3] See POWE 16/176.

[4] MAGB 1916, 14.

Although they complained at being singled out from other industries, the coalowners put up little political resistance and the Coal Price (Limitation) Act became law on 29 July 1915.[1] In fact, the 'standard' margin of 4s. was a generous average, since industry-wide unit costs, including a wages bonus and higher overheads on a smaller output, had risen by only 3s. But fine discrimination was thought to be impossible and the extra margin was designed to cover the position of the worst-placed enterprises and prevent pit closures. In the spring and summer of 1915 the Board of Trade also negotiated voluntary agreements with London wholesale merchants and coal factors in an attempt to restrain distribution margins.[2]

The question of coal prices which had led to the flurry of government activity in the first half of 1915 reflected both a 'real' problem and a problem of morale and politics. In the autumn of the same year, a similar range of issues returned to the surface—this time in response to a hardening of miners' attitudes towards their employers. In September–November a Cabinet Committee on 'Industrial Control' considered a range of interventionist policies for coal, even extending to the direct control of production, with the object (in Redmayne's words) of removing 'the sources of unrest amongst the miners from the belief that large profits are being made by the owners'.

This was in many respects an anticipation of the forces which were to lead to the imposition of government control of production in December 1916. For even though (as was pointed out by a tart Board of Trade memorandum) the economic objectives of control might easily be attained by less 'heroic' measures, the problem of industrial relations was central to the discussions of autumn 1915. Some officials even contemplated the take-over of the South Wales field, or at least of the 28 collieries on the Admiralty List since they were concentrated in the Rhondda and neighbouring valleys, 'which have proved the storm centre of recent troubles'. So serious were the discussions that the Monmouthshire and South Wales Coal Owners' Association proposed

---

[1] The Coal Mining Organisation Committee's report and the subsequent Act are reproduced in Redmayne 1923. The legislation was discussed by the Mining Association of Great Britain on 8, 12, and 14 July (*MAGB* 1916). The Liberal MP and maverick coalowner Sir Arthur Markham had proposed price limitation at the pithead as early as Feb., and was given credit for this by Runciman in the House of Commons on 8 June.

[2] Some 300 local authorities were urged to secure similar agreements, and although only 67 managed to do so, they included some of the largest cities (Edinburgh, Glasgow, Leeds, Manchester, Sheffield, and Swansea): Runciman Papers, WR 147 ('Regulation of Retail Coal Prices', c.Oct. 1915).

a form of control (by the industry itself) to satisfy domestic demands and administer exports.[1]

In the event, there was no immediate experiment with drastic forms of intervention. Yet the economic problems of the industry still awaited solution. The mounting tempo of war production in 1915–16 placed strains on the mechanisms of market allocation, and led the *Colliery Guardian* to advocate a form of managed distribution.[2] As the tide of complaints from manufacturers and public utilities rose, government departments (the Board of Trade, the Home Office, and the Ministry of Munitions) cooperated, in January and February 1916, to create a network of district committees of coalowners to ease and coordinate coal distribution. The owners were reluctant to share their authority with other groups, but government departments retained ultimate control and the system worked fairly well, in that customers' needs were identified, adjudicated, and satisfied.[3] In contrast, the official attempt to coordinate the means of transport was much less successful.

Coal was shipped by rail with the aid of some 600,000 private coal wagons, access to which was jealously guarded by their owners (many of them coalowners). The constant sorting and empty journeys led, in Redmayne's words, to 'a considerable squandering of power and labour', and even the *Colliery Guardian* was moved to condemn the system as 'inadequate and wasteful'. Nevertheless, official efforts to interpose central administrative control of the use of wagons were greeted with a 'storm of opposition' and the MAGB blocked every effort to rationalize the physical side of coal distribution. Its Chairman's preference for 'leaving well alone' won the day: in 1916 the railway department of the Board of Trade 'concluded that it was not advisable to proceed further in this direction'.[4]

The lack of success in relation to the pooling of private wagons was, however, an exception to the general effectiveness of government intervention in the pricing and distribution of coal in the first two years of the War. An advisory and semi-executive body (the Coal Mining Organisation Committee) had been created; a network of committees allocated domestic supplies and controlled exports; legislation restrained domestic pithead prices; informal but effective agreements limited distribution margins. Even so, as had been shown by the committee

[1] Runciman Papers, WR 147 (Sept.–Nov. 1915).
[2] *CG* 20 Aug. 1915, 377–8.
[3] POWE 16/166; POWE 16/176; Redmayne 1923, 36–8; *CMOC* II, 477–8; *MAGB* 1916, 32 ff.
[4] *CMOC* II, 477–8; *CG* 21 Jan. 1916, 125; *MAGB* 1916, 27–32.

inquiries of the spring of 1915 and the discussions of industrial control in the autumn, the essential problems of coal supply originated in the mines themselves. The most enduringly important aspect of the industry's wartime history therefore concerned production and manpower.

iii. Manpower and production

Although the principal policy departures of 1915–16 concerned the coal trade, the question of its supply was constantly in the background. 'If you have not got the coal to meet the demand', the Chairman of the Coal Mining Organisation Committee told a conference of owners and miners in September 1915, 'it does not matter what the price is.'[1] And behind the question of supply lay the size of the effective labour force and the loss of manpower which had drained the industry of some of its best workers in the first year of the War. The resulting discussion of the length of the working day or the increased employment of boys and women proved inconclusive, and relatively little good resulted from attempts to concentrate work-places or recruit Belgium refugees and expatriate British miners.[2] Somewhat larger benefits flowed from appeals to miners to work during their traditional holidays (one such appeal from the War Office and Lord Kitchener led to voluntary restriction of the Easter and Whitsun breaks in 1915 in England, and in Scotland the July holiday was almost eliminated). But the limitation of holidays was a short-term and modest device, precariously dependent on miners' goodwill, and not always successful.[3]

As was to be the case in the Second World War, given the shortage of men, the pervasive controversial issue with respect to labour supply was 'voluntary' or 'avoidable' absenteeism—the absence from work beyond the 5 per cent of miners who were assumed, on average, to be unable to attend for any particular shift because of illness or injury. (Absenteeism

---

[1] *Miners' Federation of Great Britain. Coal Mining Organisation . . . 2 September 1915. Conference . . . on Matters arising out of the Report of the Coal Mining Committee* (NRO 759/28), 5.

[2] CMOC III, 477.

[3] Lanarkshire miners agreed to work an eleven-day fortnight instead of a five-day week. *CMOC* I, 18; *CMOC* II, 310; *CMOC* III, 476; *MFGB* 1916, Executive Committee, 18 Mar. 1915. In South Wales, miners insisted on a two-day holiday at Easter and a three-day holiday at Whitsun in 1915, although in Aug. 1916 (having originally resisted official appeals and the offer of a bonus of 6s. per shift) South Wales miners acceded to the appeal of Admiralty and union representatives in a secret session, and postponed all summer holidays. *The Times* 31 May 1915, 8b; *CG* 4 Aug. 1916, 225; 11 Aug. 1916, 272.

was the number of manshifts not worked expressed as a percentage of manshifts possible.) In fact, considered generally, absenteeism was not a 'problem' in the sense that it grew appreciably worse. Indeed, in the early years of the War it fell slightly, from about 10 or 11 per cent in peacetime to just over 9 per cent in 1916—a significant achievement in view of the increase in the average age of the labour force and the rise in shift wages.[1]

Nevertheless, absenteeism in wartime remained an unpalatable fact for many observers. And it was the more so because the national averages masked great variation: hewers and haulage workers, on whose efforts output critically depended, were much more likely to be absent; there were sharp contrasts in district rates (Lancashire, for example, experienced twice the absenteeism of Durham); and on particular days (Mondays and the day after pay day) absenteeism might shoot up to 20 or 30 per cent.[2] The worst examples were obviously not representative, but, particularly in the early stages of the War, they were bound to excite not merely the gentle exhortations of Asquith, appealing for 'regularity of attendance' as an emblem of patriotism, but more vigorous criticism from those prepared to pillory the miners for being 'content to let others fight their battles' while they pursued 'leisure, treasure and pleasure'.[3] Not surprisingly, the miners vehemently resented the accusation of general absenteeism or slacking, and in July 1915 their union President, Robert Smillie, refused to make a public appeal for harder work on the grounds that 'the mining community worked excessively hard as it is'.[4]

In practice, of course, the issue of absenteeism and the associated question of the rhythm and control of work patterns were complex and subtle. The deliberations of the Coal Mining Organisation Committee showed an awareness of their complexity, as well as of their political sensitivity. Coalmining was simply not an occupation in which intense efforts could be continuously expended. Before mechanization it could be a cripplingly fatiguing task. There was in any case an extremely powerful social inertia surrounding traditional rest days, and owners and managers were frequently sympathetic not simply to the physical demands of mining or the touchiness of miners, but to the distinctive

---

[1] POWE 16/176.
[2] CMOC I, 11; CMOC II, 310; CMOC III, 11-13.
[3] CG 19 Feb. 1915, 391-2; 19 Mar. 1915, 603; 23 Apr. 1915, 865, 876-7.
[4] CG 6 Aug. 1915, 268. In Mar. 1915 Aberdare miners threatened to strike if the Chairman of Powell Duffryn repeated his allegations of absenteeism: CG 26 Mar. 1915, 666.

and inflexible characteristics of mining communities that would need to be reversed if the traditions of leisure preference were to be abandoned, even in the face of a World War. Recreation was of enormous importance to mining communities, so that work as well as leisure incurred opportunity costs. In the Lancashire phrase, 'a pennyworth of ease is worth a penny'.[1]

Considered unemotionally, three main points stand out in relation to absenteeism. First, the essence of the problem lay not with the generality of miners but with a comparatively small number of habitual offenders, whose absence seriously affected the work of many more men. It followed that it might be difficult, or at least very costly, to reduce absenteeism by offering financial incentives, since any bonus for regular attendance would also have to go to those who were already working continuously. In any case, the absentee already had a financial incentive to amend his behaviour: he lost pay by not working. Second, therefore, voluntary absenteeism was much more a political than an economic problem, and its solution could only have been found in an alteration of miners' attitudes—either towards the companies which employed them or towards the urgency of the country's war needs. Certainly, neither the miners nor many politicians nor the public at large had grasped the true seriousness of the War even by the summer of 1915.[2]

The third aspect of the problem illustrated another layer of meaning to the term 'political'. In any appeal to the miners the role of the union and its leadership was indispensable. For, however much other miners might criticize absentees, they were unwilling to expose them to attack from outside the industry, or amend in any significant way the autonomy of the worker with respect to his attendance at the pit. The Coal Mining Organisation Committee was therefore constrained to agree with the MFGB President that exhortation was not even a matter for joint action, but would have to be 'left to the miners' side when they were convinced that the matter of absenteeism was capable of improvement'.[3]

Given the initial loss of men, therefore, there were no easy remedies for labour supply problems in the industry. And given the nature of the

---

[1] CMOC QQ 440, 1036–7, 2311. The Lancashire aphorism was quoted by the mining agent of Chatterley–Whitfield Collieries: Q 4312.

[2] CMOC QQ 2075, 3221 ff. (Evidence of Hugh Bramwell, General Manager of Great Western Collieries and Chairman of the Monmouthshire & South Wales Coal Owners' Association); E. S. Montagu to H. A. Asquith, 3 July 1915, Asquith Papers 83/98.

[3] CMOC QQ 2317–18; CMOC I, 17.

industry's organization and industrial relations, any realistic labour policy had to be based on voluntarism, exhortation, and union initiative. Within broad limits, the work process was, in the last resort, controlled by the labour force.

Officialdom could do little more than dramatize the issues. This was done largely through public gestures and emotional appeals of the sort most theatrically exemplified in July 1915, when 2,500 miners, owners, and managers were assembled in the London Opera House in 'one of the most remarkable gatherings in the industrial history of the United Kingdom'.[1] Even so, the conference had had to be postponed because of the alarming deterioration of industrial relations in South Wales, while the miners' union only agreed to cooperate on condition that controversy was avoided. The ritualistic nature of such events was made the more apparent by the official briefing to government ministers: in their analyses of the industry's problems, they were to avoid any mention of drink, wages, prices, profits, mining organization, or the eight-hour day.[2]

The July meeting was, ostensibly, a propaganda success, with a characteristically engaging and inspiring performance from David Lloyd George, expressions of profound cooperation from the union's leadership, and a culmination marked by 'loud and prolonged cheers and the singing of the national anthem'.[3] But the actual results were to confirm the existence of powerful obstacles to change. In September, the Coal Mining Organisation Committee called a meeting of representatives of the MAGB and the MFGB to consider the length of the working day, absenteeism, holidays and rest days—only to find that the union leaders were still adamantly opposed to any change in hours (Smillie said that the MFGB would oppose an increase in a particular district even if the local miners wished it) and reluctant to make any strong statements about absenteeism. For their part, the owners were extremely sensitive to the political as well as practical disadvantages of trying to secure an increase in the length of the working day. They doubted if more output would result and were in any case anxious to avoid the impression (in the *Colliery Guardian*'s words) that the miners were 'in the bondage of their plutocratic employers'.[4]

---

[1] *CG* 6 Aug. 1915, 267.

[2] *The Times* 1 July 1915, 9f; *CG* 25 June 1915, 1333; MUN 5/79/341/11; Arnot 1975, 38; *MFGB* 1915, Executive Committee, 8 June 1915.

[3] *CG* 6 Aug. 1915, 267–8; *The Times* 30 July 1915, 8a. A quarter of a million copies of the transcript were distributed in the coalfields: *MFGB* 1915, Executive Committee, 21 July 1915.

[4] *Miners' Federation of Great Britain. Coal Mining Organisation ... 2 September 1915. Conference*

There was another strong thread running through the discussions of 1915–16: manpower losses arising from the enlistment of miners into the forces. Both the committees appointed in March 1915 had warned that the time might come when such recruitment might have to be discouraged. And in July the Home Secretary and the newly appointed Director-General of Recruiting (Lord Derby) agreed to 'bar' (from the pressure to enlist) all underground and strategic surface workers in the industry. In effect, active recruiting ceased and by the late summer men were being prevented from leaving the Admiralty pits. Further, when the Derby scheme for voluntary registration was introduced in late 1915 most miners were 'starred' as being in a reserved occupation, and local tribunals (supervised by the Coal Mining Organisation Committee) were established to decide if miners who had 'attested' themselves as willing to enlist, might be recruited.

The same principles were applied when the Military Service Act introduced conscription in 1916: the original tribunals were transformed into Colliery Recruiting Courts (thus giving their miner representatives a special status) and the more vital categories of pitmen were exempted from conscription.[1] Indeed, as the need for coal for strategic exports and the munitions industries mounted in 1916 so there arose a pressure to release miners from the Army for work in the mines. In June the Cabinet's War Committee both strengthened the controls over the allocation of coal and agreed in principle to release between 90,000 and 100,000 men—although the War Office continued to drag its feet on this highly sensitive subject, and the issue was still not resolved in September.[2]

In the opening years of the War, therefore, a general anxiety about the balance of supply and demand led to a wide variety of expedients being adopted. In addition to those already mentioned, Daylight Saving was adopted in 1916, an economy campaign was introduced (although it came to be appreciated that significant savings might only be attained with compulsion, which would be politically inadvisable), technical advice produced economies in the distribution of electrical energy (and therefore the use of coal), and Redmayne's concern to enlist the help of

. . . on Matters arising out of the Report of the Coal Mining Committee (NRO 759/28); MAGB 1916, 37–9; Asquith Papers, 119/110 (Report by Walter Runciman, 19 Aug. 1915); CG 19 Sept. 1915, 527.

[1] Redmayne 1923, 49–51; CAB 37/149/16 (8 June 1916); Asquith Papers, 119/108–16 (19 Sept. 1915). Volunteers for military tunnelling work continued to be called for.

[2] CAB 42/16/8, App. 101 (June and July 1916); CAB 37/149/16, 29 (8 and 13 June 1926); CAB 42/19/6 (12 Sept. 1916).

the miners with the problem of absenteeism led somewhat haltingly to the creation of fairly ineffective Pit Committees, 'to watch and deal with absenteeism'.[1] There was, however, no transformation of the industry's position, although the control of marketing and the marginal consequences of productive efforts fended off any severe difficulties. In fact, the real basis of crisis in the industry in these years came not from a threatened failure of 'normal' operations, but from the frictions and dislocations associated with the problems of wage determination and labour relations.

iv. Labour: wages and industrial relations

As has been seen, the complicated and hesitant construction of a new machinery of state intervention in the coal trade in 1915 and 1916 was associated with a number of undercurrents deriving from the problems of labour supply. Initially, these problems did not include any severe threat of labour unrest. As with industry in general, disputes seemed to fade away with the opening of hostilities. But the *Colliery Guardian's* anticipation of a future 'spirit of sweet reasonableness' was ill-founded.[2] Two strains in particular began to be felt. First, as has been seen, in 1913 the MFGB had stipulated that all district Conciliation Board agreements should be negotiated and agreed at the same time, and fixed 1 April 1915 as the date on which notice to terminate old agreements should be given—although it was only in South Wales that the negotiation of a new wage agreement provoked a major crisis of industrial relations.[3] But this crisis, which occurred in the summer of 1915, was preceded by a second, and more general, problem which was provoked by the rapid inflation of the first months of the War.

As prices rose (between July 1914 and 1 March 1915 food costs had increased by 24 per cent and working-class living costs by 20 per cent), so the industrial truce was disrupted by a widespread restlessness about the level of wages. In January and February 1915 industrial stoppages occurred in shipbuilding, engineering, jute manufacture, and on the railways. And on 23 February a delegate conference of miners urged a consideration of wages in relation to prices. Significantly, the MFGB Executive Committee formulated its claim—for a 20 per cent increase in

[1] Redmayne 1923, 77 ff.

[2] *CG* 1 Jan. 1915, 28; Redmayne 1923, 57; *CG* 21 Jan. 1915, 243 and 12 Feb. 1915, 343. The exception to the industrial truce of the first months of the War was a prolonged dispute in West Yorkshire.

[3] Below, 66–9.

national earnings—on 16 March, at the same meeting which considered the choice of witnesses at the Coal Mining Organisation Committee and delegates to the Treasury Conference which had been called by the government to secure the relaxation of restrictive practices and the use of arbitration in disputes. The various pressures of the War were converging, although the miners rapidly withdrew from the Treasury Conference in order to retain freedom of action on restrictive practices and use of the strike weapon. How far the War was transforming industrial relations was reflected in novel features of the miners' wage claim—which was national (rather than district based), related to total earnings (rather than basic rates), and based on the cost of living (rather than the price of coal).[1]

The national wage claim was spurned by the owners on the grounds that wages were matters for local negotiation. And, in spite of the government's initial slothfulness, the dispute was an irresistible stimulus to state intervention.[2] The MFGB leadership fended off a South Wales proposal to threaten strike action, but also pressed the government to act on the grounds that the miners would find it difficult to respond to appeals for more intensive effort if their demand for a national settlement were ignored. At a meeting under the Prime Minister's chairmanship on 26 April, the MFGB tried to calm the owners' fears that uniform wage movements would place less profitable areas, such as eastern Scotland and Northumberland, at a disadvantage. At the same time they reiterated that the claim would not be used as a precedent for national settlements in normal times, and warned Asquith and the owners that 'For some months now the leaders of the miners had been standing between them and taking a forward movement.' After a further inconclusive round of negotiations, and a further conference at which the leadership beat off another assault by the militant South Wales delegates, the MFGB agreed to accept the Prime Minister's arbitration in preference to an unthinkable national wartime strike, with problematic support.

The Prime Minister's decision, published on 5 May, bore out the forebodings of the South Wales miners that the foundations for truly national action had been eroded. For, although Asquith freely conceded the case for a wages increase, he asserted that the amount could not be fixed uniformly for all fields. District Conciliation Boards and sliding-scale committees were therefore adjured to settle the size of bonuses

---

[1] *CG* 12 Mar. 1915, 558; *MFGB* 1915, Executive Committee, 16 Mar. 1915.
[2] The course of the dispute can be traced in the pages of the *Colliery Guardian*, the annual report of the MFGB for 1915, and *The Times*.

within a week (failing which the government would appoint umpires). The final settlements averaged about 10 per cent on earnings—half the original claim, but not far behind what the MFGB had offered as a basis of settlement in earlier negotiations with the owners. The disappointing feature from the union's viewpoint was the variation in the war bonuses between districts—ranging from just over 9 per cent in Northumberland (and a little more in Durham and Scotland) to 11 per cent in South Wales and about 17.5 per cent in the English Federated Area.[1]

In national terms this dispute did not threaten any sensational consequences, if only because rank and file support for strike action was unlikely.[2] But the story was quite different in South Wales. There, the purely regional problem of a new Conciliation Board agreement threatened to have dramatic, even disastrous, consequences for the nation as a whole, precisely because the participants were adamantly behind a challenge to national authority. The origins of the crisis were significant at two levels. Within Wales, they revolved around the labour force's assertion of the right to determine the patterns and hierarchies of work and reward. On the national scene, they embodied a direct challenge to the state's faltering attempts to control industrial relations and working practices, and to the central arm of its industrial policy—the Munitions of War Act.

Along with the MFGB in other areas, the South Wales Miners' Federation had formulated its claim for a new wages agreement in early February 1915: a higher basic wages standard, a minimum wage 10 per cent above standard, no upper limit on wage rates, a daily minimum of 5 s. for underground and surface workers, the payment of six 'turns' for every five shifts worked in a week by men on the afternoon and night shifts, and a term for the agreement which would ensure its duration into peacetime.[3]

The extent of these demands, and the militancy with which they were pursued, were obviously influenced by the socialists and syndicalists who were so influential in the South Wales coalfield. But they were also very deeply embedded in the South Wales miner's attitude to his economic situation. First, there was a general dislike of the previous agreement (of 1910) which, it was felt, had been accepted under duress

---

[1] *CG* 21 May 1915, 1075, and 28 May 1915, 1131. The absolute amounts per shift were 9 d. in the North-East and Scotland, between 10 d. and 1 s. in South Wales, and between 1 s. and 1 s. 3 d. in the English Federated Area.

[2] *The Times* 21 Apr. 1915, 5a.

[3] *CG* 12 Feb. 1915, 343; *CG* 9 Apr. 1915, 767; Wrigley 1976, ch. VII, Appendix.

('forced down the throats of the men by the coalowners' threat of a lockout').[1] Second, there was a widespread sense of frustration that the maximum-wage provision of the 1910 agreement had prevented any increase in wage rates since 1913 (actual earnings had grown with more regular employment). Third, and related to this point, the miners felt particularly aggrieved in so far as prices and profits in the South Wales industry seemed to be buoyant and rising with no prospect of wages being able to join in the presumed bonanza.

The Welsh miners' composure was not improved by the reaction of the Monmouthshire & South Wales Coal Owners' Association. For weeks after the SWMF's claim (first made in February), the employers refused to meet or negotiate, arguing that a new agreement was inappropriate during wartime, and offering a simple 10 per cent bonus (on the 1879 standard) on account of inflation. Such obduracy only aggravated the situation, inflamed the miners, and lost the owners any public sympathy they might have enjoyed—especially in the context of the 'enormous profits' that they were thought to be making and, it was widely held, concealing.[2] As so often happened in South Wales, the owners therefore bore a large part of the responsibility for their own humiliation. In the summer of 1915 their provocations helped explain why their employees, even in the face of opposition to strike action from the national union and local officials, never swerved from the militancy of their demands—and secured virtually all of them.[3]

The impasse of the spring gave way to a flurry of activity at the approach of the deadline of 30 June (when the old agreement would terminate). Meetings with the President of the Board of Trade on 22–6 June came to nothing. And when the matter was referred to the Chief Industrial Commissioner (George Askwith) his report—which acknowledged the equity of the Welsh miners' case but did not concede the argument for a new agreement—had to be suppressed, at the urging of the SWMF, on the grounds that 'nothing could prevent a stoppage' if it were made public.[4]

Meanwhile, the Minister of Munitions, Lloyd George, was meeting the MFGB's national Executive Committee (on 24, 25 and 28 June) in an

---

[1] Vernon Hartshorn, quoted in Arnot 1975, 54 n.

[2] Asquith to the King, 19 July 1915: CAB 37/131/26; Riddell to Lloyd George, 19 July 1915; Lloyd George Papers, HLRO D/18/7/3.

[3] For the strike and the settlement, see Wrigley 1976, ch. VII; *History of the Ministry of Munitions* IV, II. The story can also be traced, in great detail and with more colour, in the pages of the *Colliery Guardian* for Feb.–July 1915.

[4] *History of the Ministry of Munitions* IV, II, 6; Askwith 1920, 394.

attempt to accommodate coalmining's industrial relations within the regulatory framework of the Munitions of War Act (which was to become law on 2 July 1915). This provided for the regulation of labour and the limitation of profits in 'controlled establishments', the outlawing of strikes and lockouts, and the imposition of compulsory arbitration in industries relating to the war effort. These discussions also came to nothing. The miners' representatives were unyielding in their opposition not simply to compulsory arbitration, but even to the embodying of their voluntary commitment (with 'no pains and penalties') in the Bill. Lloyd George was utterly frank in his concession: 'I am not going to have any conflict with the Miners.'[1] His statement was soon to come home with a vengeance, as the miners made good their claim that 'whatever may be said of other industries, the miners were capable of managing their own affairs'.[2]

In the two weeks from the end of June the situation in South Wales deteriorated rapidly. On the day of the deadline, Runciman, the President of the Board of Trade, was persuaded by the former SWMF leader, William Brace (who had joined the government at the end of May), to agree to a variety of wage concessions and to oblige the owners 'to accept conditions which are very distasteful to them'. Nevertheless, a delegate conference in Cardiff insisted on further negotiations and concessions. Runciman, arming himself with the possibility of applying the Munitions of War Act to South Wales in the event of a strike, declined to adjust the semi-official terms of settlement, and in South Wales the delegate conference abandoned any posture of compromise.

On 12 July, incensed by the refusal of the government to accept their claim for a minimum wage rate, and rejecting the advice of their officials to keep negotiating and ballot the membership, the delegates voted by almost two to one to 'stop all the collieries' on 15 July 'until their demands are conceded'. Events unfolded remorselessly. On 13 July a proclamation declared the projected stoppage to be illegal. On Thursday 15 July 1915 the huge South Wales coal industry was brought to a complete halt. In the midst of the greatest war in British history—a war in which coal was as essential as munitions or soldiers—some 700 coalmines and 200,000 coalminers stopped working.

Confronted with such a show of solidarity, the government could resolve its unprecedented dilemma in only one way. Even though the Cabinet, on Monday 19 July, appeared to decide to face down the

[1] MUN 5/48/300/7-8.
[2] William Straker, quoted in CG 25 June 1915, 1339.

strikers and attach the union's funds, its decision to send Lloyd George to South Wales to make a final appeal 'on patriotic grounds' opened the way to capitulation.[1] For no one knew better than the Minister of Munitions how inadvisable was any sustained dispute with the miners at such a time. The government, which had commenced as an apparently disinterested arbitrator, had become, in Balfour's words, 'by the very force of circumstances parties to the dispute'.

Lloyd George, accompanied by two senior members of the Labour Party, Henderson and Roberts, travelled to Cardiff on the evening of the 19 July, met the union and owners on the 20th, produced a settlement which in effect conceded all the men's demands, and on 22 July addressed an understandably enthusiastic open meeting of miners, praising their potential and urging them to close ranks and work hard. The need for coal had proved much greater than the need to assert the government's sovereignty. And even those, like the *Colliery Guardian*, who considered the strike to have reflected 'a perverted and sordid democracy', sensed that Lloyd George 'had to save something from the wreck, and he succeeded as well as the wit of man could conceive'. The miners gained all their main demands, including new minimum wages, the application of the agreement to SWMF members only, and the long duration of the settlement. The owners, who had placed themselves 'unreservedly' in the hands of the government, had to accept defeat with grace and expressions of gratitude from the President of the Board of Trade and the King.[2]

The events of July 1915 may well have shown the Munitions of War Act 'to be a thing of clay',[3] and they must have encouraged the upsurge of wage demands which began to affect the government's general industrial policy.[4] But their principal historical significance lay in their exposure of important aspects of the coal industry's problems.

[1] Draft of letter from Asquith to King, 19 July 1915: CAB 37/131/26.

[2] H. H. Asquith to the King, 19 July 1915: CAB 37/131/26; Balfour to Asquith, 7 July 1915: Asquith Papers, 14/113–16; *The Times* 19 July 1915, 8c and 8d; 20 July 1915, 7 f.; 22 July 1915, 7; *CG* 25 July 1915, 173. The *Colliery Guardian's* Editorial opened: 'The strike in South Wales has been ended and the men have gone back to the pits, but the stink remains. Mr Lloyd George went down to Cardiff and told the Welsh miners what a fine lot of fellows they were, and they fervently acquiesced.'

[3] *CG* 25 July 1915, 173.

[4] This was certainly George Askwith's view. He subsequently argued that 'The so-called settlement did more to cause unrest during the succeeding years than almost any other factor in the War.' (Askwith 1920, 395.) In Aug. the South Wales miners demanded that the agreement be applied to craftsmen, and Lloyd George overcame Runciman's inhibitions. In the latter's words, 'The effect on other trades will be deplorable, but there we are in the men's hands and humiliating as it is, I see no end to it but Lloyd George surrendering to them.' Quoted in Wrigley 1976, 128.

First among these was the position of the South Wales coalfield, not merely because of the vital importance of its coal for the Admiralty and the Allies, but also because of the special radicalism of its miners and the uniquely bad relationships between them and their unyielding and stiff-necked employers. Indeed, the resulting tendency to constant and hostile deadlock in South Wales was to be the ultimate cause of government control of the industry towards the end of 1916. At the same time, however, these attitudes were based on observation and experience.

To the members of the SWMF it was naturally galling that theirs should have been the only district in which the owners declined even to discuss a new agreement, while making very large profits and holding down wages under the pre-existing agreement. Compounded by their powerful political independence ('the South Wales miner recognises no law but himself. If he agrees, it must be on his own terms, unmodified by employers or State'),[1] and by their failure to persuade the national union to threaten a strike over the 20 per cent wage claim in the spring, the SWMF was determined to fight its own fight and have its own way when the issue was the district wages agreement. The national Federation was firmly warned not to interfere in the dispute.[2]

By this time, of course, even the SWMF Executive Committee was hardly in control of events in the coalfield,[3] and the question was naturally raised as to how far rank-and-file syndicalist and socialist influences were more effectively in command. Certainly, to judge from the tenor of debates, it was tempting to attribute a disproportionate influence to radicals who wished to engineer a large degree of government interference, or to 'extremists' and class-conscious militants who demanded (in the later words of the Commission on Industrial Unrest) industrial or political action 'involving the reconstitution of the whole basis of society'.[4]

It was perhaps in the nature of things that vigorous young men of commitment and 'advanced views' should have been overrepresented in conference delegations and in lodge discussions, at the expense of 'the

[1] CG 16 July 1915, 123.

[2] MFGB 1915, Executive Committee, 12-13 July 1915.

[3] The Times 19 July 1915, 6c-d.

[4] For attacks on 'violent and treasonable elements' or 'hot heads' in South Wales, and on 'bombastic threats, which are the product of Ruskin College', see The Times 19 July 1915, 7b; CG 23 Apr. 1915, 876 and 16 July 1915, 123. For a more considered analysis, see Commission of Enquiry into Industrial Unrest. No. 7 Division. Report of the Commissioners for Wales, Including Monmouthshire (Cd. 8668. 1917), 17. The report was printed in PP 1917-18 XV.

chapel lot', especially if selection meetings were held in public houses.[1] And to this extent it may well have been that a ballot (which the SWMF delegate conference rejected) might have reflected alternative views derived from 'the silent and strong backbone of the Federation—the steadying influence against extremists'.[2] But the situation in South Wales made it very unlikely that the mass of its miners were simply puppets of a small number of agitators. The radical elements could not go further than the negotiating situation, the attitudes of the mass of their colleagues, and the politically inept stance of the owners allowed them to go—and that was quite far enough.

To some extent, of course, the crisis in South Wales reflected the deterioration in industrial relations generally in the country in 1915. During that year wage-earners began to voice more strident dissatisfaction with the growth of profits, the rise of prices, and the conciliatory attitudes of their trade-union leaders. But the problem in the Welsh coalfield was a very special one. For it was rooted in the 'appalling bitterness' towards the owners, itself the product of years of bruising conflict, and a deep resentment at the fact that the owners were profiting from the shortage of coal while the miners were accused of lack of patriotism in declining to continue to work the pits under peacetime conditions. The complexity of the men's mood, torn between a basic patriotism and an unwillingness to strike on the one hand, and a determination not to surrender on the other, was caught by *The Times'* Special Correspondent, who wrote of a coalfield 'full of wretchedness' where the mass of the men were 'longing to be back in the pit, but . . . determined not to go back until their demands or something like them are satisfied.'[3] Many of the articulate young miners who dominated events for a traumatic fortnight were no doubt the sort of 'red-hot Syndicalists' so unwelcome to senior members of the SWMF Executive.[4] But in terms of industrial demands and action they were swimming with a powerful tide of genuine grievance and enormous solidarity.

Given these attitudes, two things followed in relation to the role of the state. First, government intervention in South Wales was inevitable. Second, 'intervention' could only have one politically realistic outcome:

---

[1] *CG* 23 July 1915, 181.

[2] *CG* 16 July 1915, 130. Cf. *CG* 9 July 1915, 81: 'The ballot brings out the men who do not attend lodge meetings, in which delegates are selected, elderly men, some of whom object to public houses . . . and most of them well pleased with present-day conditions.'

[3] *The Times* 19 July 1915, 6a, 20 July 1915, 7f, 21 July 1915, 7f.

[4] Report by the Brigade Major in charge of Troops of Strike Area, South Wales Coalfields, 19 July 1915 in Runciman Papers, WR 147.

the state had to compel the owners to accept the miners' terms. A sufficiently large-scale flouting of the law was bound to be successful, since it was obviously 'impossible to summon and try 200,000 men'.[1] Whatever the merit of the miners' case, therefore, the experience of July 1915 helped establish and publicize their new-found power and established the foundation of future, and more far-reaching, demands. And it confirmed the experience of industrial policy since February 1915. Just as the state had lost its faith in market forces as the arbiters of munitions supply, so it had to concern itself with manpower needs, labour conditions, labour rewards—and labour troubles.

In many industries more or less connected with munitions, all this had been accompanied by attempts (using voluntary as well as compulsory techniques) to amend the freedom of industrial action, negotiation, and the trade-union control of work processes and skills. It was, therefore, of some significance that throughout this period, and indeed throughout the War, there was never any serious question of the state being able to override the wishes of the miners or amend the organization of their work or otherwise adjust their 'privileges'. Above all (and even though the original eight-hour legislation provided for suspension in time of national emergency), the limit on underground hours remained sacrosanct. The South Wales situation was, after all, merely an extreme example of the very special political and structural position of the coal industry as a whole. In the course of 1916, the result was widespread political exasperation and a major extension of government control.

v. The move towards government control

By 1916 the distribution and allocation of coal were fairly effectively overseen by a variety of official and informal devices. These, however, did not touch the problems of production, and as the War continued attention increasingly turned to the conditions of supply and manpower, which had been the subject of investigation and exhortation ever since the appointment of the Coal Mining Organisation Committee in the spring of 1915.

In the early months of 1916 a good deal of anxiety had been generated by the issue of enlistment and conscription. The miners, although strongly opposed to the Military Service Act, had trodden carefully in

[1] Robert Wallace (Lloyd George's choice as Chairman of a putative South Wales Munitions Tribunal) to Lloyd George, 17 July 1915: Lloyd George Papers, HLRO D/11/1/6.

the public expression of that opposition. On the other hand, and in spite of the labour shortage in the mines, there was an undercurrent of resentment at the miners' position, with the Director-General of Recruiting asserting in the House of Lords that some men had gone down the pit in order to avoid military service, and others arguing that persistent absentees should be sent into the forces.[1] There was, nevertheless, an element of shadow-boxing about all this. On the one hand, the MFGB's opposition to military conscription was intimately bound up with their apprehension that industrial 'conscription' might follow. On the other hand, it was clear that the shortage of manpower in the mines was potentially a more severe handicap to the war effort than the shortage of men in the Army. Absenteeism, effort, and morale were, therefore, far more important points of policy focus than was the question of whether miners should be called up.[2]

In May 1916, for example, in response to a letter from the Chairman of the CMOC (Sir Richard Redmayne), urging the vital need to increase output, the miners' Executive Committee agreed to a meeting with the owners to discuss absenteeism and the duration of holidays—but absolutely declined to consider the length of the working day and expressed adamant hostility to the idea of increasing the labour force by reducing the age at which boys could work underground. The principal outcome was an agreement to refer the question of absenteeism to the various districts on the understanding that committees would be established, at individual pits, in an attempt to secure regular attendance.[3] But in the First, as in the Second, World War, such joint pit committees were to prove inadequate means of reducing absenteeism. The miners wished to use them as sounding-boards for more general complaints, and avenues to a greater role in management affairs, and were in any case most reluctant to invest them with any disciplinary powers. It took some months to form committees, and the MFGB dragged its heels on the question of giving them effective power, preferring them to use 'moral pressure'. (The Lancashire and Cheshire district was unique in providing for the withdrawal of exemption under the Military Service Act from persistent absentees.)

By October 1916, however, most districts had formed networks of

[1] *MFGB* 1916, conferences on 8, 9, and 13 Jan. 1916, and meeting with Prime Minister, 21 Jan. 1916; *CG* 14 Jan. 1916, 76, and 17 Mar. 1916, 84.

[2] For the story of production and manpower problems in the War see Redmayne 1923 and Cole 1923.

[3] *MFGB* 1916, Executive Committee, 8 and 16 May 1916.

local committees. Even so, very few had been effectively formed in South Wales, where industrial relations continued to be bad, and considering the nation as a whole, very little improvement in attendance resulted. Another national representative conference was therefore arranged (on 25 October 1916), and the MFGB, anxious to fend off the growing demand for the withdrawal of exemption certificates from persistent absentees, agreed to permit pit committees to impose fines on offenders as long as procedures conformed to rules agreed with the union. The public-relations element in all this was quite marked. Thus, at a delegate conference on 22–3 November Robert Smillie, the union's President, defended himself against radical charges of being too accommodating by arguing that, by cooperating with government, he and the Executive had saved the miners from something much worse (amendments to the Eight Hours Act or inclusion in the Munitions of War Act). Compromise on fines, he argued, was vital so that control of the issue of absenteeism should remain the prerogative of the MFGB.[1]

The problem of absenteeism led, therefore, to prolonged, painstaking, but only partially successful deliberations. And even when the miners reluctantly agreed to a system of fines, there was little promise of any substantial increase in output resulting from the experiment in institutional reform. The fact was that the wartime problem of manpower and effort in coalmining had now evolved into a matter of labour attitudes, morale, and industrial relations, rather than the recruitment of more men or the application of minatory controls on the intensity of work.

At the same time, however, many of the issues which were approached with such anguish were relatively marginal to the central problem of war supply. Thus, any feasible reduction in absenteeism could only have increased output by one or two percentage points at a time when the normal level of production never really threatened the war effort—at least before 1918. Although the CMOC, in March 1916, calculated that there might be a deficit of 15 million tons in that year, that assumed a fairly high level of exports and did not take into account possible improvements in output and economies in use. Later in the year the 'deficit' was identified with a shortfall of exports below a total overseas demand of 48.53 million tons, and in any case the Board of

[1] *MFGB* 1916, Conferences and Executive Committee meetings on 9–11 May; 11 July; 16–18 Aug.; 5, 23, 26 Oct.; 22–3 Nov.; 5–6 Dec. Among the procedural conditions laid down by the MFGB was the provision that a fine could be 'worked off' by a month's regular attendance.

Trade suggested that the figure was exaggerated—3 million tons being nearer the mark.[1]

On the other hand, modest optimism depended on reliability and continuity of production. That optimism had been briefly shattered by the South Wales strike of July 1915. And even after the resolution of the strike, although much had been done to bring the coal industry into a semblance of official and coordinated oversight, the fact remained that the industry's central problem—labour dissatisfaction and unrest, and its threat to continuity of production—was still unresolved. This had been a cause of official anxiety in September and October 1915.[2] And the resulting discussions anticipated not merely the causes, location, and arrangements for the control of the coal industry which came a year later, but also the fact that, in the words of a senior civil servant, even if the coal mines were taken over by the state, 'South Wales being South Wales, it is impossible to say what other causes of unrest may not arise at any moment.'[3]

In the coal industry, as in politics and the economic management of the War generally, events moved towards a catharsis late in 1916. At one level, that movement, as with other experiments late in Asquith's administration, involved a refinement of the oversight which had begun in 1915. The CMOC, the Exports Committee and the Central Coal and Coke Supplies Committee were only loosely linked by overlapping membership, and responsibility for them was divided between two departments of state. In July 1916, therefore, the task of coordinating their activities was given to Lord Milner, who set about it with his usual vigour—consulting widely, listening sympathetically to the miners' case, pushing for clarification of his role.[4]

Yet Milner was very soon frustrated by the situation in the coal industry. By early November he had concluded that, while the committees were working well individually, no amount of 'coordination' could lead to a satisfactory policy because there was no 'paramount idea' behind their various endeavours. The government, he urged, lacked a guiding principle; it must review the situation as a whole, since there were 'great possibilities of mischief lurking in the present state of affairs'. He also made it clear that that 'mischief', and the greatest danger to the maintenance of an ample supply of coal, resided in the men's

[1] Redmayne 1923, 67; CAB 37/149/16, 25 and 29 (memoranda of 8, 10, and 13 June 1916).
[2] Above, 55.
[3] Runciman Papers, WR 147 (11 Sept. 1915).
[4] Gollin 1964, 350–3; Milner papers, 44/169–71, 193–4, 207–12; and 353/75–6, 99–117, 129–34.

resentment at its high price and 'the piling up of profits by their employers'. In a despairing note to Samuel, he advocated at the least the firm enforcement of the price-limitation statute, and at the most extreme government appropriation of the entire output at lower prices and, therefore, restrained wage levels.[1]

In the course of his memorandum, Milner identified the problem which was to induce a much more radical institutional change than had been involved in his own appointment. For in South Wales, where the settlement of July–August 1915 had done nothing to resolve the fundamental dispute between owners and miners, the two sides remained locked in combat throughout 1916. Indeed, the problem had been aggravated by the fact that the 1915 agreement had failed to stipulate an 'equivalent price' for coal which would correspond to minimum wage levels, with the result that there were no guidelines for the resolution of the conflicting claims for wage alterations (within the terms of the agreement) which arose every few months.

The miners' resentment at the high prices and the owners' presumed profits, and their frustration in relation to their own wage levels, found outlets in continuous industrial-relations conflict, in a refusal to reduce their holidays in the interest of greater output (a refusal which was temporarily overcome in the summer by an appeal by the Admiralty), and in leading an MFGB assault on a proposed increase in the export prices to be charged by South Wales owners ('these people are simply shovelling up money', claimed one Welsh member of the union's Executive Committee).[2] Admittedly, in June, by dint of a further interposition of government arbitration, the South Wales miners gained a 15 per cent increase.[3] But this was followed by a further seemingly provocative price increase (which was, in fact, based on increases in production costs) and a renewed wage claim. The real point was that *ad hoc* wage settlements could not eradicate what *The Times* referred to as 'The Curse of South Wales' and the virtual private feud which was imperilling the nation's safety.[4]

The SWMF's new claim (for a further 15 per cent wage increase) was

[1] Milner to Samuel, 6 Nov. 1916, Milner Papers, 353/102–7.
[2] *MFGB* 1916, 19 July 1916. The story of the continuous wage disputes and the deterioration of industrial relations in South Wales is told in Cole, *Labour in the Coal-Mining Industry*. CAB 37/160/14 (23 Nov. 1916) summarized recent history and the claim which precipitated the final crisis. Also see *CG* 24 Dec. 1915, 20 Apr. 1916, 5 May 1916, 9 June 1916, 30 June 1916, 4 Aug. 1916, 11 Aug. 1916, 22 Sept. 1916.
[3] *CG* 9 June 1916, 1095, 1106.
[4] *The Times* 22 Nov. 1916, 9b.

submitted on 31 October 1916 and the union indicated that if it were refused they would insist on a joint audit of the collieries' books to resolve the vexed question of the true level of profits. The owners countered with a claim for a 10 per cent reduction on the grounds that production costs had risen sharply, and a bleak refusal to throw open their accounts. By 10 November the Conciliation Board was deadlocked and the miners refused to allow the case to be referred to its independent chairman. Instead, they made a direct approach to the government, threatening strike action. The owners' agreement to an independent (but not a joint) audit failed to solve the crisis, and by the last week of November 1916 the time was ripe for the radical departure that had been tentatively examined a year earlier.

The long-running dispute in South Wales had at last persuaded all shades of political opinion that something needed to be done. That something would not be against the interests of the miners. The South Wales owners had made the worst of a poor case, and alienated their erstwhile supporters; the authorities were blamed for not consulting the miners about the recent price increase; and South Wales seemed on the brink of another, even more explosive, strike. On 27 November *The Times*, having already drawn attention to the problem in a series of documentary articles, published a leader attacking the South Wales owners for their mismanagement, obstinacy, and selfishness:

in no other coalfield is there such strife and distrust of the owners. . . . They have taken upon themselves to conduct the industry and they have drawn immense wealth from it. They are trustees of it to the nation. If they cannot conduct it, the sooner it is transferred to someone who can the better. We are aware that the men are influenced by revolutionary theorists who are quite irreconcilable and wish to bring the trade to a standstill; but, we are also aware that these theorists would never have gained the ear of the bulk of the men if the owners had not played into their hands by a grasping policy.[1]

By the time that these words were published, government departments were already persuaded that drastic action was necessary. On 28 November 1916, with the support of the Admiralty, the President of the Board of Trade—which now asserted a departmental primacy in official dealings with the industry which it was not to relinquish until the formation of the Ministry of Fuel and Power in 1942—circulated a draft

---

[1] See *The Times* 20–4 and 27 Nov. 1916, 9b.

regulation to his Cabinet colleagues, providing for government control of the South Wales district:

The recurrent disputes and unrest in the coalfield which practically every three months threaten an interruption in essential supplies of coal for the Navy, for munitions, and for the national industry, can in the judgement of the Board of Trade be put an end to in no other way than by assuming control over the coal-field in the national interest.[1]

The next day (29 November) the government issued the necessary orders under the Defence of the Realm Act, which empowered it to assume control over any of the country's collieries, and immediately applied its authority to South Wales.[2] In a startling move, Britain's lead-ing coal-producing district came under state supervision. More than this, it proved impossible to confine the official control to the South Wales field: although the rest of the British coalmining industry was not brought within the control until February 1917, the enlargement of the area of state action was contemplated from December 1916 and officially agreed early in January 1917—the result, it was said, of pressure from the miners, but also intervention from Lord Milner, whose experience as informal coordinator of coal policy had persuaded him of the need for much more explicit government intervention.[3]

In any case, the control of the coal industry was unique among various examples of state intervention in major industries in that labour unrest, rather than the direct problem of supply, was the root cause of intervention. The state was called in because the industry's work-force was apparently unwilling to continue its cooperation with the private administration of the mines. The South Wales owners' management, in the words of the President of the Board of Trade, 'was leading straight to a general strike'.[4] Control had become necessary not because of defi-ciencies in the piecemeal system of committee oversight which had been constructed in 1915-16, but because important parts of the industry were becoming ungovernable.

The bad relationships that had been inherited from prewar conflicts in South Wales were aggravated by the miners' suspicions about war-time profiteering and their own desire to secure balancing wage

---

[1] CAB 37/160/23 (28 Nov. 1916).
[2] Asquith to the King, 30 Nov. 1916: CAB 37/160/30.
[3] CG 16 Feb. 1917, 337. Also see Lloyd George's first Commons statement as Prime Minister (*Hansard* 19 Dec. 1916, col. 1346) and the War Cabinet Minute for 8 Jan. 1917 (CAB 23/1/114-15).
[4] CAB 37/160/23 (28 Nov. 1916).

increases. The resulting tensions could not be contained within the industry or by a series of *ad hoc* government concessions. Instead, financial control proved to be the only way of diminishing the explosive pressures which, by November 1916, threatened to jeopardize the continuity of production and therefore of the war effort.

To that extent, the exercise of control was certainly successful. Yet, as events were swiftly to demonstrate, the drama of the coal industry did not subside with the achievement of control. Within days of government intervention the miners' full claim for 15 per cent had been granted. More significantly, as far as the war effort and manpower problems were concerned, the institutional reform of control simply shifted the *locus* of tension nearer the centre of government. The problems had been reorientated rather than eradicated, and the coal-mining industry became a directly political issue. As was to be demonstrated in 1917–18, the War involved a readjustment of power relationships rather than a resolution of industrial conflict.

CHAPTER 3

The State and the Necessities of War
1916–1918

The government's assumption of control in the coal industry—first in South Wales on 1 December 1916 and then throughout Great Britain on 1 March 1917—meant that the state was now drawn much more directly and continuously into the oversight of prices, profits, wages, manpower, and distribution. Formal control lasted until the end of March 1921. But the experiences of the control period, variously interpreted by rival schools of thought, were to be cited as benign or dreadful precedents in the controversy about the appropriate roles of the state and private enterprise in coal production and distribution which began in 1919 and hardly ceased until the industry was nationalized 27 years later. Indeed, after 1921, whatever their ideological predilections, governments would never again be able to shed a concern with questions of wages, costs, and industrial organization in coalmining. For these reasons, then, the experience of the war years provides an indispensable foundation for the interwar history of the industry, influencing as it did attitudes as well as performance, policies as well as institutions.

In spite of the importance of government regulation to the economic history of the coal industry after 1916, it is as well to remember that the performance of the industry and the longer-term consequences of these years were also the outcome of the pressures of an unprecedented war upon a particular industry with distinctive characteristics. There was an acute shortage of manpower and a spectacular enhancement of the bargaining power of the labour force and its principal trade union; a disjunction of demand and supply which market forces either could not, or could not be allowed to, 'solve'; a transformation of wages and profits; and a new pattern of economic and ideological incentives for coal-owners and coalminers alike. In this chapter, the basic tasks and organization of the control system will be considered first. Then the problems and performance of the industry, and the mounting degree of government intervention in the supply and use of its resources in the latter stages of the War will be discussed. This leads logically to a consideration of the effects of the War, first on the rewards to and political position of labour, and then on the business, profitability, and outlook of coalmining.

i. The Coal Control: means and ends[1]

As has already been seen, the apparent abrupt control of the South Wales coalfield on 1 December 1916 was the consequence of the government's realization that only such direct intervention could salve the destructively abrasive industrial relationships which threatened economic and social stability in the Principality. Indeed, the need to provide a greater representation for the public interest and a more coherent degree of industrial coordination, had been recognized by some civil servants a year earlier. The foundations for the radical step of state control were therefore laid by the Asquith administration, as was the case with other measures of control in food and shipping.[2]

In spite of this fact, however, and although the prospect of extending formal regulation to all the nation's coalfields was being freely discussed even while South Wales was being brought under control, there was as yet no explicit concept as to how best to administer the industry. (On 2 December 1916 Lord Milner, who had declined the Food Controllership on the previous day, gave an indeterminate answer to the offer of the job of 'trying to tackle the Coal Question' on the grounds that he had first to 'know what the policy is, which I am asked to carry out'.)[3] Nevertheless, contemplation of national control indicated an awareness of the need to come to grips with the economic problems of wartime production as well as the political problems of industrial power. For industrial relations in the coal industry outside South Wales were nowhere near a state of crisis. If, as seems to have been the case, the control of the Welsh industry was occasioned by the collapse of orderly industrial relations there, it was extended to other fields 'so that the

[1] The 'Coal Control' was the generally employed phrase for the department of the Board of Trade which was established early in 1917 to oversee the coal industry. It was sometimes referred to as the 'Coal Mines Department', although that designation was to be more accurately employed when a regular, peacetime sub-Ministry, under a Secretary for Mines, was created by legislation in 1920.

[2] Redmayne 1942, 190–1; and above, 52–7.

[3] Milner Papers, 353/129–34. Milner was already keen on Lloyd George overturning Asquith's 'pure squashiness'. For the acceptance of the idea of national control in late Nov./early Dec. 1916, see *CG* 16 Feb. 1917, 337; Lloyd George's first Commons statement as Prime Minister (*Hansard* 19 Dec. 1916, col. 1345) and the War Cabinet Minute for 8 Jan. 1917 (CAB 23/1/114–15). Also Bonar Law, in *Hansard* 12 Nov. 1917.

Government might have complete control over the whole production and distribution of the entire output of all the coal mines', with the transport and allocation of the mineral a particular problem.

Lloyd George announced the government's intention to control the entire industry on 19 December, on the grounds that coal supply was 'an essential ingredient of our military and industrial efficiency', and preparations for the take-over began in the first weeks of the new administration. Initially, it had been intended to exercise control through a three-man interdepartmental committee representing the Board of Trade, the Admiralty, and the Home Office. And this committee was responsible for granting the 15 per cent increase in wage rates which settled the immediate dispute in South Wales. But according to Redmayne (who was the Home Office's representative), it only met three times and never received terms of reference.[1] The idea of an interdepartmental committee was intrinsically unsatisfactory if the control of the industry was to be effective: there had to be a unique point of responsibility and a department independent of the other (potentially conflicting) interests concerned with the use of scarce resources. As early as 8 January, therefore, the Cabinet agreed that the industry should be controlled by a single department within the Board of Trade, headed by a Coal Controller—although it was over a month before an official announcement of the decision, and of the associated appointment, was made.[2]

The government's first choice for Controller had been Sir Gilbert Claughton, Chairman of the London & North Western Railway, but he was apparently vetoed by the Miners' Federation on the grounds that his business interests were too closely identified with the mining industry.[3] No such objections were raised to the man actually appointed—Guy Calthrop, General Manager of the same company. Quite apart from the need to allay the suspicions of the mineworkers, there were obvious strategic advantages in choosing an ousider, who might be expected to stand above the inter-district and inter-firm rivalries of the fragmented coal industry. And in the event Calthrop (who was knighted in 1918 and served as Coal Controller until his death in the same year) seems to have earned the sincere respect and support of those with whom he worked. In any case, his senior aides were men

[1] Redmayne 1923, 63; id., 1942, 121–2.
[2] CAB 23/1/114–17 (8 Jan. 1917); CG 16 Feb. 1917, 342. The allocation of departmental responsibility to the Board of Trade, rather than the Home Office, reflected the broader economic concerns which lay behind the control.   [3] Redmayne 1942, 194.

of considerable experience. They included Sir Richard Redmayne, whose technical expertise as Chief Inspector of Mines had been augmented by his work with the Coal Mining Organisation Committee, and A. Lowes Dickinson, an eminent accountant who took charge of the Control's financial branch.

By the standards of wartime administration, the Coal Control was not huge. In September 1917 it employed about 330 people (including railway clerks seconded by their companies, but not railway employees still in their companies' pay).[1] Initially, it was divided into four departments or branches: production, finance, distribution, and a secretariat. Subsequently, in the summer of 1917, when it extended its operations to the rationing of domestic fuel supplies, a fifth branch was formed to supervise the allocation of coal.[2]

In an industry as large, complex, and sensitively structured as coal-mining, however, it was not possible to apply control simply through a conventional departmental system. And just as the government's original attempt to oversee production through the Coal Mining Organisation Committee in the spring of 1915 had entailed extensive and continuous consultation, so the new Coal Control had to be equipped with a formal and elaborate means of gathering advice and associating the industry's principal interest groups with its decisions. This took the form of the Coal Controller's Advisory Board, which was announced in February 1917 and established when the industry was officially taken over in March. The Advisory Board (which was intended to meet weekly, although it did not quite manage that goal) consisted of equal numbers of representatives of owners and miners—or, more exactly, of the Mining Association of Great Britain and the Miners' Federation of Great Britain, for the Board's membership was exclusive. Thus, when the MFGB objected to the inclusion on the committee of representatives of the aggrieved surface workers' union not affiliated to the MFGB, the committee unanimously agreed that the MFGB should be the sole representative organization for workers in the industry. It was symptomatic of the Board's importance that the original members (five from each side, rising ultimately to seven) should have been the chief officeholders of the respective associations.[3]

[1] 'Statement of the Cost of the Coal Mines Department', Sept. 1917: POWE 10/12. The numbers grew to 432 in Oct. 1918 and 859 in Nov. 1919: 'Committee of Staffs Report on Coal Mines Department', Oct. 1918: POWE 10/13; *Hansard* 25 Nov. 1919, col. 1630.

[2] The organization of the Coal Control is described in POWE 10/12–13, and in Redmayne 1923, 93 ff.

[3] The Minutes of the Advisory Board are in BT 189/1. Its original members were, for the

The existence and formal role of the Advisory Board suggests that the advent of control also marked the introduction of a 'corporatist' or consultative–collective element into the management of the industry. But in practice, the Board's function was advisory rather than policy-making or executive. Thus, in relation to matters of vital importance to the miners—wages and recruitment policy being outstanding examples—the MFGB insisted, throughout the War, on direct negotiations with the Coal Controller.[1] And both the owners and the miners firmly declined the Controller's invitation to appoint personal advisers to help him tackle the crisis of supply that was looming in the last months of the War. Until its demise in 1919, the Advisory Board remained in an anomalous position: constantly consulted, but very rarely willing to accept any responsibility for policy or decisions.

As we have seen, government control had been instituted with two principal objectives: to oversee production and distribution in the national interest, and to remove a chief cause of industrial unrest 'by making it possible for men to feel that they were working for the community and not to earn excessive profits for the owners'.[2] It was not immediately apparent how these were to be achieved in terms of designating actual tasks for the new department. But one point was clear: the government did not intend to get involved in the actual running of pits or companies, or even in the direct sale of coal. These were to remain the responsibility of colliery owners and merchants. Instead, the new arrangements for control were to evolve from the administrative bases established in the first 18 months of the War: national wage-bargaining, the general oversight of manpower and the effectiveness of its use, price control, and the allocation of overseas and domestic sales. In the first instance the most pressing need was to rationalize distribution, and the Controller's first major task was therefore the prosaic but vital one of tracing the flow of all coal from pit to final consumer—although the initial parliamentary announcement also referred to discussions with the Director-General of Recruiting concerning the industry's manpower shortage.[3]

There were, however, two levels at which the implications of its original tasks extended the depth and range of the government's

MAGB: Hugh Bramwell, Sir Thomas Ratcliffe-Ellis, Adam Nimmo, A. F. Pease, and C. E. Rhodes; for the MFGB: Vernon Hartshorn, Robert Smillie, Herbert Smith, William Straker, and Stephen Walsh. Exclusiveness was confirmed on 27 June 1917.

[1] Below, 108–9.   [2] CAB 24/21/96–107 (26 July 1917).
[3] *Hansard* 22 Mar. 1917, cols. 2048–9 and 27 Mar. 1917, col. 202; *CG* 5 Apr. 1917, 677.

responsibilities for the administration of the coal industry. First, as will be discussed below, as the War dragged on its exigencies drew the Coal Control more and more into collateral areas of the industry and trade: into domestic rationing (introduced for London households in the summer of 1917, and into the rest of the country a year later); into a more diffused and insistent concern with national manpower planning, wages, recruitment, absenteeism, consultative procedures, export and shipping; and even (although the instance was an isolated and indirect move) into an attempt, in March 1918, to restrain the use of resources for development. Such an extension of its activities inevitably brought the Coal Control into contact, and occasional conflict, with other departments (the Ministries of Munitions, Labour, National Service, and Shipping, the War Office, and the Admiralty), and meant that the coal industry came to occupy a disproportionate amount of the War Cabinet's time. The second elaboration of the original area of the Coal Control's responsibility derived from the need to settle the terms on which the government would oversee the industry's finances. This was important not merely because of the state's now explicit responsibility for prices and wages, and therefore profits; but also because the administration of the industry as a whole necessitated some form of unified accounting.

Government intervention inevitably distorted the industry's finances. This was because the essence of control was the making of *administrative* decisions about the pattern of production and allocation of coal. But this could, and did, mean the generation of unusual profits for some collieries, and enforced profit-reductions or losses for others—which might be denied access to the hyper-profits of export markets, or obliged to sell (for example, to the Navy) at prices below the best available, or compelled to remain in production even though their costs exceeded their proceeds. It was therefore important as well as equitable to try to ensure that where proceeds were unevenly distributed because of wartime policy, they should be reallocated between undertakings earning fortuitously high profits and those earning subnormal ones. By the same token, since wage negotiations, and wage improvements, were now settled nationally (i.e. irrespective of the different economic circumstances of the various districts), and in part on the basis of political criteria, some reallocation of funds was necessary to allow less efficient collieries to pay the uniform increases without excessive distortions in cost–price relationships.

In the summer of 1918, for example, the Board of Trade assumed responsibility for financing the two war wages (amounting to a total of 3s. per shift for adult miners) granted in 1917 and 1918. These were met by a price increase and a levy of 4s. per ton on colliery output—the collieries paying out the actual money and returning to the Coal Control any receipts above the costs of the awards. The Coal Control then used these payments to compensate collieries whose costs exceeded the levy.[1] In effect, then, control presupposed the pooling of profits, as a result of which the Controller would have a free hand to adjust production and distribution, and issue directives as to transport.[2] As we shall see, the idea of a national profits pool, and therefore national wage bargaining (favoured by the MFGB as a means of securing better wages for the poorer areas, and resisted by the owners as an erosion of their economic independence), was to dog much of the immediate postwar history of the industry.

As far as the owners were concerned, the government's arrangements for finance were to be the principal area in which the effects of control were to be felt. But in spite of the early announcement that there would be a guarantee of the profits of individual companies commensurate with prewar earnings, the serious business of negotiating the exact terms took some time to begin and months to complete. The process was controversial as well as prolonged. The coalowners' case was handled by a 15-man committee of the MAGB; but the jealousy and suspicions entertained by individual districts and enterprises towards any degree of centralized decision-making led to dissension within the Mining Association.

At one level, for example, some of the poorer districts within the Federated Area successfully threatened to break away and undertake separate negotiations unless they were granted specific representation on the Committee.[3] At another level, individual colliery owners (particularly in South Wales) objected to the form as well as the terms of the proposed agreement. Here, the lead was taken by a South Wales owner and merchant, Sir Clifford Cory—at the MAGB, at protest meetings, and in the House of Commons. Cory and his fellow dissidents criticized (among other things) the use of a negotiated settlement rather than parliamentary guarantees, the proposal to tax excess profits at a rate of 95 per cent (as against 80 per cent for most other industries), and the

---

[1] Below, 91.

[2] CAB 24/21/96–107 (26 July 1917).

[3] *MAGB* 1918, 11. The districts involved were South Staffordshire, Warwickshire, Shropshire, Leicestershire, South Derbyshire, and Cannock Chase.

'negotiating other men's property away' by secret deliberations facilitated (he held) by the appointment of MAGB officials to the Coal Controller's Advisory Board, where they had been 'nobbled'.[1] On the other side, quite apart from that tiny minority of coalowners who took an entirely altruistic view of the matter (Sir Arthur Markham, for example, had advocated a 100 per cent excess profits tax)[2] the majority seem to have acquiesced in the control agreement—either because they recognized the government's determination or because they acknowledged the force of the argument that in the case of the coal industry it was logical to treat it as a whole and reallocate the abundance that War had brought to it.[3]

The control agreement was finally signed on 20 July 1917.[4] Its details were extremely complicated, and when it ultimately came to be embodied in a Bill, much parliamentary time was consumed by its critics attacking, and its defenders acknowledging but excusing, its apparent incomprehensibility. But its essential principles were fairly straightforward. An excess profits duty had been applied to business generally in 1915, and by 1917 it had been raised to 80 per cent of all profits above the best level of the immediate prewar years. Within these general arrangements, coalmining received a further allowance of 9 per cent (for companies) and 10 per cent (for individuals) on the grounds that its business was based on a 'wasting asset' for which it would be difficult to make provision as normal depreciation. Under the Coal Mines Control Agreement, however, this special allowance was abolished (it being feared that colliery companies might sink their surplus allowance in the acquisition of further mineral reserves or capital development of their pits).[5]

The industry was also to be treated differently as regards excess profits: having paid the 'normal' 80 per cent, individual colliery companies then had to pay three-quarters of the remainder (i.e. 15 per cent of surplus profits above prewar levels) to the Inland Revenue. These Coal Mines Excess Payments would then be transferred to the Board of Trade to be used to compensate those undertakings which experienced reduced profits, or actual losses, owing to the policy and directives of

[1] *MAGB* 1918, 16; *Hansard* 8 Nov. 1917, cols. 2428–30. For discussions about financial guarantees between the government and Cory and his associates, see Slaughter and May to Runciman, 15 Nov. 1917: Runciman Papers, WR 161.

[2] Stamp 1932, 85.

[3] *MAGB* 1918, 16; Sir J. Harmood-Banner in *Hansard* 8 Nov. 1917, 2438.

[4] *PP* 1920 XXVII, 125–6.

[5] *Sankey Evidence* I, 406.

the Coal Control. Provision was also made for firms whose production fell below prewar levels (for any fall up to 35 per cent, the standard profit level would be reduced by 75 per cent of the same percentage).

No sooner had this agreement been reached in the early summer of 1917, than an intractable legal difficulty was discovered. For negotiations had been undertaken by representatives of the Mining Association of Great Britain, which had no power of enforcement on its members. The agreement was, in effect, a voluntary instrument and it was clear from the violent responses of people like Sir Clifford Cory that the necessary measure of goodwill was completely lacking. Reluctantly, therefore, the War Cabinet concluded that it would be necessary to devote precious parliamentary time to making the agreement legally enforceable.[1] Even so, having begun its Second Reading on 25 October 1917, the Coal Mines Control Agreement (Confirmation) Bill did not receive the Royal Assent until 6 February 1918—a full year and more after discussions of financial arrangements had begun. It was, however, backdated to the beginning of coal control, and in practice those concerned had been able to assume the existence of the agreement from early in the summer of 1917.

In the event, the financial operations of control were not as self-sufficient as had been predicted, or promised, to Parliament. In the first two years, 1917/18 and 1918/19, the Inland Revenue was reported to have collected £563,064 in Coal Mines Excess Payments and the Board of Trade made compensation payments of some £2,268,825. The deficiency was made up partly from a surplus on the levy imposed on collieries to cover the war wage in the summer of 1918, and partly from a drawing of £1,250,508 from the Civil Contingency Fund.[2] But all things considered, and largely because of the rise in the price of coal, the burden on government finances involved in the huge step of control, was extremely small.

ii. Output, prices, and allocation

During the first two years of the War the principal causes of anxiety about coal supplies had derived from the disruption of the distribution

---

[1] CAB 23/3/12 and 142 (7 June and 31 July 1917); CAB 24/21/96–107 (26 July 1917) CAB 24/22/141 (7 Aug. 1917).

[2] These figures are rounded to the nearest £1. The precise accounting is in *Accounts of Receipts and Payments by the Board of Trade and the Commissioners of Inland Revenue respectively, under the Coal Mines Control Agreement (Confirmation) Act, 1918, for the period 1st April, 1917, to 31st March, 1919 (PP 1920 XXVII, 125–8)*. The surplus of the war wage levy above the outlays of firms whose costs were less than the levy was £1,202,015; of this the Coal Control paid out £657,922 to firms which were unable to cover their costs from the price increase (equal to the levy).

system and the problems of pricing and labour relations. The question of total production was less urgent. Indeed, in 1916 output (256.4 million tons) was greater, by about 3 million tons, than in 1915 and the amount available for home consumption was 12 million tons greater than in 1913. The last two years of the War, however, became a race between shrinking coal supplies and mounting strategic needs, and the industry's affairs therefore became objects of sustained and increasing concern.

The broad statistical characteristics of the industry's wartime performance have already been summarized in Table 2.1. The declining trend in production, although not precipitous, was significant. However, there was some compensation in the dramatic fall in exports, so that the amount of coal available for domestic consumption rose until the penultimate year of the War. Nevertheless, domestic demand also increased and by 1918 the situation had reached crisis proportions. Domestic prices were controlled (from the summer of 1915) at a level which covered rising costs, but did not reflect market scarcities. On the other hand, export prices were maintained at very high levels indeed, although Britain's French and Italian Allies were treated more favourably than neutral consumers.

Yet such simple aggregates and averages are more than usually misleading, not merely because they conceal variations,[1] but also because they distort the relevant emphases. Thus, the decline in exports, which helped maintain domestic supplies, was by no means wholly welcomed: it involved a weakening of the military potential of Britain's Allies and a diminution in Britain's access to vital foreign exchange. As a result, the pattern as well as the amount of exports was subject to strict control, and as the supply situation worsened towards the end of the War, Allies' needs were more stringently compared with those of the domestic economy, and neutral markets outside Europe were starved in order to maintain home and continental supplies. (The French and Italian markets took 30 per cent of shipments in 1913, 60 per cent in 1916, and 65 per cent in 1918.)[2]

At the same time, transport difficulties, especially the scarcity of shipping for Welsh and Scottish coals, occasionally produced severe local problems. (During the 1917 submarine blockade, the export trade

---

[1] Average prices cover an extremely wide range of grades of coal, and individual prices. In a schedule of export prices issued by the Coal Controller in June 1917, for example, those for the Midland field varied from 20s. per ton for 'unwashed smalls' to 30s. for large screened coals: POWE 26/8 (28 June 1917).

[2] ARSM 1927, 118.

from South Wales, where the Severn tunnel presented a bottleneck for land transport, was 'absolutely throttled'.)[1] At another level, the man-power figures, which in aggregate reflected a serious enough situation, masked a huge and enfeebling turnover. The industry lost 400,000 of its fittest men to the Forces, and generally replaced them with less suitable workers. Finally, the War affected patterns of demand: the need for steam coal for munitions factories, and for coke and such by-products as benzol and toluol, kept the mines of Yorkshire (with their large production of 'steam nuts')[2] and Durham (which produced coking and gas coals) very busy, while east Scotland suffered from export restraints.

But in the last resort, all production had to adapt to the drastic change in circumstances brought about by the War. The heavy drain on the labour force, quite apart from its direct effects, involved dislocation in the flow and organization of mining. In the Northern Division, for example, where almost 100,000 men enlisted, many face workers had to depart from the traditional division of labour and undertake putters' tasks as well; development work on new pits or seams had to be post-poned, although shortages as the War progressed led to some relaxation of such restrictions; shift systems were revised, principally to reduce the number of cutting shifts and thereby concentrate inputs; and the War also introduced some acceleration, albeit a marginal one, in mechaniza-tion and economy in the use of hand labour and horse power.[3]

The framework for all these pressures and adaptations was, of course, the regulatory oversight of coalmining. 'The whole history of the coal trade', asserted the *Colliery Guardian* in its review of 1917, 'has been an experiment in Government control of a great industry.'[4] In the last resort, as we shall see, the most serious problem for the Coal Control was the manpower shortage, and it was this which drew the government into the most contentious areas of policy-making. But the Control was also concerned with immediate issues of demand and distribution. Indeed, the Control's first priority task, and perhaps its most unam-biguous success, was logistical: to rationalize the use of the country's rail

---

[1] *Sankey Evidence* I, 401, 404. At one time late in 1917 there were 11,000 wagon-loads of coal blocked in South Wales, unable to find shipping. With the shortage of storage space in the valleys, the Control contemplated closing the district's pits. The Admiralty then succeeded in finding enough vessels to relieve the industry, and within two weeks ships were queuing for coal instead of the other way round.

[2] *CG* 4 Jan. 1918, 26.

[3] For a general, if somewhat vague, description of the effects of the War on production in the different coalfields, see the Divisional Inspectors' reports in *Mines and Quarries, General Report for 1918*.

[4] *CG* 4 Jan. 1918, 25.

network for the carriage of coal. It was largely the pressure of a huge coal traffic on an already overloaded land transport system which produced a virtual 'coal famine' in the South during the winter of 1916–17.[1] Easing this situation would solve two problems: shortages in the supply of consumers and disruptions to production because of the inability to provide empty wagons to the pithead.

The basic prerequisite for the necessary rationalization was statistical data. The Coal Control's Distribution Branch, headed by Edwin Davies, former district Goods Manager of the London & North Western Railway, therefore immediately set about gathering information on the amount, types, and channels through which coal was distributed. And four months after Calthrop assumed office, he was able to produce a 'Coal Transport Reorganization Scheme', which divided the country into 20 areas (all but two of which contained coalmines) and set strict limits as to which geographical markets might be supplied by rail from which areas. The objective was to reduce the total amount of coal traffic, while concentrating as much as possible on the trunk lines with the best facilities.[2]

The Coal Control had estimated that the scheme would save 700 million ton-miles of railway resources, and although it was never possible to provide an accurate measure of the economies attained, Davies subsequently attested to the validity of the estimate—which was in any case probably too low, since it related to savings on the carriage of coal only and not to the cost of hauling the deadweight of wagons. This, he argued in 1919, before the Sankey Commission (where the owners were concerned to deny the value of central direction of transport, let alone mining) was equivalent to an annual saving of 50,000 trains each carrying 350 tons of coal 40 miles. He also contested the claim of some owners to the Commission that the saving had been purchased at the cost of obliging customers to accept inappropriate grades of coal. Far from being 'a complete fiasco', as many in the coal trade had anticipated, the scheme had proved its worth and 'should be maintained as a means to effecting national economy'.[3] It

---

[1] Ibid.

[2] The necessary information was gathered through the District Coal and Coke Supply Committees which had existed since 1915. The scheme is described in POWE 26/8 (4 July 1917); Redmayne 1923, ch. VI; and Davies's evidence to the Sankey Commission (*Sankey Evidence* I, QQ 1887–93, 2120–24). Redmayne and Davies, both of whom vigorously defended the scheme, claimed that it would have been perfectly possible to apply similar controls to trade *within* the areas, but that staff shortages precluded the necessary administrative effort.

[3] Even the *Colliery Guardian* praised the scheme, and the Divisional Inspector of Mines for the

was an argument eagerly (if unsuccessfully) adopted by those who favoured nationalization in 1919.

The Coal Control was therefore undoubtedly successful in its oversight of market allocation; but it had much less success in tackling the potential waste involved in the private ownership, and exclusive use, of railway wagons. It was estimated that apart from 800,000 wagons owned by railway companies, there were about 600,000 wagons in private ownership, of which 400,000 belonged to colliery companies. Earlier attempts to persuade coalowners to pool their wagons, so as to avoid the extensive running of part-full or empty wagons, had failed.[1] Now, the Coal Control, which in the spring of 1917 took powers under the Defence of the Realm Regulations, had no more success. The problem of securing the agreement of coalowners and railway companies to financial terms, the threat of disorganization, and the fact that merchants and collieries tended to use wagons as mobile storage bunkers, proved obstacles to any national scheme, or even to an experiment which the Coal Control wished to conduct in Lancashire.[2] After the War, Davies argued that one-third of all wagons could have been saved if they had been pooled—an estimate which was greeted with disingenuous shock by such advocates of a single coal enterprise as Sidney Webb and R. H. Tawney.[3]

Price controls were also a leading feature of government intervention in the coal industry. They had, of course, been the first example of intervention in 1915, when the Price of Coal (Limitation) Act had set a maximum of 4s. per ton above the prewar price of comparable coals sold on the domestic market.[4] (Export prices were allowed to go much higher, and coal for the Admiralty was purchased below the domestic levels.) In June 1917, arguing that it was necessary to prevent undue price fluctuations, the Coal Controller ordered that the maxima of the Act should also be the minima, and tightened his grip on the price of exports and on distribution margins.[5] Broadly speaking, it was assumed

Yorkshire and North Midland Division asserted that the rail congestion which had led to pit stoppages in the early part of the War was overcome by control: *Mines and Quarries. General Report for 1918*, 45.

[1] Above, ch. 2, sect. ii.

[2] *Sankey Evidence* I, QQ 1897–2110; *MAGB* 1918, 26–41; BT 189/1, 13 June 1917. The Scottish railways operated a limited, and successful, pooling scheme.

[3] *Sankey Evidence* I, QQ 2050–2.

[4] Above, 55.

[5] POWE 26/8 (28 June and 5 Sept. 1917). There were instances of export coals selling at up to four times their inland price: Redmayne 1923, 263.

that domestic price increases should not exceed the increase in costs of production.

This was certainly the presumed basis of the legislation of 1915, and further increases were allowed on the same assumption—first in the autumn of 1917 (2s. 6d. on domestic sales when adult miners received a flat-rate bonus of 1s. 6d. per shift, and juveniles 9d.), then in June 1918 (2s. 6d. to cover increases in non-wage costs), and finally in July 1918 (a further 1s. 6d. to compensate for another wage bonus). The result, it was estimated, was a doubling of average pithead prices for domestic coal, from 9s. 10d. to 20s. 4d. per ton between 1914 and 1918. Meanwhile, export prices, especially to neutral countries, were allowed to rise much more freely, ranging up to 50s. per ton for best Welsh bituminous coal and 70s. for large screened Midlands fuel.[1]

All this was based on the need to cover costs and to make the controlled industry self-supporting. But, as Lowes Dickinson, the Head of the Finance Branch, subsequently admitted to the Sankey Commission, the Coal Control had very little clear idea of the actual cost increases, or (therefore) of the very high profits being made by some colliery companies. In 1917, the new prices which collieries were allowed to charge, were set at a level which would keep the least efficient undertakings in business. And this had the inevitable result that the more productive firms were able to earn very substantial profits. Admittedly, in 1918 the Control instituted a form of 'claw-back' of any surplus between the cost of the war wages and the higher prices and the presumed increase in costs. But even then, as Dickinson admitted under fierce cross-questioning by the miners' representatives on the Commission, the extent of the price increase was substantially more than was warranted by the actual—as distinct from the claimed—increase in operating costs: 'on the information we have now [in 1919] it is extremely improbable that the 2s. 6d. [price increase] would have gone

---

[1] POWE 26/8 (domestic price orders of 12 Oct. 1917, 21 June, and 5 July 1918); CAB 23/6/189 (21 June 1918); MUN 4/3806 (10 July 1918); POWE 26/8 (export prices: 26 Oct. 1918). For actual prices (proceeds), see CYB 1932, 598. Domestic increases were not uniform. In recognition of the special cost problems of South Wales & Monmouthshire and the Forest of Dean they were allowed to sell coal at 2s. 6d. more than the national margin above prewar prices—13s. as against 10s. 6d. from July 1918. The administration of price increases varied over time. Initially, they were at the free disposal of colliery companies. But from the summer of 1918, as has been indicated, the Coal Control assumed formal responsibility for the war wage awards. Colliery companies were credited with the payment of the war wages on behalf of Control, and were debited with a levy of 4s. per ton (equivalent to the notional price increases). If their war wage costs fell below 4s. per ton, the balance was to be paid to the Control and used as a pool to compensate those firms whose wage costs exceeded the levy.

on'. Between 1913 and 1916 average profits per ton virtually doubled, and aggregate profits (on a smaller tonnage) rose by over 50 per cent.[1]

Although the Coal Control's responsibilities in relation to distribution and prices were clearly important, as the War proceeded it became apparent that the vital problems related to the contrast between the mounting demand for fuel and its by-products, and the diminishing supply. As far as the domestic economy was concerned, the situation was eased by the fall in overseas shipments, from 98.3 million tons in 1913 to 43.4 million in 1918 (however, as has been seen, the war-induced dislocation of exports impaired the war effort through its effects on Allies and the earning of foreign exchange). Yet even though the amount of coal available for home consumption grew from 189 million tons in 1913 to 200 million tons in 1917, the generally higher level of domestic economic activity, and the sustained expansion of the munitions and related industries,[2] put an increasing strain on coal supplies. When, in 1918, supplies dropped below prewar levels, the threat not merely to munitions production, but to civilian morale, labour relations, and public order, became a prime consideration for the War Cabinet.[3] Even before then, however, the severity of the 1916–17 winter and the shortage of carters had provoked a flurry of activity to increase supplies to the London poor. And by the summer of 1917 the need to allocate household coal in an equitable way led to the introduction of domestic rationing in London.[4]

Active and successful as the Coal Control had been in its oversight of distribution and prices, the latent problem of production (which had led to the creation of the Coal Mining Organisation Committee in 1915) was to become dramatically manifest in the last year of the War. At its root lay the difficulty which had also existed since 1914–15: a shortage of manpower. And just as that had been occasioned by the voluntary enlistment of miners, so the Coal Control's knottiest problems were generated by the need to balance the mines' demand for men and the nation's recruitment system.[5]

[1] *Sankey Evidence* I, 403–9 (Evidence of Sir Arthur Lowes Dickinson), Appendix 5; *CYB* 1932, 598.

[2] In June 1918 it was estimated that the Ministry of Munitions had an interest in 120 million tons of coal, or 60% of the nation's output. Steel production alone took 32 million tons. See MUN 4/3806 (10 June and 9 Sept. 1918).

[3] Below, 94–7.

[4] CAB 21/87 (8 Feb. 1917); POWE 26/8 ('Household Coal Distribution Order', 10 Aug. 1917 and 'Notice to Consumers' 1 Sept. 1917). The maximum annual entitlement ranged from 3 tons 18 cwt for a dwelling of up to 4 rooms, to 12 tons 13 cwt for one of 9 or 10 rooms, and 22 tons to 10 cwt for one of more than 15 rooms.

[See opposite page for n. 5]

As we have seen, towards the end of 1915, when the gravity of the coal industry's manpower losses were properly appreciated, mining occupations had been 'barred', and when compulsory military service was introduced in 1916, underground and some surface occupations had been certified as of national importance, and their workers exempted from the call-up. Questions of deregistration (e.g. to secure a supply of tunnellers for military duty) were handled by Colliery Recruiting Courts, on which miners' representatives had a powerful voice. But, in any case, policy oscillated. Thus, in the recruiting drive of the spring of 1916 there was a review of the circumstances of all those who had joined the industry since 15 August 1915, with a view to a 'comb-out' of recent entrants (this date was later amended to include all those who had joined since the War). On the other hand, by the summer of the same year the threatened shortage of coal led to an absolute ban on the recruitment of miners and a recall of ex-miners in home military units who were unfit for overseas service.[1]

In any event, by January 1917, as the Coal Control commenced, some 26 per cent of the industry's original labour force of some 1.1 million had joined or been recruited into the Forces, and had been largely replaced by new entrants from other industries or from the schools. But the War's appetite for men was insatiable, and the coalmining industry was one of the last big reservoirs of young, fit men. In January 1917, therefore, the War Cabinet decided to call up 20,000 miners—starting with the unskilled (primarily surface workers) and those who had joined the industry since the outbreak of the War. This led to protests by the MFGB, and active resistance in South Wales. But although the War Office suspended the notices for two months in the hope that volunteers would make up the numbers, strategic needs soon enforced a call for a further 20,000.

The national union, but not the South Wales Federation, subsequently endorsed the idea of a comb-out of newer entrants and it was agreed that the Controller would allocate quotas to individual districts, where they would be filled according to lists drawn up by joint committees of owners and men. Even so, the results of the comb-out were

[5] For the recruitment of miners, see Redmayne 1923, 49–55, 146–8, 192–5; and Cole 1923, *passim*.

[1] Redmayne 1923, 54; CAB 42/16/8 (16 June 1916). There was some disagreement between the Home and War Offices as to the number of former miners in the Forces. The War Office estimate was significantly lower than that of the Home Office (or than was, in fact, the case)—either because of problems of occupational definition or because miners did not declare their jobs with any precise accuracy on joining the Army.

disappointing, as a pessimistic Coal Controller reported to the War Cabinet in July, while simultaneously warning its members of the need to handle the MFGB with great tact.[1] Throughout the autumn of 1917 controversy raged over the government's attempts to introduce effective conscription for miners. Indeed, only the combined effect of General Smuts's oratory and the persuasive power of the MFGB Executive prevented a general strike on the issue in South Wales (where the Miners' Federation held a strike ballot on the issue), while the national union vigorously opposed the War Cabinet's move to deny the MFGB its previous right of dealing directly with the Coal Control on matters relating to recruitment.[2]

But the War had not stopped consuming men—or coal. In January 1918 the War Cabinet was obliged to accede to Geddes's request for 50,000 recruits from the mines, with a further 50,000 to be held in reserve for later conscription. Now the MFGB itself was stirred (partly under pressure from the South Wales Federation) to protest and action: it arranged for a national ballot to gauge the attitude of its members to conscription. Yet the military situation grew so much more threatening that the War Cabinet decided to press ahead with recruitment on the government's own terms (whereupon the MFGB predicted strikes and 'anarchy').

In the event, although the miners' ballot showed a narrow margin against the comb-out, the miners were persuaded not to oppose it—principally because of the crisis provoked by the German spring offensive, together with some very plain speaking by the Director of Military Operations and the Prime Minister. The Germans might soon be at Calais, Lloyd George said on 21 March, 'and the only answer we

[1] CAB 23/1/120 (19 Jan. 1917); BT 189/1 (28 Mar. and 27 June 1917); CAB 24/19/101–2 (3 July 1917); CAB 24/20/440–2 (20 July 1917). For the South Wales Miners' Federation continuing opposition to the comb-out, see *The Times* 17 Apr. 1917, 3e. It was as well that the miners were not privy to a eugenicist outburst by Auckland Geddes, Minister for National Service, on 13 July (CAB 23/3/104–6). He complained that 3.9 million men of military age were still in civilian employment, and that a disproportionate burden of recruitment was being placed upon older men, and those from the professions or independent business. Those still in civilian life 'contained a large number of syndicalists, cowards, cranks of all sorts, and unskilled men'. The War was therefore 'destroying the independent class of the nation and protecting those not so worthy of being preserved'. Later in the discussion, Geddes claimed that the mining industry contained just over 500,000 men of military age—the largest pool of potential soldiers in the country.

[2] CAB 24/28/134 (8 Oct. 1917); CAB 23/4/106 (18 Oct. 1917); BT 189/1 (31 Oct. 1917). The Minister of National Service, Geddes, had urged the War Cabinet to change its policy. The miners on the Coal Controller's Advisory Board were particularly anxious 'to keep out of the hands of the Ministry of National Service'.

have to give, is a vote of the Miners' Federation to say that they are not prepared to fight. You cannot give that answer.' As the possibility of a major battlefield defeat loomed, Geddes asked for the second batch of 50,000 miners. The political economy of coal in wartime appeared to have taken a new turn. The loss of miners might have to be accepted, and household rationing extended to the entire country, while the Controller was requested to draw up contingency plans for industrial rationing of coal.[1]

In fact, the industrial implications of the decisions taken under the pressure of events on the Western Front in the early spring of 1918 were more serious than were appreciated at the time. By May, the Coal Controller sensed the existence of a potential crisis of coal supplies that was likely to become even more serious than the crisis of military manpower. He argued that the situation had changed significantly since the beginning of the year. Then, he had agreed to an extensive comb-out of working miners because production was relatively buoyant at the end of 1917, and because shipping shortages were in any case impeding exports to Britain's European Allies. Now, however, there was a rapidly mounting scarcity of coal in France, aggravated by the loss of output in the Pas-de-Calais following the German advance. Further, shipping was available and the comb-out was having unexpectedly disruptive effects on production. He therefore asked for a reduction in the recruitment target.

Reluctantly, the War Cabinet lowered it to 75,000. Even so, the coal situation was still sufficiently serious for the government to order that Allied markets should have absolute priority over neutral ones; that domestic rationing should be severely extended to the whole country (this was done in June) and plans for industrial rationing advanced; and that 25,000 medically 'low-grade' miners should be returned from the Army to the industry. Meanwhile, the Prime Minister arranged to meet managers and miners in order to exhort them to greater efforts; and the Controller once more tried, and once more failed, to persuade the MFGB that the crisis warranted the suspension of the Eight Hours Act (on the Advisory Board even the owners concluded that the miners' likely hostile reaction would nullify the effects of a longer working day).[2]

---

[1] See Redmayne 1923, 193–4; CAB 24/44/20, 285–7 (4 and 12 Mar. 1918); BT 189/1 (6 Mar. 1918); CAB 23/5/177, 186 (22 and 25 Mar. 1918); CAB 24/61/36 (15 Aug. 1918). For the attitudes and policies of the South Wales Miners' Federation, see Woodhouse 1969, 142–4. Lloyd George's 'straight and burning words' were reported in *The Times* 23 Mar. 1918, 4c, 6c.

[2] CAB 24/52/36–9 (22 May 1918); CAB 23/6/126 (24 May 1918); CAB 24/53/69 (31 May 1918);

The decision to extend the rationing of household coal was designed to save about 25 per cent of the 35 or 36 million tons consumed annually in private dwellings. But this eight or nine million tons—which was the most obvious economy—was quite insufficient to bridge the now alarming gap between new needs and declining production. And throughout the summer of 1918 tortured discussion of the shortfall, and of the least harmful way of meeting it, continued at the War Cabinet, its War Priorities Committee, the Coal Control, and the Ministry of Munitions Coal Supply Committee (created in June to tackle shortages of supply to munitions works).[1]

The essence of the problem was that the likely production in 1918 was estimated at 230 million tons—reflecting a reduction, compared with 1917, of 18 million tons (caused principally by the loss of manpower to the Forces, but also by the influenza epidemic which, by increasing involuntary absenteeism, reduced output by about three million tons in July). On the other hand, there was likely to be an increase in demand of some 20 million tons: nine million for crucial exports, five million for the munitions industry, five million for the Admiralty and the American Expeditionary Forces, and one million for agriculture and the food industries. Against this, recent policies (household rationing, a cut of 4.5 million tons in extra-European exports, and stock reductions) could only generate savings of 15.5 million tons. All estimates of the gap agreed on its gravity. There was likely to be a shortage of between 20 and 25 million tons, or some 10 per cent of annual output.[2]

From late summer of 1918, therefore, the coal industry experienced its most threatening wartime crisis. Its severity was exemplified by the response to the claim for a further wage award of 1s. 6d. per shift which the miners, sensing an opportunity favourable to their case, submitted in June. The Coal Controller, desperate above all to avoid a stoppage, privately urged the owners not to resist the demand. The imminent shortage of coal was so obvious and severe that the claim would *have* to be granted, and speedily.[3] But the avoidance of a strike simply maintained an unsatisfactory situation. The government's dilemma was that

CAB 24/54/140–8 (13 June 1918); CAB 24/61/39 (15 Aug. 1918); BT 189/1 (discussion of Eight Hours Act on 30 May, 6 June, and 25 Sept. 1918); POWE 26/8 ('The Household Fuel and Lighting Order', 28 June 1918).

[1] MUN 4/3806.

[2] Detailed calculations are in CAB 24/62/274 (31 Aug. 1918). Discussions are in MUN 4/3811 (17 June 1918); CAB 24/54/313 (18 June 1918); CAB 23/6/188 (21 June 1918); CAB 23/7/92–3, Appendix I (30 Aug. 1918).

[3] BT 189/1 (14 June 1918).

the only area in which there was realistic scope for economy was in the supply of coal to industry, and if industrial rationing were to be in any way commensurate with the problem, it would throw a huge number out of work (a figure of 500,000 was generally accepted). Even though the Ministry of Munitions was willing to forgo its claim for an additional five million tons, the likely cost of rationing in terms of worsening morale, bad industrial relations, higher unemployment benefit, and possible public disorder would still have been considerable. And the only alternative to industrial rationing was the release of fit and experienced former miners from the Army.

Throughout August and September a consequential controversy raged in government circles. On the one side, as the military position grew more tense and the supply of armed manpower more critical, the proposal that the Army be robbed of soldiers was fiercely resisted by the Service Chiefs and only with the greatest reluctance contemplated by the War Cabinet. (Indeed, as late as the beginning of August the War Cabinet had turned down a proposal of its own War Priorities Committee that the recruiting of coalminers be suspended until spring 1919.)[1] On the other side, those directly concerned with the coal industry were conscious of an inescapable logic: neither exhortations to greater effort nor swingeing economies would suffice to produce the vital supplies.

In mid-August, the Coal Controller urged the War Cabinet to release 25,000 Grade 'A' men to dig coal (as well as to expedite the release of the 18,000 lower-grade men still remaining from the June quota of 25,000). To others, more experienced in the industry, even this was insufficient. The MAGB argued that the need was for 50,000 more men; and Sir Adam Nimmo (a leading Scottish owner who had just become expert adviser to the Coal Control) confirmed this to the War Cabinet, warning that the Controller's request was inadequate, and that no amount of extra effort would alone meet the problem.[2] In September Nimmo wrote a powerful letter to the Prime Minister, reminding him that propaganda for more output was a two-edged sword (since it served to

[1] CAB 24/59/198–200 (30 July 1918); CAB 23/7/55 (7 Aug. 1918).
[2] CAB 23/7/70–1 (16 Aug. 1918); *MAGB* 1919, 16, 21–2. Both the owners and the miners had rejected the Controller's plea for them to second a representative to help him through the crisis, and relations with the MFGB in particular were growing very strained. Nimmo served in a private capacity. By the late summer, the MAGB were complaining of lack of consultation and excessive interference in management problems by miners' representatives on the Advisory Board, and the MFGB was pressing for a much greater executive role for the Board and far more detailed information about the business activities of coalmining. See *MAGB* 1919, 16, 19–20; BT 189/1 (25 Sept. 1918).

remind the miners of the strength of their bargaining position) and pointing out that the shortages were 'too great to be overcome by any temporising expedient'.[1]

For as long as they could, and even after recognizing the political obstacles to industrial rationing, leading Ministers, and Lloyd George in particular, clung to the empty belief that exhortation might turn the tide: on 10 August the Prime Minister was pleading with Welsh miners to 'sling coal at them ... hurl it in wagon loads', and almost a month later, on the very brink of a disaster of coal supplies, the War Cabinet still postponed a decision in order to allow Lloyd George to make a personal and private appeal to miners' leaders.[2] But by October even this, now desperate, expedient had been exposed as useless. On 7 October the President of the Board of Trade and the Coal Controller presented what amounted to an ultimatum to the War Cabinet: it *had* to choose quickly between industrial rationing, with the concomitant risk of 500,000 unemployed, and the release of 50,000 miners from the Forces. And a week later, after a sorely troubled discussion, torn between the strength of the Army and the morale of civilians, the War Cabinet surrendered. Plans for industrial rationing were abandoned and the Armed Forces were told to transfer the necessary number of Grade 'A' miners to the Reserve with a view to releasing them to the coal-mining industry. By 7 November, within four days of the Armistice, almost 38,000 former miners had been released from the Army.[3]

The War therefore came to an end just as the government had taken the extreme step of releasing serving fighting men, in the fittest and most active grades—a step which was to be resisted in the Second World War.[4] Yet the significance of the move was never put to the test, for it was taken just as the German war effort was about to collapse. The advent of peace therefore prevented an assessment of whether the addition of 50,000 working miners would have maintained the supply of coal at an adequate level while not seriously handicapping the military effort which it had been designed to serve.[5] But at

[1] CAB 24/61/34–9, 45, 48–51 (15 Aug. 1918); CAB 23/7/70–1, 92–3 (16 and 30 Aug. 1918); CAB 24/62/100–4, 274 (29 and 31 Aug. 1918); CAB 24/64/106–8 (Nimmo to Lloyd George, 16 Sept. 1918).

[2] *CG* 16 Aug. 1918, 341; Redmayne 1923, 190; CAB 23/7/96–7 (3 Sept. 1918).

[3] CAB 24/66/6–10 (7 Oct. 1918); CAB 23/8/29–31 (15 Oct. 1918); MUN 4/3806 (23 Oct. 1918); POWE 20/11 (7 Nov. 1918).

[4] Below, ch. 11, sect. v; ch. 12, sect. iv.

[5] In the weeks after the Armistice the coal shortage was, if anything, worse. Anxious about the diminished supply of fuel in the United Kingdom ('there might be a revolution') and the slow rate of demobilization of miners, a ministerial committee under Lloyd George pressed for much more

least the War had been successfully negotiated without a crippling shortage of fuel.

Whatever the fortuitous elements in that success—and it is difficult to imagine that the coal problem would have been easily solved if hostilities had lasted into 1919—the Coal Control had attained its principal goal. By a combination of compromise, exhortation, concession, and painful effort, it had guided the industry through the last two years of the War without a disastrous loss of coal supplies, or any very serious dislocation of prices of distribution. Instead, the brunt of the War's distortion had been borne by wages, profits, and industrial relations. And in these respects the consequences of the War and the way coal was controlled were to be irresistibly long-lasting.

iii. Mining labour in the Great War

As far as the coal industry was concerned, the principal effect of the particular form of state control that was adopted was to enhance the influence and power of the miners in matters relating to wages, hours, conditions of work, the control of the labour supply, and direct access to government authority. If only temporarily, the War transformed the expectations and ambitions of the miners as a group.

Even before control, in South Wales through the strike of July 1915 and more generally by less dramatic pressure, the Miners' Federation of Great Britain had preserved and even extended its precious privileges—as its President (in the face of radical criticism of the Executive) had pointed out to the Annual Conference in 1916.[1] The miners had gained a degree of control over work processes and recruitment policy, had successfully obstructed changes which might have increased the supply of juvenile labour below ground or female labour at the surface, had preserved the Eight Hours Act inviolate, had excluded themselves from the operations of the Munitions of War Act, and prevented the application of compulsory arbitration in the industry. Even the advent of control can be seen as a victory for the South Wales miners, unwittingly aided by the obstinate owners, in making private ownership virtually unworkable in wartime conditions. From the outset the miners secured a commitment from Lloyd George that control would not bring any

urgency and dispatched Lord Milner to France to ensure that the government's orders were fulfilled. By the end of the third week in December about 100,000 miners had been demobilized. CAB 24/70/238 (25 Nov. 1918); CAB 23/8/102 (6 Dec. 1918); BT 189/1 (18 Dec. 1918).

[1] *MFGB* 1916 (Annual Conference, 11 July).

legal discipline to pit labour or involve a reduction of wages (which might have happened if coal prices had been reduced and local wage agreements had been activated).[1]

In general, the miners' wartime achievements were, perhaps, unavoidable concessions. In any case, state control and financial oversight did, indeed, secure much of the government's initial objective: they greatly reduced the more disruptive manifestations of resentment on the part of the miners which had earlier been fed by the existence of untrammelled private ownership and profits. Admittedly, price controls and an excess profits duty existed before December 1917. But both as symbols and because they entailed a further levy on collieries and a degree of reallocation of profits, the new arrangements made a considerable psychological difference in persuading the miners that they were not simply working on behalf of the owners' private profit.

On the other hand, the existence of control by no means eliminated unrest among miners or secured their unconditional commitment to the war effort. (In this respect, some official pronouncements were excessively sanguine.)[2] Their material aspirations and anxieties still determined their attitudes to the industry and work. This was most obviously the case as far as wages were concerned, particularly in so far as wartime inflation threatened living standards. As we saw in Chapter 2, the successful wage claim of 1915 had been primarily related to the cost of living, and the possibility of future claims on the same grounds was brought forward by the MFGB at the introduction of control. Meanwhile, however, throughout 1916 local Conciliation Board Agreements continued to apply, leading mostly to wage increases, but occasionally to a reduction (as in Northumberland in February 1917, when the miners asserted that they would not repeat the experience).[3] By the summer of 1917, however, prices had moved up sufficiently far for the miners to initiate a national, concerted move to adjust wage levels.

In May, the miners had complained to the Prime Minister about 'shameful profiteering', and demanded government control and rationing of food. By 1 June 1917 food costs had risen 100 per cent above their

---

[1] F200/1 (meeting of 21 Dec. 1915); BT 189/1 (7 Mar. 1917); *Hansard* 22 Mar. 1917, cols. 2048–9; POWE 20/10 (26 Feb. 1917).

[2] See the review of the Coal Control's Production Branch in 1917 ('Control of Coal Mines', 2 Jan. 1918) in POWE 10/12: the experience 'justifies the assertion that the men now realise that they are working for their country rather than for the private profit of their employers, with the result that there has been a marked decrease in industrial unrest.'

[3] POWE 20/10 (20 Feb. 1917). Later that year the Coal Controller ordered that there should be no further reductions in export areas: POWE 20/10 (6 Sept. 1917).

level of 8 August 1914 (although government officials estimated that adjustments of diet to reduce the consumption of eggs, butter, and sugar would imply a cost-of-food increase of only two-thirds). And at the end of July a special conference of the MFGB decided to press for a national wage increase of 25 per cent to match the wartime rise in the cost of living. Within government circles, it was accepted that the miners' case was moderately strong, since their full claim would just about match the rise in the overall cost of living (including non-food items) of about 75 per cent between July 1914 and 1 August 1917. More than this, it was also accepted that (especially in comparison with workers in munitions and allied industries) the miners had 'played the game', and not made a wage demand in 1917. Further, as was to be the case in the Second World War, instances were cited of miners' children bringing home bigger wage packets than their fathers, from easier, if more time-consuming, work in munitions factories.[1]

In spite of this mood, the Coal Control and the government were at first disinclined to concede any very large increase. But the MFGB's leaders were now adamant. Their claim (for 1s. 10d. per shift), they argued, transcended the conventional cost-of-living index and the achievement of other industries was irrelevant. The miners, they asserted, had a special case for a social wage.

By late September the issue had been brought to the verge of a national strike, with the Executive of the union asserting that it could hardly restrain the men, who were 'in no mood to brook delay'. With the munitions industry having a mere 10 days' supply of fuel, 'the men out of hand', and the possibility that Britain might not be in a position to prosecute the War, the War Cabinet had to concede. 'The government', it was understandably minuted, 'could not embark on a conflict with the miners unless they were certain to bring it to a victorious issue', and that was judged to be unlikely. Public opinion would not easily be convinced that the government 'were justified in permitting a colossal dislocation of the nation's industries in the midst of war for the sake of a difference of half-a-crown'.

The issue was settled on 28 September, by an award of 1s. 6d. per shift ('boys' received 9d. but the age at which 'boys' became adults was lowered from 18 to 16). In addition, the miners secured two important concessions: the payment for idle days when there was no work available, and the bonus payment for six afternoon or night shifts even where

---

[1] The May Conference is touched on in CAB 24/13/240-1 (18 May 1917). The wage claim is dealt with in POWE 20/10 (Sept.) and POWE 26/11 (Nimmo to Calthrop, 30 Aug. 1917).

the customary work week was less than six days. The total cost of the award was estimated at £22 million and, although this averaged 2s. per ton on inland sales, prices were raised by 2s. 6d. to allow for the variety of local conditions.[1]

After the 1917 award a 'marked tranquillity' was detected 'among mining labour'.[2] But given wartime circumstances it was only a matter of time before the industrial-relations trauma was repeated. By June 1918, in the midst of a profound crisis of coal supply,[3] the MFGB put forward a claim for a doubling of the bonus awarded in September 1917. And this time the atmosphere was even less propitious for official resistance. The shortage of coal loomed disastrously, the miners were in a position of extraordinary strategic strength and appeared quite ready to use it. Hence, a mere two days after the claim was submitted to the Coal Controller he met the owners and informed them that a strike had to be avoided at all costs. The owners were therefore told to keep in the background, and on 28 June, when the War Cabinet met in sombre mood, it was obliged to accept the argument that shipping traffic and the munitions industries might be stopped, and France and Italy driven out of the War, if the miners' demands were not accepted. The Cabinet therefore declined 'to go to war with the miners', and surrendered, with a vacuous attempt to save a little face by attaching an unenforceable condition 'that the miners should increase their output'.[4]

As a result of the adjustment of wage standards in 1915, the myriad changes in standards and rates throughout the War, and the flat-rate bonuses of 1917 and 1918, miners' actual earnings rose appreciably between June 1914 and November 1918. Even so, the average increase (which varied from 92.5 per cent for piecework getters to 98.75 per cent for unskilled dayworkers) lagged behind the increase in the average cost of living, which was about 120 or 125 per cent.[5] However, some further points need to be made about this situation.

First, the comparison which implies a fall in real wages may be misleading in so far as changes in working-class expenditures in wartime

[1] Material relating to the dispute is in POWE 20/10; CAB 23/4/64, 67, 86, 100 (26–7 Sept., 8 and 16 Oct. 1917); CAB 24/28/62 (5 Oct. 1917).

[2] MUN 10/20 (2 Jan. 1918).

[3] Above, 95.

[4] BT 189/1 (14 June 1918); CAB 24/55/209, 219 (26–7 June 1918); CAB 23/6/199–200 (28 June 1918). Within a week the MFGB (insisting on the utmost speed) also obliged the government to pay the increased rates to its members (i.e. other sorts of miners) working in munitions industries.

[5] Rowe 1923, 88 ff. Wages for June 1914 and July/Sept. 1918 are also given in *ARSM* 1922, 122. These suggest a national average increase of from 6s. 5½d. to 12s. 6½d. (6s. 9d. to 14s. for SWM and 6s. 2d. to 12s. 6d. for Northumberland).

appear to have enabled many wage-earners to enhance their standard of comfort with a less than proportionate increase in spending.[1] Second, there was the usual variation in wage movements as between districts (of the leading fields, Northumberland, Scotland, and South Wales did significantly better than average). Third, as the average figures imply, the War witnessed a narrowing of the pay differential between skilled and unskilled mineworkers—a narrowing which occurred almost entirely after the summer of 1917 since it was based on the universal flat-rate bonuses of September 1917 and June 1918. (The gap was to be further reduced in 1919 and 1920, when additional bonuses were awarded.) Finally, although the two successful wage claims of 1917 and 1918 had not represented any unique assertiveness on the part of miners (throughout the last two years of the War there had been general pressure on wages, especially in war-related industries), they *had* exemplified their special political and economic position.

As has already been made abundantly clear, however, the strengthened position of the miners was not exemplified in wage bargaining alone. Indeed, as far as the union leadership was concerned, much of their attention was given to the protection of the privileges which prewar legislation had given their members, and with the wartime rulings and adjustments they had secured. The miners therefore managed to retain control of their hours of work, the supply of labour, a good deal of recruiting policy, and the publicity in favour of more sustained effort which was an integral part of the war effort.

To those charged with the responsibility of mobilizing Britain's resources for the War, many of the miners' attitudes—and in particular their unwillingness to extend working hours or adapt working practices and conventions—were bound to seem exasperating, wilful, and even selfish. Admittedly, the Coal Controller, who had to make the best use of the material and situation to hand, tended to be quite extraordinarily tolerant. To others accustomed to a different perspective, in so far as labour harmony existed in coalmining, it appeared to have been purchased by large, and too easily gained, concessions. There was a widespread feeling that, after the miners had succeeded in excluding themselves from the operations of the Munitions of War Act in 1915, they had abused their position. And this was exemplified in journalists' complaints about 'a tribute to be paid by the nation' to the miners, and in the Minister of Labour's argument that they 'have felt that they have

[1] Winter 1986, ch. 7; *Report of the Committee . . . the Cost of Living* (Cd. 8980. 1918), 7, 20.

the whip hand of the government' and used their position to 'force concession after concession without encountering any effective opposition'.[1]

In practice, of course, the coal industry presented a superficial appearance of relative harmony. But the infrequency of widespread national or regional stoppages did not reflect any powerlessness on the part of the miners' union, or any conciliatory desire to subsume their individual concerns in the service of official policy. Rather, it was an indication of the relative ease with which the strategic scarcity of coal enabled the miners to defend what they took to be their industrial interests.

On many issues the question of a dispute did not arise: the MFGB simply withheld its cooperation and government and owners alike realized that it would be futile to press the point. In any case, the incidence of national or even large regional strikes is a poor index of the state of industrial relations in the coal industry. Coal's open conflicts were more characteristically fragmented and local, diffused and erratic. Hence, even though there was no national stoppage (and only one serious district strike—in South Wales in 1915) the statistics of strikes indicate that the coalmining industry remained far and away the most susceptible to disputes during the War. It was true that there was a reduced strike proneness during the War, which was greater in the case of coal than any other major industry except transport. But coal's overall record remained the worst. Working days lost through strikes in the industry accounted for 13 per cent of the national total in 1913 (it had exceeded 75 per cent in 1912), over one-third in 1914, about 55 per cent in 1915, 13 per cent in 1916, and some 20 per cent in each of 1917 and 1918.[2]

This strike record is one indication of the constant background of potential disaffection among many workers in the industry. Meanwhile, union membership grew during the war years (according to one source, MFGB membership rose from some 645,000 at the end of 1913 to 754,000 in 1918 and 805,000 in 1919—and there were thousands of members of other mining unions).[3] And the unstable character of

---

[1] *The Times* 26 Sept. 1917, 4a and 4b; and 28 Sept. 1917, 4a; CAB 24/60/157–61 (13 Aug. 1918). Cf. CAB 24/62/100–4 (28 Aug. 1918).

[2] Department of Employment and Productivity 1971, Table 197. Cf. Knowles 1954, 162.

[3] Arnot 1953, 545. Arnot's figures for the MFGB are probably underestimates: the Registrar of Friendly Societies' returns of mining unions exceeding 5,000 members in 1913 suggested that there were well in excess of 700,000 in England and Wales alone and Church (1986, 690–1)

industrial relations in the industry lent considerable strength to the arguments of the union's national leadership that theirs was a precarious control, needing powerful reinforcement through the granting of concessions and the avoidance of provocation on the part of the state. As a result, it was only very rarely and in moments of extreme hazard—as with the recruiting crisis of the spring of 1918—that the government was able freely to assert its will against the determination of the miners.

In many respects, however, the War merely served to strengthen the more permanent forces which shaped the social outlook of mining communities.

This obviously applied to the determinants of the general 'militancy' and sensitivity of mining communities: their geographical isolation and concentration, the character of underground work, the antipathy to hierarchical intrusion and anxiety about relative autonomy within the work process—all of which would have been affected by official wartime pressure for increased production.[1] But it also related to the continued regional contrasts within the mining industry. As a result, while there was greater scope for more autonomous action on the part of the miners as a group, the War also reinforced the individual characteristics of the various districts. Correspondingly, for example, the industrial and political radicalism of South Wales, and to a slighter extent of South Yorkshire, continued to stand out against the more conventional and cautious attitudes of, say, the North-East.

The balance of forces making for industrial unrest or relative tranquillity in the coalfields was outlined in the various reports of commissions of inquiry charged with investigating industrial unrest in the summer of 1917.[2] In the North-East, for example, the universal causes of dissatisfaction and unrest were undoubtedly present. (They included high food prices, housing shortages, restrictions on personal liberty through wartime regulations and conscription, suspicions of government procrastination, industrial fatigue, etc.) Yet the Commissioners for Northumberland and Durham concluded that industrial relations there were generally fairly good, and that in coal in particular

estimates that total union membership in Britain in that year was some 885,000—roughly 80% of the total work-force.

[1] For a discussion of the social outlook of mining communities, see below, ch. 10, sect. vii.

[2] *Commission of Inquiry into Industrial Unrest* (PP 1917–18 XV). This contains the various reports, by groups of 3 Commissioners, on each of 8 regional divisions (there was also a special report on the Sheffield district), together with a summary by the Minister of Labour, G. N. Barnes.

speaking generally there is no unrest in the mining community. There exists an arrangement between employers and employees which for a long period of years has secured amicable settlement of contentious questions, and we can suggest no method of dealing with disputes which is likely to meet with more success in this very important field.[1]

In Yorkshire and (perhaps surprisingly) the East Midlands, by contrast, although the coal industry was not specifically considered at any length, the atmosphere was reported to be much worse, and the prevailing mood was said to be one of 'weariness, sorrow, disappointment and suspicion'.[2] But the most systematic and penetrating analysis was embodied in the remarkable report from the Commissioners for South Wales & Monmouthshire.

The report on South Wales was, in effect, a small monograph, substantiated by statistical and social analysis, on the economic, social, cultural, and political institutions and conditions of the region. Even allowing for the fact that the Commissioners represented strong preconceptions about the position of the working classes in South Wales, and took evidence from a very limited (and fairly radical) group of miners' representatives,[3] they produced a document which would have been persuasively sobering for a government to receive at any time—let alone in the middle of a great war.

The Commissioners emphasized the extraordinary concentration of labour and the recent violent growth of the coalmining industry, especially in the context of grim social and working conditions in the constricted valleys. They paid particular attention to the fierceness of class antagonisms, tracing the evolution of the trade union movement from the status of a defensive club, in a moderate and liberal setting, to a vehicle for a 'class-conscious programme', aiming at 'the reconstruction of the whole basis of society', so that the miners' lodges had become centres of purposeful educational, political, and social activities which infused much of community life. More than this, the Commissioners

---

[1] *Commission of Inquiry into Industrial Unrest* (*PP* 1917–18 XV, 10.

[2] Ibid., 53.

[3] The 3 Commissioners for South Wales were: D. Lleufer Thomas, Thomas Evans, and Vernon Hartshorn (who was an active member of the South Wales Miners' Federation). The only 2 members of the South Wales Miners' Federation to give evidence were Noah Ablett and Frank Hodges—both very able spokesmen for the left-wing section of the union, and with a prewar history of commitment to the Unofficial Reform Movement. The only spokesman for the anthracite section of the SWMF was S. O. Davies, another strong left-winger. However, considering the general gathering of evidence, the Commissioners could not be accused of restrictive bias: they heard 144 witnesses and received a vast amount of written submissions.

pointed out that the same spirit, magnified by disaffection and argument, had led the more 'advanced' men to deny the efficacy or validity of conventional political action, and to advocate a root and branch reform of the union, leading to industrial unionism and the aim of direct control of production.

The outcome was an impasse: 'Thus between the employer and the worker a great gulf is fixed'. And the War, the report argued, had accentuated all this by leading the miners to an even keener appreciation of the importance of education and their sectional interests, and by encouraging the trade union to pursue better organization not simply against the employer but also, if necessary, against the government.

On such an analysis, it was not war but history which had led to the deterioration of industrial relations, to class antagonism and a 'sense of irresponsibility', to unofficial strikes breaking out 'on the slightest pretext', and to the fact that 'unrest has become almost a permanent condition'. The consequences of war (apparent profiteering, unreliable government promises, overwork, narrowing differentials, controls) served merely to aggravate the traditional issues of wages, poor living conditions, stressful work organization, and mutual hostility between owners and miners which had long soured the South Wales industry. On the other hand, the Commissioners also emphasized that they did not envisage a breakdown during the War (the patriotism of the miners and the adjustment of wages or prices to maintain real wages would guard against that).[1] Rather, the threat of social dislocation, they felt, would become manifest in the immediate postwar period.

The South Wales & Monmouthshire Commissioners, as they acknowledged, were dealing with a distinctive area of industrial Britain. More than this, like many men in the midst of a crisis, they exaggerated the durability, representativeness, and strength of the more extreme or strident forces they were describing. Yet those forces *were* important, even if their importance derived not from the fact that they had a mass following, but from the extent to which their disaffection fell on temporarily fertile soil.

When all was said and done, and even though it had less permanent consequences than predicted, the labour unrest of 1917 was both serious and indicative of a significant mood. Momentarily, at least, it

---

[1] The Commissioners recommended that industrial unrest in South Wales might be assuaged by policies more favourable to labour's case: improved institutional arrangements and living standards, social reforms, more participation in decision-making, the overhaul of industrial-relations machinery.

transcended dissatisfaction with munitions work or immediate material ambitions, and reflected a diffused sense of labour's important position in society and new possibilities for wage-earners and institutions. In the words of the Minister of Labour, summarizing the various reports of 1917, behind the complaints of wage-earners about prices and wages lay a lack of confidence in their leaders or the future. As a result,

The feeling in the minds of the workers that their conditions of work and destinies are being determined by a distant authority over which they have no influence requires to be taken into consideration not only by the Government, but by the Unions themselves.[1]

As far as the mass of British miners were concerned, the War involved a heightened perception of their relationship with the systems of authority and control which so closely touched their working and social lives. This led not so much to an elaborate programme of institutional reform as to a determined defence of what they took to be their privileges; and since the point at which they could assert this defence was where changes were proposed the result was an apparent—and frequently a very real—militant conservatism. This was exemplified in an insistence on traditional hours of work and weekly work patterns (in many Scottish pits, for example, an eleven-day fortnight was customary—and miners' representatives fiercely resisted any change to a twelve-day fortnight throughout the War); in a resistance to changes in regulations concerning the employment of boys or women; in the successful campaign to be excluded from the operations of the Munitions of War legislation; and in a persistently uncooperative attitude towards the recruitment or conscription of miners. More positively, starting with the South Wales Miners' Federation, they also insisted that the hours of surface workers should be reduced from 11 (including $1\frac{1}{2}$ hours for meals) to $8\frac{1}{2}$ (plus 20 minutes for meals), and enforced their demands on a reluctant government, which was not allowed to rest content with a promise to use its good offices with the owners.[2]

At the same time, the miners' union was obviously concerned with the broader questions of decision-taking and industrial management

---

[1] For a somewhat exaggerated view (by an American visitor) of the labour movement's potential and achievement in this regard, see Gleason 1917. Gleason was excessively optimistic about the promise of 'the machinery of joint boards, workshop councils, imperial conferences and franchise extension … minimum wage, limitation of hours, choice of work, control within industry' (284).

[2] POWE 26/11 (23 Oct. 1918); CAB 24/66/313–14 (23 Oct. 1918); CAB 23/8/44 (24 Oct. 1918). For Scotland, see SCOA for the war years.

that had been raised by the War. As part of its defensive posture, for example, it insisted on using much more direct and overtly political means of negotiation than would have been provided by a consultative machinery. This affected the miners' attitudes to the Coal Controller's Advisory Board (which was not used as a forum for important decisions) and led to their campaign to keep away from the Ministry of Labour in matters relating to industrial disputes, and from the Ministry of National Service in matters of recruitment. Instead, they attempted to insist on direct dealings with the Coal Control or (where issues of wage determination were concerned) representatives of the War Cabinet.[1]

In addition to the short-run policy brought into prominence by the War, there was also the question of the long-run ownership and management of the industry, and the miners' role within it. Here, the accretion of power to the labour force, and the expectations engendered by the experience of war and wartime control, led to the discussion of quite radical demands—albeit intermingled with new claims for higher wages, favourable terms for demobilization, and reduced hours. In the wartime context, these matters came to a head at the MFGB's annual conference at Southport in August 1918. There, in addition to formulating prospective demands concerning wages and demobilization, the delegates unanimously accepted a South Wales motion in favour of the state ownership of coal mines 'with joint control and administration by the workmen and the State'. The apprehensions about 'bureaucracy' which had led to the argument in favour of direct control, were also reflected in the attitude to the wartime system of Coal Control. And the conference accepted the view that

the present form of Government control of the mines tends to develop into pure bureaucratic administration, which is in itself equally inimical to the interests of the workmen and of the industry as was the uncontrolled form of private ownership.

Pending nationalization (which was acknowledged to be a more distant objective) there was a demand that the joint advisory committee 'should be vested with power jointly with the Coal Controller'. To this end, the

---

[1] For the MFGB's reluctance (and generally, if not completely, successful resistance) to being involved with the Ministry of Labour or the Ministry of National Service, see BT 189/1 (7 Mar., 9 May, 13 June, 13 June, 27 June, 31 Oct. 1917); CAB 24/28/134 (8 Oct. 1918); CAB 23/4/106 (18 Oct. 1917). Ultimately, the responsible Minister, Auckland Geddes, was able to secure a War Cabinet ruling that recruitment was a matter solely for the Ministry of National Service.

MFGB formulated demands for a new role and more detailed information about the industry's affairs.

In the event, the Coal Controller interpreted the demands relating to the Board's functions as principally a request for more detailed information about the outcome of the advice given him by the industry's representatives. Such a request (which was not what the miners had had in mind) could in large part be conceded, and the Controller's civil-service advisers expressed the hope that, as complex matters of industrial policy were discussed, the MFGB resolution might be allowed 'to drift into oblivion'.[1] This degree of prevarication appeared to have succeeded—as did the official resistance (primarily on legal grounds) to the miners' request for the dissemination of detailed statistics of profits and other financial affairs within the industry.

The matter came to a head in December 1918 and January 1919, when the MFGB was already preparing for its postwar attempt to transform the economic position as well as the industrial role of its members. And the implications of the campaign were exposed when the Coal Controller offered information about profits on condition that the Advisory Board maintained strict confidentiality about them—an offer rejected by the MFGB. In the words of the Advisory Board's Minutes. 'The miners' side said that if the Owners were not getting the profit the Government were and the miners did not want the Government to get it, they wanted it themselves.' As became clear, the union's desire for information concerning the financial operations of the industry related less to a judgement on its ideal structure than to an impending wage claim, which was to be based on the inflation of profits, the rise in the cost of living, and the merits of the miners' case for a social wage.[2]

As the War came to an end, therefore the miners' leaders could look back on a sustained and reasonably successful campaign to protect their members' economic interests and to prepare the ground for further changes. Those changes were designed not simply to extend the miners' wartime gains, but also to transform the structure of the coal industry, and their political and industrial power within that structure. In this respect, the War had served to bolster expectations and confidence as well as to augment shorter-run economic power.

As events were to turn out, those expectations and the confident

[1] POWE 26/11 (7 Nov. 1918). For the pressure by the MFGB on the Advisory Board, see POWE 26/11 (4 Sept. 1918); BT 189/1 (25 Sept., 9 Oct. and 6 Nov. 1918, 8 Jan. 1919).
[2] BT 189/1 (8 Jan. 1919). For the advice of the Law Officers concerning the legality of publicizing information gathered under the Coal Mines Control Act, see POWE 26/11 (18 Dec. 1918).

psychology which sustained them, proved misplaced. The miners' relative autonomy only lasted as long as the brief postwar boom. More than this, as we shall see, there proved to be political limits to its exercise even in the circumstances of coal shortages in 1919 and 1920. Whether this could have been otherwise is not certain. But what was clear was that the admixture of short-run demands relating to wages and hours, and longer-run aspirations concerning public ownership and joint control was an enfeebling rather than a strengthening characteristic of the miners' case. The pursuit of immediate material improvements diverted energies, their attainment sapped political application, and the coincidence persuaded many that the proposals for structural reforms were secondary and fleeting compared with those for higher wages and lower hours.[1] All that was to emerge in the heady debates and disputes of 1919–20. But it was already implicit in the relative autonomy and dialectical authority with which the War had endowed the miners by 1917–18.

iv. The business of coalmining during the War

The War had a somewhat more ambiguous effect on the business of coalmining. For one thing, government intervention was neither consistent in its incidence nor uniform in its application as between different collieries. For another, although the financial outcome of wartime operations was generally very favourable to coalowners, postwar circumstances—economic as well as political—were uncertain and therefore risky.

Even after February 1917 government control of the industry operated in a selective way. In particular, it was exercised primarily through legal limits on the maximum pithead price of coal intended for British consumers; regulation of the markets to which output might be sent; state intervention in wage settlements; and a system of financial levies and allocations designed to limit excessive profits, protect vulnerable firms against losses, and generally 'recycle' abnormal profits to potentially disadvantaged colliery firms.

Yet even though the marketing and many of the financial functions of private enterprise in the coal industry ceased to be determined autonomously, the actual process of coal production—the management of the individual mines and enterprises—was left almost completely in private hands. Indeed, it was only about a year after the introduction of

[1] Below, ch. 4, sect. ii, vi.

control that the Controller took a direct and positive step relating to the operation of colliery enterprises: in March 1918 he issued a notice forbidding any colliery development work without prior notice to the Control, and similarly restraining any increase in the wages of officials or the fees of directors. This move was apparently designed to prevent owners making use of the system of guaranteed but limited profits to devote proceeds (and, in part, scarce labour) to bolstering the long-term position of the enterprise.[1]

Such direct intervention remained rare. As was pointed out in 1942, 'the Government took over complete financial responsibility for the industry, while leaving the running of the mines in the hands of the colliery owners'.[2] Nevertheless, the state's general assumption of responsibility for marketing and financial arrangements, together with the sustained demand for coal, created the determining framework for business enterprise in mining during the War years. And in spite of the owners' restlessness with a system of financial pooling and subsidy (in spite, too, of their distaste for the government's conciliatory attitude to the miners' union), the business outcome was generally very favourable.

Although taxes and levies (which took a higher proportion of gross income than in most other industries) diminished net profits, coal-mining in wartime turned out to be a very profitable activity. This was for two reasons. At a general level, the sustained demand for coal enabled collieries to work near full capacity and to sell all they produced to eager consumers. As far as export sales were concerned, there was the added advantage of extremely high prices; but, as we have seen, even in the case of production for the British market (where the legislation of 1915 had limited pithead prices, and where producers were often required to sell their coal in lower-priced markets), the Coal Control Agreement compensated for loss of proceeds.

More critically, as far as the industry as a whole was concerned, the government's oversight of costs and prices was sufficiently 'broad-brush', and even negligent, to ensure that price limitation was rarely an uncomfortable policy for producers. As we have already seen, the attempt to adjust allowable price increases to the extent of cost increases was vitiated by an official ignorance of the exact extent and pattern of

[1] Redmayne 1923, 199–200. On the other side, however, one owner wrote to *The Times* in the same month, complaining that since the Coal Mines Control Agreement made retainable profits dependent on output, owners had too great an incentive to concentrate on the most accessible and easily worked seams: 'it means picking the eyes out of the mines during control'. Quoted in *CG* 28 Mar. 1918, 648.

[2] Memorandum by Secretary for Mines, quoted in CAB 87/92/3 (24 May 1942).

rising costs—an ignorance which tended to exaggerate costs, and therefore inflate prices (and profits). An equally telling deficiency in the control system was its lack of discrimination: for much of the time price increases (which were uniform either nationally or within districts) were allowed in relation to the costs of the least efficient collieries. This was designed to enable them to keep in production. But beneath this umbrella the more productive and therefore lower-cost colliery enterprises were naturally able to make very substantial profits.[1] Table 3.1 provides a rough indication of the growth of profits up to and during the War.

Table 3.1. *Estimated profits of coalmining*[a]
(£ m.)

Financial year	Gross profits[b]	Net profits[c]
1908–9	21.4	15.6
1909–10	14.7	8.6
1910–11	15.1	8.8
1911–12	13.1	6.7
1912–13	22.4	16.3
1913–14	26.9	20.5
1914–15	19.0	12.4
1915–16	31.2	21.5
1916–17	46.6	28.5
1917–18	34.2	10.5

[a] Profits including coking and by-product profits.
[b] Net estimated profits, less wear and tear.
[c] Profits less royalties, mineral rights, duty, excess profits duty, coalmines excess payments, and income tax.

Source: SRO *CB* 5 Dec. 1919, 1505.

The figures in Table 3.1 relate to the industry as a whole. Profits per ton, on the other hand, showed even larger increases: whereas the amount for 1912–13 was a record at 1s. 4.5 d. the figures for the years 1914, 1915, 1916, and 1917 were 1s. 1.5 d., 1s. 8 d., 2s. 11 d., and 2s. 2.5 d. For the quarter July–September 1918, the figure jumped to 3s. 6.5 d.[2] Such figures of

---

[1] Above, 91.
[2] *Sankey Evidence* I, 400 ff. Within these profits there was a very large disparity between the profitability of export and inland sales. In the quarter ending Mar. 1918, for example, when average profits per ton were 1s. 11½ d., profits on domestic sales were 8.24 d. and on export sales 6s. 6.8 d. (*Sankey* I, 5).

profitability (which, being averages for a very disparate industry, masked really spectacular instances of profitability as well as examples of trading losses) were said to be innocuous since taxation and excess profits duty retrieved much of the gain for public use. But the fact remained that gains were sufficiently large for leading firms to accumulate very big reserves.[1] And in any case, the existence of large wartime profits was a constant irritant to industrial relations in coalmining (it was, of course, one reason why the industry had to be taken into control in 1916) and a subsequent cause of widespread and profound criticism of the industry's owners at the time of the Sankey Commission's inquiries in 1919.

In contrast to the situation at the end of the Second World War,[2] the owners had relatively few doubts about the future in 1917 and 1918. This relative optimism was no doubt based on the scale of their wartime profits and a belief in the transitory nature of wartime realignments of industrial power. While the experience of war led them to appreciate the need for a greater measure of consultation with their work-force, they could hardly envisage the political storm that would almost engulf them in 1919. And, although government control was to continue for some years, it was not envisaged as a threat to private enterprise—being based primarily on the political need to restrain domestic prices, secure national benefits from a world coal shortage, and provide an orderly oversight of the industry's finances.

In market terms, too, there were few obvious grounds for anxiety. Future demand (at home and abroad) was assumed to be assured, and a departmental committee (composed largely of leading owners) on the postwar coal trade, although obviously concerned with costs and productivity, gave little sign of trepidation about long-run competition.[3] There might, then, have been some grounds for complacency on the

[1] It was estimated that in the two months Nov.–Dec. 1917 31% of collieries produced 62% of the nation's output of coal at a profit and 15% of collieries produced 13% of the total output at a loss: *Sankey Evidence* I, Q 612. Representative figures for individual companies are difficult to adduce. However, there were various impressive performances which were not, apparently, exceptional. And colliery companies frequently managed to accumulate large reserves and increases in capitalization—especially those which combined coalmining with metallurgical and coking business. Thus, between 1913 or 1914 and 1918 Baldwins Ltd., Dorman Long & Co., and the Ebbw Vale Steel, Iron & Coal Co. all succeeded in doubling or more than doubling their capital and reserves carried forward—which virtually doubled again by 1921. See Neuman 1934, 65.

[2] Below, ch. 13, sect. v.

[3] *Report of the Departmental Committee Appointed by the President of the Board of Trade to Consider the Position of the Coal Trade after the War. PP* 1918 XIII (Cd. 9093. 1918). The committee had reported on 25 Apr. 1917.

part of the owners—a complacency which would have been greatly reinforced by the growth of profits and the accumulation of reserves during the War years. It was to be on the basis of this performance and its continuation in 1919–20 that leading companies expanded their capital base by the division and bonus distribution of shares, and the realignment of corporate relationships.[1]

As will be seen in subsequent chapters, it was not long before this complacency was shown to be misplaced—first, by the miners' campaign for substantial improvements in wages and conditions, and for nationalization and joint control; and subsequently, by the deterioration in markets and the intensification of competition which settled over the industry by the mid-1920s. It then became clear that the owners had greatly underestimated the effect of the War on the competitive power of foreign coal producers, and had misjudged the course of world demand for fuel.[2] That much, however, was common and probably understandable: the forecasting of business environments is notoriously difficult, and neither the complete stagnation in the world demand for coal, nor the long-run downward trend in the international economy, could have been reasonably anticipated in, say, 1917–18.

A more pertinent question as far as concerns the effects of the War on the enterprise of British coalowners is the extent to which complacency was transmuted into culpable conservatism in matters of innovation, organization, and investment. Given the extent of wartime profits, did the coalowners neglect opportunities for modernization which might reasonably have been taken and which, if taken, would have improved the industry's postwar competitive power?

There can be no easy answer to such a question: neither the need for, nor the availability of, relevant investment funds can be accurately estimated, nor is it at all easy to assess what might have been the effects of hypothetical investment programmes on long-run productivity. However, two principal points *are* fairly clear. On the one hand, the exigencies of wartime production—the need for coal and the shortage of manpower—necessarily involved the postponement of development and perhaps even maintenance work, with the result that Britain's coalmines faced peacetime conditions with a large backlog of incidental and preparatory work to do. (Sir Richard Redmayne estimated that the industry would need five to seven years to catch

[1] Below, ch. 5, sect. v.
[2] For the postwar political and economic challenges to the industry and its businessmen, see below, ch. 4 and 5.

up.)[1] On the other hand, in the years that followed the War the degree of technical change and corporate productive reorganization were fairly modest when compared with what occurred in continental coalfields or with what might have been financed by the accumulated profits of war-time operations.

Investment certainly did take place—both in existing operations and in new fields (notably Nottinghamshire and North Derbyshire).[2] But the fact was that the industry experienced nothing like the reconstruction undertaken by Germany and France in the postwar years. Structurally, as we shall see, coalmining changed only slowly; technically, it began to fall behind its competitors; and measured in terms of the definitive criterion of productivity, the business performance of the 1920s gave grounds for both anxiety and disappointment.[3] To this extent, then, the coalowners can be blamed: reinvestment in the industry was incommensurate with the funds available.

And yet, it is still not obvious that the relative lack of vigorous industrial renewal was an irrational or unrealistic response to the circumstances then being experienced. Shortages of coal at the end of the War must have suggested that expensive capital programmes to reduce unit costs need not be given the highest priority. Then, the end of the War was accompanied by the assertion of trade-union power and a political crisis which persuaded many people (among coalowners as well as less interested sections of society) that nationalization or some drastic measure of public or workers' control was inevitable. Such uncertainty must have inhibited development plans. On the other hand, as will be seen, quite apart from political instability, market conditions changed with such volatility in the immediate postwar years that an orderly perception of the need for long-run development and innovation might have been very difficult—for, either the booming demand for coal appeared to diminish the need to invest very substantially in improvements, or the abrupt collapse of markets produced a debilitating pessimism about economic prospects. As in many other spheres of the nation's economic life, the War had changed things so drastically, that men were for some time unable to grasp the character and implications of the new world around them.

---

[1] Redmayne 1923, 208-14.
[2] Below, 183-4.
[3] Below, ch. 5, sect. iii; ch. 9, sect. iii.

CHAPTER 4

The Political Economy of Coal, 1918–1921

The three years immediately after the end of the First World War form a particularly important episode in the twentieth-century history of the coalmining history. In the course of the 1920s, as will be seen in Chapter 5, the prewar bases of the industry's prosperity were to be destroyed and near-intolerable burdens imposed on the material welfare and social relations of those engaged, or formerly engaged, in it. But the stagnation of domestic, and the collapse of overseas, demand, did not begin immediately the War ended. Rather, for two years after the Armistice, the market for British coal remained buoyant and its values greatly inflated. Against that background, the internal pressures which had originated during the War intensified, traditional institutional forms and relationships were questioned, and there was an unprecedented controversy about industrial policy and nationalization.

Even when the issue of public ownership was resolved, tensions within the industry and between the work-force and the government, continued—only to be abated in 1921 when the market for coal disintegrated, government control was withdrawn, and wages were reduced after the miners had been defeated in a protracted and bitter stoppage. In effect, the years 1918–21 were a turning-point in economic and political trends. Market forces, in a much more threatening form, reasserted themselves and frustrated what had been a far-reaching attempt to establish the industry on a new basis.

That attempt was made possible by the character of the market for coal in 1919–20, and was rooted in the experience of wartime industrial relations. But it was largely shaped by the political environment of 1919 and the power and attitudes of the various interest groups involved in the industry. Thus, government control of the industry's wages, prices, and profits continued beyond the War, not because of any official plans for major industrial or social reform, but for the same transient reasons that had produced it in 1916–17: the precariousness of industrial relations under private enterprise during a period of coal scarcity, and the political desire to restrain home prices.

Equally, those concerned with the business aspects of coalmining, although they felt little reason to doubt the ultimate return of prewar market conditions and industrial relations, also accepted control as a temporary necessity. In effect, the essential initiative in 1919-20 lay with the miners, who had experienced a transformation of their bargaining position as a result of wartime conditions. Given the economic, and even more the political, situation at the end of the War they had some reason for believing that the industry's new power relationships might continue into the peace, and be used to enhance their material welfare, attain a system of national wage determination which would redistribute proceeds between profitable and less profitable districts, and even secure a radical change in the ownership and control of the mines. Structural change, social experiment, and a new role for the state in the industry seemed feasible as well as desirable. Their pursuit and frustration form the principal subject-matter of the industry's 'adjustment' to the immediate postwar world. The unstable character of that adjustment is exemplified in Table 4.1.

i. Postwar issues and possibilities

The ending of hostilities in November 1918 did not immediately mitigate the sense of a practical crisis of production which had characterized official thinking about the coal industry throughout the previous year. While the urgent demand from the munitions industry came to an end, continental shortages, now aggravated by institutional breakdown in central Europe, gave cause for great anxiety. There was also a politically worrying scarcity of coal for domestic purposes within Britain, and the preoccupation with short-term issues (and especially the supply of manpower), continued to dominate policy discussions. In the sombre words of a Cabinet minute:

unless the supplies of coal in this country were increased, it was not impossible that there might be a revolution. Even now the spirit of lawlessness was apparent, and no one could say what might happen if, for instance, there was no coal in the East End in December.

Pressed by the Coal Controller, the War Cabinet managed to secure the release of 100,000 miners from the Forces by mid-December, and fend off the immediate threat of scarcity.[1]

---

[1] CAB 24/70/238 (25 Nov. 1918). Also see CAB 24/69/295 (15 Nov. 1918); BT 189/1 (20 Nov. and 18 Dec. 1918); CAB 23/8/102 (6 Dec. 1918).

Table 4.1. *The United Kingdom coal industry: output, exports, prices, profits, employment, and productivity, 1913-1922*

	1913	June 1914	1918	1919	1920	1921[a]	1922[b]
1. Coal raised (ooo tons)	287,430	—	227,749	229,780	229,532	163,251	249,607
2. Export of coal, coke, man. fuel (ooo tons)	76,688	—	34,174	36,759	28,863	26,247	67,939
3. Total shipped abroad (incl. bunkers) (ooo tons)	98,338	—	43,390	51,323	43,667	37,597	87,352
4. Average selling value at pit (per ton)	10s. 1½d.	—	20s. 4½d.	27s. 0¼d.	33s. 8d.	25s. 6d.	17s. 6d.
5. Average profit (per ton)	1s. 6d.	—	2s. 2½d.	2s. 8d.	2s. 11¼d.	−2s. 9½d.	0s. 10½d.
6. Number of persons employed (ooo)	1,118	—	1,009	1,191	1,248	1,144	1,163
7. Output per manshift (cwt)	—	20.32	17.75[c]	15.60[d]	14.57	14.46[e] 17.73[f]	18.02
8. Average declared value of coal shipped at Sunderland	12s. 11d.	—	32s. 3d.	54s. 4d.	79s. 9d.	34s. 3d.	22s. 3d.
9. Average declared value of coal shipped at Cardiff	15s. 10d.	—	28s. 2d.	43s. 1d.	83s. 4d.	36s. 6d.	23s. 9d.

[a] National stoppage April–July 1921.
[b] Great Britain only.
[c] July–Dec. 1918.
[d] Length of maximum underground shift reduced by one hour.
[e] Jan.–Mar. 1921.
[f] Oct.–Dec. 1921.

Sources:

1–5: *CYB* 1932, §98 ff.
6 and 7: *Samuel Evidence*, QQ 20–1; *Samuel Appendices*, App. 8, Table 1 and App. 18, Table 14.
8 and 9: *CYB* 1948, 579.

Given the extreme shortage of coal abroad, and the government's determination to avoid political crisis at home, there was no alternative to its continuing control of the industry. In this way it managed exports so as to maximize Britain's financial benefits from high overseas prices, while ensuring that adequate supplies were available to domestic consumers at prices restrained by official regulation. At the same time, it could adjust the industry's finances so as to prevent excessive gains or losses falling on collieries which were allowed or obliged to supply one or other of the two types of market. Government control therefore continued to have little to do with the management of production or long-range planning. It was concerned, rather, with the administration of a two-tier system of distribution.

Surprisingly, the problems of low production and shortages of coal which so dominated the last months of the Great War, were not accompanied by any very extensive consideration of the character and needs of the industry's likely postwar environment. There had, of course, been some wartime discussions under the general umbrella of the Ministry of Reconstruction, whose Coal Conservation Committee proposed the creation of a Ministry of Mines and Minerals (to integrate the government's existing functions), a greater state role in exploration, and extensive measures to economize in the use and mining of coal.[1] But these bore little relationship to the future market for coal or the problems of its production. Even the Board of Trade's Departmental Committee on Britain's postwar coal trade (which was appointed in June 1916 and reported in April 1917), while it drew attention to Britain's slow rate of productivity growth compared with the United States and Germany, was non-committal about the nature of postwar problems, other than the likely need to reduce wages. And there was in general a curious lack of appreciation of the possibility that the War would introduce fundamental changes into the economics of the coal-mining industry.[2]

This is not to say that important issues concerning the structure of the industry were entirely ignored. Thus, some of the officials concerned with the Coal Control used the advent of peace to emphasize the need to enhance efficiency and avoid waste (in underground barriers

---

[1] *PP* 1917–18 XVII, *PP* 1918 VII.

[2] *PP* 1918 XIII. There was also a detailed and serious investigation of the practical and legal problems flowing from the fragmented private ownership of mineral rights, but no action flowed from this. See *Third Report of the Acquisition and Valuation of Land Committee of the Ministry of Reconstruction*, *PP* 1919 XXIX.

and dead areas) by reducing the number of companies, since 'it is evident that it is only the large companies which, on the average, can carry on with any measure of success'. They therefore advocated the formation of district- and even nation-wide enterprises.[1] Yet such opinions were not widely echoed or discussed. The central economic issue exposed by the War was that of industrial relations, rather than organizational structures.[2]

Certainly, little in the industry's recent past gave great cause for comfort on the question of internal harmony. During the War the miners had extended their autonomy and their power. Those involved in coalmining had ostensibly welcomed the Whitley Report (which proposed the creation of joint industrial councils throughout the economy), but had assumed that the industry's existing conciliation machinery could be made to fit the Whitley mould with little adjustment of structures or attitudes. The owners (at least as represented by the MAGB's Parliamentary Committee) had begun to consider the post-war situation as early as October 1916; but when they finally circulated a report to the district associations, it appeared to place excessive reliance on a putative 'spirit of harmony and cooperation', proffering a relatively superficial structural solution—a network of consultative committees at pit and district levels—for an endemic problem. Admittedly, the MAGB did suggest that wages should be determined in each district by reference to net proceeds (after the payment of minimum wages, non-wage costs, and interest on capital). But this scheme was to be based on individual areas, with proceeds divided between wages and profits in proportions to be decided by district negotiations.[3]

Such proposals were clearly based on a sensitivity to the miners' new-found ambitions, but they proved inadequate to their purposes. The miners had always insisted that consultation without participation in management decisions was unacceptable to them, and were profoundly reluctant to give up the system of nation-wide bargaining and *de facto*

[1] A. Lowes Dickinson *et al.*, draft memorandum on the termination of the control of coalmines, 13 Dec. 1918: POWE 10/12. Lowes Dickinson was Head of the Coal Control's Financial Branch. He and his colleagues adduced figures showing that in the two-month period Nov.–Dec. 1917 two-thirds of the national tonnage was produced by one-third of the colliery firms at an average profit of 2s. 3d. per ton, and the balance by two-thirds of the firms at an average loss of 2s. per ton. This memorandum may be connected with an undated memorandum advocating a National Coal Corporation, under joint control, as an alternative to nationalization: POWE 26/14.

[2] This contrasts with the experience of the Second World War, which resulted in a major reconsideration of the structure, investment, and efficiency of the industry. Below, ch. 12 and 13.

[3] *A Suggested Scheme of Reconstruction for the Coal Mining Industry* (1919). Various editions (the first being dated 15 Feb.) are in SRO CB6/2.

profit pooling that had been among their biggest gains from the War. In any case, their thinking had gone well beyond a tinkering with the industry's institutions. Their long-term advocacy of public ownership had taken an altogether more purposeful turn; as their President said in November 1917, the miners 'want the State to have the ownership and full control of the mines'.[1] And eight months later, at their annual conference, the MFGB delegates had voted unanimously in favour of nationalization, pending which reform they demanded a direct role in the Coal Control.[2]

The social, political, and economic upheavals of the War, and the intangible promises of the imminent Peace, readily explain why the demand for a major experiment in industrial ownership and control should have been so attractive in 1918. 'The War did much more than destroy Kings and Emperors', one miners' MP was to claim in December 1919; it 'has created an absolutely new school of economic thought amongst the workmen of this country.'[3] But these influences were profoundly reinforced by the optimism with which the miners could now contemplate their economic aspirations and, above all, by their newly forged power. In the Minister of Labour's words, 'the experience of the miners has convinced them of the overwhelming strength of their economic position'—as a result of which they had been able to win practically all their wartime conflicts with the government.[4] Such an analysis was certainly a more realistic indication of the politics of industrial relations than the Colliery Guardian's claim, in January 1919, that in the new mood after the General Election of December 1918, there might be an end to 'the virus of class hatred' and 'the stiff-necked reactionary battling for the employers'.[5] Indeed, even as these words were published, the miners' union was submitting a set of claims which were to provoke a national crisis.

The origins of the MFGB's demands lay in resolutions accepted at its annual conference in the previous year, and largely held over to the Peace. On 9 January 1919 the union submitted a claim to the Coal Controller, asking for an increase of 30 per cent on basic earnings plus the war wage of 3s. per shift, and preferential treatment for miners with

---

[1] See Interim Report of the Mining Sub-Committee of the Coal Conservation Committee, Minority Report by Robert Smillie (7 Nov. 1917), published as Appendix II to the Committee's Final Report: PP 1918 VII, 662–4.

[2] Above, 109.

[3] William Brace in Hansard 11 Dec. 1919, col. 1718.

[4] CAB 24/62/100 (28 Aug. 1918).

[5] CG 10 Jan. 1919, 87, and 17 Jan. 1919, 144.

regard to demobilization. The wages claim was of particular importance since it transcended arguments about the cost of living or the performance of the industry, and was based on the presumed social needs and moral standing of mining communities. Its essence was, quite simply, that the miners 'are entitled to a higher standard of living'.[1] By the end of the month, after a special conference on 14–16 January, the MFGB had augmented their formal claim (which was now made to the Minister of Labour, the President of the Board of Trade, and the Home Secretary) to include a shorter working day underground (a maximum of six as against eight hours) and an agreement by the government that the industry should be nationalized. They insisted on receiving an answer within a week, and threatened strike action if their demands were not accepted.[2]

To the industry's trade journal, all this appeared to be a 'flouting of economic virtues';[3] but it was immediately clear that the matter was not one that could be settled at this level of argument. All elements in the claim had to be taken seriously—partly because they were seriously meant and backed by the threat of an immediate national strike, and partly because they coincided with, and were an integral part of, a period of intense social upheaval and labour troubles. In January and February 1919 there were riots by soldiers demanding demobilization, serious unrest in Glasgow and Belfast, the threat of a disastrous strike on London's tube trains and in the capital's generating stations, and the strong likelihood of disruption on the railways.[4] All these events and prospects darkened the political sky with the prospect of a major, and perhaps unprecedented, national crisis. And in such a context, wide-ranging and extreme demands from the strongest and most determined union of all were of the utmost political significance.

ii. The Sankey Commission: the first stage

The strength of the miners' bargaining position and the War Cabinet's fear of provoking a national strike and profound social unrest lent

---

[1] Evidence of the miners' President, Robert Smillie, to the Sankey Commission: *Sankey Evidence* I, Q 6893. Between July 1914 and Feb. 1919 underground and surface labourers in the mines had received wage increases of just over 100%, and hewers of just under 100%. Retail prices had risen by about 100%. If the full claim had been granted in February, it would have resulted in an increase of 160% since July 1914—compared with increases of between 95 and 145% for workers in engineering and shipbuilding. See CAB 24/74/213 (4 Feb. 1919).

[2] CAB 23/9/36 (31 Jan. 1919); CAB 24/74/210ff. (4 Feb. 1919).

[3] *CG* 24 Jan. 1919, 199–200.

[4] See Wrigley 1976, ch. 5.

authority to the proposal (emanating from the Minister of Labour, Sir Robert Horne) that the union should be offered an interim cost-of-living wage increase and a court of arbitration with a carefully balanced, and directly representative, membership.[1] In fact, although this initial offer was rejected out of hand by the MFGB (another delegate conference called for a ballot on strike action to commence on 15 March), it contained the seeds of the provisional solution to the social and political crisis. That solution was the appointment of a Royal Commission of Inquiry—the Sankey Commission—equally representative of miners and owners, and armed with unrestricted terms of reference to investigate all aspects of the industry and extensive powers to call witnesses and secure official information. In the circumstances, such an inquiry had an obvious appeal for the government: it avoided the dangerous precedent of granting either wage concessions without preliminary investigations or political concessions under the threat of direct action. More than this, however, senior Ministers (and Lloyd George in particular) were well aware of the need to propitiate wage-earners, who had high expectations of rapid improvements in social and industrial conditions. As the Prime Minister told his Cabinet, genuine measures of social reform were necessary

to guarantee the social peace of the country.... Nothing struck me more in the conversations I had with the miners, than the part this plays in the general irritation that has made them unreasonable.... [Y]ou have to win back their confidence. Until we have that confidence back we shall have unrest.[2]

Underpinning such arguments was the realization that it might be reasonable as well as politic to explore the facts of the case. As *The Times* put it, 'We want all the cards on the table', for the industry's organization was 'neither scientific nor economical'.[3] Certainly, this was the line taken by Lloyd George in a characteristically emotional and eloquent address to the MFGB Executive on 20 February, when he appealed for the avoidance of a direct confrontation given the general acceptance of the strength of much of the miners' case.[4]

There is, of course, an alternative and more cynical explanation of the

---

[1] CAB 24/74/215 (4 Feb. 1919); CAB 23/9/58 (7 Feb. 1919).

[2] Quoted in Johnson 1968, 370 ff. Also see memorandum on industrial unrest by Tom Jones (Assistant Secretary to the War Cabinet) in Jones, *Whitehall Diary* I, 73–4.

[3] *The Times* 13 Feb. 1919, 9b; 17 Feb. 1919, 12a. *The Times* toyed with the idea of the government conceding the principles of shorter hours and public ownership, and using the Inquiry to assess their likely effects.

[4] *The Times* 21 Feb. 1919, 11f.

creation of the Sankey Commission. As some of the miners feared, the government might have been concerned simply to prevaricate until the political atmosphere grew calmer, the miners' determination waned, and the more extreme demands could be rejected without fear of a militant reaction. Such a consideration could hardly have been absent from the Cabinet's mind. It was, after all, the mirror image of the miners' assumption that in the circumstances of early 1919 they could extract maximum gains from direct confrontation rather than prolonged negotiation. Time is never on the side of ultimatums. Yet the granting of the miners' wages and hours demands, together with the concession of the principle of nationalization, on such evidence as was available in February 1919, would have been inconceivable. Nor is the fact that the government was taking steps to maintain essential supplies in the event of a strike a necessary indication of any particularly sinister intent. The Lloyd George administration was a long way from objectivity in the matter of the miners' claim, but the measures it put in hand reflected no more than an understandable sense of being on the brink of a catastrophe of industrial and social relations.[1]

In any event, the more ruthless language used in contemplation of a national strike proved irrelevant to the immediate problem. Once the statutory inquiry had been proposed, the initiative lay with the government. Having laid the ground with the MFGB Executive, the Prime Minister then persuaded Beatrice and Sidney Webb (the latter being a well-known supporter of the miners' cause) of his intention to create a Royal Commission whether or not the union cooperated. In their turn, the Webbs (mistrusting Lloyd George but suspecting that the union did not have sufficient rank-and-file support to win a direct confrontation on the issue of public ownership) helped persuade the MFGB that a Commission was essential to advance their cause.[2]

---

[1] CAB 23/9/59–60, 62 (7 and 10 Feb. 1919). Preparations to run essential services in the event of a strike were undertaken by a Committee on Industrial Unrest (formed on 4 Feb.), which was subsequently renamed the Supply and Transport Committee. Taken in isolation, the Prime Minister's notorious argument in Cabinet on 10 Feb. (if the miners 'chose starvation as a weapon they must not complain if society made use of the same weapon') and some of the associated responses which were canvassed, seem unfitting—especially for a Prime Minister. In context, however, they indicated a mental preparation for the worst (by a government with no experience of the sort of universal unrest that was felt to be imminent), while hoping for better things. (Quoted in Johnson 1968, 374.) On the other hand, the Cabinet was neither indifferent to the outcome of the dispute, nor a neutral arbitrator. It is relevant to emphasize that Sir Adam Nimmo, a leading Scottish coalowner and then adviser to the Coal Controller, was present at the Cabinet discussions of how to respond to the miners' claims.

[2] The story of the Webbs' role is in Cole 1952, 146 ff.

On 24 February Lloyd George introduced the Coal Industry Commission Bill into the Commons, forcefully emphasizing its powers, his sympathies for the miners, and the need for a thorough investigation of their case. The legislation received the Royal Assent on 26 February. The next day, after a compromise on the timetable (the Commission was to produce an interim report on wages and hours by 20 March—the Cabinet preferring 30 March, the MFGB the 15th), an MFGB delegate conference, sustained by an overwhelming vote in favour of a strike, was persuaded by Smillie and the Executive to postpone the strike notices and cooperate with the Commission.[1] To the owners, who felt that any large concession to the miners would be unwarranted, the atmosphere in which the Commission was created seemed unhealthy and even hysterical. But to the Cabinet and opinion at large it offered a precious breathing space.

The membership of the Royal Commission of 1919 was much as had been predicted. The chairman Sir John Sankey was a High Court Judge who could, it was felt, hold the ring between the opposing sides. The MFGB was directly represented by its President, Secretary, and Yorkshire Vice-President (Robert Smillie, Frank Hodges, and Herbert Smith). Three other members were nominated by the miners: Sir Leo Chiozza Money, R. H. Tawney, and Sidney Webb. The owners' association had three representatives (Evan Williams, R. W. Cooper, and J. T. Forgie). And there were three independent businessmen: Arthur Balfour, Sir Arthur Duckham, and Sir Thomas Royden.

The first stage of the Sankey Inquiry marked the high point of an exceptionally dramatic year. The Commission met in public, wrestling with fundamental ideological and detailed practical questions in the King's Robing Room of the House of Lords. Its hearings soon turned into a bruising adversarial contest. Its members were aligned, in their seating as well as their attitudes, into contesting 'sides'. Its dialectic was determined by the principles of prosecution and defence, question and cross-examination. Yet it was largely a one-sided contest. The coalowners were thrown off balance by the pugnacity as well as effectiveness with which the union men mounted their onslaught on private ownership and its presumed social consequences. And the miners' successful mixture of technical insight and emotional force was powerfully supported by the formidable intellects and forensic skills of those

---

[1] The creation of the Sankey Commission coincided with moves to tackle the broader issues of industrial unrest, by means of a National Industrial Conference, which was convened on 27 Feb. See Lowe 1978.

whom the *Colliery Guardian* sourly but not inaccurately called their 'socio-political abettors'.[1]

Neither the businessmen on the Commission, nor the business and official witnesses proved a match for the miners and their appointees. Tawney thought that the owners and steelmakers who took the stand were 'extraordinarily incompetent, not to say stupid'; and Sankey confided to his diary that the owners were 'hopeless'. *The Times* felt that, while the owners 'cut a sorry figure', this was not simply a matter of demeanour since the miners' 'case was better presented, but it was also a better case'. The printed evidence confirms such judgements: the owners' questioning was pallid and unproductive, their defence of the existing system of private enterprise banal, their knowledge of social conditions clearly limited, and their lack of sympathy with the miners' welfare objectives manifest. 'The other side', wrote Beatrice Webb in her diary, 'are absurdly outclassed', with 'not the remotest inkling of the wider political and social issues.'[2]

This last point was of considerable importance. For the owners were clearly caught out by the direction taken by the first stage of the Inquiry. In their *naïveté* they were quite unprepared for fundamental discussion of the social responsibilities of businessmen, let alone questions of nationalization and control. They imagined, but were soon disillusioned, that the Commission would adhere to the original stipulation that its first stage would be confined to the issue of wages and hours. Yet whatever their excuse for ineptitude, the absence of a well-prepared case or of any sign of a tendency to self-reform, gave their erstwhile sympathizers grounds for disappointment. 'By refusing to organise itself to the common advantage', the *Colliery Guardian* complained, the coal trade 'not only has played into the hands of the enemy, but . . . has invited the dubious alternative of nationalization.'[3]

In sharp contrast, the miners' spokesmen had a well-prepared and powerfully argued viewpoint. They rested most of their case in favour of higher wages on social arguments—they needed 'higher wages in order

[1] *CG* 21 Mar. 1919, 663.

[2] Tawney: Tom Jones to Lloyd George, 14 Mar. 1919: HLRO F/23/4/34; Sankey: quoted in Morgan 1979, 63; *The Times* 18 Mar. 1919, 11b; Cole 1952, 152–3 (12 Mar. 1919). For an example of the owners' poor showing see the evidence of Wallace Thorneycroft (a leading Scottish owner and Chairman of the MAGB's Propaganda Committee), who was humiliated by Smillie's attack on the quality of company housing in Scotland, by Webb's exposure of his ignorance of industrial conditions, and by Money's criticisms of his use of statistics. Nor was Thorneycroft's standing much helped by such claims as 'The standard of health in the mining industry is high and there is little room for improvement.' See *Sankey Evidence* I, QQ 6810ff., 7101ff., and 7812ff.

[3] *CG* 28 Feb. 1919, 487.

to give their wives and children the living which they are entitled to expect'. In their President's words, they were 'really claiming, because of their usefulness to the State, because of the dangerous nature of their employment, that they are entitled to a higher standard of life.'[1] This was the essence of the argument, and the dictates of justice were often contrasted with those of the market. Nevertheless, the miners' representatives also urged that the problems of wages and hours could not be divorced from those of conditions and ownership; that the War had demonstrated the economic advantages of central control and coordination; that the miners' entitlement to environmental improvement rested on economic as well as moral grounds; and that the industry's ability to pay higher wages or support lower hours depended on reorganization, public ownership, and joint control.

The miners' tactics were not, therefore, simply a question of embarrassing opposing witnesses by exposing their traditionalist views or analytical *naïveté*. Sir Arthur Lowes Dickinson (responsible for the Coal Control's Financial Branch) was forced to concede that wartime profits had been very large and official price increases excessively generous to some firms. Edwin Davies (in charge of the Control's supplies section) acknowledged that the unification and central control of transport and distribution had brought about considerable savings in railway resources. Sir Richard Redmayne (Chief Inspector of Mines and in charge of the Control's Production Branch), while firmly opposed to nationalization, admitted that in his opinion 'the present system of individual ownership of collieries is extravagant and wasteful' and that 'collective production' was desirable. And a host of witnesses were pressed on the low quality of housing; the fatiguing, uncomfortable, and dangerous conditions of work; the poverty and deserving character of miners; and the misery and high infant mortality of mining communities. There was, in all this, an emotional division of labour. The miners pressed the moral justice of their claim, and their intellectual allies pursued economic arguments concerning the advantages of unification under public ownership, the potential for greater efficiency, and the presumed weakness of the owners' counter-case that higher wages would impair coal's competitiveness in the world's markets and raise costs for British industry generally.

---

[1] *Sankey Evidence* I, QQ 4353, 6893. Also see evidence of Vernon Hartshorn, MP (of the South Wales Miners' Federation): 'Even if ... the other side can prove that ... wages have kept pace with the increase in the cost [of living], yet the miners still say that the pre-war standard of living was so inadequate that they must insist upon a substantial advance in wages.'

Read soberly, there was little on either side of the *economic* arguments about the relative advantages of private and public ownership which was analytically and empirically persuasive. But considered as political discourse and emotional dialectic, the miners' case had enormous force. And in this respect it was greatly helped by the MFGB's formidable management of public relations, which earned the owners' grudging respect (and ultimate imitation). The great success of the Sankey Commission, as far as the miners were concerned, was not its logical but its *moral* impact. It was not only committed newspapers like the *Daily Herald* which came to feel that 'there is blood on the coal'. The public at large learned of appalling housing in mining communities, of the extremes and dangers of working conditions. As a result, the miners' representatives succeeded in establishing the emotional argument in favour of improved pay, and the concept of a 'social wage' effectively dates from the controversies of 1919.

More than this, pity for the miners naturally welled over into sympathy for their economic assertions and resentment at the owners, and at evidence of their large wartime profits. Public opinion, Tom Jones told Lloyd George, had swung right round to the miners' side as a result of the prominence given to their case by newspapers. On 12 March Beatrice Webb gleefully confided to her diary that the Sankey Commission had been transmuted into 'a revolutionary tribunal', and its daily business into 'a state trial of the coal owners and the royalty owners, culminating in the question, "Why not nationalize the mines?"' As its first stage came to an end, Lloyd George was well aware that the Commission was 'arousing the social conscience in a way that no enquiry of modern times has succeeded in doing'.[1]

Perhaps of even greater importance, the Inquiry aroused the conscience of its influential members. On 20 March the Commission published three separate interim reports: one by the Chairman and the three independent businessmen, one by the miners and their allies, and one by the coalowners. All recommended a large increase in wages and a reduction in the maximum of hours which could be worked underground. The Chairman's report, which was the one officially adopted, proposed an increase of 2s. per shift for adults and 1s. for boys (the

[1] *Daily Herald* 15 Mar. 1919, 4. On public opinion: Tom Jones to Lloyd George, 14 and 17 Mar. 1919: HLRO F/23/4/34; Cole 1952, 152–3 (12 Mar. 1919); Lloyd George to Tom Jones, 17 Mar. 1919: HLRO F/23/4/37. *The Times* also welcomed the fact of the Inquiry ('most instructive . . . it has thrown much light on dark places'), and felt that it had established a useful precedent: 18 Mar. 1919, 11a–b.

equivalent of about 20 per cent on earnings, as against the 30 per cent claim); a limitation of profits to 1 s. 2 d. per ton (in large part to pay for the wage increase); and a reduction of maximum hours from eight to seven, with effect from July 1919, plus a further reduction to six hours in July 1921 if the industry's circumstances warranted it. The miners' group were, of course, unconditionally in favour of the full claim. The owners, although they grudgingly argued that the result would be 'seriously prejudicial to the economic life of the country', advocated an increase in pay of 1 s. 6 d. for men and 9 d. for boys, and also a reduction in hours to a maximum of seven.[1]

In the context of the original claim, and given the prevailing atmosphere of crisis and sympathy, such recommendations were only to be expected. And the same might be said of other important aspects of the interim reports. For in spite of the fact that the Commission's initial remit had confined its first stage to a consideration of hours and wages, the Chairman and the independent businessmen, like the miners, went out of their way to pass judgement on the industry and its management. In words which were to be quoted again and again as a verdict on the industry as it emerged from the First World War, they asserted that

Even upon the evidence already given, the present system of ownership and working in the coal industry stands condemned, and some other system must be substituted for it, either nationalisation or a method of unification by national purchase and/or by joint control.

To almost everyone except the leaders of the Mining Association of Great Britain, such a verdict came as little surprise. Indeed, even close supporters of the coalowners initially felt that their representatives on the Sankey Commission had blundered in not signing that section of the interim report: 'no enlightened employer can regard the present system, which is none of his making, as anything but unsatisfactory'.[2] There was

[1] The interim reports are in *PP* 1919 XI. Working hours underground are usually specified in somewhat misleading terms. This is partly because the figures used normally derive from the legislative stipulation of the *maximum* length of underground shifts, and not all coalfields worked to the maximum. More important, hours were conventionally measured from the last man down to the first man up and a 'legal' shift would therefore last eight (or, from 1919, seven) hours *plus* one 'winding time' (the time needed to lower an entire shift of men to the bottom of the shaft). The average winding time was some 37 minues (*Sankey Evidence* I, QQ 5119ff.). On the other hand, once underground, miners had to travel to their work-places so that the actual time spent working might be significantly less. If underground hours were reduced by, say, one, the reduction in the time spent hewing or putting could therefore be proportionately more, since the time taken in underground travel was obviously *not* reduced.

[2] *CG* 21 Mar. 1919, 66. *The Times* (21 Mar. 1919, 11a) also felt that the owners should have made 'the painful admission' indicated by Sankey's remarks. Later, the *Colliery Guardian*

even a belief that many of the coalowners actually sympathized with Sankey's adverse conclusion, but were reluctant to confess it 'for fear of damaging their future bargaining position with the government'—and certainly in the discussions in the various district associations many owners took the view that nationalization in some form was almost inevitable.[1] The fact is, however, that the firm and uncompromising condemnation in the Sankey report had largely emotional overtones.

While public opinion had been shocked by the industrial and social conditions exposed in the Inquiry, and understandably attached most blame to those responsible for the business management of the industry, empirical observation and rational deduction were not the only forces at work. The Commission's hearings were conducted under the direct threat of a national strike. And the owners' subsequent observation that at every private sitting of the Commission Sidney Webb ('the stage manager for the other side') reminded its members 'that all we had to do was to prevent a strike' was a jaundiced but substantially accurate indication of the prevailing political mood.[2] Indeed, as the Commission began to discuss its interim report in the third week of March, Ministers and their advisers were seriously worried lest the outcome would not go far enough to cool the miners' wrath and avoid a crisis. To avoid 'a Strike ... of such magnitude as might lead to something like a social revolution', the Chairman and the independent businessmen were officially pressed to accept the principle of 'national ownership'. And Sankey and Lloyd George ensured that the Scott Report (on the private ownership of royalties) should not be published at that juncture since it discussed alternatives to nationalization and might therefore be considered by the miners as provocative.[3]

The essentially political overtones of the Inquiry and its outcome were decisively illustrated in the relief which the interim reports engendered, and the eagerness with which the government's acceptance of their principal terms were received. Even the *Colliery Guardian*
apologized to the owners for its first pronouncement on the grounds that it had learned that their representatives on the Commission were presented with the draft report only hours before publication was necessary: *CG* 2 May 1919, 1026.

[1] Lloyd George to Bonar Law, 20 Mar. 1919: HLRO F/30/3/33 (also in CAB 23/9/18). For the district association discussions, see below, 135.

[2] 'Deputation of the Coal Owners' Association to the Prime Minister', 14 Nov. 1919: British Coal (Hobart House) Library, P622:338, 3. The shadow of the threatened strike did hang over the Commission. See *Sankey Evidence* I, Q 5820.

[3] Tom Jones to Lloyd George, 14 and 18 Mar. 1919: HLRO F/23/4/34 and 38. On the Scott Report, see HLRO F/45/3/2–3 (17 Mar. 1919) and F/30/3/31 (19 Mar. 1919). For the confidential negotiations which preceded the final drafting, see Cole 1952, 154–6.

welcomed Sankey's report as 'a statesmanlike attempt to deal with the crisis', while *The Times* gave it an equally good reception and the Commons announcement (in Lloyd George's absence at the Peace Conference) by Bonar Law that the government accepted Sankey's report was 'received with joy by the whole House'. The government had declined to go further than Sankey's interim report. But this granted most of the miners' claims, and with the second stage of the Inquiry still to come, it was not likely that the miners would strike on the issue of nationalization. What Lloyd George referred to as 'the flow of healing testimony' could continue.[1]

In accepting the Chairman's interim report, Bonar Law had said that this was done 'in the spirit as well as in the letter'. This seemed a sufficiently explicit phrase, and was widely interpreted as an acceptance of the principle espoused by Sankey—public ownership or the direct social control of the industry. Yet Bonar Law's statement contained fertile seeds of ambiguity, and therefore future controversy, precisely because the report was negative rather than positive about the system of ownership and control on coalmining. There was, however, no room for controversy about the recommendations concerning wages, hours, and profits. The Sankey wage award was granted and backdated to 9 January (the date of the official submission of the claim); the commitment to a seven-hour day was translated into law on 15 August; and the government began to prepare for a limitation on profits.[2] The miners called off their strike and all concerned awaited, with varying expectations, the Sankey Commission's second stage—the detailed examination of the issue of nationalization.

iii. The Sankey Commission: the second stage

Very clearly, the coalowners were thrown on to the defensive by the tone of the first stage of the Sankey Inquiry and by its outcome. It so happens that just before the Commission had been appointed, the Mining Association had produced its own *Suggested Scheme of Recon-*

---

[1] *CG* 21 Mar. 1919, 66; *The Times* 22 Mar. 1919, 13a ('The Road to Peace'); 'Deputation of the Coal Owners' Association to the Prime Minister', 14 Nov. 1919: British Coal (Hobart House) Library P622:338, 48 ('received with joy'). Lloyd George resisted pleas from Sankey and Bonar Law, declining to return from the Paris Peace Conference on the grounds that the Conference was at a particularly sensitive point so that to leave it would run the risk of failure and 'world catastrophe'. For this, and his comment about 'healing testimony' see Lloyd George to Tom Jones, 17 Mar. 1919: HLRO F/23/4/37.

[2] Below, 141–2.

struction for the Coal Mining Industry, which in its first draft, dated 15 February 1919, proposed not only a new system of consultation and wage-determination,[1] but also a radical scheme for a single national sales corporation to handle the country's entire output. In his Introduction, Sir Adam Nimmo had placed this plan in the context of the government's moves towards an inquiry, which he saw as 'a distinct turning-point in the industry': 'We stand today facing a new order of things', he argued. 'We cannot go back to the past, even if we would.' But this turned out to be a minority as well as a premature view. Before the document's publication on 21 February, all references to a reorganization of marketing had been eliminated—an omission which was the occasion for the *Colliery Guardian*'s subsequent regret that the coal trade had sacrificed 'an excellent chance of redeeming its character on business lines'.[2] What was left in the document played little part in the Sankey hearings. In the shock of the interim reports at the end of March the MAGB withdrew its industrial-relations proposals entirely, although they were to be reintroduced for the second stage, after the owners had failed to agree on an alternative strategy.[3]

As public discussion and the Sankey Inquiry continued after March 1919, although the MAGB could not secure agreement on any counter-proposals, it began to assert itself—spurred on by the adamant opposition of rank-and-file members to any voluntary cooperation with the government in the matter of profit limitation, or in any attempt to get the owners to bear the cost of the wage increase. In London, its national officials put their case forcibly to the President of the Board of Trade and his colleagues. They absolutely refused to negotiate about the industry's financial agreements. And after a certain amount of bluster by their senior representative, Sir Adam Nimmo, they persuaded the government to accept responsibility for finding the back pay generated by the Sankey award (i.e. for the period 9 January to 1 April), although they had to accept the government's ruling that the colliery firms should meet all future wage costs. The MAGB also created a Propaganda Committee and a Central Committee to oversee publicity and political strategy generally, as well as to manage the owners' presentation to the second stage of the Sankey Inquiry.[4]

---

[1] Above, 121.

[2] 28 Feb. 1919, 487.

[3] For the MAGB's failure to secure internal agreement to an industrial plan after the discussion of 20 drafts, see *The Times* 10 Apr. 1919, 13d.

[4] *MAGB* 1920, 14, 21.

Meanwhile, the MAGB was mobilizing opinion in its constituent district associations. At meetings called to discuss the Sankey interim reports, district after district rejected both joint control and nationalization as solutions for the problems of coalmining. Significantly, however, they also claimed that, if obliged to choose, they would prefer to accept outright public ownership. In the words of the Chairman of the Scottish Coal Owners' Association

the Owners should tell the Government that in their view the Industry should remain as at present, and the Owners are willing to co-operate with the Workmen and give them the information they desire, and that wages should be based on the results of the industry. Further, they are willing to establish Pit Committees as Advisory Committees. . . . These Committees, however, would not have the power to decide how the Collieries would be worked. If the Government decided that this was not acceptable and the only alternative was joint control or nationalisation, then the Owners would recommend that nationalisation should be carried out.[1]

This view was to become MAGB official policy: joint control was unworkable, even unthinkable, and 'the State ... purchase [of] the collieries at their fair selling values' was the only alternative reform.[2] Hence when Lord Gainford, a leading Durham owner, came to give official evidence to the second stage of the Sankey Inquiry he made the following notorious statement:

I am authorised to say, on behalf of the Mining Association, that if the owners are not to be left complete executive control, they will decline to accept the responsibility of carrying on the industry, and though they regard nationalisation as disastrous to the country, they feel they would, in such event, be driven to the only alternative—nationalisation on fair terms.[3]

There was an obvious note of bullying defiance about this sort of response—a confident challenge to the rest of the community to run the coalmining industry without the help of its businessmen and managers.[4] Yet at the same time, given the political atmosphere in the spring of 1919, it also contained an element of shrewd realism. For it seemed to many informed observers, including a number of coalowners, that coal nationalization might well be inevitable. The nationalization of the rail-

[1] SCOA, 31 Mar. 1919. Also see MSWCOA, 29 Mar. 1919.
[2] *MAGB* 1919, 90.
[3] *Sankey Evidence* II, 810.
[4] Colliery managers were said to be equally vehement in their opposition to joint control: *CG* 23 May 1919, 1219.

ways had already been officially canvassed; leading Tory members of the Coalition Government were neither horrified nor surprised at the idea of nationalizing the collieries (the Conservative Party established a working party on the subject in the following winter); and men such as *The Times*'s industrial correspondent, Arthur Shadwell, were coming round to the view that some form of public corporation was the only answer to the industry's problems.[1]

In these circumstances it was hardly surprising that the coalowners themselves should discuss public ownership as a distinct possibility, nor that they should assume that it would be in their interest to ensure that nationalization, if it were to prove unavoidable, took place while their assets were more or less intact. And the value of their assets, they assumed, might well be threatened by the long continuance of the Sankey wages and hours award—let alone by sharing control with a work-force seeking short-run benefits. Given such an assumption, a minority came to an uncomfortable conclusion: 'the owners desired to have nationalization now, rather than five years hence when the Collieries have been reduced to a ruinous condition.'[2]

Of course, none of this persuaded the generality of owners to welcome or encourage the idea of nationalization. And their sectional resolve was strengthened by broader arguments, which reminded them that in the matter of public ownership at such a time, they 'merely occupy the front trench'.[3] They succeeded in mounting a powerful counter-attack from that front trench. The fortuitous withdrawal of two members of the Sankey Commission enabled them to strengthen its anti-public ownership representation with Sir Adam Nimmo and Sir Allan Smith (the forthright and confident Chairman of the Engineering Employers' Federation). The MAGB also mustered and prepared its

---

[1] Conservative Party committee on nationalization: Arthur Steel-Maitland Papers, SRO GD 193/317/77 ff. Bonar Law and Baldwin on coal nationalization: Jones to Lloyd George, 18 Mar. 1919, in HLRO F/23/4/38. Arthur Shadwell 1919. In April Lloyd George had told an anxious Bonar Law that even if the government were forced into a policy of nationalization 'that will not be very serious', since public ownership would be unavoidable sooner or later. Riddell 1933, I (11 Apr. 1919).

[2] SCOA, 31 Mar. 1919. Also see *MAGB* 1919, 92.

[3] *CG* 27 June 1919, 1554. Also see the remarks of the MAGB's President Evan Williams to the Monmouthshire & South Wales Coal Owners' Association in March (MSWCOA, 29 Mar. 1919): 'In regard to Nationalisation there are certain owners who think it would be advisable to accept Nationalisation. There is, to an extent, an amount of justification for this, but it must be remembered that it is not in the Nation's interests, as well as in the Owners' interests, that this should be resorted to.' In early April, however, *The Times* had entertained the suspicion that the owners might be 'prepared for nationalisation in the assurance that the present House of Commons will secure for them generous terms of compensation'. (10 Apr. 1919, 13d.)

witnesses to much better purpose during the Inquiry's second stage, which lasted two months. Meanwhile, the Propaganda Committee and the newly formed 'Coal Association' initiated an active publicity campaign. 'We did not understand the [*propaganda*] game', it was said in May 1919, 'but we are now beginning to learn it.'[1]

By June, therefore, the crisis atmosphere had been dissipated, and when the Commission produced four contrasting reports, the government was presented with a number of options. Sir John Sankey wrote an individual report, which advocated nationalization less because of its direct economic benefits than because it might dispel 'the present atmosphere of distrust and recrimination' and achieve harmony in industrial relations by abolishing private ownership. His was a forthright if naïve document, relying on 'the honour of the men's leaders and the men' to maintain output. The miners and their allies also argued in favour of nationalization, while rejecting Sankey's proposal for compulsory conciliation in the event of industrial disputes. Sir Arthur Duckham broke the business ranks by recommending a system of large-scale amalgamations on a regional basis, together with profit limitations, government oversight, and worker representation at board level. The coalowners and the two remaining independent businessmen rejected public ownership and supported the MAGB proposal for consultation and a diluted form of profit-sharing. The first three reports discussed the need for improvements in welfare, and advocated substantial extensions in pithead baths. And all four recommended the nationalization of the actual mineral, on the grounds that the fragmentation of private ownership and decision-making led to inefficiency in the use of a natural resource.[2]

In the event, neither the second-stage hearings nor the final reports excited public attention or private anguish in quite the same way as those of the first stage. Given the changed mood of public opinion and the variety of the reports, radical experiment seemed much less likely in the summer than it had done in the spring of 1919. And the probability was further diminished as a result of the MAGB's greatly strengthened publicity and the rallying of anti-nationalization forces generally. The

[1] Wallace Thorneycroft (Chairman of the Propaganda Committee) to the MAGB annual meeting: *MAGB* 1919, 115.

[2] The Reports and Minutes of Evidence of the second stage of the Sankey Commission are in *PP* 1919 XI and XIII. In advocating the nationalization of mineral royalties the owners had taken an apparently radical step, from which they drew back in later years, explaining that it had been an aberration brought about by the febrile atmosphere of 1919, and that legislation in 1923 had sufficiently clarified property rights and obligations.

owners produced some 1.5 million pamphlets opposing public ownership, and organized a memorial signed by about 300 MPs, mostly Tory
members of the Coalition, which was held to have 'considerably influenced Lloyd George and the Government'. Many Liberals were also
unwilling to support public ownership. Clearly, the threat to the unity
of the government posed by the question of the nationalization of the
coal industry, was an important influence on the Prime Minister's
thinking.[1]

   In addition to these considerations, even labour support for nationalization was flagging. Late in July, it became clear that the miners' allies
(the railwaymen and transport workers) would not condone a strike to
enforce any part of the Sankey Report, and an MFGB conference had
even declined to give its Executive Committee any authority to strike
without first consulting its various districts. The rank and file, as well as
officials, of the miners' union were in fact much preoccupied with securing adjustments to piece rates, so as to minimize the effects on wages of
the reduction in hours. And their political cause was weakened, on the
one hand, by a tense strike in Yorkshire on the issue of piece rates
(which could be represented as an undisciplined act of material ambition); and, on the other hand, by an abrupt increase in the price of coal in
the second week of July. The latter, coinciding with publicity about
falling labour productivity, was put forward by the government as the
cost of the Sankey award at a time of low output—but could with equal
plausibility be interpreted as a propaganda stunt on the eve of a by-
election. As prolonged controversy eroded public confidence in nationalization as a solution for the industry's problems, so the events of the
summer lost the miners much of the sympathy they had attracted earlier
in the year.[2]

   The absence of any direct industrial or political pressures on the

---

[1] MAGB publicity and the Commons memorial: Wallace Thorneycroft to Lord Gainford,
10 Sept. 1919: Gainford Papers, 98; *The Times* 14 July 1919, 8b; CAB 24/85/315–18 (12 July 1919);
CAB/24/85/240–1 (6 Aug. 1919). Bonar Law had raised the political problem of nationalization in
the context of the Coalition Government on the eve of the Commission's interim reports: Tom
Jones to Lloyd George, 18 Mar. 1919: HLRO F/23/4/38. Lloyd George was also influenced by a
dinner with 18 MPs (mostly Coalition Liberals)—all but one of whom accepted the idea of nationalizing the railways, but rejected public ownership of the coalmines (while advocating worker
representation on boards of management): CAB 23/11/57–8 (23 July 1919); HLRO F/21/4/7
(22 July 1919).

[2] Declining union support: CAB 24/84/319–20 (23 July 1919); *The Times* 13 Aug. 1919, 10a. Falling productivity: *Hansard* 26 Nov. 1919, col. 1829. Also see CAB 24/83/78–91 (3 July 1919); CG
11 July 1919, 101; *The Times* 10 and 11 July 1919, 13a and 13f; *Hansard* 14 July 1919, cols. 77 ff.; *Report
by Messrs. Tongue & Co., Chartered Accountants, on the Coal Industry*. Cmd. 555. 1920 (*PP* 1920 XIII).

government, or any obvious economic justification, pointed inexorably towards an official rejection of Sir John Sankey's proposals for outright public ownership of the coalmining industry. There was a certain amount of prevarication in the War Cabinet, and in the first two weeks of August some Ministers continued to propose fairly drastic solutions (e.g. an experiment in public ownership in one district) for the industry's problems.[1] Nevertheless, the outcome was never really in doubt. On 18 August Lloyd George, in a Commons statement on the economic situation in general, rejected the proposals to nationalize the coalmines. Instead, he announced that the government would seek public owner-ship of royalties and foster regional mergers of colliery companies along the lines advocated by Duckham (although he avoided any reference to Duckham's proposals for profit restrictions, and implied that the state's role would extend to sponsoring schemes rather than overseeing administration). The Prime Minister also accepted the idea of worker representation on area boards (but not in the direct management of individual pits) and the creation of a welfare fund, financed by a levy on royalty payments and to be directed to ameliorating social and working conditions.

At any other time and in other circumstances, this might have been considered a fairly radical programme. But in the context of 1919 its tone disappointed political observers and outraged the miners, whose parliamentary representatives argued that they had been duped and deceived, and that the government had gone back on a virtual commit-ment to nationalization.[2] Indeed, given the immediate history of the problem, Lloyd George's statement *was* prosaic and unimaginative, and its moral force was weakened by his demagogic attacks on members of the Sankey Commission. At the same time, however, taken at their face value, the government proposals appeared to offer the industry the possibility of very extensive reform. Yet that possibility was imme-diately clouded by the profound disappointment of the MFGB, and by its consequence unwillingness to cooperate with the government's

[1] For criticism of the government's equivocation, see *CG* 4 July 1919, 33. War Cabinet discus-sions are in: CAB 24/85/399–402, 407–8, 420–1 (2, 5, and 6 Aug. 1919); CAB 24/80/171–9 (7 and 14 Aug. 1919); CAB 23/15/177 ff. (7 Aug. 1919).

[2] *Hansard* 18 Aug. 1919, cols. 1979 ff.; *The Times* 19 Aug. 1919, 10b and 11b; *Nation* 23 Aug. 1919, 609. There was a certain amount of fruitless controversy about the exact meaning of Bonar Law's words about accepting the Sankey interim report in the letter and in the spirit. Liberally interpreted, they could be taken as encouragement to believe that the government was largely committed to public ownership in March. But, as even some opponents of the government conceded, the miners did not have a 'letter-perfect case' (*Nation* 23 Aug. 1919, 609). Also see Bonar Law's statement in the Commons on 20 and 21 Feb. 1920.

proposed programme. In its turn, this must have come as a relief to the War Cabinet, which was never more than half-hearted, and certainly far from spontaneous, in its proposals for structural change. Even its diluted plans could now be shelved.

The miners' reaction to Lloyd George's proposals operated at two levels. First, they objected to a blueprint for the industry which appeared to reinforce private enterprise in a more grandiose form. The government's plan, their Secretary said, amounted to no more than 'trustification', and two months later their President told an exasperated Lloyd George that he would prefer the old system 'to setting up trusts which might be trusts between the miners and the mineowners ... against the general public'.[1] On the other hand, they were also deter-mined to avoid compromise, and to pursue their original objective of nationalization in its pristine form. Yet theirs was a determination with-out any very powerful impetus. In the autumn the MFGB shelved, and therefore in effect abandoned, the threat of direct action. Instead, it embarked on a belated publicity campaign—designated 'Mines for the Nation'—in favour of public ownership.

The MFGB leadership's efforts made very little impression on the public at large, while within the mining industry the achievement of substantial improvements in wages and hours, together with a further wage increase of 20 per cent in March 1920, cooled the rank and file's general enthusiasm for organizational change or ideological politics. In January 1920, union officials in Derbyshire were complaining about their members' indolence and indifference to the question of national-ization. And two months later the steam went out of the campaign completely, as the lack of public concern became manifest, an MFGB delegate conference displayed only moderate enthusiasm for drastic action, and the TUC overwhelmingly rejected the idea of strike action in support of public ownership.[2]

Thus, twelve months after the first stage of the Sankey Inquiry had appeared to presage huge structural transformations of the coalmining industry, its radical possibilities had disappeared. Nevertheless, the events of 1919 were not without historical resonance. Chief among these was, perhaps, the miners' sense of having been cheated out of their prize.

[1] *The Times* 19 Aug. 1919, 10b; Smillie quoted in Johnson 1968, 477.

[2] J. E. Williams 1962, 627; Arnot 1953, 218. It has been argued that the MFGB's error was to seek orthodox and bureaucratic nationalization instead of genuine workers' control: Woodhouse 1978. But it is difficult to see why this should have had a more wholesome attraction to the public—or even to the rank-and-file miners whose concern was far more keenly with issues of wages and hours.

A characteristic reaction was that of William Straker, the far from extreme Northumberland union leader: 'the offer to the miners was merely for the purpose of deception so as to get over a difficult situation for the time being. That trick can only be played once.'[1] These emotions played an important psychological role for decades—until nationalization was finally achieved in 1946/7.

Yet the resulting mythic character of discussions of 1919 is not entirely well-founded. The only thing of which the miners were 'cheated' was full-scale nationalization—a demand which they alone originated, which they allowed to obstruct all other avenues of organizational reform, and which was entertained by other people only in so far as it was presented as the sole answer to a crisis of industrial disharmony and social unrest. Political choice rather than class duplicity denied them their preferred outcome. The miners had begun the process which lent some justification to Baldwin's subsequent judgement that they 'lost all because they would not be content with less than all'.[2] Moreover the perspective of 'betrayal' is also misleading to the extent that it distracts attention from other consequences which flowed from the Sankey inquiries and reports, from the decision to accept many of the recommendations, and from the unstable market environment within which the industry had to operate. These consequences can be considered, first, in terms of the Commission's implications for the industry's finances and the associated need to define the government's future role; second, in terms of the repercussions for the representative institutions and attitudes of the coalowners; and third, and most important, in terms of wages and markets.

iv. Financial control and industrial policy

The government's unconditional acceptance of the wages, hours, and profits recommendations of the interim Sankey report in March 1919 was primarily a political decision, based on the desire to maintain 'peace in the coalfields'.[3] Their economic implications had to be worked out in the following months, albeit still in a political context. As has already been seen, the owners' vehement opposition to having to bear the cost of the wages increase was only partly successful: the government assumed liability solely for the 'back-pay' element (from 9 January to

[1] Quoted in Davison 1973.
[2] Baldwin to Lloyd George, 30 Jan. 1922: POWE 221/13.
[3] *Hansard* 11 Dec. 1919, col. 1674.

1 April), although even this involved an expenditure of some £7 million. Yet, whoever paid for it, the flat-rate award was a further complication for wage settlements across the disparate districts, while a more immediate problem loomed in the form of falling output per manshift, and was exacerbated by the reduction in the length of underground shifts.[1]

The combination of declining productivity, the yawning gap between high export prices (attuned to a booming world demand) and restricted inland prices, and the politically motivated desire to bring home to the public the presumed costs of the miners' demands led the War Cabinet to increase the price of domestic coal by 6s. per ton in July. This was greeted with widespread doubt and criticism, and confidence in the government's grasp of events was further shaken when four months later it announced a *decrease* (of 10s.) in the price of household and public utility coal, on the grounds that there had been an unexpected surge in average export prices, from 38s. in the spring to 62s. 5d. in October. And it was symptomatic of the confusion and policy anomalies of 1919 that both the miners and the trade journal attacked the price reduction—the former because it would produce losses and chaos and 'queer the pitch for nationalization', the latter because it was 'playing to the gallery' and was part of a conspiracy to demoralize business so that 'nationalization may be achieved as a bloodless victory over the body of a moribund industry'. The volatility of controlled prices proved so difficult to explain that the government had to appoint a firm of accountants to investigate the matter—with results that were uncomplimentary to officials of the Coal Control.[2]

The sense that the government was living on a hand-to-mouth basis as far as a coal industry policy was concerned was further confirmed when it came to deal with Sir John Sankey's recommendation that profits be limited to 1s. 2d. per ton. Here, the owners were even more vehement in their opposition, since it would have entailed an effective reduction of more than 40 per cent in permissible profits under the Coal Mines Agreement Act. They argued, with some justice, that they were expected privately to bear the cost of securing the public benefit of social peace. In spite of fierce grass-roots opposition, led by Sir Clifford Cory (who urged that MAGB officials should not deal with Ministers,

---

[1] See 'History of Financial Control': POWE 26/51 (wage award) and *Hansard* 13 Nov. 1919, cols. 502ff. and 24 Nov. 1919, cols. 1418ff. (output).

[2] A miners' MP (William Brace) 28 Nov. 1919, col. 2009. For the subsequent reduction, see CAB 23/18/136–40 (21 Nov. 1919); *Hansard* 28 Nov. 1919, cols. 2012ff., 2059; *CG* 28 Nov. 1919, 1437; and (for protests of district coalowners) LCOA, 8 Dec. 1919 and 7 Jan. 1920.

but should rely on Parliament where 'the owning Classes' were capable of protecting the industry against 'confiscation'), the MAGB made determined representations to Lloyd George and other Ministers. The pledge to limit profits, they argued, had been extracted 'at the point of a bayonet' and could therefore be repudiated with honour. The Prime Minister, although sympathetic, accepted that the government had an inescapable commitment to the policy. Nevertheless, he indicated that every effort would be made to diminish the impact of the measure, and cannily urged the owners not to insist on any public statements: 'I think the less said about it the better ... the less you say the more you will get.'[1]

Yet once again (as had happened over the issue of structural reform in August) the War Cabinet and the owners were saved from a distasteful prospect by the all-or-nothing attitude of the miners' union. For in the Commons their spokesmen refused to accept the '1s. 2d. Bill' as an adequate fulfilment of the government's commitments in the absence of any fundamental reorganization of the control of the industry. A relieved War Cabinet needed no further encouragement. The government announced that it considered itself free to reconsider its earlier pledge and that it would therefore withdraw the Bill.[2]

The failure to introduce structural reforms or profit limitations by no means exculpated the government for the lack of a systematic new policy for the coal industry. Certainly, the industry would now have to be decontrolled. Indeed, much of the original framework of control had been overtaken by the events of 1919. In August the transport management scheme was abandoned, and in November the miners (disgusted at the lack of consultation before the decision to reduce prices) resigned from the Coal Controller's Advisory Board—which had in any case hardly met for months and had 'ceased to form any useful function'.[3]

Meanwhile, Sir Richard Redmayne resigned as head of the Produc-

---

[1] See 'Deputation of the Coal Owners' Association to the Prime Minister', 14 Nov. 1919: British Coal Library, P622:388, 3; *MAGB* 1919, 99; CAB 24/93/391–8 (25 Nov. 1919); *Hansard* 11 Dec. 1919, cols. 1668, 1675. Cory had also led the opposition (within the MAGB) to the 'voluntary' financial agreement of 1917–18. See above, 84. It was proposed to attain profit limitation by changing the basis of the profits standard. Under the wartime control this had been derived from the choice by *individual collieries* of their best prewar years. This meant that total (and therefore average) standard profits reflected the total of each enterprise's *best* years. The proposal in Nov. 1919 was that the profits standard should be based on an *industry-wide average* of prewar experience—which, at £12.8 million would generate an average of 1s. 2d. per ton of the estimated 1919 output of 225 million tons.

[2] *Hansard* 11 Dec. 1919, cols. 1675, 1715–18, and 22 Dec. 1919, cols. 967–70.

[3] *Hansard* 28 Nov. 1919, cols. 2010–1.

tion Branch. Yet *financial* control could not be abandoned so easily. Decontrol in that sense was out of the question in 1919. The huge disparity between free-market export prices and controlled inland prices meant that decontrol would have led to a sharp increase in prices and widespread unemployment—'utter and complete chaos' in the words of the President of the Board of Trade (Auckland Geddes). On the other hand, the growing differential in prices threatened the existing system of financial control since the export collieries (having 'a valuable monopoly conferred upon them by the state') were making enormous profits, while those obliged to sell within Britain were incurring heavy losses which had to be met from the Exchequer.

Hence, as Geddes argued, although decontrol would come, the industry could not yet be left to the free play of market forces and collective bargaining. Before control was abandoned, it would be necessary to readjust the industry's finances and give more purposeful direction to the government's feeble and fragmented role. This was especially important because the uncertainty which had characterized the industry throughout 1919 was already having a serious effect on investment decisions, and miners as well as owners and politicians were extremely worried by the neglect of development work. National stability itself, the President of the Board of Trade urged, depended on a solution to the problems of the industry.[1] With the more 'extreme' Sankey proposals out of the way, this process could be accompanied by more congenial and fruitful consultations with the coalowners.[2]   The new financial basis for control was embodied in the Coal Mines (Emergency) Act of 31 March 1920, which was initially to run until 31 August 1920. It provided for the retrospective repeal of the existing legislation and for the more genuine pooling of colliery profits from 31 March 1919. Under the original (1918) agreement, each colliery had 'stood by itself', either retaining a portion of its profits above its prewar standard or having any deficiency below that standard made up by the state. Now, the entire

---

[1] For the President of the Board of Trade on the chaos that might follow decontrol and the industry's financial structure, see *Hansard* 11 Dec. 1919, col. 1671; and 22 Dec. 1919, cols. 967–70. Geddes also put the arguments in favour of retaining control yet redefining policy in CAB 24/95/22–22A (17 Dec. 1919). Also see 'History of Financial Control': POWE 26/51. The comment on national stability is in CAB 24/96/26 (6 Jan. 1920). For the postponement of investment (it was claimed that £58 million of capital projects were being postponed) see 'Deputation of the Coal Owners' Association to the Prime Minister', 14 Nov. 1919: British Coal Library, P622:388, 3; *Hansard* 28 Nov. 1919, cols. 2013, 2019, 2026, 2077; *Hansard* 14 Dec. 1919, cols. 571–2; President of the Board of Trade to War Cabinet, 27 Jan. 1920: POWE 26/44.

[2] *MAGB* 1920, 18–21; POWE 26/14 (27 Jan. 1920); CAB 24/97/58–76 (27 Jan. 1920); CAB 23/20/128–31 (11 Feb. 1920); HLRO F/188/1/8 (27 Jan. 1920).

industry's excess profits were to be pooled, and the pool used to pay up to the guaranteed level of 90 per cent of the prewar standard to collieries with a shortfall. Only if aggregate profits exceeded aggregate standards, therefore, would there be any surplus for further payments—and such surplus payments would be limited to 10 per cent of the excess. In contrast to the previous situation, each firm which might otherwise lose money would receive a deficiency payment from the pool before any firm was allowed to retain any excess profit. No longer could a sizeable part of the industry make 'enormous profits' from 'absurd monopoly prices' (albeit these proceeds were heavily taxed), while another sizeable part, selling at controlled prices, lost money and had to be subsidized from the Exchequer.[1]

Meanwhile, the longer-run future of the state's involvement with the industry was also being settled. In the spring of 1920 Sir Robert Horne (who had replaced Geddes as President of the Board of Trade) reiterated the official intention to return the industry to private enterprise—although not until the summer of 1921. And in order to prepare the way by enhancing the profitability of inland sales, domestic prices were raised (the 10s. price cut of the previous November was reinstated and a further 4s. 2d. imposed) and price controls loosened. At the same time, some strengthening and coordination of the government's permanent role was obviously necessary. For most of 1919 the Coal Control, which never had the authority of departmental status, had struggled against large pressures with inadequate resources. (The stress of the job was said to have hastened the death of the first Coal Controller and led to the demoralization and premature resignation of the second.) By January 1920, therefore, wartime proposals for a Ministry of Mines were revived, although the resurgence of the owners' political influence enabled them to prevent its being established as a department in its own right. Instead, it was to become a subordinate branch of the Board of Trade, in the charge of a Secretary for Mines, whose proposed status and salary were reduced by a Lords amendment.[2]

[1] 'History of Financial Control': POWE 26/51; CAB 24/97/77–88 (26 Jan. 1920). The quotations concerning excess profits are from a speech by Bonar Law: *Hansard* 11 Dec. 1919, col. 1716.

[2] For the increase in the price of coal and the loosening of price controls, see CAB 23/21/73–6, 83, 208–10 (6 and 10 May, 3 June 1920); CAB 24/196/136A–137 (25 May 1920). For the inadequacies and stresses of the Coal Control, see Geddes to Lloyd George, 28 Aug. 1919: HLRO F/17/5/51; *Hansard* 28 Nov. 1919, col. 2061. Sir Guy Calthrop had died in the influenza epidemic in 1918. His successor Sir Evan Jones (a civil engineer) resigned in Oct. 1919. He was succeeded by Andrew Duncan. For the Ministry of Mines, see POWE 26/14 (27 Jan. 1920); CAB 24/97/58–76 (27 Jan. 1920); HLRO F/188/1/8 (27 Jan. 1920); CAB 23/20/77–80 (4 Feb. 1920); CAB 24/98/21–3 (11 Feb. 1920); Bridgeman Diaries, 42 (Aug. 1920); *The Times* 17 Aug. 1920, 11c.

The government's new policy was embodied in the Mining Industry Act of 1920, which was introduced on 21 June and received the Royal Assent on 16 August. Apart from provisions for collective drainage schemes, it dealt with four aspects of the industry. First, it created a Mines Department within the Board of Trade. Second, it continued the existing arrangements for the control of the industry's prices, exports, and financial affairs, but established an ultimate deadline of 31 August 1921 for complete decontrol. Third, with a vestigial gesture towards the fundamental discussions of 1919, the Act provided for a network of consultative committees to represent miners and management, stretching from individual pit committees through district and area boards to the national level. (In the event, these powerless bodies were never established, since first the miners and then the owners refused to cooperate with the system.)[1] Finally, the government provided for a Miners' Welfare Fund (as had been promised by Lloyd George in August 1919), based on a levy of 1 d. per ton of output. The Fund was to be administered by a Miners' Welfare Committee in the interest of the 'social well-being, recreation and conditions of living' of miners and their communities—including education and research, but excluding housing.[2]

The outcome of the fierce postwar debates was, therefore, negligible. The government's promise to nationalize the minerals was quietly dropped, a small step towards the collective provision of welfare facilities was attempted, a government department was established but was denied independent status, and the financial affairs of the industry were rearranged with an eye to its inevitable decontrol. Meanwhile, the economic performance of the industry was proving inadequate. The postwar situation and the policy which emerged were described with the cynicism of hindsight by the Secretary for Mines in his first report:

it became clear that the industry was in an alarming condition. Enterprise and initiative were stifled. Output fell off and quality deteriorated. Capital was shy

---

[1] For the initial discussions of the consultative machinery, see CAB 24/98/21–3 and CAB 23/20/128–31 (11 Feb. 1920); CAB 24/98/197–8 (14 Feb. 1920). The MFGB was originally opposed to the committees because it feared that the district basis of representation would preclude the *national* scheme for wage determination for which it had been pressing since the War. The union changed its mind after its complete defeat on the wage-determination issue in 1921. But by that time the newly confident owners saw no need to cooperate. To the chagrin of the government they now refused to participate in the consultative machinery. See *Correspondence Between the Mining Association and the Mines Department Regarding the Operation of Part II of the Mining Industry Act, 1920* (Cmd. 1551. 1921) *PP* 1921 XXXI.

[2] Below, ch. 10, sect. v.

and development by private enterprise was almost wholly suspended. Demand still greatly exceeded supply and the machinery of artificial distribution was perpetually on the verge of disaster. The hybrid system of regulating the industry had clearly become intolerable and it was necessary to go either forward to nationalisation or back to private enterprise.[1]

There was, no doubt, a degree of rationalization in this verdict. But it captured the unsatisfactory character of compromise, and perhaps the inevitability of decontrol.

v. Mobilizing representation: the coalowners after Sankey

The repercussions of the Sankey Inquiry and its sharp political and ideological confrontations were felt within the industry as well as on the national stage. The miners had begun their struggle with enthusiasm and from a position of apparent strength. They were, nevertheless, grievously disappointed by events, while their determination to avoid compromise on structural or financial issues denied them many partial victories. Although they gained very substantial material successes in 1919 and 1920, the memory of the Sankey Commission and their larger frustrations became an emotional bank on which they henceforth drew in adversity. But it was an inadequate substitute for genuine achievement.

In contrast, the owners' attitudes and morale traced a reverse trajectory in 1919–20: from defensiveness and disarray to assertive confidence in their political strength. The tone of desperate resentment which had characterized the district associations' first reactions to the Sankey Inquiry was, within a year or so, replaced by a new mood, as the President of the MAGB was able to congratulate his members on two grand successes: 'putting nationalisation to sleep' and 'avoiding the financial proposals' of Sir John Sankey's Report.[2] This transformation flowed from large changes in the balance of political and economic power. But it was also a matter of institutional attitudes and reforms which were stimulated by the upheavals of 1919, and laid the basis of the MAGB's public role for the next 25 years.

From one viewpoint, the reorganization of the MAGB, entailing as it did a much greater degree of centralization and an extension of formal political action, was simply part of a broader trend towards corporate coalescence which affected employers' and workmen's associations as a result of the First World War and its aftermath. (In 1918 the miners'

---

[1] ARSM 1922, 4.   [2] MAGB 1920, 57.

union had established a permanent London headquarters and provided that its President and Secretary should be full-time officials.) From another, it was directly related to the Sankey Inquiry. The appointment of a Propaganda and a Central Committee (the latter within 24 hours of the Commission's interim reports) reflected the need for more effective policy formulation than could be provided by the large and unwieldy Executive Committee. Although they were envisaged as temporary arrangements, it was soon clear that they could not be discarded. In June the Central Committee's life was extended 'to sweep up all the debris that had been caused or would be caused by the Sankey Commission'. More important, by the second half of 1919 it was obvious that the new political climate and the emerging links with the state had called into question the structure and purpose of the MAGB as it had evolved in the nineteenth century.   Under its 1894 constitution the MAGB had been merely a loose federation of local associations, circumscribed in its authority and powers of initiative and negotiation, and largely confined to keeping a watching brief on traditional legislation. During the War, of course, government control and the central determination of wages and prices, had obliged the Association to assume a more active national role. In 1919, and in spite of the continuing apprehension of local associations (jealous of their distinctive positions with regard to wage systems, marketing, and business conditions), it was realized that a more enduring adjustment was required. In the face of the new public discussion of coalmining, the owners knew that they needed a stronger and more authoritative representation at national level. Propaganda work had to be continuous and the MAGB needed a London office with 'some permanent officials who could be trusted to look after our varied interests'.[1]

In the winter of 1919–20, therefore, the MAGB moved to reorganize itself. W. A. Lee, who had previously worked for the Coal Control, was appointed Assistant Secretary (he was the Association's first full-time official), and after careful consultation with district associations, a new constitution was accepted. Henceforth, membership was confined to district coalowner associations (before this, individuals had been eligible), and 25 such associations were named in the first instance. The formal purposes of the MAGB were extended from those of a parliamentary watchdog to embrace the functions of a modern interest group: the collection and dissemination of detailed statistics, propaganda, and publicity, general representation, and the encouragement of research and scientific work.

[1] Lord Gainford to T. Ratcliffe Ellis, 17 Sept. 1919: Gainford papers, 98.

At the same time, the interests of district associations were protected in that the MAGB was still precluded from a concern with any local questions relating to wages or conditions of employment or commercial price regulation. A permanent office and officials were provided for, and internal structures were strengthened by the creation of the Central Committee, the Propaganda and Statistical Committee (whose activities were financed by levies on district outputs), a Parliamentary Committee, and a Finance Committee. At the same time, the role of the MAGB as a pressure group was enlarged by the emergence of the office of President as a permanent and virtually full-time official. The first occupant of the new post was Evan Williams, a formidable South Wales coalowner, who had been elected under the old constitution, and in 1919 shared much of the work of negotiation with Sir Adam Nimmo. In 1920, when Williams had completed two years as President and should, by convention, have retired, he was re-elected—and continued to be re-elected until his formal retirement in 1944. This unofficial permanency apparently resulted from Williams's outstanding powers of representation and negotiation, and his quite extraordinary force of personality. Over 20 years later, Hugh Gaitskell was to describe him to the President of the Board of Trade as 'a pure Galsworthy type'.[1] From the owners' side, he was to dominate the politics of coal for 25 years, and his accession to power marked an entirely new phase in the public role and impact of the MAGB.[2]

vi. Wages and the economics of coal, 1919-1920

The political and administrative developments of 1919-20 took place in the context of the peculiar economics of coal and the successful pursuit by the miners of improvements in their earnings. The extraordinary character of both years consisted in the combination of falling productivity, stagnating output and exports, restrained inland prices and profits, and huge windfall gains on overseas sales. The tonnage of coal raised had been 287.4 million in 1913, but had fallen below 230 million

---

[1] *Dalton Diary*, 392 (11 Mar. 1942).

[2] In 1921 Williams was awarded an honorarium of £5,000 in recognition of his work for the MAGB. (He had been paid £3,000 annually as President of the Monmouthshire & South Wales Coal Owners' Association.) The gift was to be repeated in future years. The transformation of the MAGB was echoed in various district coalowners' associations, which created standing and propaganda committees, and statistical departments. The Scottish owners had, since 1916, given their Chairman (Sir Adam Nimmo) an annual honorarium of £1,000. See SCOA, 11 Dec. 1917, 16 Dec. 1918, 22 Dec. 1919: UGD 161/4/4-5.

by 1919 and 1920–in spite of an increase in manpower. Between 1913 and 1920 output per man-year fell from 226 to 183 tons.

Yet world shortages were pushing export prices even higher. At Newcastle, for example, they rose by about 60 per cent between 1918 and 1919, and by 75 per cent in the next year; and at Cardiff they virtually doubled in 1919–20. As a result, although the tonnage exported in 1920 was only about one-third of the 1913 total, its value rose from £53.7 to £120.3 million. (These sharp changes in values are demonstrated in Table 1.1.) The dominant consideration for all parties was, therefore, the vast financial surplus on exports, initially appropriated by the government through the limitation on retained business profits. In particular, the surplus was in the forefront of the miners' concern about the industry as a whole. For it offered them both the opportunity of increased earnings and a means of ensuring that the industry's finances, and particularly its wages system, might remain national in scope—to the benefit of miners in the potentially less profitable districts.

Early in January 1920 the MFGB urged the government to lower the price of coal or raise wages to meet the increase in living costs. And later that month the War Cabinet was advised that exports were proving so profitable that, even after meeting deficiencies on domestic sales, the industry was likely to have a surplus of £11 or £12 million in the four months April–August, so that some wage increase might be afforded.[1] Against this background, and with their political campaign for nationalization flagging, the MFGB turned to more orthodox industrial pressures. On 12 March, the day after the TUC had rejected their call for direct action in aid of nationalization, they put in a claim for an extra 3s. per shift. Successful in their assertion that it was not feasible to discuss a national wage claim with the owners (who had no national negotiating machinery), they were also successful in securing a share of the industry's bloated surplus: in April the government conceded the equivalent of 20 per cent on basic earnings.

But the economics of coal were once again amended by the government's determination to move towards decontrol. That inescapably meant an adjustment of prices (to narrow the gap in profitability between home and overseas sales). As we have already seen, the 10s. per ton which had been cut from the price of household coal in November 1919 was reinstated, and a further 4s. 2d. was imposed on all types of coal. The controls on distribution and of wholesale and retail margins

[1] Ministerial conference, 27 Jan. 1920: HLRO F/188/1/8.

were also relaxed.[1] The coexistence of enormous export profits and an increase in the price of coal (as well as the cost of living generally) turned the attention of the miners to the related questions of decontrol, prices, and wages. And on 7 July they submitted a double-barrelled claim which was designed, in the words of their Executive Committee, to cut 'right at the roots of the policy of the government'.

The MFGB demanded that the addition of 14s. 2d. to the price of household coal be withdrawn and that wages be increased by 2s. per shift for adults, 1s. for youths of 16 and 17, and 9d. for boys. Although the total cost (£63 million) could just be met from the industry's export surplus, the 'indivisible' claim, according to Smillie, would prevent control by diminishing the industry's financial viability for most private undertakings. The miners were 'not prepared to allow the coal trade to be decontrolled and each colliery to stand on its own legs'.[2]

At first, the government was adamant in resisting both claims. The price cut would impede movement towards economic operations for inland collieries (and therefore towards decontrol), and would expend the adventitious export surplus on a purely sectional interest. In any case, the wages claim exceeded the movement in the cost of living since Sankey, while the miners' gains in real income since 1913 already exceeded those of all other groups except builders and railwaymen. For their part, the miners were equally adamant, and in a ballot in August voted by a very large majority to commence a strike on 25 September. This threat was taken very seriously by the government—which prepared for a military as well as a civil emergency—although the actual prospect of a national coal strike was faced more stoically than had been the case in February 1919. If Damocles had been an Englishman, wrote *The Times*, 'he might have said "Confound the sword! . . . If it is going to fall, let it fall!"'[3]

---

[1] CAB 24/104/288–95 (26 Apr. 1920); CAB 23/21/73–6, 83, 208–10 (6 and 10 May, 3 June 1920).

[2] Events are summarized in *MAGB* 1921, 34 ff. Also see *MFGB* 1920 for July. The quotations are cited in Arnot 1953, 237–8. The initial negotiations are discussed in CAB 24/109/281–90 (19 July 1920); CAB 23/22/175–6 (26 July 1920).

[3] *The Times* 28 July 1920, 17c. For the War Cabinet's determination, see *The Times* 17 Aug. 1920, 11c, and for public opinion's opposition to the miners, 13 Sept. 1920, 11b. Cabinet deliberations and preparations included the proposed recall of troops from Ireland and the Rhine, the activation of the Supply and Transport Committee, and instructions to the Treasury to consider strike-related expenditure as if the threatened strike were analogous to a war. See: CAB 23/22/124–5 (17 Aug. 1920); Churchill to Lloyd George, 26 Aug. 1920: HLRO F/9/2/4; CAB 24/111/460 (14 Sept. 1920); CAB 23/22/156 (14 Sept. 1920); CAB 24/111/551–2 (23 Sept. 1920); CAB 23/22/244 (30 Sept. 1920).

In the face of the possibility of a stoppage and of declining output (to the alarm of the Coal Controller, production fell by 4 per cent between the first and third quarters of 1920), the government's resolution wavered. The miners were offered a wage increase contingent on an increase in output beyond a basic (or 'datum') line. And since by this time the MFGB had abandoned its determination to obtain a price reduction and was willing to discuss earnings in relation to production, a settlement seemed possible. But in spite of the postponement of a stoppage as a result of Lloyd George's persuasive intervention, the miners rejected both their own President's advice to accept arbitration and the government proposals for a conditional wage increase. After yet another overwhelmingly favourable ballot, the stoppage began on 16 October.[1]

The 'datum line' strike was potentially more serious than the situation that had given rise to it. Public support for 'firmness' waned in the face of reality, and *The Times* now deplored the militant language of those opposed to the miners: talk of 'settling the issue between them [Labour and Capital] once and for all is nonsense'—the 'capitalist counterpart of syndicalism'.[2] In any case, so much had been conceded in negotiations, that it was most unlikely that the government would contest the strike for long. Spurred by the fear that the railwaymen would support the miners by industrial action, Lloyd George renewed negotiations, and arrived at an agreement which was signed by the miners' Executive on 28 October. (Although a national ballot narrowly failed to endorse the settlement, the contrary vote lacked the two-thirds majority needed to continue a strike and the MFGB's rules therefore allowed a delegate conference to abandon it.)

Superficially, the settlement was a victory for the miners, for it conceded their full claim. At the same time, however, such a verdict presupposed (as did the MFGB) that the market for coal would remain unchanged. For the advances were only guaranteed until 3 January 1921. Thenceforth the maintenance (or decrease or increase) of the additional wages would be linked with output and determined by the price of exports compared with the base or datum line of the September quarter of 1920. The production incentives were generous, and the outcome for

---

[1] For the sequence of events, see Arnot 1953, 252 ff. Also: *MAGB* 1921, 34 ff.; HLRO F/188/2/7 (1 Oct. 1920); CAB 24/111/551–2 (23 Sept. 1920); CAB 23/22/244, 278–80, 280–91A (30 Sept., 15 and 26 Oct. 1920); CAB 24/112/369–76, 530–40 (14 and 21 Oct. 1920); CAB 24/114/151–6 (28 Oct. 1920).

[2] *The Times* 18 Oct. 1920, 13b.

January was an increase (3*s. 6d.* per shift for adults) very much greater than the original claim. But this declined to 1*s. 6d.* in February and in March, as the collapse of the export market came into the reckoning, the advance disappeared entirely.[1] In effect, then, the miners had allowed their wage increase to be tied not simply to their productivity (in a fairly undemanding fashion) but also to the market forces which determined the price of exports. It was a symbolic, and ultimately a real, victory for the owners' argument that wages must depend on the economic potential of the industry rather than a concept of social worth.

The settlement of October 1920 also contained two other provisions of some significance. First, the owners were obliged to participate in the risks of variations in earnings accepted by the miners. Their entitlement to the 10 per cent of standard profits under the Coal Mines (Emergency) Act which was not guaranteed, was to be varied up or down by one-quarter for each 6*d.* by which the men's advance was increased or decreased. Second, owners and miners agreed explicitly that the prosperity of all depended on increasing output, and that the wages system had to be overhauled. They therefore agreed to establish national and district committees for cooperation on the problem of production (this had been anticipated by informal consultations in a joint committee earlier in the year) and to produce a scheme for a new system of settling wages no later than 31 March 1921.[2]

The miners had obviously travelled a long road since 1918. In material terms—which was their principal *continuing* preoccupation—all miners had gained important improvements in real wages by the spring of 1920. Inflation then eroded the gains of skilled pitmen, but the less skilled remained significantly better off. Compared with June 1914 the cost of living had risen by 176 per cent by November 1920 and the average shift

[1] The formula was very complicated. 'Export coal' was defined as *output* (whether or not exported) in excess of an annual rate of 219 million tons. This excess was then multiplied by the prevailing f.o.b. price of actual export coal, and the amount compared, on an average weekly basis, with the export values of the Sept. quarter 1920. If the proceeds for the 5 weeks to 18 Dec. were only the same as those for the datum period, then the advance from 3 Jan. would be limited to 1*s.* for adults, 6*d.* for youths, and 4½*d.* for boys (i.e. 50% of the original claim). But it would be increased by 6*d.* 3*d.* and 2*d.* for every £288,000 by which net proceeds (proceeds less 15*s.* per ton to allow for costs) exceeded those for Sept. From 31 Jan. new calculations would be made on the basis of the 4 weeks since the last test period.

[2] In the face of falling output, the Coal Controller in Aug. 1920 had appealed to the owners and miners to reconstitute the old Advisory Board or form a new Joint Committee to consider the issue. Informal discussions between the MAGB and the MFGB led to the creation of a committee which was reconstituted under the terms of the strike settlement. *MAGB* 1921, 34; 'Report of a Conference between the Government, representatives of the MAGB and of the Executive of the MFGB', 1 Oct. 1920: HLRO F/188/2/7.

wage of the four main grades of workmen had risen by 169 per cent for hewers, 170.5 per cent for firemen, 192 per cent for putters, and 203 per cent for unskilled labourers.[1] Had the world market for coal justified even a fraction of the miners' optimism, their gains in 1921 would have been considerable. But this was not to be.

vii. Descending into the market-place, 1921

The events of 1920 had finally persuaded the miners that their postwar hopes for public ownership had been misplaced. Had they been willing to compromise in 1919, they might have been able to secure a large degree of structural change and government intervention in the industry. Failing this, however, even their attempts to postpone decontrol were frustrated. By late 1920, therefore, although still in a powerful bargaining position *vis-à-vis* wages, they were obliged to accept that private enterprise would continue and that the remuneration of those involved in the coalmining industry would depend primarily on output and prices.[2]

On the other hand, they were still not ready to accept that the primacy of market forces need mean anything other than an improvement in their material position—first, because they persuaded themselves that the export boom could and would continue; second, because they still felt that they could secure a system of settling wages which would protect the distributive gains of state control. In this regard, their aim was to secure a *national* wages agreement, which would have to be

[1] Trends in shift earnings in particular districts are summarized in Table 10.2. These naturally varied from region to region. In the period under consideration the percentage change for piece-work hewers varied from 233 in Somerset and 208 in South Staffordshire to 153 in West Yorkshire and 145 in South Yorkshire (although the last was still among the best paid at both dates). See Rowe 1923, 95–6. Long-run national averages are in ibid., 93:

Percentage increase in shift earnings since June 1914

	Cost of living	Skilled (hewers)	Skilled (firemen)	Semi-skilled	Unskilled (putters)
Sep. 1917	80/85	55.5	46.75	48.0	42.0
Nov. 1918	120/125	92.5	89.0	98.75	98.5
Jan. 1919	120	115.0	115.0	130.0	133.0
Mar. 1920	130	146.0	144.5	161.0	168.0
Nov. 1920	176	169.0	170.5	192.0	203.0

[2] For the miners' new attitudes, see *MAGB* 1921, 78–80; CAB 23/22/286–91A.

based on some form of inter-district 'pooling' of profits, so that the better-placed collieries might continue to subsidize work in the poorer-placed. Admittedly, the principles as well as the details of a new wages system still had to be negotiated, and the owners remained unswervingly opposed to pooling. Yet there were some grounds for optimism in that the government appeared willing to guarantee the continuation of the control until an agreement was reached, and the owners and miners were willing to seek an agreement in a positive spirit.

Yet all this (including the expectation that joint discussions would produce a solution by the end of March 1921) was based on assumptions about market trends and export prices which proved hopelessly unrealistic. In December 1920 the general economic slump which marked the end of the bubble of 1919-20 finally caught up with the coal trade: the average price of export coal tumbled from about £4 to about £2 per ton.

The market for coal had already suffered through American competition as a result of the datum line strike and French government action to keep out British coal on the grounds that its high price had exploited French consumers. In the early months of 1921 the situation deteriorated even further as European sales collapsed and depression in the heavy industries at home began to bite. Ironically, all this happened just as the incentives to increased output, which were part of the 1920 settlement, began to work.[1] As the datum line advance was eroded by falling export sales, as depression squeezed the industry remorselessly until the government felt obliged to abandon control with no attempt to adjust the industry's institutions, as the owners reasserted their power and rejected out of hand the idea of cross-subsidy involved in a national pool for wages, so the mutual accommodation of October and November 1920 was shattered beyond repair. The willingness to adjust wages to output and therefore to market forces had been only as enduring as the short-lived boom.

Wages and profits felt the blow of depression almost immediately. The wage increases derived from datum line settlement disappeared entirely, and the industry's costs reverted to those of the previous September. Nevertheless, although the rich Midland fields could still cover costs and produce a small profit, the halving of export prices between October and the end of January meant that South Wales and

---

[1] Between Sept. 1920 and Jan. 1921 the annualized rate of production rose from 237 to 260 million tons: CAB 24/118/451-67 (27 Jan. 1921). For the invasion of European markets by American coal as a result of the strike, and the reaction of the French to high British prices, see *The Times* 16 Feb. 1921, 11f; HLRO F/189/1/1 (27 May 1921).

Scottish collieries were losing almost 6s. and over 3s. per ton respectively.

Initially, the strain was taken by the government, since the Coal
Mines (Emergency) Act of 1920 guaranteed collieries not merely against
losses but also against any shortfall of profits below 90 per cent of their
prewar standards. But, as the President of the Board of Trade (Sir
Robert Horne) warned the War Cabinet, although the surpluses accumulated from the boom months of 1920 would see the Exchequer
through until the end of March, after that it would be faced with the
alarming, even inconceivable, prospect of having to cover a monthly
deficit of £5 million to keep the industry going. Once this fact became
apparent, then decontrol well before the deadline of 31 August became
inevitable. Conventional economic solutions within control were precluded by circumstances—since inland coal prices could not be raised in
the middle of a domestic slump, and wage reductions below September
levels ('the only sound course', according to Horne) would be difficult
to attain and were politically inadvisable as long as profits were
guaranteed. The only possible unconventional alternative was a continuing Exchequer subsidy. But it seemed out of the question to use public
monies to guarantee profits 'at a time when every other industry in the
country is working either without much profit or at a loss'. As the
Permanent Secretary to the Coal Mines Department said, a subsidy was
'unthinkable'.[1]

A measure of the official apprehension about the costs of existing
policies was the political humiliation which was accepted in deciding on
a precipitate rather than an orderly and well-prepared measure of
decontrol. The President of the Board of Trade had to confess to the
miners and owners that the government, in taking a risk based on its
expectations about prices, 'had been hopelessly wrong'. And although in
January the miners refused to discuss decontrol until the joint report on
the future of the industry was available, the government pressed ahead
with their decision, in the words of *The Times* 'to wash their hands of
control' even at the price of 'chaos' in the five main districts which were
'heavily insolvent'. On 28 January it was decided that the control of
prices and exports would cease on 1 March 1921 and financial control on
31 March.[2]

---

[1] The President of the Board of Trade's memorandum on the plight of the industry and the
limited scope for government action is in CAB 24/118/464 (27 Jan. 1921). Also see *MAGB* 1921, 40.
The Permanent Secretary's opinion is in Gowers to Dimbleby, 2 Feb. 1921: POWE 16/508II.

[2] Quotations are from Armitage 1969, 143; *The Times* 13 Jan. 1921, 10b. For the Cabinet

The latter decision was not announced until 23 February. And the threat of such an abrupt exposure to market forces provoked industry-wide consternation. The miners were the more alarmed. After the 1920 strike they had felt, with some justification, that the process of negotiation might take them some way towards their goal of a national wages agreement and even some pooling of profits. Now, the government guarantees which had underpinned the discussions were to be withdrawn and the new market circumstances would simultaneously render any such agreement impossible and destroy the basis of *existing* wages. Whether or not they really believed their own claim that agreement was feasible if the government would only agree to continue the subsidy for a little longer (and this seems unlikely in view of the owners' position on pooling and national wage agreements), they left the Cabinet in no doubt that 'they will never willingly agree to the termination of the present pooling system unless there is some other pooling scheme to take its place'.[1]   The position of the owners was less clear-cut. They wished for decontrol, but disliked intensely the circumstances in which it was to be thrust upon them. They complained, for example, that the government had taken over a solvent industry, had insisted on pursuing policies which had increased its labour costs and rendered it insolvent, and now insisted on handing it back, like someone who pushes a man into a pond and then 'helps him back to terra firma, but refuses to provide him with dry apparel'.[2] But the core of their grievance and anxiety lay in the level of wage costs they were about to inherit. Like the miners, they had some hope of a new wages agreement (albeit along different lines), but they were also persuaded that the new economic conditions must necessarily enforce a substantial fall in wages. And since the proposed new timetable meant that such a reduction must be draconian and occur before any new agreement, they felt that the

decision see CAB 24/118/449–67 (27 Jan. 1921) and CAB 23/24/35–6 (28 Jan. 1921). Material on the events and discussions leading up to decontrol (as well as the strike which followed) is in POWE 16/508II. Tom Jones (*Whitehall Diary* I, 136–7 (5 Apr. 1921)) argued that in the previous Nov., government policy had stressed the need for increased output and taken the risk of a fall in prices, but that when the miners responded and produced more coal while prices fell, the government 'ran away from that bargain' and suddenly introduced decontrol. Jones guessed that the probable reason was the realization that decontrol at the time originally planned (Aug.) would occur at the same time as the return of railways to private enterprise—an unfortunate political coincidence.

[1] CAB 24/118/449–67 (27 Jan. 1921).

[2] *CG* 11 Mar. 1921, 726–7. It was, however, noted that the owners, who had clamoured for decontrol when profits were high, lost their enthusiasm for it when the market slumped. See *The Times* 9 Mar. 1921, 13d (arguing that it was 'time for the industry to stand on its own two feet').

government should bear the entire responsibility for the painful transition. These points were made by the President of the MAGB in February 1921 in a report which was a grimly accurate prediction of future events:

A large number of collieries will have to close, and men will be thrown out of employment. The Government should either themselves take off the wage increases they have put on before they hand back the collieries to the owners, or they should see the industry through the transition period that must elapse until the operation of an agreed scheme brings wages to their proper level. If they do neither of these, there appears to be no alternative but for each district to determine in some way or other what wages it can afford to pay.[1]

In spite of the vehemence with which such arguments were expressed, the fact that the owners were known to favour decontrol on principle, together with the weakness of their political position (even the coal-owner MPs were unwilling to oppose the government to the extent of demanding a subsidy), meant that they were effectively resigned to decontrol. And since it would have been politically impossible for the government to cut wages, the MAGB was reduced to the arguments that the state should not interfere when the owners came to make the necessary cuts.[2]

The negotiations between owners and miners were, of course, wrecked by prospect of a disastrous slump. Admittedly, by the spring there was substantial agreement on some important principles: that the industry's performance should be the most important determinant of pay; that there should be standard (minimum) wage rates and profit levels; that the net 'proceeds' of the industry (i.e. sales less standard profits and wages and other costs), having been ascertained by a joint audit, should be divided proportionately between wages and profits. But the points of disagreement proved insuperable. They included the levels of standard wages and profits, the extent to which the flat-rate wage increases of 1917–19 should be incorporated in basic wages, and the desirable proportions for the division of proceeds.

Of more far-ranging significance, however, was the profound disagreement over the appropriate unit for the calculation of proceeds, and the

---

[1] Evan Williams, 'Report on the Present Position of the Industry', 26 Feb. 1921: *MAGB* 1921, 99–100. The economic circumstances of different fields varied. The Midland producers, it was said, could afford to stand on their own feet at the end of March, whereas Lancashire and the South-West were doing so badly that they were prepared to contemplate indefinite control. See memorandum by the President of the Board of Trade in POWE 16/508II.

[2] WYCOA, 11 Jan. 1921; DCOA, Annual meeting, 1922.

desirability of pooling profits within such a unit. The owners insisted that the only relevant accounting unit was the district, since the coalfields varied so much in geological and commercial terms, and that there be absolutely no pooling. The miners, aware of the advantages of a national system, insisted that the unit be the nation as a whole and that there should be either 'complete financial unification of the industry' or a profits pool to support the poorer collieries (and their wage payments) from the better results of the richer mines.[1] So critical was this last range of issues, and so determined were the owners in their aversion to a system of national pooling which would inevitably retain a large measure of political decision-making in the industry, that it seems most unlikely that a negotiated agreement would have been reached no matter how long the government postponed decontrol and irrespective of the market for coal. As the MAGB's members were informed by their officials:

The men's representatives were informed that the owners would not, in any circumstances, agree to a national settlement of wages; that they could not even think of considering a national pool, or any form of unification of finance in the industry, either nationally or in the districts; that they stood absolutely for individualism in the industry, and for every colliery company to stand or fall by its own results.[2]

Given these contrasting attitudes, the outcome was inevitable. At the moment of decontrol (31 March 1921) the owners terminated earlier district contracts and offered new, and much lower, rates of pay. The MFGB immediately announced a general stoppage, and the miners ceased work on 1 April.[3] But if the central issue appeared to be the dispute about the principle of a national pool, that was only because its acceptance was made a precondition of negotiation or settlement. The fact is that the origin of the stoppage—bitter, prolonged, and with terrible memories—lay in the district-based wage cuts which the owners envisaged as the only way to economic salvation in a falling market (in

[1] The position of both sides is fairly summarized in *MAGB* 1921, 93-107.

[2] *MAGB* 1921, 43. See ibid., 78: The opposition to a national pool and a national settlement of wages 'was [the] one point which we ourselves had determined that we were going to fight and to stick to the very last, because we were bound to realise that the establishment of a national pool, a national control of wages, was but a step which would make the subsequent step to nationalisation of the mines an easy one.'

[3] Since the owners had to terminate existing contracts in order to offer revised wages, the stoppage was, strictly speaking a lockout, with the miners declining to work at the newly posted rates of pay.

February, almost 90 per cent of South Wales's output was produced at a loss).[1]

Although the extent of the proposed wage reductions varied between districts, they were in many instances so extreme—ranging up to more than 45 per cent in South Wales—that they excited unease even among erstwhile supporters of the owners. And they shocked public opinion as well as outraging the miners. Even Sir Robert Horne, generally in favour of 'realism', questioned their justification; and in the War Cabinet Edwin Montagu complained that they were 'indefensible'. Yet reductions on this scale were inevitable if it was assumed that the industry had to absorb its losses without external help, and the prevailing political mood on deflation offered few alternatives. The 'very big issue involved', held the Prime Minister, was 'the readiness or otherwise of workmen to accept an economic basis for their wages. . . . It is essential to bring it home to the miners.'[2]

For their part, and contrary to the opinion of their opponents, the miners were not completely deaf to the appeal to market logic. They appreciated that *some* reduction of wages was necessary (particularly since the cost of living was falling rapidly with general deflation), and early in the stoppage they offered to accept a cut of 2s. per shift. On the other hand, strong as their case appeared on humanitarian grounds, the miners' anxieties led them to commit errors of approach and tactics. Well placed to focus public attention on low wages, the MFGB managed to divert it by calling for the sort of complete stoppage which (since it might include safety men) placed the pits at risk. It raised the issue of a subsidy in a climate which was bound to be hostile to such an expedient; and insisted on the acceptance of a national wages board and a national pool as a precondition even of a temporary settlement.

Yet in retrospect it seems clear that none of these considerations was particularly relevant to the circumstances of spring 1921. The economic collapse which had been described by Lloyd George without too much exaggeration as 'the worst trade depression which has ever been known', had destroyed the foundations on which the financial values and institutions of the coal industry had been based over the previous seven years. The disintegrating market for coal and the beleaguered

---

[1] Riddell to Davies, 14 Apr. 1921: HLRO F/43/7/17.

[2] For anxieties about the extent of the proposed cuts, see *CG* 24 Mar. 1924, 877; *The Times* 1 Apr. 1921, 9b, 2 Apr. 1921, 9b, 4 Apr. 1921, 9b. For Horne and Montagu, see POWE 16/508II (30 Mar. 1921) and CAB 24/122/218 (19 Apr. 1921). Also see Jones, *Whitehall Diary* I, 134, 137, 145. For the Prime Minister's comment see ibid., 161 (24 May 1921).

position of their fellow trade unionists denied the miners an adequate, let alone a strong, bargaining position. And the determination of government weakened their appeal to the state. Lloyd George and his Ministers now set their face against either any continuance of control or a subsidy. Although they could envisage a national wages settlement, they favoured district standards and rejected both the idea of a national pool (which, they argued, would erode incentives and lead to the introduction of 'complete and permanent' state control) and any form of 'dole' to the industry.[1] The political economy of the 1920s was beginning to enmesh the miners. After three months of a desperate stoppage it was to conquer them.

For one million miners and their families those three months were increasingly traumatic. For the rest of the nation, however, the effects of the stoppage were less serious than had been anticipated. The possibility of social disruption and a challenge to the political order through the participation of railwaymen and transport workers, seemed at one point real. But the economic climate and the resentment of other trade unionists at the miners' obstinate opposition to either arbitration or a temporary settlement, made an all-out strike unlikely. It was obviously with some relief that on 15 April—'Black Friday'—the other members of the Triple Alliance called off their threatened stike when the MFGB Executive refused to seize the lifeline (of a temporary settlement on a district basis) offered by some obscure remarks by the miners' Secretary in the course of a meeting at the Commons. Sensing his initiative, Lloyd George was patently relieved at the disappearance of the chance of compromise and felt that he could now scotch the miners' 'idea that they can strangle the community'. As late as May he shocked Churchill with the confession: 'I do not feel myself in a hurry to settle.'[2]

Once more, the miners' attitude had weakened their case rather than intimidated their opponents. They were left to fight their lonely and ultimately hungry battle with no very effective weapon other than their own mounting desperation. In April, still insisting on a national pool and system, they had rejected an offer (district settlements, a graduated reduction, a subsidy of £10 million to cushion the cuts) which was along lines they were obliged to accept in July. And in mid-June a national

---

[1] Lloyd George on the slump: HLRO F/221/7/21 (9 Nov. 1921). Government statement on the dispute (12 Apr. 1921): quoted in *MAGB* 1921, 46. Also see Jones, *Whitehall Diary* I, 145. Christopher Addison, however, argued in Cabinet that, 'I have never been able to understand on what grounds we have taken up the attitude that a Pool necessarily means the continuation of State Control and subsidy.' CAB 24/123/159–60 (5 May 1921).

[2] Jones, *Whitehall Diary* I, 148, 161.

ballot rejected a slightly improved offer. But by the last week of June, with no alternative strategy to hand and their membership poverty-stricken and wracked with tribulation, the union had to surrender. On 28 June the Executive agreed to provisional terms: 'Economic and political factors', they confessed, 'are dead against us.' The overwhelming bulk of their membership agreed. As Beatrice Webb put it, they accepted 'the existing order of society ... lest worse befall them'. Wage levels were now the most vulnerable element in the industry. In addition to reduced earnings, the miners had to accept the fact that there was now no chance of the further reduction in the length of underground shifts which had been envisaged in 1919. The promises of that extraordinary year had been almost completely frustrated. The market had won.[1]

viii. Facing the market, 1921–1922

The terms of the National Wages Agreement of 1921 are worth considering because they were the foundations of wage structures in the industry until the Second World War. For an initial period of three months the government was to provide a subsidy (limited to £10 million) which was to be used to restrain the speed at which wages were reduced. Over the longer run, in each district a standard wage was to be established equivalent to the basis wage of 31 March 1921 augmented by the percentage additions payable in July 1914.

The 'basis' rates were determined locally, and ranged from agreements concerning the rate for piecework in a particular pit or even seam, to district-wide rates for whole categories of day-wage workers.[2] Percentage additions were determined for the district as a whole. These percentage additions were ultimately determined by the profitability of the districts' mines, but the agreement provided for a minimum: no miner was to be paid less than the relevant standard wage for his grade, plus 20 per cent. The effect of this complex formula was a minimum wage rate which exceeded the actual wage rates of June 1914 by about 43 per cent, as against a 92 per cent increase in the cost of living. (In practice, of course, miners frequently, but by no means invariably,

---

[1] Cole 1952, 219. The course of the 1921 stoppage is traced in 'Decontrol of the Coal Mining Industry and the Stoppage of 1921', in POWE 16/508II; 'Diary. Coal Mining' in LAB 27/1: 'History of National Coal Stoppage, 1921' in POWE 26/83 (from which the MFGB Executive's quotation is taken).

[2] For a fuller description of wage-payment systems, see ch. 1, sect. iv.

earned more than the minimum.)[1] Low-paid men were to be paid locally determined subsistence allowances if necessary. In each district a joint audit would ascertain the industry's 'proceeds' by deducting, from total sales, the standard wages, non-wage costs of production, and a standard profit equivalent to 17 per cent of the standard wages. (If there were insufficient funds to pay profits, the deficiency might be carried forward to set against possible future surpluses.) The net proceeds of the ascertainment, if any, would then be divided between wages and profits in the ratio 83:17. The system was to be overseen, and unresolved details settled, by a National Board, with equal membership of miners and owners, and a neutral Chairman.[2]

The owners had won a clear industrial-relations victory, and the strength of their position also enabled them to spurn the government's efforts to establish the consultative committtees envisaged by the Mining Industry Act of 1920. According to an exasperated Secretary for Mines, they were 'on top of the wave', and by February 1922 the Cabinet, like the miners before them, had to concede defeat.[3] However, the 1921 settlement involved a degree of compromise for some owners.

This was because the less well-placed, or the poorly organized, collieries would now find their wage commitments adversely influenced by the superior results of the more profitable enterprises. For the latter's profitability would increase a district's proceeds and therefore entitle miners to higher rates of pay, which would have to be paid by unprofitable and profitable collieries alike. As a result, the composition of the districts for ascertainment purposes—especially in the huge Eastern Federated Area—was a question of some sensitivity. Even before the stoppage, as decontrol loomed, districts like Lancashire, Cheshire, North Wales, and South Staffordshire sought to extricate themselves so as to be considered separate districts for purposes of wage determination. And the vulnerable West Yorkshire industry, directly threatened by its booming neighbour, decided unanimously that the District Association 'should absolutely refuse to be merged with South York-

---

[1] Rowe 1923, 100; Department of Employment and Productivity 1971, 166-7. For the concept of the basis wage, see above, ch. 1, sect. iv.

[2] Compared with the owners' original offer of Mar. 1921, the settlement contained 3 improvements: the £10 million subsidy, the 20% increase in the minimum wage, and the subsistence wage for low-paid men.

[3] *Correspondence Between the Mining Association and the Mines Department Regarding the Operation of Part II of the Mining Industry Act, 1920* (Cmd. 1551. 1921) *PP* 1921 XXXI. CAB 24/133/49-67 (10 Feb. 1922).

shire for wages purposes'. During the stoppage, however, as a result of extreme pressure from the government and the MAGB, the West Yorkshire owners reluctantly agreed to merge with others from the old Federated Area (including South Yorkshire)—although Lancashire, Cheshire, and North Staffordshire attained their aim of forming a separate district, as did North Wales (alone) and South Staffordshire and Shropshire.[1]

How did the settlement of July 1921 affect the business results of coal-mining? During the last three months of control, when the slump was intensifying, all the main export districts had lost huge amounts of money and even the inland collieries did not quite cover their costs. Such losses were obviously reduced by the wage cuts, although the much greater fall in wage *costs* (per ton) than actual shift *earnings* suggests that a large part of the difference was made by an increase in productivity. (Output per manshift rose by just over 20 per cent between the first and last quarters of 1921.) Overall, 1921 was a disastrous year. However, taking the first quarter of 1922 as a new standard of 'normalcy', the industry as a whole, although still very depressed, was at least not losing money: prices and costs had, however violently, adjusted to the extraordinary distortions of the unexpected slump. Average profits (proceeds less costs) were 1s. 1¼d. per ton—as against the horrendous loss of 6s. 11¼d. a year earlier and profits of 5s. 2d. in the halcyon first quarter of 1920. Tables 4.2(a) and 4.2(b) show the volatility of costs, prices, and proceeds in the industry as a whole, and exemplify the even greater volatility in particular districts. Northumberland and South Wales benefited most from the boom to 1920, and lost most in the following slump; Scotland suffered in the depression, without having secured very much benefit from the preceding boom; and the great Midland and Yorkshire field withstood the worst ravages of the collapse and survived into 1922 with significantly higher wages than all other districts, and higher profits than most.

To many of the miners, of course, the slump and the wage settlement came as unmitigated disasters (especially in the export districts) although the full consequences were not experienced until the autumn of 1921, when the subsidy ceased. Thus, between March and November

---

[1] The other districts were to be: Scotland, Northumberland, Durham, Monmouthshire & South Wales, Cumberland, Bristol, the Forest of Dean, Somerset, and Kent. For West Yorkshire: WYCOA, 7 and 22 Mar. 1921, 30 June 1921; *MAGB* 1921, 81. West Yorkshire was praised by the President of the MAGB for its 'sacrifice' and extracted a disproportionate share of the £10 million subsidy as the price for its cooperation.

Table 4.2(a). *Quarterly earnings and proceeds in British coalmining, national averages, 1918-1922*

		(i) s. d.	(ii) s. d.	(iii) s. d.
1918	Jan.–Mar.	—	19 $7\frac{1}{4}$	1 $8\frac{1}{4}$
	Apr.–June	—	20 2	1 $6\frac{3}{4}$
	July–Sept.	12 $6\frac{3}{4}$	24 10	3 $8\frac{1}{2}$
	Oct.–Dec.	12 6	24 $10\frac{1}{4}$	3 $3\frac{1}{2}$
1919	Jan.–Mar.	14 3	24 $11\frac{1}{2}$	0 $10\frac{1}{4}$
	Apr.–June	14 $2\frac{1}{4}$	26 6	0 $10\frac{3}{4}$
	July–Sept.	14 4	32 $7\frac{1}{4}$	4 $2\frac{3}{4}$
	Oct.–Dec.	14 $5\frac{1}{4}$	34 $5\frac{1}{2}$	5 10
1920	Jan.–Mar.	15 $1\frac{1}{2}$	34 7	5 2
	Apr.–June	16 $10\frac{1}{2}$	36 $7\frac{1}{4}$	4 $0\frac{1}{4}$
	July–Sept.	16 $11\frac{1}{4}$	39 7	4 $10\frac{1}{4}$
	Oct.–Dec.	18 $5\frac{3}{4}$	39 $3\frac{1}{2}$	−0 $6\frac{1}{4}$
1921	Jan.–Mar.	19 2	33 $1\frac{1}{4}$	−6 $11\frac{3}{4}$
	Apr.–June	—	—	—
	July–Sept.	—	29 $0\frac{3}{4}$	2 $3\frac{3}{4}$
	Oct.–Dec.	12 8	23 0	0 $3\frac{1}{2}$
1922	Jan.–Mar.	11 $0\frac{1}{4}$	20 10	1 $1\frac{3}{4}$
	Apr.–June	10 $2\frac{1}{2}$	18 $11\frac{1}{4}$	−0 $0\frac{1}{4}$
	July–Sept.	9 4	18 3	1 1
	Oct.–Dec.	9 $5\frac{1}{4}$	18 $6\frac{1}{4}$	1 $6\frac{1}{2}$

(i): Earnings per shift.
(ii): Total proceeds ('price') per ton.
(iii): Total proceeds less total costs per ton.

Sources: ARSM 1922, 122–3; ARSM 1923, 114–17.

1921 earnings in South Wales, Scotland, and Durham fell by about 50, 40, and 33 per cent respectively—although in the more profitable Midlands fields the reduction was only 16 per cent.[1] By the first quarter of 1922 the average earnings per shift (counting men and boys together) in the country as a whole were barely more than 11 s. This represented a fall of 43 per cent over the previous year, during which time the cost of living had only fallen by 24 per cent.

[1] Estimates provided for the Prime Minister in preparation for a meeting with the MFGB, 8 Nov. 1921: POWE 16/508II.

Table 4.2(b). *Quarterly earnings and proceeds in British coalmining, selected districts, 1918–1922*

	Northumberland			Durham			South Wales and Monmouthshire		
	(i)	(ii)	(iii)	(i)	(ii)	(iii)	(i)	(ii)	(iii)
	s. d.	*s. d.*	*s. d.*	*s. d.*	*s. d.*	*s. d.*	*s. d.*	*s. d.*	*s. d.*
1918	n/a	21 6¼	2 7¼	n/a	19 6½	1 6¼	n/a	23 4	1 6
1919	14 0	31 6¼	6 2½	13 8½	26 1½	1 10	15 5¼	29 3¼	1 6¼
1920	14 10	48 3	18 5¼	14 7½	37 7	8 6¾	16 4¾	54 11	18 7½
1921	19 0	34 1¼	−9 9¾	18 9½	34 4½	−4 2½	21 6½	38 1¾	−19 9¼
1922	8 6½	18 11¾	1 9	9 2¾	18 11	1 0¾	9 8½	20 10½	0 4½

Table 4.2(b) (cont)

	Yorkshire			Derbyshire, Nottinghamshire, Leicestershire			Scotland		
	(i) s. d.	(ii) s. d.	(iii) s. d.	(i) s. d.	(ii) s. d.	(iii) s. d.	(i) s. d.	(ii) s. d.	(iii) s. d.
1918	n/a	18 4	2 7¾	n/a	17 4	3 0½	n/a	19 1¼	1 2½
1919	14 5¼	22 5	1 1	13 7	21 1	2 0½	15 1	24 3½	0 2
1920	15 7¾	25 8½	0 10¼	14 10½	23 0½	—0 6	15 11	29 3	—0 2¼
1921	18 11	31 6	—0 6½	18 6½	30 0	—0 0½	19 4	32 1½	—7 7

a

	(i) s. d.	(ii) s. d.	(iii) s. d.
1922	13 11½	21 8½	1 8

	(i) s. d.	(ii) s. d.	(iii) s. d.
1922	10 2¼	18 2½	0 10¾

(i): Earnings per shift.
(ii): Total proceeds ('price') per ton.
(iii): Total proceeds less total costs per ton.

a Plus Cannock Chase and Warwickshire

n/a = not available.

Sources: ARSM 1922, 122–3; *ARSM* 1923, 114–17.

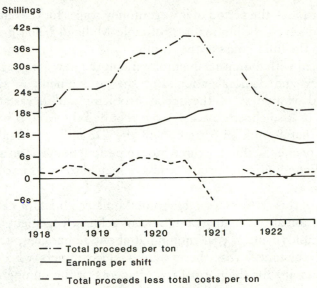

Fig. 4.1. Quarterly earnings and proceeds in British coalmining, 1918–1922

Put another way, since June 1914 money wages had increased by only 60 per cent, as against a rise in living costs of about 90 per cent. Even allowing for concessionary coal and, in some areas, housing, the miners' living standards had been subject to a large, and occasionally precipitous, decline. Area after area was reduced to paying wages at or near the exiguous minimum stipulated in 1921, and for low-paid men the bare subsistence wage had to be activated.[1] As Table 4.2(b) shows, by the late

---

[1] Rowe 1923, 99–100. In Durham, the subsistence clause was activated from 1 Dec. 1921 and gave a daily wage of 7s. 1d. to the low-paid. Even hewers' wages, which had been £1 per day in Jan. and 16s. 6½d. in Mar., fell to the settlement minimum of 8s. 7½d. in Feb. 1922. See DCOA, 26 Feb. 1926. For the poignant appeals of the local union on behalf of the low-paid, many of whom were 'on the verge of starvation and had had to apply for parish relief', see DCOA, 3 and 31 Mar. 1922, 11 Apr. 1922, 2 June 1922 (quotation from last of these). The wage of £1 per shift had been fairly common before the 1921 stoppage, and reactions to it during the stoppage induced Siegfried Sassoon to write 'The Case for the Miners':

> 'Why should a miner earn six pounds a week?
> Leisure! They'd only spend it in a bar!
> Standard of Life! You'll never teach them Greek,
> Or make them more contented than they are!'
> That's how my port-flushed friends discuss the Strike.

> And that's the reason why I shout and splutter
> And that's the reason why I'd almost like
> To see them hawking matches in the gutter.

summer of 1922—the period of lowest money wages for the entire inter-war period—even the normally profitable Midland fields finally succumbed to the full rigours of the slump.

Combined with mounting unemployment, the new low wages generated misery and demoralization. But the government, in spite of a widespread awareness of the social problems and devastation, felt powerless or disinclined to act. It even rebuffed the MFGB when they proposed that £3 million (that part of the £10 million subsidy which was not expended within the three-month period) be spent on aiding the industry. Economic equilibrium, it was held, had to be attained in a less 'artificial' way.

In spite of this ruthlessness, the Prime Minister's brief for his meeting with the union also contained a significant acknowledgement of reality. With unemployment in coal running at about 20 per cent, it could be 'reasonably assumed' that there were 125,000 miners who were no longer necessary for the normal requirements of the mining industry; even so, wages in the industry were so low that other trades must 'reduce their own costs of production by other means than a [further] reduction in miners' wages'. As we shall see, transitory developments later in 1922 and in 1923 were to reintroduce a brief, hothouse prosperity in coalmining. But 1921, which the *Colliery Guardian* rightly called 'the year of the great disillusionment', had witnessed a fundamental transition to the monetary values of depression and to the much lower levels of activity which, with brief exceptions, were going to characterize the next 15 years.[1]

---

[1] See POWE 16/508II, especially memorandum from President of the Board of Trade, 21 Oct. 1921, and meeting between Prime Minister and MFGB, 9 Nov. 1921. Also CAB 24/129/225–8 (21 Oct. 1921); *CG* 6 Jan. 1922, 35.

PART C

ADJUSTING TO A NEW REALITY
COAL IN THE 1920s

CHAPTER 5

The New Economics of Coal, 1919–1929

Dramatic as were the consequences of the First World War for the coal industry, neither the nature nor the permanence of the changes it introduced were clear to contemporaries. As has already been seen, they entertained diverse economic and political hopes for the future, but based them all upon optimistic expectations about a favourable market environment for the British industry. In the event, of course, none of their expectations was justified. The industry was on the verge of economic developments for which there was no precedent. Throughout most of the interwar period (although the new situation did not become continuously manifest until after 1923–4) there was a secular stagnation in the demand for coal, in both the world and home markets. The combination of a break in the trend of world economic development and prolonged depression in Britain's heavy industries confronted British collieries with enormous pressures on prices and profitability, wages and employment. And, as economic forces attempted to compress the coalmining industry into a more viable size, shape, and cost-structure, so problems of business failure, social misery, industrial strife, and government intervention came to dominate its affairs.

Initially, the postwar problem appeared to be one of short-run, if violent, fluctuations. Only with the passage of time—as the elimination of one crisis merely ushered in another, or as transient bouts of prosperity gave way to further misery—did those involved come to appreciate the underlying realities of the new conditions of demand and supply, and (more slowly and less universally) the need for novelty in attitudes and policy.

This chapter will be primarily concerned with the economic and business trends which came to be so painfully experienced in the 1920s. The first three sections will consider the general performance of the industry, the varying experiences of different coalfields, and the proximate causes of the long-run depression of coalmining. The fourth section will discuss the effects of stagnation on wages, prices, and profits; and the final section the extent of structural adaptation to adversity.[1]

i. Economic trends

The notorious instability of the coalmining industry was at no time better illustrated than in the years after the First World War. And the chronology of postwar decline is, therefore, instructive.

Initially, in 1919–20, there was an acute shortage of coal, especially on the continent, and the price and profitability of British exports rose very rapidly. But, while export prices more than doubled, output tonnage remained more or less constant, and productivity low. At the same time, in 1919, the miners' demands for higher wages, a shorter working day, and nationalization thrust the industry into a political and social controversy—as a result of which they secured their first two objectives, but failed utterly in their attempt to force structural change. An abrupt and calamitous slump in export markets in the winter of 1920–1 (which more or less coincided with a slump within Britain) led not merely to the precipitous withdrawal of government control, but to a deflationary squeeze on wages which provoked a bitter three-month stoppage in April–June 1921. The industry emerged from this upheaval with money wages greatly reduced, but business prospects still very bleak.

Fortuitously, in 1923 and 1924 some market buoyancy was introduced, first by a 16-week coal strike in the United States, and then by the French occupation of the Ruhr, each of which reduced output in one of the world's major coal producers. Profitability and wages began to recover some of the lost ground in Britain. (In 1924 earnings were helped by a revision of the 1921 national wages agreement which was favourable to low-paid groups.) But the more forbidding underlying trends inexorably reasserted themselves from the summer of 1924: ruthless competition overseas, stagnation in the home market, surplus capacity, falling prices, pit closures. By 1925 adversity and controversy once more came to dominate the industry's affairs. Time (purchased by a government subsidy of £23 million, and utilized by the Samuel Commission of 1925–6) soon ran out and once more a move to cut wages produced a major stoppage.

The strike/lockout of 1926—a wound that never healed—led to

---

[1] Subsequent chapters will deal with official and business responses to the industry's vicissitudes and their social implications.

another defeat for the miners, another reduction in wages, and an increase in the length of the working day. Once more, however, the crumbling of the market was too great for such accommodation. And in 1927 and 1928, in spite of the reduction in labour costs implied in the 1926 settlements, the industry entered the gloomiest trough of a troubled decade. Admittedly, a mild upsurge of exports in 1929 (when average unemployment exceeded 13 per cent and the industry barely covered its costs) was interpreted by some as the beginning of a decisive change—only to be exposed as a false dawn when output and employment slipped back in 1930, preparatory to even greater disasters in the following two or three years. By the end of the 1920s opinion within the industry and in government had to acknowledge that the industry, having had to 'pass through the Valley of the Shadow of Death',[1] still had to face the problem of secular stagnation, a permanent reduction in the level of viable capacity rather than a temporary crisis; and that new policies were needed to deal with overproduction, surplus manpower, inefficiency, and unfettered competition.

The downward trend of the 1920s reflected a fundamental imbalance of capacity and demand in the coal industry as a whole. But the instability which it exemplified also arose from the peculiarities of the markets facing the different types of coal, and from the fact that prices and values were inordinately volatile. Thus, in the immediate aftermath of war output fell to about 230 million tons compared to an average of 270 million tons in the five prewar years, yet absolute and relative prices (especially of exports) were extremely high. The resulting growth of profits and wages probably restrained rather than encouraged productive effort, and thereby further increased the demand for labour. Combined with the reduction of hours in 1919, this endowed the industry with a record labour force: over 1.2 million men and boys in 1920. By 1922, however, coal prices had fallen to 50 per cent of their 1920 level. There was then a brief recovery in the artificial circumstances of 1922–3 (in 1923 production even exceeded the prewar average). But the dismal trend soon reappeared: between 1922–4 and 1927–9 output fell by 6 per cent and prices by 27 per cent.[2] The new international standing of the British coal industry was now manifest. Between 1913 and 1929 its share of world output had declined from 23.2 to 18.8 per cent, and of world trade from 55 to 45.3 per cent.[3]

---

[1] CG 4 Jan. 1929, 50.

[2] Price fluctuations varied according to the type of coal. Industrial coal fared worst and household coal held up best. This was, presumably, a reflection of different demand elasticities. See Neuman 1934, 95–6.   [3] ARSM 1936, 8.

Table 5.1(a). *Output, exports, prices, and profits in British coalmining, 1913-1930*
(until 1921 the figures relate to the United Kingdom)

	Coal raised[a]		(iii) Exports[b]			(iv) Average selling value per ton at	(v) Cost & royalties per ton	(vi) Profits per ton
			Total (coal, coke, manufactured fuel, bunkers)	Coal exports				
	(i) Tons (m.)	(ii) £ (m.)	Tons (m.)	Tons (m.)	£ m.	*s. d.*	*s. d.*	*s. d.*
1909–13 (av.)	269.59	—	88.3	66.1	40.0	8 8¾	7 9¼	0 11½
1913	287.43	145.53	98.3	73.4	50.7	10 1½	8 7½	1 6
1914 (June)	265.66	132.60	—	—	—	—	—	—
1919	229.78	314.11	51.3	35.2	83.2	27 0¼	24 4¼	2 8
1920	229.53	396.87	43.7	24.9	—	33 8	30 8¼	2 11¾
1921	163.25[c]	213.75	37.7	24.7	43.0	25 6	28 3¼[d]	2 9¼[d]

1922	249.61	220.00	87.3	64.2	72.5	17	6	16	$7\frac{1}{2}$	0	$10\frac{1}{2}$
1923	276.00	259.23	104.5	79.5	99.9	18	$2\frac{3}{4}$	16	$2\frac{3}{4}$	2	0
1924	267.12	251.67	84.5	61.7	72.1	18	$2\frac{1}{4}$	17	$1\frac{1}{4}$	1	1
1925	243.18	198.98	71.5	50.8	50.5	15	$8\frac{1}{4}$	15	$5\frac{1}{4}$[d]	0	3[d]
1926	126.23[c]	123.39	—	20.6	19.1	14	6	13	4	1	2[d]
1927	251.23	183.54	71.9	51.2	45.5	13	$11\frac{3}{4}$	14	5	−0	$5\frac{1}{4}$
1928	237.47	152.52	71.6	50.1	39.0	12	$3\frac{1}{2}$	13	$1\frac{3}{4}$	−0	$10\frac{1}{4}$
1929	257.91	173.23	82.2	60.3	48.6	12	$11\frac{1}{2}$	12	$7\frac{1}{2}$	0	4
1930	243.88	165.73	75.1	54.9	45.7	13	1	12	9	0	4

[a] 'Coal raised' includes estimated value of fuel used at collieries or by miners until 1917. Thenceforth, based on proceeds of coal actually sold.

[b] Export statistics from 1923 include shipments to the Irish Free State (about 2.5 million tons in most normal years), but those before 1923 do not include sales to Ireland.

[c] There was a three-month stoppage in 1921 and a six-month stoppage in 1926.

[d] Figures include the effects of the various subsidies (9s. ¼d. per ton in 1921, 11s. ¼d. per ton in 1925, and 2s. 6¼d. per ton in 1926). Without them, costs would have been greater and profits smaller.

Sources:

(i), (iv), (v), and (vi): CYB 1932.

(ii): 1913 (total value): Home Office, Mines and Quarries. General Report and Statistics, 1913, Part III, 221; 1919–30: ARSM, various years.

(iii): 'Total' tonnage: ARSM 1931, Table 29. 'Coal exports': 1909–19: POWE 26/14; 1921–30: ARSM, various years. (Coal tonnage for all: CYB 1931, 604–5.)

Table 5.1(b). *Employment, productivity, and earnings in British coalmining 1913–1930* (until 1921 the figures relate to the United Kingdom)

	Employment (000)		(ii) Output per man-year (tons)	(iii) Output per manshift (cwt)	(iv) Average annual % unemployment[b]			(v) Total number of days lost through want of trade	(vi) Average earnings		Wages (1909–13 = 100)
	(i)	(i')			wholly	tempo-rarily	total		Per shift (s. d.)	Per year (£ s. d.)	
1909–13 (ann. av.)	—	1,048	257	n/a	—	—	—	—	—	—	100
1913	1,117	1,106	260		—	—	—	—	—	—	108.5
1914 (June)	—	—	—	20.32	—	—	—	—	6 5¼	—	
1919	1,176	1,171	196	15.64	—	—	0.2	—	14 3¾	—	237.9
1920	1,233	1,227	187	14.55	—	—	0.1	—	16 10¼	—	304.6
1921	1,132	1,132	144	14.46[a] 17.73[a]	—	—	8.1	29.1	19 2[a] 12 8[a]	—	
1922	1,148	1,148	217	18.02	—	—	10.6 (6.8)	24.51	9 11¾	125 2 0	155.5
1923	1,203	1,203	229	17.83	—	—	2.2	9.40	10 1	134 6 1	169.3

Year													
1924	1,192	1,213	220	17.59	—	—	5.7	19.31	10	7¾	138	4	7	174.4
1925	1,074	1,102	221	18.46	—	—	15.8	31.02	10	6	131	15	9	172.0
1926 (Mar.)	1,116		n/a	n/a										
(Dec.)	944		n/a	n/a										
1926	925	—	n/a	n/a	—	—	9.1ᵇ	—	10	5	99	17	9	n/a
1927	1,005	1,024	245	20.61	10.7	0.4	18.1	46.12	10	0¾	122	12	2	158.6
1928	921	939	253	21.29	14.4	7.5	21.9	47.91	9	3½	113	16	7	152.1
1929	939	957	270	21.60	11.8	4.2	16.0	32.37	9	2¾	118	6	4	152.1
1930	914	931	262	21.62	13.3	7.1	20.4	44.54	9	3½	113	18	2	153.5

ᵃ Figures for output per manshift and earnings in 1921: first line refers to first quarter, second line to last quarter.

ᵇ Figures for 1919–23 are averages of quarterly data of a (small) sample of trade union members. For 1921 they exclude the quarter during which there was a stoppage. The figure for 1922 is particularly suspect: the figure of 6.8 in brackets is a quarterly average of unemployment insurance books deposited in labour exchanges. Figures from 1924 are averages of monthly totals. The data exclude those who ceased work on account of the dispute of 1926.

Sources:

(i): to 1920: Home Office, *Mines and Quarries. General Report and Statistics*, various years; from 1921: *ARSM*, various years.

(i'): *CYB* 1932, 639.

(ii): *CYB* 1931, 631.

(iii): *ARSM*, various years.

(iv): *Ministry of Labour Gazette*, various years, and *CYB*, various issues.

(v): Ministry of Labour, *Eighteenth Abstract of Labour Statistics* (Cmd. 2740. 1926), 100; *Twentieth Abstract of Labour Statistics* (Cmd. 3831. 1931), 74; *Twenty-First Abstract of Labour Statistics* (Cmd. 4625. 1934), 70.

(vi): Average earnings per shift and year: *ARSM*, various years; wage index: *CYB* 1932, 639.

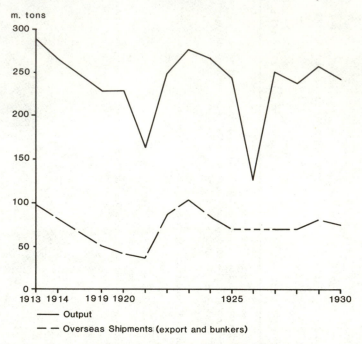

Fig. 5.1. Output and overseas shipments of British coal, 1913–1930

The onset of chronic depression combined with the higher labour productivity which resulted from lower wage rates to reduce the demand for labour, and by the end of the decade the 'normal' labour force was barely 950,000, having averaged almost 1.2 million in 1919–24.[1] Moreover, as capacity stood idle, unemployment rose. The average number of shifts worked per week declined from 5.48 in 1923 to 4.78 in 1928 and unemployment grew from 11.2 per cent in December 1925 (in which year it had for the first time exceeded the national average among the insured work-force)[2] to 17.3 per cent two years later.

By 25 June 1928 virtually 300,000 miners were out of work. This represented one-sixth of *all* the insured unemployed in the country and 25.7 per cent of the total of insured employees in the mines—although unemployment statistics in coalmining need careful interpretation

[1] Estimates of the labour force for individual years are misleading since the numbers employed obviously varied markedly within any year. Until 1925, figures quoted as relating to a particular year were derived from the owners' returns of the numbers 'ordinarily employed'; thenceforth they were averages of four dates within the year.

[2] The percentage figures for postwar unemployed (wholly and temporarily) in Dec. of each year between 1920 and 1924 in coalmining (and among all insured workers) were: 0.3 (7.8), 11.2 (17.7), 4.6 (12.2), 2.4 (10.5), 7.8 (10.6). Source: Clay 1929, 41.

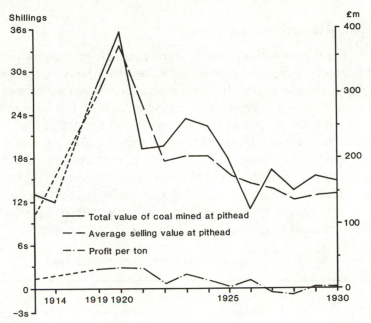

Fig. 5.2. Total value, average selling value, and profit per ton of British coal, 1913–1930

because of the unusual incidence of part-time and occasional work (in June 1928 14.5 per cent of miners were wholly, and 11.2 per cent temporarily, unemployed).[1] The premonition that there might be a permanent surplus of manpower in the industry had crossed some minds in the depression of 1921. By 1927–8 it had given way to the virtual certainty that there had been an irreversible decline in capacity of anything between 100,000 and 250,000 jobs.[2] The miners, the *Colliery Guardian* acknowledged in January 1929, were 'the victims of an economic debacle'.[3]

[1] It was possible to register as unemployed even while working for 3 days per week (entitlement under the insurance scheme could be generated if the member was unemployed for 3 days out of any 6), and some collieries arranged work-sharing rotas which allowed miners to combine part-time work with the receipt of insurance benefits. Hence, while the Ministry of Labour's insurance data indicated that the number of unemployed miners grew by 254,000 between 1924 and 1925, according to the Mines Department, using more direct measures, the figure was 58,000 (*Samuel Evidence* QQ 628, 1256). In addition, the category of 'temporary unemployed' accounted for a large proportion of the miners returned as out of work (see Table 10.3). It consisted of workers who were working part time or who (like many in mining) had been stood off on the understanding that they would be able to return to work within 6 weeks.

[2] Below, ch. 6, sect. v.

[3] *CG* 4 Jan. 1929, 50.

ii. Regional diversity in the 1920s

Any description of national trends in the coal industry conceals important differences of regional experience, although in the 1920s the forces of
depression were so strong that all districts succumbed to them to some
extent. As Table 5.2 suggests, the principal contrast was between coalfields dependent on the keenly competitive export trade and those
serving inland markets. More than this, there were contrasts *within* each
of these groupings. Given the economic characteristics of the industry,
its variety was manifested less in changes in the relative levels of production (collieries supplying overseas markets attempted to hang on to customers by accepting low prices) than in values, profitability,
employment, and wage levels.

Table 5.2. *Output by coalmining districts, 1914-1929*

	1913		1923		1929	
	m. tons	%	m. tons	%	m. tons	%
Northumberland	14.8	5.1	14.3	5.2	14.5	5.6
Durham	41.5	14.4	34.9	12.6	39.0	15.1
Yorkshire	43.7	15.2	46.5	16.8	46.4	18.0
Lancs., Cheshire, & North Wales	28.1	9.8	23.5	8.5	19.1	7.4
Derby, Notts. & Leicestershire	33.7	11.7	34.9	12.6	32.7	12.7
Stafford, Salop, Worcester, & Warwickshire	20.8	7.2	20.3	7.4	18.2	7.1
Other English Districts	5.4	1.9	5.5	2.0	5.6	2.2
Monmouthshire & South Wales	56.8	19.8	54.3	19.7	48.1	18.7
Scotland	42.5	14.8	38.5	13.9	34.2	13.3
TOTAL	287.4	100.0	276.0	100.0	257.9	100.0

Source: Output: *CYB* 1948, 518–19.

Taking the export fields first, between 1913 and the late 1920s there
was only a modest fall in the share of total output produced by the

North-East, South Wales, and Scottish districts, but a far more telling decline in their share of the *value* of national output, as well as greater pressure on their profitability. By the same token, unemployment was much more severe in the export fields,[1] and the numbers they employed declined by over 20 per cent, while those at work in Yorkshire and the great Midland fields actually rose by 9 per cent. Moreover, there were significant differences *within* the export sector. Between 1913 and 1928,

Table 5.3. *Exports of coal, coke, and manufactured fuel, 1913-1928*
(million tons)

Ports	1913	1928
East Scotland	8.3	4.2
West Scotland	2.2	0.9
Humber	8.8	3.8
Bristol Channel	29.9	20.9
North-East	23.0	17.5

Source: ARSM 1928, 119.

[1] The uneven distribution of unemployment in the various districts is illustrated by the following (see Table 10.3 for a more detailed breakdown):

Average percentage unemployment in various coalfields in March and September, 1927-9

	1927		1928		1929	
	Mar.	Sept.	Mar.	Sept.	Mar.	Sept.
Yorkshire	20.5	10.7	10.6	16.2	8.9	9.6
Derbyshire	16.4	10.2	9.1	11.4	5.0	11.0
Notts. & Leics.	9.9	6.3	7.4	10.3	4.7	7.7
Lancs. and Cheshire	12.8	18.7	16.4	27.9	12.1	24.2
Northumberland	12.8	26.3	20.4	20.5	13.3	10.6
Durham	21.1	23.9	22.2	22.7	17.3	11.2
South Wales & Mons.	22.0	31.7	27.3	30.3	19.5	21.1
Scotland	13.9	13.5	14.5	18.5	13.1	14.8
GREAT BRITAIN	16.8	18.6	17.2	21.6	13.2	14.6

Source: *Ministry of Labour Gazette*, various years. Note that Lancashire & Cheshire, although not among the export fields, fared about as badly as they did.

for example, shipments from Scotland and the Humber ports (the latter were served in part from Yorkshire) each fell by about 50 per cent; those from the Bristol Channel ports declined by about one-third; and those from the North-East coast by just under 25 per cent.

Such variety was in large part based on market patterns and peculiarities: sales from Scotland and the Humber ports were heavily dependent on the Baltic market, which was adversely affected by the virtual closing of the Soviet Union to coal imports and, in the second half of the decade, by the invasion of cheap Polish coal. Exports from the North-East did relatively better (its inland market was shattered through the collapse of heavy industry) because the demand for gas coal, one of Durham's specialities, held up better than that for steam coal.[1]

Economic variety also existed within the major districts: in Scotland, the experience of Fife collieries, applying an exceptional degree of mechanization and internal reorganization to their more modern pits and exploiting richer seams, was more favourable than Lanarkshire's, with its older pits and greater geological and marketing problems; and in South Wales the anthracite collieries held up better than the steam-coal pits. Nor did all values march in step: South Wales & Monmouthshire made the least profits in relatively good years (1923 or 1929) and lost the most in bad times, but Welsh wages exceeded those of other export districts (except for Scotland in the early 1920s). Yet even at their most favourable, signs of better achievement were no more than the flickering of uncertain beacons. The export districts enjoyed little but misery for most of the 1920s.

The inland fields comprised even less of a unity than the export districts. On average they fared better, but they were far from immune to extreme adversity. Thus, quite apart from small areas with high costs and poor markets (Cumberland, North Wales, Bristol, the Forest of Dean, Somerset), the old and geologically troubled field in Lancashire and Cheshire, which was already in difficulty before the War, suffered the further handicap of being tied to Lancashire's manufacturing industry. The depression in cotton, and the rising competition of Yorkshire coal, compounded the crippling problem of thin, faulted seams where working conditions were rapidly deteriorating.[2] As a result, between 1913 and 1929 the Lancashire and Cheshire field's output fell from over 24 million to less than 15.7 million tons and its labour force declined by 30 per cent. Throughout the 1920s it made minuscule or

---

[1] 'Notes on the basis of inter-district tonnages', 6 Aug. 1929: POWE 16/180; Garside 1968, 6, 16.
[2] See Prest 1937, 287–96.

negative profits and paid the lowest wages of all the principal inland districts. West Yorkshire was another old field, serving an industrial area, which suffered from the long depression.

In contrast to this story of decline, the coalfields of Leicestershire and the West Midlands (Shropshire, Staffordshire, Warwickshire, and Worcestershire), which in 1913 were collectively slightly less important than Lancashire and Cheshire, performed somewhat better in the 1920s. With an annual output in excess of 20 million tons, they maintained their share (just over 8 per cent) of national production. More important, helped by relatively high pithead prices and relatively buoyant markets, their finances were relatively healthy: in the disastrous years 1927–9 the combined results of South Derbyshire, Leicestershire, Cannock Chase, and Warwickshire were the best in the country,[1] and they also suffered less from the blight of unemployment. Even so, it is well to emphasize that it was only in comparison with the export districts that the traditional inland fields appeared to do well.

There was less ambiguity about the economic performance of the newer collieries in South Yorkshire and the East Midlands. There, the successful development of such fertile seams as the Barnsley Bed, or Top Hard, and the Silkstone which straddled North Derbyshire, Nottinghamshire, and South Yorkshire, had begun before the Great War. In this eastward extension the seams dipped sharply and were therefore expensive, if rewarding, to reach: new mines had to be sunk to between 2,000 and 3,000 feet. But the coal was thick, easily worked, and much in demand for household, steam-locomotives, and coking uses. It therefore warranted the substantial investment needed to reach it, while the very fact that costly shafts had to be sunk made it necessary to extend the underground operations of each pit so as to spread the initial investment over as large an output as possible. On the eve of the War the deep pits around Doncaster were among the most advanced in the world (at least in terms of layout and organization—they were not highly mechanized, since their coal was easily cut). Even during 1919, when political uncertainties retarded investment in the industry generally, it was possible to find funds to renew and extend the sinkings in South Yorkshire.[2]

However, the most striking example of new development was under Sherwood Forest in the Dukeries area of Nottinghamshire. There,

---

[1] In 1929 the area's profit was 1 s. 2¼d. per ton, when the national average was only 4½d. *ARSM 1927*, 10 and *ARSM 1929*, 12.

[2] *Home Office, Mines and Quarries. Reports of Divisional Inspectors: York & North Midland Division*, 1919, 83.

between 1919 and 1925, a handful of major colliery and iron and steel companies from Derbyshire and Yorkshire began the sinking of seven huge pits, which reached workable coal seams between 1922 and 1928. Modern in conception and advanced in layout and ancillary equipment, using centralized services and fully integrated into complex business organization, building their own extensive housing and developing their own communities—these giant mines were spectacular examples of a distinctive phase of industrialism.[1] They each cost between £1.5 and £2 million, and were designed to produce roughly one million tons annually.

To some contemporaries, sensitive to the 'permanent change in the character of colliery enterprises' in the decade after 1914, such capital expenditure and organizational integration were signs of progress, 'the only means of preserving the integrity' of coalmining companies.[2] To others, more critical of modern capitalism, their economic success and the apparent dependency of their labour force represented the social threat of 'a new industrial feudalism'.[3] But all were struck by their potential for producing very large amounts of coal at a profit, and changing the balance of mining activity in Britain. Altogether, between 1913 and 1929 South Yorkshire and Nottinghamshire increased their share of British coal production from 14 to almost 19 per cent, and of the mining labour force from 12 to over 18 per cent.

Successful as were the Midlands mining enterprises, the deadweight of depression was a restraining influence on new investment in the second half of the 1920s.[4] Admittedly, the production of the tiny Kent field, stimulated by a Treasury guarantee for much of its investment, grew throughout the 1920s; but the amount of coal involved was negligible (1.3 million tons in 1930). And as stagnation became manifest in the

---

[1] The companies (and the associated pits) involved were: Barber Walker & Co. Ltd. (Harworth), Butterley Co. Ltd. (Ollerton), Bolsover Colliery Co. Ltd. (Thoresby and Clipstone), Stanton Iron Works Co. Ltd. (Bilsthorpe), Staveley Coal and Iron Co. Ltd. (Blidworth), and Staveley together with Sheepbridge Coal and Iron Co. Ltd. (Firbeck Main). There were, of course, other smaller developments in the county, while comparable and even bigger pits existed in South Yorkshire (where 7 or 8 mines employed over 3,000 men in 1924). For the development of the Nottinghamshire field see Waller 1983; Griffin 1971b; *ARSM* 1924, 18–21; *Samuel Report*, 46 and *Samuel Evidence*, evidence of Charles Markham and Appendix 46. Between 1919 and 1925 South Yorkshire and Nottinghamshire accounted for over 40% of all new housing built by or for colliery undertakings in Great Britain: *Samuel Appendices*, Appendix 18, 248.

[2] *CG* 2 Jan. 1925, 35. Colliery companies in Lancashire and the North-East also provided capital for new developments in Nottinghamshire and South Yorkshire: *CG* 6 Jan. 1928, 46.

[3] *New Statesman*, 24 Dec. 1924, 352.

[4] *RCSM Evidence* Q 3277; *Annual Report, 1930 of the Mines Inspector for the Midlands and Southern Division*.

industry as a whole, so the number of new mines completed fell—from an average of 38 in 1921–5 to 10 in 1927–31.[1]

iii. Markets, costs, and competition

Given the unsatisfactory performance of British coalmining between the Wars, the determinants of its lack of success are of considerable interest to historians. In recent years, a good deal of attention has therefore been paid to the presumed structural deficiencies of the interwar coal industry, to the quality of its management and the slow pace of technical modernization, to the possible inhibiting effects of the royalty system, and to the disadvantages of the age of many of its mines.[2] Such lines of argument mostly relate to explanations of the industry's sluggish response to extreme adversity. But it is important to remember that the initial cause of its troubles lay less in structures or postures than in what amounted to a world economic crisis. The blight which settled on most of the British coal industry in the third decade of the twentieth century was in large part the product of a stagnation in the international demand for coal, aggravated by an enhancement of the competitive power of other producers.[3]

The First World War, by disrupting normal trade and increasing the demand for coal, provoked a selective but intensive development of new sources of supply. Thus, in the United States output rose from 517 million tons in 1913 to 597 million in 1920; and consuming countries attempted, if possible, to reduce their dependence on others (the combined production of South Africa, Spain, the Netherlands, India, and Japan rose by almost 25 per cent during the War).[4] In the 1920s, although American production slipped back, the world's new and larger capacity was maintained.

In particular, once the drastic postwar economic and financial adjustments had taken place, Britain's position was the more threatened as German and Polish production grew. Admittedly, the growth in the world's total output of coal was modest, but Britain's standing had

[1] Calculated from lists printed in *ARSM* annually.

[2] Buxton 1970; Kirby 1972; Greasley 1982, 246–68; Trevor Evans & Ben Fine, 'Economies of Scale in the British Inter-War Coal Industry' (unpublished); Trevor Evans & Ben Fine, 'The Diffusion of Mechanical Cutting in the British Inter-War Coal Industry' (unpublished).

[3] The view that the origins of the industry's problems were exogenous not simply to the industry but to the British economy was put forward by Neuman 1934, 18, writing in the context of contemporaneous criticism of the coal industry's organization and businessmen.

[4] League of Nations 1929, 20 ff.

deteriorated sharply. Her coal exports as a proportion of world consumption fell from 17 per cent in 1913 to 10.5 per cent in 1928. Above this, the deadweight of idle capacity had increased substantially. By the end of the decade it was estimated that about 25 per cent of the capacity of the German and British coal industries was surplus to market requirements (the Polish figure was at least twice that much).[1]

The problems of surplus capacity were severely aggravated by the inadequacy of world demand for coal. For almost 30 years before the outbreak of the First World War there had been an average annual increase of over 4 per cent in the international consumption of coal. But after 1913, denied the stimulus which had come from the expansion of the nineteenth-century international economy or of its great coal-using technologies (steam-powered factories, locomotives, and ships), that boom decelerated. In the decade and a half between 1913 and 1928, international demand rose by barely the equivalent of a single year of prewar growth. This retardation was largely due to the drastic slowing down of the world's leading economies.

Demand for coal also suffered because of the growing popularity of alternative fuels and the application of more efficient techniques to the use of coal. Thus, between 1914 and 1924 coal-burning ships registered at Lloyd's fell from 89 to 66 per cent of the total (vessels with oil-burning installations rose from 3 to 31 per cent). Meanwhile, in the steel industry large fuel economies resulted from the use of scrap rather than pig iron, and in the basic iron industry between 1914 and 1929 the amount of coke needed to produce a ton of pig iron was reduced by 10 per cent; while in the gas industry in the 20 years to 1924 there was a saving of 15 per cent in the use of coal. Fuel economy in electricity was the most spectacular of all—a saving of 40 per cent in the 1920s.[2]

Restrictive trends were also at work within the British market. Industrial production rose by a mere 15 per cent between 1913 and 1929; fuel savings and substitution reduced the potential market for coal; and the heavy industries, which had been particularly large consumers of coal

[1] The world production of coal and lignite (coal equivalent) was 1,215.7 million metric tons in 1913 and 1,245.3 million metric tons in 1928. By the mid-1920s when Britain's output was some 6% below the prewar average, the rest of the world's was about 13% above. 'The British Coal Mining Industry', 1928: POWE 16/180/22. British exports and world consumption: MSWCOA, Box File 729, 'World Trade—Coal', Appendix D. Capacity estimates: League of Nations 1929, 8–9.

[2] 'Committee on Industry and Trade. Memorandum on the British Coal Export Trade': SRO GD 193/425. Samuel Report, 12; Samuel Evidence QQ 2977 ff.; Political & Economic Planning 1936, 115–16; Buxton & Aldcroft 1979, 110. In the United States, where industrial production rose by more than 80% between 1913 and the late 1920s, the consumption of coal increased by a mere 3%: League of Nations 1929, 7.

and coke, underwent a disproportionately prolonged stagnation (between 1913 and 1927–9 the metallurgical industries' consumption of coal fell by 8 million tons). Among other large consumers, only the booming electrical supply industry demanded significantly more coal, but since the amount of coal used per unit of electricity fell from 3.47 lb. in 1920 to 1.5 lb. in 1929, the enormous expansion of electricity output involved an increase of only some 5 million tons in its coal needs. For the rest, and in spite of a 10 per cent increase in national income between 1913 and 1929, consumption remained fairly steady (the railways at about 13 million tons, gas manufacturing at about 17 million tons, and general manufacturing and household use together amounting to between 95 and 98 million tons). As a result, home consumption never quite regained the 183.4 million tons of 1913, and slipped back to 172.3 million in 1927–9.

Table 5.4. *Consumption of coal in Britain, 1913 and 1929*

	Amount (m. tons)		% of total	
	1913	1929	1913	1929
General manufacturing	40.0	40.0	21.8	23.0
Household	57.7	55.0	31.4	31.7
Iron and steel	31.4	23.4	17.0	13.5
Coalmines	18.0	13.7	9.8	7.9
Gas	16.7	16.8	9.1	9.7
Railways	13.2	13.4	7.2	7.7
Electricity	4.9	9.8	2.5	5.7
Coastal steamers	1.9	1.4	1.0	0.8
TOTAL	183.8	173.5	100.0	100.0

Source: CYB 1934, 624–5.

Throughout the interwar period economies reduced the demand for coal by just under 3 per cent annually, and national income growth just about counterbalanced this reduction.[1] Only the immunity of the

[1] Figures of coal consumption are from *CYB* 1934, 624–5. Pig iron production in the 1920s was generally only 70 or 75% of its 1913 level: Mitchell Abstract, 131–2. For the figures on the use of coal in the electrical supply industry, as well as a discussion of fuel efficiency generally, see Coal

British market to foreign competition protected the inland fields— although some experienced very severe difficulties, either because they were associated with depressed manufacturing industries (cotton in Lancashire, metallurgical and heavy engineering in the North-East), or because they were exposed to new competition from the rich seams of South Yorkshire and Nottinghamshire or even from export districts such as Fife and Durham with surplus supplies which could be relatively easily thrown on to the domestic market.[1] In spite of such problems, however, the home market at least remained fairly stable. 'The seat of our present troubles', in the words of the Samuel Commission, lay in the export trade.[2]

The decline of overseas sales was erratic. Indeed, owing to the exceptional circumstances of 1923 the average exports for 1922–4 (68.4 million tons) exceeded those for 1911–13 (67.5 million tons). But the underlying trend asserted itself in 1924 and 1925 when (even with the help of a substantial wage subsidy) exports plummeted to an annual rate of just over 56 million tons. By the last years of the decade they were stuck at about 51 million tons—a mere 76 per cent of the prewar level. And bunker shipments fell by almost as much. Not surprisingly, then, Britain did worse than the generality of other coal exporters, and her share of the world's coal trade fell from the 50 per cent or more of the prewar years to just under 40 per cent in 1925–9.[3]

There were, of course, diffused and long-run causes of the weakness of the British coal trade. Before considering these, however, it is

Industry Nationalisation Compensation Tribunal, Proof of Evidence of Sir Harold Hartley (1946): POWE 28/240. The calculations of the mutually cancelling effects of economies in the use of coal and increases in national income are in Richard Stone, 'The Internal Demand for Coal in the United Kingdom in the Period between the two Wars' (Apr. 1946): POWE 28/235. Curiously, the demand for household fuel failed to grow even though population rose by 10% and the number of houses by 1.75 million (1913–31). This was attributed to the elasticity of demand in the face of relatively high coal prices in the early 1920s, and to the substitution of gas and electricity for solid fuel in domestic appliances: Neuman 1934, 97–105.

[1] SRO CB7/2/10 (Minutes of meetings of representatives of the 4 Scottish areas); Garside 1968, 16.

[2] Samuel Report, 4.

[3] Export figures from: Home Office, Mines & Quarries. General Report, 1913, Table 172; ARSM 1931, 130–1. Calculations for 1927–9 exclude about 2.5 million tons exported to the Irish Free State to ensure comparability with official figures for the period before 1923, which excluded intra-United Kingdom trade. Britain's share of world coal trade: Kahn 1946, 86. Britain's coal exports as a proportion of total non-British consumption fell from 9.9% in 1909–13 to 6.7% in 1925–9: Neuman 1934, 38. The fall in overseas bunkers (from 19.5 million to 1911–13 to 16.6 million in 1927–9) was brought about not simply by changes in the technology of ships and the level of world trade, but also by the decline in coal exports themselves, since coal accounted for some 80% of the total tonnage of British shipments.

necessary to emphasize that, as the pattern of decline represented in Table 5.5 suggests, exports were affected by a number of abrupt exogenous 'shocks'. For example, the most severe loss was experienced in the Baltic market, which accounted for some 22 per cent of British sales in 1913 and less than 12 per cent in 1929. Initially damaged by the dislocations attendant on the Russian Revolution and subsequent import prohibitions, Britain's Baltic exports were further eroded, in the late 1920s, when Polish coal (denied access to Germany and spurred by government subsidies) invaded the Scandinavian market. Some disruption worked to Britain's temporary advantage (in 1922-3, for example) but on balance Britain probably lost from such events. Thus, the coal stoppages of 1920 enticed American coal into Europe and, even more seriously, that of 1926 gave a decisive and enduring impetus to German and Polish coal production and export competitiveness.[1]

Table 5.5. *Distribution of British coal exports (excluding manufactured fuel), 1913-1929 (%)*

	1913	1922	1923	1927	1929
Baltic	21.7	12.8	12.1	13.7	11.6
North Sea	35.3	49.5	60.6	32.7	45.3
Western Mediterranean	21.7	17.1	14.8	24.6	22.2
Eastern Mediterranean	7.7	4.0	3.2	6.8	5.6
Arabia, Indian Ocean, etc.	1.1	2.5	0.6	1.0	1.8
North and Central America	0.2	6.5	1.6	2.2	2.0
South America & Atlantic	9.6	5.9	5.4	10.5	9.4
Total exports (m. tons):	73.4	64.2	78.0	48.7	57.8

Baltic includes Russia, Finland, Estonia, Scandinavia.
North Sea includes Germany, Netherlands, Belgium, France, Switzerland, Channel Islands.
Arabia, Indian Ocean, etc. includes India, Malaysia, Oceania, Further Asia.

Source: ARSM, various years.

Behind 'random' disruptions such as these, however, lay the more fundamental issue of the heightened competitiveness of the stagnant international market for coal. In particular, continental capacity grew as

[1] Russian market: *ARSM* 1930, 28; Asteris 1971, 22-4; *Samuel Report*, 251. American exports to Europe (14 million tons in 1920 as against 1 million in 1912-13): SRO GD 193/425/60 ff. The 1926 stoppage: Political and Economic Planning 1936, 152-3. Between 1925 and 1926 Germany's exports rose from 22.5 to 38 million metric tons and Poland's from 8.25 to 14.75 million tons.

a consequence of the shortages of 1914–20, of 'autonomous' business activity in the early 1920s, and of conscious public policy in the form of import restrictions (as happened in France, Spain, and Germany); subsidies and preferential freight rates (the last were used in France, Germany, Poland, and Belgium); and selective price controls provoked by resentment at what was assumed to be British profiteering in 1919–20 and 1923.[1]

The results of all this were impressive. In postwar France, for example, the mining industry was modernized and reorganized in a major programme of reconstruction. By 1924 it had regained its 1913 levels of output (at pithead prices which equalled, instead of greatly exceeding, British prices) and by 1928 it was producing 20 per cent more coal.[2] The recovery of German coalmining was even more significant. Wartime shortages encouraged the development of huge supplies of lignite ('brown coal'), equivalent to about 15 million tons of bituminous coal. Taking coal and lignite together, Germany produced 141.8 million metric tons within its postwar boundaries in 1913 and 187.1 million tons in 1927. This expansion was facilitated by determination and reorganization. Regional syndicates or cartels (of which the Rhenish–Westphalian, controlling 101 of the Ruhr's 145 million tons, was the best known) had been encouraged by legislation in 1919, and adjusted the output, sales, and prices of their constituents. But the reorganization of the mines themselves, and the advance of mechanization (in 1926 66 per cent of the Ruhr's output was cut mechanically as against 22 per cent in Britain) were the really potent forces.

By 1925, output per manshift in the Ruhr had overtaken Britain's, and Germany was on the way to becoming an effective competitor to Britain in Italian, French, and Scandinavian markets. Although the Peace Treaty restricted Germany's exports until 1924, by the late 1920s they were 85 per cent of their 1913 level (as against Britain's 75 per cent)—and this in spite of the postwar expropriation of 26 per cent of Germany's resources in favour of France and Poland.[3]

---

[1] For the encouragement of continental production by various states, see *Samuel Report*, 253 and Annex, section 2; *Samuel Evidence* Q 8394; and (in detail) 'The British Coal Mining Industry' (1928) in POWE 16/180, 9–11. The British government also subsidized the mining industry, albeit for slightly different reasons. Temporary subsidies to cushion wages against reductions amounted to £10 million in 1921 and £23 million in 1925–6. Below, 224.

[2] SRO GD 193/425/49.

[3] On output per manshift: Political and Economic Planning 1936, 153–4. For a discussion of the comparative efficiency of mining operations, see below, ch. 7, sect. v; ch. 9, sect. ii. With the exception of Scotland, the principal export fields in Britain tended to have output per manshift figures at, or slightly below, the national average. On Germany's industry in the 1920s: *Samuel*

Germany's competitiveness was the more keenly felt because of the terms of the Peace and subsequent reparations, which were occasionally interpreted as an unfair threat to British sales. At the Peace, Germany had been obliged to give options to France to purchase 7 million tons of coal, to Belgium to purchase 8 million tons, and to Italy to purchase a total rising from $4\frac{1}{2}$ to $8\frac{1}{2}$ million tons—all at cost price. Further, from 1924, under the Dawes Plan, it was possible for reparations to be paid in kind—including coal and coke shipments. The direct consequences for British trade could not have been serious in the early 1920s, since deliveries were not up to their maximum levels. But by the late 1920s German shipments to France and Italy were substantial, while British exports were about 30 per cent below those of 1913. Even so, as most informed observers confirmed, it seems unlikely that the effect on total British exports was very great. For one thing, 40 per cent or more of reparations shipments were in the form of metallurgical coke, which was a negligible item in Britain's trade. On the other hand, there was some feeling that they had a disturbing effect on the South Wales coalfield through its particular relationship with the French and Italian markets, which took more German and less British coal. More than this, the specific arrangement for reparations probably did help the more general recovery of the German industry, and established commercial links which proved useful for the sale of non-reparations coal or coke in subsequent years.[1]

An altogether more obvious and serious consequence of Germany's position as a defeated nation occurred later in the decade. Under the terms of the Peace Treaty, Germany's Upper Silesian mines were ceded to Poland, and from 1922, as a result of the Geneva Convention, Poland was given guaranteed access to the German market to the extent of 500,000 metric tons per month. But in 1925, as part of the trade war, Germany terminated the Convention, and thus presented Poland with the urgent task of finding outlets for six or seven million tons of coal annually. It found them in markets served by Britain. Polish exports (encouraged by a tax rebate and subsidized freight charges which allowed them to undercut British coal in spite of a 400-mile haul to the coast) invaded the Baltic market with vigour and success, especially in

Report, 7-8, 243-6, Annex 2; League of Nations 1927, I, 19; League of Nations 1929, 20-3; SRO GD 193/425/48-9; Asteris 1971, 38.

[1] Henderson 1955, 93-5. Other material on reparations is in *Samuel Evidence* QQ 1936 ff. and 8091; Political & Economic Planning 1936, 153; SRO GD 193/425/Appendix II. Under the Young Plan of 1929 reparations payments were eased and Italy agreed to contract to buy British coal for its state railway.

Scandinavia. And their initial footholds were greatly strengthened by the effects of Britain's coal stoppage in 1926.

Clearly, the course of international and labour history in the 1920s did not much favour the competitive power of Britain's coal exporters. Yet, underlying and reinforcing such adverse developments was a fundamental problem of prices and quality. In prewar years the trading strength of British coal had been its relatively high labour productivity, low prices, and good profitability. In the 1920s, however, new competitors increased their labour productivity significantly faster than did British coalmining, and by the end of the decade, as Table 5.6 shows, it had been overtaken by its principal trade rivals.

Table 5.6. *Output of coal per manshift in various countries, 1913-1929* (cwt)

Year	Great Britain	Ruhr	Polish Upper Silesia	Pas-de-Calais	Belgium	Holland
1913	21.5	18.6	23.6	14.9	10.4	16.2
1924	17.6[a]	16.9	14.3	11.4	9.1	14.6
1927	20.6	22.3	25.1	12.7	10.1	20.0
1929	21.7	25.0	26.4	14.2	11.3	24.5
Increase 1913–29	1%	34%	12%	10%	9%	52%

[a] In 1919 the normal underground shift was reduced by an hour in most districts.

Source: Political & Economic Planning 1936, 153.

These differential rates of productivity change were largely explained by the rapid postwar reorganization of continental industries, and the associated investment programmes, especially as they facilitated the extension of mechanical cutting and conveying.[1] Admittedly, many owners claimed that there was less scope for a similar investment programme in Britain—principally because of the age, adverse geology, and engrained underground organization of her collieries. 'Mechanization' involved more than the introduction of machines: to be fully effective, it would have to be accompanied by extensive amendments of existing

[1] Between 1913 and 1929 the proportion of coal won by mechanical means (mostly mechanized picks on the continent and coal cutters in Britain) rose from 8% to 29% in Britain, 2% to 91% in Germany, 0% to 31% in Polish Upper Silesia, and 10% to 89% in Belgium: Political and Economic Planning 1936, 154.

practices, layouts, and techniques throughout the relevant mines. But whether or not this was so (and the later investigations of the Reid Committee emphasized the enormous costs that would have been involved),[1] the consequent improvements in competitors' industries were keenly felt by British mines.

There were, of course, other contributory factors in changing cost structures: British owners blamed relatively high wages (although wage reductions helped very little in the late 1920s); British collieries and exporters were slow to appreciate the need to maintain the quality of their product (by cleaning and grading coal) or to attract sales by guaranteeing its chemical characteristics;[2] and output per manshift alone was an inadequate measure of cost-efficiency—which also depended on wage rates, capital charges, industrial organization, the cost of materials, etc. Nevertheless, there was little doubt that the relative competitiveness of continental coalmining was greatly improved in the decade after the First World War.

At the same time, the coal trade was also caught up in the dislocations which flowed from rapid changes in money values and exchange rates in the 1920s. In the early years, when sterling had been floated, the exchange rate appears to have played only a minor role in the coal industry's changing fortunes. In 1924, however, the coincidence of an official determination to return to the prewar parity of $4.86 and favourable market circumstances for the pound resulted in an increase in the rate of exchange just as continental competition in the coal trade intensified. Coalmining, along with other 'unsheltered' industries, was already under pressure from the distorted pattern of prices and wages (which enforced low world prices on export trades but allowed 'sheltered' industries to sustain inflated values and pass on inflated costs). Now, a rise in the exchanges had the effect of further increasing the money cost, and therefore reducing the profitability, of British coal exports.

As the exchange and competition rose in 1924, coal export prices fell by 12 per cent. By the spring of 1925, when Britain returned to the Gold Standard at the prewar parity, it was fairly clear that, as far as Britain's staple exports were concerned, the pound was overvalued, and the deleterious consequences of that overvaluation were to be felt for the rest of the decade. Keynes, in his polemic against the government's

---

[1] Below, 617–18.

[2] See *Samuel Report*, 94–5 and *Samuel Evidence* QQ 8008 ff.; *Hansard* 15 June 1926, col. 2187; Mines Department, *Report of the British Coal Delegation to Sweden, Norway, and Denmark*. Cmd. 3702. 1930 (*PP* 1930–1 XV).

policy, assumed that the overvaluation was of the order of 10 per cent and that there would be an inevitable squeeze on the prices, and therefore labour costs, of the export industries in order to maintain some semblance of international competitiveness. Coal, Keynes argued, would be 'above all others a victim of our monetary policy' and the miners 'the victims of the economic juggernaut'.[1]

Subsequent events justified Keynes's warnings about the prolongation of unemployment, the deterioration of industrial relations, and the political impossibility of pushing home the deflationary policies implied in the return to the Gold Standard. By the same token, it soon became clear that the authorities' concentration on the dollar exchange rate in 1925 had led them to underestimate the importance of the currency situation on the continent, where British coal had to find its most important overseas market. In fact, the German currency stabilization of 1923-4 and the French and Belgian stabilization two years later, all produced 'undervalued' currencies, and reinforced the strength of their competition as against commodities priced in sterling. Of course, had Britain returned to the Gold Standard at a significantly lower parity, other countries might well have retaliated by devaluing their own currencies even further, thereby cancelling the effect of Britain's move or generating even more instability in international trade. But the fact remains that in 1924-5 the coal industry received a severe competitive jolt because of monetary developments, and that it was only partly (and temporarily) protected by the wages subsidy offered by the government between August 1925 and April 1926.

Nevertheless, the events of 1924-5, and of the stoppage which followed, must be seen in the context of an industry which was already weakened, depressed, and declining.[2] The return to Gold aggravated rather than caused the stressful trends of the 1920s. Market forces exerted enormous pressures; the coal industry had to take the strain.

iv. Taking the strain in the 1920s: prices and profits, wages and unemployment

The demand for British coal in export markets in the 1920s was highly elastic. Certainly no individual exporter or even large group could

[1] *JMK* IX, 222-3. Also see Moggridge 1972, ch. 4. For export prices in 1924, see *Joint Sub-Committee, 1925*, Appendix.

[2] Both Keynes and Sir Josiah Stamp (who agreed with him about the harmful effects of the return to Gold) fully appreciated that the weakness of the coal industry pre-dated the rise in the exchange rate. *JMK* IX, 222 and XIX, Pt. I, 399; Note by Stamp in *Buckmaster Report*, 22-3.

afford to offer coal at prices above those of Britain's competitors. And although some observers implied that British supply *as a whole* might 'set the world price', so that the use of cartel arrangements might increase income without a commensurate reduction in sales,[1] no such experiment was tried in the 1920s. British collieries continued to find it increasingly difficult to meet foreign prices and were encountering extreme competition in the home market.

In the face of surplus production and low prices, there were four main strategies that the industry might have adopted: a direct attempt to lower costs by reducing wages or increasing hours, the formation of selling associations or quota schemes to mitigate competition, investment and industrial reorganization to increase efficiency, and rationalization to eliminate excess capacity. In the event, the most notorious response to adversity was the first of these—a logical, if short-sighted, consequence of the fact that labour accounted for about three-quarters of total costs in 1919–20 (about two-thirds even after the drastic wage reductions of 1921). Certainly for much of the interwar years most owners rejected the view that there were substantial but unrealized economies to be derived from widespread colliery reorganization or unification; and until the years 1927–8 they also opposed any form of inter-company cooperation for marketing purposes. As will be seen in the next section, there *were* structural changes. But their overall effects were limited. The strains of stagnation were taken by prices, profits, earnings, and employment. As a result, by the late 1920s the coalmining industry embodied one of the country's most severe social as well as economic problems: some of its proudest communities were devastated by chronic unemployment and desperate poverty.[2]

The economic distress which overcame large parts of the coal industry was the more painful in that it followed a brief period of unprecedented prosperity. Between 1909/13 and 1919/21 nominal profits per ton doubled (they were 2s. 11¾d. in 1920), while their real value, allowing for price increases, was maintained.[3] Because of control most of the profits of coalmining found their way into government hands, but retained profits were high enough to provoke resentment among the miners and

---

[1] *JMK* XIX, Pt. 2, 535–6 (15 May 1926). For subsequent discussion of a possible export cartel, see below, 287–8.

[2] The various responses to the vicissitudes of the decade are considered in more detail in ch. 6, which deals with government policy as well as industrial relations. More general issues relating to business history and the social problems of mining communities are considered in ch. 9 and 10.

[3] *CYB* 1932, 598; *Samuel Report*, 218. For the bases and outcome of financial control (which lasted until 12 Mar. 1921), see above, ch. 3, sect. iv; ch. 4, sect. iv.

induce a wave of mergers, a boom in colliery shares, and a large number of bonus share issues, by which means colliery companies could capitalize their growing assets.[1]

For their part, the miners found that the scarcity of coal and their own bargaining power within a threatening climate of industrial relations, enabled them to achieve a distinct improvement in material welfare. The length of the working day was reduced by about one hour in 1919, and a series of wage increases in 1919 and 1920 lifted their earnings above the levels of 1914 and those of workers in comparable industries. By early 1921, shift earnings were three times those of July 1914, and 20 per cent higher in terms of purchasing power.[2]

This diffused prosperity was, nevertheless, insecurely based, and came to an abrupt end with the collapse of the export boom during the winter of 1920-1. Prices and profits slumped, followed—after a bitter dispute from April to June 1921—by wages. The National Wages Agreement which ended the 1921 dispute gave some support to basic earnings. But the low minima and the poor performance of the industry led inexorably to a fall in money wages and real incomes. Between the first quarter of 1921 and the summer of 1922 shift earnings were reduced by 50 per cent, which represented a decline of about 32 per cent in real terms and a much steeper reduction than in other export industries. Meanwhile, however, the price of coal fell even faster than coalminers' wages, so that profits shrank drastically—from almost 3s. per ton in 1920 to $10\frac{1}{2}d.$ in 1922.[3] Yet even when wages in 1922 were driven to their lowest levels of the interwar period, the price of coal relative to other commodities was still greater than it had been in 1913 (relative prices only began to fall from 1925).

The brief revival of trade late in 1922 and 1923 increased prices,

[1] For (incomplete) lists of bonus share issues by colliery companies in the years after 1917, see the Labour Research Department's publications 1934, 21; Fox 1935a, 27; Williams 1937, 19. Among the most spectacular examples were, in South Wales: Ocean Coal & Wilson's (£2 million, or $66\frac{2}{3}$%), Guest, Keen & Nettlefolds (£675,065, or 100%), and Great Western Colliery (over £300,000, or 40%); in Yorkshire: Carlton Main Colliery (over £1 million, or some 150%), Newton Chambers (£306,400, or 100%), and Wharncliffe Woodmoor Colliery (£295,680, or 350%); and in Northumberland: Ashington Coal (£391,680), Mickley Coal (£324,000), and Bedlington Coal (£224,000).

[2] Shift earnings: *ARSM* 1923, 110-11; cost of living: Department of Employment and Productivity 1971, 166-7. Details of quarterly shift earnings in Britain in the postwar period are given in Tables 4.2(a) and 4.2(b) and in the various districts throughout the interwar period in Table 10.2.

[3] These figures were derived from accounts obtained under the National Wages Agreement. The MFGB, however, challenged their reliability and asserted that they underestimated true profits.

profits, and (after an interval) wages. By 1924–5 shift earnings had risen by about 10 per cent (8 per cent in real terms) from the trough of 1922, but were still below their prewar levels. Although all miners fared substantially worse than workers in sheltered industries, compared with other export industries unskilled miners had lost ground since 1913 and skilled miners had advanced.[1] But even these new positions could not be held. By the spring of 1925 the maturing of international competition and the appreciation of sterling introduced a new note of crisis, and a new strain on wages and profits. By May 1925 some 60 per cent of the industry's output was produced at a loss. 'The industry', said the President of the MAGB, 'is not in a position to continue'; and his opposite number in the MFGB agreed that it was 'crumbling to pieces'.[2]

Against this background, the owners succeeded in increasing hours and reducing pay, but only after the government had purchased a delay by the Royal Commission and wages subsidy of 1925/6 and the miners had resisted throughout the prolonged and desperate stoppage of 1926. But even when the owners had gone as far as they dared, and in spite of higher output per manshift and lower wages and unit costs (all of which brought the *relative* price of coal back to or below prewar levels),[3] the business troubles of the coal industry were not much nearer a definitive solution, as Table 5.7 suggests.

[1] *Samuel Report*, 155–9. The variety of geographical circumstances and the range of grades of labour make such industry-wide averages very misleading. This can be illustrated from figures for Sept. 1923, when the MAGB took a wages census, which can be compared with the averages (irrespective of grades) produced in *ARSM* 1923 (Table 22). Average shift earnings for the industry as a whole were then 10s. 3d. (to the nearest penny), and district figures for the principal fields varied from 8s. 10d. for Lancashire & Cheshire to 10s. 11d. for Scotland. According to the wages census (*Samuel Appendices*, Appendix 26), the average in Sept. for all workers (10s. 6d.) was composed of such disparate figures (each one an average of differing district amounts) as 14s. 5d. for hewers, 11s. for winding enginemen, 9s. 8d. for underground labourers, 8s. 4d. for surface labourers, 5s. 9d. for boys working underground, and 4s. 6d. for boys working on the surface. Adult wages averaged 11s. 8d.—with those underground earning 12s. 5d. and those on the surface 8s. 10d.

[2] *Macmillan Court*, 59 (60% of the industry operating at a loss); *Joint Sub-Committee*, 1925, 886, 156 (quotations).

[3] The position with regard to relative price movements is brought out in the following comparison of price indices (1913 = 100):

	1920	1924	1927	1929
Coal	333	180	138	128
Food and raw materials	295	164	144	135
Wholesale prices	307	166	142	137

Sources: *ARSM*, various years; Mitchell, *Abstract*, 475–7.

The problem was that the market for British coal was simply not available. Prices tumbled further in the early months of 1927, and the Permanent Secretary to the Mines Department, Sir Ernest Gowers, almost wearily affirmed that 'the task of securing enough of the world's markets to satisfy the present capacity of the industry is beyond the reach of the coal owners'. The industry as a whole operated at a loss in both the grim years of 1927 and 1928, and in the latter year pithead prices fell to 12s. 3½d. (a decline of over 60 per cent since 1920) and unemployment rose to a peak of 25 per cent in the summer. Between 1924 and 1929, miners' earnings were reduced by 12 per cent in nominal terms and 6 per cent in real terms, at a time when nearly all other industrial groups showed an improvement. The effect on mining communities now appeared cataclysmic, and stirred both public and political opinion.[1]

Obviously, such a bald summary neglects very large differences between different districts and firms. Yet, although the profit performance of export areas (especially of South Wales) was worse than that of the inland fields, the differences diminished in the second half of the 1920s, as desperate export collieries, having seen their prices tumble by one-third between 1924 and January 1928, unloaded their output on home markets. As a result, *all* districts made large losses in 1928 and the fall in employment in the opening months of that year was as heavily concentrated in the inland fields of Yorkshire, the Midlands, and the North-West as the earlier decline had been in Scotland, the North-East, and South Wales.[2] On the other hand, individual firms occasionally made profits in adversity—not merely in North Derbyshire and Nottinghamshire (where the Bolsover, Butterley, Sheepbridge, and Staveley colliery companies continued to pay modest dividends throughout the late 1920s) but also, although more rarely, in West Yorkshire, Scotland, and South Wales, where Henry Briggs & Son, the Fife Coal Co., and Ocean & Wilson's did the same (except for the last in 1928). Generally, however, even normally powerful undertakings in South Wales and the North-East (e.g. Amalgamated Anthracite, the Cambrian Combine,

---

[1] Gowers: 'The Present Position of the Coal Mining Industry', 17 June 1927, in Baldwin Papers 17/15. Data on prices and profits: *CYB* 1932, 598; on unemployment: *Ministry of Labour Gazette*, 1928, 251, 258–9; on earnings: *ARSM*, various years, and Mitchell, *Abstract*, 352–3. Most important groups of wage-earners experienced an increase of between 5 and 15% in real earnings. Real wages in iron and steel remained fairly steady.

[2] In 1925–7 over 70% of the fall in employment occurred in the principal export fields; in early 1928 about 75% of the fall in employment occurred in the main inland fields. Secretary for Mines, 'British Coal Mining Industry': POWE 16/180/13.

Table 5.7. *Profits, earnings, and unemployment in selected coalmining districts, 1920–1928*

	Profits per ton (proceeds minus costs)			Average quarterly earnings			Percentage unemployment			
	July/Sept. 1920 *s. d.*	Apr./June 1925 *s. d.*	July/Sept. 1928 *s. d.*	July/Sept. 1920 £ *s. d.*	Apr./June 1925 £ *s. d.*	July/Sept. 1928 £ *s. d.*	22 March 1926 wholly	22 March 1926 temporarily	25 June 1928 wholly	25 June 1928 temporarily
Northumberland	12 3¼	−1 9½	−1 4	57 4 8	27 12 10	22 10 3	8.0	1.5	16.3	4.3
Durham	7 0¾	−1 5¼	−1 0¾	56 11 2	29 7 2	24 10 10	15.7	0.2	19.2	3.3
Yorkshire	4 3		−1 4			26 18 11	2.2	0.4	8.5	16.1
Derbyshire,							1.0	0.3	6.0	18.4
Nottinghamshire,										
Leicestershire,	5 2¾	−0 3¼	n/a	56 17 6	31 19 8	n/a	0.8	0.6	6.0	17.5
Cannock Chase, &							n/a	n/a	n/a	n/a
Warwickshire							1.2	n/a	9.8	1.9
Nottinghamshire	n/a	n/a	−0 9¾	n/a	n/a	28 0 1	n/a	n/a	n/a	n/a
North Derbyshire	n/a	n/a		n/a	n/a		n/a	n/a	n/a	n/a
Monmouthshire & South Wales	11 7½	−1 3¾	−1 8	66 19 7	34 4 11	31 8 6	10.0	3.2	21.1	8.7
Scotland	−0 4¾	−1 3¼	−1 1½	60 11 7	33 17 6	31 17 4	9.9	1.4	20.0	1.4
Great Britain	4 10¼	−0 11¾	−1 4¼	58 17 10	31 10 4	27 6 9	7.5	1.8	14.5	11.2

n/a = not available.

Sources: Earnings: *ARSM*, various years; unemployment: *Ministry of Labour Gazette*, various years.

Consett Iron, Ebbw Vale Steel, Iron and Coal, Pease & Partners, Powell Duffryn Steam Coal), as well as the Wigan Coal & Iron Co. in Lancashire, paid no dividends on ordinary shares after 1925.

Miners' earnings also varied between districts. Those in Northumberland and Durham earned least of all, although, as Table 5.7 shows, it was by no means always the wage-earners in export districts who did badly: wages in Scotland and South Wales remained among the highest in the country. On the other hand, some of the most severe strains of depression were felt in figures of the wholly unemployed, as pits reduced their output or closed altogether (pits employing 123,700 men were closed between 1924 and 1928). And the resulting contrasts in the regional experience of worklessness were more or less accurate indications of the constraints of market conditions. In September 1928 the (unweighted) average of unemployment in the three leading export areas exceeded 22 per cent; that of Derby, Nottinghamshire, and Leicester was less than 11 per cent.[1]

Unemployment was, indeed, the principal symptom of the industry's marketing difficulties and organizational rigidities. Coalmining simply had too many workers. In 1921–2 and after 1924 it could not provide a continuous living for all the men who, in the years of its peak prosperity, had been attracted into it. The sad continuance of this fact was partly attributable to the notorious immobility of mining labour. In the words of a contemporary, 'the expulsive power, even of relatively low wage rates and heavy unemployment . . . worked . . . in a slow and hesitant manner'. Yet, even if miners had been sufficiently rootless to wish to migrate rapidly and in large numbers, the arrangements (including trade-union opinion) in other industries, sheltered or unsheltered, would not have made it easy for them to absorb more labour or accept lower wages.[2]

Coalmining remained an overmanned industry with too large a capacity. This was recognized as early as the autumn of 1921, and by 1925 opinion in the MFGB was willing to acknowledge that there were 'too many men in the mines and . . . too many mines at work'. Legislation in

---

[1] Pit closures: Secretary for Mines, 'British Coal Mining Industry': POWE 10/180/13. Statistics of unemployment by district: Table 10.3. The average number of shifts worked by those in employment also fell: from 266 in 1923 to 244 in 1927. ARSM 1927.

[2] Quotation: Pigou 1947, 52. For the low 'exit mobility' of miners also see Pilgrim Trust 1938, 79–80. The coalowners advocated a reduction of wage levels in sheltered industries, in large part in order to reduce the costs of production of coal. See Samuel Evidence, 929 ff. For the miners' and transport workers' responses, see ibid., Q 16378 and 895–909. For interwar migration, see below, 490–1.

1926 allowed for some restriction on new recruitment to the industry, but such an enactment only touched the fringes of a problem which grew worse in the next two years. In 1927, as desperation spread, the Minister of Labour argued that there was a surplus of at least 200,000 men in the industry and the government established an Industrial Transference Board in an attempt to demonstrate its commitment to help the unemployed. In its first report, in 1928, the Board expressed what had now become a consensus:

We regard the existence of a surplus of labour in some of the heavy industries as a fact, and we think that too much reliance should not be placed on a reduction in this surplus by measures taken within the industries. . . . In certain of the industries, and particularly in coal mining, there exists a definite surplus of labour. . . . The resulting unemployment involving upwards of 200,000 workers, constitutes a tragic problem, necessitating the urgent and sympathetic attention of the entire country.[1]

In the event, the Industrial Transference Board's powers were restricted and its achievements limited. Much more migration occurred on a 'spontaneous' basis. The personal upheaval must have been considerable, and very large numbers remained unemployed. Nevertheless, such migration remained perhaps the least painful sort of adjustment to the strains of decline in the coal industry in the 1920s. For in this respect economic pressures were unforgiving: the transient bubble of prosperity had burst; business losses and mass unemployment, anguished argument and social misery, inevitably followed.

v. Taking the strain: structural change

Thus far, we have only considered the deflationary consequences and strains of industrial decline. But, as Keynes had predicted in his assault on the Gold-Standard policy of 1925, political and social inhibitions meant that deflationary pressures could not be carried to their logical conclusion. Not surprisingly, the owners in the export districts ultimately had to confess that there was no longer scope for wage reductions. This happened in 1927, when the industry's crisis was deepening. It therefore opened the way to a discussion of alternative devices for

---

[1] For the issue of surplus labour in 1921 and the views of the MFGB, see Prime Minister's brief, 8 Nov. 1921: POWE 16/508II; *Joint Sub-Committee, 1925*, 55. For later assumptions about excess manpower, see Sir Alfred Mond in Baldwin Papers, 13/181-5 (17 Apr. 1926) and 21/53-4 (30 Apr. 1926); Morgan 1926, 536-75; CG 6 Jan. 1928, 49; Secretary for Mines, 'The British Coal Mining Industry': POWE 16/180/15; CAB 30/21-39 (13 Feb. 1929). Minister of Labour (Sir Arthur Steel-Maitland): SRO GD 196/661 (22 June 1927). *Industrial Transference Board Report*: Cmd. 3156. 1928.

adapting the industry to new necessities. Until then, those primarily responsible for conducting the coalmining industry had largely confined themselves (at least in public) to emphasizing uncompetitive wages and hours as the 'causes' of the industry's problems.

This argument was naturally met with fierce resistance by the miners, who countered the suggestion that wages be reduced and hours increased with the assertion that the industry needed far-reaching reform: its costs were high not because its work-force was paid too much, but because its management was low grade, its investment needs neglected, and its structures inflexible and atomized.[1] The miners' view had dialectical and political overtones, and they were unspecific as to where managerial or organizational savings might lie. But even though their assertions lacked empirical detail, their views converged with those of many observers who concluded that the industry could be rendered viable only by extensive reorganization of production (to lower costs or eliminate marginal units) and/or of distribution (to limit competition and maintain prices).[2] Certainly, the economic adversity which had reduced output, profits, and wages, also imposed pressures on the structure of the industry. How far did it succeed in adapting itself to the new situation?

In spite of the fact that throughout the 1920s the owners offered implacable opposition to arguments in favour of any extensive programme of amalgamation,[3] there *was* a degree of structural adaptation to the new economic circumstances of the period. In the first instance, however, that adaptation was associated with prosperity rather than adversity.

During the War and its immediate aftermath, as we have seen, colliery undertakings had accumulated very large profits and reserves. And once the War was over, these were applied not simply to the development of new mines (as happened in Nottinghamshire) but also to the acquisition of existing capacity through merger or purchase. This was particularly marked in South Wales, where in 1920–1 the Powell Duffryn Steam Coal Co. purchased the Rhymney Iron Co., including its five pits and one million tons of annual capacity; Guest, Keen & Nettlefold acquired two colliery firms and a large selling agency (L. Gueret, Ltd.); and the Ebbw

---

[1] Below, ch. 6, sect. ii and iii.
[2] Ibid.
[3] In the late 1920s the owners did accept the need for experiment with marketing associations. For this and the widespread advocacy (by private interests, official inquiries, and Cabinet Ministers) of a policy of industrial concentration in coalmining in the 1920s, see below, ch. 6, sect. v.

Vale Steel, Iron & Coal Co. completed the absorption of four colliery undertakings with a combined capacity of 2.5 million tons annually. In Durham at about the same time Pease & Partners extended its operations through major acquisitions; and in South Yorkshire in 1919 a distinctive business realignment took place when four large companies (Brodsworth Main, Bullcroft Main, Hickleton Main, and Yorkshire Main), all controlled by the Staveley Coal & Iron Co., formed the Doncaster Collieries Association to undertake their marketing and the purchase of their supplies. The DCA was an impressive and effective example of coordination and economy, and was joined by another Staveley-dominated company, Markham Main, when the latter began production later in the 1920s.

Other important restructurings took place in 1923–4, presumably in response to the temporary boom of 1922–3. In 1923 Guest, Keen & Nettlefold purchased Consolidated Cambrian and D. Davis & Sons (together accounting for 5 million tons of output annually); and in the hitherto fragmented South Wales anthracite field, two mergers were effected: Amalgamated Anthracite Collieries, floated by Sir Alfred Mond, and United Anthracite Collieries. (Their joint output accounted for 25 per cent of South Wales anthracite production, and in 1926 they too were to merge.) In 1924 in Durham, Lambton & Hetton Collieries joined forces with James Joicey & Co. to create an undertaking controlling over 20 mines and about 4 million tons of coal annually.[1]

Developments such as these were based on large profits rather than shrinking markets. Presumably, however, as with the accumulation of real capital which resulted from prosperity (it was estimated that the industry invested £45 million in 1914–21, and a further £15 million on capital projects between April 1921 and 1925),[2] most of them must have strengthened the industry. But some were simply financial juggling, and altogether they fell short of the radical reorganization envisaged by many critics. This was partly because the mergers which did take place were, in the context of the vast extent of coalmining activity, relatively limited in scope; and partly because few of the 'mergers' amounted to the sort of coalescing of operations which could have produced a large increase in the economies of scale. In practice, amalgamations rarely led to a speedy concentration of production. In most instances the constituent companies retained their legal existence, and pursued economies

[1] Neuman 1934, 62 ff., 139 ff.; *Stock Exchange Year Book*, various years; Williams 1924; Fox 1935a; Hare 1940, 40–53.

[2] *Buckmaster Proceedings*, 136–7; *Samuel Report*, 122; *Joint Sub-Committee*, 1925 III, 705–6.

and profits through the coordination of various commercial and financial functions, and the planning of investment. Beneficial as such steps
might have been for the strong companies which took them, they were
unlikely to transform the cost structures of coalmining as a whole. And
in any case there were felt to be limits to the size of the undertaking that
a single management team might effectively control.[1]

In economic terms, then, the growth of large-scale production in its
conventional sense (the emergence of substantial and *unified* enterprises) registered only a modest increase, albeit a measurable one. Thus,
between 1913 and 1924, while the proportion of miners in pits employing 1,000 or more rose from 47 to 55 per cent, the proportion in colliery
firms with 5,000 or more workers increased from 26 to 33 per cent. On
the other hand, the number of companies in this category rose from 36
to 49, so that the trend hardly amounted to 'concentration' in the
normal sense of the word.[2]

In *business* terms, by way of contrast, the importance of large-scale
groupings which linked legally distinct entities, was more extensive,
although difficult to measure nationally. To take an example from the
coalfield underlying South Yorkshire, Nottinghamshire, and North
Derbyshire, in 1924 the Staveley Coal & Iron Co. appeared in the Mines
Department's *List of Mines* as operating five pits, worked by 6,617
miners. Yet it also exercised complete or near-dominating control of
seven other colliery firms, each of which was listed separately in the official statistics, and some of which were grouped for selling and purchasing purposes in the Doncaster Collieries Association. They employed
nearly 20,000 men. Moreover, Staveley had close links with other companies, including the Sheepbridge Coal & Iron Co., which employed
4,200 miners in its own pits, and in turn controlled three other companies employing over 5,500 men. Charles Markham, the leading

---

[1] See evidence of Charles Markham (Chairman and Managing Director of Staveley Coal &
Iron Co. and 4 other large colliery companies) to the Samuel Commission: *Samuel Evidence* QQ
11220 ff. In 1932 R. A. Burrows (Deputy Chairman of the newly formed Manchester Collieries)
argued that it needed a man of very rare ability to manage an undertaking which produced as
much as 5 million tons annually, and that above that level managerial efficiency would suffer. See
notes of conversation, HC and Burrows, 19 Apr. 1932 in SMT 6/7.

[2] Colliery firms employing 3,000 or more miners employed 46% of all the work-force in 1913
and 52% in 1924. There were more striking changes in some individual districts. Thus, considering
colliery undertakings employing over 5,000 men, between 1913 and 1924 those in South Wales
increased their share of the area's work-force from 40 to only 41%, whereas those in South Yorkshire, Nottinghamshire, and Derbyshire rose from 18 to 30% of the work-force, and those in the
North-East from 41 to 55%. In Scotland the share increased from 28 to 34%. Statistics calculated
from Mines Department, *List of Mines in Great Britain and the Isle of Man*, for 1913 and 1924.

businessman in the Staveley enterprise, told the Samuel Commission that the colliery undertakings with which he was associated produced 10 million tons—almost 4 per cent of the national output, and four times the output of the Staveley Company.

In fact, of course, the coalmining industry as a whole, as well as its collateral business in coke, by-products, iron and steel, was characterized by an extensive interlocking of interests and shareholdings, although much of this was constrained within business boundaries. In 1925, in a survey of 572 firms producing 200 million tons of coal, it was found that over half the 2,365 directors involved were also on the boards of other colliery companies, and that 320 were on the boards of undertakings in which the parent company had a controlling or substantial interest.[1]

The trends towards mergers and 'tighter' business relationships which had been based on intermittent prosperity in the years after 1917, were checked by the decisive collapse in the market for coal in 1924. Once the stoppage of 1926 was over, however, there was scope and pressure for further realignment in the new circumstances of relative stagnation. This was particularly so in so far as the stronger companies were well placed to join forces, strengthen their organization, and acquire businesses which now found it difficult to stand alone. In the late 1920s, therefore, business restructuring was the outcome of economic difficulties. And this took place at two levels. On the one hand, there was a spate of corporate amalgamations in 1926–30; on the other, in 1927–8 owners in virtually all the principal coal-producing districts agreed to join voluntary marketing schemes to limit competition.

Two important mergers in this period made use of the modest possibilities of legal encouragement embodied in the Mining Industry Act of 1926. First, Amalgamated Anthracite Collieries and United Anthracite Collieries were merged in 1926 (the new company retained the name Amalgamated Anthracite and controlled 20 pits and 40 per cent of the industry). Second, in 1927 a new firm, Yorkshire Amalgamated Collieries, united the interests of four of the county's leading colliery enterprises.[2]

---

[1] *Samuel Appendices*, 182 (Appendix 18). For a further discussion of the structure of the coal-mining industry, see below, ch. 9, sect. i.

[2] For the Mining Industry Act, see below, ch. 6, sect. iv. In 1928 Amalgamated Collieries acquired two other anthracite undertakings and controlled 75% of the industry. The Yorkshire merger encompassed Rossington Main, Dinnington Main, Maltby Main, and Denaby & Cadeby Main Collieries. The first three of these had been effectively controlled by the Sheepbridge Coal & Iron Co., which owned one-third of the shares of the new company.

Beyond these, Powell Duffryn bought up a series of bankrupt colliery enterprises (the Windsor Steam Co., the Lewis Merthyr Colliery Co., a large pit from the Taff Rhondda Navigation Steam Coal Co.) as well as some going concerns and a selling agency. By 1928 the combine owned 36 pits and employed 25,000 miners. Other spectacular mergers occurred elsewhere in South Wales and in South Yorkshire in 1926–8, and the amalgamations of those years (which involved 17 schemes, 172 pits, and 176,000 men) were heavily concentrated in those two districts. But in 1929–30 there were also two major mergers in hard-hit Lancashire: Manchester Collieries, which united 20 pits ('the more progressive colliery owners', it was subsequently claimed, sensed the disaster which would flow from 'unrestricted competition in a depressed market'), and the Wigan Coal Corporation, financed in part by the Bank of England's Securities Management Trust, which united the colliery interests of the Wigan Coal & Iron Co. and Pearson & Knowles Coal & Iron Co., and possessed an annual capacity of 3.3 million tons.[1]

The business effects of all this activity were augmented by the attainment of full production by the giant new mines of Nottinghamshire and the extension of mechanization in such leading Scottish firms as the Fife Coal Co. and William Bairds. But how far they changed the essential structure of British coalmining is debatable. Even though some 75 per cent of district output was controlled by seven undertakings in South Wales and by 20 in Scotland,[2] there was still only a relatively small degree of genuine massing and concentration of productive capacity. And the problems of fragmentation, excess capacity, and marginal firms remained to dog the industry. The obstacle to genuine 'rationalization'—the fact that it was rarely in any particular undertaking's private interest to spend money in buying up surplus productive capacity just to close it—remained.[3]

As far as business strategies *within* individual firms were concerned, whatever the entrepreneurial failings of the owners in the long run, it may be altogether unrealistic to look for any large amendment of economic performance in a period of only a few years. The technical transformation of an individual colliery needed integrated changes, detailed planning, and heavy investment over a long period. For it involved not

---

[1] For merger activity generally: *First Report by the Board of Trade under Section 12 on the Working of Part I of the Mining Industry Act*. Cmd. 3214. 1929 (*PP* VIII 1928–9). For Manchester Collieries: POWE 28/239/2.

[2] Kirby 1977, citing *The Economist* 22 Aug. 1931, 341.

[3] Below, ch. 8, sect. iii; ch. 9, sect. iii.

merely re-equipment but large alterations in layout and underground and surface facilities. Nor were the technical difficulties greatly eased by the mere fact of corporate acquisitions: the units of production involved were not always adjacent, and even when they were sufficiently near for unified control and operation to be envisaged, expensive and prolonged programmes, together with rare management skills, would have been needed for modernization. Thus, looking back on its enormous acquisitions after 1927, a representative of the Powell Duffryn company pointed out that

To convert a colliery from a losing to a profitable undertaking is generally an expensive and protracted business. In some cases underground roads and airways, and in fact the whole underground lay-out and method of mining may have to be replanned and reorganized. Thus, losses are likely to increase before they diminish.... This was certainly the case with the Windsor, Lewis Merthyr, Albion and Great Western properties, but the average pre-acquisition losses of over £285,000 per annum were in 1933 turned into a profit of nearly £160,000.

Tedious as the process of reorganization must have been for Powell Duffryn, it was exceptional in achieving it within five or six years. Mergers often generated their own handicaps—as in the case of Manchester Collieries, where 'the price of amalgamation was a Board of 22 Directors, of whom 14 were employed as full-time executives although some of them did not possess the specialised knowledge necessary to exercise a suitable executive function in the new Company'. In such circumstances, it was not until 1937, seven years after its formation, and when trade conditions had begun to improve, that the company could begin 'the major work of colliery re-organisation'.[1]

There were, then, limits to the reform of British coalmining in the 1920s. This is not to say that technical change ceased: in the ten years after 1923 between £10 and £20 million was invested in equipment to wash and grade coal for marketing; and in the 1920s the amount of electricity used in mines rose by two-thirds, the number of face conveyors trebled, and the proportion of coal cut mechanically increased from 14 to 28 per cent. Yet in the Ruhr, where only 2 per cent had been cut mechanically in 1913, the proportion rose to 66 per cent in 1926 and

[1] For Powell Duffryn, see POWE 28/239/5. For Manchester Collieries, see POWE 35/247/3. Sir Robert Burrows (of Manchester Collieries) pointed out that other benefits of the merger could be attained in the interim. These included the reallocation of coal areas between mines, improving selling arrangements and coal preparation, the centralization of workshops and power distribution, and the standardization of equipment and stores.

91 per cent in 1929.[1] The relative slowness of organizational change as well as capital investment was presumably responsible for the fact that British labour productivity lagged behind its continental rivals'. If we take the crucial measure of output per manshift of underground workers, the British performance in 1922–9 was fairly respectable (a growth of 20 per cent). But this was largely accounted for by the 14 per cent increase in the legal duration of the underground shift in 1926. A comparison of 1913 and 1929 (when hours worked were broadly similar) suggests that average productivity growth was very modest—6.6 per cent over 16 years.[2]

Business policy towards production was, therefore, slow to change in the industry as a whole. For most of the 1920s the same was true of attitudes to marketing. But in the later years of the decade there was an abrupt and important change in this respect. For some time the coalowners had been unavailingly urged to cooperate in order to mitigate competition, to use marketing agreements to restrict and apportion output to satisfy a diminished demand while avoiding desperate price competition. More elaborate versions of such schemes also involved the use of levies (on colliery companies which remained in production), the proceeds of which could be used to compensate those companies which had to sell less coal or to deal in more competitive markets.

It so happened that in 1919 the Mining Association of Great Britain had itself advocated a single national corporation to market the entire output of coal in order to avoid the burden of 'unfettered competition'.[3] But this was quickly abandoned in the face of the political turmoil which led up to the Sankey Inquiry, and the generality of owners returned to the reliance on individualism and free competition, and to the suspicious aversion to cooperation, which had long characterized

[1] Neuman 1934, 27; *ARSM* 1921, 129 and *ARSM* 1929, 145; Political & Economic Planning 1936, 154. The incidence of mechanization in Britain in the 1920s was very unequal. By 1929 some two-thirds of Scottish and 55% of Northumberland's output was mechanically cut, as against 9% in South Wales and 13% in South Yorkshire. The percentage in most important districts grew at a rate similar to the average. The exceptions were Northumberland (where the proportion mechanically cut rose from 20 to 55%) and Warwickshire & Leicestershire (from 6 to 40%).

[2] Figures for output per manshift underground in 1913 are in *Joint Sub-Committee, 1925*, Appendix, 36; for 1922 and 1929 in *Buckmaster Report*, 13. On the basis of 1913–29 Northumberland, South Wales, and Lancashire did particularly well (12.5%, 16.1%, and 13.3% respectively). No doubt the Depression helps explain part of the improvement since it must have squeezed out less efficient firms (South Wales and Lancashire both lost 25% of their output over this period).

[3] *A Suggested Scheme for the Reconstruction of the Coal Mining Industry* (15 Feb. 1919): SRO CB6/2 MAGB. Schemes to control sales by national or regional cartels had been propounded in the late nineteenth century. See Neuman 1934, 16 n.

their business attitudes. Hence, in the crisis of 1925–6, when they were pressed to control competition and limit production by forming selling organizations, their representatives firmly rejected the idea—even as it applied to export markets—on the grounds that it would diminish competitiveness and sales.

As long as the owners saw some prospect of cost reductions by lowering wages or increasing the length of the working day, the official response of their national and district associations to the possibility of market cooperation was to resist argument and ignore adverse publicity. And it was this posture which, in the words of the Permanent Secretary to the Mines Department, 'almost makes one despair', and which for Keynes was 'one of several indications that we are dealing with a decadent, third-generation industry'.[1] Yet even the most obstinate coal-owners could not deny the emerging reality: the wage cuts and increased hours which were the fruits of their victory in 1926 did not transform the industry's competitive situation. Indeed, even during the disputes of that year, colliery owners in the Midlands toyed with the idea of forming a marketing association. And although the proposed inter-county scheme did not materialize, the West Yorkshire owners, spurred by W. A. Archer (Managing Director of the South Kirby, Featherstone, and Hemsworth Collieries), pursued the idea and in the spring of 1927 formed the West Yorkshire Collieries Sales Organization, which was primarily concerned to secure agreement to establish a minimum price for coal.[2]

By 1927 the economic lessons were being driven home with great force. British coal still faced a disastrously low and dislocated level of demand, the various districts could no longer advocate further reductions in wage costs, and they therefore had to consider alternative strategies. This was exemplified in Scotland and South Wales, where earlier opposition to selling schemes had been strongest. There, such stalwarts of the 1926 assault on wages and hours as Sir Adam Nimmo and Wallace Thorneycroft, in Scotland, and Sir Evan Williams (President of the MAGB), in South Wales, had to acknowledge that, while wage levels could not be depressed any further, the coal trade was in a 'deplorable state', different in kind from anything known hitherto. The owners discussed the possibility of some relief from local rates, social

---

[1] Sir Ernest Gowers to Chancellor of the Exchequer, 17 June 1927: Baldwin Papers, 17/15; *JMK* XIX, Pt. 2, 528 (24 Apr. 1924).

[2] LCOA 19D 55/2 (11 June and 15 Sept. 1926); WYCOA, 22 June 1926. For the West Yorkshire scheme: WYCOA, 15 Nov. and 2 Dec. 1927.

security charges, and railway freight rates. But the most dramatic outcome of the dilemma in the two leading export fields was the formation of schemes to limit competition. As Thorneycroft put it, they were plans to 'convert part of our trade into a Sheltered Industry'.[1]

The Scottish Coal Marketing Scheme began on 6 March 1928. It was followed in April by the South Wales Coal Marketing Association (which had been formed in November 1927 with the objective of 'steadying the market and stabilising prices'), and by the Central Collieries Commercial Association, which united the great central coalfields in the Midlands, Yorkshire, Lancashire, and Cheshire.[2]

The various district schemes differed from each other in important respects. Thus, the South Wales Association, which was supported by owners of about 80 per cent of the district's capacity, was initially concerned with the setting of minimum prices for different grades of coal and with applying a levy on output to compensate those firms which lost trade because of their use of minimum prices. But the plan was still vulnerable to excess output, as well as to competition from non-members. As a result, there was a policy review in January 1929, which resulted in a proposal for production quotas. This, however, did not secure sufficient support and the scheme limped along (with minimum prices applied only to steam coal) until the introduction of statutory marketing arrangements in 1930.

In Scotland, where owners of about 90 per cent of the productive capacity originally supported the plan, prices were raised, a levy was imposed on pits producing for the inland market, and subsidies were paid to marginal firms to restrict output (this was what Thorneycroft had meant by treating part of the field as a sheltered industry). It was thought that the scheme served to 'stiffen' the market during the worst of the depression,[3] but it had clear weaknesses. There was no way to

[1] SCOA, 9 May and 9 July 1927; MSWCOA, 21 June 1926, 19 Aug., and Nov. 1927. Rate relief and an accompanying reduction in freight rates were actually achieved. Although the average savings were not very large (some 3*d.* per ton on the total output) the effect on export coal (7*d.* per ton) and on coal destined for the iron and steel industry (10*d.* per ton) was significant. *ARSM* 1928, 6 and *ARSM* 1929, 5; below, 263–4

[2] The various schemes are described in Neuman 1934, 158–69; Kirby 1977, 115–23; *ARSM* 1928, 3–5 and *ARSM* 1929, 3–4; Memorandum from Secretary for Mines, 12 June 1928: POWE 16/180. Lancashire entered the Midlands scheme belatedly, its coal trade being described by a leading owner (Arthur Colegate) as 'wholly disorganised and . . . therefore a great weakness to us all'. Colegate urged the Governor of the Bank of England to use his good offices to ensure that Lancashire owners acted collectively. He also wanted the banks to advise their colliery debtors 'to temper their individualism with common sense'. See SMT 2/272, correspondence between Colegate and Norman, 3 Nov., 5, 8, 9, and 10 Dec. 1927.

[3] Neuman 1934, 167.

ensure a permanent reduction in capacity, the cost of keeping marginal pits closed was high, and the inland pits resented the costs and anomalies of the differential 'tax' on their activities. As a result, and as inland pits, especially in Lanarkshire, opposed further support of exporters, it proved impossible to renew or amend the scheme and it lapsed in March 1929.

The Central Collieries (or 'Five Counties') scheme, an 'enormous cartel' whose members controlled about 90 per cent of the region's 100 million tons of output, proved a somewhat more durable association (although even it effectively ceased operations early in 1930). Given its greater geographic scope, it was obviously an improvement on the tenuous experiment of the West Yorkshire owners in 1927.

The CCCA scheme involved a levy on all producers, from which a subsidy on exports was paid, and a set of quotas designed to limit total production. But it lacked any element of price control. In addition, the 'basic tonnages' used to establish the proportionate allocation of quotas between collieries, being designated by individual collieries by reference to their best output of the previous fifteen years, were too generous for comfort and greatly handicapped new or developing pits. The rules therefore threatened either over-production or, more commonly, excessively low individual quotas (in order to reduce total output), which in turn meant an increase in average costs for large and potentially efficient mines operating well below capacity.[1]

Between them, the three principal marketing associations encompassed firms producing over 75 per cent of the country's coal. Even in Northumberland and Durham, which had been traditionally the most reluctant to interfere with competition in exports (a reluctance which extended to the local MFGB leaders), the owners agreed to oversee prices and regulate competition between the two counties. Indeed, it was from the North-East, in mid-1928, that there came pressure for the MAGB to devise a scheme to coordinate and centralize marketing policy on a national basis, in order to eliminate the greatest weakness of the district agreements. At a meeting in July 1928 (blessed by the Secretary for Mines) 50 representatives from all districts agreed that 'co-operation was absolutely necessary and that price-cutting should cease'. A national committee was formed to examine the possibility of an inter-district marketing agreement, and by late 1928 there was some optimism that a workable plan might be accepted. Yet, when it came to the point, there was insufficient enthusiasm for the plan actually

[1] *The Times* 25 March 1929, 20d; Neuman 1934, 169 ff.

proposed (in March 1929) and the national initiative for voluntary action foundered.[1]

Yet the weakness of the schemes of 1927–8 is perhaps less important than the fact that they were floated at all. Given the traditional, entrenched attitudes of the owners, they reflected a remarkable transformation of business policy—an indication, no doubt, of the dimensions of the crisis which faced the industry, but also an attempt at structural reform of potentially far-reaching significance.

Such voluntary arrangements for coordinated marketing were obviously vulnerable to competition from non-members, unable to restrict output, and at the mercy of inter-district trade. Indeed, the official opinion was that the various district schemes were inherently 'antagonistic' to each other and collectively 'doomed to failure'.[2] Doomed or not, however, the marketing innovations of the late 1920s, like the less extensive colliery amalgamations of the same period (the one designed to avoid, and the other to ensure, changes in the structure of production) were both important examples of adaptive responses to the strains of an unprecedented depression. In the event, both types of structural adjustment were frustrated by the limitations of a collective action which could not be universal, because it was voluntary.

The voluntary principle was obviously inadequate for industry-wide control. In production, the economics of the coalmining industry in depression precluded any far-reaching rationalization by private initiative.[3] In marketing, neither the desperation of the weak nor the ambitions of the strong could be sufficiently curbed to prevent destabilization: it would always pay some firms to undercut marketing associations. Hence the ultimate failure of the adjustments of 1927–9.

Meanwhile, the economic climate threatened all those involved. It was not, therefore, surprising that in the last months of the Conservative Administration of 1924–9 some of its senior members should have contemplated drastic measures of state intervention to introduce a measure of rationalization, reduce capacity, and enforce marketing

[1] DCOA 43 (13 Feb. 1928); CAB 24/194/204 ff. (21 Apr. 1928); POWE 16/180/4 (12 June 1928); Neuman 1934, 167. For the discussions of a possible national scheme see John Craig to Lord Kylsant, 27 July 1928 (File 'Lord Kylsant, 1928 to 1929', in British Steel Corporation, Scottish Regional Records Office, Glasgow. I am indebted to Dr Clemens Wurm for this reference); POWE 16/180 ('Committee on Inter-District Co-operation', July 1928, and 'HWC' to Faulkner, 16 Nov. 1928); Kirby 1977, 119.

[2] 'Trade Outlook', Mar. 1928 and 19 June 1928: CAB 24/193/152–91 and CAB 24/194/204–32; Secretary for Mines to President of the Board of Trade, 12 June 1928: POWE 16/180.

[3] Below, ch. 8, sect. iii; ch. 9, sect. iii.

schemes in the coal industry—nor that even the feeble minority Labour Government which followed at last grasped the nettle of enforced control. By the late 1920s the manifest deficiencies of private action had begun to present the arguments for collective intervention in a new light.[1]

[1] Below, ch. 6, sect. v.

CHAPTER 6

Responses to Stagnation, 1921–1929

After the coal industry's high drama of 1919–21, the economic strains and political controversies which followed ensured that the institutional history of coal in the 1920s was anything but tranquil. Rather, the transition aroused fierce passions and an intense concentration of public and political attention. It ultimately demonstrated that a solution for the industry's long-term problems could not be found in either the market-based system of 1913 or in any derivative of the hybrid state intervention of 1917–21.

The story is complicated because of the variety of levels at which it unfolded. The first section of this chapter will deal with the fluctuations in earnings which accompanied the instability after decontrol in 1921, and with the consequent renegotiations of the Wages Agreement in 1924 and the beginning of a broadening of the discussion of the industry's performance. From 1924, however, it became clear that the industry was embedded in a prolonged crisis, and the second section will consider the resulting deterioration of industrial relations, the more elaborate discussion of possible remedies, and the renewed intervention of government (both directly and with yet another Royal Commission) in 1925–6. The critical Samuel Inquiry and the subsequent stoppage of 1926—an indication of the impossibility of any agreement on basic interpretations—will be discussed in the third and fourth sections. Finally, given the failure of the defeat of the miners to transform the industry, the fifth section will consider the new situation of the industry in the late 1920s.

i. Towards a precipice, 1921–1925

The sudden disengagement of the state from financial control of the coal industry in the spring of 1921 seemed to many observers a brutal step. And the settlement that the miners were forced to accept, together with the government's expression of helplessness in the face of pit closures and mass unemployment,[1] must have confirmed the despair of a

[1] Above, ch. 4, sect. viii.

demoralized work-force. Yet the more profound brutality lay in the collapse of overseas markets; and the threatening losses of the industry were such as to make any sustained official intervention inconceivably costly—at least in the political and ideological context of 1921–2. On the other hand, there was by no means a complete reversion to *laissez-faire*: the National Wages Agreement of July 1921 provided universal guidelines for district settlements, for the division of proceeds between wages and profits, and for the levels of minimum and subsistence wages. It also established a National Board for the Coal Industry, within which general issues of principle (such as accounting conventions) could be negotiated and, if necessary, referred to an independent Chairman.[1] Further, the Mining Industry Act of 1920 provided for some amelioration of the social conditions in mining communities through its creation of a Miners' Welfare Fund, financed by a tonnage levy on royalty owners.[2]

Nevertheless, the postwar expectations of the MFGB had been sorely frustrated and the gains of 1917–20 largely destroyed. By the late summer of 1922 wage levels had been forced down to the minima provided for in the 1921 agreement. In the North-East and in Lancashire and Cheshire average shift earnings even fell below 9s. As a result, by the winter of 1922–3, the MFGB presented a helpless appearance as it appealed to the government to protect the miners' earnings. Through no fault of their own, they complained, their average real earnings per shift had fallen by more than 25 per cent since 1914; and after a year of accepting lower wages (representing, in some instances, a cut of 50 per cent) many miners were below the poverty line. They simply wanted a 'living wage', and the country had a duty to alleviate their 'unjust agony', since the owners were 'helpless', or, rather, 'have developed resistance to change to a very fine art'.

These were themes which the miners were to refine through the desperate controversies of 1924–6: wages should be set (or protected) by social and 'civilized' criteria and take precedence over profits; the industry's capacity to pay decent wages depended on managerial efficiency; and structural changes, in their turn, might depend on government action, could be helped by a move to joint control, and would certainly be stimulated by a higher level of earnings (and neglected if wage reductions were allowed to stand). In general, if coal was an

[1] *Proceedings of the National Board for the Coal Industry* (3 volumes, 1921–3; copy in British Coal Library).
[2] Below, ch. 10, sect. v.

important industry, the country at large must somehow ensure that it paid adequate wages. In the winter of 1922–3, however, the MFGB met only an expression of sympathetic helplessness on the part of Bonar Law (who had replaced Lloyd George as Prime Minister in October 1922). By February 1923, with the Prime Minister counselling patience on the grounds that the trade upturn would soon be automatically reflected in higher wages, Herbert Smith struck a lugubrious note: 'We have nothing to expect from each other. We have to save ourselves now.'[1]

For once, the promise of better times was justified—if only temporarily and after a painful delay. Largely owing to the French occupation of the Ruhr in January 1923, the market for British coal began to improve. And as the industry's proceeds rose, so wage levels drifted upwards. Even so, this happened very slowly since the MFGB had earlier insisted that the periodic 'ascertainments' of the industry's business results, which determined wages, should be based on two months' experience and be applied after a lapse of a further two months—thus introducing a delay of four months between a change in profitability and a change in wages. (The arrangement was based on the miners' profound suspicion of accounting procedures, their desire to have complete information before accepting an outcome, and, no doubt, their feeling that they would thus delay any *reduction* in wages.)[2] The national average for shift earnings rose from its low point of 9s. 4d. in July–September 1922 to 10s. 7¼d. a year later, before sagging slightly, as labour productivity and net proceeds fell back.

The modest increase in average shift earnings was not sufficient to calm the miners' anxieties about the level and variability of wages. In the first four months of 1924 average shift earnings in South Wales, Lancashire, Cheshire, and North Staffordshire were still at the minimum level;[3] and throughout the country the lower-paid day-wage employees were in a particularly pinched position. In November 1923 the MFGB took advantage of trade recovery to request changes in the Agreement. When these were refused, the union gave the necessary three months notice (on 17 January 1924) of its termination. Their new claim had three main elements: a reduction in the ratio of 'standard' profits to 'standard'

---

[1] CAB 23/31/62/351–3 (10 Oct. 1922); CAB 24/140/246–83 (2 Dec. 1922); CAB 24/159/264–97 (27 Feb. 1922).

[2] On the other hand, there was nothing to prevent their accepting *interim* ascertainments, and their obstinate failure to do so greatly puzzled the chairman of a wages inquiry in 1924: 'There are some things which pass human comprehension, and this is one.' (*Buckmaster Proceedings*, 150–1.)

[3] *Buckmaster Report*, 11.

wages (from 17:100 to 13:100); an increase in the share of wages in any 'surplus' proceeds (from 83 to 88.5 per cent); and an increase in the percentage addition to standard wages to provide for district minima (from 20 to 40 per cent).

The miners' bargaining position was obviously strengthened by the industry's temporary prosperity. In addition they could look for support to the first Labour Government (formed in January 1924), ready to lend such weight to the MFGB's claim as its minority position allowed. In the background, too, there was not merely a good deal of public sympathy, but the threat of minimum-wage legislation. In later years, the owners complained that political pressure had forced them to concede an unrealistically high settlement in 1924,[1] and both the Secretary for Mines (Emanuel Shinwell) and the Prime Minister (Ramsay MacDonald) played active roles in the negotiations. Yet the owners seem to have adopted a generally conciliatory attitude throughout the early months of 1924, and their counter-offer included substantial concessions (although this itself might have been the outcome of a sense of political necessity). Indeed, the owners' offer was only narrowly rejected by the miners in a national ballot early in April. When a Court of Inquiry was appointed on 15 April, it was able to conclude that a resumption of negotiations offered an 'immediate and practicable means' of arriving at a new wages agreement.[2]

Although its recommendation led to a settlement, the hearings of the Buckmaster Court were somewhat confused. The Inquiry's hoped-for clarification was clouded not merely by the almost hysterical perplexity which was the customary accompaniment of any attempt to explain the industry's wage system to laymen,[3] but by disagreement between the two sides as to what the grounds of their controversy were. Ostensibly, the Court had assembled to consider some specific percentage claims. But the MFGB could not resist presenting its larger case: the miners were 'always in the trenches' and were entitled to a 'respectable wage'. This meant, they now argued, a level of earnings equivalent to 1914 plus an allowance for the increased cost of living *plus* the sort of allowance awarded by Sankey in 1919 to reflect a necessary improvement in living standards.[4] In the words of A. J. Cook, 'the industry must adapt itself to the needs of procuring a living wage for the men engaged in it' and that

---

[1] CAB 24/180/57 (21 May 1926); Memorandum by Evan Williams in MSWCOA Box 1002.
[2] *Buckmaster Report*, 14. The Buckmaster Inquiry reported in early May 1924.
[3] Above, 38.
[4] *Buckmaster Proceedings*, 9, 31, 88, 279; *Buckmaster Report*, 10, 13–14.

meant unification of enterprises, reorganization, and improved management. Better wages would *oblige* owners to reform their businesses. Moreover, if, after all this, the industry could still not pay adequate wages then there should be some form of social subsidy in recognition of the industry's importance to the economy as a whole.[1]

The MFGB representatives also took the opportunity of rehearsing their growing grievances at the accounting conventions of the Wages Agreement: they feared that investment was debited to current costs and therefore reduced proceeds and wages, they suspected that 'transfer prices' (where coal was supplied to another department within a composite enterprise) were kept too low, and they wished to incorporate the profits of associated businesses (wagon hire, coke ovens, by-products) in the ascertainments.[2]

In many respects, then, the Buckmaster hearings were a rehearsal for the more elaborate arguments which the miners were to raise as they resisted attempts to reduce wage levels and increase hours in 1925 and 1926. Equally, the owners began to assemble their own case concerning the primacy of labour costs in the industry's troubles, the problems consequent on the reduction of hours in 1919, the severe limitations on any large-scale reorganization as a means of enhancing competitiveness, and the impossibility of accepting the level of wages in 1914 as an overriding criterion for postwar earnings.

In any event, a week after the Report's publication, negotiations between the two sides had produced a provisional agreement (15 May 1924), which was ultimately confirmed on 18 June. It supported wages at the three points originally claimed: the share of standard profits was reduced from 17 to 15 per cent of standard wages; wages' share in net proceeds rose from 83 to 88 per cent; and the district percentage additions for minimum wages was increased from 20 to 33 per cent. Since the most distinct improvement related to minimum wages, while wage levels above the minimum were still largely determined by the industry's performance, the application of the new Agreement had its greatest effect in the districts at or near the minima under the previous Agreement. Hence, while wages in the Eastern Federated Districts (mostly the Midlands and Yorkshire), Scotland, Northumberland, and Durham, being significantly above the minimum in early 1924, benefited only by

---

[1] *Buckmaster Proceedings*, 250–2, 256; *Buckmaster Report*, 13–14.

[2] *Buckmaster Proceedings*, 257, 280. Herbert Smith claimed that when the miners were 'down and out' after the 1921 stoppage, the government and the owners 'filched away from this industry everything that was a paying proposition'.

2 or 3 per cent, those in South Wales, Lancashire, Cheshire, and North Staffordshire rose appreciably—by about 10 or 11 per cent.[1]

In its short life, the Labour Government of 1924 also tried to reform other aspects of the industry. For example, it considered the nationalization of mining royalties, as well as legislation to make the provision of pithead baths compulsory and to permit municipal retail trading in coal.[2] However, all the discussions were rendered abortive—principally by the government's political weakness (it was finally defeated in October 1924). Moreover, even the results of its support for the National Wages Agreement of 1924 were limited in effect and duration. For the Agreement was signed just as the market for coal once again began to crumble: from the spring of 1924 rising foreign competition and falling prices and profits (the latter the further squeezed by the new Agreement) imposed intense, and ultimately irresistible, pressure on labour costs in the industry.[3]

In the last eight months of 1924 in the Eastern District, irregularity of work almost wiped out a modest increase in wages over the first four months; Scottish earnings fell as the district went on to minimum rates from August and experienced more unemployment; there was a similar decline in earnings in the North-East; and in South Wales and the North-West the new minimum rates (admittedly higher than those of 1921–3) operated throughout the year, and living standards were eroded by unemployment. More than this, with wages already under pressure, profits were fast disappearing. In March 1925 the Board of Trade's advisory committee received an ominous and no doubt carefully phrased warning from Sir Adam Nimmo, the leading Lanarkshire coalowner and one of the principal protagonists in the industrial-relations clash of 1925–6: the industry must 'come down to French and Belgian wages' and 'German workers ... seemed ... disposed to accommodate themselves for the time being to prevailing conditions'.[4]

[1] ARSM 1924, 9–12.

[2] CAB 24/166/724–36 (7 May 1924); CAB 24/167/468–72) 9 July 1924); CAB 24/168/37–40 (23 July 1924); CAB 24/168/317–406 (3 Oct. 1924). The Secretary for Mines Emanuel Shinwell also brought pressure to bear on coal merchants and cooperative societies, in order to try to reduce distributive costs: Mines Department. Retail Prices and Qualities of Household Coal. Correspondence between the Mines Department and the Coal Merchants' Federation of Great Britain, together with the Report of a Conference between the Secretary for Mines and the Federation (Cmd. 2117. 1924); Mines Department Retail Prices and Qualities of Household Coal. Report of a Conference between the Secretary for Mines and Representatives of the Co-operative Societies (Cmd. 2185. 1924).

[3] Above, 172–9.

[4] CAB 24/172/239 (12 Mar. 1925).

ii. On the brink, 1925–1926

The industrial history of 1925 and 1926 is more than usually tangled. Yet throughout the bitter skein of events and arguments which surrounded the negotiations and inquiries of 1925–6 and the seven-month stoppage which followed, and which finally destroyed the miners' will, there ran a single thread: the proposal to meet the collapse of markets by a direct reduction in labour costs. To the owners' unswerving belief that lower wages and/or longer hours were the only way forward, was opposed the fierce resistance of the miners, determined to eschew the slightest concession on these points, and counter-attacking on the issue of the industry's efficiency and organization. Two larger themes were also involved: a prolonged and unresolved debate about the economics of the coal industry, its structure, size, and efficiency; and a contest of wills and power within the industry which was ultimately, if not inevitably, 'won' by the group and viewpoint which had initiated it, and 'lost' by the group which (against the urgings of its friends, as well as its opponents) refused to offer any concessions on its initial stand.

The proximate economic origins of the struggle lay in the market deterioration of the last months of 1924. By November, the owners concluded that the situation was becoming untenable; and the MAGB invited the MFGB to join a small committee to examine the parlous state of the industry. Although reluctant, the union was in no position to refuse, since the existing Wages Agreement would be open to termination on one month's notice from 30 June 1925. On 18 March 1925, therefore, the Joint Sub-Committee met. It consisted of ten representatives from each side.[1] And its first meeting took place just as the economic storm which was to turn the industry's troubles into tragedy began to gather force.

Meeting in private, the owners and miners were no less unyielding, bruisingly frank, and mutually critical than when they succumbed to the temptations of propaganda and the spur of public combat. For 13 meetings between mid-March and mid-June 1925 the two sides pursued a tedious, circuitously argumentative, and occasionally intemperate 'discussion'. Nor was the gladiatorial nature of the meetings tempered by

---

[1] The proceedings of the Committee (hereafter referred to as *Joint Sub-Committee, 1925*) were transcribed and reproduced (copy in British Coal Library): The Mining Association of Great Britain. The Miners' Federation of Great Britain. *Minutes of Proceedings of a Joint Sub-Committee appointed to investigate the Economic Position of the Coal Industry* (3 volumes. 18 Mar. to 23 June 1925).

the fact that the two Presidents—Evan Williams and Herbert Smith—were such dominating personalities. (The MFGB presentation was virtually deflated when Smith was away ill; and Williams, while clearly respecting Smith, was easily capable of seeing off most other miners, including the quicksilver A. J. Cook.)

The Joint Committee's deliberations were distorted from the start because in the coal industry the distinctions between 'facts' and 'causes' and 'prescriptions' were unclear. The miners, of course, agreed that the situation of the industry was disastrous. If it continued, Herbert Smith said, 'we shall watch the boat go down, safe as houses'.[1] Nevertheless, they challenged the very structure of the MAGB's presentation. In part, this was a spoiling tactic, which owed something to a dislike of the consequences of an 'objective' analysis of the industry's economic problems. But it also owed something to the miners' sense of a certain disingenuousness on the part of the owners. For the latter were in very little doubt about what was wrong with the industry: its labour costs were too high and had to be reduced by lower wages and, ideally, longer hours, which would mitigate the need for wage reductions. To accept their premiss, therefore, would be to make it very difficult to avoid their conclusion.

From the outset the miners wished to establish the impossibility of wage reductions or alterations in hours. Indeed, they urged that even in the current situation, better wages could be paid, since the accounting conventions under which earnings were determined by the Wages Agreement were unfair—artificially reducing proceeds and siphoning off the real profits of coalmining.[2] In any case, the MFGB argued that proposals to cut wages or increase hours amounted to nothing more than a 'fetish', with no relevance to the basic problems of the industry. Wages and hours were 'untouchable'. In Smith's pugnacious words, 'We are not going back to where you want us.' The owners' proposal (and, *ipso facto*, their agenda) was both irrelevant and unacceptable.[3]

The MFGB did, of course, have some comments on the current commercial problems of the coal industry (they blamed low exports on reparations and what they took to be a politically biased refusal to trade with the Soviet Union, although on both issues they could not sustain an argument against the better informed owners).[4] But in the main their

---

[1] *Joint Sub-Committee, 1925*, 156.
[2] Below, 234–5.
[3] *Joint Sub-Committee, 1925*, 396, 752, 761, 936.
[4] For reparations, see above, 191.

positive contributions augmented their earlier campaigns for improvements in their earnings: the industry's problems, and its apparent inability to pay decent wages, were attributable to poor management, deficient organization, and costly distribution. It was necessary to reduce costs by 'an elaborate and ruthless reorganization of your [*i.e. the owners'*] side of the industry'. And to help bring *that* about, the MFGB urged (it was, in fact their only *concrete* proposal), a form of 'co-partnership' was needed: Part II of the 1920 Mining Industry Act, providing for joint consultative machinery, should be activated 'to get our brains into the movement'.[1] In any case, they argued, their earnings should be sustained on social grounds, irrespective of the economics of the industry. '[I]t is the country's duty', Smith asserted, 'to keep the backbone of the country in a fit condition to do its work'.[2]

In fact, at no point during the three months of discussion was there any indication of a possible accommodation between the two sides. After their last meeting the initiative lay with the owners. Giving advance warning of their intention to terminate the 1924 Wages Agreement, they appealed to the miners to join in a petition to revoke the Seven Hours Act.[3] On 30 July the MAGB gave formal notice and on the next day published proposals for new wage levels which went beyond the miners' worst expectations. Earnings were to be determined on a district basis as heretofore, but (with the exception of the relatively prosperous Eastern Federated District) there were to be no minimum percentage additions to basis rates. Wages would no longer have overriding priority over profits. Instead, non-wage costs would be deducted from proceeds, and 87 per cent of the balance apportioned to wages (each district determining subsistence wages for low-paid day-wage men, which would have first call on this 87 per cent). In effect, the proposals were for an element of profit (averaging 13 per cent of the balance beyond non-wage costs) to be guaranteed, while apparently there was to be no floor to wages. (This feature was subsequently judged by an official inquiry to be 'unacceptable'.)[4]

The MFGB rejected not only the proposals but also the idea of any

[1] *Joint Sub-Committee, 1925*, 303, 781.

[2] *Joint Sub-Committee, 1925*, 759 ff., 781 ff., 931. Although miners' earnings had fallen considerably since the winter of 1920-1, they were (in 1924-5) still higher than those in other export industries when compared with their prewar level.

[3] *CG* 26 June 1925, 1573. The *Colliery Guardian* expressed uneasiness at the situation created by this approach.

[4] *Industrial Courts Act 1919. Report by a Court of Inquiry Concerning the Coal Mining Industry Dispute, 1925* (Cmd. 2478. 1925), 18. The owner's proposals are in Appendix III.

further discussions with the owners until they had been withdrawn. At the same time, it extended and strengthened its trade-union support, forming in effect a Quadruple Alliance with the railwaymen, the transport workers, and seamen. As the elements of a new and drastic industrial crisis took threatening shape early in July 1925 government Ministers (notably W. C. Bridgemen, formerly Secretary for Mines and now First Lord of the Admiralty, Arthur Steel-Maitland, Minister of Labour, and George Lane-Fox, Secretary for Mines) joined the discussions, which did little more than circumnavigate the same irreconcilable issues. On 13 July, in some desperation, the government announced the setting-up of yet another Court of Inquiry under H. P. Macmillan, KC.

The Macmillan Court (which was boycotted by the MFGB on the grounds that the proceedings were 'designed to justify the present attack upon the mineworkers' standard of living') began its hearings on 20 July and reported within a week. As with so many other outside commentators the report emphasized that the dispute was only superficially about wages: 'The origin of the trouble is much more deep-seated and is to be found in the deplorable condition of the industry itself.' This was exemplified in the commercial disintegration which had led to the closure of 508 pits, employing over 110,000 men, in the previous twelve months, and which had intensified to a point at which 60 per cent of the coal raised in May 1925 was produced at a loss.

The Court accepted the owners' argument that a return to an eight-hour day would substantially increase output, but was doubtful if this could be disposed in a 'depressed and disturbed market' while simultaneously raising earnings and profits.[1] It went on to criticize the owners' proposals for wage reductions, and to emphasize the need for a minimum wage and drew attention to the apparent clash between 'the economic wage which the coal industry can afford to pay, and the social wage which the worker can be asked to accept'. The Report also raised more general issues of principle about the autonomy of market forces, although it was beyond the Court's power to resolve them. Nor was its main conclusion as reassuring as it was well-meaning: the industry's crisis 'is due to causes not within the control of either party . . . [and] . . . which may continue to operate for some considerable time to come' and

---

[1] This aspect of the owners' case (their assumption that an increase in the working day would bring about a saving in labour costs, which would increase average proceeds *and* sales) was also severely questioned by the Samuel Commission (below, 233). On the other hand, their historical observation was clearly valid; the decrease in hours of 1919, accompanied by a commensurate raising of piece rates and no alteration in day rates, had significantly increased labour costs.

that, being a 'common calamity', it should be met by the antagonists 'taking common counsel together'.[1]

The Macmillan Report's combination of well-meaning vagueness and its sympathy for the miners had, if anything, brought a breakdown in negotiation nearer, since it probably stiffened the MFGB's determination to make no concession, while enraging the owners.[2] And behind the threat of industrial conflict unprecedented in scope and duration, lay an impending economic disaster. The Prime Minister was thereupon brought into two hectic days of negotiation (29–30 July 1925), having rashly given the Cabinet a promise that 'there will be no question of any subsidy'.[3] As a result, the owners were prevailed upon to accept the principle of a minimum wage.[4] But the miners stoutly maintained their complete opposition to any amendment of wages or hours, and their case was now officially supported by the TUC's General Council, which, fearing a more general attempt to reduce wages, issued orders for a national union agreement to prevent the movement of coal.

The crisis now assumed a threatening political as well as industrial dimension, and it was a measure of the seriousness of the situation that the government beat an ignominious retreat. After firm denials that financial help was feasible, it drew back from the brink of a general strike at the last moment by offering a nine-month subsidy to bridge the gap between the wage rates of July and the lower rates (implied in the owners' later offer) needed to ensure a profit of 1s. 6d. per ton.[5] The breathing-space thus created was to be filled by a full-scale inquiry into the industry.

[1] In an addendum, one of the three members, Josiah Stamp, blamed the plight of the industry, and especially the deterioration since March 1925, on the appreciation of the exchanges and the return to gold at the prewar par, leading to a 'one-sided deflation'.

[2] Macmillan himself succeeded in depressing the Secretary for Mines—to whom he 'could suggest no remedy'. Lane-Fox Diary, 23 July 1925.

[3] Lane-Fox Diary, 28 July 1925 et seq. The President of the Board of Trade, Philip Cunliffe-Lister, excused himself from any participation in the coal negotiation since he had extensive family investments in the industry. Touchingly, the Secretary for Mines George Lane-Fox, a congenial and humane but essentially lightweight politician, offered to resign to make way for a stronger man, but Baldwin declined to accept the resignation. Lane-Fox Diary, 14 Aug. 1925; 16 Aug. 1925; 19 Dec. 1925.

[4] Report by Secretary for Mines, 24 Nov. 1925: CAB 24/175/503–14; Jones, *Whitehall Diary* I, 234.

[5] There was stiff opposition to the subsidy in the Cabinet. But the Prime Minister was effectively supported by Churchill and Neville Chamberlain (Minister of Health). Strictly speaking, the subsidy was intended to guarantee the *percentage additions* to basic wages. In the following months there was some controversy as the owners claimed that basic wage rates remained subject to negotiation. Ultimately, however, in response to pressure from the MFGB, the government agreed to comply with the spirit of its offer by guaranteeing actual wages.

This outcome was announced on 31 July 1925—heralded as 'Red Friday' in contrast to the 'Black Friday' of 1921. Consternation within the Conservative Party at what appeared to be appeasement of the TUC, and wounding parliamentary gibes by Lloyd George, were misplaced even on a cynical interpretation of events. The government was badly placed to run essential services if there had been a major strike. The need to buy time and Baldwin's sense that an inquiry was necessary to inform a wider public, were probably the two most powerful motives for the official volte-face.[1] On the other hand, the owners appear to have been genuinely outraged. The MAGB's President, having in June welcomed the opportunity for the owners to exercise their 'free will' and run their industry without 'outside interference', now complained bitterly that the subsidy was 'a complete capitulation to pressure and threats from extremists', and predicted, more or less accurately, that a general strike would begin the day the subsidy ended.[2]

It took a month to settle the composition and terms of reference of the Royal Commission, which was officially appointed on 5 September to 'inquire into and report upon the economic position of the Coal Industry and the conditions affecting it and to make any recommendations for the improvement thereof'. The miners' demand that the membership should be directly representative of the interests involved was rejected. The four members of the Commission were therefore, in the words of one of them, 'all unspotted by previous knowledge of coalmining'.[3] The Commission itself declined to accept the owners' argument that it should meet in private. On the other hand, as was almost invariably the case in such inquiries, the MAGB and the MFGB were given an exclusive status: only the Commission members and their representatives could examine and cross-examine witnesses.[4]

The Chairman of the Royal Commission was the leading Liberal politician and statesman, Sir Herbert Samuel (the government's first choice, Earl Grey, having declined on the grounds of age, infirmity, and inexperience).[5] The other members were: General Sir Herbert Lawrence, a

[1] For the view that the lack of preparedness for a strike was a dominant motive, see Lane-Fox Diary, 30 July 1925.

[2] MSWCOA MG17 (16 June and 5 Aug. 1925); Middlemas and Barnes 1969, 388.

[3] Beveridge 1953, 216.

[4] Ibid., 217; Lane-Fox to Baldwin, 12 Aug. 1925: Baldwin Papers, 13/44; Lane-Fox Diary, 11–14 Aug. 1925. On the first day of its hearings, the Samuel Commission noted that neither the Mineral Owners' Association nor the National Federation of Colliery Enginemen, Boilermen, and Mechanics could have the same rights.

[5] Baldwin Papers, 13/44 (12 Aug. 1925); Jones, *Whitehall Diary* I, 327–8. The membership was chosen by Churchill, Steel-Maitland, and Lane-Fox (Baldwin being out of the country on holiday).

banker; Sir William Beveridge, a social scientist and administrator, then Director of the LSE; and Kenneth Lee, a businessman, of Tootals, Broadhurst, Lee and Co. For the next six months (the Samuel Commission reported on 6 March 1926 in order to allow adequate time for public discussion before the expiry of the subsidy on 30 April) the public controversy marked time, and the Commission's proceedings occupied the centre of the stage.[1]

iii. The Judgement of Samuel

The Samuel Commission's Inquiry and Report represent the high point of the heated deliberations about the coal industry's problems which had glowed and spluttered intermittently throughout the years since the Great War. It served to lend much greater clarity to the central issues of that controversy and to provide authoritative if inconclusive information on important points of fact. Yet it failed to leave any enduring mark on events, and years later its leading member felt that his service had been 'lost endeavour'.[2] Neither the owners nor the miners were persuaded by its advocacy. In the short run it was followed by disastrous industrial strife of the most uncompromising sort.

The historical significance of the Samuel Commission therefore lies not in its positive influence, but in its convenient presentation of broad issues, and its role in a politico-industrial drama. In fact, the true deadlock of the industry's postwar history had been reached in July 1925, and the Commission simply collated the various issues integral to that deadlock—and postponed an inevitable stoppage for nine months. The problem was simply not susceptible to solution by rational argumentation. None of this came as a surprise to informed observers. In November 1925 Lane-Fox, the Secretary for Mines (presumably guided by his officials, and particularly by the well-informed and influential Ernest Gowers), reported on the coal situation to the Cabinet. The burden of his report was simple, accurate, and devastating: since the miners were absolutely adamant about the inviolability of wages and hours (Lane-

---

[1] In the winter of 1925–6 the government entertained overtures from the Ruhr coal industry (in particular the Rhenish–Westphalian Syndicate) on the possibility of an Anglo-German agreement on exports. But the proposal foundered on the reluctance of British exporters to form a selling association and on the risk of alienating France and the USA. However, Steel-Maitland, in cooperation with Sir Alfred Mond, did arrange for the delegates from the Rhenish–Westphalian Syndicate to meet the Samuel Commission. CAB 24/175/509 (24 Nov. 1925); CAB 24/178/8–11 (4 Jan. 1926); Lane-Fox Diary, 17 Nov. 1925; Baldwin Papers, 8/6 (30 May 1926).

[2] Beveridge 1953, 221.

Fox argued that their leaders saw the force of the argument about the need to reduce labour costs but were unwilling to commit 'official suicide' by saying so), there could be no reduction in wages or increase in hours until a stoppage had taken place. The Royal Commission, then in session, would be powerless to help. It would most likely propose, like other Inquiries before it, extensive reorganization of the industry to improve efficiency; the nationalization of royalties, to facilitate production and improve psychology; and an interim wage reduction of modest proportions. But, Lane-Fox advised the Cabinet, restructuring the industry would take years to effect and meanwhile the MFGB would not accept wage cuts. The industry was therefore bound to come to a shuddering halt at the end of April 1926, as it had done at the end of March 1921.[1] His scenario could hardly have been more accurate.

Given the politics of industrial relations in the coal industry, such a cynical view was, perhaps, unavoidable (the MAGB were even more negative: asserting the uselessness of the delay, the viciousness of government intervention, and the waste of the subsidy). Nevertheless, in the summer of 1925 the industry had, indeed, been brought to an unprecedented crisis, and the appointment of a Royal Commission which, unlike its predecessor of 1919, could explore the issues in a systematic and fairly leisurely way, did provide a final (and politically necessary) opportunity to exhaust the question of whether the industry's problems could ever be set out and resolved in a way which might avoid conflict. Certainly, the Samuel Commission was more adequately briefed and under less political and public pressure than the Sankey Commission. Its deliberations, in themselves and in their reception, were commensurately less sensational; and its proceedings (in spite of the unavoidable intrusion of bitter controversy) were decidedly less warped by ideological clashes. This was mostly due to the well-informed and well-prepared nature of its members (Beveridge in particular played a vital and searching role), who succeeded in being objective without becoming anodyne. But it was also no doubt influenced by the looming economic crisis and by the absence of the public mood of near-hysteria which had rendered the spring of 1919 such an inauspicious setting for a 'factual' investigation.

The Commission made extensive visits to the coalfields and took evidence from 76 witnesses in 323 public sittings between 15 October 1925 and 14 January 1926. In addition, of course, it also went to great pains to accumulate its own information. As with its proceedings, so the

---

[1] CAB 24/175/503–14 (24 Nov. 1925).

THE PROMISE OF MAY.

COAL OWNER } (together). "WHAT HAPPENS WHEN OUR CRUTCH IS TAKEN AWAY?"
MINER

DR. SAMUEL. "WITH THE HELP OF MY TONIC YOU SUPPORT ONE ANOTHER."

2. 'The Promise of May' (*Punch*, 17 March 1926)

Commission's Report was substantial, extremely detailed, and exhaustive in topical coverage.[1] Yet, the number of really vital issues was strictly limited: how much scope was there for improvement in efficiency (and therefore an increase in net proceeds) through reorganization of production and distribution? Did the state have a role to play? Were the miners' complaints about the existing system of wage-determination justified? Was it necessary or desirable to alter wages or hours?

Each of these topics obviously implied a variety of subsidiary issues; and there were many other aspects of the industry which could usefully be examined. But the Commission's main business was naturally determined by the principal claims and counter-claims of the two sides to the dispute which had precipitated the crisis: on the one hand, that British coal could be made competitive only by an increase in hours worked and the restraint or reduction of wages; on the other, that wages and hours were inviolable (indeed, that wages were being artificially diminished by sharp practice in the wage ascertainment's accounting procedures), but that the industry was inefficient and had great scope for improvement in terms of its management, ownership, and organization.

The core issue clearly related to the structural efficiency of the industry, for this offered the best, perhaps the only, hope of avoiding economic disaster or industrial warfare. And here Samuel and his colleagues were unambiguous and decisive: there were 'powerful economic forces' outside the industry which had weakened it, but 'we cannot agree with the view presented to us by the mine-owners that little can be done to improve the organisation of the industry, and that the only practicable course is to lengthen hours and to lower wages'.[2] Instead, the Commission concluded that too many collieries 'are on too small a scale to be good units of production', and that there were defects of equipment and management, while selling and transport methods were excessively costly. Labour relations and the wages system needed reform. Rejecting nationalization of the mines as a remedy for these defects,[3]

[1] The Commission took about 6 weeks to write its Report. Ernest Gowers saw drafts of various sections of the Report, and commented on them with, apparently, some effect: see various letters and memoranda dated Feb. 1926 in POWE 16/5141.

[2] This and other indications of the Commission's conclusions on general issues, are from the Summary in the *Samuel Report*, 232–7. The owners made a relatively poor showing when presenting their own case to the Commission (see quotation from the *Sunday Observer* in Lubin & Everett 1927, 269–70 n.)

[3] Beveridge felt that the Commission was 'open-minded' on the general principle of nationalization, but could not accept the miners' proposal, which was 'too syndicalist'. Nor was it inclined to try to devise an alternative proposal for public ownership, which would not be acceptable to the miners. *Power and Influence*, 219.

the Commission advocated public ownership of royalties; extensive amalgamations of existing mines, with a restrained role for government, but no full-blown compulsion;[1] a closer integration of mining with allied industries; the formation of cooperative selling agencies and other methods to economize in distribution and transport; and reforms in industrial relations (an overhaul of the wage ascertainment conventions, no alteration in hours, joint pit committees, family allowances, profit-sharing, etc.).

In asserting, as it did in its detailed discussion, that 'there are great advantages in large-scale production which are not now being realised' the Samuel Commission was addressing itself to the issue of the size of colliery companies, rather than of individual mines; and it was relying on a body of statistics concerning scale, output, and productivity for recent years. It was not, strictly speaking, deriving its conclusions from the broad thrust of expert opinion—nor from a precise examination of the constituent elements of efficiency. Indeed, most witnesses from among managers and owners, as well as the official MAGB submission, denied that there were *any* very marked economies of scale as yet unrealized, and often went out of their way to warn of the *dis*economies (especially the managerial limitations) of too large an enterprise.[2] To the Commission, this was evidence of the owners' apprehensions about nationalization, and it rather disingenuously claimed that it had not bothered to pursue this line of questioning since the Sankey Commission had gone into the matter fully, and the owners there had given decisive support to the argument in favour of scale (in fact, the 1919 witnesses cited by the Samuel Report, were by no means as whole-hearted as it implied).[3]

The extent to which a very large improvement in British coal's com-

[1] In difficult cases, the Commission favoured the combination of mines, not mine-owners: where some owners wanted to effect a desirable amalgamation but were frustrated by others, the latter's leases could be compulsorily transferred (with appropriate compensation) to the former; where the owners of a group of mines were unwilling to pursue a progressive course, but others might be willing to acquire their interests, the proposed legislation should provide that after an interval of three years from its passing, there might be a compulsory transfer of relevant leases.

[2] See, for example, *Samuel Evidence* QQ 4932, 50112 ff., 11032 ff., 12202, 15781 ff.

[3] The Commission examined two particular witnesses on this subject. Sir Richard Redmayne advocated further mergers but was rattled by persistent questioning by the MAGB's President Evan Williams. Charles Markham (the formidable Managing Director of the Staveley Coal & Iron Co.) argued that it was only feasible to combine mines with similar working conditions and techniques, and that there were in any case severe managerial constraints. *Samuel Evidence* QQ 3502 ff., 4836 ff., 9998 ff., 1128 ff. The MAGB requested its district associations to consider Redmayne's evidence and provide it with ammunition to counter his arguments: DCOA 41 (20 Nov. and 5 Dec. 1925); LCOA 19D 55/2 (21 Nov. 1925); SDCOA N9/B10 (25 Nov. 1925).

petitiveness could have been secured (let alone secured expeditiously) by a reorganization of existing collieries and undertakings, is not readily apparent.[1] The pattern of achievement of the existing structures (e.g. any tendency for bigger firms to be more efficient) was no necessary indication that similar advantages would be derived from rapidly *extending* concentration. There may well have been force in a point made by Evan Williams (admittedly putting the MAGB case against enforced amalgamations and therefore summoning every feasible argument against an unpalatable proposal) that 'successful companies have become big because they are efficient, and not efficient because they are big'. On the other side, however, the weight of statistical evidence as well as the actual tendency to amalgamation (combined with the patent advantages of large size in certain technical and many commercial functions) suggest that in an industry which was as fragmented as coalmining there were indeed unrealized economies of scale—coexisting with unrealized (and possibly bigger) economies to be derived from technical modernization of existing undertakings. Economies of scale could, therefore, still be obtained, but how large they might be and how easily secured, remained obscure questions. In any case, there were abundant instances of small undertakings which were very profitable and large colliery firms which did badly.

The Commission's discussions of the economies of scale were significant for two other reasons. First, irrespective of their validity or business implications, its conclusions were very influential outside the ranks of the coalowners. They had political resonance when coal was becoming decisively a political matter; and they generated a good deal of sympathy for the miners' case that structural reform should be tried before the miners were called on to make wage sacrifices.[2] Second, there was little in the Report to indicate that the potential economies of scale in the context of the industry as a whole were large in relation to current losses, and nothing to show that they could be secured in sufficient

[1] For a general discussion of this issue, see below, ch. 8, sect. iii; ch. 9, sect. iii.

[2] See the comments of a publicist, Sydney Walton, writing to Sir Harry Brittain, MP on 17 June 1926, when the coal stoppage was intensifying (SRO GD 193/109/5/331–3): 'In my opinion the crisis in the coal industry is not really a problem of labour ... but a problem of Britain's reluctance to reorganise and readjust to meet the demands of a new age. ... The problem is how to shake certain coalowners out of old ruts. ... Quite frankly, I think the miners are right in their instincts (tragically led though they've been) namely, that we ask them to sacrifice in the dark. To them the present proposals have the look of the confidence trick. They fear the vested interests which may thwart real reform. Yet the economic urge of a new industrial era the world over makes the reorganisation of the coal industry as inevitable as fate. Why not reorganise now and win peace and prosperity for the whole nation?'

amount and sufficiently quickly to save the industry from extremely painful decisions.

There was, however, less doubt about the Commission's conclusions concerning the advantages of selling agencies and associations (it expressed a particular and justified admiration for the Doncaster Collieries Association):

The industry as a whole has so far failed to realise the benefits to be obtained by a readiness to co-operate [*in distribution*]. Large financial advantages might be gained by the formation, in particular, of co-operative selling agencies. They are especially needed in the export trade.

This line of argument was to be constantly reiterated, and marketing associations ultimately came to characterize the industry even more than did amalgamations. Yet this, too, was no panacea: the thought that British coalmining might increase its income by forming an effective cartel was premature, and the actual cost-savings to be won by commercial integration was still a very small part of the huge losses of the mid-1920s.[1]

Of course, it could well be argued that such reorganizations were vital elements in any long-run programme, and that, together with other proposals, they comprised a 'package' which, through its psychological as well as economic effects, could help transform the industry. Nevertheless, on any realistic views the Samuel Commission's structural observations, vague and cautious as they were, hardly engaged very directly with the industrial-relations crisis which gripped the industry. Equally disheartening from the viewpoint of the MFGB was the Commission's conclusion that nationalization of the mines in the form advocated by the MFGB (albeit without the fervour, or expectations, of 1919) held out no prospect of social gains and carried grave economic risks. On the other side, however, the Commission *did* advocate the nationalization of royalties. This, it was felt, would have the twin advantages of facilitating more efficient underground workings (and incidentally help the state to encourage amalgamations) and of applying a salve to one of the industry's principal irritants—the miners' deep resentment of the royalty owners' unearned incomes. Even this step,

---

[1] As an example of the economies involved, the Doncaster Collieries Association, the best-known and possibly most efficient selling agency, handled 5 million tons annually at a flat rate of 6d. per ton (say £125,000), and returned a dividend of £45,000–£70,000 to its owners. Assuming that its dividend payments were generated by its coal transactions (in fact, it also handled purchases on commission, but presumably earned more profits than it paid in dividends), that indicates a fairly modest saving, although it must have been the case that the DCA retained valuable and usable assets (it was also used as a finance company).

however, could hardly defend wage levels in 1926, nor bring the industry much nearer to solvency within the necessary time-scale.

Indeed, whatever the respective merits of the arguments of the owners and miners about organization and ownership, the problem of solvency was perhaps the most urgent. In the last quarter of 1925 modest wages and a middling level of average profits (of about 1s. 7d. per ton) were only being maintained by a subsidy of some 3s. per ton. Without the subsidy almost 75 per cent of all coal would have been raised at a loss (in South Wales the figure was 80 per cent, in Durham 90 per cent, in Northumberland 99 per cent).[1] Hence, even if all profits were to disappear, it would still have been necessary to save costs (or secure further income) of about 1s. 5d. per ton if wages and/or employment were not to deteriorate dramatically. To the owners, neither reorganization nor technical change offered a way out. The whole burden of adjustment would have to be borne by wages—including, possibly, a reduction in railwaymen's wages to allow a saving on the cost of transporting coal. Politically, and in terms of public relations, this was an utterly dogmatic posture. Yet the dimensions of the economic crisis were such as to concentrate attention on the biggest item of costs. How did the Samuel Commission respond to matters relating to wages and hours?

The Commissioners' *general* conclusions on hours, wages, and welfare were much more explicitly favourable to the miners' claims. Most important of all, they firmly rejected the owners' case that a return to an eight-hour day was essential.[2] This was a direct challenge to the owners, who sought an increase in hours in the hope of securing greater output with a less than proportionate increase in costs, thereby bringing a reduction in unit costs and an increase in net proceeds. In the Commissioners' view, however, the putative savings of 2s. per ton (which assumed a recovery of the reduction in daily output which had taken place when underground hours were reduced in 1919) depended on

---

[1] *Samuel Report*, 226. The subsidy, bridging the gap between actual and offered wages in the summer of 1925, was extended to *districts* which made losses, irrespective of the position of individual collieries within those districts. However, all collieries then shared in the subsidies, so that the more profitable/efficient collieries could cut prices. Prices *were* cut (export prices fell by 10% in the year Apr. 1925–Apr. 1926), but it is significant that no more coal was sold as a result.

[2] However, they did recommend that the notional week's allocation of 6 days at 7 hours might be reallocated to 5 days of 8 hours, and that minor adjustments might be made if a strict adherence to a seven-hour day prevented two-shift working. The Commissioners also treated with pained aversion the owners' ill-advised attempts to attribute the industry's problems to 'extremism and 'ca'canny': *Samuel Evidence* QQ 6229 ff., 6620–3, 6549. Occasionally, both Beveridge and Samuel demonstrated a fastidious exasperation with the more opaque arguments of some owners' representatives.

weak assumptions about the psychological reaction of the work-force and the physical capability of the pits.

More seriously, while the 2s. alone would not be sufficient to put the industry on a sound footing, the presumed increase in output to 250 million tons annually (which would, in any case, still leave some 100,000 men unemployed) would have to be sold on an overstocked market. And to do that, in the circumstances of 1925–6, it would be absolutely necessary to reduce prices, thus absorbing the 'savings' derived from an eight-hour day. The 'economies' would be corre-spondingly less available to prop up either profits or wages. On logical grounds, therefore, as Beveridge brought out in the hearings, the proposal to secure a longer day's work for the same pay was 'a ludi-crous plan'.[1] In an alternative formulation, an increase in hours with no fall in price or increase in production would reduce the labour force, thus producing more social distress and unemployment: 1926 was 'a bad time' to expel the labour sucked in by the boom of 1919–20.

If the Samuel Commission provided perceptive economic argu-ments to stiffen the miners' moral and psychological opposition to an increase in hours, it also lent weight to the MFGB's presuppositions about the existing wage agreements. It insisted that the general prin-ciples behind the agreements were sound, and that *national* wage agreements should continue.[2] More specifically, it accepted at least some of the miners' complaints that the profits of ancillary operations (coke ovens, wagon transport, by-product and manufactured-fuel plants) and of selling agencies were excluded from 'proceeds' and therefore from the wages fund; that Directors' fees and the colliery companies' insurance premiums for workmen's compensation were charged against the industry's proceeds; and that they were being cheated by devices which reduced the perceived profitability of coal-mining. The miners felt, in particular, that items of capital investment were being charged to revenue,[3] and that 'transfer prices' (used to

---

[1] *Samuel Report*, 173–5; *Samuel Evidence* QQ 5788 ff., 16052 ff. Cf. *JMK* XIX, Pt. II, 534, 562. In one respect, however, the owners' assumptions were better than the Commission's which assumed that prices would not fall. In the event pithead prices fell by over 10% between 1925 and 1927 and by about 22% between 1925 and 1928.

[2] Members of the Commission were outraged when the MAGB subsequently appeared to seek justification for its insistence on purely district settlements in the Commission's own Report.

[3] The problem of accounting procedures as far as investment was concerned was a particularly knotty one in coalmining since the distinction between 'investment' and the normal costs of rou-tine production is vague. Digging new 'roads' or 'headings', supporting roofs with expensive labour and timber, maintaining the workings in an effective and safe form, opening up new areas

account for coal that was transferred to another department within a composite enterprise, or sold to an associated firm) were too low.

Admittedly, the Commission judged that the separation of the profits of ancillary production activities was reasonable. But selling agencies and associations were a different matter: they were normally formed by colliery companies to undertake a function which was otherwise an integral part of coalmining; the extent of their profit was in a sense arbitrary, since it comprised a commission on sales; and the payment of dividends to their parent colliery companies was excluded from the official ascertainments.[1] In this case, therefore, the Commission recommended that the profits of selling agencies *should* be brought into the ascertainments. (The Commissioners also felt that it would 'disarm a great deal of criticism' if Directors' fees, although only accounting for ½d. per ton, were treated as profits rather than costs.)

As far as wage determination was concerned, however, their most important gesture in the miners' direction related to transfer prices. About one-third of all coal produced was not sold competitively on the open market, but went to processing firms, blast-furnaces, and selling agencies, where there was either a direct link with the supplying colliery or a substantial overlap of ownership or directorships. Although the Commission had been advised that the ascertainments 'are fairly and accurately made', it felt that the need to allay suspicion was sufficiently great to leave transfer prices out of account altogether, and instead to use an informed assessment of 'true' market prices for the relevant grade of coal.[2]

Finally, the Commission also made extensive proposals for improvements in the industry's welfare provisions. Payments systems should be altered to give non-face-workers a direct interest in output; profit-sharing should be obligatory; pithead baths should be generally established; annual holidays with pay should be introduced when prosperity returned to the industry; and, in spite of the MFGB's bleak opposition to the principle, family allowances should be established, since they were 'one of the most valuable measures that can be adopted for adding to the well-being and contentment of the mining population'.

for exploitation—were all essential to current production but could also be classed as investment in future output.

[1] Thus, the Doncaster Associated Collieries' agency was exclusively owned by 5 collieries connected with Charles Markham's Staveley group, and marketed their output at a charge of 6d. per ton. In the early 1920s it was paying a dividend of 10% or 15% on a capital of some £460,000: *Samuel Evidence* QQ 11291 ff.

[2] *Samuel Report*, 135–40; *Samuel Evidence* QQ 5409 ff.; POWE 16/46.

Attractive as much of this might have been to the miners, when the Commission's report addressed the immediate crisis, its analysis and conclusions proved much less palatable. The Commission could not ignore the fact that without the subsidy the great bulk of Britain's coal output was being produced at a loss. Moreover, since the output in 1924 was roughly comparable to the annual average of 1909–13, but the work-force had grown by over 15 per cent, 'You have seven people trying to live where six people did before'—and claiming the right to live equally well. The sobering implications of this were drawn in the report: 'This is an account that no good will and no fine words can balance; the gap [between costs and prices] must be filled in one of three ways: by a marked rise of coal prices, by better organisation leading to a greater output, or by acceptance of a lower standard of living.' The first was improbable, the second would take time, the third 'is a price that must be paid in wages or hours of employment'.

Since the Commission had rejected the idea of increasing hours, this left only a reduction in wages, by an alteration of the minimum per-centage addition to wages that had been negotiated in 1924. The Samuel Commissioners were unhelpfully vague as to their calculation of the necessary wages cut; but by implication it amounted to an average, although not uniform, reduction of 10 per cent. Such an adjustment was the only way to avoid the 'disaster [which] is impending over the indus-try'.[1] In any case, the Commissioners argued, the reduction would affect only the somewhat better-paid men (the lower-paid were protected by 'subsistence' wages which should *not* be reduced). The principle that real wages should never fall below the level of 1914 was not economi-cally tenable, had been abandoned in other staple industries (where wages, especially those of skilled workers, were already below those of miners), and if retained in coalmining would 'mean violent contraction of the industry and a disastrous degree of unemployment'.

Taken by itself, all this was a powerful argument for wage reductions, and one which threaded its path ingeniously between the owners' one-sided views on wages and hours, and the miners' publicly and privately embarrassing refusal to suggest *any* remedy for the industry's imme-diate crisis.[2] Yet taken in the political and economic context of the

[1] *Samuel Evidence* QQ 231–4; *Samuel Report*, 130, 227, 236.

[2] At the hearings MFGB witnesses declined to make any proposal concerning current prob-lems. And in a fruitless private meeting with Smith and Cook on wages and hours, three of the Commissioners failed to initiate any useful discussion. Beveridge found Smith's mind 'granite' and Cook's as having 'the motions of a drunken dragon-fly'. *Samuel Evidence* QQ 16942, 17, 153; Beveridge 1953, 220.

Inquiry, the Report as a whole was inadequate to the problems for which it was designed. From the perspective of long-run reorganization and modernization the proposals were too vague as to realization, effect, and timing. Yet as long as the future of the industry was still left obscure, the miners could claim—as, later, men otherwise unsympathetic to their position claimed on their behalf—that they were being asked to make immediate and specific material sacrifices, in return for remote possibilities of structural reform.[1] Moreover, the Commission's own dogmatism about a subvention ('The subsidy should stop at the end of its authorised term and should never be repeated') implied a *naïveté* about the relationship between the timetable of structural change and the pressing economic and political dilemma of the industry.

From another perspective, however, although the Commission's conclusion that labour costs had to be reduced by wage cuts seemed explicit enough, it was in fact hedged and conditioned in ways which reduced the practical impact of the arguments. Above all, it was made part of a 'package' which included full acceptance of all the Report's main recommendations, whereas the logic of the argument was that it was necessary *irrespective* of the shape (if any) taken by longer-run policies. Here, there was much force in Keynes's criticism of the Report as 'weak and woolly', containing 'too much diplomacy' because it did not deal squarely and decisively with the fact that the industry was too large and employed too many men.[2]

The tone of the Samuel Report was scrupulously fair; its assessment of the situation finely balanced. Yet, precisely because it possessed these virtues, it also suffered from the characteristic vice of idealism in an imperfect world: it ignored political realities. As a consequence, it alienated both sides while not offering policies which either obliged or tempted the government to action. The success of the Commission's prescriptions depended on an eventuality which the form of its proposals made impossible—voluntary cooperation. Moreover, each disputant was provided with an escape route: the owners because the Report embodied no compulsion or timetable or incentive, and (in its central portions on organization) could too easily be dismissed as tentative and ambiguous; the miners because the wording of the Report implied that wage reductions were dependent on structural reforms which were improbable. The resulting impasse was inevitable.

[1] See the comments of Sydney Walton, above, p. 230 n. 2, and Ernest Gowers, below, 348.
[2] *JMK* XIX, Pt. 2, 532 (May 1926).

iv. Into the abyss, 1926

Ever since 1920, said Ernest Gowers in his evidence to the Samuel Commission in October 1925, a major depression 'has been lying in wait for the coalmining industry'.[1] In spite of the first instalment in 1921, the same might have been said of the prolonged stoppage in the coal industry which followed the hopelessly abortive discussions of the Samuel Report in the spring of 1926. It is just conceivable that, if the government had been able to muster the ideological flexibility, and political will, the owners might have been bludgeoned into accepting a radical programme of reorganization. But no government could have coerced the industry into sustained profitability; and there is absolutely no evidence that in the spring of 1926 the miners would have been *willing* to accept either wage reductions or increases in the working day. The 'package' proposed by Samuel and by many would-be mediators who followed him was never a realistic option. The only alternatives—and neither was politically feasible—would have been either to support the industry with huge subsidies over many years or, without government support, to maintain wages and hours at levels that would have ensured the sort of industrial shrinkage and mass unemployment that the Samuel Commission and the government found unthinkable.[2] Apart from such inconceivable possibilities, wage reductions (with or without a stoppage or lockout) were unavoidable. But if the broad outcome of 1926 was tragically inevitable, its configurations and implications were susceptible to choices and strategies. All three sides to the dispute had various options between which they could, at least in principle, discriminate. None did so particularly well.

The events of March–December 1926 form perhaps the most tortuous, as well as depressing, chapter in the modern history of British industrial relations.[3] Initially, events turned on government initiative. In March, that meant the response of the Cabinet to the Samuel Commission's proposals. After preliminary discussions within Departments, a Cabinet Committee, chaired by the Prime Minister, was appointed on

---

[1]   *Samuel Evidence*, 4.

[2]   In Apr. 1926 the Prime Minister asked Herbert Smith whether an immediate increase in unemployment of a least 200,000 was unacceptable, the MFGB President said that they were prepared for that, and preferred it to varying the industry's wages and hours—although one observer (Tom Jones) felt that, when brought up sharply against the fact, the miners would prefer a compromise. See Jones, *Whitehall Diary* II, 18–19.

[3]   For the detailed history of these events, see Phillips 1976; Middlemas and Barnes 1969; *ARSM* 1926, 8 ff.

THE SOFT-WORD PUZZLE.

MR. BALDWIN. "CAN ANYBODY THINK OF ANOTHER WORD FOR 'SUBSIDY'?"

3. 'The Soft-Word Puzzle' (*Punch*, 24 March 1926)

17 March to consider the Report (this Committee, informally referred to as the Cabinet Coal Committee, met about 50 times, and continued in existence throughout 1926, overseeing policy towards the coal industry). Clearly, there was a good deal of official reluctance to commit the government to the nationalization of royalties, municipal trading, subsidizing redundant miners seeking work elsewhere, or intervention in amalgamations. Nevertheless, a positive response was politically necessary, and on 24 March Baldwin announced that the government was willing, 'for the sake of a general settlement', to pursue the policies recommended by the Commissioners provided that those involved in the industry also accepted the Report *in its entirety*. The government would even provide a limited subsidy to cushion the blow, if those concerned agreed to a settlement by the end of April. For the Cabinet dissidents the offer was undoubtedly a risk worth taking, if only because the principal condition—a speedy acceptance by the owners and miners of the entire Report—was most unlikely.[1]

In the course of the negotiations which followed, the owners, although opposed to the Report, were reluctant to run foul of public opinion by rejecting it too precipitately. The balance of opinion, apparently guided by the strong views of Scottish owners (who urged prevarication and felt that many of their southern colleagues were not sufficiently sensitive to the dangers of the Report),[2] contented itself with the expression of a vacuous goodwill. The MAGB insisted that the basic wage settlements would have to be arrived at within the various districts, even if made subject to ratification by a national conference. They also served notice to terminate the existing national wage agreement at the end of April.

For its part, the MFGB, guided by a delegate conference, formally reiterated the stand that it was to maintain until poverty and demoralization enforced concessions in the autumn: there must be no deterioration of pay or hours ('not a cent off the pay, not a second on the day'); and wage agreements must be national in scope and provide for a uniform nation-wide minimum percentage addition to (district) basic wages. Once more the miners said that they were willing to accept very heavy unemployment rather than lower wages,[3] and insisted that reorganiza-

---

[1] The records of the Cabinet Coal Committee (including memoranda submitted to it) are in CAB 27/316–19. Cabinet proceedings in Mar.: CAB 23/52/11/185–6 (17 Mar. 1926); CAB 23/52/12/ 206–8 (22 Mar. 1926); CAB 23/52/13/213 (24 Mar. 1926); CAB 24/179/302–11, 340 (20 and 23 Mar. 1926). For the Treasury attitude to the nationalization of royalties and opposition within the Cabinet, also see Baldwin Papers, 13/152 (16 Mar. 1926) and 18/158–61 (22 Mar. 1926).

[2] SCOA UGD 161/1/7 (20 Mar. and 7 Apr. 1926). Also see WYCOA, 29 Mar. 1926.

[3] Lane-Fox Diary, 23 and 24 Apr. 1926.

tion must have absolute precedence in any policy to deal with the economic crisis.

The seriousness of the deadlock was aggravated when, on 21 April, the owners' district offers finally became available, and were seen to imply widespread reductions in wages (ranging to 25 per cent in the leading export areas, and generally involving rates below 1921 levels). Such offers justified the Minister of Labour's fears that the proposed levels of earnings would shock public opinion.[1] Further government pressure elicited a grudging agreement by the owners to a *national* minimum percentage, in return for which they were persuaded that the government would suspend the Seven Hours Act.[2] But, as the MAGB had predicted, since the offer had to cover the situation in the poorer districts, it was extraordinarily low: a return to the minimum of 1921 (20 per cent on basic rates) *plus* an increase of an hour in the working day—a proposal which two of the Samuel Commissioners felt to be 'astonishing' and 'wholly unreasonable'.[3]

Although this offer was an improvement on the owners' original proposals, it was insufficient to prevent a definitive breakdown in direct negotiations. The MFGB placed its case in the hands of the TUC. Yet the discussions were utterly constrained by the TUC's commitment to a general strike (which had been called for the night of 3-4 May) if negotiations failed; by the owners' unyielding insistence on their own terms; by the Cabinet's increasingly determined resistance to pressure from other unions outside the coal industry; and by the miners' refusal (in spite of fraternal attempts to dissuade them) to entertain the idea of any reduction in wages. On the night of 2-3 May the final rupture was precipitated by an apparently wilful show of strength on the part of Cabinet negotiators. They rejected further discussions unless the TUC withdrew its instructions for a strike and repudiated the action of compositors at the *Daily Mail*, who had refused to set an editorial entitled 'For King and Country'. Negotiations ceased. The General Strike began at midnight on 3-4 May, 1926.

The nine peaceful days of the General Strike (or, more accurately, the strike against most essential services)[4] were costly to the labour

---

[1] CAB 23/52/50/243-5 (14 Apr. 1926); SRO GD 193/426 (15 Apr. 1925).

[2] WYCOA, 3 May 1926; SCOA UGD 161/1/7 (13 May 1926); SCOA, 19 May 1926.

[3] Beveridge to Steel-Maitland, 30 Apr. 1926; SRO GD 193/109/5/245-7; Attorney-General (on behalf of Lawrence) to Baldwin, 3 May 1926: Baldwin Papers, 13/217. They also contested the owners' view of the need for district settlements and reiterated the Commission's insistence on a national settlement.

[4] The strike call went to workers in all modes of transport, printing, iron and steel, metal and heavy chemical industries, and power supplies, as well as most building trades.

movement and to the country at large, without in any way affecting the position of the coal industry. As was pointed out by two foreign observers, a much more effective and less self-defeating tactic might have been to confine strike action to the handling and transport of coal.[1] As it was, however, the labour movement had embarked on a course which the government and many citizens were bound to resent and resist to their fullest extent; which the miners had not fully expected (they, too, imagined that selective action might be best); and which, given its overt political overtones, the TUC was at a loss to know how to manage—particularly in the face of the government's unmovable refusal to negotiate about the strike action or a return to work. It was perhaps symptomatic of the whole affair that it came to an end unilaterally and amid misunderstanding. Acting unofficially, Herbert Samuel offered a formula linking wage reductions with an agreement on reorganization, a National Wages Tribunal, and—somewhat perversely, in the light of the Samuel Commission's Report—a temporary subsidy. In spite of the government's determined assertion that the proposals were 'not clothed in even a vestige of official character'[2] and the MFGB's subsequent predictable rejection of its implications, the TUC, with a pathetic eagerness, seized the 'offer' as a basis for renewed negotiations about coal. The General Strike came to an ignominious end on 12 May. Its cessation, like its inception, solved nothing.

The loss of TUC support merely stiffened the miners' refusal to contemplate any change in their hours or wages. And the near-farce of the General Strike was followed by the tragedy of the coal lockout, which bore out the *Colliery Guardian*'s prediction that, with the end of the General Strike, 'the mining problem remains as it was, a bitter conflict of irreconcilable opinion which, it would seem, can only be ended by sheer exhaustion'.[3] The war of attrition was, of course, punctuated by flurries of activity at various levels: a government initiative in mid-May, which was rejected by both sides; legislation in June–August which introduced most of Samuel's less sensitive proposals but also attained the owners' objective of legitimizing the eight-hour day; an unavailing attempt at mediation by religious leaders in July; a brief and angry attempt to reopen negotiations in mid-August; and a major effort by Winston

---

[1] Lubin and Everett 1927, 102.

[2] Correspondence between Samuel and Steel-Maitland, 8 and 9 May 1926, reprinted in *The Times* 14 May 1926. The Cabinet were determined to end what it viewed as an 'unconstitutional and illegal' General Strike without any bargaining.

[3] *CG* 7–21 May 1926, 1101.

Churchill to secure a settlement at the end of August and the beginning of September, which was sabotaged by the owners' insistence on using their power, but which marked the beginning of decisive concessions by the miners. After yet another unsuccessful attempt at a government solution in mid-September there was nothing left except to wait until time and poverty forced the miners to concede.

By the early autumn, significant numbers had begun to return to the pits (on owners' terms) in the search for work and earnings: about 70,000 by the end of August, more than twice that number a month later, some 230,000 by the end of October, 400,000 by the third week in November. The stoppage crumbled under its own internal pressures, although the crumbling was accompanied by persistent government attempts to intervene to dampen the shocks. On 19 November the MFGB advised its districts to make their own settlements, and as December opened the union acknowledged its bitter defeat. The men returned to work on the basis of district agreements, at increased hours, and with the likelihood (but not yet the universal certainty) of lower pay.

In spite of the occasional outbursts by the Prime Minister, and other Cabinet Ministers, against the MAGB's dogmatism and patronizing self-righteousness[1] neither Baldwin nor his senior Cabinet colleagues withdrew their sympathies from the owners.[2] And throughout the summer, as in the spring, there was a strong contrast in the attitudes and preconceptions of Cabinet members towards the owners as compared with the miners: 'Ministers are at ease at once with the former, they are friends jointly exploring a situation'.[3] The government's sense of the owners' inspired ability to lose public respect and to neglect important avenues of industrial development, was consistently outweighed by an official reluctance to compel the MAGB to pursue distasteful policies. Above all, although some members of the government (notably Winston Churchill) were uncomfortable with a policy of attrition, the government had concluded that a reduction in wage costs *was* a vital necessity, and that the miners, by refusing to acknowledge this, were ultimately responsible for the prolongation of the stoppage. In fact, the Cabinet did intervene again in June. In return for a revised wage offer by the MAGB, it agreed to legislate for an increase in the working day up to

[1] See the Prime Minister's correspondence with the owners and miners on 20–22 May 1926 in: CAB 23/53/31/7, 12–13; CAB 24/180/9–11, 54 ff. Also see *CG* 7–12 May 1926, 1101.

[2] For examples of this in May 1926, see Phillips 1976, 251–2. On 14 May Baldwin warned the owners that he was 'a little anxious . . . lest the miners' delegates should adopt the formula [put forward by the government itself] and want to negotiate on it'.

[3] Jones, *Whitehall Diary* II, 19 (23 Apr. 1926).

a maximum of eight hours. On 15 June the Prime Minister announced two legislative initiatives.[1]

In the context of the dispute the first was the more important: the Coal Mines Bill (which received its Second Reading on 28 June and became law on 8 July) raised the permissible length of the underground working day to eight hours (plus one winding time). Such a move seemed to promise some abatement of the humanitarian and political costs of the very low wages which might be necessary if the seven-hour limit were maintained. And the government publicized the owners' assurances that the July–September wages for half the work-force would be unchanged from those of April and in the case of many of the rest could be reduced by less than 10 per cent. It was also privately hoped—officially as well as within the MAGB—that the responses to such offers would help promote 'cleavages' between different districts of the miners' union.[2]

The second piece of legislation enacted those recommendations of the Samuel Commission that the Cabinet felt to be politically acceptable and administratively feasible. The Mining Industry Act (which became law on 4 August) provided carefully restricted procedures for the use of compulsion where desirable mergers were being prevented by some of the potential parties; introduced reforms into the Mines (Working Facilities and Support) legislation of 1923, which removed restrictions inherent in the earlier Act; imposed a further levy of 5 per cent on coal royalties to provide pithead baths and drying accommodation at collieries; and empowered the Minister of Labour (after consultation with owners and miners) to issue regulations restricting the recruitment into the industry of adult workers not employed therein on 30 April 1926.

It was a useful, but hardly very radical, package of reform. The question of selling associations was to be referred to a departmental committee, which reported later in the year.[3] But the opposition within the Cabinet to the nationalization of royalties or to municipal trading in coal had its way and they were dropped or sidetracked. In the case even of the provision for amalgamations (which was described in the *Colliery*

---

[1] CAB 27/318 (26 May 1926); *WSC* V, 725–6 (21 May 1926), 728–9 (9 June 1926), 730–1 (14 June 1926); Lane-Fox Diary, 31 May, 11 and 14 June 1926; SRO GD 193/417 (15 June 1926); *ARSM* 1926, 15; *Hansard* 15 June 1926, cols. 2138 ff.; Evan Williams in MSWCOA MG 17 (21 June 1926).

[2] Churchill to Baldwin, 26 June 1926: Baldwin Papers, 18/41–4. Subsequently, there was some disagreement as to whether the owners had also agreed to keep open the possibility of national as well as district settlements in return for the legislation: below, 248.

[3] *Report of the Departmental Committee on Co-operative Selling in the Coal Mining Industry*: Cmd. 2770. 1926 (*PP* 1926 XIII).

Guardian as no more than 'a pious injunction'), the original intention to set a time limit of three years before adopting more stringent measures, was abandoned, and the Board of Trade was merely requested to report on the outcome of the legislation after two years.[1]

These rather attenuated efforts were the government's main contribution to the problems of the coal industry in the summer of 1926. As far as the dispute was concerned it had set its face grimly against any offer of further financial assistance to the industry, thus rendering impossible any return to work at pre-stoppage wage rates, or even a *temporary* return pending a new settlement. It now simply assumed that the eight-hour legislation, by making possible less draconian wage reductions, would bring nearer the unavoidable concession of *some* cuts. At the end of June it used its control of the impending legislation to press a reluctant MAGB to make the new offers.[2]

In effect, the government appeared to assume that, with the new laws, the dispute would have to solve itself. And Cabinet Ministers responded ambiguously to the attempts of third parties to mediate in the dispute. Some—notably those by Lord Wimborne, a conciliatory coalowner, and by Seebohm Rowntree and W. T. Layton—were certainly not discouraged.[3] Others, however, were strongly resented, since they usually involved an element of subsidy and, in the view of senior Ministers, raised expectations which merely postponed the inevitable acceptance by the miners of the hopelessness of their position. This was the case with a well-publicized and widely supported proposal by several Anglican Bishops and representatives of the Nonconformist Churches. In July, the Prime Minister and the Minister of Labour were obliged to meet a delegation to discuss the plan, which involved a hefty subsidy and full acceptance of the Samuel Report.

[1] CAB 23/53/147 ff. and 183 ff. (21 and 24 June 1926); CAB 24/180/280 ff., 304 ff., and 326–7 (22 and 25 June, 6 July 1926). Also see *CG* 2 July 1926, 29, quoted in Lubin and Everett 1927, 104. The Cabinet was prepared to allocate £250,000 to research on low temperature carbonization. In July, when the issue of the costs of maintenance of pithead baths was raised, it was decided that these should not be a charge on the Miners Welfare Fund, but must be borne by the relevant coalowners: CAB 23/53/243 (21 July 1926).

[2] CAB 23/53/166 (30 June 1926). The Cabinet was 'profoundly dissatisfied' with the owners' tardiness and insisted on seeing particulars before parting with control of the Bill. The owners had wanted to avoid making the offers until the passage of the Bill was certain. LCMA UGD 159/1/6 (25 June 1926). Also see SCOA UGD 161/1/7 (21 June 1926). In fact there is some indication that the offers were only made public when there was some guarantee that the Bill was being passed: SCOA UGD 161/1/7 (2 July 1926).

[3] For such attempts see Middlemas and Barnes 1969, 429–32. These, and other less likely, proposals are touched on in SRO GD 193/407/107 ff. (22 June 1926); SRO GD 193/811/228–9 (28 June 1926); Baldwin Papers, 16/7 (2 July 1926).

At the meeting, on 20 July, Baldwin lectured the clergymen on their presumed innocence in matters of finance and industrial relations; on what he took to be the cynicism of Arthur Cook (who, Baldwin claimed, had imagined that he had scared the government into a subsidy in 1925 and could do so again); on the tenuous promise of reorganization; and, most important of all, on the utter impossibility of the government providing any more money. The objective, he told his pious audience with a homely use of metaphor, must be 'to wean this great industry from the breast of the State, where it has been for ten years'. Both sides were 'equally stupid and equally bigoted' but the only way forward lay in a change of heart on the part of the miners, and this could probably not come under the present leadership.[1]

This last point reflected a strong feeling on the part of the Cabinet, and centred principally on a derogatory and widely shared interpretation of A. J. Cook's personality. Steel-Maitland went so far as to leave a note in his papers to the effect that by July he had concluded that Cook was 'an essentially unstable character (a study in dual personality)' who was moderate when talking with moderate men and in other surroundings 'carried away either by the extremist statements of others or his own eloquence'.[2] In spite of this, however, there is evidence that the MFGB President, Herbert Smith, was the stronger character, and that by the end of the summer his determined presence tempered Cook's desire to arrive at a settlement. In any event, the two together seemed to the government a formidable roadblock, and in August the Minister of Labour, Steel-Maitland, argued that, in addition to a fair and economic settlement, a prime objective should be 'the elimination of Herbert Smith and Cook'.[3]

Yet in this respect at least, the Bishops were less naïve than some Ministers, for in their tense meeting with the Prime Minister they had gone out of their way to emphasize the loyalty of the miners behind their leadership: 'it is not a question of dealing with Cook, but of dealing with the extraordinary solidarity of the miners'. Moreover, the Cabinet was placed in an unhealthily compromised position by virtue of its

[1] For the Bishops' initiative, see Baldwin Papers, 17/135 ff.

[2] SRO GD 193/81/1 (29 Jan. 1929). Also see Baldwin Papers, 17/174–5; Beveridge 1953, 220. For a more favourable view of Cook, see Sir Oswald Mosley's verdict, cited in Mosley 1982, 90.

[3] On the respective roles of Cook and Smith see Samuel to Baldwin, c. 11 May 1926: SRO GD 193/81/1/35–40; Steel-Maitland to Baldwin, 14 Aug. 1926: Baldwin Papers, 15/296–7; Jones to Baldwin, 26 Aug. 1926: Baldwin Papers, 18/218–22; Lane-Fox Diary, 26 and 28 Aug. 1926. To some unsophisticated observers Smith and Cook assumed an emblematically diabolic role, especially as the dispute dragged on. See Lord Londonderry to Churchill, 11 Sept. 1926: WSC V, 824–5.

relationships with the owners. Indeed, the government and the Conservative Party—tied to the owners' side by social sympathy as well as economic predilection—were, often against their will, obliged to take the lead in publicizing the case against the miners' claims because the inept owners besides being 'absurdly suspicious' of any suggestions, did their propaganda work 'abominably badly'.[1]

Yet the resulting political situation, so inimical to the miners' position, was partly of their own making. For their utterly dogged refusal to discuss changes in wages or hours throughout the spring and early summer of 1926 offered no counterpoise against the owners' side of the argument. It was this, as Tom Jones argued in September, that had led the miners time and again to fail to exploit the situation in their own interest: they did not 'arm the Government with terms good enough to enable the Government to go ahead in spite of the owners'.[2] The *only* circumstances in which the MFGB would have accepted some official negotiating help was one which the Cabinet would not contemplate: the protection of existing wage levels and the working day. And by the end of the summer, when the miners showed some faint and hesitant sign of a willingness to discuss a compromise on wages, it was politically too late. Cabinet opinion had hardened against them.[3]

All this was exemplified in the bout of feverish activity which accompanied Churchill's attempt to end the dispute in late August and early September. With Baldwin—seemingly on the verge of a breakdown—dispatched by his colleagues for an extended holiday in Aix-les-Bains, and Steel-Maitland almost equally exhausted by his efforts during the summer, the Chancellor of the Exchequer took characteristically vigorous command of the situation.[4]

After the union had rejected the Bishops' proposals (in a vote announced on 16 August) the MFGB had attempted to renew negotiations with the owners on 19 August. They tentatively offered a return to work at the minimum rates of 1921 but with a seven-hour day and

[1] Steel-Maitland to B. Hudson Lyall, 11 June 1926; SRO GD 193/420/38–9. There was a good deal of 'education' work undertaken by Ministers and Conservative Party during the stoppage, as well as liaison between them and propagandists or such owners as Wallace Thorneycroft of Scotland: Lane-Fox Diary, 24 June and 12 and 19 Aug. 1926; SRO GD 193/422/60 (6 Sept. 1926), 193/428/347–50 (17 June 1926), 193/419/61–3, and 193/412 (Steel-Maitland's 'Diary of General Strike and Coal Dispute').

[2] Jones to Baldwin, 109 Sept. 1926: *WSC* V, 822.

[3] Lane-Fox to Churchill, 8 Sept. 1926: *WSC* V, 816; Jones, *Whitehall Diary* II, 86 (22 Sept. 1926).

[4] For Baldwin's and Steel-Maitland's frailty see Jones, *Whitehall Diary* II, 62–4; *WSC* V, 773; Middlemas and Barnes 1969, 433–4. Documents relating to Churchill's initiative are in *WSC* and Jones, *Whitehall Diary* as well as the Baldwin Papers and, of course, Cabinet records.

priority given to reorganization. However, the miners had stormed out of the meeting when they realized that the owners were absolutely unwilling to change their minds on the need for district settlements.[1]

There followed a meeting between the MFGB and the Cabinet Committee, and over the next two weeks Churchill offered conciliation and encouragement to the miners both in a successful Commons speech on 31 August, and privately. The result, after mediation by Ramsay MacDonald, was a formula by which the union offered an important concession: 'to enter into negotiations for a new national agreement with a view to a reduction of labour costs to meet the immediate necessities of the industry'.

However, this scheme foundered, amid recriminations from Churchill, on the MAGB's steadfast refusal to enter into any *national* discussion of wages or hours. (At an acrimonious meeting Evan Williams lectured Churchill at length on the loose, federal structure of the Association and its powerlessness to discuss wages or hours without the express permission of its constituent district members.)

The Chancellor was furious at the volte-face in negotiating policy; and his colleagues were alarmed by his warm assault on the owners, accompanied by accusations of bad faith (he felt that the new Eight Hours Act had been passed on the assumption that the MAGB would still entertain the possibility of a national settlement) and by threats to use government power to bring the owners into line. Steel-Maitland, for example, attacked the Chancellor for 'impulsiveness and combativeness' and afterwards felt that 'we jumped too soon. . . . The miners were nearly down and out and ready to agree to anything.'[2]

Yet, as if to demonstrate the reinforced strength of the owners' posi-

---

[1] SCOA UGD 161/1/7 (10 Sept. 1926).

[2] CAB 24/181/294–5 (4 Sept. 1926); *CG* 3 Sept. 1926, 521; Williams to Lane-Fox, 29 Aug. 1926: Baldwin Papers, 18/245–7; Jones to Baldwin, 30 Aug. 1926, in Jones, *Whitehall Diary* II, 69–70; *WSC* V, 819–20. For other criticisms of Churchill see ibid., 816, 824–5, 826 (Lord Birkenhead sent a telegram from Biarritz: 'Why should we impose upon owners national settlement if they are strong enough to obtain district settlements'), 849–50; SRO GD 193/428/129–35, 283; Baldwin Papers, 18/149–54, 20/205–6. For the MAGB's 'consultations' with its district members, see MSWCOA MG17 (10 Sept. 1926); SRO GD 193/403/156–7 (13 Sept. 1926). For praise of Evan Williams's extemporaneous defence of the owners and his counter-attack on the Cabinet, see: MSWCOA MG17 (10 Sept. 1926); SCOA UGD 161/1/7 (10 Sept. 1926). Steel-Maitland, however, still tried his best to persuade the owners to accept national negotiations. The contrast between Churchill's pugnacity during the General Strike and his attempts at conciliation during the coal stoppage was explained by his different assessment of the two. On 10 Sept. he wrote to the King's Secretary saying that he was never frightened of a General Strike, which could be fought and taken by the throat, but that the coal stoppage could last very much longer and do enormous damage to the economy. It was 'like a ship slowly sinking in a calm sea'. *WSC* V, 822–3.

tion, the Cabinet could do nothing. In response to Churchill's pleading, the MAGB 'consulted' its members, but the balance of opinion was overwhelmingly against national negotiations, and was helped in this orchestrated response by the MAGB's formulation of the question (it ignored Churchill's request for tripartite discussions and asked, instead, whether the districts favoured 'reconstituting' the MAGB as a national negotiating body). As a result Evan Williams could definitively reject Churchill's plea, claim that the district associations had withdrawn the MAGB's authority to negotiate, and reiterate his assertion that wages settlements 'can only be made in the light of the circumstances of the districts'.[1]

The failure of Churchill's initiative in September marked a substantial narrowing of the scope for official action. The Cabinet continued to explore possible solutions in a half-hearted manner, and the news that the miners had turned them down was received with some relief.[2] By this time, the owners' official posture was the critical factor in deliberations. It began to seem to some observers that they were determined 'to be left to themselves even if the men would not cave in until the crack of doom'.[3]

Of course, as with other groups, the solidarity of the owners' public position masked uneasiness and disagreement in private. Throughout 1926 Cabinet Ministers attempted to enlist the support of individual owners in bringing pressure to bear on district associations to secure 'reasonable' wage offers, to restrain increases in hours, or to secure national negotiations.[4] More specifically, when consulted about Churchill's September proposals, for example, the owners' associations in both Durham and West Yorkshire were reluctant to rule out tripartite discussion and were prepared to accept some sort of national ratification of, or national principles for, district agreements. Indeed, in West Yorkshire a motion proposed by A. W. Archer (Managing Director of

[1] Evan Williams to Winston Churchill, 13 Sept. 1926: GD193/403/156.
[2] Evan Williams to MSWCOA MG17 (29 Sept. 1926). Jones, *Whitehall Diary* II, 88: 'In their heart of hearts the Cabinet hate this offer and are dreadfully afraid that it may be accepted.' Cunliffe-Lister was instrumental in pressing for national arbitration as a means of achieving the miners' national principles: Lane-Fox Diary, 14 and 15 Sept. 1926.
[3] CPD to Davidson, 9 Sept. 1926: Baldwin Papers, 18/232–3; MSWCOA MG17 (10 Sept. 1926). The owners were also supported by extreme opinion within the Conservative Party: SCOA UGD 161/1/7 (10 Sept. 1926); Boothby to Churchill, 9 Oct. 1926, in *WSC* V, 852–3; Baldwin Papers, 20/205–8 (14 and 29 Sept. 1926).
[4] This particularly applied to Steel-Maitland, in spite of his mounting pessimism. See his letters to the Earl of Crawford, 16 Apr., and R. A. Burrows, 7 Aug. and 3 Sept.: SRO GD 193/428/5–7, 29, 30. Also Cunliffe-Lister to A. W. Archer, 19 Aug.: SRO GD 193/422/72.

the giant South Kirby, Featherstone, and Hemsworth Collieries) calling for joint meetings nationally and uniformity for wages and hours
settlement was only narrowly defeated. Archer himself—having, in
August, expressed sympathy for the Bishops' proposals and advocated
the formation of selling associations and a settlement along the lines of
the Samuel Report—briefed Ministers on the mistaken character of the
owners' eight-hour policy, and on the illogicalities and inconsistencies
of the MAGB's position on national negotiations.[1] And it was clear
that a considerable minority of owners in various districts would have
been ready to negotiate on the basis of a 7½-hour day, national agreements and local variations.[2] Politically and strategically, the owners
were as one.

On their side, the miners experienced a crumbling of support only
after the most prolonged erosion of their material standards. Indeed, the
work-force displayed an unexpectedly cohesive and determined forti-
tude. In part, this was because the resources available to support the
miners, and more particularly their families, were more abundant and
more flexible than had been predicted. Strike benefit was itself negligible
and soon exhausted. But miners' dependants could turn to the Poor Law
authorities for contributions to subsistence (normally 10s. per week for
wives, and just under half that per child), while in districts where politically sympathetic authorities existed, rates of relief might be particularly
favourable, free school meals could be extended to include breakfasts
and an evening meal, and arrangements could be made for the communal provision of food (of which, it was said by cynics, the men themselves might take advantage).[3] At the beginning of the dispute the
numbers in receipt of Poor Law relief were about the same as at the *end*
of the 1921 dispute (some 1.2 million). By June 1926 that number had
reached the 'absolutely unprecedented figure' of 2.3 million.[4] Altogether, between March and December the borrowings of Poor Law
Unions in England and Wales had jumped from £9.3 to £16 million; and
in the year to March 1927 the total spent on outdoor relief in England

[1] DCOA 41 (6 and 11 Sept. 1926); WYCOA, 10 Sept. 1926; Archer to Steel-Maitland, 8 Aug.
1926 and Cunliffe-Lister, 20 Aug. and 9 Sept. 1926; SRO GD 193/428/1, 422/78–85, 422/49–59;
Lane-Fox Diary, 21 Oct. 1926.

[2] Jones, *Whitehall Diary* II, 70 (30 Aug. 1926); Burrows to Steel-Maitland, 27 Aug. and 8 Oct.
1926; SRO GD 193/428/33–4, 27–8.

[3] Two Poor Law Unions in mining communities (Bedwellty in South Wales, and Chester-le-
Street in Durham) were so 'generous' to miners' families in 1926 that ultimately (in 1927) the
Minister of Health replaced their Guardians with ministry nominees.

[4] Minister of Health, *Hansard* 13 July 1926, col. 264.

and Wales, which had averaged £14.5 million in 1924–6, rose to almost £24 million.[1]

Churchill was only slightly exaggerating when he pointed out to the King's Private Secretary that 'with the modern methods of local relief there is no decisive pressure upon them [the miners] to return' to work.[2] Moreover, these resources and methods were supplemented by public appeals (which were matched by government grants)[3] and by an extensive drawing on the support of formal and informal community institutions: the purchase of goods on credit from cooperative stores; the non-payment of rent (often allowed by colliery companies which owned houses); neighbourly help and mutual aid; outcrop working; and the absorption of savings.[4]

Yet such support, although it undoubtedly facilitated a prolonged stoppage, could not maintain an indefinite one. Nor, indeed, could it have maintained the stoppage that did take place had it not been for the determination and solidarity of the miners themselves. In spite of its isolation within the Labour movement and the extreme material pressures on its members' families, the MFGB had, throughout the summer of 1926, fought the dispute with no intention of yielding to the slightest extent on hours or wages. Moreover, and contrary to the views of their critics, this was not a posture imposed by a remote leadership, but reflected an almost mystical conviction on the part of a majority of the men: coalfield ballots rejected both the Bishops' emollient proposals in August and (against the leadership's advice) the Cabinet's plans for settlement in November.[5] In this fervour, the commitment to the gains of 1919 with regard to hours was particularly critical, although the fact that the attachment to a seven-hour day was so deeply felt, and that the associated resistance to wage reductions became so emotional and cogent a posture, did not make them any the more realistic—or even wise.

In practice, and in the light of their ultimate surrender, the miners' strategy of unyielding resistance proved a profound handicap. For some

---

[1] Daley 1978, 55; Williams 1981, 172. In many instances Poor Law Unions lent money to miners on relief. Some £228,000 of such debts were outstanding in 1930: POWE 10/80.

[2] 10 Sept. 1926 in WSC V, 822.

[3] As was to be the case in 1928: below, 262.

[4] Lubin and Everett 1927, 103 n.; CAB 24/179/863–5 (4 May 1926); Baldwin Papers, 21/20 (June 1926); SRO GD 193/420/20–2 (23 July 1926); SRO GD 193/424/5–7 (28 July 1926); CAB 24/181/470 (2 Nov. 1926); CAB 23/53/55/370–1 (3 Nov. 1926).

[5] In Durham the men even voted against the final local settlement, negotiated by the leaders, but the majority was insufficient to prevent a return to work.

weeks before the stoppage began, and until at least mid-June, an offer by the miners to compromise on the issue of wages would in all probability have secured a protection of the seven-hour day and a more active government policy towards reorganization. Above all, it would have maintained the national framework of negotiation and settlement—and, therefore, the national influence of the union. Instead, the miners' continuing obstinacy over the summer weakened their credibility and narrowed the ground on which they could stand, while giving their opponents a chance to muster and regroup.[1] And their one bargaining point (that there should be no discussion of wages or hours until industrial reorganization had been not merely discussed and agreed but, by implication, put into effect) was so extreme as to be unrealistic. Moreover, the Prime Minister was not unreasonable in pointing out that 'we none of us know what is meant by reorganization'.[2] The MFGB had in fact created an impossible situation. And although there was considerable force in the miners' argument that wage reductions not accompanied by the determined, official pursuit of structural change would inevitably lead to complacency and inactivity on the part of the owners,[3] in the context of 1926 their stand on wages and hours was utopian, and self-defeating. Its outcome was a worse and a more humiliating surrender.

The miners' defeat was slow and painful but none the less inexorable in coming. When, on 24 September, Baldwin reported that they were 'beaten and rattled', well over 100,000 men were already back at work.[4] The drift to work was an ever-widening chink in the MFGB's armour. And when the miners, in October, issued a desperate call for the withdrawal of the safety men, the appeal fell largely on deaf ears. It was a sign of impending defeat rather than renewed aggression. The union no longer had much to offer its members. By the end of October nearly a quarter of a million men were back in the mines. Two weeks later the Nottinghamshire miners, led by George Spencer in a break-away union, had signed an agreement with the owners.[5] The MFGB was on the point of surrender. On 19 November a delegate conference instructed its members to seek district settlements. The collapse was soon complete.

As district after district settled at the end of November (although the

[1] For signs of uncertainty and disarray among the owners in the spring of 1926, see MSWCOA MG17 (22 Mar. 1926), SCOA UGD 161/1/7 (22 Mar. 1926).
[2] Baldwin Papers, 17/182 (20 July 1926).
[3] See below, 348.
[4] *WSC* V, 842–3; *ARSM* 1926, 18. Defections were heavily concentrated in the Midlands.
[5] Griffin 1977.

final signature of the new agreements was frequently postponed for weeks or even months), it was clear that the resolution of the conflict, although not perhaps the 'Carthaginian Peace' that Churchill had said the owners were trying to impose,[1] was severe enough. First, the miners were denied the use of any national machinery or agreements: settlements were entirely local and this—together with the exhaustion and humiliation of the MFGB—was a severe setback to the cause of the national union. Second, in spite of the determination of the miners to protect hours even above wages, the length of the working day was increased throughout the coalfields, although (as some owners had predicted) this did not mean a uniform eight-hour day. Hours for all underground workers in Yorkshire, Nottinghamshire, and Derbyshire, and for hewers in the North-East, were to be $7\frac{1}{2}$; other workers and fields were to have an eight-hour day, although Saturday shifts in various districts were somewhat shorter (usually six hours).

The wages aspects of the new settlements are not easy to assess. District agreements provided for a return to work at temporary rates, providing a sufficient period of working to allow for the ascertainment of proceeds (for all the district agreements retained the basic *principles* of the 1921 and 1924 agreements). And except in Northumberland and Durham, where temporary rates of pay were set at 1921 levels (i.e. about 10 per cent less than on the eve of the lockout) all districts established provisional levels at least equal to those of April 1926, and in the case of Nottinghamshire, Derbyshire, Leicestershire, Warwickshire, and Staffordshire, above those of the spring. Moreover, when the new agreements came into force, the division of net proceeds between wages and profits were not very different from pre-stoppage rates (87:13 in the case of export fields, but 85:15 in most other districts). However, the true extent of the miners' defeat was demonstrated by two elements in the new agreements which were forced on local unions.

First, local organizational practices and the accounting conventions used to calculate net proceeds were revised in the owners' favour. In South Wales, for example, management were given the unencumbered right to impose double shifts, and in Durham the miners' customary controls of jobs and job allocation were eroded. In general, subsistence wages were to be counted against the wages total rather than as a cost, as was free or concessionary coal and housing in the North-East, and the owners took the opportunity of arranging for deficiencies in relation to profits to be carried forward to subsequent years, so that 'lost' profit

[1] CAB 27/316 (11 Nov. 1926).

could be recovered.[1] Second, and most important of all, the minimum percentage addition to basic rates, to be used once the initial period of working was passed, was set at 1921 levels in all but the Midlands fields. In effect, the miners were forced to accept a longer working day *and* a universal wage cut.[2] For in the event, these minima soon became operational: wages in all districts except Worcestershire and Leicestershire were at the minimum by August 1927, and those two fell to it by the end of the year. Hence, although in the first three months of 1927 average earnings per shift (10s. 7d.) and per week (£2 11s. 6d.) were about the same as in 1925 and early 1926, by the end of the year shift earnings had fallen to levels only just above the 1921 agreement minimum (reached in the summer of 1922) and irregularity of work reduced weekly earnings even more. Durham, Scotland, Lancashire and Cheshire, and South Wales did worst of all.[3]

The balance sheet for 1926 therefore made gloomy reading for the miners. Nor, however, did it bring much good economic news to the owners. Admittedly, they had their way in that hours were increased and wages reduced, and their predictions that productivity would rise and costs fall were borne out: between 1925 and 1927, as the length of the working day increased and the miners' financial needs grew, output per manshift rose from 18 to 20.5 cwt; and labour costs fell by 12 per cent.[4] Yet the economic climate continued to worsen. Prices fell and sales stagnated; higher productivity simply reduced the numbers in employment; and within months the owners were obliged to turn to more radical structural experiments in an effort to fend off commercial collapse.[5] It is true that, as a result of the stoppage, the MFGB ceased—at least temporarily—to be an effective national force. But it is by no means certain

[1] For examples of local settlements see DCOA 42, Annual Report, 1927; WYCOA, 30 Nov. 1926; MSWCOA MG17 (16 Nov. 1926); SDCOA, N9/B11 (24 Nov. and 2 Dec. 1926); SCOA UGD 161/1/7 (8, 25, and 29 Nov. 1926).

[2] Wages and hours under the new agreements are listed in the *ARSM* 1927, Tables 18 and 19. Under the 1921 agreement the addition had been 32% to basic rates in Yorkshire, Nottinghamshire, Leicestershire, Cannock Chase, and Warwickshire. Under the settlements of 1926–7, they were: Yorkshire, 36% (plus 6.1% for hewers); Nottinghamshire, 38% (plus 7% for hewers); North Derbyshire, 38% (plus 7% for hewers); South Derbyshire, 35%; Warwickshire, 43%.

[3] 'The British Coal Mining Industry': POWE 16/180; *ARSM* 1927, 106–7. The effect of these changes was reduced by the fall in the cost of living—which declined by 23% between the time of the negotiation of the 1921 agreement and the end of 1927; and by 7% between the previous nadir of wages (the summer of 1922) and Dec. 1927.

[4] This national average covered a range, in the important areas, from 6 or 7% in Yorkshire and Nottinghamshire, to 14% in Scotland and 16% in Northumberland, Durham, and South Wales and Monmouthshire: *ARSM* 1927, 11–12.

[5] Above, ch. 5, sect. v; and below, 259–6.

that the fragmentation and enfeeblement of the union, which also occurred *within* districts as 'non-political' unions broke away, was in the interests even of the owners, particularly since the owners made no substantial move towards industrial reform or change.[1] And in any case, the long-run health of the industry had been eroded by the stoppage. The competition from Germany and Poland which moved to fill the gap left by the effective cessation of British exports was not subsequently driven back. Markets were lost never to be completely regained.[2]

v. Reactions and strategies, 1927–1929

Throughout the 1920s the dominant political opinion was averse to state intervention in economic affairs in general, and in the formidable problems of coalmining in particular. 'Most of our party', wrote the Conservative Secretary for Mines in September 1926, 'dislike Government interference'.[3] Yet neither ideological nor pragmatic preference could prevent governments being dragged into the affairs of the ailing coal industry. Structural and commercial problems were too insistent, industrial strife too threatening, and the growing realization that the problem of a chronic surplus of at least 200,000 miners had to be tackled or at least accommodated,[4] meant that the coalmining industry could not be removed from the political arena.

One measure of this tendency had been the use of Treasury funds to support the industry. But the principal symptom was the pressure on the state to produce longer-run policies for the twin issues of structural reform and unemployment in the industry.

The question of industrial reorganization had been raised by officials of the Coal Control within a few weeks of the end of the Great War, and was discussed before the Sankey Commission in 1919. Nevertheless, apart from the possibility of nationalization, arguments that there should be regional or even national unification of colliery firms to secure the industry's unrealized economies of scale, were not persistently canvassed in the immediate postwar years.

Even in 1921, when the postwar market collapse first became a threat to stability in the industry, most discussion concentrated on the level of

[1] See Lubin and Everett 1927, 349–50.

[2] Between 1925 and 1926 Germany's exports rose from 22.5 to 38 million tonnes, Poland's from 8.25 to 14.75 million.

[3] Lane-Fox to Lord Irwin, 29 Sept. 1926; *WSC* V, 849.

[4] Minister of Labour 'Unemployment in the Coal Industry', 22 June 1927: SRO GD 193/661/91; *Industrial Transference Board Report* (Cmd. 3156. 1928), 7–8.

wages and the methods of paying them. And in spite of a number of significant examples of amalgamations and mergers in the early 1920s and after 1926, within the industry, throughout most of the 1920s, the owners' representatives hewed to the line that their critics saw as a 'pathetic' loyalty to a prewar dogma:[1] that efficiency and competitiveness were to be sought primarily in lower wages and a longer working day. Hence, when the question of economies of scale came to be more systematically discussed in relation to the Samuel Commission in 1925–6, the owners were thrown on to the defensive, emphasizing the negligible scope for such savings, the unreliability of statistics which ignored differences in the circumstances of collieries, the difficulties of managing huge colliery enterprises, the possibility of attaining commercial economies without formal mergers, and the grave disadvantages of compulsory amalgamations (which would be 'fatal to progress, development and efficiency').[2]

Nevertheless, as we have seen, the Samuel Commission concluded that there *was* an important correlation between efficiency and size.[3] The Commission therefore advocated a gentle effort by the state, allowing ample time for voluntary initiatives, to stimulate desirable 'fusions and absorptions' that might be neglected by the parties concerned. The Commission's support for a programme of reorganization was very influential outside the ranks of the owners (even within them there were a few—notably Sir Alfred Mond—who also urged a major programme of restructuring), and the miners seized on to this apparent confirmation of their own view to insist on reorganization as a prerequisite of wage negotiations.

Yet both in 1926 and the troubled years that followed, there were two insuperable obstacles to decisive state action. On the one hand, extensive intervention in private enterprise against the wishes of those involved encountered powerful inhibitions, on both practical and ideological grounds—the more so in that the outcome was uncertain. On the other, any effective policy of restructuring would need both time and money. Given the enfeebled condition of the industry by the mid-1920s, and with so little incentive even to conventional investment, it was diffi-

[1] Smart 1930, 47. Cf. Clay 1929, 174 ff.

[2] *Samuel Evidence*, Appendix A, 935 ff. For the discussion of amalgamations in 1925–6, see above, 230–1.

[3] *Samuel Report*, 53–60, 259–65. The Commission's statistics, which were challenged by the MAGB, principally related to undertakings and only partially to mines. They therefore did not distinguish between large undertakings with many small- or medium-sized mines, and large undertakings with a few big mines.

cult to envisage funds becoming available for the massive reorganization and re-equipment implied in the more optimistic statements about the industry's potential. It was certainly impossible to envisage that they might have come from the Treasury.[1] In any case, the Cabinet insisted that minatory action was inappropriate and unacceptable.

As a result, even proposals for the acceleration of mergers were deflated by financial and ideological limitations. And the only outcome of the debate was the innocuous Mining Industry Act of 1926. This stipulated that where a majority of colliery owners in a potential grouping were frustrated by a minority, they could appeal to the Board of Trade, which might then (if it felt that a prima-facie case had been established) submit the proposal to a judicial body, the Railway and Canal Commission. Before enforcing the amalgamation, however, the Court had to be satisfied that the scheme was not merely in the national interest but was 'fair and equitable' to all concerned. This was a degree of protection for minority interests which virtually ensured that little use would be made of the law (equitable financial treatment of less efficient pits was precisely the costly step which prevented extensive private, voluntary mergers). The legislation was less the vehicle of determined government intervention than a signal to the industry: a breathing-space designed to encourage private initiatives. Under the terms of the Act, the Board of Trade was to report on *all* mergers in the industry after two years. The basic principle of voluntary action therefore emerged relatively unscathed from the traumas of 1926.[2]

There was, of course, an alternative approach to the problems of costs and prices in the coal industry. Instead of labouring to control production and increase productivity by rationalization, merger, and heavy investment, the coalowners were frequently urged to control competition in marketing and, by using selling associations, to restrict and apportion output to a diminished demand and to set minimum prices. But since such a scheme was vulnerable to undercutting, proposals for marketing cooperation normally also involved means of limiting and

---

[1] In 1929 a full national programme backed by government guarantees was estimated to cost £100 million, although it was felt that £25 million might make a significant difference. See Cunliffe-Lister to Baldwin, and associated documents, 13 Feb. 1929, Baldwin Papers, 30/21–39; also in CAB 24/202/179–97 (covering note 24 Feb. 1929). Clay (1929, 198) argued that a figure equal to the wage subsidy paid in 1925–6 (£23 million) 'would probably have covered all the improvements that correct technique would suggest'. However both suggestions seemed to relate to rationalization (i.e. closures and concentration of production) rather than the reorganization and improvement of existing capacity.

[2] For the trend to voluntary amalgamation, see above, ch. 5, sect. v.

allocating production between firms (to prevent excess capacity under-cutting the market) and even levies on those firms remaining in production (to compensate those with no quota or having to sell in more competitive markets).

Again, this reflected an approach which, in the heady days at the end of the Great War, had been seriously entertained within the industry: in February 1919 an MAGB Committee recommended the creation of a single national corporation to market the entire output of coal and by a 'scientific' handling of the output avoid the costs of 'unfettered competition'.[1] But this proposal had been lost, or abandoned, in the political confusion and anxiety of the spring of 1919 and when, in 1925-6, there was renewed pressure to form selling organizations, the MAGB rejected the idea (especially in relation to the export market) on the grounds that by raising prices it would diminish the industry's competitiveness and sales.

In fact, however, support for the idea of marketing associations came from all quarters. The Samuel Commission certainly favoured the idea in the spring of 1926 and both Ministers and the Commission's members met representatives of the leading German cartel to discuss the principles of such an association. Moreover, a number of coalowners were powerful advocates: in West Yorkshire, for example, A. W. Archer told the Minister of Labour that he attached 'the greatest importance' to a marketing scheme to promote 'cohesion and common sense'; pressure was exerted by the Chairman of the North Staffordshire Colliery Owners' Association and, in South Wales, by Sir Samuel Instone; while Sir Alfred Mond bombarded Ministers, Parliament, and the public with his passionately held view that, rather than desperate and self-defeating attempts to cut wages, the industry should be pursuing (and might justifiably be *forced* to pursue) the example of the Rhenish–Westphalian Syndicate, which marketed 70 per cent of the Ruhr's output, adjusted sales to local demand conditions, and deployed production quotas for its associated colliery enterprises. In Germany, Mond argued, 'coal is not sold by a disorderly mob of people throwing their coal into the market without any relation to consumption or the demands of the market'.[2]

[1] *A Suggested Scheme of Reconstruction for the Coal Mining Industry*, 15 Feb. 1919 (copy in SRO CB6/2).

[2] For Archer, see SRO GD 193/416/13 ff. (15 July 1926); for North Staffordshire: *Samuel Evidence* Q 16370; for Instone: SRO GD 193/416/52 (13 Apr. 1926), MSWCOA, 21 June 1926. For Mond: *Hansard* 15 June 1926, col. 2186. Cf. ibid., cols. 2196-7. Mond's advocacy, according to *The Economist* 'is resented more than it is appreciated' (quoted in Neuman 1934, 158). For his

Once again, however, as with schemes for the amalgamation of mines, political and ideological inhibitions deflected the government from energetic initiatives, although behind the scenes Steel-Maitland urged leading owners to persuade their local associations to act.[1] Admittedly, in the summer of 1926 the Cabinet established a Departmental Committee on cooperative selling which concluded that 'there are worse evils than a monopoly' and (with its three coalowner members dissenting) advocated district-based 'organised marketing' to counter 'excessive individualism', with legal powers for the owners of 75 per cent of the output in a district to oblige owners of the remaining 25 per cent to participate.[2] Yet, the idea of *external* compulsion was still shunned and the government decided to postpone a consideration of policy for a further two years, at which time it would also examine the issue of amalgamation.

In the two years after 1926 the context for industrial policy changed in various important respects. The most important development was the failure of the wages and hours settlements to arrest the industry's economic decline. As we have already seen, the appreciation of this fact produced an abrupt volte-face on the part of the owners—who in 1927-8, in all the major districts, formed voluntary marketing associations in an attempt to control supply and maintain prices.[3] At the same time, however, neither these structural reforms nor the coincident increase in industrial concentration had very much effect on the depression. Unemployment, in early 1926, had averaged just under 10 per cent (wholly and partly unemployed); in 1927 it did not fall below 16 per cent

campaign, see Baldwin Papers, 13/181-5 (17 Apr. 1926), 21/48-51 (23 Apr. 1926), and 21/53-5 (30 Apr. 1926); Mond 1927, 222 ff. (especially 230-1). Mond organized a visit by representatives of The Rhenish–Westphalian Syndicate in Apr. 1926: SRO GD 193/146/17-22 (18 Apr. 1926); *Industry and Politics*, 230. He also organized a private meeting of coalowners to consider the problem and claimed that many (including Evan Williams) were sympathetic, but that the move was frustrated by opposition by two Scottish representatives, Sir Adam Nimmo and Wallace Thorneycroft: Baldwin Papers, 21/48-51 (23 Apr. 1926). The Rhenish–Westphalian Syndicate was widely quoted as an example and model (German legislation of 1919 had extended the coverage and powers of such marketing syndicates), and was described in detail by the Samuel Commission and the Departmental Committee of 1926. However, there was a certain amount of loose thinking by those who cited it as a precedent without reservations, since the Ruhr was a single coalfield, producing a narrow range of coal (predominantly coking coal) for more homogeneous markets—and thereby much easier to administer than Britain's disparate and scattered fields. See the comments in *Britain's Industrial Future, being the Report of the Liberal Industrial Inquiry* (1928), 347.

[1] SRO GD 193/421/54-6 (15 Apr. 1926).
[2] *Report of the Departmental Committee on Co-operative Selling in the Coal Mining Industry*, PP 1926 XIII, 771-6. Also see *Hansard* 22 Feb. 1927, cols. 1689-1729.
[3] Above, ch. 5, sect. v.

and averaged 20 per cent in June–September; a year later (June–November 1928) it rose to 26 per cent,[1] and the Cabinet was fearful of social as well as economic disintegration.

Such anxieties appeared in the spring and summer of 1927, when it became apparent that the 1926 settlements had failed to rescue the industry. Spurred by the Minister of Labour (Steel-Maitland), the Cabinet Committee on Civil Research looked into the problem of unemployment in coalmining[2] and was made vividly aware of its uneven geographical incidence (the export areas were particularly badly hit)[3] and the extraordinary pressure on the system of Poor Law relief. Of the 80 Poor Law Unions providing relief to an above-average proportion of their population, coalmining districts accounted for 35, representing about half of all coalmining Unions.[4] From 1 August 1927 the provision of the 1926 Mining Industry Act which enabled recruitment of adults to the industry to be restricted to those who had been in the industry in April 1926 was activated. But otherwise, nothing very specific came of these deliberations, although the Committee appears to have toyed with the curious idea of raising the school-leaving age for miners' sons.[5] Certainly, as far as industrial (as against relief) policy was concerned, the government had boxed itself into a corner by precluding any major legislative initiative for two years after 1926.[6]

Yet political perturbation about the problem of unemployment continued to mount (a Commons debate on the subject on 16 November 1927 had to be suspended in uproar) and when Steel-Maitland once more warned the Cabinet of the seriousness of the crisis and the need to counter the alarming concentration of surplus manpower by a policy of 'disintegration', the Cabinet appointed a Committee on unemployment in the coalfields. There, the President of the Board of Trade (Cunliffe-

---

[1] *CYB* 1934, 632.

[2] CAB 24/186/279–81 (10 May 1927), SRO GD 193/661/80–93 (22 June 1927).

[3] On 25 July 1927 the national average of coalminers wholly unemployed was 10.8%. The figures for Northumberland, Durham, South Wales, and Scotland were 18.4%, 21.0%, 15.0%, and 12.4%. *CYB* 1928, 692.

[4] Memorandum by Minister of Health (Neville Chamberlain): 'Pauperism in the Coal Mining Areas', 24 June 1927: SRO GD 193/661/4. Chamberlain pointed out that the problem was not simply one of over-generous Guardians: 'the continuing high figures for instance in Bedwellty, which has been administered by nominees of the Minister for the past three months, indicate the real difficulty of dealing with a population which is surplus to the openings for employment in the area'.

[5] Memorandum by Secretary of State for Scotland, 1 July 1927: Baldwin Papers, 11/7.

[6] Gowers to Chancellor of Exchequer, 17 June 1927: Baldwin Papers, 11/5. Gowers argued that the industry's problem was a chronic excess of capacity—and that the two vital needs were 'co-operation in selling' and 'some centralised organization' to control supply.

Lister) argued that 'no government could contemplate 100,000 or 200,000 men completely without work however they were maintained'.

The Cabinet Committee concluded that the problem of surplus man-power was by no means 'ephemeral' and, following arguments from the Minister of Health, Neville Chamberlain, advocated government help in the transference of labour out of the chronically depressed mining areas.[1] This was, in effect, a modest enough proposal, and although it led to the speedy creation of an Industrial Transference Board (announced on 7 December 1927 and appointed on 6 January 1928) the Board had only a negligible budget and a largely coordinating and investigatory role. Yet it was, at least, a form of action—and one which was to excite a certain amount of interest.[2] In its first Report the Board served to emphasize the problem of surplus manpower—which it confirmed as being at least 200,000—in staple industries which were regionally con-centrated. Accepting the main outlines of industrial and financial policy as given (and therefore excluding consideration of industrial reorganiza-tion, subsidies, tariffs, reflation, or government investment), the Board concentrated solely on the means by which 'the rapid transfer of workpeople from the depressed areas' might be facilitated.[3]

In the course of 1928, however, the problem of unemployment and social distress reached crisis proportions, and the government began to show signs of desperation. Some Ministers were even obliged to re-examine fundamental assumptions: Steel-Maitland, for example, almost stumbled on cost-benefit analysis by exploring the savings in relief and other social expenditure that might come from public stimulus to employment, while Cunliffe-Lister reminded his Cabinet colleagues of the costs of doing nothing about the workless.[4] Nevertheless, experience and ideology both militated against radical experiment or substantial

[1] Memorandum by Minister of Labour, 23 Nov. 1927: CAB 24/189/268-73; Cabinet Commit-tee on Unemployment in the Coal Trade, 2 and 6 Dec. 1927: CAB/27/358. In the course of the Committee's discussions, Chamberlain also advocated arrangements for the relief of the long-term unemployed separate from the Poor Law; and the President of the Board of Education argued in favour of a reduction of the burden of rates on the coal industry—anticipating the pro-visions of 1928-9.

[2] For admiring comments by an American on the provisions for training and transference, see Morris 1934, 234 ff. The Industrial Transfer programme placed 10,000 miners in 1928, 32,000 in 1929, and 30,000 in 1930. The numbers then dropped as the depression spread to other areas. These were gross numbers. Up to 40% returned home.

[3] *Industrial Transference Board Report*, July 1928. (Cmd. 3156. 1928) 6. The Board's first report contrasted unemployment levels (in May 1928) of 2.5 to 5% in London and Midland counties with 24.2% in Glamorgan, 21% in Durham, and, in smaller coal districts, 62.3% in Merthyr Tydfil, 48.6% in Blaina, and 42% in Bishop Auckland.

[4] SRO GD 193/504 (1 and 19 Mar. 1928); CAB 24/196/88 ff. (24 June 1928).

action—with lugubrious results. 'Imagine our charge sheet on the Day of Judgement', wrote Steel-Maitland helplessly to the Prime Minister in October; '"The greatest material evil of your day was worklessness. Did you try to diagnose it?" What could we say?'[1]

Yet complete passivity was an impossible posture, if only because lack of work and mounting poverty in distressed areas, and especially in the increasingly notorious coalmining districts of South Wales and the North-East, threatened actual malnutrition and social collapse. In the spring of 1928 the government encouraged the private initiatives which led to the creation of the Lord Mayors' Fund for the Relief of Distressed Mining Areas. In the summer a Board of Education survey showed only that 'On the whole ... there is no alarming amount of malnutrition among school children' in South Wales and Durham, but acknowledged that even that precarious situation might deteriorate. And later in the year, after the Minister of Health had expressed anxiety about food consumption in the two areas, and arranged for further surveys of nutrition and health, the Cabinet responded to pressure to do more to ward off privation.

Public money was to be used to help organize communal feeding under the auspices of the Lord Mayors' Fund, government administrative resources were placed at the Fund's disposal, and the Treasury was to provide matching grants for the money raised by public appeal. The government even secured the patronage of the Prince of Wales, who in a remarkable Christmas broadcast on behalf of the Fund spoke of the 'cruel torture' experienced by a quarter of a million miners and their families: 'helpless distress, starvation face to face, nothing left, and few places to go for help'. This had an immediate effect on the sums raised. Yet the Fund's resources (the public contributed £800,300 in the Fund's first, and only, year, and that was matched by the government contribution) hardly touched the core of the problem, and the campaign even managed to excite opposition from those (often themselves in want) who still resented the miners' prolonged and seemingly destructive stoppage in 1926.[2]

---

[1] Baldwin Papers, 130/10 (22 Oct. 1928).

[2] *PP* 1928–9 XIV, 162–9; Baldwin Papers, 19/42 ff. (27 Mar. 1928); CAB 24/196 (19 July 1928); CAB 27/381 (14 Dec. 1928); MH 79/304 (15 Dec. 1928), which pointed out that the wages of those in employment in South Wales collieries were often lower than the exiguous Poor Law rates of relief; *Interim Report of the Central Joint Committees for the Administration of the Lord Mayors' Fund for Relief of Distressed Mining Areas, July 1929* (copy in MH 79/304); *The Times* 27 Dec. 1928, 7b. Baldwin Papers, 12/8 (27 Jan. and 19 Mar. 1929). The Fund was inaugurated on 1 Apr. 1928 by the Lord Mayors of London, Cardiff, and Newcastle. Its scope was greatly extended towards the end

Meanwhile, following the first report of the Industrial Transference Board in July 1928 the government also moved towards a more direct, although still very limited, assault on the problem of worklessness. Retraining, the provision of 'forest holidays', and the Board's help to migration were all to be extended; and, again following the Board's recommendation, the Prime Minister sent a personal appeal to 120,000 employers exhorting each to offer a job to a man or boy from the depressed areas.[1]

Yet these efforts barely touched the problem of unemployment in the coal industry, let alone more generally. And, in the absence of any official acceptance of more reflationary policies or of a broad-based policy of protection, Ministers could only really contemplate restricted action relating to specific industries. As far as coal was concerned, the problem was lent an air of urgency by the near-panic among owners, who appreciated that wages could not be driven any lower. Hence, while turning 'almost in desperation' to the possibility of restructuring the marketing side of the industry,[2] the owners also began to emphasize the deleterious effects of the costs of taxes, social services, and railway rates. Even in South Wales, erstwhile individualists (including Evan Williams) began to look to government for some sort of help. A small minority were prepared to contemplate financial aid, and a majority pressed for an official appeal for help and (in line with the MAGB's national policy) state action to reduce rates and railway charges.[3]

Partly in response to such pressures, the Chancellor of the Exchequer formulated a scheme (announced in the 1928 Budget) for extensive rating relief, via central government grants, to encourage industry and agriculture. The reduction of local rates on railways and industry by 75 per cent was due to come into effect on 1 October 1929, and the railway relief would be passed on as lower freight charges. But in response to the immediate industrial crisis, and after powerful representation from the coal industry as well as Steel-Maitland and the Unemployment Policy

of the year. The bulk of its expenditure went on boots and clothing. In Jan. 1929 the Secretary for Mines successfully resisted proposals that the Miners' Welfare Fund be diverted to supply the immediate necessities of mining areas: CAB 24/201/235–43 (15 Jan. 1929).

[1] CAB 24/192/88–133 (29 June 1928); CAB 27/34 (20 July 1928). For the modest activity of the Unemployment Grants Committee, 1920–32 see *Final Report of the Unemployment Grants Committee, 20th December 1920 to 31st August 1932* (Cmd. 4354. 1933). There was, of course, an awareness that public works might generate employment. But on the whole the predominance of the 'Treasury View' prevented the formulation of any counter-cyclical public works programme.

[2] See memorandum by Secretary for Mines, May 1928 (revision of Nov. 1928); POWE 16/80.

[3] MSWCOA MG18 (1 and 10 Nov. and 19 Dec. 1927).

Committee, it was agreed to expedite and focus the new measures. The rating relief for railways was therefore brought forward to 1 December 1928, and the relief itself was concentrated (as far as coal was concerned) on fuel destined for exports, foreign bunkers, and the iron and steel industry.[1]

At a more general and more important level, the Cabinet returned to the major question of the economics of coalmining and to the problem of industrial reorganization. In July 1928 the Cabinet Unemployment Policy Committee reiterated the previous year's proposal that the government might guarantee loans to underwrite approved amalgamations in the coal, iron and steel, and cotton industries (to a limit of £10 million).[2] Nothing came of this, but it was indicative of a new concern with 'rationalization'—the elimination of surplus capacity and the concentration of productive units. Indeed, by 1928–9 it was clear that neither the Mining Industry Act of 1926 nor the pressure of market forces had (as far as advocates of extensive reconstruction were concerned) made a sufficiently reassuring difference to the industry's structure,[3] while the industry's own district marketing schemes were proving inadequate to their task.[4] Even within the government, it seemed to some that the two-year breathing-space had not worked. In June 1928 the Secretary for Mines (Douglas-King) even advocated a plan for the compulsory limitation of output by individual firms,[5] but once again nothing came of the suggestions for government action.

As such stillborn proposals suggest, the feeling that piecemeal changes might not suffice was related to an enhanced emphasis of surplus capacity as the industry's central problem. This was hardly surprising, given the failure of the reduced wages and increased hours of 1926 to have any perceptible ameliorative effect and the fact that potentially efficient firms were often obliged to work below capacity, and therefore at high average costs.[6] And this reinforced perception, in its turn, meant

---

[1] CAB 24/196/207–8, 393–7 (9 and 20 July 1928); CAB 27/34 (20 July 1928); *MAGB* 1929, 27–8, MSWCOA MG18 (26 Mar. 1928 and 5 June 1928). In the discussions at the Monmouthshire & South Wales Coal Owners' Association, Evan Williams estimated that for South Wales the concentration of railway relief on export coal would save about 1s. per ton and that this, together with the relief on rate payments by the collieries themselves, would just about equal the trading loss in coal in South Wales: MSWCOA MG18 (5 June 1928).

[2] CAB 27/34 (20 July 1928).

[3] See the disappointed comments in Clay 1929, 179–80.

[4] Above, 210–12.

[5] Secretary for Mines to President of the Board of Trade, 12 June 1928: POWE 16/180.

[6] In addition, since voluntary marketing schemes often meant that efficient firms were kept operating below capacity, they frequently increased costs.

that the discussion of coal was incorporated into the broader vision of rationalization of Britain's staple industries—the need to coordinate, concentrate, streamline—which was a characteristic of the late 1920s.[1]

In fact, of course, rationalization would not improve employment prospects. On the contrary, it was designed to *reduce* capacity. But those who advocated reorganization urged that a smaller industry was bound to come, and that it was better to reduce capacity in an orderly, conscious fashion than to leave it to the harsh processes of impersonal markets. In effect, the social problem of unemployment was to be relieved by social policies; the economic problem of coal by stream-lining. The need to reduce capacity by restricting the operations of in-efficient pits had been argued in 1925-7. And in 1925 there had even been some informal proposals (involving the Ministry of Labour and the Governor of the Bank of England) that the joint-stock banks might bring pressure to bear to eliminate 'obsolete and extravagant plants' in coalmining, iron and steel.[2] But a widespread persuasion that systematic public initiative and finance might be needed did not come until the last years of the decade.

By this time, the discussion of costs in the coal industry had therefore got beyond the consideration of the economies of scale: rationalization was taken to mean the eradication of the least efficient units and the concentration of output in the most efficient—thus achieving the twin advantages of diminishing competition and lowering average costs even without an increase in the size of enterprises. It was essentially an exer-cise in scaling-down. As the Secretary for Mines put it, 'The anticipated closing down of the inefficient pits through the natural play of eco-nomic forces has not happened and is not happening quickly enough to save the situation. The pruning of the mining industry has still to be done.' Hence his proposal for government intervention.[3]

Yet the cause of this situation also explained why it was difficult to tackle. It lay in the 'amazing capacity' of marginal firms to hang on in bad times, preferring either to sell at a loss of 1s. or 2s. a ton, rather than bear the costs of closing down altogether (with little chance of realizing many of their assets), or to close down temporarily, only to open when

---

[1] For the rationalization movement see Hannah 1976, ch. 3; Mond 1927, 210-21; the reports of the Balfour Committee on Industry and Trade (*Factors in Industrial and Commercial Efficiency*, 1927 and *Final Report*, Cmd. 3282, 1929); and *Britain's Industrial Future*, 128-30.

[2] Baldwin Papers, 13/181 (17 Apr. 1926), 21/53-4 (30 Apr. 1926), 17/15 (17 June 1927); *Samuel Evidence* Q 16023; *Hansard* 15 June 1926, col. 2185 (Sir Alfred Mond); *Britain's Industrial Future*, 353; E. R. Peacock to Montagu Norman, 21 Aug. 1925: SMT 2/272.

[3] Memorandum to President of the Board of Trade, 12 June 1928: POWE 16/180.

the market showed any sign of revival. Such firms were sustained by overdrafts from banks which were themselves fearful of losing existing loans, and hopeful of recovering some of their money when (and if) trade picked up. They were thought to damage the industry 'out of all proportion to the relative quantity of coal they produce'.[1] The problem was general to the staple industries, but others had been more drastically and successfully pruned since the War,[2] and the coal industry was especially notorious for the number and range of its businesses and the painful slowness with which adversity extruded the unprofitable firm. 'Certain collieries may have to close down', argued one Lanarkshire coalowner ruefully in the dreadful year 1927, 'but only after all Owners have lost considerably'.[3]

Here, then, was the problem: the benefit of reducing capacity would be general, but without a national policy the costs would have to be borne privately, by firms which might not necessarily benefit at all. As the Secretary for Mines phrased it when pointing out that no firm would buy up 'superfluous' pits simply to close them: 'Why should they? The shutting is not for their own benefit alone. Why then should they pay for it?'[4] Here, too, lay the rationale for government intervention and even coercion. Many men in power may well have sympathized with the view that 'It is living in a fool's paradise . . . to wait for the industry to reorganise itself' since the owners lacked 'the will or the power' to do it.[5] And yet outsiders, whether bankers or politicians, were unable to do much about it. For, in spite of official proposals in 1927–9,[6] it was virtually impossible to envisage such a reorganization of the industry on a national basis: the political will, the necessary investment funds, the practical expertise, the likely cooperation of businessmen who were

---

[1] Sir Ernest Gowers to Chancellor of Exchequer: Baldwin Papers, 17/15 (17 June 1927); Clay 1929, 181. Also memorandum by 'H. W. C[ole]' in POWE 16/180 (23 May 1928): 'The brute cause of the trouble is that too many pits are being kept in existence in the hope that prices will improve.' For a description of the 'extraordinary' tenacity of loss-making firms in staple industries and the necessity of 'cutting out the dead wood' through consolidation rather than competition, see the *Final Report of the Committee on Industry and Trade* (Cmd. 3282. 1929), 179.

[2] Memorandum by H. W. C[ole], 23 May 1928: POWE 16/180: 'The mining industry has escaped from the pruning that the other major industries have experienced since the War.'

[3] Lanarkshire Coal Masters' Association, 9 June 1927. Bankruptcies and closures *did* take place—but painfully slowly.

[4] Memorandum to President of the Board of Trade, 12 June 1928: POWE 16/180.

[5] Clay 1929, 174 ff. He advocated government intervention and the use of public funds, comparing the British situation with the effective postwar reconstruction of the French and German coal industries which, he argued, had been facilitated by reparations and inflation, respectively.

[6] Above, 264.

sceptical of such a policy, and even the necessary reasonable prospect of economic success—all were lacking.

By 1929, therefore, the Cabinet hardly knew which way to turn. In February Cunliffe-Lister gave grudging approval to the revived idea of government support for investment in merger schemes, only to have the proposal undermined by the authoritative accountant, Sir William McLintock. At the same time, he proposed that the provisions of the 1926 Mining Industry Act (by which the Board of Trade might oblige recalcitrant minorities to accept merger schemes) be extended to selling schemes.[1] Again, however, nothing came of the discussions. And although coal exports in 1929 were sufficiently buoyant to improve the industry's performance, it was still extremely depressed.

Nevertheless, in spite of the lack of any major policy initiatives, it was clear that the situation could not continue indefinitely. And it is difficult not to agree with a contemporary economist, Henry Clay, who in 1929 argued that the economic stress of decline, having failed to produce any effective private responses, would, through corresponding political pressures, enforce major departures in policy. He published a warning prophecy: when the current wage agreements came to be renegotiated at the end of the year, the owners would deny the possibility of paying higher wages or the feasibility of structural change; and the miners would urge both the necessity of such payments and the possibility of funding them by restructuring the industry. The debates of 1926 would have to be restaged. And Clay's prediction of the outcome was to prove remarkably accurate:

The issue was 'settled' in 1921 by a lock-out, which exaggerated the effects and delayed recovery after the initial slump; it was 'settled' again in 1926 by a lock-out, which exaggerated the check to activity and delayed recovery after the final return to the Gold Standard. Whatever Government is in power when the decision arises, if the industry has no alternative to offer except a third 'settlement' of this expensive character, it is hard to believe that some compulsion will not be applied.[2]

---

[1] Cunliffe-Lister to Baldwin, 13 Feb. 1929, and attached documents: Baldwin Papers, 30/21–39. Also in CAB 24/202/179–97 (24 Feb. 1929). For McLintock's memorandum, 22 Feb. 1929, see Baldwin Papers, 18/4.

[2] Clay 1929, 205.

PART D

DEPRESSION AND RECOVERY
COAL IN THE 1930s

CHAPTER 7

Coal in Depression and Recovery
1929–1938

As was the case with British industry in general, the coal industry's history in the 1930s was a matter of sharply contrasting phases. Even so, there was little ambiguity about the secular trend of production: in spite of the fairly steep recovery from the collapse of the early part of the decade, the industry was adjusting to a permanently lower level of output and reward than it once had enjoyed. In one respect, therefore, the unhappy experiences of the 1920s were continued and aggravated—especially in the disastrous fall in output in 1930–3. Indeed, even in the subsequent recovery the coal industry never regained the levels of output of 1929 or even 1930. On the other hand, the fluctuations in total output were accompanied by a far greater degree of price and wage stability (and therefore industrial harmony) than had been the case in the 1920s.

Related to these new elements, the 1930s also witnessed significant changes in public policy and industrial and commercial structure which together marked an important stage in the industry's history. This chapter will be concerned with the broad features of the industry's performance, with the explanation of its problems, with reaction to its vicissitudes, and with the adaptations of its marketing and industrial structures. The next chapter will be devoted to a closer consideration of the underlying issues of policy and welfare which both shaped, and flowed from, trends in output and organization.

i. The vicissitudes of the market: output and incomes in the 1930s

Shocking as the plight of the coal industry in 1927–8 had seemed,[1] worse was to come. For the unprecedented crisis of world depression after 1930 had particularly adverse consequences for the British coal industry's markets both overseas and in the heavy industries at home.

[1] Above, 260–2.

Of these, the effect on exports was the worse: between 1929 and 1933 they fell by some 30 per cent (home demand fell by 15 per cent in the same period). Even in 1927–8, total coal shipments (cargo, bunker, and manufactured fuel) had averaged about 71.5 million tons. Having reached 82 million in the mild boom of 1929, they fell precipitously to some 57 million tons in 1932–3. This dramatic collapse was a grim augury: the export trade remained stagnant in the ensuing years, falling to a bare 50 million tons in each of 1936 and 1938.[1] The halcyon year (in 1913 shipments were just over 98 million tons) were never to return. In the early 1930s, however, the decline was aggravated by the erosion of the home market. Between 1929 and 1931 British industrial production fell by 16 per cent; in 1930–1 the output of the iron and steel industry—a particularly important customer for coal—fell by one-third. By 1932 the average consumption of coal per capita in Britain was 67 cwt—the lowest for 32 years (with the exception of the years of major stoppages in 1921 and 1926) and a full 20 cwt less than in 1913.

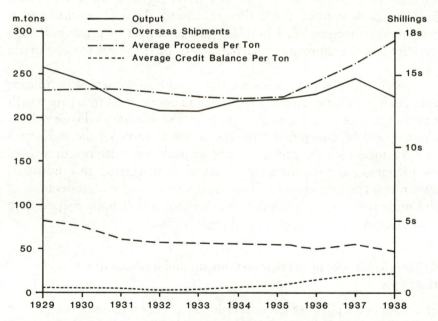

Fig. 7.1. Output, overseas shipments, and proceeds in British coalmining, 1929–1938

[1] *CYB* 1948, 623.

Table 7.1. *Output, overseas shipments, proceeds, costs, and wages in British coalmining, 1929–1938*

	(i) Output (saleable)	(ii) Exports etc. (1) Coal	(ii) Exports etc. (2) Coal, coke, man. fuel, bunkers	(iii) Available for home consumption	(iv) Average proceeds per ton disposable commercially	(v) Balance per ton disposable commercially	(vi) Output of saleable coal per manshift worked	(vii) No. of manshifts worked	(viii) Cash earnings per manshift	(ix) Average earnings per annum: Cash	(ix) Average earnings per annum: Real earnings
	(000 tons)	(000 tons)	(000 tons)	(000 tons)	*s. d.*	*s. d.*			*s. d.*	£ *s. d.*	
1929	257,907	60,267	82,149	173,500	13 11	0 4½	21.69	257	9 2¾	118 6 4	100.0
1930	243,882	54,874	75,103	166,580	14 1	0 4¼	21.62	245	9 3½	113 18 2	100.0
1931	219,459	42,750	61,647	155,680	14 0¼	0 3½	21.61	243	9 2¼	111 10 9	104.8
1932	208,733	38,899	57,147	149,500	13 10	0 2	21.99	239	9 2	109 8 5	105.8
1933	207,112	39,068	56,685	148,370	13 6½	0 2¾	22.47	242	9 1½	110 5 10	109.1
1934	220,726	39,660	57,094	161,480	13 4¼	0 5	22.94	253	9 1¾	115 11 6	113.6
1935	222,249	38,714	55,545	164,470	13 6	0 6¼	23.35	256	9 3½	118 8 1	114.8
1936	228,448	34,519	50,342	175,900	14 7½	0 11½	23.54	262	10 0¼	131 4 1	112.5
1937	240,409	40,338	56,296	181,780	15 10½	1 2¾	23.35	270	10 8	144 3 3	129.8
1938	227,015	35,856	49,633	175,142	17 4¼	1 4	22.96	259	11 2¾	145 7 5	129.2

The financial results of the industry (iv)–(vii) are presented in a revised form in unpublished *Statistical Summaries* compiled by Peat, Marwick, Mitchell and Co. in British Coal's Library. The adjustments are relatively minor.

Sources: (i), (ii) (2), (iii), (iv), (v), (vi), (viii): *CYB* 1948; 572, 584, 623, 653. (vii) *ARSM*, various years. (ix) *ARSM*, various years, adjusted by Cost of Living Index from Mitchell, *Abstract*, 345.

The consequences of these trends for the coal industry were cata-strophic. Output fell from an annual average of 249 million tons in 1927–8, and 257.9 million in 1929, to 207.9 million in the depression's depths, 1932–3. The 1933 level was the lowest (again with the exception of 1921 and 1926) since 1898, while the numbers employed, which were just under 950,000 at the end of 1929, fell to 770,000 in September 1933;[1] and the average percentage of unemployed miners (both wholly and tempor-arily unemployed), which had seemed bad enough at 21.9 per cent in 1928, reached 34 per cent in 1932.[2] On the other hand, a feature of these years which distinguished them from the 1920s was the relative stability of prices: pithead proceeds fell by less than one per cent per annum between 1929–33, compared with over 6 per cent for wholesale prices (including coal) in the same years, and an annual fall of 5.7 per cent in pithead prices in 1924–9.[3]

This reversal of historic tendencies was attributable to two principal factors. First, in 1929 costs were already low and wages were already at the minimum under existing district agreements. This meant that there was very little scope for direct cost reduction. Second, the Coal Mines Act of 1930, in order to facilitate the maintenance of wages while hours were reduced, had introduced schemes for the control of output and sales, and this had naturally opened the way to cartelization and price maintenance.[4] There was, in effect, a trade-off between levels of prices, profits, and wages on the one hand, and levels of activity, output, and

[1] *ARSM* 1929, 9; *ARSM* 1933, 11.

[2] Unemployment statistics from *Ministry of Labour Gazette*, various years. The coal industry was able to ensure a more extensive sharing of the existing work than most others, so that there was always a relatively high proportion of miners temporarily out of work. The figures in the text relate to annual averages: they were exceeded in some months of the relevant years. Figures for unemployment percentages at a specific date in the second or third week of June in selected years are as follows:

	Coalmining (GB)			All Industry (UK)		
	Wholly	Temporarily	Total	Wholly	Temporarily	Total
1928	14.5	11.2	25.7	7.7	1.9	9.6
1932	21.0	19.6	40.6	17.5	3.3	20.8
1933	22.4	14.4	36.8	18.0	4.0	22.0
1935	18.8	11.8	30.6	14.0	2.5	16.5
1938	9.9	8.1	18.0	10.4	2.5	12.9

Also see Table 10.3.

[3] Jones 1939, 147–8.   [4] Below, 296–30.

employment on the other. As a result, the slump was felt more keenly in the waste of idle men and capital than in the returns to those who managed to stay active.

This was exemplified in the fact that minimum wages under district agreements continued to be paid although less regular work reduced *annual* cash earnings by about 7 per cent in 1929–33 (however, retail prices fell by 15 per cent, so that the *real* wages of those in employment actually rose). For the owners, the combination of sticky prices and falling costs meant that even in the worst years they appeared to earn a small positive credit balance, although this was on a severely declining tonnage and was in any case insufficient for the owners to pay interest on debentures and other loans. Further, being a national average, it masked significant losses in particular districts. In part because of economic inflexibility, therefore, and in part because of the combination of the 'social' determination of wages and the effects of government-inspired 'social control' of markets, the real (relative) price of coal, which had been forced down during the 1920s, once more shot up. Between 1929 and 1933 wholesale coal prices fell by about 2 per cent; but wholesale prices in general (*including* coal prices) fell by just over 25 per cent.[1] Significantly, the devaluation which accompanied Britain's leaving the Gold Standard in September 1931 had a major deflationary effect on coal prices in other countries, while enabling prices expressed in sterling to remain almost stationary.[2] Moreover, the operation of marketing schemes supported the price of coal throughout the 1930s, albeit at the probable cost of a loss of sales. Between 1930 and 1938 wholesale prices in general rose by a mere one per cent; those of coal increased by over 20 per cent.[3]

In common with the larger economy, the coal industry experienced a marked recovery from 1934; and, as with that broader movement, the upward trend was largely based on the buoyancy of home markets, where the demand for coal increased very rapidly before falling back in the brief recession of 1938. Yet the failure of exports to recover was a serious impediment to long-run health: the annual average production of 1936–8 was still only 232 million tons, compared with 249 million tons in the poor years at the end of the previous decade and 273 million in 1911–13. Further, although unemployment declined, it remained

[1] Mitchell, *Abstract*, 477. As a result, in 1933 the average price of coal was some 22% above that of 1913, although wholesale prices generally were more or less exactly the same.

[2] International Labour Office 1938, I, 190–1, 199.

[3] Mitchell, *Abstract*, 477. For the 'trade-off' between prices and output, see Prest 1936.

uncomfortably high, and even in 1937—a relatively 'prosperous' year—
11.4 per cent of insured miners were wholly out of work and 7.5 per cent
were on short time. The industry was blighted by secular stagnation,
seemingly unable to eliminate its chronically surplus capacity. Employment, which had been 956,700 in 1929 stayed below 800,000 throughout
the recovery; and even with a growing demand, the excess of supply
held down prices until the winter of 1935–6, when a successful wage
demand raised both costs and prices.

Two measures indicate the increasing rewards which went to those
still active in the industry as a result of the combination of industrial
revival and the semi-official controls of output and prices. On the one
hand, between 1934 and 1938 average coal prices rose by 30 per cent,
which was distinctly faster than costs, so that the owners' credit balances,
which averaged a mere 2d. or 3d. per ton in 1931–3, reached 11½d. in 1936
and 1s. 4d. in 1938.[1] On the other, employed miners also gained—initially
from the greater regularity of work, which meant that annual earnings
rose by more than shift earnings, and then from the wage settlement of
1935–6. Thus while shift wages were almost unchanged between 1933 and
1935, annual earnings increased from £110 5s. 10d. to £118 8s. 1d.; and in
the subsequent three years the former rose from 9s. 3d. to 11s. 2d. and the
latter from £118 8s. 1d. to £145 7s. 5d.[11]

In some important respects, therefore, the experiences of the coal
industry in the 1930s contrasted with that of the 1920s: its output trends
were sharply defined; legislative and institutional experiment replaced
purely competitive forces in the determination of output and price
levels and patterns; and in the course of a fairly well-sustained revival
there was a not insubstantial increase in the rewards to the employed
factors of production. Yet these developments coincided with an
enforced accommodation of the industry to the lower level of activity
which had been violently anticipated in the previous decade. For, even
though the amount of coal available for home consumption by 1936–8
was more or less the same as in 1909–13 and in the best years of the
1920s, the persistent stagnation of the export trade defeated the industry. At the end of the 1930s overseas sales were less than 60 per cent
of the levels obtained before the First World War. This painful contrac-

[1] Between 1933 and 1938 the relative price of coal remained unchanged: the indices of coal
prices and general wholesale prices both rose by just over and just under 20% respectively:
Mitchell, *Abstract*, 477.

[2] *ARSM*, various years. These figures (which are national averages) relate to cash earnings only.
In 1938 the average value of payments in kind (which were made in only a handful of districts)
were estimated at 5d. per shift and £5 12s. per annum.

tion of a great staple industry was, as we shall see, partly the result of secular changes in the role of solid fuel in the world economy. But it also reflected the long-run decline in Britain's competitive position.

Between 1929 and 1938, while Britain's share of world output remained more or less stable at about 18 or 19 per cent, her share of the world's *trade* in coal fell significantly: from some 45 to 37 per cent, according to the Secretary for Mines.[1] Associated with this decline was a significant increase in the relative price of British coal.[2] Such an increase hindered sales, but it undoubtedly helped sustain the rewards of employed labour and capital in the late 1930s and in that respect 'justified' the schemes for the control of output and sales which were given legislative effect from 1930, and strengthened in 1934 and 1936.[3] At the same time, relative prices also reflected relative costs, for the lag in British efficiency which had appeared in the 1920s, was continued into the next decade. In 1934, for example, a pessimistic Secretary for Mines noted that between 1930 and 1934 output per manshift in different continental countries had grown between four and seven times the rate (just under 6 per cent) at which British OMS had grown.[4] Even allowing for the imprecision involved in the international differences and chronological changes in the length of a shift, these were startling indications of the deterioration in Britain's competitive position.[5]

Once again, however, it is misleading to imagine that the costs and benefits of change were shared uniformly between the various coalfields in the country. As in the 1920s, the combination of differential movements in export and domestic sales, and the uneven geographical process of development and ageing, generated significant contrasts in the economic experience of different districts.

The fields which had been more dependent on overseas sales naturally had to bear the most severe strains between 1929 and 1938. The combined output of South Wales, Northumberland and Durham, and Scotland fell by some 19 per cent, which was three times the rate at which that of the more recently developed mines in South Yorkshire,

---

[1] *ARSM* 1936, 8; *ARSM* 1938, 10. In 1913 British coal had accounted for 23% of world output and 55% of world exports. A somewhat steeper fall (to 29% of world trade) is suggested in Darmstadter (see Table 7.2).

[2] Below, 285.

[3] Below, 296–301.

[4] *ARSM* 1934, 14. He also pointed out that the Ruhr mines had increased their OMS (by 23.5%) with no significant change in the proportions cut and conveyed mechanically—i.e. presumably by improvements in organization, layout, and concentration of production. Also see below, 284–5.

[5] Below, 284.

North Derbyshire, and Nottinghamshire declined. In the early 1930s the main export areas, while exemplifying horrific rates of unemployment,[1] had also been producing at a distinct loss. But later in the decade Scotland and even more the North-East recovered much lost financial ground—measured in terms of profits per ton produced—as they benefited from bilateral trade agreements and also from an increasing diversion of their output to satisfy the rapidly recovering demand from British heavy industries. South Wales, by contrast, and especially in the bituminous coal sector, had a persistently unhappy experience. With the lowest OMS of all the principal fields (except for Lancashire and Cheshire), the highest labour costs, and the weakest markets (its steam coal was particularly hit by the rise of oil-powered shipping), South Wales experienced industrial stagnation, losses or negligible profits, and the highest rates of unemployment throughout the decade. (Even in 1935–8 the average percentage of wholly unemployed in South Wales exceeded 21 per cent of the labour force, at a time when the national figure was just over 15 per cent.)

On the other hand, the complexities of wage-determination meant that this situation was not matched in terms of the earnings of miners employed in the export fields. Thus, throughout the period Scottish miners, whose average shift earnings fell below all other major fields except for the North-East, received the highest annual incomes—principally because they worked the most shifts and the longest hours and had the highest OMS of all but the Yorkshire–Nottinghamshire–North Derbyshire field.[2] Even South Wales and Monmouthshire, where labour productivity (OMS) was almost the lowest in the country, had the second highest level of annual earnings in the slump of the early 1930s, although its persistent economic troubles meant that by the second half of the decade its earnings had fallen below those of the inland fields. There was, however, no doubt about the position of miners in the North-East: both shift and annual average earnings in Northumberland and Durham were the lowest in the country, and even allowing for the

---

[1] In 1933 the percentages of *wholly* unemployed miners were 26.8 in Scotland, 30.1 in Durham, and 26.7 in South Wales & Monmouthshire, as against figures of between 9 and 17% in Yorkshire, Derbyshire, Nottinghamshire, Leicestershire, Staffordshire, Shropshire, Worcestershire, and Warwickshire.

[2] Scottish miners also received lower allowances in kind than miners in most other districts. For a discussion of the factors mitigating the wage superiority of Scottish miners, see Long 1978, 238 ff. (There were, of course, very important contrasts even within such a disparate district as 'Scotland'.) In the 1930s (1930–8) the annual average number of manshifts worked was 297 in Scotland and 252 in Britain as a whole: *ARSM*, various years.

fact that the average value of allowances in kind were far and away the highest (they were estimated at some £14 or £15 in 1937—as against a national average of just over £5) the estimated total income was still less than any other major field. Nevertheless, the fact remained that, on average, between 1929 and 1938 the annual cash earnings of British miners rose by 23 per cent, while retail prices fell by 5 per cent.

Considered in general terms, the main beneficiaries of the changes in demand and supply in the course of the 1930s were, of course, the inland districts (although, as with the 'export districts', specialization was not complete: coal from the Midland field (Yorkshire, for example) found its way to overseas markets via the Humber ports).

Sustained by rich seams and large-scale and intensive deep mining, and (after 1933) by the expanding home market, the South Yorkshire–North Derbyshire–Nottinghamshire field continued its relative growth. By 1938 it was producing 26 per cent of the national output, and having made credit balances of just under 1s. per ton even in the slump of the early 1930s, it returned good profits and the country's highest wages (after Scotland) in the second half of the decade. The somewhat smaller inland 'district' of South Derbyshire, Leicestershire, Cannock Chase, and Warwickshire (which was about one-fifth of the size of the South Yorkshire–North Derbyshire–Nottinghamshire field) did even better in terms of credit balance per ton, which averaged over 2s. in 1936–8, and almost as well in terms of miners' earnings. Except for the traditional problem of seasonal unemployment, the Yorkshire and Midland pits also had relatively good employment records; and in 1938 their unemployment rate was only about 6 per cent (wholly out of work), as against a national average of 10 per cent. (Warwickshire's record was outstanding, and even in the terrible years 1932–3 its percentage of unemployed miners was less than 10.) The new, but minuscule, Kent field continued to expand even in the slump, but from 1933 its share of total output (still less than one per cent) remained more or less unchanged.

In the Lancashire and Cheshire field, which had been the Cinderella of the inland districts in the 1920s,[1] the instabilities of the 1930s were met with somewhat more vigour. Although proceeds (i.e. average prices) fell drastically in the slump of 1932–3, as the small export market of the Irish Free State was virtually closed by a tariff and as other British inland districts desperately sought outlets, average costs on Lancashire and Cheshire were also greatly reduced, so that the losses of 1929–30 were

[1] Above, ch. 5, sect. ii.

turned into tiny gains in 1932–3. The district (data come from Lanca-shire, Cheshire, and North Staffordshire) appears to have benefited from the pioneering use of a central selling organization, and intensive efforts to improve techniques. Some benefits may also have come (at least initially) from the reorganization associated with the formation of Manchester Collieries Ltd. (1929)[1] and the Wigan Coal Company (1930). This improvement was accelerated in the later 1930s, as home markets revived. By 1938 the average net profit per ton in the combined field exceeded those of Yorkshire, Nottinghamshire, and North Derbyshire. On the other hand, and in spite of *relatively* good annual earnings for most of the 1930s, unemployment remained very high (an average of about 15 per cent wholly, and 8 per cent temporarily, unemployed even in 1936–8). As a result, Lancashire and Cheshire continued to produce about 6 per cent of the nation's coal output in both depression and recovery.[2]

ii. The context of long-run stagnation

Such gains as accrued to the British coal industry in the 1930s were, as has been seen, severely conditioned by their unequal distribution between districts and over time, and by the fact that the industry was never able to regain the level of activity (and employment) which it had known in 1924, let alone 1913. The long-run stagnation, which was beginning to be apparent in the 1920s, now had to be accepted.

The most important context for that stagnation was international: the industrial and financial collapse in the world economy of the early 1930s also brought about a collapse in the world's consumption of, and trade in, coal, and the 1929 levels were not recovered, even in the relatively prosperous year of 1937. In fact, the retardation of the world's coal industry was more marked in the 1930s than the 1920s. Taking the period 1929–38 as a whole, there was an annual average *decline* of almost one per cent in world coal production and of 3.5 per cent in world coal exports.[3] Within this, as we have seen, Britain's share of world trade continued to fall.

What lay behind these trends? The foundation, of course, was the

---

[1] For subsequent caveats concerning Manchester Collieries' performance, see below, 313.

[2] For Lancashire and Cheshire see Jones 1939, 75, 80; Prest 1937, 296.

[3] Darmstadter 1971, 732. Whereas the annual rate of growth of world demand for coal had been about 4% for some decades before 1914, between 1913 and 1929 it was 0.7%, and between 1913 and 1937 a mere 0.3%. International Labour Office 1938, I, 75–6.

Table 7.2. *The international coal industry, 1929-1938*
(Volumes in ooo metric tons of coal equivalent)

	1929	1933	1937	1938
World				
output of primary energy	1,847,910	1,466,198	1,974,278	1,867,563
output of solid fuel	1,437,567	1,079,703	1,417,385	1,323,774
as % primary energy	77.8	73.6	71.8	70.9
output of hard coal	1,345,086	1,005,169	1,310,787	1,213,358
as % primary energy	72.8	68.6	66.4	65.0
exports of solid fuel	168,343	113,488	142,341	125,691
as % primary energy exports	60.4	51.4	47.5	43.3
bunkers:				
all	73,892	56,397	66,135	60,077
solid fuel	41,023	27,756	30,729	27,965
solid fuel as % all bunkers	55.5	49.2	46.5	46.5
Germany				
output of solid fuel	231,595	159,998	242,310	247,165
as % world output	16.1	14.8	17.1	18.7
exports of solid fuel	45,347	30,664	48,830	38,536
as % world exports	26.9	27.0	34.3	30.1
UK				
output of solid fuel	262,045	210,436	244,252	230,636
as % world output	18.2	19.5	17.2	17.4
exports of solid fuel	65,434	42,824	44,160	38,796
as % world exports	38.9	37.7	31.0	29.3
solid fuel bunkers	16,655	13,675	11,891	10,657
as % world solid fuel bunkers	40.6	49.3	38.7	38.1
Poland				
output of solid fuel	46,258	27,306	36,223	38,107
as % world output	3.2	2.5	2.6	2.9
exports of solid fuel	13,643	8,982	10,228	10,141
as % world exports	8.1	7.9	7.2	7.7

Source: J. Darmstadter, *Energy in the World Economy* (Baltimore, 1971), 224 ff., 263 ff., 423 ff., 588 ff.

relatively poor performance of most of the world economies in the 1930s. The output of, and even more the trade in, coal was dragged down and its fall exaggerated by the great depression which broke in 1929–30; and from the trough of 1932–3 it proved impossible to regain all the lost ground. But the demand for coal was also eroded by the growth of protectionist policies in response to slump and dislocation, and by continuance of developments which had been at work for some time: the increased efficiency with which coal was consumed and the growth of substitute fuels. Protectionist policies—tariffs, import quotas, bilateral trading agreements, subsidies[1]—had a much greater effect on trade than production, since their object was, precisely, to limit commercial competition by restricting access to domestic markets. Economies and substitutions, by contrast, affected consumption in general (i.e. even within protected markets).

Those involved in the coal industry were perhaps most sensitive to the competition of petroleum products with coal. This was certainly not trivial: between 1929 and 1937 the proportion of the world's gross shipping tonnage which was coal-fired declined from 60.8 to 48.6 per cent.[2] Yet the decline from 1913 to 1929 had been even more marked (from about 90 to 60.8 per cent) and part of the fall in coal bunkers in the 1930s was in any case attributable to the fall in world trade.[3] Moreover, the general fall in the proportion of the world's primary energy derived from solid fuels (from 77.8 per cent in 1929 to 70.9 per cent in 1938)[4] was composed of some trends which had only a marginal effect on coal—notably the growth of the motor car and the aeroplane which used petroleum products.

Much more serious for the factors of production committed to the coalmining industry—although of considerable benefit to final consumers and industry in general—was the extensive attainment of continuing economies in the *direct use* of coal as a fuel and raw material. This occurred most obviously in the production of gas, electricity, iron and steel, and in the driving of steam locomotives, but was also evident throughout industry more broadly considered. In the United States, for example, the total output of goods and services hardly changed between 1929 and 1938, whereas the average annual consumption of solid fuel fell by 4.6 per cent (and of primary energy by 2.2 per cent). In the same period, the coal consumed per kilowatt-hour of electricity fell by 16 per

---

[1] Jones 1939, ch. X.

[2] International Labour Office 1938, I, 86. The proportion of *new* coal-fired tonnage in 1937 was only 19.6%.

[3] Between 1929 and 1937 the international use of solid fuel bunkers declined by some 10.3 million tons, but that of bunkers as a whole (i.e. including fuel oil) fell from 73.9 million to 66.1 million (i.e. about 11%): above, Table 7.2. Of course, given the earlier existence of specialist coal-producing districts, the decline in coal bunkers would have a concentrated and serious effect—as it did in the Monmouthshire & South Wales field.

[4] Darmstadter 1971, 224.

cent and there was a somewhat smaller increase (4 or 5 per cent in 1929–35) in the efficiency with which coal was used in steam railways and the production of pig iron.[1] In Britain, in 1929–38 the gross domestic product grew by 24 per cent but the home use of coal by only just over one per cent; while industrial production rose by 24 per cent between 1929 and 1937, but the consumption of coal in manufacturing industry increased by merely 4.7 per cent. Again at the level of the economy in general, it was estimated that between 1924 and 1935 the *annual* saving in the use of coal per unit of output was 2.5 per cent—and of that saving some 80 per cent was accounted for by 'direct' economies rather than the use of alternative fuels.[2] Some of these savings were very large: the amount of coal per ton of pig iron produced in 1930–6 fell by 12 per cent (it had fallen by 8 per cent in 1913–30); and in electricity supply between 1929 and 1938 the coal used per kilowatt-hour fell by over 30 per cent (it had fallen by 42 per cent in 1920–9).[3]

Against such a background even the existence of substantial economic growth would have imposed some demand constraints on the coal industry. It was only to be expected, therefore, that the combination of international economic depression and technical progress after 1929 had a particularly severe effect on the world's coalmining industry—an industry which was already weakened by a deadweight of excess capacity. Moreover, in the course of the depressed decade of the 1930s, that excess capacity was further enlarged, and at the same time intensified by improvements in the use of fuel which enabled the much more extensive use of 'small' coal in railways, electricity generation, and steam-raising generally (thereby increasing the level of 'economic' output for any given level of 'physical' capacity, since small coals had formerly had a much smaller market).[4]

---

[1] US Department of Commerce 1960, 139, 507–8; Darmstadter 1971, 733; International Labour Office 1938, I, 96.

[2] GDP: Feinstein 1976, T10. Industrial production: Monmouthshire & South Wales Coal Owners' Association, *Survey of the Position of the South Wales Coal Trade* (26 Jan. 1939), 15, in MSWCOA Box File 729. Fuel savings: Singer 1940–1, 166–77. Professor Singer pointed out that changes in the industrial structure (and therefore in the relative importance of different consumers of coal) *also* led to a decline in the potential demand for coal—although this was only about one-fifth or one-sixth of the 'savings' generated by economies and substitutions (i.e. 7.5 million tons as against some 38 million tons).

[3] Railways and iron: International Labour Office 1938, I, 96–7; electricity: Hannah 1979, 432–3. At the levels of 1929 the electricity output of 1938 would have used 8 million more tons than it actually did—and the growth in electricity's demand for coal would have been 13 million tons rather than the actual 5 million tons.

[4] International Labour Office 1938, I, 105, 111–112.

In such a setting, British coal exporters found themselves particularly badly placed as their ability to compete declined even faster than the available market. Two problems in particular plagued British exports. On the one hand, protectionism and the use of overt and hidden subsidies to production and transport of coal by Britain's rivals narrowed the potential demand for British coal.[1] Against these, the modest help offered by the British government (notably the derating of industry and railways which had taken place in 1929) had only a small, albeit not negligible, effect—estimated, in the late 1930s at about 1s. per ton.[2] On the other hand, however, and underlying Britain's chronic export problem, was the decline in its relative productivity. Between 1929 and 1936–7, when the average UK output per manshift increased by a mere 8.4 per cent (and that of its principal export districts by considerably less), OMS in the Ruhr, Belgium, and Polish East Upper Silesia increased by 34.5 per cent, 38.1 per cent, and 52.9 per cent respectively.[3] Nor was this simply a matter of mechanization; for Britain had doubled the proportion of coal mechanically cut (albeit it was still under 60 per cent) whereas the Ruhr had seen hardly any change in its level of mechanization (which was over 90 per cent as early as 1929), while the increase in mechanization in Poland was relatively small (from 32 to 40 per cent).[4]

[1] Germany and Poland in particular, deployed heavily subsidized freight rates, bonuses, and subsidies to exports, and inflated domestic coal prices, to keep down the costs of their overseas sales. For the range of policies, see ibid., I, 179 ff.; Jones 1939, ch. X–XIV; Monmouthshire & South Wales Coal Owners' Association, *Survey of the Position of the South Wales Coal Trade* (MSWCOA Box File 729), 2–9. According to the latter source, the subsidized freight rate for export coal carried from Katowice to Gdynia in 1935 was just over 3s. for a journey of over 300 miles. This was generally less than the cost of bringing coal over the average journey of 25 miles between South Wales' pits and tidewater.

[2] International Labour Office 1938, I, 185; above, 264 n. The 1930s saw no equivalent to the massive wage subsidy of over £23 million of 1925–6.

[3] Ibid., 109. However, on a different basis of computation the figures for the UK, Germany, Belgium, and Poland were 8.5, 29.4, 37.8, and 45.5%. Ibid., 211. The *Reid Report* gave the following indices for OMS:

	UK	Ruhr	Belgium	Netherlands	Poland
1913	100	100	100	100	100
1929	107	135	107	152	111
1936	116	181	148	223	161
1938	113	164	140	201	159

[4] International Labour Office 1938, I, 17. Such aggregate figures of 'mechanization' are somewhat misleading. First, there was considerable regional variety (see below, Table 7.7); second, such averages leave out of account data on coal mechanically conveyed (which are not available in

Rather, the superiority of performance on the continent—especially in the Ruhr—is to be attributed to improvements in layout and organization; the systematic grouping of mines and undertakings; the concentration of production in the best mines and, within those mines, in the best seams, and extensive improvements in haulage and winding.[1]

The upshot of that general superiority, together of course with the result of various non-market policies, was severe price competition for British coal, which before 1913 had enjoyed a distinct cost advantage. Thus, between 1929 and 1936 the export prices (measured in sterling at current exchange rates) of British coal rose by 5.5 per cent, whereas those of German coal fell by 22.4 per cent and of Polish by 7.4 per cent.[2] This differential appeared as early as the onset of the depression in 1929–31. Subsequently, British exporters found themselves unable to take full advantage of two potentially favourable developments: the moratorium and then ending of Reparations (1931 and 1932), and the effective devaluation of sterling as Britain left the Gold Standard in September 1931.

The ending of Reparations, which, in principle, extended Britain's marketing possibilities, was nullified by low prices elsewhere, by the growth in trade restrictions, and by the commercial relationships established by German exporters.[3] The abandonment of Gold—which was followed by a fall in the dollar value of sterling by between 20 and 30 per cent—might have been imagined to give a big boost to such staple exports as coal (especially bearing in mind the arguments which had attended the resumption of the Gold Standard at an inflated sterling rate in 1925).[4] But no such consequence flowed from devaluation. Quite apart from the inauspicious circumstances, sterling's fall produced a

comparable detail); third, technical methods varied, with the pneumatic pick being much favoured on the continent and the cutting machine in Britain.

[1] The *Reid Report*, 16–18, pointed out that improvements in OMS did *not* depend on intensified mechanization.

[2] International Labour Office 1938, I, 203. Expressed in *national currencies* British export prices rose by about 1% in 1929–31, while Germany's, Belgium's, and Poland's fell by 11%, 15%, and 11% respectively. Ibid., 201.

[3] *ARSM* 1931, 5; *ARSM* 1932, 6; POWE 16/210 Annex D. The Young Plan (1929) had already reduced and diminished credits, with the result that Germany's reparation shipments fell from 9.274 million tons of coal (and 3.126 million tons of coke) in 1929 to 4.081 million (0.739 million) the next year. Yet, such was the competitiveness of German coal, including the 'good will and commercial connections' that had been created in the late 1920s, that Germany's 'free' exports to France more than compensated for the decline in Reparations (i.e. total shipments to France *rose* from 5,520,000 to 5,521,000 tons in 1929–30).

[4] Above, ch. 5, sect. iii.

rapid deflation on the continent, the effects of which were augmented by currency adjustments and exchange restrictions—especially in Germany. To take Britain's two main trading competitors, between 1931 and 1933 the average pithead price of coal, measured in national currencies, fell by about 20 per cent in Germany and Poland, as against a 3.5 per cent fall in the United Kingdom. And the fall in continental f.o.b. export prices was even greater.

As a result of these shifts in the structure of prices (and costs), and in spite of the intervening devaluation, by 1933 both Germany and Poland were selling coal *in sterling* at *lower* prices than 1929 (reductions of 6.4 and 2.1 per cent respectively), while Britain's f.o.b. prices were almost exactly the same (−0.1 per cent). Nor did the situation improve. As we have seen, the combined result of a more rapid increase in productivity, a more successful pressure on wage rates, and a more effective deployment of subsidizing policies gave Germany and Poland (and, indeed, *all* main continental producers) a price advantage over Britain.[1] Between 1929 and 1937 (two years of relatively buoyant exports) the world's exports of solid fuel grew by about 4 per cent, yet British sales declined by 20 per cent. Admittedly, Poland's sales suffered even more than Britain's, but an even more telling measure of adaptation to the new circumstances was the export growth from the depth of the slump in 1933 to 1937: 3 per cent for Britain, 59 per cent for Germany, and 13.9 per cent for Poland.[2]

Against such a background, it was no wonder that the export trade—once the foundation of the coal industry's prosperity—had by the 1930s become an almost crippling handicap. Whether or not a determined technical or organizational response to competition in a declining market could have reduced British costs sufficiently to remedy the situation was a matter of unresolved controversy, especially given the apparent inelasticity of demand for coal.[3] But it was inconceivable that such an increase in productivity could have taken place without an even more drastic reduction in the size, and therefore the labour force, of the industry. There was, however, no such response (although technical improvements *did* take place). Rather, the problem of Britain's exports was approached with an eye less to technical change than to the possibility of securing financial or market adjustments. These could take three forms: first, subsidizing exports; second, raising the price of coal

[1] International Labour Office 1938, I, 201–3.
[2] Darmstadter 1971, 423 ff. For exports, see above, Table 7.2.
[3] Below, 313–19; Jones 1939, 153–5.

by encouraging cooperation and collusion; third, stabilizing markets through bilateral trade agreements.

The first of these (the provision of direct financial aid) was perennially attractive if only because of the extent of subsidy and price manipulation on the continent. In 1930 some form of direct help had been advocated (given the failure to secure protective trade agreements) in a report by a trade delegation which included the Labour Secretary for Mines. And in later years the matter was raised officially and insistently. Indeed, in 1936 even South Wales owners, abandoning their sturdy individualism, joined with their employees to plead for a subsidy, and were subsequently supported by the Joint Standing Consultative Committee of the industry. Nevertheless, for most of the 1930s the political, ideological, and economic obstacles to a subsidy were too great. The government feared an unhealthy precedent, the effect on taxpayers and industrial consumers, and the likely need to offer subsidized prices to markets where demand was guaranteed by trade agreements.

While the state was always reluctant to contemplate direct financial help to the coal industry, until the very end of the decade the industry itself was unable to secure the agreement of the inland owners to the alternative possibility—the raising of export subsidies by levies on coal destined for the home market.[1] Only in the summer of 1938, with the 'recovery' of the industry arrested and renewed fears that an export surplus might once again spill over into the inland market, did the owners muster sufficient support for the idea of a 'trade maintenance fund' (financed by a levy on inland sales) which might be used to support overseas sales in 'contested' markets. By that time, too, the President of the Board of Trade and the Mines Department were sympathetic to such manipulation and willing to urge not merely open government support but also official financial help.[2]

The second alternative (sales cooperation and attempts at market

[1] Mines Department, *Report of the British Coal Delegation to Sweden, Norway and Denmark, 13 to 25 Sept. 1930* (Cmd. 3702. 1930); CAB 24/263/284–90 (6 Aug. 1936); POWE 16/216 (cutting from the *Western Mail*, 30 July 1936); CAB 24/268/167–76 (20 Feb. 1937); 'Brief ... for Debate ...' (26 July 1937): POWE 16/224. Arguments in favour of subsidies were normally buttressed by the claim that they were necessary prerequisites to international trade agreements. In contrast to the 1s. per ton estimated value of the rating relief of 1929 (above, 284), subsidies to German coal exports were estimated to be worth 5s. to 7s. per ton in 1934 ('Brief ... Debate on Coal Mines Department Estimates', 17 July 1934: POWE 16/216).

[2] CAB 24/278/64–75 (15 July 1938); *MAGB* 1939, 21. Action was to be postponed until the autumn, while international negotiations proceeded. Events were therefore overtaken by the War. The Secretary for Mines made two sympathetic, albeit non-committal, statements in the Commons, on 26 July 1938 and 31 Jan. 1939.

control) was frequently urged upon the coal industry from 1925–6 and did produce schemes (voluntary and partial in 1927–8, compulsory and complete from 1930) to control output, prices, and (eventually) sales.[1] But owners in the export fields were hindered in their overseas sales by minimum price regulations, and in their access to inland markets by quotas after 1934. In any case, having to face world markets and world prices, British exporters were clearly less able to determine prices or sales. Hence, in the face of what was interpreted as a 'state of economic war'[2] there was a widespread feeling, officially supported by the Mines Department, that the only permanent solution lay in an international coal agreement or cartel.[3] In the event, however, the efforts of the early 1930s to produce some comprehensive European agreement foundered,[4] in part because of the reservations and conservatism of British coal-owners, who were anxious about their share of any controlled market and found difficulty in speaking with one voice.[5]

On the other hand, an Anglo-Polish Coal Export Agreement, signed at the end of 1934 and renewed in 1937, did offer stability to British sales in north-west Europe and the Mediterranean while shielding the Poles from price pressures (flowing from sterling devaluation) and affording them a minimum proportion of British sales to specified markets.[6] And in 1937 the leading European producers (after years of negotiation) joined an international coke cartel which created reserved markets, provided for minimum prices, and allocated quotas between Germany (48 per cent), Britain (21 per cent), the Netherlands (18 per cent), Belgium (10 per cent), and Poland (3 per cent).[7] By that time, too, the British experience of cooperative market control at home, and the growth of representative institutions to oversee output, prices, and sales, made the possibility of international agreement both more palatable and more realistic. In 1938 the exporters—who a few years earlier would have considered such a step anathema—approached German and Polish owners' organizations with a view to forming an international coal cartel. But this policy initiative was frustrated by the outbreak of war the next year. In spite of it, the fact remains that throughout the

---

[1] Above, 209–12; below, 296–30.

[2] POWE 16/216, cutting from *Western Mail*, 30 July 1936.

[3] POWE 16/216 (1934); POWE 16/224 (1937); cf. *Hansard* 17 July 1934, col. 955, and 26 July 1937, col. 2692.

[4] *ARSM* 1932, 6; *ARSM* 1933, 8–9; International Labour Office 1938, I, 248 ff.

[5] Political and Economic Planning 1936, 165–6; *ARSM* 1933, 8–9.

[6] Political and Economic Planning 1936, 164; International Labour Office 1938, I, 249–50.

[7] Ibid., 250–1. The percentages in the text are rounded to the nearest whole number.

1930s there had been little effective international control of the coal trade.

This left the third response to shrinking international markets—bilateral agreements—and here Britain was very active indeed, although the results were not always clear cut.[1] The origin of Britain's bilateral trading agreements lay in the competition from Polish coal in Scandinavian markets in particular. This was perceived by a delegation of coal-owners and exporters, led by the Secretary for Mines, which visited Scandinavia in 1930. They argued that Polish competition was derived not merely from Germany's abrogation of the agreement to accept Upper Silesian coal in 1925 and by the British coal stoppage in 1926, but was also supported by low production costs, massive freight-rate subsidies, and differential pricing.[2] Flowing from this sort of appraisal was a recognition that formal steps were needed to recoup some of the serious losses of market shares in Scandinavia and in the Baltic generally (the British share of the Estonian market had fallen from 84 per cent in 1929 to 38 per cent in 1931 before recovering to 68 per cent in 1932).[3]

With the formal abandonment of Free Trade in 1932 the way to negotiations with British suppliers and customers was clear. The MAGB and coal exporters played an important part in these negotiations in 1932–3, and in 1933 there was a series of agreements with Denmark, Norway, Sweden, Iceland, and Finland. Each country guaranteed British coal a minimum percentage of the market (ranging from 70 to 80 per cent, except for Sweden where the percentage was 47). Trade agreements with Argentina and Germany were also signed in 1933, and in the next year, agreements with Estonia, Latvia, and Lithuania (again with quotas for British coal—ranging from 70 to 85 per cent of those markets), and with France. Canada had already extended preferential tariffs to British anthracite in 1932. In 1935 a livestock agreement with the Irish Free State revived Britain's dominant position in the supply of coal to that country after a period when poor political relationships had led to a collapse of British exports to the Republic. Less important quota agreements were also arranged with Italy (1936), Holland (1934), and Belgium (1931). The direct effect of all these arrangements was beneficial: between 1930 and 1934 the proportion of British exports going to

---

[1] *ARSM* 1933, 3–6; *ARSM* 1934, 7–9; POWE 16/215–16; International Labour Office 1938, I, 188 ff.

[2] Mines Department, *Report of the British Coal Delegation to Sweden, Norway and Denmark, 13th to 25th September 1930* (Cmd. 3702. 1936). In 1913 Britain had supplied 93% of Denmark's needs, 95% of Sweden's, and 98% of Norway's. By 1929 these had fallen to 54%, 47%, and 62% (and Poland's shares had risen to 28%, 28%, and 33%). [3] POWE 16/216.

the countries with which trade agreements had been signed rose from 16.7 to 31.0 per cent.[1]

Yet in many instances these agreements were either modest in extent or two-edged in effect. Overall, total British exports to the 16 non-Commonwealth countries involved fell by 19 million tons (26 per cent) between 1929 and 1937, while German and Polish exports grew by some 4.8 million tons.[2] Only in the Baltic were the quotas significant, and there the volume of British sales to the relevant countries (Scandinavia in particular) grew. Even within the Baltic, however, the absolute amounts could be quite small. The Lithuanian agreement, for example, was estimated to provide only an extra 400 jobs, the Estonian an extra 42.[3] More seriously, such gains were in part counterbalanced by indirect costs. Polish coal in particular, but German coal as well, faced with the minor renaissance of British exports to northern Europe, turned elsewhere for needed outlets and began to bite more deeply into markets in southern Europe and the Mediterranean. Indeed, while the most important of the bilateral agreements favoured coal exports from the North-East and eastern Scotland, that was in part at the expense of sales from South Wales to other markets. Of the various agreements, only that with Argentina was of any significant benefit to South Wales and the importance of the agreements therefore helped depress the South Wales industry by enhancing competition and price-cutting in some of *its* main markets.[4]

Nor was Britain the only country to extend bilateral arrangements. Germany, for example, signed agreements with countries in central Europe, the Balkans, and Latin America, and the strengthening ties between Nazi Germany and Fascist Italy also handicapped Britain's access to the latter market. Without bilateral agreements, Britain's export position would no doubt have been worse in a world in which trading and currency restrictions were multiplying; but they were essentially defensive measures, doing more to mitigate losses than achieve

[1] *ARSM* 1934, 7. *MAGB* 1933, 32; *MAGB* 1934, 31; *MAGB* 1935, 28–9. The countries involved were Canada (where preferential tariffs had been arranged in 1932 at the Ottawa Conference), Scandinavia, Iceland, the three Baltic countries, and Argentina. Scandinavia and Iceland were particularly buoyant: their purchases of British coal rose from 3.6 million tons in 1931 to 8.0 million in 1934. By contrast, import restrictions in France, Germany, Belgium, the Netherlands, Italy, and Switzerland were blamed for a decline in the proportion of Britain's exports going to those markets, from 57.4% in 1930 to 44.6% in 1934: *ARSM* 1934, 6.

[2] MSWCOA *Survey*, 7–8 (Box File 729).

[3] 'Brief ... Debate on Mines Department estimates. 17 July 1934': POWE 16/216. These gains were reckoned from a baseline of the low levels of exports of 1932.

[4] Secretary for Mines, *Hansard* 17 July 1934, cols. 953–4. Cf. *Hansard* 26 July 1937, col. 2692.

gains. The picture of a major export industry in decline remained unaffected. And as Table 7.3 indicates, the effects on the volume and pattern of British trade were striking: between the relative peak years of 1929 and 1938 cargo exports fell by almost 30 per cent. Sales to the Baltic countries, however, *increased* and thereby their proportion of all British coal exports rose sharply from some 11 to 25 per cent. On the other hand, the biggest fall in absolute terms came in Britain's most important markets—essentially western Europe along the North Sea coast—which accounted for 11 million tons of the total decline of 20 million tons in exports. Worryingly, these countries, even while reducing their imports of coal, purchased more from Britain's main trading rivals. A similar blow (resulting in the loss of about 7 million tons of exports) came, and for similar reasons, in the western Mediterranean markets.[1] The adjustment had, indeed, been fundamental.

The critical importance of the decline in the export trade justifies the attention devoted to it in the foregoing pages. Nevertheless, as has already been indicated, some compensation for this gloomy tale was to be found in the domestic market. Of course, even within Britain the slump of the early 1930s, and in particular the decline of heavy industry, drove down the levels of demand. By 1933 the fall in domestic sales of coal accounted for half the absolute decline in output (of 50 million tons) since 1929, and the violent depression in iron and steel accounted for half the home loss. From this miserable trough, however, home consumption rose 'by leaps and bounds'[2] and the average of home consumption in 1936–8 (just over 177.5 million tons) almost reached the levels of the best years of the 1920s. The basis of this recovery was the general revival of the economy, reinforced by the role within that revival of the rearmament 'boom', which had particularly expansionary consequences for the relatively heavy industrial users of coal. Yet the

---

[1] The pattern of decline and adjustment was apparent in the slump:

British cargo exports (000 tons)

	1929	1934	Difference
Total	60,267	39,660	−21,407
Baltic Sea	6,686	8,575	+1,889
North Sea etc.	28,629	14,266	−14,363
Western Mediterranean	12,809	9,086	−3,723

[2] *ARSM* 1936, 10.

Table 7.3. *Patterns of Briti*

Destinations	Ports (% to relevant market)							
	Eastern Scotland		North-East		Humber		Bristol Channel (mostly Wels	
	1929	1937	1929	1937	1929	1937	1929	1937
Baltic Sea	31.4	68.3	16.4	36.8	20.3	42.0	1.0	2.3
North Sea etc.	49.0	24.5	56.4	43.2	57.2	40.2	34.5	44.6
Western Mediterr.	12.0	3.3	21.5	14.3	5.8	4.7	27.6	18.5
Eastern Mediterr.	1.8	0.2	2.6	2.4	2.2	1.3	9.0	7.4
West Coast of Africa	0.1	0.3	1.0	1.3	0.2	1.0	3.7	2.8
East Coast of Africa	—	0.0	—	0.3	—	—	0.4	0.5
Arabia, Indian Ocean, Asia	0.6	—	0.8	0.2	6.5	0.1	1.7	1.0
North and Central America	3.3	2.5	0.2	0.9	0.3	1.0	3.2	6.0
South America etc.	1.8	0.9	1.1	0.6	7.5	9.7	18.3	16.9
All regions: 000 tons	4,829	4,014	20,674	13,302	6,500	4,169	24,716	16,2.
% from each group of ports	8.0	9.9	34.3	33.0	10.8	10.3	41.0	40.2
Foreign bunkers: 000 tons	1,265	1,026	3,316	1,820	2,516	2,572	4,080	3,0
% from each group of ports	7.7	8.8	20.2	15.6	15.3	22.0	24.9	25.8

Baltic Sea: USSR, Finland, Estonia, Latvia, Lithuania, Poland, Sweden, Norway, Denmark.
North Sea etc.: Germany, Netherlands, Belgium, France, Switzerland, Channel Islands, Eire.
Western Mediterranean: Portugal, Spain, Italy, Malta, Gibraltar, Morocco, North African coast.
Eastern Mediterranean: includes Austria, Hungary, Balkans, Yugoslavia.
South America etc.: includes Falkland Islands, Greenland, Iceland.

Source: *ARSM* 1930, Appendix A, Table 28; *ARSM* 1937, Appendix A, Table 29.

coal exports, 1929 and 1937

North-West		Western Scotland		Total cargo exports from GB			
				1929		1937	
				ooo tons	% to relevant market	ooo tons	% to relevant market
1929	1937	1929	1937				
0.4	0.0	5.1	18.6	6,688	11.1	10,219	25.3
88.1	96.9	48.8	50.2	28,629	47.5	17,302	43.0
0.6	0.0	31.9	17.4	12,809	21.3	5,456	13.5
7.9	2.3	1.3	1.5	3,257	5.4	1,632	4.1
0.4	0.0	—	0.4	1,135	1.8	685	1.7
—	—	—	0.7	87	0.2	130	0.3
1.1	0.2	0.3	0.2	1,067	1.8	197	0.5
0.4	0.1	8.0	10.9	1,168	1.9	1,390	3.5
1.1	0.5	4.6	0.1	5,429	9.0	3,268	8.1
1,229	978	1,835	1,309	60,267	100.0	40,338	100.0
2.0	2.4	3.0	3.2	—	—	—	—
2,513	1,652	1,199	940	16,394	100.0	11,703	100.0
15.3	14.1	7.3	8.0	—	—	—	—

Table 7.4. *Principal categories of home consumption of coal, 1913–1938*

	1913		1929		1933		1938	
	m. tons	%	m. tons	%	m. tons	%	m. tons	%
Gas works	16.7	9.1	16.75	9.7	16.16	10.9	18.20	10.4
Electricity generation	4.9	2.7	9.84	5.7	10.33	7.0	14.93	8.5
Railways (locomotives)	13.2	7.2	13.41	7.7	11.67	7.8	12.52	7.1
Blast furnaces	21.2	11.5	14.51	8.4	7.37	5.0	11.56	6.6
Other iron and steel	10.2	5.5	8.92	5.1	5.92	4.0	7.18	4.0
Collieries (engine fuel)	18.0	9.8	13.69	7.9	11.59	7.8	11.86	6.8
Domestic	40.0	21.8	40.00	23.0	84.12	56.7	96.87	54.4
General manufacturing etc.	57.7	31.4	55.01	31.7				
TOTAL	183.8	100.0	173.50	100.0	148.37	100.0	175.14	100.0

Source: CYB 1948, 624–5. The Ministry of Fuel and Power's *Statistical Digest 1946 and 1947* contains slightly different estimates for some categories in 1938. Its estimates are also in some respects more finely broken down (coke ovens: 19.1 million tons; domestic use: 45.8 million tons; miners' coal: 4.6 million tons).

beneficial effect of general economic recovery was mitigated by the improvements in the efficiency with which coal was used. Some indication of the extent of those savings in particular industries has already been given.[1] For Britain, a more precise measure of fuel efficiency (and therefore of possible demand forgone) can be derived from the Censuses of Production in 1924 and 1935. Between those two dates the coal used per unit of industrial output declined by some 28 per cent. Obviously, if those economies had not been available it is unlikely that industrial production in 1935 would have been exactly the same. But it is relevant to note that, to produce the industrial output of 1935 with the levels of fuel efficiency of 1924 would have necessitated an extra 38 million tons of coal—a 'saving' of which one-third might be attributed to the iron and steel industries and 15 per cent to the generation of electricity and gas.[2]

The performance of the coal industry within Britain cannot be considered in terms of market forces alone. In 1930 legislation obliged coalowners to formulate schemes by which output quotas were to be allocated to districts and to individual colliery undertakings; in 1934 separate inland and export quotas had to be used; and in 1936 the government made it compulsory for districts to create organized selling schemes. The industry therefore had increasingly to operate within a managed framework (whose bases and operations will be discussed in the next chapter). That framework was in large part responsible for the stability of British coal prices, and to some extent for the fall in output. In other words, it introduced an element of rigidity into the industry's structure, and it seems likely that it was inimical to 'progressive' changes and cost-reduction. On the other hand, its protection of costs against market pressures also meant a protection of wage agreements—and thereby helped account for the relative tranquillity of industrial relations in the 1930s. Whether in the long run the possible price in terms of inefficiency was worth the benefit will have to be considered later.

iii. The organization of marketing

The reverberations of the coal industry's decline in the 1930s touched many aspects of political as well as economic behaviour. And they did so much more systematically than had been the case in the 1920s. Although it will be necessary to consider the principal determinants and outcomes

---

[1] Above, 282-3.   [2] Singer 1940-1, 166-77.

of public policy in this and the next section, the detailed history of coal policy in the 1930s will be examined in the following chapter. As will be seen, throughout the decade there were persistent attempts to harness public policy to the amelioration of the plight of the depressed coal-producing areas, to the revival or creation of demand for the industry's products, to drastic reform in the ownership of its assets, to the lowering of its business costs. Few of these had any significant effects. On the other hand, from 1930 there was extensive, and fairly effective, legislative intervention in the industry's distributive and marketing structures, and a legislative framework (nullified in practice) which might have stimulated far-reaching changes in the industry's productive organization.

Such reforms or attempted reforms were themselves part of the institutional changes associated with the decisive decrease in the industry's size and in the employment it was able to offer. Output fell by about seven per cent between the late 1920s and the late 1930s, and average employment and the number of mines in operation each fell by some 20 per cent. As this last figure suggests, there were adaptations at the levels of labour productivity and industrial concentration: the average output per manshift rose by about 10 per cent and, while the average mine continued to employ about 365 men, the average output per mine rose by 15 per cent (from 95,549 tons to 110,157 tons).[1] The continued trend towards concentration among colliery firms will be discussed in Section iv. First, however, it is necessary to consider the changes in the organization of distribution and marketing.

In 1927–9 the industry's principal response to trade depression had been to form voluntary associations for controlling output and marketing. These had failed,[2] and in the event it was the political need to protect wages which led to government intervention. The minority Labour Government which came to power in May 1929 was committed to reduce the length of the miners' working day, and in order to achieve that aim while maintaining earnings, it was necessary to increase the industry's proceeds. Here, political necessity coincided with that part of business opinion which was in favour of a cartel arrangement to mitigate competition in the coal industry.[3] Part I of the Coal Mines Act of 1930

[1] For data on employment, output, and number of mines, see *ARSM*, various years, and *CYB* 1932, 680 and *CYB* 1947, 520.

[2] Above, ch. 5, sect. v.

[3] The export areas were strongly opposed to the control schemes propounded in 1929–30. For a fuller consideration of government action in the 1930s, see below, ch. 8, sects. ii and iii.

obliged the industry to formulate schemes (in which membership would be compulsory) for central and district committees to regulate output and, in the case of the districts, minimum prices.[1] This was done in 17 districts (five of the original 21 districts subsequently forming the Midland (Amalgamated) District) and the schemes began operations on 1 January 1931. The Central Council laid down quotas for each district; and the Executive Boards in each district established 'standard tonnages', based on production in the 'normal' years of the 1920s for their colliery undertakings. Depending on the district allocations, those undertakings were then awarded output quotas proportionate to their standard tonnages (provision was made for the sale of surplus quota tonnages within each district to collieries wanting an increase), and the districts—but not the central authority—were empowered to establish minimum prices for coal from their undertakings.

These embryonic cartels were much less effective than had been hoped. This was in part because the procedure was too monolithic as to allocation and pricing, but principally because evasion of the minimum price regulations proved to be ridiculously easy (with the result, it was claimed, that some export areas, where competitive pressures were fiercest, were in 'a state of utter and absolute demoralisation').[2] In addition, however, the Central Council was precluded from any attempt to coordinate prices, so that the individual districts could set their own, and sometimes unrealistically low, minima—thus enhancing rather than controlling inter-district competition. This was a particularly serious matter since the export area, desperately short of sales in the early 1930s, were able to invade and undercut the markets of inland areas.

As a result, when the legislation was renewed in 1932, the government stipulated that the industry should put its house in order. For two years, however, the coalowners failed to secure the requisite majority (proposals had to be supported by 85 per cent of the industry) and it was only after the threat of further legislation that extensive reforms of the scheme were instituted. From 1934 the administration of the procedures was tightened; the Central Council was authorized to issue directives as to minimum prices; and (most important of all) provision was made for *separate* quotas for inland and export sales—thus ensuring the better coordination of production and regulation of competition. Inland areas in particular benefited, although the export areas, which had strongly

---

[1] The various schemes and their evolution in the 1930s are described in *ARSM* 1931, 10ff.; Jones 1939, ch. VI; Kirby 1971, ch. IX; and International Labour Office 1938, I, 232ff.

[2] J. P. Dickie, in House of Commons: *Hansard* 1 Mar. 1933, col. 460, quoted in Kirby 1971, 186.

opposed the reform, were given a concession in that the main basis of the new inland quotas was to be the existing pattern of distribution, in which such erstwhile specialist export areas as Scotland and the North-East had managed to establish a strong position.

Even after 1934, however, the more disciplined coordination of prices was still vulnerable to market forces, and in particular to private contracting. To make price control effective, it was necessary to take a further step: to reduce competition by centralizing sales. And this further move towards the industry's cartelization came in 1936. Once again pressure from the miners (a national wage claim for 2s. per shift in the autumn of 1935) was an element in the structural change. In a compromise settlement, prices and wages were both raised and the owners agreed to establish district selling organizations (i.e. syndicates to control contracts within areas) to be coordinated by the national authority. The new comprehensive schemes came into effect in July 1936 (the Lancashire and Cheshire district had voluntarily instituted its own selling organization a year earlier). Nominally, sales competition within the industry ceased.[1]

The sharp fluctuations of market conditions which coincided with the evolving social control of sales in the 1930s make it difficult to assess the effects of the new arrangements. But clearly, the structure of the industry (at least in its marketing aspects) had been profoundly affected. To its defenders the cartel scheme had two vital and related benefits: prices and proceeds were supported at levels which obviated a business and social disaster and in ways which shared out available demand in a relatively orderly fashion; and employment as well as rewards was maintained and spread. As the Secretary for Mines claimed in 1934, without such a scheme to guard against the 'unleashing' of excess capacity and the ensuing cut-throat competition, available employment would be concentrated and a further 150,000 miners would lose their jobs.[2]

On the other hand, however, prices were higher than they would otherwise have been, and from time to time important consumer groups complained about the costs of getting supplies. Further, some economists argued that output and employment were obliged to take all the strain of the slump, while prices were unnecessarily maintained (in

---

[1] The actual institutions used varied. Some districts established a single selling agency; others controlled all significant sales through permits which specified prices, conditions, and amounts; and the Midland district obliged the existing selling agents working for groups of collieries to conform to the coordinating authority of the district.

[2] Memorandum, 1 Feb. 1934: CAB 24/247/40–52.

1929-33 output fell by 19.7 per cent, pithead prices by only 3.1 per cent).[1] The former point was, of course, tacitly accepted since it was, precisely, the function of the selling schemes to maintain prices: in June 1932 the Secretary for Mines estimated the effect as 2s. per ton.[2] But there was little agreement as to the consequences for output. Both at the time and since, the notorious inelasticity of demand for coal together with the obvious collapse of markets in the early 1930s have been offered as reasons for believing that even drastic price reductions (assuming that they could have been socially acceptable in view of their effects upon wages) would hardly have stimulated sales and output.[3] Even so, the fact was that, especially abroad, British coal did have to meet price competition, in which rival supplies undoubtedly benefited from their ability to reduce prices. Furthermore, we have seen that falling living costs were not matched by falling money wages so that *in principle* there *was* scope for cost-saving of a reasonable magnitude— even if the political and social reverberations might have been unacceptable.

A more subtle and perhaps important point, however, related to the consequences of the control of output and sales for the general efficiency of the industry. There was, in the first instance, the possibility of bureaucratic error in the prediction of particular sectors of demand, compounded by the tendency to operate at a high level of aggregation. The allocations to districts, for example, were in terms of total tonnage of 'coal', whereas they had to produce according to a changing pattern of demand in terms of different types of coal product. More significant was the question of the incentives to optimize investment and improve efficiency. For the quota scheme was essentially a system of protection for existing interests: minimum-price and sales guarantees were hardly likely to 'discipline' low-productivity firms, or encourage growth among the most efficient. Admittedly, the schemes made provision for the sale of surplus quotas (although not between different districts) and also for changes in standard tonnages. Yet the former was an expensive

---

[1] Jones 1939, 167. Similarly, employment fell by 17.5% and average money shift earnings by only 1.1%.

[2] Cited in Jones 1939, 151.

[3] These issues are discussed in Jones 1939, ch. IX; Kirby 1971, 225 ff.; Kirby 1973. The Mines Department argued that allocations were generally very liberal and that actual output usually fell below stipulated levels. However, this ignores the genuine inefficiencies and friction which, in a controlled system, disturbed the balance between demand and output—especially in relation to specific categories of coal. The Secretary for Mines, in arguing that price competition would have reduced employment, clearly believed either that demand was inelastic or that costs would not decline significantly with increases in output.

and unwieldy way of changing market shares; and there is little evidence of any reduction of standard tonnages (i.e. in the case of inefficient firms).

The fact was that the new structures were *designed* to protect the relatively inefficient areas and firms, and to prevent the existence of spare capacity driving down prices or concentrating the reduction of output. The remuneration of those factors of production fortunate enough to retain employment were being sheltered from the consequences of inefficiency as well as from the harsh winds of economic stagnation. That there should be an economic price to be paid is hardly surprising, since such cartel arrangements necessarily involve an element of enforced subsidy.

On the other hand if, as some observers strongly felt, the alternatives would have been excessively costly—in terms of further social dislocation, more intense pockets of unemployment, provocative pressures on wages, and the renewal of industrial-relations warfare—then a less efficient allocation of national resources may have been a price worth paying, particularly in the early 1930s when the depths of the general slump would have made a renewal of the bitter strife of 1925–6 even more socially dangerous.[1] After all, the consequences of unregulated competition in the 1920s (increased capacity in the face of falling demand, downward pressures on wages as well as prices, severe industrial strife) were hardly reassuring.

There are, in addition, two further considerations in the context of the industry's long-run history. First, there was a real danger that the coal industry could be completely demoralized. Its experience in the 1920s had been bad enough. By the 1930s market conditions had deteriorated—and it may have been that those involved in the industry (owners as well as miners) were approaching the sustainable limit of a more or less orderly response to violent competition, rapid changes in values, and declining sales. Control schemes of the sort devised after 1929 may, therefore, have been needed to redress the balance. Certainly, they appear to have worked well for the sense of well-being among owners—in Lancashire for example, where a voluntary central selling organization was created with good effect in July 1935. In that sense, laissez-faire seemed to offer only 'an appalling chaos' whose workings 'would be virtually intolerable'.[2]

The second consideration also relates to a point of psychology and social behaviour. The coal industry was notoriously individualistic, and

----

[1] See below, 326–30.   [2] *Financial Times* 6 Dec. 1933.

throughout most of the 1920s its leading members fiercely resisted attempts to persuade them towards more cooperative (indeed, less anarchic) behaviour. The severity of trade depression in the late 1920s had gone *some* way to introducing a new, and more 'realistic' spirit. But, it could be argued, the owners still needed a much more prolonged 'education in cooperative action'.[1] That might have been provided by the phased introduction of increasingly systematic control schemes. As one leading Yorkshire owner put it in retrospect, 'if we could keep that gang under control we had some hope of getting better prices'.[2] As a result, on this argument, not only did the industry come to accept the sorts of sales organization which, in the mid-1920s it had almost contemptuously rejected, but the experience of the new sales agencies from 1936 made it more likely that the owners would be much more amenable to the process of *industrial* concentration—the mergers which would change the *productive* structure of the industry. The fact that, in the event, the owners remained quite as opposed to government intervention or to any external pressure towards structural reform could not have been anticipated by reasonable men.

iv. Industrial structure

Whatever the expectations, the reality of industrial reorganization in coalmining in the 1930s was less striking than the contemporaneous changes in the organization of marketing and selling. As with the latter, there were continuous official efforts to stimulate structural change—in this instance the amalgamations and industrial concentration which, since the mid-1920s, had seemed to offer the best chance of improvements in efficiency and cost-competitiveness.[3] Part II of the Coal Mines Act of 1930 empowered a Coal Mines Reorganisation Commission to propound merger schemes which might be given the force of law. But the sustained hostility of most owners to the Commission, and the emergence of serious legal deficiencies in its powers, rendered it almost completely powerless. After much heart-searching, new legislation in 1938 transmuted it into the Coal Commission, which was to oversee the public acquisition of mineral royalties and to deploy greater power

---

[1] Jones 1939, 378–80.

[2] Roland Addy (Chairman and Managing Director of Carlton Main Colliery) in evidence to the Central Valuation Board, 6 July 1948: POWE 42/11/17.

[3] The evolution of public policy and the controversies to which it gave rise are discussed in ch. 8.

within a more amenable set of legal criteria in order to compel colliery undertakings to amalgamate. However, the industry was granted a delay (in the hope that it would begin to reform itself), and the Commission's powers were not to be exercised before 1 January 1940. As a result, the outbreak of War prevented these aspirations being put to the test (although the nationalization of royalties went ahead in 1942).

In spite of evidence that the owners were proving somewhat more cooperative to the main thrust of the Commission's preparatory work in 1938-9, the fact remains that such structural change as took place in the 1930s was not directly influenced by public policy.[1] Indeed, in spite of Sir Ernest Gowers's argument that the owners were coming to appreciate that the degree of cooperation in marketing which they desired might be facilitated if there were fewer units of production, it is possible that the attainment of market control through selling schemes actually *lessened* the incentive to voluntary mergers.[2]

Relative to the major industries, the structure of coalmining remained superficially very fragmented: in 1938 the number of firms was still 1,034, and the number of mines 1,870. Admittedly, many of these were very small (57 per cent of the undertakings employed less than 100 workers), and there had been a significant decrease since the mid-1920s (in 1924 there were 1,411 undertakings and 2,507 mines).[3] But the numbers remaining were still large by normal industrial standards. Given this, how far did the structure of the industry change?[4]

As Table 7.5 indicates, there was a modest but significant trend in favour of the largest firms (although it is likely that much of the change after 1924 took place in the 1920s rather than the 1930s). Thus, firms employing 5,000 or more miners accounted for 33 and 34 per cent of the labour force in both 1924 and 1938—but the proportion of all *firms* which was in this category declined from 5 to 3 per cent (however, they retained control of the same proportion of the country's *mines*). Moreover, in spite of the drastic fall in the total size of the industry, there was a sharp increase in the proportion of miners employed in firms of 10,000 or more. At the other end of the scale there was little change in the

---

[1] *Reports of the Coal Commission for the Years 1938 and 1939: PP* 1939-40 V.

[2] See Memorandum by Gowers (who was Chairman of the Coal Commission) of Nov. 1938: COAL 17/178 (Meeting 10, Paper 3, Agenda 4).

[3] Data refer to undertakings and mines in production throughout the relevant years. All calculations relating to structure are derived (unless otherwise indicated) from data in the *List of Mines* for 1913, 1924, and 1938.

[4] The course and determinants of changing industrial structure are discussed more fully in ch. 9.

Table 7.5. *Size distribution of British colliery undertakings by labour force: 1913, 1924, 1938*

Size of undertakings: no. of miners	Undertakings		Mines belonging to those undertakings		Labour force	
	No.	%	No.	%	No.	%
1913						
1–99	681	47.3	759	28.7	17,561	1.6
100–499	293	20.4	430	16.2	74,207	6.8
500–999	160	11.1	289	10.9	114,562	10.5
1,000–2,999	211	14.7	563	21.3	376,258	34.6
3,000–4,999	58	4.0	248	9.4	225,468	20.7
5,000–9,999	31	2.2	264	10.7	216,837	19.9
10,000 and over	5	0.3	95	3.9	63,534	5.8
	1439	100.0	2648	100.0	1,088,427	100.0
1924						
1–99	707	50.1	789	31.5	16,386	1.3
100–499	237	16.8	333	13.3	59,756	4.9
500–999	137	9.7	232	9.3	100,321	8.3
1,000–2,999	222	15.7	511	20.4	308,887	25.4
3,000–4,999	59	4.2	250	10.0	233,592	19.2
5,000–9,999	40	2.8	270	10.8	274,989	22.6
10,000 and over	9	0.6	122	4.9	121,753	10.0
	1411	100.0	2507	100.0	1,215,684	100.0
1938						
1–99	589	57.0	722	38.6	12,546	1.6
100–499	129	12.5	220	11.8	31,266	3.9
500–999	102	9.9	149	8.0	73,857	9.2
1,000–2,999	148	14.3	329	17.6	257,960	32.3
3,000–4,999	39	3.8	152	8.1	151,989	19.0
5,000–9,999	18	1.7	143	7.6	126,816	15.9
10,000 and over	9	0.9	155	8.3	144,113	18.0
	1034	100.0	1870	100.0	798,547	100.0

Sources: List of Mines for 1913, 1924, 1938.

relative importance of small firms (almost 60 per cent of firms employed under 500 miners, yet accounted for a mere 6 or 7 per cent of the labour force) so that it was the middling-size firm, of 500–2,999 employees, which became relatively less important. There were, of course, differences between districts. Thus, considering undertakings which employed over 5,000, in Glamorgan and Monmouthshire they accounted for 40 per cent or so of the labour force in each of 1913 and 1924, but 57 per cent in 1938 (the proportions for firms of 7,500 or more were 20, 23, and 50 per cent); there was also a substantial rise in the rich Midland and South Yorkshire district (17 per cent in firms of 7,500 or more in 1924, 28 per cent in 1938); but in the North-East, the largest firms declined in importance (firms of 7,500 or more employed 34 per cent of the labour force in 1924 and 27 per cent in 1938).

Although equivalent measurements based on output are more difficult to derive, estimates by the Samuel Commission for 1925 and by the Coal Mines Reorganisation Commission for 1935 confirm the general picture (Table 7.6).[1] Between the two dates undertakings producing 2 million tons or more (although they grew in number) increased their share of national tonnage quite dramatically—from 10.6 to 30.7 per cent of the total; while the importance of those producing 1–2 million tons stayed more or less constant, sagging slightly from 26.2 to 24.3 per cent of output. On the other hand, whereas in 1925 some 40 per cent of tonnage was raised by firms producing under 600,000 tons, ten years later those producing under 500,000 tons (the categories of the two surveys were different) accounted for only 23 per cent of the national output. The industry was still far from monolithic, but the move towards business concentration had been significant.

Changes in industrial structure were, however, much less marked when considered in terms of the unit of production (i.e. mines rather than undertakings). Indeed, the largest mines—those employing 2,000 or more—having increased in importance from 1913 to 1924, had fallen back by 1938: they accounted for 17, 26, and 17 per cent of the labour force at the three dates. This was roughly proportionate to the decline of the industry as a whole and no doubt reflected the diffusion of excess capacity and unemployment. On the other hand, medium-sized mines

---

[1] *Samuel Report*, 54; COAL 17/18 (Coal Mines Reorganisation Commission Meeting 5, Paper 4, Agenda 5: 20 Nov. 1936). As far as numbers and proportions of firms are concerned, these are not quite comparable with each other or with the figures derived from the *Lists of Mines* since both Samuel and the CMRC used samples. And although the firms selected accounted for virtually all the industry's output, they fell far short of the total number of firms in the industry at the time.

Table 7.6. *Size distribution of British colliery undertakings by output, 1925 and 1935* (based on samples)

Output (000 tons)	Undertakings		Tonnage raised	
	No.	% of total	Amount (000 tons)	%
A. JANUARY–JUNE 1925 (annual rates)				
Under 5	10	1.6	32	negl.
5–under 200	307	50.1	27,360	12.7
200–under 400	126	20.6	36,394	16.9
400–under 600	72	11.7	35,118	16.3
600–under 800	28	4.6	19,132	8.9
800–under 1,000	20	3.3	17,992	8.4
1,000–under 2,000	42	6.9	56,280	26.2
2,000 and over	8	1.3	22,744	10.6
Total of sample	613	100	215,052	100.0
B. 1935				
Under 10	522	53.7	1,168	0.5
10–100	149	15.4	5,867	2.6
100–500	172	17.5	44,649	20.1
500–1,000	68	7.0	48,446	21.8
1,000–2,000	40	4.1	53,950	24.3
2,000 +	21	2.1	68,157	30.7
Total of sample	972	100	222,237	100.0

Sources: *Samuel Report*, 54; COAL 17/18 (Coal Mines Reorganisation Commission Meeting 5, Paper 4, Agenda 5, 20 Nov. 1935).

(500–1,999 miners), having declined slightly in significance from 1913 to 1924, grew from 1924 to 1938: they accounted for 59, 56, and 66 per cent of the labour force in those years. Again, there were telling regional contrasts. Even in the rich and successful Midland fields the proportion of miners employed in pits of 2,000 or more rose from 31 to 52 per cent in 1913–24, but fell back to 33 per cent in 1938 (those in mines of 1,000–1,999, however, travelled an inverse route: 41, 30, and 44 per cent). And in Monmouthshire and South Wales there was an even more abrupt decline after 1924: employment in mines exceeding 2,000 fell from 30 to 9 per cent, while those in mines of 1,000–1,999 rose from 30 to 43 per cent.

In sum, there was no trend towards concentration in the unit of production (the individual pit)[1] and only a modest tendency to concentration in the unit of organization (the colliery firm or undertaking). Hence, although there were large-scale firms, and the largest among them grew distinctly bigger, it was far from the case (except in some specialist products or one or two regions) that the industry as a whole was dominated by them. On the other hand, however, this fragmentation was misleading in two important respects.

First, firms in the industry were linked by a multiplicity of business relationships (overlapping shareholding and directorships, informal and formal cooperation in marketing, mutual ownership by holding companies). This no doubt made a substantial difference to competition and to commercial and financial *dealings*—even though the *economic* effects of such arrangements, in terms of cost-reduction or scale economies, were limited.[2] A second, and perhaps more important, caveat to generalizations about the extent of fragmentation of enterprises is the variation between districts and products. In South Wales, for example, in 1935, the anthracite section of the industry was overwhelmingly dominated by one firm; and the three largest firms in the bituminous field (each producing more than 3 million tons) were responsible for 48 per cent of the industry's output (60 per cent of South Wales's output came from the five biggest firms). In Scotland the four largest undertakings produced over 2 million tons each, and accounted for 35 per cent of the region's coal, and there was even more concentration within particular Scottish counties. In Lancashire and Cheshire the two local giants (Manchester Collieries and Wigan Coal Corporation) were responsible for 43 per cent of the field's production.[3] Even so, of course, large numbers of firms accounted for substantial proportions of

[1] Official calculations of the size distributions of mines in relation to employment and output confirm the decrease in the size of the biggest mines. Thus, mines employing more than 2,000 miners numbered 118 in 1924 and 39 in 1942. And between those two dates their share of the labour force fell from 26% (314,782) to 14% (97,941), and of output from 27% (72 million tons) to 14% (28.7 million tons). Calculated from data in *Samuel Appendices*, 177 ff. and Ministry of Fuel and Power, *Statistical Digest from 1938* (Cmd. 6538. 1944), 11.

[2] In Nov. 1936 the Coal Mines Reorganisation Commission estimated that there were 1,075 separate colliery concerns, but that if those with overlapping ownership or control were eliminated, the number would be reduced to 953: COAL 17/178 (Meeting 5, Paper 4, Agenda 5).

[3] COAL 17/178 (Coal Mines Reorganisation Commission Meeting 5, Paper 4, Agenda 5: 20 Nov. 1936). In 1938–9 the Coal Commission also surveyed the degree of concentration: COAL 17/178 (Coal Commission Meeting 10, Paper 3, Agenda 4). In Fife, the Fife Coal Company accounted for 41% of the output, the Wemyss Coal Company for 27%. A later survey in COAL 17/178 (Coal Commission Meeting 18, Paper 1, Agenda 2: 21 Apr. 1939) showed that in Northumberland 4 colliery groups produced 70% of the county's output and 4 colliery firms in South Wales produced two-thirds of the bituminous output.

the remaining outputs and coalmining remained highly fragmented by the standards of most large and important industries.[1] More than this, although there had been some shift in favour of the largest firms between the 1920s and the 1930s, a good deal of this must have been attained by the distinct if limited merger boom of the late 1920s.[2]

Left-wing critics of the coal industry in the 1930s were emphatic in their comments on the extent of combines and the web of shared interests between different concerns. Their literature is replete with large numbers, sarcastic comments on gross accumulations of private wealth, and complicated diagrams representing the multifarious links between legally separate firms.[3] Critical reference was made to the looming presence of Powell Duffryn and (before the two merged in 1935) the Welsh Associated Collieries in the South Wales steam-coal field; the almost complete domination of the anthracite field in South Wales by Amalgamated Anthracite, whose 53 pits controlled 80 per cent of the output in the mid-1930s; the extensive intertwining of the members of the Staveley–Sheepbridge–Yorkshire Amalgamated Collieries groupings in South Yorkshire; the powerful position of firms like the Fife Coal Company, the Wemyss Coal Co., and Bairds and Dalmellington in Scotland; the continuing success of large-scale colliery companies like Butterley, Bolsover, and Stanton in the relatively new Nottinghamshire and the North Derbyshire fields; the importance of firms like Ashington, Hartley Main, Broomhill, Dorman Long, Hordern Collieries, Pease and Partners, and Londonderry Collieries in the North-East; and the emergence of the giants of the Lancashire field (Manchester Collieries in 1929 and the Wigan Coal Corporation in 1930).[4]

[1] In South Wales & Monmouthshire (which was the district with the greatest degree of concentration) in 1935 some 30% of the output came from 40 firms each producing between 50,000 and 1 million tons annually: COAL 17/178 (Coal Mines Reorganisation Commission Meeting 5, Paper 4, Agenda 5: 20 Nov. 1936).

[2] Above, ch. 5, sect. v.

[3] See, especially, the publications of the Labour Research Department 1934; Fox 1935a; Fox 1935b; Williams 1937, 1938, and 1939. Such exposés (they were mostly based on publicly available information gleaned from company reports and stock-exchange publications) were, of course, part of a tradition—which looked forward (e.g. Heinemann 1944) as well as backward (e.g. Williams 1924).

[4] In 1935 the 9 largest colliery firms (or *closely* knit groups) were: Powell Duffryn Associated Collieries (10.1 m. tons), William Baird and Co. and Bairds and Dalmellington (4.6 m. tons); Lambton, Hetton, and Joicey Collieries (4.0 m. tons); Amalgamated Anthracite, Henderson's Welsh Anthracite, and Welsh Anthracite (3.7 m. tons); Manchester Collieries (3.6 m. tons); Bolsover Colliery (3.4 m. tons); Amalgamated Denaby Collieries (3.4 m. tons); Fife Coal (3.4 m. tons); and Ocean Coal, Burnyeat Brown, and United National Collieries (3.1 m. tons): 'Colliery Undertakings in Great Britain ... 1935' Statement B: POWE 22/85.

Yet, as most of these names imply, the essential foundations for large-scale enterprise in coal had been laid and consolidated in the first two decades of the century, and particularly in the merger 'booms' following the Great War and after 1926. Indeed, it was the circumstances of the late 1920s rather than the new depths of depression of the early 1930s, which gave rise to the two principal amalgamations of 1930: the Wigan Coal Corporation (a subsidiary of the Lancashire Steel Corporation, formed with the help of the Bank of England to 'rationalize' the collieries of the Wigan Coal and Iron Co. and three other colliery firms) and Welsh Associated Collieries (which united the coal interests of Guest, Keen and Nettlefold and Sir D. R. Llewellyn, and accounted for some 20 per cent of South Wales's bituminous output).[1]

Naturally, as the Board of Trade reports indicate,[2] corporate regrouping did not cease in the new circumstances of the 1930s, and even though some examples were almost ritualistic in character (the creation of Doncaster Amalgamated Collieries in 1937 simply united six companies which were already intimately connected by ties of ownership and management),[3] there were a few genuine corporate innovations which had considerable local effects. The leading example was the creation of Powell Duffryn Associated Collieries in 1935, which absorbed the extensive interests of the Powell Duffryn Steam Coal Co. and Welsh Associated Collieries, thus forming the country's biggest colliery enterprise. By 1938 it controlled 50 pits, employed 37,507 men, and produced almost 12 million tons of coal, or roughly one-third of the South Wales steam-coal output.[4] Another instance was the formation in 1931 of Bairds and Dalmellington to acquire the coal interest in Ayrshire and Dumfriesshire belonging to William Baird and Co., its subsidiary the Sanquhar and Kirkconnel Collieries, and the Dalmellington Iron Co. The new company, with 24 pits, controlled 9 per cent of Scotland's output in 1934 and 12 per cent in 1939.[5]

Yet these *were* exceptional. Moreover, the 'amalgamations' listed by the Board of Trade frequently included minor acquisitions, very small-

[1] For the mergers of 1928–30, see above, 205–8.

[2] Between 1928 and 1939 the Board of Trade published 11 *Reports... under Section 12* [of the Mining Industry Act, 1926] *on the Working of Part I of the Act*. These provided details of voluntary as well as official amalgamations. The Reports are reproduced in the Parliamentary Papers. Also see summaries in *ARSM*, various years.

[3] The 6 were: Brodsworth Main, Bullcroft Main, Firbeck Main, Hickleton Main, Markham Main, and Yorkshire Main. Firbeck Main was in Nottinghamshire. All these colliery firms worked the rich Barnsley Bed.

[4] POWE 28/239/17.

[5] COAL 37/30. The firm's output was 2.8 million tons in 1934 and 3.7 million in 1939.

scale mergers, the creation of joint enterprises for non-mining purposes (selling or the purchase of minerals), or the formalization of existing corporate links. Hence, the number of genuine and large-scale mergers was very small. And even though the numbers are misleading for the early years, there was a distinct decline in the extent and significance of amalgamations between the late 1920s and the 1930s.[1] The principal lineaments of concentration in the coalmining industry had been largely established by 1930. Indeed, much of the structural change which did take place appears to have been the result not so much of the formal commercial uniting of enterprises as of the commercial success of already large-scale firms, making no moves towards further major acquisitions, but strengthening their share of the industry's output by increasing or merely maintaining their output in a falling market.[2] Moreover, in every instance of 'autonomous' growth—relative or absolute— the maintenance or even increase in output was accompanied by a *reduction* in manpower. In effect, 'rationalization' in so far as it occurred at all, was an individual, private, and internalized—rather than a public and social—matter.

The point is that in matters of structural reform the focus of attention had shifted. In the mid-1920s, the discussion of industrial reorganization in coalmining had been largely concerned with the presumed economies of scale which might be attained by amalgamations. But by the early 1930s the crippling problems of excess productive capacity meant that structural change was now seen almost exclusively in terms of the need

---

[1] Figures reported by the Board of Trade (which in the early years appear to contain double-counting, when a merged firm took part in a subsequent scheme) or other statistical errors (counting all employees of a large-scale firm which simply purchased a small undertaking) were:

	1926–30	1931–8
Schemes	26 (reduced to 22 by sub-sequent amalgamations)	64 (43)
Miners involved	212,260	94,740

Source: PP 1930–1 XV, 1102–3; ARSM 1938.

[2] The following are examples of large-scale firms whose corporate entity was little changed but whose output rose, or only fell by a small amount, between 1929 and 1939: Ashington (3.0 and 4.0 m. tons), Bolsover (4.0 and 5.5 m.), Henry Briggs (1.5 m. tons at both dates), Butterley (almost 3.0 and 3.0–3.5 m.), Consett Iron (2.35 and 2.0 m.), Fife Coal Co. (4.0 and 3.5 m.), Ocean Coal and Wilson's (2.75 and 2.5 m.), Sheepbridge (1.2 and 1.5 m.), Staveley (2.5 m. at both dates). All data from the *Colliery Year Book* for each year. National output at the two dates fell from 258 m. tons to 231 m. tons.

to reduce capacity by concentrating output in a smaller number of units. 'Rationalization' now meant the closure of seams, collieries, or entire firms, so as to match stagnant demand with a reduced supply and a lowering of average costs by the concentration of output.

Yet as far as *public* policy was concerned, the pursuit of a smaller industry was handicapped not merely by the impossibility of making public funds available or by the legal, administrative, and political difficulties which nullified the work of the Coal Mines Reorganisation Commission, but by the central social scandal of unemployment. For reorganization would not only entail, it would actually *seek*, a reduction in employment at a time of severe depression. Thus, in 1934 there were still 200,000 miners wholly unemployed. The government could hardly be expected to intensify that problem by a wholehearted support of the Reorganisation Commission's plans to streamline the industry.[1] By the same token, in the mid-1930s the miners' union (which, in the discussions of 1924–6, had been prepared to contemplate radical industrial reorganization) was opposed to extensive amalgamations on the grounds that large-scale unemployment would be involved.[2] Nor did it need an undue cynicism on the part of the owners' organization to oppose the activities of the Reorganisation Commission in 1933 on the grounds that its proposed amalgamations would so concentrate available employment that hypothetical savings in costs of production would be outweighed by the substantial social costs involved in a leap in unemployment and the creation of yet more derelict communities.[3]

Yet if a determined official programme of industrial concentration was inconceivable for most of the 1930s, there were precious few incentives for similar ends to be pursued by private enterprise. For one thing, Part I of the 1930 Act reduced market pressures towards economy through merger since it protected potentially weak firms against failure by guaranteeing sales and made it more difficult for successful firms to acquire less efficient collieries by raising the latter's value. But in any case, the possibilities of an effective reduction in

---

[1] The Chairman of the Commission (Sir Ernest Gowers) argued that an administered and orderly reduction of capacity was preferable to a painful, perhaps anarchic market-induced reduction such as would be inevitable in an unreformed industry (below, 343). Yet even while pressing for action by the newly constituted and strengthened Coal Commission in 1938, Gowers acknowledged that Parliament recognized the economic necessity for reorganization but feared its social consequences: COAL 17/128 (Coal Commission. Paper by Chairman: 1 Sept. 1938).

[2] Kirby 1973, 281–2.

[3] Appendix by Mining Association of Great Britain to Mines Department. *Coal Mines Reorganisation Commission. Report to the Secretary for Mines. December 1933*. Cmd. 4468. 1933; COAL 12/171.

surplus capacity through acquisition and closure was, as we have seen, very remote: in competitive conditions such as obtained in the coal industry, and with 'the unconscionable tenacity' of a small firm 'which enables it to keep a semblance of life almost irrespective of its economic condition',[1] the private costs to an acquiring firm were likely to be in excess of any benefit that *it* could secure in terms of a greater share of the market. Hence, if the principal economic argument in favour of amalgamation was a reduction of industry-wide capacity, it was most unlikely to come about simply through private decision-making.

Although elaborate changes in industrial structure were therefore unlikely, the circumstances of the 1930s nevertheless did produce a certain amount of 'autonomous' rationalization. First, the official selling schemes meant that the easiest route to expansion was frequently the purchase of another colliery enterprise in order to acquire its 'standard tonnage' (and therefore quotas) under Part I of the Act. In 1935–9, for example, Manchester Collieries Ltd. purchased four other undertakings, which secured it a further 500,000 of standard tonnages (it then closed down three of the collieries).[2] Second, however, many big undertakings which also operated a large number of pits streamlined their operations, closing marginal or less efficient collieries and concentrating a shrinking work-force. Examples here were: Powell Duffryn (between 1928 and 1938 the firms composing it at the latter date reduced the number of operating pits from 86 to 49, and their employment from 52,079 to 37,507—while holding output steady at just under 12 million tons); Lambton, Hetton, and Joicey Collieries of Durham (between 1931 and 1939, with a relatively unchanged output of 5 million tons, it closed 5 of its 23 pits and reduced its work-force from 22,636 to 13,559); the Fife Coal Co. (between 1929 and 1939 it reduced its pits from 32 to 15, its manpower from 11,646 to 7,592, and its output from 4 to 3.5 million tons); Manchester Collieries (between 1930 and 1938 its output rose from 3.4 to 4.2 million tons, and its labour force fell from 17,275 to 15,208); and Pease and Partners of Durham (between 1929 and 1939 its pits fell from 18 to 8, its labour force from 8,816 to 4,841, and its output only from 2 million to 1.65 million tons).[3]

---

[1] Lubin and Everett 1927, 305.

[2] POWE 28/239/3.

[3] Powell Duffryn and Manchester Collieries: POWE 28/239/17 and 24. Other data are from the relevant *Colliery Year Books*. The Secretary of the Coal Mines Reorganisation Commission estimated that between 1930 and 1936 in South Wales the constituent companies of Powell Duffryn ceased work at 42 mines and Amalgamated Anthracite at 12; in Scotland, Wilson and Clyde ceased mining at 13 pits, Bairds and Dalmellington at 9, the Fife Coal Company at 8,

Such examples were indicative of one response to the 1930s, even though they were far from universal. In general, however, the number of pits working declined from 2,419 in 1929 to 2,158 in 1932 and 2,080 in 1936.[1]

In any case, the closing down of uneconomic capacity or the concentration of work on superior seams and pits, were only part—if the most obvious part—of a new business strategy. Later, in 1944, Sir Ernest Gowers argued that amalgamation was not a *panacea*, nor more than an 'insignificant' beginning; but that the formation of bigger units with larger resources was a fundamental prerequisite of a progressive industrial policy—of the *technical* reorganization, modernization, and investment needed to revive the industry.[2] That was an aspect of public discussion which was much more common in the last years of the Second World War than in the 1930s. Nevertheless, it reflected a situation which was no less relevant to the problems of the 1930s. The real issue of efficiency lay beyond simple alterations of corporate structures.

v. Performance and production

The nature of the problem was exemplified by the time, and in some instances the difficulties, involved in the revival of fortunes of merged enterprises. That there were economies of scale available for larger colliery firms and, in certain circumstances, for individual mines, can hardly be denied.[3] But the ease with which they could be attained by the merger of existing mines and companies *was* open to debate. There were, in any case, very obviously managerial problems attendant on the growth in scale—problems of skills to administer complex institutions or of sheer control. And any significant advance in productivity (beyond minor economies of shared or centralized services, or beyond the more continuous working which came from concentration of production)

Colville at 8, and United Collieries at 7; in Lancashire the Wigan Coal Corporation closed 7; in Durham, Dorman Long, Pease and Partners, and Lambton, Hetton, and Joicey 5 each; and in the Midlands, Clay Cross closed 6, New Hucknall 5, and Butterley and Staveley 2 each. See C. S. Hurst to W. G. Nott-Bower, 10 July 1936: POWE 22/85.

[1] *CYB* 1947, 521. The size of the pits which went out of business is not known. But it is probable that they were not the very smallest. Thus, over a somewhat longer period (1924–38) when the number of pits in operation fell by just over 600, those employing under 20 miners actually *rose* in number (from 535 to 537). But 136 of the fall were accounted for by pits employing between 20 and 99 miners; 274 by pits with a labour force between 100 and 499; and 163 by pits with between 500 and 1,499 miners. (Calculated from *List of Mines* 1924 and 1938).

[2] Draft report of the Coal Commission, 15 Nov. 1944: COAL 17/179.

[3] Below, 398–9.

usually presupposed expensive investment and prolonged reorganization. Nor was it always possible to distinguish the effects of changes in markets and market control. Hence, while the management of Powell Duffryn could point with pride to the success of their enlarged operations in the 1930s, that considerable financial achievement took place within (an admittedly modest) trade revival and as the result of enormous outlays—and substantial social costs through closures.[1]

In other instances the immediate advantages of large-scale operations were less clear. Manchester Collieries, for example, 17 years after its creation in 1929, confessed that it had proved very difficult to overcome labour problems inherited with its initial constituent companies; that there were initial serious organizational shortcomings because of the need to accommodate the numerous directors of the various firms involved; and that because of the trade depression and the social disadvantages of concentration the major work of colliery reorganization could not commence until 1937.[2] The firm, however, *did* make profits. Yet in 1940 the Chairman could still complain that the original objectives of the amalgamation in terms of significant cost reductions had not been attained (in spite of the greater scale of operations and the transfer of production between pits), that the large expenditure and mechanization programmes after 1936 had not been justified, and that output per manshift had actually declined.[3]

Such complaints raise, in a dramatic form, some important and unresolved issues: could efficiency have been materially enhanced by increasing the average size of mines or colliery undertakings? What was the connection between mechanization, reorganization, and productivity? Was the relatively poor productivity performance of the British coal industry the fault of 'bad' entrepreneurship?

In terms of the industry as a whole, it is not easy to adduce the

---

[1] See the memorandum submitted to the Coal Industry Nationalisation Compensation Tribunal, Mar. 1946: POWE 28/239.

[2] 'Manchester Collieries Limited, General Statement of History and Progress' (1946): POWE 28/239. Profits rose from £118,495 in the year to 31 Mar. 1930, to £219,202 in 1935 and £340,131 in 1938. On the other hand, labour productivity (OMS) between 1930 and 1938 rose by 17% (while national OMS rose by 6%).

[3] 'Mining Policy, Manchester Collieries Limited, October 31st 1940' Lancashire Records Office, NCMc 4/6. The Company's OMS in the years 1936-40 was: 19.9, 19.9, 20.3, 20.2, 19.8 cwt. (POWE: 28/239). In his 1940 memorandum, Burrows blamed lack of control (by the Board of Directors) of development expenditure. Significantly, he described the motives for the original merger in terms of non-technical economies: the restraint of 'senseless' competition, the ability to control markets and adjust outputs, the pooling of managerial knowledge, and the prospect of enhancing the average quality of coal produced.

relevant information nor even specify the appropriate evidence.[1] Certainly, mechanization was likely to increase labour productivity, and statistical studies suggest that it might have been a more important element than increasing scale of operations in improving efficiency.[2] Yet it was not uniformly beneficial and the cost implications (in terms of labour responses and higher wage rates as well as capital outlay) were not negligible. Hence, although the technical and economic arguments in favour of mechanization were unambiguous, and the pace of new installations was quite rapid, the *business* problems were not always easily solved.

As far as the attainment of economies of scale was concerned, most of the detailed statistical information relates to mines rather than under-takings. And to that extent the potential to be realized from mergers and business growth might have been very limited. Admittedly, in relation to the individual pit there does appear to have been some correlation between size and productivity—although it did not follow that the largest pits were the most productive. In the case of the superficially most persuasive argument, precise measurement is vitiated by the use of the average output of pits (nationally or in districts) as a proxy for size, and output per man-year as an indicator of productivity.[3] Yet the potential could only be realized painfully slowly, and it was far from clear that *starting with the mines as they actually were* there was much scope for the sort of increase in average size which would have transformed pro-ductivity (apart, that is, from a drastic programme of closures and concentration, joined with massive new investments). And on the other side—the increase in scale of operations of colliery *undertakings*—the economies of scale in production were severely limited (apart, again, from ruthless and expensive internal regrouping). On either side, in the context of the 1930s the social and private financial costs would have been considerable—in excess, perhaps, of the social and private gains to be derived from the risky transformations.

Looking at productive organization of the industry in very general terms, the 1930s saw relatively little change: between 1929 and 1938 the average output per mine was virtually constant, while the number of miners per pit fell slightly. That, in turn, is consistent with two of the

---

[1] These issues are discussed in more detail in ch. 9.

[2] Buxton 1970; Kirby 1972; Evans & Fine, 'Economies of Scale in the British Inter-War Coal Industry' (unpublished); Evans & Fine, 'The Diffusion of Mechanical Cutting in the British Inter-War Coal Industry' (unpublished); Greasley 1979; Paull 1968; Rhodes 1945.

[3] Evans and Fine, 'Economies of Scale'. Output per man-year neglects important differences in the number of shifts worked.

most notorious features of the interwar performance of the British coal industry: the fact that it was carried on on a much smaller scale than its continental competitors and the almost painful slowness with which labour productivity (output per manshift) rose.[1] As we have seen, output per manshift in British coalmining increased by a mere 6 per cent in the 1930s (the increase to 1936 was somewhat greater—8.8 per cent—but was followed by a decline). Even bearing in mind the very limited extent of industrial reorganization in the period, this was distinctly disappointing—first, because the overall reduction in demand (and therefore in output and manpower) should have led to some statistical improvement if only through the increased scope for concentrating on more productive seams and places; second, because the gentle increase in OMS was in fact accompanied by an impressive extension of mechanization. Between 1929 and 1938 the proportion of coal cut mechanically doubled (from 28 to 59 per cent), while the amount of coal conveyed mechanically (along the face or between the line of the face and other parts of the mine) increased from 37.1 million tons to 122.9 million tons. Data on conveying are uncertain but there can be no doubt about the significance of the measures of mechanized cutting.[2]

Superficially, then, the rapid growth in mechanized cutting, assuming that it led to significant advances in efficiency, barely compensated for forces making for deterioration in labour productivity (increasing age of mines, antiquated equipment, geological difficulties, labour problems, institutional rigidities). Some clue as to the direction in which an explanation might lie is provided by a finer measurement of output per manshift, to take account of the function (undercutting) principally involved in mechanization. In a study, on a district basis, of the relationship between the degree of face mechanization and the productivity of *face-workers*, it was found that in many instances the latter increased with the former—although sometimes slightly and by no means invariably.[3] Certainly, the experience of productivity improvement at the face

[1] In 1936 OMS (in kilogrammes) was 1,195 in Britain, 1,710 in the Ruhr, 1,781 in the Netherlands, and 2,073 in Polish Upper Silesia: International Labour Office 1938, I, 109.

[2] The measurement of mechanized conveying is uncertain, since it is not clear how account was taken of the extension of conveying systems within one mine (e.g. did the addition of non-face to face conveyors increase the tonnage recorded as being conveyed?), nor of how much of the distances underground were traversed by the new techniques. Official data were subsequently translated into proportion of total output. See Ministry of Fuel and Power, *Statistical Digest from 1938* (Cmd. 6538. 1944), 12, which translates the 122.9 million tons conveyed in 1938 into 54% of output.

[3] Rhodes 1945, 101-10. The positive link was fairly well marked in the 1920s in Northumberland, South Wales, and Scotland, and in the 1930s in Durham, Yorkshire (from 1927),

was much more marked than total labour productivity: output per man-shift *worked at the face* rose by about 12.4 per cent between 1929 and 1938, which was by no means spectacular, but considerably more than the figure for workers elsewhere underground (5.5 per cent) or for surface workers (whose output per manshift *declined* by 4.2 per cent). And the obvious implication (subsequently elaborated by the Reid Committee)[1] was that the problems of the coal industry were more marked (or less successfully tackled) away from the face: in transport and organization underground, or in the overall integration of colliery activities.[2]

Yet, suggestive as such data are, there is, as usual, a fundamental problem in accepting national averages as indicative of an extremely varied situation. This problem is even more obvious in this case because of the importance of different geological conditions—including not merely the size and condition of the seams but the nature of the coal and the effect on it, and its marketability, of different cutting methods.[3] Whatever the explanation, however, there *was* great variety in the different coalfields, with respect to both the pace at which mechanized cutting was extended and the achievement by the late 1930s. In the principal districts, as Table 7.7 shows, the latter varied from 26 per cent of output in South Wales to 91 per cent in Northumberland.

By the same token, there were also wide and significant contrasts in the levels and changes of output per manshift. In this respect it is pre-sumably relevant to note the contrast between export and inland fields. Output per manshift for all the labour force actually declined in the principal export areas (except for Northumberland, where the excep-tional degree of mechanization no doubt helped), while in the great

Nottinghamshire and North Derby (from 1927), and Lancashire and Cheshire and North Staf-fordshire (from 1927); and slight in Northumberland in 1927–30 and Scotland and South Derbyshire; Leicestershire, Cannock Chase and Warwickshire (both in 1927–30).

[1] Below, 616.

[2] This was in part, perhaps, the consequences of the fall in the industry's size, since overheads and the number of 'on cost' workmen did not fall in line with production. Thus, between 1929 and 1938 the proportion of surface-worker manshifts rose from 21 to 23%.

[3] Where seams were thick or where the roof and the coal seams themselves were unstable or where the product was intended for carbonization (so that round coal was not important), there were likely to be delays in the introduction of mechanical cutting. This was the most likely explanation for the relatively low (even by British standards) proportion of coal cut mechanically in South Yorkshire, South Wales, and Durham. For a discussion of the circumstances in which mechanization was more, or less, likely, see Greasley 1979, Ch. 2. However, considering *general* trends Dr Greasley concludes that mechanization proceeded more slowly than circumstances warranted and that entrepreneurial decision-making was most probably at fault.

Table 7.7. *Mechanization and labour productivity in British coalmining, 1929 and 1938*

	Proportion of output mechanically cut		OMS (underground labour) cwt.			OMS (all labour) cwt.		
	1929	1938	1929	1938	% increase	1929	1938	% increase
Great Britain	28	59	27.47	29.91	8.9	21.69	22.96	5.9
Scotland	63	79[a]	27.13	30.61	12.8	23.74	23.30	−1.9
Northumberland	55	91	28.71	30.17	5.1	22.54	22.86	1.4
Durham	22	42	29.72	27.26	−8.3	21.65	21.48	−0.8
South Wales & Mons.	9	26	24.44	24.75	1.3	20.46	20.13	−1.6
South Yorkshire	13	56	29.59	33.33	12.6	23.49	25.58	8.9
West Yorkshire	32	55						
Nottinghamshire	27	70	31.39	38.59	22.9	24.29	28.78	18.5
North Derbyshire	30	88						
North Staffordshire	43	92		33.17		17.62	20.48	16.2
Lancashire & Cheshire	23	68		26.39				
Leicestershire	5	84						
Warwickshire	29	69		35.82				

[a] = 1937

Sources: ARSM 1929, 124–5, 145; *ARSM* 1938, 182–3, 203.

Table 7.8. District proceeds in British coalmining 1930–1938

	1930		1931		1932		1933		1934		1935		1936		1937		1938	
	(i)	(ii)	(i)	(ii)	(i)	(ii)	(i)	(ii)	(i)	(ii)	(i)	(ii)	(i)	(ii)	(i)	(ii)	(i)	(ii)
Scotland	48.2	—0/1	62.4	—0/2	69.3	—0/5	46.3	—0/0	27.3	0/6	16.0	0/11	12.9	1/5	8.3	1/10	11.8	1/10
Northumberland		0/8		0/1		0/5		—0/3		—0/1		0/2		0/6		1/1		1/5
Durham		0/4		—0/1		—0/5		—0/5		—0/3		—0/4		0/1		0/6		0/11
SWM	56.7	0/2	55.0	0/0	58.8	0/1	61.6	—0/2	60.8	—0/1	42.9	—0/1	33.4	—0/1	20.0	0/5	29.1	0/5
Yorkshire	31.4	0/7	38.9	0/6	32.9	0/6	22.5	0/9	17.8	0/11	24.3	0/10	19.5	1/2	11.6	1/4	16.2	1/3
Nottinghamshire	33.8	0/8	10.1	1/4	12.2	1/2	9.5	1/1	12.2	1/3	11.2	1/4	1.1	2/1	2.9	2/1	2.4	1/11
North Derbyshire	18.2	0/7	32.5	0/10	27.8	0/10	19.3	0/9	18.1	0/10	8.9	0/12	4.3	1/11	2.4	1/9	4.2	1/7
North Staffs.		0/6	15.1	0/9	17.1	0/9	15.8	0/9	17.8	0/10	12.1	0/11	25.9	1/3	7.6	1/1	3.2	1/9
Leicestershire	18.3	0/5	nil	1/2	23.0	0/10	20.1	0/7	9.8	1/5	8.6	1/4	8.6	1/10	9.7	1/10	nil	1/9
Warwickshire	10.7	1/10	19.7	2/2	15.8	1/8	16.1	1/6	15.6	1/11	15.0	1/11	10.5	2/4	13.0	2/6	9.2	2/9

(i): Percentage output showing debit balance.
(ii): Average credit per ton (nearest 1d.).

Source: SRO CB7/3/19 ff.

Midland districts and even in Lancashire and Cheshire it rose at two or three times the national average. Differences between inland and export districts as far as OMS at the face or underground was concerned were also marked—although the Scottish fields were an exception to the dismal story of those fields relying on exports.

In general, it is difficult to avoid the conclusion that to a small extent the degree of mechanized cutting, and to a larger extent the achievement of overall labour productivity (calling for more extensive investment and reorganization), depended on the profitability of operations and the pace of output growth—with the relatively poor performance of export collieries, and the relatively good performance of inland collieries, explaining the contrasts in their productivity, rather than the other way round. Districts in decline found it very difficult to undertake the transformations necessary to overhaul their productivity. Moreover, at the general level, the costs of thorough reorganization, together with the alternative avenues to profitability (through cartel and price-maintenance arrangements) must have reduced the incentives to technical and structural change.

In all but isolated pockets, therefore, the productive achievements of British coalmining in the 1930s were disappointing. And this was no doubt for the reasons that the Reid Committee adduced in 1945: mechanization alone was not an adequate strategy; to secure the largest benefits it had to be associated with fundamental reorganization—of layout, underground transport systems (of men as well as coal), shafts and roadways, entire mines.[1] And in the context of the depressed 1930s, and of purely private decision-making, such measures were risky, time-consuming, and expensive, while the incentive to adopt them must have been lessened by the availability of alternative and easier ways of making money (or reducing losses), through cartel arrangements and the ability to manipulate markets and sustain prices. Market structures and institutions, the balancing of costs and benefits, go further than entrepreneurial deficiencies to explain economic performance.

[1] For the Reid Committee, see below, 615–19.

CHAPTER 8

Towards the Social Control of Industry
1929–1939

As was seen in the previous chapter, during the 1930s the coal industry's persistent problems—unemployment, surplus capacity, the threat of economic decay and social dislocation, the insistent demands of labour and capital—combined to elicit a new pattern of government intervention. In many respects this was simply a series of *ad hoc* responses to social problems and political pressures. But it was also part of a more general phenomenon. For in the course of the decade there was a distinct change in ideological outlook and expectations, and a more limited set of legislative and administrative innovations. Even though the extent and enthusiasm of state interventionism fell short of the aspirations of its principal advocates, it was in the 1930s that a self-conscious *laissez-faire* was finally, in Harold Macmillan's words, relegated to the 'limbo of forgotten things'.[1]

In the 1930s, as far as the staple export industries were concerned, the two most potent reasons for state intervention were mass unemployment, with its fearful social problem of 'derelict communities', and the economic deadweight of surplus capacity and low productivity, with their concomitant pressure towards fundamental reorganization. These two issues were closely related. This was not merely because of their interactions (surplus capacity created depressed areas). It was also the result of the dilemmas of policy. On the one hand, official scepticism as to the possibility of an effective macro-economic unemployment policy (deficit spending, an extensive public works programme, etc.) led to attempts to sustain markets and prices, and to a discussion of the ways in which a presumed core of 'structural unemployment' might be dissipated through a policy of industrial reorganization. On the other, the pursuit of economic efficiency inevitably clashed with the immediate prerequisites of social welfare.

---

[1] Harold Macmillan, in *Hansard* 3 Apr. 1935, col. 442.

i. Markets and jobs

At one level, there was little distinction between the government posture towards coalmining in the 1920s and the 1930s. In both decades policy was primarily concerned with sustaining the industry's sales and potential for employment. Initially, however, this was a long-run goal, to be approached by indirect means. Until the late 1920s political principles and excessive optimism as to the industry's 'natural' potential for recovery made for a reluctance to intervene in its affairs. Only crises of industrial relations (in 1919–20 and 1925–6, for example) forced the government's hand. After about 1927, however, the chronic nature of the industry's position, and its unresponsiveness to the return to the Gold Standard and consequent wage cuts, became almost universally apparent. Quite apart from the resulting discussion of fundamental structural reform, this led to a consideration of ways in which the market for coal might be more directly increased within the existing organizational framework.

However, in the circumstances of the time there was very little scope for direct action by the government to protect, let alone expand, the market for coal or (in practical terms) to reduce its costs. A partial exception to this arose in relation to exports, where the existence of official subsidies to Britain's trade rivals, and above all the growth of bilateral trading arrangements, encouraged and facilitated intervention. As has already been seen, rating relief generated a modest 'subsidy' to export coal; and—of much greater significance—in the early 1930s Britain built up a network of bilateral trade treaties, especially in northern Europe, which gave some protection to sales and therefore stimulated, as well as distorted, the export trade.[1] In the absence of such measures, British coal exports would have been even more severely affected by the events of the 1930s. And as trade restrictions and economic nationalism mounted, the government came to encourage the coalowners to join international cartels, and even, in the last years, toyed with the acceptance of the general principle of export subsidies.[2]

In other areas, however, there was considerable resistance to arguments in favour of expanding sales by direct action or indirect subsidy. Thus, the 'Back to Coal' movement of the early 1930s, even though it brought together quite disparate interest groups, had no effective success in its attempt to secure the reintroduction of coal-fired ships

---

[1] Above, 289–90.   [2] Above, 287.

into the Navy and the Mercantile Marine. And even the idea of an export subsidy was linked to the raising of funds by a levy on inland sales.

The most likely—and perhaps most 'legitimate'—avenue to explore was government aid to the development of processes by which manufactured fuel and oil and petrol could be commercially produced from raw coal. The technical basis of such processing had been established before the First World War, and one of the first acts of the Department of Scientific and Industrial Research had been to establish (in 1917) a Fuel Research Board which conducted modest experiments in carbonization and coal-processing. But at no time in the period was there any profit in the unsubsidized commercial pursuit of low temperature carbonization (which primarily produced solid fuel) or hydrogenation (which was primarily designed to produce petrol).[1] Yet, even under a Labour Government and when the unemployment problem in coal began to reach its most worrying dimensions, there was considerable official reluctance to use public funds to aid development (especially by means of commercial subsidies) in these fields.[2]

Quite apart from the general reluctance to subsidize private enterprise, it was very doubtful if the result would greatly increase net demand for coal, since the manufactured fuel which would result from low temperature carbonization would compete with sales of raw coal (it was estimated that of every 1,000 tons of coal processed, only 10 per cent would represent new business). Further, the pursuit of *high* temperature carbonization was not particularly relevant to the chronic problem of unemployment. Another estimate from 1934 suggested that if all petrol and oil products then used were to be derived from coal, the result would only be an increase of 30 to 40,000 in mining employment.[3]

The principal exception to the refusal of governments to subsidize technical innovation was the British Hydrocarbons Production Act of 1934, which guaranteed that, for a limited period, any duty on British petroleum products derived from British coal would be lower than that on imported petroleum products. This was decided after negotiations with ICI, which controlled the hydrogenation process in Britain and had been trying to secure some sort of government encouragement

[1] *Samuel Evidence*, 166 ff.; *Committee of Imperial Defence. Sub-Committee on Oil from Coal* (Cmd. 5665. 1938: *PP* 1937/8 XII); Reader 1975, II, 128–9, 162–81, 264.

[2] DSIR 8/49 (17 Dec. 1930); there was a small (and unsuccessful) joint state-private venture in low temperature carbonization with the Gas, Light, and Coke Company in 1928–31: CAB 24/220/182–96 (27 Feb. 1931).

[3] *Hansard* 21 Nov. 1934, col. 223.

since the late 1920s. On this basis, ICI went ahead with the development of a plant for the extraction of petrol from coal at Billingham. It opened in 1935, but was never a success. By 1938, when the Falmouth Committee on the production of oil from coal recommended that the 8 d. preference granted four years earlier should be renewed, ICI had in effect abandoned its hopes for oil-from-coal, while the Committee itself reported that there could be no reliance, even in wartime, on oil produced from indigenous sources.[1]

With the exception of the bilateral trade treaties, therefore, the impracticability of enlarging the market for coal by direct state intervention confirmed official policy in its resistance to policy innovation on pragmatic as well as ideological grounds. By way of contrast, however, governments found it much more difficult to avoid sustained consideration of action to alleviate unemployment, which by the late 1920s was acknowledged to be more than a transitory issue. And its most dramatic manifestation was in the coal industry, where in the autumn of 1928 some 15 per cent of the workers were wholly unemployed and 6 per cent were on short time. (In the late 1920s miners accounted for almost one-fifth of all the insured unemployed.) After a very slight respite in 1929–30, the problem worsened. By late September 1933 some 230,000 miners (21 per cent of the total) were completely without jobs and about half that number had only very intermittent work.[2]

The seriousness of the situation in coalmining was aggravated by the exceptional concentration and long-term nature of its unemployment problem, which devastated whole regions and produced the 'social tragedy of dereliction'.[3] In many districts miners accounted for over 50 per cent—and not infrequently for 70 per cent and more—of the labour force. Given the fact that in the three main export regions (Durham, Scotland, South Wales) the percentage of *wholly unemployed* miners throughout 1931–5 did not fall below 20 per cent (in 1933 the figures ranged between 25 and 30 per cent), it was hardly surprising that in many communities within these districts two-thirds and more of the entire work-force lacked jobs. Moreover, long-term unemployment was peculiarly intense in the coalfields. Thus, in Great Britain as a whole in the summer of 1934 almost one-quarter of the unemployed had been out of work for more than a year, but in south-west Durham the figure was

---

[1] Reader 1975, II, ch. 10; *Committee of Imperial Defence. Sub-Committee on Oil from Coal* (Cmd. 5665. 1938: *PP* 1937/8 XII).

[2] The figures for all insured workers in Sept. 1933 were 15% and 3%.

[3] Sharp 1935, 22.

over three-quarters. And in the principal communities of eastern South Wales over half the 50,000 miners who were wholly unemployed had been out of work for more than two years—and one-third of them for more than three years.[1] The prolonged intensity of such unemployment created, in the words of the Chief Medical Officer of Health, 'deprivation, hardship, social ill and anxiety'.[2]

Throughout the interwar years there was intermittent, and often impassioned, advocacy of government intervention to increase the demand for labour by public investment and other counter-cyclical expenditures. In general, however, this was resisted by Cabinets and the Treasury.[3] Admittedly, limited measures designed to *alleviate* unemployment had been devised in the 1920s: modest grants to local authorities to cover part of the cost of public investment; some assistance to migration; Treasury guarantees for business loans; an accelerated road-building programme; rating relief for industry. But these were all very restricted in scope and funds, were generally hedged by strict conditions and qualifications, and were, if anything, diminished from 1931. Throughout most of the years there was fairly significant public expenditure (for the construction of the electricity 'grid' for example, or the electrification of the railways), but this was neither envisaged nor presented as a policy to counter unemployment. And the bleak official opposition to extensive public works as a counter-cyclical or unemployment policy endured, with only the slightest hint of changing attitudes in the late 1930s.

In practice, therefore, the principal public response to unemployment did not aim at the direct creation of jobs. Rather, it involved the extension of direct financial assistance to the workless and their dependants—unemployment benefits, Poor Law and supplementary relief, and even (in 1928–9) official contributions to private charity funds directed to mining communities.[4] In fact, Britain's unemployment insurance system was among the most advanced and 'generous' in the world, and was continuously supplemented by payments beyond those actuarially justified by contributions. In 1931 the National Govern-

---

[1] *Reports of Investigations into the Industrial Conditions in Certain Depressed Areas* (Cmd. 4728. 1934): *Durham and Tyneside*, Tables I–III; *South Wales and Monmouthshire*, 135.

[2] *Public Health Reports, 1932. Annual Report of the Chief Medical Officer of the Ministry of Health*, 39. In spite of this acknowledgement, however, the weight of official opinion tended to argue against the view that chronic unemployment had serious deleterious effects on health. This has remained a matter of controversy. See below, ch. 10, sect. iv.

[3] Middleton 1985; Howson 1981; Pollard 1970; Winch 1969; Glynn & Howells 1980.

[4] Above, 262.

ment's economy measures reversed previous trends by reducing benefits and tightening up the conditions which had been relaxed by the Labour Government in 1930. But these cuts had been imposed at a time of falling prices and were restored in 1934. And 'transitional' payments, albeit means-tested, remained as a buffer between the lapse of insurance entitlement and resort to the Poor Law. (In the 1930s transitional payments covered virtually all the unemployed and, as a result, the numbers relieved by the Poor Law fell drastically when compared with the 1920s.)

Of course, the system had serious defects. Quite apart from the humiliation and inequity frequently experienced by the recipients of benefits (in 1924–30, the application to miners of the condition that claimants should be 'genuinely seeking work' was particularly harsh), the levels of weekly payments were hardly munificent. Thus, in 1930 a miner with a dependent wife and two children would have received 28s. per week in benefit—as against the average shift wage of 9s. per day (the average miner worked just under 5 shifts per week).[1] Nevertheless, in its historical and cultural context the insurance and relief scheme had many admirable elements and the material protection it afforded was never negligible. Above all, by the standards of the day it involved very large public expenditures: over £400 million of insurance benefits (about 85 per cent of which was covered by contributions) in the 1920s; and payments of some £700 million (including £250 million of 'transitional' benefits funded by the Exchequer) between April 1929 and March 1936.[2] Extensive and continuous support of the unemployed had become an inescapable political obligation. It far outweighed in scope—and economic effect—any of the other halting attempts to tackle unemployment.

Although governments did not entertain the idea of directly stimulating economic growth, after 1931, with the final abandonment of the Gold Standard and Free Trade, the 'policy' embodied in low interest rates, protection, and exchange-rate management *did* make a contribution to recovery. Yet, in spite of the remarkable nature of that recovery,

[1] *The Times* pointed out that for a sizeable minority of workers in 1937, both benefits and wages fell below a level of reasonable subsistence: *The Times* 4 Mar. 1937, 15c, using data in the *Ministry of Labour Gazette* Aug. 1937.

[2] *Twentieth Abstract of Labour Statistics* (Cmd. 3831. 1931), 60–1; *Twenty-Second Abstract of Labour Statistics* (Cmd. 5556. 1937), 68–9. The figures for the 1920s and 1930s are not quite comparable since those for the 1920s do not take account of Poor Law relief (paid to the unemployed who had exceeded their entitlement), whereas by the 1930s, 'transitional' benefits had taken over some of this relief.

which was largely based on the home market, some industries remained profoundly depressed, unemployment levels were still high, and the upturn threw into even sharper relief the central economic problem of the 1930s: structural and regional imbalance. In 1936, after three years of rapid growth, the national rate of full-time unemployment among insured workers was 13 per cent, and in comparisons with the South-East's 7 per cent and the Midland's 9 per cent, the percentages of wholly unemployed in the North-East was still 17 per cent and in Wales 29 per cent.

Since the late 1920s, around the staple industries in general, and the export coal industry in particular, there had grown up depressed areas—whole regions sunk in 'the pit of permanent local worklessness'.[1] It was in response to these problems that the most interesting, if still restricted, innovations in government policy were launched. In the case of one set of policies ('rationalization') their relationship to unemployment was oblique: *their* prime aim was to adjust the size and structure of the coal industry.[2] At another level however, there was a direct confrontation with the demand for and supply of jobs: these involved less decisive—but nevertheless symptomatically significant—attempts to facilitate the transfer of labour and to revive the flagging health of depressed, or 'special', areas. Again, the devastation of the coalfields lay at the centre of the government's perception of the social problem.

Industrial transference activity was a product of the 1927 depression in coalmining and the political anxieties which accompanied it. After a report from the Industrial Transference Board (1928), government policy attempted to encourage geographical and occupational mobility by publicity, grants, and retraining. And it reflected a desire not merely to 'disperse' intensely concentrated unemployment but to overcome 'rigidities' in the labour market. It was, in principle, a social policy of symbolic significance, and attracted warmly commendatory international attention.[3] In practice, however, it had unavoidable limitations. Those whom it could most easily help to leave the depressed areas were, naturally, young and single, skilled and inherently mobile; and as far as the depressed areas were concerned, it therefore exacerbated their remaining problems by leaving a less 'employable' work-force—as well as redundant social capital—behind.

There was, moreover, the difficulty of ensuring that such migration

---

[1] *The Times*, 21 Mar. 1934, 16a.
[2] Below, 341–58.
[3] Morris 1934, 234 ff.

4. David Lloyd George addressing South Wales Miners' Federation Conference, Cory Hall, Cardiff, 21 July 1915

5. Hewing at the coalface, Clay Cross Company, North Derbyshire, early twentieth century

6. Hewing and Loading, Clay Cross Company, North Derbyshire, early twentieth century

7. Miners' housing, Varteg, Monmouthshire, constructed c. 1840

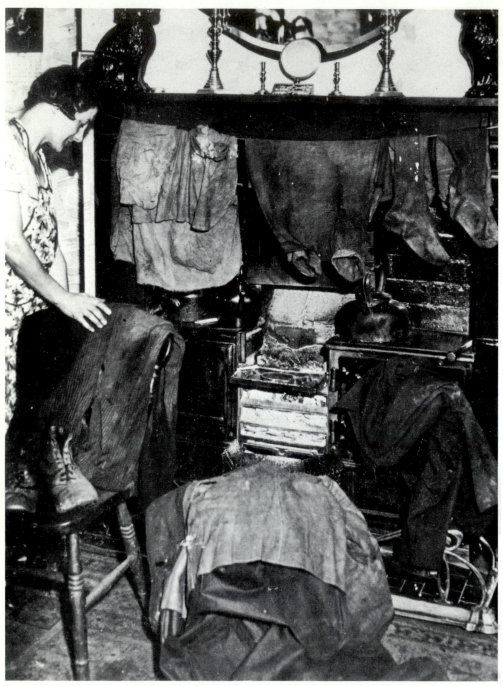

8. Drying pit clothes at home, Penallta Colliery, Rhymney Valley (Powell Duffryn Associated Collieries), 1938

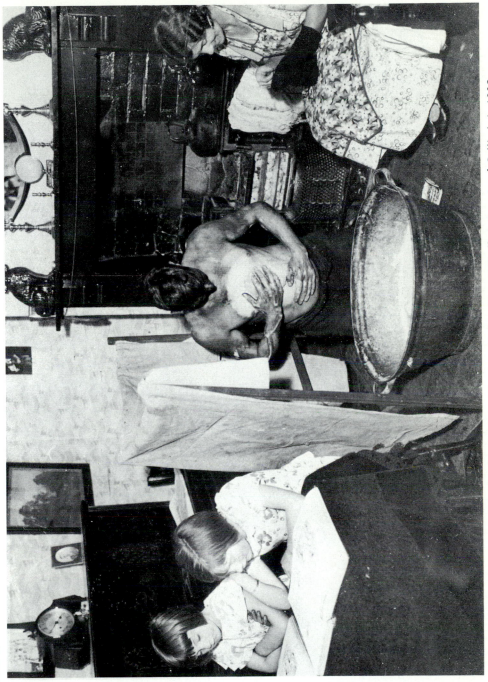

9. Bathing at home, Penallta Colliery, Rhymney Valley (Powell Duffryn Associated Collieries), 1938

10. Pithead baths, Ellington Colliery, Northumberland, 1930s

11. The National Coal Board in session, 15 July 1946

12. Public Ownership begins, 1 January 1947

was permanent. In practice many migrants returned to their home community (of the 25,000 miners who received public help in leaving South Wales in 1928–31, some 40 per cent ultimately returned[1]). Of course, the interwar years *did* see very substantial relative, and some absolute, shifts of population away from the old coalfields,[2] but most of these were privately funded. And the Transference Board's efforts had a limited, although not negligible outcome: 101,000 adults and 20,000 juveniles received assistance in 1929–33, and 82,000 adults and 54,000 juveniles in 1934–8.[3] Not surprisingly, the transference policy worked best at times of national buoyancy or recovery, when relative prosperity in other regions widened the employment and income gap between them and the coalfields. For only then were there jobs to go to. When depression was diffused—as in 1931–3—net migration slowed down or ceased.[4]

Perception of the regional distortions of the economy was obviously inversely related to the geographic extent of severe depression. By the same token, therefore, the evolution of regional policy (of which transference was an early example) was dependent on the distinctive character of the slump in the coalfields. Even so, there was precious little response to the crisis of the late 1920s, and even the genuine anxiety about the threat to health from unemployment in the distressed areas of South Wales and the North-East was absorbed in complacency and inaction.[5] The Labour Government's initiative in sponsoring independent surveys of the depression in Lancashire, Merseyside, the North-East, South Wales, and south-west Scotland resulted in no decisive action. (The surveys were commissioned early in 1931 and produced the next year.) Only after the worst of the general slump had passed, and when recovery elsewhere had begun, did the problem of the depressed areas come to the forefront of politics. By 1934, as *The Times* pointed

[1] Daley 1978, 129. For migration from mining communities, see below, ch. 10, sect. vi.

[2] Over 600,000 people left South Wales and the North-East in 1921–36: Titmuss 1938, 279–80. Between 1921 and 1937 the national population grew by 7½%, that of London and the Home Counties by 18%, and of the Midlands by 11%. Mid-Scotland, however, grew by only 4%, and Lancashire and Northumberland and Durham by 1% or less; Glamorgan and Monmouthshire experienced a decrease of 9%: *Royal Commission on the Distribution of the Industrial Population* 1940, 37; quoted in Breach and Hartwell 1972, 217.

[3] McCrone 1969, 98–9.

[4] The number of insured workers in South Wales fell by 7% in 1926–9, when the coal industry was much more depressed than many industries elsewhere, but actually rose by 1.4% in 1930–1, when the slump became more widespread (Daley 1978, 125). The numbers of adults helped by the Transference Board were 62,000 in 1929–30 and 20,000 in 1932–3. In 1932, as unemployment spread throughout the country, the government actually reduced its efforts to facilitate transference.

[5] Below, 464–8.

out some years later, their 'black features' 'began to stand out again in lonely contrast to the returning prosperity of the Midlands, and the South'. Thenceforth, 'the needs of the Special Areas dominated, like an unclimbed mountain, politics and public opinion'.[1] Although this mountain *remained* unclimbed, there was at least some semblance of activity.

By the spring of 1934 the National Government (as had happened with Baldwin's Administration in 1928) was obliged to consider the effects of long-term unemployment on health in South Wales and Durham.[2] But even though it managed to avoid any public acknowledgement that the health situation warranted serious anxiety, the whole question of the depressed coalfields received a dramatic airing in *The Times* of 20–2 March 1934. Three articles on Durham, entitled 'Places without a Future', put forward a persuasively sensational and detailed case: after six years 'of continuous, bitter poverty' the coal-producing areas had little hope:

England is beginning again to think in terms of prosperity; and may even deceive herself into imagining that at home, if only she holds what she has gained, everything, everywhere is going to come right. That is not so. There are districts of England, heavily populated, whose plight no amount of general trade recovery can ever cure, because their sole industry is not depressed but dead. It would be a failure of humanity to forget them, a failure of statesmanship to neglect them.[3]

And the leader writer drew conclusions which could not be ignored: in the face of 'the terrible persistence of an unrelieved depression . . . it is no longer a question of saving an industry, but of saving the people from a desperate plight'. Desperate and unprecedented action was therefore necessary; a 'Director of Operations' with extensive powers must be appointed for 'in the main the energy and drive, the reviving impulse, will have to come from the outside, and not casually or intermittently, but with steady and sustained direction. . . . Areas of decay must be cleared . . . the people must be rescued from an encroaching desolation . . . men must be set on their feet again and given a purpose in life.'[4]

---

[1] *The Times* 1 Nov. 1937, 15f. In 1934 the average rate of unemployment in London and the South-East was about 9%, in the North-East 22%, and in Wales 32%: McCrone 1969, 100.

[2] Below, ch. 10, sect. iv; *Report on the Investigation in the Coalfield of South Wales and Monmouthshire on the Social Condition of the Miners' Families* (Cmd. 3272. 1929); *Annual Report of the Chief Medical Officer of the Ministry of Health*, 1932–4; *Report on Maternal Mortality in Wales* (Cmd. 5423. 1937).   [3] *The Times* 20 Mar. 1934, 15f.

[4] Ibid., 15c; 22 Mar. 1934, 15b. The publication of the articles and leaders coincided with a Commons debate on the same theme.

The pressure from such public anxieties in the spring of 1934 was the direct origin of the elaboration of government policy towards the depressed coalfields. The Cabinet appointed four official investigators to report on the regions which were the principal sufferers: the North-East, South Wales, Scotland, and west Cumberland. Their Reports were delivered in October, and confirmed the grim tale of dereliction—especially in South Wales and Durham (in which instances there was telling criticism of the organization and attitudes inherent in the coal industry). Even though some of the documents' more critical comments on industrial relations were removed before publication, the government could no longer resist the clamour for positive action. In Harold Macmillan's words the reports were the result of 'a visit from Whitehall to the Passchendaele of Durham and South Wales', and contained 'passages . . . of an explosive and even a revolutionary character'.

The Special Areas (Development and Improvement) Act of 1934 designated South Wales, the North-East, west Cumberland, and south-west Scotland as 'Special Areas' (although the major towns within them were excluded from the legislation). Responsibility for a policy of stimulating economic development was given to two Commissioners: one for England and Wales, the other for Scotland. Once more, however, the potential importance of the policy innovation was negated by explicit restrictions on its scope. The Commissioners were given only small budgets and were specifically precluded from initiating policy without prior Treasury approval of its general lines. They were not to use public funds to subsidize private businesses, and could not extend financial assistance to public authorities where funds were already receivable from any other government department. The result was powerlessness at the very levels where advocates of a vigorous regional development policy had wished to see initiatives taken.

In his first Report the Commissioner for England and Wales, Sir Malcolm Stewart, went out of his way to emphasize the limitations on his activities and the restricted scope of his powers.[1] Ultimately, in the face of the Act's deficiencies, there were some official and unofficial responses. In 1936 the Bank of England, with government financial backing, established a fund to make loans to small businesses in the Special Areas, and Lord Nuffield created a £2 million trust for similar purposes. In 1937—in what The Times called an 'epoch-making departure from the State's traditional policy'[2]—new legislation amended the

[1] First Report of the Commissioner for Special Areas (England and Wales) (Cmd. 4957. 1935).
[2] The Times 1 Nov. 1937, 15f.

Special Areas Act. The Treasury was now empowered to make loans to firms in the Areas and the Special Area Commissioners were empowered to deploy tax and rates incentives, and to remit rents on the trading estates which had been created in the Special Areas.

On the eve of the Second World War, then, the instruments of regional policy, although still only embryonic, were extremely varied and the state had lost most of its principled objections to the direct encouragement of private enterprise. By the late 1930s, there was a universal recognition that important regions were simply too dependent on individual staple industries (especially on coalmining), and a near-universal sense that 'the key [*to the problem of regional unemployment*] lies, not in South Wales or Durham, but in Downing Street and Threadneedle Street'.[1] Nevertheless, the change of attitude was not yet matched by any very *effective* change of actual policy,[2] and the extent to which the instruments of policy could be used, and the potential *scale* of government intervention, were still almost painfully limited. The staple industries had to await the rearmament boom for any substantial revival.

ii. Coalmining and industrial strategy: controlling markets and prices

The inhibitions which characterized the macro-economic approach to state intervention were less influential at the level of the problems of individual industries. There, chronic depression led, almost inevitably, to attempts to disperse the core of 'structural' unemployment by reorganization and rationalization. Yet, as was indicated in Chapter 7, structural change was by no means a straightforward matter. Considered as 'rationalization', it was advocated as a means of raising productivity and lowering costs by concentrating production and by eliminating surplus capacity. More grandiosely, by the early 1930s it was coming to be seen as an instrument by which the balance of the country's industrial structure might be revised to the benefit of 'new' or more 'progressive' industries.

All this implied a degree of mobility and adaptation. Yet, as was well

[1] Harold Macmillan, in *Hansard* 22 Nov. 1934, col. 263.

[2] By Sept. 1938 the Special Commissioners had spent nearly £17 million in grants; by 1939 the Treasury had loaned just over £1 million to firms in the depressed areas. One indication of the new perception of Britain's industrial position was the appointment, in 1938, of the Royal (Barlow) Commission on the Distribution of the Industrial Population. It reported in 1940: Cmd. 6153 (*PP* 1939–40 IV).

exemplified in the case of the coal industry's selling schemes, industrial reform also implied a contradictory strategy: the mitigation of competition, the maintenance of prices, and the cushioning of staple industries, and inefficient firms, against the forces of depression by the spreading of available work and the substitution of cooperative decision-making for impersonal market forces. In the event, these opposing forces were never reconciled. Yet whatever the inconsistency of motives, the result was a profound change in the role of government and in the arrangements for industrial marketing and management. A return to 'the old conditions of unrestricted individualism' was officially judged to be 'inconceivable'.[1]

In terms of the economy as a whole, the concept of a 'middle way' between competitive individualism and socialism had important roots in the previous decade: in railway reorganization, in the development of electricity supply, in some of the proposals of the Samuel Commission, and in the political and economic debates which were reflected in the quirky radicalism of Sir Alfred Mond's *Industry and Politics* (1927) or the Liberal Party's *Britain's Industrial Future* (1928) or the views of such centrist conservatives as Robert Boothby and Harold Macmillan embodied in *Industry and State* (1927). Yet it was only in the 1930s, and especially after the trauma of 1931, that 'middle opinion', advocating systematic planning and detailed government intervention, became politically influential. Evidence for this intensification is to be found not merely in an abundant literature (e.g. *The Next Five Years: An Essay in Political Agreement* (1935), the various economic reports of Political and Economic Planning, Harold Macmillan's *Reconstruction* (1934) or his *The Middle Way* (1938)) but in a varied if still informal political movement and even a moderately well-articulated set of policies.[2]

Of course, the movement towards a mixed, let alone a quasi-planned, economy in the 1930s should not be exaggerated. Planning in its modern sense was never a political or administrative possibility; even cost-reducing rationalization was not widely accepted or broadly introduced; and government intervention and industrial self-government remained pragmatic, partial, and defensive. Nevertheless, it *is* possible to detect a new departure in the scope of public discussion and the variegated pattern of official action and private initiatives.

Of the various possible examples of this readjustment of industrial policy, the reform of coalmining was the most important and has

[1] Memorandum by Secretary for Mines, 12 Dec. 1935: PREM 1/172.
[2] For these trends, see Marwick 1964; Middlemas 1979; Beer 1965; Carpenter 1976.

remained the most frequently cited. And in the case of coal as with the general tendency, the roots of change could be discovered at two levels. On the one hand, they were entangled with the events of the post-war decade—the controversy over the nationalization of mines and royalties, modulated into discussion of corporate grouping, in 1919; the canvassing of industrial and marketing reform during and after the Samuel Commission's deliberations; the legislation of 1926 and the quasi-official exploration of coordinated amalgamations in the late 1920s; and the (unsuccessful) experiments in voluntary selling schemes in 1927–8, which suggested to the normally cynical miners' representatives that 'even the coalowners may learn from adversity'.[1] On the other hand, however, discussion and action were also pragmatic outcomes of the 1930s and derived their impetus from the persistence of chronic unemployment and unprofitability; from the need to accommodate demands for improvements in the levels of wages, hours, and prices; from the belated, if still hesitant, adjustment of business opinion to the new economic realities of the post-1913 economy.

The fact that compulsory reform of the coal industry's organization dates from 1929–30 is explained partly by the fact that the General Election of May 1929 followed a period of prolonged stagnation, and partly by the fact that the Labour Party (which then formed a minority Government) had given important policy pledges to the Miners' Federation, which sponsored 43 of its 287 MPs.[2] At the same time, its potential radicalism (at least in the matter of the coal industry) was curbed by its status as a minority government. As a result, the issue of nationalization was not seriously pursued. Instead, the immediate starting-point of the new government's industrial policy for coal was a determination to reduce the maximum permitted length of the underground working day from the eight hours stipulated in the legislation of 1926.[3]

The MFGB had placed the highest priority on reversing this consequence of its humiliating defeat three years earlier. Yet the question of hours could not be considered in isolation. There was an imminent need

---

[1] *MFGB* 1929, Executive Committee Report, June 1929, 74–7.

[2] Ibid., 71–3. Of these MPs, 32 received full financial support, and 11 a grant of £100. They were distributed as follows: 10 in South Wales, 7 in Durham, 5 in Lancashire, 9 in Yorkshire, 7 in Scotland, 2 in Northumberland, 1 each in Derby, Cumberland, and Cleveland. A. J. Cook, the MFGB Secretary, claimed that he had the Labour Party's pledge to reduce hours of work 'signed and sealed in his office desk': Neuman 1934, 317.

[3] The legal situation was complicated. The paramount Act was that of 1919 which had reduced maximum hours from the eight of 1908 to seven. The 1926 legislation had increased this to eight—but for 5 years only. In the absence of further legislation, therefore, the permitted maximum would revert to seven in July 1931.

to renegotiate the district wage agreements of 1926–7, while the precarious economic position of the industry inevitably meant that any abrupt reduction in hours (and, therefore, in labour productivity) would have to be accompanied by a reduction in costs (i.e. most likely wages) or an increase in proceeds. If not, losses would mount and unemployment be intensified. Wage reductions were 'morally impossible' in some districts and would provoke a universal industrial-relations crisis. Since hours *had* to be reduced, prices would have to rise. But this would necessitate structural change and control. There would have to be some systematic state intervention. On 2 July, therefore, the King's Speech promised not merely a reduction in hours, but a reorganization of the industry (including, it was said, the question of mineral ownership).[1]

Given the need for a rapid increase in proceeds to allow a fall in the working day, that reorganization was inevitably envisaged in a familiar mould: the various coalmining districts would have to formulate or accept schemes to stabilize markets and enforce production quotas, thus (it was hoped) permitting the maintenance of prices and allowing for a degree of economic coordination. In any case, of course, the recent experiences of the coal industry lent considerable strength to the argument in favour of marketing schemes.[2] And even the miners, although averse to restrictive arrangements and desiring more formal unification and control, ultimately acknowledged that district cartels might be the only way of augmenting revenue so as to protect wages when hours were reduced.[3]

Moreover, by October, the miners had to accept the Cabinet's pained confession that there were severe limits to radical action: maximum underground hours could only be feasibly reduced to $7\frac{1}{2}$ in the first instance (although it hoped that subsequent industrial reform might allow a further reduction to the desired 7 hours); the government could do little to create or enforce a national wages agreement to replace the district agreements imposed on the miners in 1926; and neither the nationalization of the mines nor the immediate public ownership of minerals was politically possible.[4] Not surprisingly, the government had

---

[1] CAB 24/204/221–38 (25 June 1929); CAB 23/61/63 (26 June 1929). The course of events leading to the legislation of 1930, and the legislation itself, are summarized in Neuman 1934, 315 ff.

[2] Above, 209–13; POWE 16/180.

[3] *MFGB* 1929, Annual Conference, 22 July 1929, 19–20; Proceedings of the Cabinet Committee on the British Coal Industry, 16 Oct. and 12 Nov. 1929: CAB 27/395.

[4] CAB 27/395; CAB 24/206/111–26 (4 Oct. 1929); CAB 23/62/27–9 (7 Oct. 1929); CAB 24/206/138–52 and 315–22 (12 and 29 Oct. 1929). The Yorkshire miners, however, remained unreconciled to the $7\frac{1}{2}$-hour limit (their working day was already at that level) and the MFGB's compromise

less success with the recalcitrant Mining Association. The owners were still antipathetic to the role of the state in the selling schemes and to the reduction of working hours, while remaining almost mischievously adamant in their refusal to meet or discuss wages and hours with the miners' representatives on a national basis (their decision, they said, 'was based on their long experience of the harmful consequences of negotiating with the Federation'.)[1]

In December 1929, after six months of deliberation and negotiation, the Labour Government introduced its Coal Mines Bill, which only received the Royal Assent in August 1930, after much amendment and a stormy passage. The original Bill provided for the reduction of maximum hours to $7\frac{1}{2}$; the imposition on coalmining districts of a statutory obligation to formulate, or to accept official, schemes for the control of output (to be coordinated nationally) and minimum prices; the possibility of local and national levies on output to subsidize exports; and the creation of a Coal Mines National Industrial Board to adjudicate on matters referred to it by the districts.

In the event, the proposed legislation had to be substantially adapted in order, first, to secure sufficient Liberal support in the Commons; and, subsequently, to avoid an immobilizing confrontation with the Lords, where the owners were better represented and where administrative details were subject to much closer scrutiny. The Liberals objected to the cartel arrangements and production quotas which, they argued with some force, would buttress antiquated and inefficient collieries while obliging productive firms to operate below capacity and, therefore, at higher unit costs.[2]

Given the political sensitivity of its status and the extent of unemployment, the Labour administration was reluctant to press for a

---

therefore occasioned the resignation from the national Presidency of the Yorkshire miners' leader Herbert Smith. In 1929 the Cabinet envisaged a gradual process of nationalizing minerals as need and occasion arose. But no legislation followed and in Oct. 1930 the President of the Board of Trade persuaded the Cabinet that immediate nationalization was impracticable and that gradual and piecemeal nationalization would be innocuous yet divert scarce political energies from the more important task of making the recently enacted Coal Mines Act 'a very valuable piece of legislation'. CAB 24/215/490-3 (15 Oct. 1930).

[1] CAB 27/395 (6 and 12 Nov. 1929).

[2] Liberal opinion reflected much non-political criticism. See *Hansard* 17 Dec. 1929 cols. 1243 ff.; Neuman 1934, 365–7; the Chairman of the highly productive Bolsover Colliery Company was presumably not alone among successful owners in regretting the combination of protection to the inefficient and artificial restraints on large-scale operation by productive firms. However, he also admitted that effective price control presupposed effective output control: *ICTR* 28 Feb. 1930, 398.

policy of enforced rationalization. Nevertheless, the Liberals were in a strong parliamentary position and were able to secure important amendments to the legislation: the marketing schemes were to operate for only three years in the first instance; administrative safeguards against the abuse of monopoly powers were introduced; and a central levy to help exports was precluded. But the major Liberal amendment was a provision designed to 'balance' the cartels by the pursuit of greater industrial efficiency: a Coal Mines Reorganisation Commission was to be established and empowered to initiate schemes for the compulsory amalgamation of colliery firms irrespective of the wishes of their owners. To the outraged owners this provision (which was Part II of the ultimate Act, Part I embodying the marketing schemes) was interpreted as the Samuel Commission's revenge for the 'contumely' with which its proposals for reorganization had been treated by them in 1926.[1]

Although, as we shall see, the Coal Mines Reorganisation Commission (CMRC) was said to have little effect on industrial structure, its creation marked a major departure in principle and policy. As a result of the Lords' opposition, however, its effective power was attenuated by the stipulation that compulsory amalgamation schemes had to be approved by a Court (the Railway and Canal Commission)—before which it had to be 'proved' that the proposed merger would be in the national interest, result in lower costs, and would not harm the financial interests or be unfair or unequitable to any of the parties involved. Furthermore, the Upper Chamber also excluded ancillary enterprises and greatly weakened the provision for district levies (they could now only exceptionally be proposed and needed explicit Parliamentary approval), and obliged the reluctant government and miners to accept the possibility of redistributing maximum hours to allow for the more flexible operation of pits. This 'spreadover', as it was called, permitted up to an eight-hour day in the context of a 90-hour fortnight,[2] although the Lords' original intention that it be determined solely by local agreement had to be abandoned in favour of a face-saving compromise (the MFGB being bitterly opposed to the idea) by which local agreements would be subject to the approval of, and hence to veto by, the MAGB and the miners' union.

[1] *ICTR* 7 Feb. 1930, 251. Sir Herbert Samuel was of course active in the Commons Debates in the winter of 1929–30. The Cabinet had unsuccessfully attempted to secure his agreement to the original Bill by promising yet another committee of inquiry. For the negotiations between Labour and Liberal politicians, see David Marquand, *Ramsay MacDonald* (1977), 525–31.

[2] The 'spreadover' could be achieved either by an 11-day fortnight with alternate free Saturdays or by a week of 5 long shifts of 8 hours and one short Saturday shift of 5 hours.

With the passage of the Coal Mines Act of 1930 there opened a new chapter in the history of industrial policy in the industry. For the rest of the decade its provisions with regard to marketing and industrial structure, and attempts to amend or strengthen them, determined the evolution—and ultimate intensification—of the relationship between government and coalmining. More than this, the precedent of a more 'forward' policy by government seems to have strengthened politicians' will. Even if decision and effective action did not invariably result, at least there was a perceptible readiness (even by Cabinet members who might have been imagined to be sympathetic to the coalowners' interest) to bring strong political pressure to bear on owners' representatives to get their agreement to unpalatable measures.

Initially, the Act did relatively little for the notorious industrial relationships of coalmining. Thus, conforming to the sad history of attempts at institutionalized consultation since 1918, the proposed Coal Mines National Industrial Board was emasculated through want of cooperation or goodwill. In particular, the coalowners and other business associations refused to nominate their members to the Board. And although the Labour Cabinet valiantly pressed ahead (its hope that the Yorkshire coalowners might break ranks was eventually disappointed, although some individual businessmen were appointed), the authority of the Board—which remained in existence until 1943—was almost entirely diluted by its distorted composition.[1]

A second, and more immediately serious difficulty, however, was that the Act did not provide a long-run basis for the resolution of the problem of hours and wages in a deteriorating economic environment. Indeed, when the shorter working day took effect on 1 December 1930 the fact of continuing slump and the slowness with which the proposed marketing schemes were coming into existence led some owners to propose wage reductions. This happened in Scotland and South Wales: most other fields had either never worked more than $7\frac{1}{2}$ hours or had reached agreements. Temporary arrangements to postpone a confrontation by the local introduction of 'spreadover' arrangements (initially without the formal agreement of the MFGB) were followed by extensive strike action in South Wales, and then by the refusal of an MFGB delegate meeting, against the advice of their Executive Committee, to sanction even the temporary continuance of the 'spreadover' beyond the end of March 1931.

[1] CAB 24/216/205–8 (16 Nov. 1930); CAB 23/69/330–1 (17 Nov. 1930); CAB 27/434 (21 Nov. 1930; WYCOA, 2 Dec. 1930.

The government was therefore hurtled into a new industrial-relations crisis in the spring of 1931. And, in its turn, this was absorbed into a much more threatening confrontation. The hours legislation of 1926, as amended in 1930, was due to lapse in July; but all concerned recognized that it would be 'economically impracticable' to revert to the 7-hour day of the 1919 Act.[1] The owners demanded an indefinite extension of the $7\frac{1}{2}$-hour day and in return offered to continue existing wage rates for a year (this implicit acknowledgement of the possibility of *national* bargaining was an important departure); but the miners refused to accept the longer day without an agreement or a wages guarantee which would coincide with the duration of the $7\frac{1}{2}$-hour stint. Ultimately, the Labour Government, after a reluctant realization that it might have to act to maintain public services during a national coal strike,[2] was once again obliged to resolve a problem of industrial relations: the Coal Mines Act of 1931 extended the $7\frac{1}{2}$-hour day by a year and guaranteed existing wage rates (minimum percentage additions and subsistence rates) for the same period.

By the time that the issue resurfaced—in the spring of 1932—the Labour Administration had been replaced by a National Government dominated by the Conservatives. Yet the owners' expectation that the new government would, in the MAGB President's words, 'repair the blunders' of the last was roughly disappointed as the President of the Board of Trade (Walter Runciman) told them that they should 'disillusion themselves if they had any idea that the present government were especially favourable to their case'.[3] The Cabinet was determined to avoid an eleventh-hour crisis or a settlement for a year only. Threats and cajolery persuaded the owners to cooperate. And in return for legislation extending the $7\frac{1}{2}$ hours indefinitely (or until a ratification—which never took place—of an international convention on mining hours) the individual districts, spurred by the MAGB, gave guarantees to extend wage agreements for at least a further year. This did not entirely satisfy the miners, who still wished for a longer guarantee for wages on a national basis; but they also appreciated the difficulties of the industry and the protection afforded to basic earnings since the reduction of hours in 1930 (the Secretary for Mines pointed out that Britain was the only coal producer where miners' wages had been maintained during the exceptional slump).

---

[1] Memorandum by Secretary for Mines, 4 July 1931: CAB 24/222/325–31.
[2] CAB 23/67/151 (10 June 1931); CAB 24/222/22A (15 June 1931).
[3] See letter from Evan Williams (President of the MAGB) to President of the Board of Trade, 19 Apr. 1932: CAB 27/485, and Runciman's report to the Cabinet: CAB 23/71/62–3 (20 Apr. 1932).

For their part, although the owners expressed abhorrence at the prospect of continuing state intervention in the matter of wages, they had to accept a compromise which in effect gave semi-official protection to wages nationally. Indeed, in 1931 and 1932 the MAGB had been obliged, against its will, to enter into the national discussion of wage rates—a move which they had sharply and successfully spurned since 1925 or earlier. Admittedly, the owners did not confirm the apparent change of heart: in 1933 they resisted pressure from the Secretary for Mines to meet the miners nationally to discuss wages,[1] and throughout 1933 and 1934 there was no response to the miners' pressure for them to attend the spatchcock National Board as a means of constructing national wages machinery.[2] Nevertheless, the government's action in 1932 meant that a step forward *had* been taken, and when in 1935 the miners renewed their demands for a national wages increase (in an atmosphere of trade revival and public sympathy), they were much more successful.

In the winter of 1935–6 and in the face of a threatened national strike and pressure from the government and public opinion, the MAGB and district associations were obliged to accept the case for higher wages and to participate in national consultative machinery (the Joint Standing Consultative Committee).[3] This was a move advocated by the miners since the First World War, and supported by successive governments since 1929, although the JSCC did not formally consider wage levels. The miners had secured little formal recognition of their claim that wages should be discussed and settled nationally; but they had secured a significant degree of protection for wages and hours in the face of a deepening slump and had laid the basis for advances in subsequent years.

The strengthening of the state's willingness to intervene in the affairs of the coal industry after the 1930 Act was even more significantly exemplified in relation to the amendment of the market and output controls embodied in Part I of that legislation. As already described,[4] there was considerable disappointment with the marketing schemes in the first two or three years as export coal invaded inland markets and price competition intensified. By December 1933 the price structure was

[1] *MAGB* 1933, 26.

[2] POWE 20/37.

[3] Below, 348–9. MSWCOA, 16 Dec. 1935; 6 Jan. 1936; SCOA, 1935–6 and 16 Jan. 1936; LCOA, 10 Dec. 1935, 3 Dec. 1935, 22 Dec. 1935, 1 and 14 Jan. 1936.

[4] Above, 297. The industry's marketing arrangements in the 1930s are dealt with in Kirby 1973.

said to have 'collapsed like a pricked balloon'.[1] As a result, in 1934 inter-district competition was curbed, by moves towards the national co-ordination of prices and the creation of separate quotas for inland sales. Two years later prices and proceeds were further protected by obliging the various districts to adopt schemes for centralized selling. These reforms are particularly interesting because—as was the case with wages and hours policy in 1932—they reflected a new-found determination, even among Conservative politicians, to *force* change on the industry, and to accelerate the departure from a reliance on market forces.

It so happened that by this time there was widespread support *within* the industry for output and market controls, if only because the already grave slump worsened immediately after 1930 and the selling schemes offered some protection against even more severe deflation. Indeed, by the early 1930s the continuance of Part I of the 1930 Act was said to be supported both by the miners (who were 'categorically' in its favour) and by an 'overwhelming majority' of the owners (among them various erstwhile stalwarts of individualism, like Sir Adam Nimmo who had originally opposed or dismissed such interference with the market).[2] There was, therefore, no opposition to the five-year extension of Part I in 1932. To the government, as to the owners and miners, competition now promised not so much efficiency as the reduction of prices, employment, and wages—and would lead to social dislocation and 'industrial trouble'.[3] Once again, therefore, the ultimate roots of inter-vention lay in the desire to fend off a labour crisis.

Government had learned its lesson. Part I of the 1930 Act had to be strengthened so as to avoid the destabilization of inland markets by cheap coal from export collieries, and it might not be possible to guarantee supplies to Scandinavia under the recently signed trade agreements.[4] More generally, in February 1934 the Secretary for Mines warned the Cabinet that without the protection of the law, the industry's huge excess capacity would be unleashed and available work would be so concentrated that a further 150,000 men would become wholly unemployed. 'The Coal Mines Act', he argued, was 'a buffer between the government and economic and social strife in the coal industry'.[5]

[1] *Financial News* 6 Dec. 1933, cutting in SMT 2/272.
[2] CAB 27/485 (19 Apr. 1932); CAB 24/247/40–52 (1 Feb. 1934).
[3] CAB 24/239/76–8 (16 Mar. 1933).
[4] CAB 24/239/76–8 (16 Mar. 1933); PREM 1/172 (13 Dec. 1933); CAB 24/247/40–52 (1 Feb. 1934).
[5] CAB 24/247/40–52 (1 Feb. 1934).

Yet the amendments of the 1930 Act which were accepted in 1934 and 1936 were not simply a matter of crisis avoidance in a harmonious political atmosphere. For one thing, the owners' associations found it difficult to muster the necessary large majority to secure voluntary reform, so that on each occasion the National Government had to threaten minatory legislation unless the industry put its house in order.[1] For another, there was some unease, particularly as business revived after 1933, that the owners might be neglecting their new powers. By September 1935 the Conservative Secretary for Mines (Harry Crookshank) went so far as to accept as 'unanswerable' the miners' case that wages were too low because the owners had failed to take advantage of their power to secure reasonable prices, and that the owners must be obliged to reorganize their marketing by being obliged to pay higher wages. In 1935–6, therefore, in its readiness to help the MFGB secure their wage claim, the National Government accepted his advice to adopt the union's policy and attempt an advance towards national wage-determination and 'district selling agencies under central control'.[2] Slowly, but none the less surely, and spurred by state initiative and the relaxation of official inhibitions, the industry's marketing moved from competition to control.

The process was neither simple nor uncontroversial. For example, while large-scale institutional consumers accepted higher prices in 1936, they also mounted a publicity campaign in an attempt to guard against the use of monopoly powers and exorbitant price increases. And this mood, in turn, both influenced the political debate about legislation in 1936–8 and led to the creation of a departmental committee of inquiry, under Sir Walter Monckton, into the distribution of coal, coke, and manufactured fuel.[3] Nevertheless, intervention and market control had evolved a long way. And by 1938 even the export trade—the erstwhile bastion of individualism and the competitive ethic—was pursuing the possibility of cooperation and cartelization.[4]

The growing confidence and the relative success with which the government obliged the coal industry to 'manage' its selling was the outcome of a multiplicity of developments. But the government's consistent and perhaps overriding motive was to avoid any deepening of

[1] PREM 1/172 (12 Dec. 1933). This policy was successfully pursued in 1934.
[2] CAB 24/257/19–26 (27 Sept. 1935).
[3] For the 1936–8 legislation, see below, 350–4. For the Inquiry, see CAB 24/275/313–20 (16 Mar. 1938) and *Minutes of Evidence* (HMSO 1938).
[4] Above, 288.

social distress or aggravation of industrial crisis. With unemployment high and wages still relatively low, Ministers were naturally apprehensive about the serious disruption of social peace which would be threatened by further unemployment or any keen pressure on wages. Ultimately, even the entrenched ideology of *laissez-faire* withered in the face of persistent slump.

iii. The state and industrial structure

There was a similar transformation of political and public attitudes towards the structure of production (as distinct from that of selling) in the 1930s—although it was not effectively embodied in a new policy until the very eve of the Second World War. The Coal Mines Act of 1930 had created the Coal Mines Reorganisation Commission with authority to encourage mergers and to formulate schemes for the compulsory amalgamation of collieries. The Commission was an important innovation—the first quasi-independent body charged with the reorganization of a major industry. The fact remained, however, that its efforts came to nothing. The principal obstacles to its success lay in the practical problems of a rationalization policy, the crippling deficiencies of the law, and the coalowners' extreme opposition to its activities.

Policy towards coalmining was, of course, part of a more general trend. It was fitting, therefore, that in 1930 the Labour Secretary for Mines felt obliged to consult the Governor of the Bank of England, Montague Norman, about the Chairmanship and membership of the CMRC, for the Bank was the most important agent of the tentative steps towards rationalization which, in the late 1920s, were being contemplated in various industries. Indeed, Norman went so far as to suggest that there be some geographical coordination of plans for the reorganization of coal, iron and steel, and electricity supply.[1]

Although rationalization was generally welcomed in official circles from the late 1920s, it was never purposefully adopted as the basis of industrial policy. Reluctant businessmen, economic uncertainty, and the scarcity of the necessary resources (whether public or private) were all serious obstacles. Yet, as we have already seen, the most telling *political* argument against a policy of rationalization—especially in coal—

---

[1] Clay 1957, ch. VIII; Sayers 1976, ch. 14. Material relating to Norman's role in the coal industry, is in SMT 2/273/1–25. In addition to its full-time Chairman (Sir Ernest Gowers, who had been Permanent Under-Secretary at the Mines Department in 1920–7), the Coal Mines Reorganisation Commission had 4 part-time members.

was the very likelihood of its success. The closure of excess capacity would throw even more people out of work. And in the deepening slump of the early 1930s, the price of efficiency (measured in unemployment) seemed too high.

Even before the passage of the Coal Mines Act, Sir Oswald Mosley, in a memorandum to his perplexed colleagues in the Labour Cabinet, had identified some of the difficulties inherent in the government's hesitant industrial strategy. Long-term reconstruction, he argued, was an inappropriate means of tackling the immediate crisis of unemployment (which was only susceptible to decisive action to encourage and promote immediate investment). Moreover, it was inconceivable that increased productivity in the export staples would lead to such an increase in sales (and therefore employment) as would compensate for the reduced demand for labour, per unit of output, which would result from greater productivity. Hence rationalization would aggravate not ameliorate unemployment. And he went on to reject 'the whole Fetish of the Export Trade' and 'the economics of the last century'. Instead of supporting erstwhile staple industries which were dependent on a 'diminishing and elusive demand', the government should encourage structural changes—'new industries and new productions to satisfy new demands ... the transition of Britain from a prewar to a postwar industrial basis'.[1]

Few other Ministers in the early 1930s were prepared to take such arguments to extreme lengths. But the Prime Minister acknowledged the possible unwelcome results of rationalization, and in 1930 the government's own Committee of Economists warned that rationalization was likely to increase unemployment, and that the efficiency of expanding industries was at least as important as the reorganization of the staples.[2] In the last resort, politicians were obliged to acknowledge the social and political risks of a programme of rationalization which could well aggravate the shortage of work.[3]

As far as the coal industry was concerned, the contradictions of policy were evident *within* the legislation of 1930 itself, for the selling schemes envisaged in Part I were designed to reduce competition and protect existing collieries, while the amalgamations envisaged in Part II

[1] CAB 23/209/220–59 (23 Jan. 1930); CAB 24/211/460–5 (1 May 1930). Also see memorandum by Vernon Hartshorn, 18 Aug. 1930: CAB 24/214/331.

[2] *Hansard* 28 May 1930, col. 1338; 'Report of Committee of Economists', Oct. 1930: Reprinted in Howson and Winch 1977, 191–2.

[3] See, for example, the comments of the President of the Board of Trade, Walter Runciman, on 13 June 1932: CAB 24/23/14.

were designed to eliminate less efficient firms. There was, therefore, an inevitable tension between an embryonic employment policy and an embryonic industrial policy. As a result, although in 1932–3 the Secretary for Mines was willing to defend the CMRC as imperfect but 'the best instrument we have', he was unwilling to advocate the enforcement of its powers or responsibilities. Circumstances altered cases he implied: when the Act was passed the coal industry gave employment to 960,000 miners; by December 1933 its active work-force had fallen to 750,000—and even that was vulnerable.[1]

The official choice was posed as one between dispersion and concentration of unemployment; between short-time working in a large number of collieries operating below capacity, and the streamlining of the industry to allow full-capacity working by a limited number of pits. The official decision, at least in the depths of the slump, was predictable, and it needed little urging from the owners, who, as we have seen, shrewdly played on political anxieties by suggesting that against any savings that might result from pit closures would have to be set the social costs of greater unemployment and the support of derelict communities.[2] Even in the worst year, 1933, the Chairman of the Coal Mines Reorganisation Commission was prepared to argue the contrary case: pit closures were economically inevitable, so that 'the real question is not whether concentration shall take place or not; it is whether the process shall be left to the haphazard forces of sporadic bankruptcies and casual purchases or brought about designedly by the industry's being so organized as to give the power to those who control it to adopt this policy as they think fit.'[3] But it was only in later years, as the general problem of unemployment eased in recovery, that the government was prepared to grasp the nettle of enforcing an amalgamation policy.

It was, in any case, not merely government anxiety about unemployment which inhibited the CMRC. As all contemporaries agreed, Part II of the 1930 Act was a badly drawn up and ineffective law. It presumed that the courts (rather than the government) would decide on whether specific amalgamations were in the national interest. And the conditions which had to be satisfied before a compulsory amalgamation scheme could be legally approved made it virtually impossible to secure the

[1] Memorandum of 27 Apr. 1932: POWE 22/55; discussions of 12 Dec. 1933: PREM 1/172.

[2] COAL 12/171 (15 Mar. 1933). The Minister of Labour was specifically worried about closures, and the Secretary of the CMRC complained that he had been influenced, unfairly, by the owners. See POWE 22/55 (24 and 31 Mar. 1933).

[3] Memorandum by Sir Ernest Gowers, 21 Dec. 1933: POWE 16/51711. Also see C. S. Hurst to Nott-Bower, 31 Mar. 1933: POWE 22/55.

courts' approval of *any* contested plan. There had to be 'proof' that a scheme would reduce costs, would not be financially injurious to any party, and would be 'fair and equitable' to all involved.

The fact that this made it impossible to pursue compulsory amalgamations was ultimately confirmed by the Law Officers in December 1935. But well before then the work of the CMRC (which for its first two years tried to pursue a strategy of encouraging voluntary mergers) had been crippled by the refusal of the mass of the owners to cooperate (in some districts they even refused—until threatened with an inquiry—to meet Sir Ernest Gowers) and by the relative passivity of the Labour Government and its successor.[1] Indeed, these two considerations were related, since the government's quiescence only encouraged the owners to drag their feet over the Commission's investigations and proposals, and their prevarications turned out to be a most effective delaying tactic. In September 1931 the MAGB, ostensibly on grounds of national economy, even proposed the abolition of the CMRC, which was, they claimed, 'irritating and mischievous'.[2] And it took the newly installed National Government a good six months to disabuse the owners of their expectations that the Conservative predominance would lead to the repeal or sterilization of the Act.[3]

Unfortunately, neither the circumstances of the Commission's appointment nor its initial pronouncements helped it in its task. Its public image was seriously marred by the huge salaries of its members (Gowers's salary of £7,000 more than doubled his previous earnings and exceeded that of senior Ministers, while the part-time members were paid seven guineas per day—with a guaranteed minimum of 100 payments per annum).[4] Furthermore, in spite of its extensive visits and thorough preparations, the Commission's first publication (in July 1931) suggested as 'an ultimate goal' a handful of giant amalgamations, six of which would coincide with the six main districts of coal production.

[1] See COAL 17/178. (Memorandum by Chairman for Coal Commission Meeting 10, Paper 3. Agenda 4. 1938.)

[2] For good measure, it also proposed the abolition of the Mines Department, the Welfare levy, and the Fuel Research Board. These proposals originated with the South Wales owners. See LCOA, 29 Sept. 1931.

[3] COAL 12/2 (16 Mar. 1932); POWE 22/55 (14 Apr. 1932). The Attorney General announced the government's commitment in May 1932.

[4] *The Times* 14 Mar. 1931, 6a. There was an outcry from Labour MPs, and also from business representatives (*O'Connell's Coal and Iron News*, 10 Dec. 1931, referred to the CMRC as a 'high-salaried circus': cutting in COAL 12/165). When the National Government introduced its economy measures, Gowers volunteered a 20% cut in his salary: *The Times* 2 Dec. 1931 (in SMT/273).

This memorandum was obviously simplistic, and was bound to appear slapdash and ill-informed—the product of a 'cartography complex'.

A year later, moved by criticism and its own reconsideration, the CMRC issued a supplementary note denying that it made 'a fetish of mere size' and asserting that voluntary amalgamations were the ideal.[1] But the damage had been done. In fact, the Commission's responsibilities were fulfilled with far greater expertise, conscientiousness, and caution than it was given credit for.[2] However, its relatively poor public image resulted not merely from its powerlessness in practice, but from a dilemma forced upon it by the owners' general refusal to cooperate: in private the CMRC could (and did) prepare its ground carefully, argue extremely cogently in favour of voluntary mergers, and use all its resources of 'coaxing, bluff and bullying'.[3] In public, however, given the owners' refusal to cooperate, the Commission had to adopt a note of helpless appeal or petulant cajolery.

By 1933, having unsuccessfully pursued the path of persuasion, and with the MAGB not merely refusing to cooperate but in active opposition, the Commission despaired of exhortation and opted for a more demanding line.[4] Following Gowers's lead, it envisaged a two-tier structure for the industry: large-scale mergers, linked by district groupings ('partial amalgamations') for joint action in marketing, purchasing, and the control of capacity. A plan for just such a group was formulated voluntarily in West Yorkshire, and received the Commission's blessing. Resisting the MAGB's demand that it either admit that it was powerless or await a single test case in the courts,[5] the CMRC pressed ahead with plans for 'a vigorous attack on all fronts'.[6] For example, it decided to attempt to enforce the West Yorkshire plan (which had secured the support of the owners of 70 per cent of the district's capacity, but was hamstrung by the rest); and it demanded that the owners in Durham, South Yorkshire, and Nottinghamshire and Derbyshire should produce schemes similar to West Yorkshire's.

This belated militancy coincided with the more general reappraisal of the government's coal policy in December 1933 and January 1934, which had been stimulated by the CMRC's first official report to Parliament,

[1] Neuman 1934, 399–400. The reference to a 'cartography complex' is from *O'Connell's Coal and Iron News*, 5 Nov. 1931, cutting in COAL 12/165.

[2] The principal records of its proceedings are in COAL 12 (especially Nos. 1–6 and 165–6).

[3] Memorandum by Sir Ernest Gowers, 2 May 1933: COAL 12/166.

[4] See the President of the Board of Trade (Runciman) in *Hansard* 18 May 1936, cols. 854–9.

[5] COAL 12/171 (15 Mar. 1933); *MAGB* 1933, 50–3.

[6] COAL 12/166 (3 Nov. 1933).

and also by the problem of unemployment and the imminent break-down of the marketing arrangements under Part I of the 1930 Act.[1] The resulting Ministerial deliberations led to a decision to press ahead with amendments to Part I and to appoint an interdepartmental committee to consider industrial organization, including the possible unification or nationalization of royalties.[2]

Since the mid-1920s the controversy over royalties had been primarily concerned not with their presumed inhibition of the development of reserves, but with the possible deleterious effect of the fragmented ownership of minerals on the layout of mines and the organization of enterprise. And by the early 1930s there was a widespread view that the multiplicity and independence of royalty owners were serious obstacles to amalgamation and structural efficiency.[3] Indeed, the owners themselves were becoming increasingly restless at the burden of royalties—especially of minimum or dead rents—amid the slump in sales. They pointed out that many leases had been drawn in the prewar period of profitable trade, and were now (1933) a costly handicap since profits were low and technical change had reduced the area worked. They therefore appealed to the mineral owners to reduce or eliminate rents and were attracted by the idea of unification or even nationalization.[4] Not surprisingly, therefore, the interdepartmental committee's interim report proposed the nationalization of royalties as 'a useful progressive step' to encourage mergers—although it was politically too cautious to advocate compulsory amalgamations and drew the line at the wholesale cancellation of existing mineral leases to that end.[5]

This proposal was approved in principle by the Cabinet, although it then took the committee a further year to produce a practical scheme

[1] Above, 297.

[2] See PREM 1/172 (12 and 13 Dec. 1933, 10 Jan. 1934, 2 Feb. 1934); POWE 16/5171 (21 Dec. 1933, 11 Jan. 1934).

[3] *The Economist* 24 Oct. 1936, 153.

[4] Evan Williams's statement at a meeting between MAGB and the Mineral Owners' Joint Committee, 15 Nov. 1933: COAL 12/14. The interdepartmental committee quoted leading owners (Lord Gainford and Sir Adam Nimmo) as favouring nationalization; and the President of the Board of Trade drew attention to views of Gainford and Nimmo (in 1933-4). See COAL 12/4 ('Nationalisation of Mineral Royalties') and *Hansard* 22 Nov. 1937, cols. 885-6. The South Wales owners were particularly worried about the cost of royalty payments and in 1934-5 introduced a test case before the Railway and Canal Commission in an unsuccessful attempt to secure a reduction: MSWCOA, 19 Mar., 18 June, 30 Oct. 1934; 18 Mar. 1935.

[5] CAB 24/249/73-85 (5 May 1934). Even so, the committee *favoured* amalgamations and argued that the displacement of miners, even by a programme of wholesale amalgamation, would be limited to 100,000, spread over a number of years, and liable to mitigation by industrial revival, natural wastage, and work-sharing.

for the nationalization of royalties. However, by the time it reported (April 1935) the atmosphere had changed sufficiently for it to present a more radical face to the world—pushed and persuaded by its dominant member, Sir Ernest Gowers (whose frustrations as Chairman of the CMRC were reflected in his assertion that 'public opinion is now, more than a year ago, sick of the obstructiveness of the old school of employers in coal, cotton and iron and steel').[1] In its final report the committee therefore not merely outlined a programme of nationalization for royalties, but now recommended that the CMRC (which was to administer them) *should* after all be empowered to cancel existing leases in order to further amalgamations. This proposal, supported by Runciman at the Board of Trade, was sufficiently drastic to be remitted to a Cabinet Committee, which was to remain in existence for three years (until the passage of the Coal Act of 1938), and that committee's deliberations helped broaden the scope of radical action.[2]

Radical action had become necessary because in the course of 1935, while the uselessness of Part II of the 1930 legislation was demonstrated beyond all doubt, the government came under intensified pressure to take an initiative in the coal industry. First of all, in May 1935, the CMRC's proposal to enforce the 'partial amalgamation' of West Yorkshire collieries was rejected by the courts in terms which made it clear that the CMRC was not empowered to pursue partial amalgamations. Indeed, it was implied that in *any* proposals for amalgamations they would be hard pressed to meet the stringent criteria of the 1930 Act. In desperation, CMRC withdrew its orders to other districts to produce similar schemes, and decided to pursue the enforcement of *complete* mergers. However, it was well aware that there was little chance of securing a favourable legal judgement for such a move, and in any case in July the government requested a postponement of action until the situation had been clarified.[3]

In December the Law Officers were to confirm the CMRC view that it would not be possible to secure compulsory amalgamations under the existing law. But well before then, in the summer of 1935, the government came to appreciate that it would soon be left without a policy for coal—and that on the eve of a General Election (which took place in

[1] See COAL 12/12. For Gowers's activities, see COAL 12/14. The final report is in CAB 24/254/341–5 (5 Apr. 1935).

[2] The records of the Cabinet Committee on the Organisation of the Coal Mining Industry are in CAB 27/597.

[3] CAB 24/268/2 (11 Mar. 1937).

November). Its sensitivity to Gowers's warning that the state of the coal industry was such that 'business and politics could not be kept apart'[1] was the keener because the relative improvement in trading conditions had emboldened the miners to renew their pressure for national wage bargaining in the context of a claim for a uniform national increase.

Public sympathy and economic reality made it clear that the government had to be seen to be doing something about the plight of the industry. Nor could the issue of wages be divorced from that of reorganization. The miners began to intensify their complaints about the owners' seeming failure to restructure and strengthen their industry. And the growing exasperation with the mass of the owners engendered much explicit sympathy for the miners' case. The Secretary for Mines, for example, was sympathetic; even a leading businessman with extensive coal interests (J. Frater Taylor, Chairman of Pease and Partners) criticized his fellow owners for their attitude, and urged 'real amalgamation';[2] and Gowers asserted that events had justified the miners' stand in 1926. Speaking with the frustration as well as the authority of the Chairmanship of the Coal Mines Reorganisation Commission, Gowers succeeded in broadening the attack. The 1926 stoppage, he argued, had occurred because the miners were convinced that wage cuts would remove the stimulus to change, and reorganization would be indefinitely postponed:

They were right. They made their sacrifice under duress, and for the next ten years the owners gave themselves over to an orgy of cutting their own and one another's throats, threw away with both hands the opportunities given to them by Parliament to reorganise themselves, and obstructed by every means in their power the attempts of the Coal Mines Reorganisation Commission to do it for them.[3]

The Cabinet quickly recognized the political need to respond to the miners' case for an improvement in their position. It therefore created a Royal Commission on health and safety in the industry.[4] More drastically, the government ensured that there was a satisfactory response

---

[1] CAB 27/597 (1 July 1935).

[2] Memorandum by Secretary for Mines, 26 Sept. 1935: CAB 24/257/20–6; J. Frater Taylor to Montague Norman, 1 Nov. 1935: SMT 2/272.

[3] Evidence to Cabinet Committee, 1 July 1935: CAB 27/597.

[4] Interim Report of the Cabinet Committee on the Organisation of the Coal Mining Industry, 26 July 1935: CAB 24/256. The last full-scale inquiries into health and safety in the mines had been before the First World War, and resulted in the Coal Mines Act of 1911. The Royal Commission appointed in 1936 reported in 1938, but consideration of its recommendations was interrupted by the War.

to the union's wage claim: it was instrumental in securing a payment of a flat-rate increase which was 6 *d.* or 9 *d.* per shift (for adults) in the main export areas and 1 s. per shift in the principal inland districts. More than this, it prevailed on the owners to participate in a Joint Standing Consultative Committee, and accepted some responsibility for helping find the money to pay the new wages. It supported a powerful appeal by the MAGB (which acknowledged the inevitability of a wage increase) to such large purchasers of coal as the iron and steel industry, ICI, and the public utilities,[1] who were persuaded to accept a revision of existing contracts on the specific understanding that the proceeds would go to the miners. And most significant of all, the Cabinet intervened to help reform marketing arrangements so as to support prices and increase proceeds: it obliged the owners to commit themselves to the complete control of sales by each district (with central coordination of the various agencies), as 'the most likely means of getting results quickly enough to avoid a strike'.[2]

Beyond all this, in October 1935 the Cabinet finally committed itself to the 'unification' (in effect the nationalization) of coal royalties, and decided to make this a pledge in the Election Campaign of 1935. And four months later it at long last concluded that industrial reorganization was both a necessary complement to the projected enhancement of the owners' market power, and a desirable and necessary aim of official policy. This was now a widespread view. *The Times* reminded its readers that the industry had been given considerable power to determine prices collectively, and that the consumer therefore had to be assured that costs of production would be reduced: 'the very structure of the industry' must safeguard efficiency, and that needed concentration. 'While Parliament is saving the industry from self-destruction, it must also save the community from exploitation.'[3]

Only a long accumulation of experience and political anxieties could have persuaded such a large part of conventional opinion that the nettle of state intervention in industrial reform had to be grasped. Admittedly, the official arguments in favour of a more purposeful departure from the economies of the market were part of a much broader mood, which had already reshaped the marketing of coal and influenced policy towards agricultural marketing, national transport, and the iron and steel industry—all of which had been pressed into forms of coordinated

[1] MSWCOA, 16 Dec. 1935, 6 Jan. 1936.
[2] CAB 24/260/157–65 (12 Feb. 1936); *ARSM* 1936, 326 ff.
[3] *The Times* 29 May 1936, 15b; 9 June 1936, 16c.

responses to economic problems. But coalmining was also *sui generis*: its problems more extreme and enduring, its political resonance more insistent, its moral overtones more explicit, and its entrepreneurs more resistant to cooperation. It so happened that even the exasperation and desperation which had overcome the government by 1935–6 was to prove insufficient to effect rapid or sweeping structural reform. But the attempt to secure it reflected the peculiar position of the coal industry, just as it established a stage in the evolution of a new economic role for government which formed the basis for significant departures in other fields.

In pursuit of its newly determined policy, the government in 1936 speedily introduced a Bill which, in its original form, removed most of the legal restrictions embodied in the 1930 Act and would have given the Administration and a revivified Coal Mines Reorganisation Commission effective powers to compel collieries to amalgamate. However, the proposed powers were *so* great (Sir Ernest Gowers described it as a 'terrifying' Bill which offered no legal protection to owners against 'a vindictive Commission')[1] that it provoked what was, for a Conservative-dominated administration, a politically irresistible storm of protest— not merely from the owners[2] but from the Federation of British Industries and the government's own supporters in Parliament. The outcome was what *The Economist* described as 'a lamentable capitulation' and a 'deplorable surrender'.[3] After attempts at a hurried compromise, the Bill was withdrawn for reconsideration.

That reconsideration was more prolonged than had been anticipated, and it was two years before fresh legislation was passed. The resistance of much business opinion to the original Bill had been based on anxiety about the quasi-monopoly powers of selling agencies, rather than a widespread concern about enforced mergers. And these anxieties were largely, if only temporarily, dispelled in the summer of 1936.[4] In the

---

[1] Gowers to Secretary for Mines, 8 Dec. 1936: POWE 16/517II. The CMRC and the Board of Trade would have been the effective judges of the national interest and of the equity of any schemes, which would be accepted unless subject to a negative resolution by Parliament within 21 sitting days. The courts' role would have been very limited. For the MAGB reaction, see *MAGB* 1936, 18–21.

[2] The MAGB claimed, not entirely unjustly, that they had been persuaded to commit themselves to central selling agencies on the implicit assumption that the question of compulsory amalgamations would be left in abeyance: Delegation from MAGB, 15 May 1936: POWE 16/517I.

[3] *The Economist* 23 May 1936, 417.

[4] The government promised new procedures to safeguard consumers: Third Report of the Cabinet Committee on the Organisation of the Coal Mining Industry, 11 Mar. 1937: CAB 24/268/335–70.

winter of 1936–7 the Secretary for Mines could report that not only was opposition among Conservative MPs more muted than he had feared, but that leading representatives of such large consuming industries as iron and steel, electricity generation, and gas, were distinctly in favour of compelling colliery owners to amalgamate. In effect, the development of a new view of a mixed, or at least a managerial, economy was no longer one-sided. Businessmen as well as politicians were increasingly attracted by the promise of stability, coordination, and economy inherent in large-scale enterprises whose relationships might transcend the mediation of fluctuating prices and market competition.[1] A rationalized industry like electricity, argued Sir Archibald Page of the Central Electricity Board, 'feels strongly that the industries with which they deal should have their houses in order also'.[2]

Nevertheless, a revised Coal Bill was not introduced until November 1937. This combined the public ownership of royalties and the policy of stimulating amalgamation. Both were vested in a new Coal Commission which was to replace the CMRC of 1930. Given the vast work of registration and individual valuation, the coal royalties were not to be vested until 1942—although even before the Coal Bill was introduced, a separate Act had provided for a national register of coal holdings and arbitration had settled the global compensation at £66.45 million.[3] In relation to the proposals for amalgamation, and following the pledges given in May 1936, ancillary enterprises were excluded, there was to be a two-year delay (in effect until 1 January 1940) before compulsory powers could be exercised,[4] and Parliament was to be given responsibility for condoning or vetoing an official scheme. Further, the legal conditions embodied in the 1930 Act were relaxed: questions of the national interest and likely cost savings, being matters of opinion and

[1] Hannah 1976.

[2] See notes of meetings, 12 Nov. 1936 and 4 Jan. 1937: POWE 16/517II.

[3] In 1934 the Inland Revenue's Chief Valuer had placed an 'outside' value of £80 million on the coal royalties: COAL 12/14 (15 and 17 Oct. 1934). Negotiations with the mineral owners early in 1937 had produced an agreed figure of £4.43 million for the average annual net royalty income in 1928–34. Arbitration was necessary to settle the number of years' purchase at which this figure was to be capitalized. The mineral owners claimed that the income was secure, and should be capitalized at 25-years' purchase (i.e. 4%); the government emphasized the industry's insecurity and suggested just over 11 years (i.e. 9%); the Tribunal recommended 15 years (6.3%). This gave a compensation figure (£4.43 million × 15) of £66.45 million. See *Unification of Coal Royalties. In the Matter of a Reference between the Mineral Owners Joint Committee and His Majesty's Government... 12th April–27th April 1937* (Mimeographed 1937. Copy in British Coal Library).

[4] In Oct. 1935 Sir Ernest Gowers had advocated just such a breathing-space-cum-deadline as a means of reconciling the government's desire to avoid compulsion and 'the regrettable fact that only a threat of compulsion is likely to produce results': POWE 16/517II.

impossible of legal proof, were now implicitly to be considered by Parliament. The Railway and Canal Commission had still to reassure itself that compulsory schemes were fair and equitable, and calculated to avoid financial injury and result in efficient enterprises.

The Bill seemed to promise much. Yet there were still doubts about the effect of post-amalgamation closures on coal communities,[1] while the MAGB remained bitterly opposed to what the *Colliery Guardian* called 'the vicious principle of compulsory amalgamation'.[2] The owners' pleas to protect private enterprise against government encroachment naturally found a wider echo. Even so, the very intensity of their public campaign against the Bill and their unyielding language also redounded to their disadvantage—at least in the propaganda campaign. Just as, by the mid-1930s, exasperation at their obstinacy had introduced a note of enthusiasm into official proposals to curb their independence, so by 1938 it also produced blistering attacks in the independent press on their 'Bourbonism' and on their failure to appreciate that their strident language was a provoking inducement to a 'violent and socialistic' reaction. In accepting the benefits of controlled marketing, it was argued, they had an inescapable social obligation to pursue efficiency through industrial reorganization.[3]

The vehemence of these opinions was not due simply to the owners' dialectic posture. They were also elicited by the MAGB's apparent success in forcing the government to amend their legislation once more. In the Bill's original form the Board of Trade, if it wished to sponsor or initiate a merger scheme, would have prepared an Order, subject to 'negative resolution'—i.e. unless specifically voted down within a given period, the Order would stand. And such resolutions were customarily taken after 11 p.m. in the House of Commons and uncontroversially.

---

[1] The Labour Party unsuccessfully pressed for amendments which would have obliged the Coal Commission to take account of the possible need to transfer labour and of representation from local authorities and miners concerning the possible effects of amalgamations on employment, social capital, and the general welfare of local communities.

[2] *CG* 28 Jan. 1938, 174. The Bill was warmly welcomed by a senior mining engineer, C. C. Reid of Fife Coal Company, as the best thing to happen in the industry for a decade: 'the day for individualism in the coal trade has gone'. (Quoted in *CG* 10 Dec. 1937, 1122.) Reid was to chair the Technical Advisory Committee which transformed the popular and political perception of the industry in 1945.

[3] *MAGB* 1938, 18–23; *The Economist* 5 Feb. 1938, 277 ('Bourbonism of the type deployed by the mine-owners invites a campaign to end "economic royalism" once and for all'); and *The Times* 3 Feb. 1938, 13b ('This unmeasured language is ill-suited to the mouths of those whose industry was rescued from suicide by the action of the state, and who today are relying on the state to continue to preserve it from those suicidal tendencies by re-enacting the coal-selling legislation . . . what will be adjusted [by the Bill] is excessively tenacious individualism'.)

Early in February 1938, however, at the Committee stage of the Bill, the President of the Board of Trade conceded that Orders were to be subject to scrutiny by Select-Committee procedure in both Houses of Parliament. This was, in effect, a form of public inquiry (with the representation of interested parties). It gave much greater weight to the Lords (where the owners were strongly represented), and ensured the sort of detailed consideration and repetitive political controversy which were likely to hamper the easy acceptance of compulsory schemes.

The President of the Board of Trade argued that such schemes were too controversial to be considered by the formal negative resolution procedure. But his critics—drawn from a broad ideological spectrum— were quick to detect another political capitulation to the owners and their attempts to hamper legislation for compulsion. *The Times* went so far as to claim that the government had truckled to the Mining Association, and *The Economist* referred darkly to 'surrender' and to the stultification of the principle of amalgamations by multi-layered administrative procedures.[1]

The sense that the government had capitulated in the face of the owners' determination produced a deepening gloom among the supporters of industrial reorganization. The coal industry was a test case for the embryonic mixed economy; and the compromises now accepted in the Coal Bill seemed to alter the character of growing state intervention. It was, therefore, not only MFGB spokesmen who argued that the state was protecting the coalowners rather than the coal industry.[2] Such a distinguished public servant as Sir Arthur Salter was moved to write to *The Times* expressing his alarm. He argued that the new procedures would be unworkable, that the Coal Commission would be 'reduced to almost as complete futility' as the CMRC, and that the amended legislation was an instance of the state being 'captured by sectional interests and made their instrument'. More provocatively, he asserted that if the state proved incapable of governing equitably in a mixed economy, he would prefer a system of *complete* control—State Socialism.[3]

The new legislation embodied a considerable advance on that of 1930, although its effectiveness remained to be tested and it embodied more caution than seemed warranted to most informed observers of the industry's affairs. The Coal Act received the Royal Assent in July 1938, after large consumers as well as the producers of coal had been placated.[4]

---

[1] *The Times* 4 Feb. 1938, 15c; *The Economist* 26 Mar. 1938, 679 and 2 July 1938, 8.
[2] *Hansard* 3 Feb. 1938, cols. 501–2.   [3] *The Times* 9 Feb. 1938, 8q.
[4] Industrial consumers were still anxious about monopolistic trends and prices, and in order to

Its subject-matter had been debated for at least 10 years, and the balance of opinion had found the coal industry's organization seriously deficient. It was in this context that it was so disappointing.

Admittedly, the Act removed legal obstacles which had previously *ensured* the impracticability of any attempt to bring about colliery amalgamations. Further, it nationalized private property and asserted and strengthened the obligation on a government agency to interfere extensively in market forces. On the other hand, the legislation still reflected a profound reluctance to use compulsion: the amendment of the government's original ideas had the effect of establishing a potential block to effective action. It was not, therefore, surprising that in welcoming the appointment of the Coal Commissioners, *The Economist* struck a restrained and sceptical note: much was to be expected 'if only the changes made in the Bill by the Commons have left a loophole for really effective legislation'.[1]

In the event, it was never possible to test the effectiveness of the Act's provisions as regards amalgamations. This was because war broke out before the Coal Commission was empowered to pursue a strategy of compulsion, while its wartime efforts to pursue its work were blocked by government, and subsequent consideration of the industry's structure was undertaken at a much deeper level.[2] Characteristically, however, during the winter of 1938–9, Sir Ernest Gowers had moved the Commission into an ambitious posture. While assuming that the Commission's principal aim was 'to frighten the coalowners into making their own amalgamations', he successfully argued in favour of an early and vigorous campaign of consultation (which, in January–March 1939, extended to both the MAGB and the country's leading owners from the 150 biggest undertakings); initiated a major review of the industry's structure and a comprehensive questionnaire to elicit vital data about production; and persuaded his colleagues to prepare a Report to Parliament which would have sketched comprehensive plans for amalgamations in the principal mining districts.

ease the Bill's passage the government had been obliged to establish an inquiry into the costs of distribution: CAB 24/275/313–20 (10 Mar. 1938); CAB 23/93/22 (16 Mar. 1938). The (Monckton) Committee on the Distribution of Coal, Coke, and Manufactured Fuel published its evidence but not a final report.

[1] *The Economist* 6 Aug. 1938, 274. The new Commissioners were: Sir Ernest Gowers (Chairman), G. P. Hyslop, W. M. Codrington, Joseph Jones, and Sir Felix J. C. Pole. The Act specified that two Commissioners should have had experience in the industry—one as a wage-earner. Hyslop was a mining engineer, Jones the former wage-earner.

[2] Below, 499, 621, and 611–27.

At first, the Commission was heartened by an apparent spirit of friendliness and cooperation in its meetings with the MAGB. Yet the owners retained reservations and by spring 1939, as the international situation darkened, they began to delay proceedings, and requested a postponement of activity. More tellingly, in his internal memoranda, Gowers emphasized the Commission's lack of political authority. In particular, he was apprehensive about the role of Parliament—'swayed by the contrary stresses of head and heart, recognizing the economic necessity of amalgamations, but fearing their social consequences'— where different ideological wings (one opposed to state intervention, the other to enforced redundancy) might trade on political considerations and sabotage specific schemes.[1]

In 1939 Gowers and his colleagues appeared more pessimistic than optimistic about their efforts. Yet they also appeared to be preparing vigorously and seriously for the deadline of 1 January 1940, after which—had there been no war—they could have tested their effective power before the Houses of Parliament. In their minds there was no doubt at all that the industry was still suffering from surplus capacity and that extensive amalgamations throughout the country were the only means of raising productivity, closing redundant pits, and lowering costs. It is obviously very difficult to assess what might have happened had peace continued. The Coal Commission had far more extensive powers than its predecessor and the legislation of 1938 was a major advance on that of 1930. But Sir Ernest Gowers and other commentators were surely right in detecting a fundamental flaw: those powers were still subject to parliamentary and therefore political ratification in each major *instance* of their exercise. This meant that the owners' undoubted determination to obstruct particular projects would be reinforced by those who were still opposed to an enlargement of the state's industrial role. On the other hand, the inhibitions and apprehensions of politicians (even those who were ill disposed towards the coalowners) might still determine the outcome: industrial reorganization in coal necessarily meant reducing capacity and jobs, imposing social costs on mining communities, and encouraging painful changes of structure and technique.

In other words, the development of an effective policy for coalmining was inhibited by a paradox. The depressed and demoralized condition of the industry, which itself gave rise to the pressure for reorganization,

---

[1] The principal records of the Coal Commission are in COAL 17/178. The quotations in the text are from the 4th Meeting (1 Sept. 1938). Gowers advocated a general rather than specific Report to try to secure Parliamentary approval and avoid detailed, *ad hoc*, discussion.

increased the social and political cost of reform. As we have seen, throughout the 1930s proposed policies had been assessed, in large part, in terms of their immediate effect on the level of employment in the industry and the returns to those engaged in it. On these criteria, the pursuit of efficiency and restructuring appeared to many politicians as too costly an exercise. And it was for this reason that many otherwise radical critics of the industry's business organization were reluctant to press for specific reforms. On the other hand, if economic pressures were relieved (for example, by a rising market for coal), the immediate *need* for reorganization would seem less urgent.

Of course, this is not to say that the developments in the 1930s had been negligible. Set against the position after decontrol in 1921 or the miseries of 1926, coalmining's economic arrangements had evolved rapidly and far, and it had become an emblem of the emerging new pattern of industry–state relationships.[1] It so happened that the changes had gone furthest at a level where the protection of existing interests had seemed most important. The Coal Mines Act of 1930 and the subsequent tightening of market control, culminating in the enforced abolition of much competition in 1936, were only remotely related to the reforms appropriate to the competitive disadvantages of British coal in world markets or in the rise in its relative price at home. But change there had been. The industry was now more centralized, more committed to a continuing dialogue with the state, more susceptible to further intervention, and more involved in an explicit recognition of the role of the miners' union in industrial policy.

Indeed, it could be argued that, in addition to the influence of general trends and widespread concern about the performance of the industry, it had been initiatives by the MFGB which were proximately most responsible for reform. This had certainly been the case in 1929–30, when the demand for a shorter working day had obliged the government to impose a cartel on the industry in order to increase proceeds to pay the real costs of the hours legislation. And in 1935/6 it was an irresistible wage claim which once more induced state intervention—this time to complete the process of cartelization and market control. Meanwhile, at each stage the possibility of *industrial* reorganization (to concentrate production, encourage efficiency, and reduce real cost) was pursued, partly as a goal in itself, partly as an attempt to mitigate the 'featherbedding' effects of market control.

[1] Beer 1954, ch. X–XII; Lucas 1937; Middlemas 1979, ch. 8.

Industrial reorganization foundered on a combination of political inhibition and the obstructionism of the owners. In the long run, however, the owners' attitudes and actions worked to their own disadvantage. For in the world outside the industry, and even more among politicians and civil servants who had to deal with them, a mounting sense of exasperation and grievance weakened their residual power. Increasingly, the sacrifices of 1926 appeared to have been one-sided, and the limited extent of voluntary industrial reform appeared culpable. As a result, their political position during the Second World War was eroded, and by 1944–5 it was almost universally assumed that compulsory reform of the industry was inevitable.[1]

Even so, it would be facile to assume that in 1938–9 the issue was coming to a head in a way which would have expedited enforced structural change had the emergency of the War not placed such matters in abeyance. In the first case, the *content* and *direct cost* of such change still had to be worked out. How far it should go, whether owners and managers could make a new system work if they were bitterly suspicious of its origins and purposes, how far a 1930s government could raise the huge amounts of necessary capital or oblige private enterprise to find it—these, and many other, 'technical' questions had hardly been posed, let alone tackled. And beyond this range of issues lay the one which had dogged the politics of rationalization for more than a decade: who would be sufficiently foolhardy or ruthless to pursue a restructuring of the industry when more than 12 per cent of insured miners were still unemployed?

When those with influence and authority finally accepted that the compulsory restructuring of coalmining was inevitable, they came to that conclusion on the basis of experience which included, but went well beyond, the events of the 1930s. The Second World War exposed the industry's fragility in the face of scarcity. And when the War came to an end, reconstruction appeared vital not, as in the 1930s, because of the strains of a coal surfeit, but because of the threat of shortages and high costs. In the depression years before 1940 the social control of the industry had progressed far, but with a protectionist bias and with little effective regard for its reconstruction. That reconstruction would have encountered at least a strong likelihood of political impasse had it been pursued in an unchanged economic environment. It was war, full

---

[1] Below, ch. 13, sect. vi.

employment, and the potential for growth which in 1942–6 finally opened the way to experiments which, in the prolonged depression of the interwar years, had seemed too costly in economic, political, and social terms.

PART E

OWNERS AND MINERS IN INTERWAR BRITAIN

CHAPTER 9

Coal Enterprises and Coalowners
1913–1939

The history of the coal industry in the quarter-century after 1913 was
conditioned by huge changes in output and profitability, in political
pressures and control, and in the balance of power between the various
economic interests involved in the industry's affairs. These changes,
together with the less dramatic trends in productivity and industrial
structures that were associated with them, were unevenly distributed
between the different regional coalfields of Great Britain. The resulting
variety (chronological and regional) of business experience makes it
unusually difficult to generalize about the character and attitudes of
business enterprise in coalmining up to the Second World War. Nevertheless, the centrality of the issues makes it necessary to pursue them,
even at the risk of oversimplification. In this chapter, coalmining
business will be considered from four viewpoints: the industry's structures; mechanization and its problems; business efficiency and the
'quality' of entrepreneurs and managers; and the public postures, representative associations, and 'ideological' attitudes which distinguished
the coalowners in these troubled years.

i. Industrial structure: scale and organization

Compared with most other staple industries, the number of firms and
productive units in coalmining was very great. In 1913, for example,
there were some 1,400 colliery undertakings producing coal from well
over 2,600 mines, and these figures were virtually the same in 1924. By
1938, however, after the prolonged economic difficulties of the late
1920s and the 1930s, the business 'population' of the industry had fallen
by about one-third, to just over 1,000 firms and almost 1,900 mines.[1]

[1] Statistics calculated from the annual *List of Mines*. Only mines in operation throughout the
year have been covered. It is difficult to give very precise figures for the number of mines, since
there were deficiencies in official statistics and private reporting, while the legal definition of a
'mine' was ambiguous from the economic viewpoint. The official *List of Mines* listed as separate

This was clearly a drastic decline, but it still left the industry with an exceptionally large number of productive units. Many of them were tiny: as Table 9.1 indicates, in 1935 there were over 500 collieries producing less than 10,000 tons each and accounting for a mere 0.5 per cent of the country's output, while 671 firms (70 per cent of all the firms in the industry) produced only 3 per cent of the coal. Yet there remained a significant number of medium-sized and large firms. The resulting dispersion was at its most striking among the former: there were 240 companies producing between 100,000 and 1,000,000 tons annually in 1935, and they accounted for 41.9 per cent of the coal produced. Even the giants of the industry hardly dominated it: the biggest 21 firms produced 30.7 per cent of the coal.[1]

Table 9.1. *Size distribution of British colliery undertakings by output, 1935*

Size (Output in 000 tons)	No. of undertakings	% of total saleable output
Under 10	522	0.5
10–100	149	2.6
100–250	90	6.8
250–500	82	13.3
500–750	38	10.1
750–1,000	30	11.7
1,000–2,000	40	24.3
2,000–3,000	12	13.0
Over 3,000	9	17.7

Source: POWE 22/85.

Such data exaggerate the degree of industrial proliferation—partly because of the corporate links between various nominally independent firms,[2] and principally because the industry's production was not homogeneous. Thus, in the case of anthracite, over 60 per cent of the output

mines, pits which were used primarily or solely for ancillary purposes (such as ventilation or pumping) and also pits which shared an underground work-force and manager. The former ('ancillary') mines have been excluded from the statistics used here. The *Reid Report* 3 gives the number of mines in 1914 as 2,734, but in 1938 the Royal Commission on Safety in Coal Mines (*RCSM* 47) gave the number in 1913 as 3,267 and in 1935 as 2,075.

[1] POWE 22/85. Also see COAL 17/178 (Coal Commission Meeting 5, Paper 4, Agenda 5: 12 Oct. 1938): the biggest 25 firms produced only 36% of coal output; the next 60 biggest firms produced 31.5%; and the next 201 firms produced 29.1%. In 1935 over 900 mines employed less than 30 men below ground: *RCSM* 48.   [2] Below, 372–7.

came from one group (Amalgamated Anthracite and its linked companies). But this was an extreme example. In general, the industry was much less concentrated than most 'heavy' staples. And the dispersion of output, with relatively large numbers of small and of fairly substantial firms, helps explain both the inherent instability of the industry and the importance of coordination to its economic and political management. Competition and over-production were endemic and difficult to control by market forces or private arrangements alone.

Taking first the question of coal *mines* (i.e. neglecting the size of colliery *companies*, each of which might own a number of mines), the period was characterized nationally by an initial increase and a subsequent decline in the importance of the larger pits. However, the movements in *relative* concentration were less marked since these trends were exemplified in the numbers as well as the industrial shares of the mines concerned.[1] As Table 9.2 indicates, between 1913 and 1924 the number of pits employing more than 2,000 men rose from 70 to 120 and their share of the industry's labour force increased from 17 to 27 per cent, while the smaller pits experienced a fall in their share. Big mines were, therefore, collectively more important. But since there were more of them, their average size (and, therefore, industrial concentration in its

[1] However, a better measure of industrial concentration is provided by the data on colliery *companies* (below). The statistics in the text were derived from detailed analyses of the *List of Mines* for 1913, 1924, and 1938. One difficulty with the statistics on mines is that the number of workers in two or more 'mines' was often given as a single figure (presumably because the mines were separate entities from the viewpoint of safety regulations, but shared a common labour force underground and/or on the surface). Where this occurs it has been assumed that each constituent mine *was* separate and shared equally in the total work-force involved. Such a procedure presumably underestimates the degree of concentration. In addition, the *List of Mines* also indicates employment (not output) for each mine. Nevertheless, the size of the labour force within the categories used seems to be an accurate proxy for output. The Samuel Commission's survey of 2,481 mines in 1924 (*Samuel Appendices*, 177–8) shows a close correspondence between employment and output. A similar correspondence between size distribution in terms of employment and output obtained in the 1930s. Thus, the Coal Mines Reorganisation Commission's survey of 1935 saleable output (POWE 22/85) compares with calculations of the labour force derived from the *List of Mines* for 1938 as follows:

Size distribution by output		Size distribution by labour force	
Firms	% output	Firms	% labour force
biggest 2%	30.7	biggest 2.5%	32
biggest 6%	55.0	biggest 7.4%	53

Table 9.2. *Size distribution (%) of British coalmines by labour force, 1913-1938*

Size of mines (labour force)	GREAT BRITAIN						SOUTH WALES & MONMOUTHSHIRE					
	1913		1924		1938		1913		1924		1938	
	(i)	(ii)	(i)	(ii)	(i)	(ii)	(i)	(ii)	(i)	(ii)	(i)	(ii)
1-9	39.1	2.9	40.3	2.1	46.9	2.4	42.2	2.9	43.6	2.9	45.4	2.5
100-499	32.8	21.6	27.3	15.4	21.9	14.7	33.8	20.6	28.6	17.3	20.9	20.8
500-999	16.6	28.8	16.7	25.1	18.8	27.8	11.2	18.3	14.3	24.3	15.6	29.1
1,000-1,999	8.9	30.2	10.9	30.8	11.6	37.6	8.1	28.4	8.8	28.0	10.8	39.8
2,000-2,999	2.3	13.4	3.7	18.3	2.4	13.5	4.1	24.2	4.2	23.3	1.3	7.9
3,000-4,999	0.4	3.1	1.0	8.3	0.5	4.0	0.7	5.6	0.5	4.2	—	—
5,000-	—	—	negl.	0.4	—	—	—	—	—	—	—	—
Total number of mines	2662		2506		1870		554		594		372	
Total labour force	1,087,293		1,209,869		798,585		230,072		246,654		135,689	
Average number miners per mine	408		482		427		415		415		364	

Size of mines (labour force)	Scotland						Northumberland & Durham						Nottinghamshire, Derbyshire & South Yorks.[a]					
	1913		1924		1938		1913		1924		1938		1913		1924		1938	
	(i)	(ii)	(i)	(ii)	(i)	(ii)	(i)	(ii)	(i)	(ii)	(i)	(ii)	(i)	(ii)	(i)	(ii)	(i)	(ii)
1–9	31.2	4.7	32.7	3.4	52.8	5.2	27.3	1.5	35.8	1.4	42.5	2.1	38.5	1.5	34.5	0.7	32.2	0.7
100–499	47.9	39.7	43.7	27.4	32.3	36.3	28.3	16.2	22.6	10.3	22.8	13.8	24.4	10.9	12.8	3.9	10.3	4.4
500–999	17.1	38.4	19.1	41.0	13.8	36.8	27.3	37.2	20.3	25.9	18.3	27.7	13.6	16.7	16.3	13.2	24.4	18.1
1,000–1,999	3.7	17.1	4.1	15.3	3.4	16.3	15.5	38.3	15.0	33.7	12.9	36.0	16.7	40.8	19.0	30.1	23.1	43.7
2,000–2,999	—	—	0.5	3.0	0.6	5.5	1.2	5.5	4.8	19.3	2.7	13.3	5.9	24.5	12.4	32.1	8.3	25.7
3,000–4,999	—	—	—	—	—	—	0.3	1.4	1.5	9.4	0.9	7.1	0.9	5.6	5.0	19.9	1.7	7.4
5,000–	—	—	—	—	—	—	—	—	—	—	—	—	—	—	—	—	—	—
Total number of mines	461		444		356		406		394		334		426		258		242	
Total labour force	138,781		143,865		90,922		218,865		238,995		161,177		252,620		240,925		191,673	
Average number miners per mine	301		324		255		539		606		482		593		933		792	

(i): Percentage of mines
(ii): Percentage of miners

[a] 1913: Nottinghamshire, Derbyshire, and East and West Riding of Yorkshire.

Sources: List of Mines, 1913, 1924, 1938.

Table 9.3. *Size distribution of British coalmines by output, 1924 and 1942*

Size of mines: annual output (000 tons)	1924 Mines		Labour force		Output[a]		1942 Mines		Labour Force		Output	
	No.	%	No. (000)	%	Tons	%	No.	%	No. (000)	%	Tons	%
Under 50	818	33.0	13,508	1.1	2,394,53	0.9	691	39.8	11,036	1.6	2,532,035	1.2
50–499	848	34.2	199,300	16.5	43,454,587	16.4	513	29.5	122,815	17.3	33,832,577	16.6
500–999	422	17.0	305,532	25.2	66,356,643	24.9	300	17.3	212,551	29.9	59,411,650	29.2
1,000–1,499	198	8.0	242,264	20.2	51,729,260	19.4	127	7.3	152,058	21.4	46,413,431	22.8
1,500–1,999	77	3.1	134,198	11.1	30,043,541	11.2	68	3.9	113,754	16.0	32,592,621	16.0
2,000–2,499	61	2.5	134,588	11.1	29,486,767	11.0	24	1.4	52,805	7.4	15,683,946	7.7
2,500–2,999	31	1.2	84,380	7.0	19,734,479	7.4	10	0.6	27,324	3.9	8,121,556	4.0
3000 and over	26	1.0	96,972	8.0	23,520,541	8.8	5	0.3	17,375	2.5	5,045,622	2.5
TOTAL	2,481		1,211		266,720,351		1738		709,718		203,633,438	

[a] The figures for 'output' in 1924 include about 250,000 tons of non-coal minerals.

Sources: *Samuel*, III, Appendix 18, 177; *Ministry of Fuel & Power. Statistical Digest from 1938* (Cmd. 6538), 11.

conventional meaning) did not change markedly. In any case, well over half the labour force was employed in medium-sized pits employing 500 to 1,999 miners.

As far as the importance of large-scale pits was concerned, 1924 was probably a peak. Over the next 14 years, as industrial output and employment both sagged, the relative significance of big pits also declined—as did their numbers, so that once again the *degree* of concentration hardly changed. By 1938, mines employing 2,000 or more miners accounted for roughly the same proportion of the industry as they had done in 1913, while mines employing 500 to 1,999 men had more than regained their prewar position. This slippage (which implies that in a period of adversity the industry as a whole either could not or would not attain economies of scale at the plant level) was presumably proximately explained by economic adversity and market controls, which combined to reduce the average level of output below capacity. As the largest mines reduced their production they simply slid into a smaller size category. Over the period as a whole, then, and allowing for changes in the market, there was very little alteration in the national picture of industrial concentration at the colliery level.[1]

A similar analysis of the size of mines in four of the country's principal coalfields (Table 9.2) demonstrates yet again the regional variety which characterized the industry's economics. In the South Yorkshire and East Midlands coalfields, for example, the proportionate share of the labour force of the biggest pits (over 1,999 miners) rose to 1924 and then fell—but the pits themselves and their share of the local industry were both larger than the national average.[2] In Monmouthshire

---

[1] This finding is not quite consistent with measures derived from overall averages or large categories. Thus, the Royal Commission on Safety in Mines (*RCSM* 47–50) indicated that between 1913 and 1935, when the national total number of mines fell by 36.5%, those employing over 1,000 men underground fell by merely 8%. The number of the smallest mines also held up—the largest decline came in medium-sized mines. According to the Royal Commission the average mine increased its employment from 345 to 376 miners and its output from 92,294 tons to 110,113 tons. (However, data from the *List of Mines* (see Table 9.2) show an increase from 408 in 1913 to 427 in 1938, with a sharper rise to 1924, followed by a decline.)

[2] Again, the figures do not reflect relative concentration—which decreased slightly, in the sense that in 1938 a higher proportion of mines (10.2% as against 6.8% in 1913) were in the category of 2,000 employees, and accounted for only a barely higher proportion of the local labour force (33.1% as against 30%). Big firms were somewhat more important, industrial concentration less. In South Yorkshire, Nottinghamshire, and Derbyshire in 1924, 4.4% of pits employed over 3,000 miners, and accounted for 19.5 % of the labour force and 20.9% of the output. Among other leading fields the next most important with respect to scale was Durham, where 1.8% of the mines employed over 3,000 men and accounted for some 10% of the labour force and output. (*Samuel Appendices*, Appendices 177–8.)

and South Wales, by way of contrast, there was surprisingly little change between 1913 and 1924, the biggest mines being no more important, and only those employing 500–999 miners increasing their share—from 18.3 to 24.3 per cent—of the labour force. And in the grim years that followed, the biggest Welsh pits became much less significant, while the share of those employing 1,000–1,999 grew quite sharply as the industry consolidated in the face of its economic vicissitudes.

A more consistent line of structural change was traced by the other two leading export fields. In the North-East in 1913–24 there was spectacular growth in the proportionate importance of the largest mines (over 1,999 men), but they never reached the level of significance of similar mines in South Wales. On the other hand, they held their economic ground somewhat better in the 1930s. Even so, Northumberland and Durham were pre-eminently coalfields of medium-to-large pits: in 1938 almost one-third of all mines employed 500–1,999 miners and accounted for almost two-thirds of the labour force. Finally, in Scotland (where economic pressures after the early 1920s elicited perhaps the most vigorous efforts to consolidate, and concentrate on modernizing, the industry) there was, throughout the period, a marked trend *in favour* of relatively large-scale mines (that is relative to other Scottish pits: the absolute size of Scottish mines was significantly smaller than the national average). In Scotland, mines employing more than 1,999 workers increased their share of the district's labour force from 17.1 per cent in 1913 to 18.3 per cent in 1924 and 21.4 per cent in 1938.

Data relating to collieries in isolation from the companies that controlled them are relevant to many aspects of the contemporary debate about economies of scale in production.[1] But from a broader viewpoint, and in terms of a more conventional interpretation of the concept of 'industrial structure', it is necessary to take account of the size distribution of coalmining *firms*. Quite apart from the intrinsic relevance of business units, it was generally assumed that financial and managerial control would enable large firms to secure a wide range of scale economies as well as facilitating the process of concentrating production in the most efficient mines and seams.

The various merger moments and trends have already been touched on in the chapters concerning the 1920s and 1930s. But the long-run picture derived from industry-wide statistics is less dramatic. Indeed changes in the corporate structure of the industry tended to smooth out some of the variations associated with the size of *mines*. In other words,

---

[1] Below, 397–401.

there was a more continuous trend towards a larger role for bigger firms (even when the share of the big mines was declining). However, the total effect was relatively modest (see Table 9.4). Nationally, the largest firms slightly increased their share of the labour force in 1913-24, presumably because of the mergers immediately after the First World War. They then held that share (53 per cent for those employing over 2,999 miners, 32 per cent for those employing over 4,999) until 1938. Medium-sized firms, employing 1,000-2,999 miners, fell and then grew in importance, accounting for about a third of the manpower at the beginning and end of the period. For Great Britain as a whole, then, there was relatively little change, and such change as occurred was towards a greater importance for larger firms. Yet, as with the size distribution of mines, but to a more marked extent, the national aggregates are not a good guide to trends within the different districts.

Although in the four districts under consideration large-scale mines were most important in South Yorkshire and the East Midlands (especially with the development of new pits after 1918), large *firms*, owning various mines, were of greatest *relative* importance in the North-East and in South Wales.[1] In Northumberland and Durham they accounted for the largest shares (colliery companies employing more than 2,999 miners had at least two-thirds of the region's labour force; those employing more than 4,999, between 40 and 55 per cent). But the trend towards bigger firms in the North-East was reversed after 1924. In South Wales, on the other hand, after a check in the boom years 1913-24, there was a moderately strong increase in the proportionate importance of big firms. By 1938 almost half of South Wales miners were employed in companies with a work-force in excess of 4,999—thus exemplifying the situation which led left-wing critics to attack combines in the Principality and which also led the CMRC to accept that there was no immediate need to push Welsh firms in the direction of amalgamation.

Elsewhere, concentration appears to have proceeded without interruption in South Yorkshire and the East Midlands. Indeed, the growing labour shares of the biggest firms underestimate the process since those firms represented a much smaller proportion of all companies in the region. And this process—by which a proportionately smaller number

---

[1] This is so in terms of the shares of the largest firms in total labour and output. If, however, the scale of operation (the average size of all firms) is taken into account, the districts with the largest firms were South Yorkshire, and North Derbyshire and Nottinghamshire—with the North-East a close runner-up. POWE 22/85 gives the following average output per firm in 1935 (in 000 tons): South Yorkshire, 813; North Derbyshire and Nottinghamshire, 682; Northumberland and Durham, 668; South Wales & Monmouthshire, 530; Scotland, 486.

Table 94. *Size distribution of British colliery undertakings employing more than 500 miners, 1913-1938*

	Firms employing 500-999 miners			Firms employing 1,000-2,999 miners			Firms employing 3,000-4,999 miners			Firms employing 5,000 miners and above		
	1913	1924	1938	1913	1924	1938	1913	1924	1938	1913	1924	1938
GREAT BRITAIN												
Percentage of miners	10.5	8.3	9.2	34.6	25.4	32.3	20.7	19.3	19.0	25.8	32.6	33.9
Percentage of firms	11.1	9.7	9.9	14.7	15.7	14.3	4.0	5.2	3.8	2.5	2.5	2.6
Percentage of mines	10.9	9.3	8.0	21.3	20.4	17.6	9.6	10.0	8.1	14.5	15.6	15.9
Number of miners	114,562	100,321	73,857	376,258	408,887	257,960	225,468	233,592	151,989	280,371	396,742	270,929
Number of firms	160	137	102	211	222	148	58	59	39	36	49	27
Number of mines	289	232	149	563	511	329	248	250	152	359	392	298
Average number of mines per firm	1.81	1.69	1.46	2.67	2.30	2.22	4.28	4.24	3.90	9.97	8.0	11.04
SOUTH WALES & MONMOUTHSHIRE												
Percentage of miners	8.4	7.1	6.9	23.6	32.0	24.5	18.9	15.4	14.2	38.2	37.2	48.5
Percentage of firms	8.3	7.5	6.6	8.9	12.8	9.6	3.2	3.0	2.0	3.3	3.3	1.5
Percentage of mines	9.6	8.7	5.2	16.9	19.5	12.2	6.5	8.6	6.2	14.8	14.4	22.3
Number of miners	19,118	17,414	9,121	53,820	79,020	32,375	43,126	37,936	18,751	87,203	91,777	63,972
Numbers of firms	28	25	13	30	43	19	11	10	4	11	11	3
Number of mines	53	51	20	94	114	47	36	50	24	82	84	86
Average number of mines per firm	1.89	2.0	1.54	3.13	2.65	2.47	3.27	5.0	6.0	7.45	7.6	28.67
SCOTLAND												
Percentage of miners	15.1	12.2	11.7	26.4	22.2	31.7	18.0	21.9	10.6	27.8	34.6	36.0
Percentage of firms	15.8	14.3	8.8	10.9	11.8	8.8	3.2	4.9	1.3	2.2	4.4	2.5

Percentage of mines	15.2	24.1	20.2	5.4	14.3	9.9	17.8	15.6	19.8	9.6	12.7	13.1
Number of miners	7,481	51,021	37,260	8,803	32,330	24,077	26,359	33,969	35,453	9,705	18,133	20,254
Numbers of firms	4	7	4	2	8	6	14	19	20	14	23	29
Number of mines	54	108	91	19	64	44	63	70	89	34	57	59
Average number of mines per firm	16	15.43	22.75	9.5	8	7.33	4.5	3.68	4.45	2.43	2.48	2.03
NORTHUMBERLAND & DURHAM												
Percentage of miners	39.2	54.5	40.5	38.1	15.8	25.7	23.0	22.7	24.8	5.6	3.8	6.4
Percentage of firms	4.7	7.7	6.7	7.3	4.5	8.4	13.8	17.6	17.6	7.3	6.1	12.1
Percentage of mines	19.3	29.1	27.4	17.0	11.0	17.3	13.7	16.1	19.1	5.6	4.6	7.8
Number of miners	62,003	129,459	90,328	44,427	37,545	57,091	36,369	53,817	55,223	8,878	8,986	14,210
Number of firms	7	15	11	11	9	14	21	27	29	11	12	20
Number of mines	62	114	109	55	43	69	44	63	76	18	18	31
Average number of mines per firm	8.86	7.6	9.91	5	4.78	4.93	2.1	2.33	2.62	1.64	1.5	2.07
NOTTS., DERBYSHIRE, SOUTH YORKSHIRE, ETC.[a]												
Percentage of miners	37.3	29.3	18.3	27.0	28.6	25.9	32.3	36.1	42.8	6.1	4.0	7.6
Percentage of firms	7.1	5.3	2.6	9.9	9.5	6.3	22.0	24.3	21.9	9.1	7.7	9.3
Percentage of mines	18.6	16.3	8.6	16.4	13.9	12.4	21.7	24.6	23.3	6.2	5.2	8.3
Number of miners	68,154	67,218	45,651	49,523	65,672	64,471	52,193	82,845	106,555	8,449	9,201	19,036
Number of firms	8	9	7	13	16	17	29	41	59	12	13	25
Number of mines	42	41	36	37	35	52	49	62	98	14	13	35
Average number of mines per firm	5.25	4.56	5.14	2.85	2.19	3.06	1.69	1.51	1.66	1.17	1	1.4

[a] 1913: East and West Riding of Yorkshire.

Sources: *List of Mines*, 1913, 1924, and 1938.

of firms control a large proportion of the regional industry—was also illustrated in Scotland. There, in spite of a dip in the share of firms employing 3,000–4,999 miners, the share of the very biggest firms rose throughout the period, and by the 1930s, in both categories, the proportionate number of firms and mines fell drastically—yet another indication of the streamlining of the Scottish industry. Finally, it is necessary to emphasize that in spite of the general trend to larger-scale activity, the stability of the industry's corporate structure was still vulnerable to the presence of a very large number of small firms, and there were very many medium-sized companies: those employing between 1,000 and 2,999 miners accounted for between 25 and 33 per cent of the labour force in all principal districts except for the East Midlands, where they accounted for about 40 per cent.

An official analysis of the size distribution of firms by *output* and region in 1935 (Table 9.5) corroborates the picture of large-scale activity in certain districts (although it also confirms the general significance of medium-sized firms producing between 100,000 and 1,000,000 tons). Thus, although there was a very large number of small colliery undertakings in South Wales, almost 50 per cent of its output came from the three giant combines grouped around Powell Duffryn, Amalgamated Anthracite, and Ocean Coal (which between them produced almost 17 million tons of coal). Some 60 per cent of South Wales's output came from the five largest groups. And yet, spectacular as such instances undoubtedly were[1] the largest firms were not supreme: there were still a sufficient number of undertakings, each producing substantial quantities, to maintain competition, and instability, in the industry.

The question of industrial structure and business cooperation was by no means exhausted by details of formal corporate entities. Coal was not an undifferentiated product, and the differing markets and uses for its various types led to distinctive patterns of corporate relationships. Thus, the mining of coking coal was rarely the responsibility of specialist colliery companies. At the least, they combined coalmining with the extensive ownership of coke ovens, and not infrequently with metallurgical production. Indeed, the mining undertaking was often a subsidiary element in an iron and steel combine. Thus, the Durham coal

---

[1] In relative terms, the most concentrated production in 1935 was to be found in Lancashire and Cheshire, where two firms (Manchester Collieries and Wigan Coal) were responsible for 43% of the output. In Scotland, two undertakings produced a quarter of the output, and in each of South Yorkshire and North Derbyshire–Nottinghamshire, two firms produced about one-fifth of the output. Particularly in the older fields, such giant enterprises were amalgamations of numerous individual mines.

Table 9.5. *Size distribution of British colliery undertakings by output of saleable coal, 1935*

Output (000) tons	Great Britain		South Wales & Monmouthshire		Scotland		Northumberland & Durham	
	(i)	(ii)	(i)	(ii)	(i)	(ii)	(i)	(ii)
under 10	520	0.5	134	0.5	81	0.7	67	0.4
10–100	147	2.6	30	3.7	28	4.7	22	1.7
100–250	87	6.5	12	4.6	11	6.2	8	2.9
250–500	79	13.2	10	10.1	8	9.5	8	6.4
500–750	35	9.4	2	3.1	5	10.2	6	8.2
750–1,000	21	8.3	4	9.8	3	8.7	7	13.9
1,000–2,000	39	23.3	2	7.6	5	20.7	9	28.4
2,000–3,000	15	16.8	2	12.5	2	13.7	5	29.1
over 3,000	10	19.4	3	48.1	2	25.5	1	9.0
Total no. mines	953		199		145		133	
Total output (000 tons)	222,237		35,025		31,347		44,300	

Table 9.5 (*cont.*)

Output (000) tons	Lancashire & Cheshire		South Yorkshire		North Derbyshire & Nottinghamshire	
	(i)	(ii)	(i)	(ii)	(i)	(ii)
under 10	34	0.7	24	0.2	36	1.2
10–100	16	3.2	4	0.4	3	0.2
100–250	11	13.8	2	1.0	9	5.7
250–500	6	14.1	4	4.6	9	12.3
500–750	3	11.6	9	18.5	4	8.9
750–1,000	1	6.4	8	22.9	4	13.5
1,000–2,000	1	7.1	7	31.7	7	37.7
2,000–3,000	1	17.5	1	9.1	1	8.2
over 3,000	1	25.6	1	11.7	1	13.3
Total no. mines	74		60		74	
Total output	14,146		29,314		25,994	

(i): Number of firms
(ii): Percentage of total output

Source: COAL 17/178 (Coal Mines Reorganisation Commission Meeting 5, Paper 4, Agenda 5).

industry in the 1930s was dominated by three large amalgamated colliery groups belonging to iron and steel interests: Dorman Long & Co., the Consett Iron Co., and Pease & Partners. And comparable groupings could be found in South Wales and the Midlands. It was estimated that in the 1930s just over one-fifth of all coal was produced by such 'composite' companies.[1] More broadly, the production of virtually any coal that was sold in bulk could be economically associated with linked or unified businesses devoted to sales. The Doncaster Collieries Association was perhaps the most famous instance of an integrated sales agency, but it was far from unique. It had a parallel in the Carlton Collieries Association, and many large firms controlled 'separate' export and selling agencies.[2]

Business linkages and groupings were not solely a matter of such substantial investments. Interlocking shareholdings, directorships, and business interests effectively created important alliances. This was most marked in the South Yorkshire–North Derbyshire–Nottinghamshire, and South Wales and Durham fields (where vertical combinations of coal, coke, and metallurgical enterprises characterized the industry) but was also present to some extent in all others.[3] Moreover, such groupings were the more dramatized by the personal ties of interlocking directorships: in the early 1920s well over half the directors in the 572 leading colliery concerns held directorships in other companies—in over 300

---

[1] POWE 28/44 Pt. 2 (Coal Industry Nationalisation Compensation Tribunal), Day 8 (27 June 1946), 33.

[2] For the Doncaster Collieries Association, see above, 235 n. Welsh Associated Collieries (formed in 1930) owned Gueret, Llewellyn & Merrett Ltd; Powell Duffryn had owned an export company since 1914; Ocean Coal & Wilson's had a fully owned subsidiary—Wilson Sons & Co. Ltd—with a world-wide distributive network.

[3] For example, in the Midland field, overlapping colliery networks developed around the Staveley Coal and Iron and the Sheepbridge Coal and Iron Companies. The two 'parent' concerns were themselves linked through directorships and through joint shareholdings in such colliery undertakings as the Firbeck Main and Newstead Companies. The Staveley Company controlled 5 separate colliery firms which, in turn, and together with the Firbeck Main Company, floated a selling agency, the Doncaster Collieries Association in 1919. In 1937 the 6 colliery companies merged their corporate entities into the Doncaster Associated Collieries. Sheepbridge, for its part, controlled 3 large separate colliery undertakings, which in 1927, and together with the Denaby & Cadeby Main Collieries, were merged into the Yorkshire Amalgamated Collieries. Sheepbridge owned one-third of the YAC, which in 1936 had an output of some 3.5 m. tons. (Fox 1935a; Political and Economic Planning, 1936, 56.) In South Wales, the giant Powell Duffryn concern owned a variety of colliery undertakings producing 4 or 5 m. tons in the 1920s. Apart from the joint ownership of the Taff Merthyr Steam Coal Company (with another combine, Ocean Coal & Wilsons, which in 1924 owned 9 pits and produced 2.5 m. tons) and other corporate acquisitions in the slump. Powell Duffryn in 1935 merged its colliery interests with those of Welsh Associated Collieries, which was itself the result of a 1930 merger, and separation, of the varied colliery interests of Guest, Keen & Nettlefolds.

instances in colliery companies where the 'senior' firm had a controlling or substantial interest, and in over 1,000 cases where it had a lesser interest.[1]

Given this corporate structure it might be imagined that both business collusion and operating economies would be greatly facilitated. And certainly, as far as the former was concerned the elaborate networks of corporate and financial connections, especially when set out in print and illustrated with dense charts by hostile critics, gave some warrant to the conspiracy theory of the coalmining business.[2] Yet, from the viewpoint of business decision-making the situation was too complicated, the numbers involved too great, and the range of interests (by no means all of them shared and harmonious) too wide for there to have been much chance of widespread collusion and cooperation between the multitudinous units which comprised the coal industry.

Nor, in this respect, need we rely solely on the logic of numbers. For, as the owners' critics were quick to point out, they seemed incapable of acting together for their own common good; they indulged in excessive price-cutting and inter-regional as well as inter-firm competition; they neglected opportunities of closing surplus or inefficient capacity; and even when favoured by externally imposed regulatory schemes—as with the selling schemes devised under the Coal Mines Act of 1930—they would, if left to their individual devices, further weaken the industry and its price structure. Indeed, the enforcement and subsequent official pressure to strengthen the regulation of selling in the 1930s is a demonstration of the inability of the industry's market-based structure to harmonize the interests of its constituents. For, even when most of the industry's leaders had come to appreciate the necessity (from their viewpoint) of coordination through the control of output and sales (as they did in 1927–8) they had found it impossible to ensure that a voluntary scheme was not undercut.[3]

The other possibility—that corporate links might lead to productive efficiency through large-scale operations—was equally unlikely. Finan-

---

[1] *Samuel Appendices*, Appendix 18. The most extreme examples occurred in South Wales, where 382 of 545 directors held other directorships, and in South Yorkshire (157 of 215). A smaller survey of leading firms in 1939 shows that 33 out of 43 directors of the five biggest colliery firms in South Wales held 122 directorships in other colliery companies. The figures for the 6 biggest colliery firms in Yorkshire were 32 out of 42, holding 125 directorships. In each case, the elimination of subsidiary companies reduces the number of directorships held to about 100. (Source: *CYB* 1939 and *Directory of Directors* for 1939).

[2] Above, 307 n.

[3] Above, ch. 5, sect. v.

cial interlocking was by no means the same as operational and business integration. It could hardly make possible the sort of extensive and close coordination necessary to attain economies of scale. Rather, most groupings of this period were analogous to holding companies which controlled, but did not combine or integrate, the operations of many scattered collieries. And unless the ownership of the various enterprises were unitary and complete, the reallocation and concentration of capacity needed to lower average unit costs was very difficult to attain. Admittedly, from about 1929 onwards there were more obvious signs of closer integration of some of the leading colliery groupings.[1] And in nearly every instance a large part of the declared aim of the more formal integration was to concentrate operations and streamline activity. Yet this turned out to be a slow rather than a dramatic process, and the costs and risks of private rationalization were considerable.[2] In spite of the appearance of a limited handful of very large firms, the formal structure of the industry in general hardly appeared much more concentrated in 1938 than it had done in 1924 or even 1913.

ii. Mechanization and mining systems

The question of the size of the mines and colliery undertakings often seemed to dominate contemporary discussion of the organization of coalmining. Yet, implicit in that discussion was a sense that the structure of the industry was itself functionally related to the *internal* workings and efficiency of the units of ownership and production. By the 1930s there was a growing realization that any assessment of the entrepreneurial performance of British coalowners had to take account not merely of the extension of scale and mechanization but also of administrative structures, labour processes, underground layout, and the system of mining as a whole.[3] How far and with what consequences did that system change?

The organization and techniques of mining in 1913 have already been described.[4] Its two most interesting characteristics, from a modern perspective, were the bewildering variety of 'Local customs, traditions,

---

[1] e.g.: the formation of Manchester Collieries and Welsh Associated Collieries in 1930; the merger which created Baird & Dalmellington in 1931; the combination of Powell Duffryn and the Welsh Associated Collieries in 1935; the integration of the corporate structures within the Yorkshire Amalgamated Collieries in 1936; and the formation of Doncaster Amalgamated Collieries in 1937.   [2] Below, 401–10.

[3] Below, 384–5, 400. The classic statement of this 'holistic' view is in the *Reid Report*.

[4] Above, ch. 1, sect. iii.

and methods' which 'often bore little or no relation to those prevailing in other coalfields, even where coalfields were similar',[1] and the extreme degree of labour intensity of the hewing, underground haulage, and surface treatment of coal. In neither respect did the interwar years witness sweeping changes.

Even the intensification of 'machine mining' did not radically diminish the dominance of wages in the structure of current costs, although the share of wages in total costs oscillated between 70–75 per cent in years of labour shortage (1913–20, 1923–4, 1942–6) and about 66 per cent in years of excess capacity (1921–2, 1927–39).[2] Certainly, there was nothing to compare with the transformation of techniques in the 1960s and 1970s. On the other hand, there were very significant extensions of longwall coal-getting and of the use of coal-cutters and face conveyors, and these were inevitably associated with pressures on the inherited system of work practices, shift arrangements, labour supervision, and overall organization.[3] As a result, and reinforced by changes in the length of underground shifts, there was some diminution of the industry's traditional heterogeneity of working practices, which allowed a greater role for differences in geological conditions to determine the regional variety of economic performance.[4]

Longwall working—the continuous extraction of coal along a broad coalface of tens and even hundreds of yards—had dominated a handful of districts (Yorkshire, Lancashire, Nottinghamshire, Leicestershire) before the First World War, and was fairly strongly in evidence in most other major fields. By the early 1940s it had become the principal method of extraction in the great majority of all mines. And even in the mid-1930s the main alternative system—'room and pillar' (it had numerous names and variants)—had survived to a considerable extent only in western portions of the South Wales coalfield and in parts of the North-East.[5] In many circumstances longwall working had important advantages: it lent itself more readily to the most accessible and popular forms of mechanization; it enabled profitable coal-getting (and therefore some return on investment) to begin with less delay; and it was also more

---

[1] *Reid Report*, 3.

[2] *CYB*, various years.

[3] See below, ch. 10, sect. i.

[4] This point is made by Dr David Greasley in an unpublished paper on 'Productivity and Factor Returns at the Coal Face in Great Britain, 1900–38'.

[5] *Digest of Evidence Given before the Royal Commission on Coal Supplies* (*Colliery Guardian* 1905), I, 192–220; *Reid Report*, 42; *RCSM* 241,393. The Reid Committee estimated that longwall was the main method in 74% of mines.

suited to deep mining and thin seams, since the slower rate of progress exposed 'pillar and room' workings to 'excessive crush ... a low percentage of extraction, difficulties in ventilation, and increased deadwork'.[1]

The longwall system actually introduced in this period was predominantly 'advancing' that is, the coal was extracted from the shaft pillar outwards, with roadways constructed in line with the progress of coal-getting, and the roof allowed to collapse behind the workings and around the roadways. Longwall advancing had the short-run advantage of economizing on immediate investment and accelerating the time when profits could begin. In addition, the colliery need not commit itself to a particular boundary line. The alternative was longwall retreating, by which roadways were first driven out to the boundaries of the coal and worked backwards towards the shaft. That process saved on road maintenance and ventilation during the working since, as the workings were left behind the roof could be allowed to subside around now-redundant voids and roadways. However, it involved an earlier commitment to specific boundaries, a much greater immediate investment, and a longer wait for a return on capital.[2] During the interwar period longwall advancing was defended by most mining engineers. Yet there was some criticism at this time, and in 1944-5 the Reid Committee came down decisively on the side of the alternative method, particularly since improved machinery for the driving of headings had greatly reduced the time needed to bring a 'retreating' face into operation.

Longwall working cannot be considered in isolation from the techniques used to cut and convey the coal, both of which were increasingly mechanized during this period. Mechanical coal-cutting along the line of the longwall was principally employed to *under*cut the coal, which then continued to be blasted or levered off the seam, and loaded by hand. In 1913 the proportion of coal mechanically cut was still only 8 per cent and there were 3,897 machines in the country. But the technology was stimulated during the First World War by coal shortages and the

---

[1] *Reid Report*, 39. *RSCM*, 50 pointed out that since 1913 coal-workings had been driven to thinner and deeper seams.

[2] *Samuel Appendices* Appendix 20.

[3] *Reid Report*, 41-5. The issue was discussed before the Samuel Commission. See, for example, evidence of the Institution of Mining Engineers: *Samuel Evidence* QQ 12207 ff. The economic state of the industry, including the shortage of resources and the doubtfulness of good returns to investment, go some way to explaining the reluctance of colliery undertakings to commit themselves to the time-consuming (and initially expensive) process of setting up longwall retreating systems.

Table 9.6. *Mechanization in British coalmines, 1914–1938*

	CUTTING				CONVEYING			
	No. of mines using machines	No. of machines	Quantity of coal cut (m. tons)	% of total output	No. of conveyors at face	No. of conveyors other than at face	Tonnage conveyed (m. tons)	% of total output
GREAT BRITAIN								
1914	652	3093	24.3	8	408			
1921	776	5259	23.0	14	818	n/a	n/a	n/a
1927[a]	929	7116	58.5	23	2185	653	28.0	11
1938	917	7754	142.3	61	5859	2412	133.7	57
SOUTH WALES & MONS.								
1914	58	131	0.6	1	63			
1921	71	273	0.9	3	342	n/a	n/a	n/a
1927[a]	110	425	3.2	7	761	191	7.0	15
1938	112	548	9.2	26	1016	368	17.1	48
SCOTLAND								
1914	230	913	9.2	2	128			
1921	255	1316	8.2	36	91	n/a	n/a	n/a
1927[a]	270	1619	19.3	55				
1938	237	1540	24.5	80	851	322	18.0	59
NORTHUMBERLAND								
1914	38	326	1.9	15	21			
1921	50	415	1.4	18	21	n/a	n/a	n/a
1927[a]	71	676	5.7	42	90	46	1.7	13
1938		852	11.8	92	325	184	5.7	45

DURHAM								
1914		369	1.6	4	47	n/a	n/a	n/a
1921	88	850	2.4	11	79			
1927[a]	99	1107	6.3	18	178	48	2.2	7
1938	84	1012	13.2	43	426	163	8.4	27
SOUTH YORKSHIRE								
1914		201	1.4	6	37	n/a	n/a	n/a
1921	39	279	1.5	8	78			
1927	59	486	3.5	11	122	32	2.2	7
1938	63	704	19.1	60	718	354	21.8	69
NOTTS. & DERBYSHIRE								
1914		294	3.5	12.2	29	n/a	n/a	n/a
1921	49	419	2.7	14	46			
NOTTS. & NORTH DERBYSHIRE								
1927[a]	58	626	6.1	22	130	44	2.0	7
1938	94	834	24.7	80	823	303	24.1	80
LANCASHIRE & CHESHIRE								
1914		498	2.4	8	28	n/a	n/a	n/a
1921	92	813	1.8	14	52			
1927[a]	94	831	2.8	16	99	11	1.2	7
1938	79	757	10.6	74	552	223	11.3	79

n/a = not available.

[a] '1927' figures for number of conveyors elsewhere than at face, and tonnage conveyed: based on 1928.

Sources: Metalliferous Mines & Quarries, Second Report (Cmd. 7476. 1914); *Samuel Report*, App. 18, Table 1; *ARSM* 1921, 1927, 1938.

importing of the latest chain-driven cutters from the United States. By 1920 the number of machines had risen to 5,071 and by 1927 to over 7,000. Thenceforth the power, efficiency, and utilization of coal-cutters were even more important than their numbers (which included various small-scale, percussive machines). The most effective type was the chain-driven cutter, which came to dominate the industry's cutting techno-logy and accounted for 6,005 machines out of a total of 6,331 in 1938. In the seven years after 1927, thanks to improvement in the machinery and more continuous use, as face conveyors were introduced, the output of each machine rose by 66 per cent. And between 1927 and 1939 the proportion of coal cut by machine rose from 23 to 61 per cent.[1]

As indicated in Table 9.6, the statistical importance of coal-cutting machinery varied markedly, both at any one time and in the speed at which it was adopted. Conventionally, the uneven distribution of machine mining was attributed to differences in physical conditions: the unevenness of roads, the stability of roofs, the faults and thickness of seams. The last was perhaps the most important consideration, since there were considerable relative economic advantages in mechanized cutting in thin seams. Hence, there was a noticeable inverse correlation between thickness of seams and extent of mechanization,[2] and the thin-ness of Scottish seams, together with the greater difficulty of working them, were offered as reasons for Scotland's exceptionally high use of cutting machinery (56 per cent of coal was machine-cut in 1927, as against a national average of 23 per cent). Elsewhere, West Yorkshire and Northumberland also exemplified a relationship between thin seams and an early acceptance of cutting machinery, while the lower labour cost of working the thick seams of South Yorkshire and Nottinghamshire no doubt made it unnecessarily expensive to intro-duce much machinery in the 1920s.

At the same time, other physical characteristics counted for much. In the South Wales steam-coal districts, for example, seams rarely needed much undercutting (the coal could be more or less levered off), while falls from unstable roofs constantly threatened to bury the machinery. Hand-working was also relatively easy in Durham. Markets were also influential: the introduction of machine mining tended to produce more

---

[1] For the mechanization of coal-cutting, see *Reid Report*, 4–11; *RCSM* 134; R. Shepherd and A. G. Withers, *Mechanised Cutting and Loading of Coal* (1960); articles in *ICTR* 159 (8 July 1949) and 170 (8 Apr. 1955), and *The Mining Engineer* No. 83 (Aug. 1967); *CYB* 1947, 521. Pneumatic picks were never very important in Britain, especially when compared with continental practice.

[2] *Samuel Appendices*, Appendix 18, Tables 10 and 11.

'round' coal, which was more useful for heat raising, less useful for carbonization, and higher priced.[1]

Such differences did not always run in the same direction, and from the late 1920s there were extraordinarily contrasting rates of change in the use of machines: between 1927 and 1929, the proportion of coal mechanically cut rose from 56 to 80 per cent; but in Lancashire it increased from 16 to 74 per cent, in South Yorkshire from 11 to 68 per cent, and in North Derbyshire and Nottinghamshire from 22 to 82 per cent. Only South Wales seriously lagged (cutting only just over a quarter of its coal mechanically in 1939), and Durham was the only other major field where the proportion fell below 50 per cent. In spite of geological differences, some of the most striking of the earlier gaps were closed. By the late 1930s there was a large-scale acceptance of machine mining on a very broad geographical front—although the increase in the use of cutters tended to be achieved by their extension *within* mines rather than by the widespread conversion of hand-getting mines to machine cutting. The generality of the change implies that there were indeed, broad economic advantages, or hopes, which induced owners and engineers to pursue this line of technical change after the mid-1920s.[2]

This was certainly the case with the other and interdependent aspect of the 'new' system of machine mining with longwall faces: the use of conveyors. The great majority of conveyors were introduced along the coalface, to reduce the grinding physical effort of shifting the coal (often by brute force in an atrocious environment) to the nearest main 'gate' where it could be loaded into tubs for transport to the shaft bottom. At the same time, face conveyors, precisely because they substituted for human effort, increased the length of face which could 'feed' one collecting point for the coal—i.e. it reduced the number of roads or gates which had to be constructed to the face. Conveyors were also advantageous both in thin seams, where the difficulties were especially great, and thick seams where they enabled cutters to be used to their full capacity by removing the full 'web' of coal without choking the supply line.[3]

Even more than mechanical cutting, the mechanization of face conveying was a product of interwar technological diffusion. Indeed, its

---

[1] For a discussion of the pace of introduction of mechanized cutting (which is judged to have been primarily determined by local geological conditions and technical adaptations) see Greasley 1982, 246–68.

[2] For a detailed statistical and analytical discussion, see Greasley 1979.

[3] *Final Report of the Departmental Committee Appointed to Inquire into the Probable Economic Effects of a Limit of Eight Hours to the Working Day of Coal Miners*, Pt. II (*PP* 1907 XIV) Q 17050; *RCSM* 134.

acceptance was particularly marked from 1927, when the full realization of Britain's deteriorating competitive condition coincided with the exhaustion of the strategy of wage reductions. Between 1927 and 1939 the number of face conveyors almost trebled (from 2,078 to 5,859) and the proportion of output carried on them rose sharply—from about 12 to 58 per cent.[1] The diffusion of conveyors was also more *extensive* than that of cutters, for whereas new cutters tended to be adopted in mines which already had experience of their use and to generate a demand for face conveyors, the face conveyors were also adopted in new situations and could be profitably used in association with hand-cutting.[2]

What came to be known as the 'conventional' system of mining (the use of machines to undercut and convey the coal, the use of explosives and hand tools to get and load it)[3] promised a significant decrease in the need for animal and human effort at a critical moment in the history of the industry. It was also associated with the use of electricity for ancillary tasks.[4] But, extensive as mechanization was, it resulted in a relatively small effect on overall labour productivity: between 1927 and 1939 output per manshift in the mines rose by a mere 11 per cent (face OMS rose by 16 per cent). Nor was there any encouraging pattern in the different districts. Admittedly, North Derbyshire & Nottinghamshire experienced a substantial rise in the degree of mechanization and OMS. But in the export areas there was only a tiny increase (Durham, South Wales) or even a decrease (Scotland) of OMS at the face, and there were other inconsistencies.[5] More complex measures of face productivity also confirm that mechanization was associated with only a modest increase

---

[1] *Reid Report*, 8, 11.

[2] Hence in 1939 South Wales was relatively unmechanized in terms of cutting, but employed face conveyors for almost half its output: Table 9.6; and *Reid Report*, 11. The important fields which used face conveyors to an extent significantly below the national average (Durham with 27% of its output, West Yorkshire with 39%, Northumberland with 45%, and South Wales with 48%) tended to be those with old, and presumably difficult, workings. With the exception of Northumberland, those districts which experienced the most dramatic increase in machine cutting (Lancashire, South Yorkshire, North Derbyshire & Nottinghamshire) also attained very high levels of face conveying.

[3] Power-loading and cutter-loading were still at their experimental stages in the 1930s, although the firm of Meco-Moore had successfully devised a cutter-loader. In 1945 only 2% of output was power-loaded: *The Mining Engineer* No. 83 (Aug. 1967), 783. For power-loaders, see below, ch. 12, sect. iii.

[4] Between 1912 and 1937 the electrical horsepower used in British mines rose from just over 500,000 to almost 2.2 million—an increase of some 1.6 million hp, of which cutting and conveying accounted for 227,000, but haulage, ventilation, and pumping over 700,000 (Nelson 1939, 602). The number of ponies working underground fell from 73,000 in 1913 to 33,000 in 1937 (Nelson 1939, 602).

[5] *Reid Report*, 9–10.

in efficiency.[1] This was no doubt because other considerations (physical conditions, the length of the underground shift, work intensity) were of greater importance. But it also derived from the fact that mechanization at the face, alone and in the form which it took, was probably insufficient to transform the efficiency of the mining system as a whole. As with all partial innovations within a complex system, it exposed bottlenecks elsewhere which prevented the full realization of its productive potential.

This was the line taken by the Reid Committee in its familiar appraisal of the industry's technical position in the winter of 1944-5. It attributed the relatively poor results of interwar mechanization to two main deficiencies: the neglect of the rest of the operations of mining and particularly of the haulage systems (which were extravagant of manpower), and the failure to appreciate that mechanization requires properly trained men and officials to get the best results.[2] Certainly, there is little interwar evidence either of innovations in haulage systems or of effective training and reorientation programmes, and to that extent the potential benefits of mechanization would be all too easily dissipated—most obviously by inefficient operations in other parts of the mine, but perhaps most poignantly in the effects of machine mining on the work, skills, and morale of the labour force. For the most immediate consequence of the new systems was their repercussions for the organization of labour and the working systems of face mining.[3]

These repercussions affected the quality, organization and supervision of underground work in ways which led to serious complaints about the neglect of 'man management' and the calibre of administration. Such complaints were part of a general dissatisfaction with the quality of entrepreneurial and managerial skills in coalmining. Yet they related to an area—mechanization and the introduction of new working practices—where the coalowners *had* been faintly energetic and even enterprising, even if they had achieved less than their American or continental counterparts.[4] A more sustained and serious criticism of businessmen in mining was that they failed to transform the *structure* of the industry. This question will be considered in the next section.

---

[1] Greasley 1979.

[2] *Reid Report*, 5-6. The Committee pointed out that when power-loaders were more extensively introduced during the War the increased output at the face immediately exposed the inadequacy of underground transport systems.   [3] Below, ch. 10, sect. i.

[4] In 1929 some 28% of British coal was mechanically cut, compared with 75% of American and 91% in the Ruhr. By 1936, after a distinct increase in the British percentage, the figures were 55%, 79%, and 97% (International Labour Office 1938, I, 196).

iii. Business performance and entrepreneurial quality

Throughout the interwar years the limited extent of structural change in coalmining was interpreted as a weakness attributable to the entrepreneurial failings of the owners—who were compared unfavourably with their rivals abroad. It seemed indisputable that the leading continental countries had benefited from the scale, concentration, and restructuring at which their postwar policies had aimed with a determined vigour. In the Ruhr in the mid-1920s, for example, there was 'a ruthless concentration of production effort irrespective of ... social consequences', so that by 1926, 20 undertakings controlled 90 per cent of the 100 million tons of output, and there were merely 237 mines. By 1938 output had risen and the number of mines fallen to 161. *Within* their diminishing number, there was a dramatic reduction in the number of 'working places' in the Ruhr. Between 1925 and 1936 output per manshift underground rose by 86 per cent.[1] In comparison with such trends, the lethargic amendment of the structure of the British coal industry was bound to seem extraordinarily cautious.

Of course, considered in isolation, neither the degree of structural concentration nor the extent of mechanization is an unambiguous indication of economic efficiency. Like all selective comparisons this one was potentially misleading. Thus, the structure of the American industry was more fragmented than the British; the fearsomely competitive Polish industry in the 1920s was no more mechanized;[2] and in certain British coalfields a high degree of concentration *had* been achieved. More than this, no single pattern of industrial organization and techniques is universally appropriate to national circumstances. Variations of costs, geography, geology, and institutions between countries may render large differences in business structures and technology perfectly 'rational'. Nevertheless, the performance of the British coal industry for most of the interwar years *did* appear lamentably disappointing. Other than for brief periods of artificial shortages overseas (as happened in 1918–20 or 1923–4), it could not sustain its export competitiveness; for much of the time it seemed incapable of providing continuous employment or an adequate return to the capital and labour invested in it; and (perhaps the most telling point) its labour productivity grew with painful slowness, and at a rate substantially below that of all other leading producers.[3]

---

[1] *Reid Report*, 16–18. For the much greater degree of industrial concentration on the continent, see Political & Economic Planning 1936, 154.

[2] International Labour Office 1938, I, 222; Political & Economic Planning 1936, 154.

[See opposite page for n. 3]

Admittedly, all this is to accept at their face value the indicators of success (especially overall output per manshift) quoted by contemporaries. A more subtle attempt to assess productivity, by measuring output per man-*hour* at the face, and also the total (combined) productivity of labour and capital at the coalface, results in a rather better picture of a reasonable growth in productivity. From this viewpoint, the coal industry's productivity performance was comparable to many other sectors of the economy in the period.[2] There are, however, problems relating to the adequacy of the data and calculations used in such exercises, and the returns to the factors were hardly munificent.

An alternative measure of the entrepreneurial performance of the coalowners is provided by its profit record.[2] In approaching this question, however, it must be emphasized that some of the most important determinants of variations in the profitability of coalmining were rarely within the control of coalowners: complex geological variety, the sharp fluctuations in prices in the 1920s, the weakness of export prices in the 1930s, wage agreements and hours legislation which introduced a rigidity into labour costs, and differences in the quality and trends of different markets.

The most comprehensive indicators of profitability were the figures of 'credit' and 'debit' per ton derived from the ascertainments of proceeds and costs under the wage agreement of 1921 and its successors. Quite apart from the regional variations, which reduce the utility of national averages, the figures themselves were open to criticism because of accounting conventions which might underestimate profits by stipulating excessively low transfer prices within composite enterprises. Further, costs might be unduly inflated since business records did not always ensure that expenditure on capital account (e.g. labour costs to develop headings or a new face) was not charged to revenue or current account.[3]

[3] In 1913–38 output per manshift in Britain grew by 13%. The figures for the United States (where the length of the shift was drastically reduced), Belgium, Poland, the Ruhr, and the Netherlands were: 36%, 40%, 59%, 64%, and 101% (*Reid Report*, 141).

[1] Greasley, 'Productivity and Factor Returns'.

[2] Since it is in principle possible to make high profits when productivity is low (and vice versa) profitability was not necessarily a good indication of efficiency. However, the wage agreements of the coal industry (basic and minimum wages, the division of proceeds above basic costs) ensured that profits were related to physical productivity and the scope for sales at reasonable prices. In any case, profits, or the prospects of profits, clearly shaped investment policies and determined the level of activity (and therefore employment) in the industry.

[3] On the other side, the owners pointed out that their profits were exaggerated because the official ascertainments did not take account of interest charges and some other costs. For these points see above, 234–5.

There is, unfortunately, no way of allowing for these drawbacks to the published data. Nor is it possible to derive an acceptable measure of capital invested in the industry, against which profits could be set so as to estimate a return on capital. Indeed, given the ambiguous distinction between 'production' and 'development' as far as miners' work is concerned, the very concept of capital investment is indeterminate.[1] Considering only plant and machinery, the Mining Association of Great Britain estimated that some £97.5 million had been invested in the period 1919–38. In the 1930s the nominal amount invested annually (about £3.09 million) had fallen by almost 60 per cent of its level in 1919–25 (about £7.57 m.).[2]

Fortunately, the suspect conceptual basis of the industry's profit statistics matters very little—at least in the aggregate. For it is most unlikely that any feasible adjustment to compensate for misleading accounting conventions could *significantly* alter the general picture of very low or negative profits (see Table 9.7). In the period 1920–38 average profits per ton fell below the 1913 level in all but two years, were minuscule (under 6*d.*) for six years, and disappeared entirely for five. Even allowing for changes in general wholesale prices, the 'real' value of profits fell below that of 1913 in all but six years. Given the fall in output, *total* profits also slumped disastrously. After 1920, with the exceptions of 1923–4 and 1936–8 the industry's commercial record was abysmal.[3]

Of course, as has already been suggested, the picture is considerably more complicated when viewed from the perspective of the different

[1] This is because so much 'investment' took the form of underground developments using labour and techniques identical with that employed to produce the coal on a day-to-day basis. Above, 234 n.

[2] POWE 22/180 (11 Jan. 1945). All figures exclude replacements and renewals due to normal wear and tear and are adjusted to allow for the fact that not all pits were surveyed. The data for 1919–25 were gathered by the Samuel Commission: *Samuel Appendices*, Appendix 26. Those for 1929–38 resulted from a survey by the MAGB, for which 'collieries were instructed to exclude expenditure at new collieries on sinking, opening out, and equipment during the development period; but to include such expenditure as that in connection with the opening out of a new seam to replace output from a seam to be abandoned, or the sinking of a new shaft at an existing pit to shorten travel time underground.' Expenditure for 1925–8 was estimated from the average rate of the other two periods. 'Other capital expenditure' was estimated at about £9.5 million in 1929–38 (over half of it on surface works), as against £31 million on plant and machinery. The memorandum in POWE 22/180 appears to underestimate investment in that there is no figure for 'other capital expenditure' (i.e. other than plant and machinery) in the Samuel estimate for 1919–25.

[3] A comparison of gross profits in coalmining and in manufacturing industry (see Hart 1965, I, 21) not only shows that profits in manufacturing industry never fell below 50% of their 1920 level (for all but five years they ranged between 75% and 120% of the figure), but also indicates that in virtually every year coalmining did substantially less well, compared to 1920, than manufacturing.

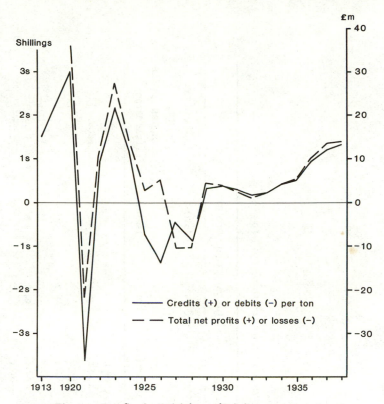

Fig. 9.1. Profits in British coalmining, 1913–1938

regions, and even more varied when individual firms are considered. Thus, national averages were considerably reduced by the very low profits of the export districts (especially in the North-East and South-West) after the artificial booms of 1919–20 and 1923. Admittedly, the Scottish industry, although it lost money fairly steadily between 1927 and 1933, found better markets (in part at home) in the late 1930s, and was therefore able to return a much better profit level: whereas between 1930 and 1932 the proportion of Scottish output produced at a profit tumbled from 52 to 31 per cent, it rose to 73 per cent in 1934 and exceeded 84 per cent from 1935 until the War. But in Durham colliery undertakings lost money for seven out of the nine years 1927–35, and in the remaining two earned a negligible 4d. or so per ton.

Northumberland did almost as badly. And South Wales had a virtually unmitigated record of losses and negligible profitability: between 1924 and 1938 there was only one year in which its profits

Table 9.7. *Profits in British coalmining 1913–1938*

	(i) Credits (debits) per ton			(ii) Aggregate profits		
	Amounts	Index of credits in constant prices[a]		Net	Gross	Index of net profits in constant prices[a]
	s. d.	1913=100	1920=100	(£ m.)	(£ m.)	(1920=100)
1913	1 6	100.0	64.6			
1920	2 11¾	154.8	100.0	36.1	47.6	100.0
1921	−3 7½ᵇ	−294.0	−189.9	−21.8ᶜ	−17.9ᶜ	−94.2
1922	0 11½	96.4	62.3	10.9	20.1	58.4
1923	2 2	226.0	146.0	27.7	39.7	148.4
1924	1 2	122.3	72.5	14.2	24.4	72.6
1925	−0 8¾ᵇ	−72.0	−46.5	2.9ᶜ	11.2ᶜ	15.4
1926[d]	−1 4¼ᵇ	−146.1	−94.4	5.1ᶜ	9.6ᶜ	29.3
1927	−0 5¼	−49.4	−31.9	−10.3	−3.1	−61.8

1928	—0 10¼	—97.2	—62.8	—10.1	—2.9	—61.3
1919	0 4	39.0	25.2	4.4	14.0	27.5
1930	0 4½	50.1	32.4	3.9	13.3	27.8
1931	0 3½	44.7	28.9	2.7	12.2	22.1
1932	0 2	26.2	16.9	1.5	11.0	12.7
1933	0 2¾	36.4	23.5	2.2	11.7	18.6
1934	0 5	63.9	41.3	4.3	14.4	35.1
1935	0 6¼	80.0	52.2	5.4	16.0	44.8
1936	0 11½	135.8	87.7	10.1	21.2	76.3
1937	1 2¾	151.1	97.6	13.8	23.2	90.3
1938	1 4	176.0	113.7	14.0	24.8	98.5

[a] Amounts deflated by Board of Trade Wholesale Price Index: Mitchell, *Abstract*, 477.
[b] Before adjustment by government subsidy.
[c] Includes subsidy.
[d] 4 months.

Sources:

(i) *CYB* 1932, 598; *ARSM*, various years. After payment of royalties, depreciation, changes, etc.
(ii) P. E. Hart, *Studies in Profit, Business Savings and Investment in the UK, 1920–1962* I (1965), 60, 64. Net profits include losses; gross profits include royalty payments and depreciation, and exclude losses.

exceeded 1 s. per ton, and in the twelve years 1927–38 there were six of losses, four when profits were 2 d. per ton or less, and another two (1937–8 when the industry as a whole was doing quite well) when they stood at a mere 5 d. In the 1930s there were five years when more than 55 per cent of the South Wales output was produced at a loss, and seven when the figure exceeded 33 per cent. No wonder that, at the end of the period, the Monmouthshire & South Wales Coal Owners' Association undertook almost desperate surveys of the regional industry's commercial collapse.[1]

On the other hand, some of the most important inland fields performed adequately or well. Thus, the Midlands generally had a fairly good profits record in the early 1920s, and in the richest areas (South Yorkshire, Nottinghamshire, North Derbyshire) aggregate losses occurred only in the very trough of 1927–8. Moreover, in Nottinghamshire, sustained by the new productive developments of the 1920s, average profits per ton were in excess of 1 s. for every year from 1931. Warwickshire did even better—earning 1 s. 10 d. or more per ton in each of seven years during 1930–8. In the Midlands, even in the worst years of the 1930s (1931–2) the great bulk of output was produced at a profit, and from 1933 more than 80 per cent, and frequently more than 90 per cent, of production came from collieries which made profits.

As far as individual colliery undertakings are concerned there are no representative indicators of their commercial performance—partly because of their number and variety, partly because of the obscurities of published accounts, and partly because many firms (and not always the least significant) retained their status as private companies and therefore divulged little information on their profits. Nevertheless, using annual dividends on ordinary shares as indices of profitability (Table 9.8), and examining an arbitrary (rather than a random) small selection of large undertakings, various characteristics, made familiar by other data, are apparent.

First, there was a tendency to abrupt fluctuations (these are even more marked in the underlying figures of trading profits—variations in which were somewhat smoothed out by policy with regard to dividends and reserves). Second, regional contrasts are very marked. The worst

[1] These and the following figures of profits per ton on a district basis are taken from the *ARSM* for various years and (for the 1930s) from the geographically more detailed summaries in SRO CB/3/1934 and printed *Statistical Summaries of the Costs of Production. Proceeds and Profits of the Coal Mining Industry during the years 1930 to 1945* by Peat, Marwick, Mitchell & Co. (British Coal Library).

performances came from firms in South Wales and the North-East where dependence on exports and, even more tellingly, on links with the heavy iron and steel industry, dragged down profits, brought enterprises to the verge of bankruptcy, and led to extensive writing-down of capital.[1] Dividends were passed for years in succession. Among the most parlous examples were Amalgamated Anthracite, Cambrian Collieries and its successor, Welsh Associated Collieries, the Consett Iron Co., Dorman Long and Co., Ebbw Vale Steel, Iron & Coal Co., Pease & Partners, and Powell Duffryn Associated Collieries. Similarly, the recovery of heavy industry in the North-East during the rearmament boom at the end of the 1930s is also exemplified in the dividend payments of such firms as Consett, Dorman Long, Pease and Partners. Other firms in these districts—Ocean Coal & Wilsons in South Wales for example, or Ashington in Northumberland—fended off the worst blasts of depression, although their profits still fell drastically.

In the other principal export region, Scotland, the figures of dividends (like those of district profits per ton) indicate a more successful response to adversity. The Fife Coal Company was the outstanding example here (its dividend never fell below 3 per cent, and by 1934–8 it averaged virtually 10 per cent), but the good record of Scottish coalmining in the late 1930s was also reflected in the high dividends of the new merger of Bairds & Dalmellington. The most consistently profitable groups of firms, however, were those with mines in Yorkshire and the Midlands. Even in the older areas of Yorkshire, compact and well-organized enterprises like Airedale Collieries and Henry Briggs, Son & Co. Ltd. maintained their profits and dividends well. But perhaps the most interesting business achievements were those of companies with extensive interests in South Yorkshire, Nottinghamshire, and North Derbyshire—companies like Bolsover Colliery Co., Butterley Co., Sheepbridge Coal & Iron Co., and Staveley Coal & Iron Co.

These relatively good results were, however, clearly exceptional. The industry's mixed experience embraced a preponderance of loss-making or barely profitable enterprises. In spite of the occasional spectacular exception, the numerous colliery undertakings of the interwar period exemplified inadequate achievement, and within the distribution the long 'tail' of unprofitability demonstrated beyond doubt the excess capacity which persistently depressed the coalmining industry. The unresolved issue which dominated discussion was whether those inadequacies were also due to entrepreneurial failings.

[1] Neuman 1934, 64–6.

Table 9.8. *Dividends on ordinary shares: selected colliery companies, 1913-1939 (%)*

Years[a]	A	B	C	D	E	F	G	H	I	J	K	L	M	N	O	P	Q	R
1913					20		10	60	8½	10	27½		12	20[b]	20	25[b]	7	
1920				20	10	10	10	12½	10[b]	5	17½[b]	12[b]	14	20	10	11¼	10	
1921				13	7½	8⅓	2½	10	5	nil	10	7	5	10		10	4	
1922	10			3½	10	11⅔	nil	4	nil	nil	12½[b]	6	6	7½	6	7½	4	
1923	10			16	15[b]	15	nil	7½	nil	nil	20	7	8	12½	7½	7½[b]	5½	
1924	7½	10[b]		14	15	12½	nil	2½	nil	nil	10	7½	1½	10	7½	7½[b]	4	
1925	5	7½		8	10	6⅔[b]	nil	nil	nil	nil	10	8	nil	6	5	7½	nil	
1926	5	nil[b]		15	10	6⅔[b]	nil	nil	nil	nil	5	5	nil	2½	2½	5	nil	
1927	2½	nil		6½	10	5	nil	nil	nil	nil	5	5	nil	nil	7½	7½	nil	
1928	5	nil		1½	7½	2½	nil	nil	nil	nil	3	nil	nil	nil	2½	5	nil	
1929	5	nil		3¾	10	5		nil	nil	nil	8	5	nil	nil	2½	5	nil	3¾
1930	5	nil		2½	7½	5		nil	nil	nil	6	4	nil	nil	5	6	nil	2½
1931	5	nil		7	7½	5½		nil	nil	nil	3	2	nil	nil		6	nil	nil
1932	5	nil	3	7½	7½	5		nil	nil	nil	3	nil	nil	nil	5	5	nil	nil

Year	A	B	C	D	E	F	G	H	I	J	K	L	M	N	O	P	Q	R
1933	7½	nil	3	7	7½	5	nil	nil	nil	5	3	nil	6½	5	5	nil	nil	
1934	7½	nil	6	8	7½	5	nil	nil	nil	7½	2	nil	6	5	6½	nil	2	
1935	7½	nil	8	9	7½	6½	nil	nil	nil	7½	nil	nil	6	6¼	8	2	4	
1936	10	nil	12½	9b	7½	8	7½	6	nil	10	2	5	7	10	9	2¾	5	
1937	10	nil	16	10b	7½b	8	10	10	10	12½	3½	10	7½	10	10b	3½	5½	
1938	7½b	nil	16	10b	7½	6½	7½	10	10	11	1½	10		12½	11	2½	7½	
1939	8	nil	16	10b	7½b	10½	7½	10	10	9	5	10		12½	10	3	7½	

A: Airedale Collieries Ltd.
B: Amalgamated Anthracite Collieries Ltd.
C: Bairds & Dalmellington Ltd.
D: Bolsover Colliery Co. Ltd.
E: H. Briggs, Son & Co. Ltd.
F: Butterley Co. Ltd.

G: Cambrian Collieries Ltd.
H: Consett Iron Co. Ltd.
I: Dorman Long & Co.
J: Ebbw Vale Steel Iron & Coal Co.
K: Fife Coal Co. Ltd.
L: Ocean Coal & Wilsons

M: Pease & Partners Ltd.
N: Powell Duffryn Steam Coal Co.
O: Sheepbridge Coal & Iron Co.
P: Staveley Coal & Iron Co.
Q: Wigan Coal & Iron Co.
R: Yorkshire Amalgamated Collieries

[a] Where accounts refer to the year ending March, April, or May, the year indicated in the Table is the previous one. E.g. year to 30 April 1922 is given as 1921. Data ignore changes in Capitalization.
[b] Indicates bonus in addition to indicated dividend.

Source: Stock Exchange Year Book, various years.

Certainly, the coal industry was *perceived* as a failure in nearly all the major commentaries on its record and position in the 1920s and 1930s. Even the owners' representatives, while remaining adamant that the explanation lay in political interference or trade union power or unfair competition from overseas, could hardly deny the industry's economic plight. But the keenest critiques came in the context of the dense sequence of inquiries into the industry's affairs—beginning with the Coal Mining Organisation Committee of 1915, continuing with the Sankey Commission (1919), the Buckmaster, Macmillan, and Samuel Inquiries of 1925–6, multitudinous official discussions of the late 1920s and 1930s, the feverish investigations of wartime, and culminating with the Reid Committee of 1944–5.[1]

Again and again the owners were attacked for either neglecting investment or constructing 'equipment that would last 100 years and be obsolete in ten', and for seeing 'no need for a change in their methods'.[2] They were accused of a persistent conservatism in the face of technical, organizational, and market pressures, and (by the 1930s) of not increasing efficiency as a quid pro quo for the powers of self-regulation and market control delegated to them by legislative and administrative innovation. Ultimately, even within the MAGB (where for much of the period self-criticism by deviant owners was muted and peripheral), senior voices were raised to acknowledge that instances of individual success and efficiency were not enough. Some form of cooperative action was needed to present the industry as 'definitely self-supporting'.[3]

Inevitably, the failure of the industry was attributed to a failure of its entrepreneurs. Given the existence of structures, organizations, and techniques (whether in a few places in Britain or in other countries) which seemed to be superior to those which characterized the British industry generally, it was natural, if not always logical, to conclude that obstinacy, or poverty of imagination and business ability, was preventing British coalowners from adopting them. As so often happens, dissatisfaction with an institution focused critical attention on the people who ran it. Nor was their situation helped by the coalowners' unyielding and hostile response to criticisms, and to collateral controversies concerning industrial relations and public policy. Thus, after the owners'

---

[1] In addition to the official Inquiries listed in the text, and press comment, see Lubin & Everett 1927; Clay 1929; Smart 1930; Neuman 1934; Political & Economic Planning 1936.

[2] Lubin & Everett 1927, 152, 159.

[3] Sir Adam Nimmo in *MAGB* 1933, 10–11.

almost contemptuous rejection of criticism before the Samuel Commission, the *Sunday Observer* took the greatest exception to their apparent complacency. The MAGB's 'plan' (no change in business behaviour, extensive cuts in wages and employment), the newspaper argued, 'could not have been much more perfunctory and unconvincing if it had been the plan of men who had washed their hands of the business and were waiting to be bought out'.[1] The inevitable result was political and public exasperation, and a predictable reinforcement of the view that they were, indeed, to blame for their own situation and that of their employees.[2]

The interwar debate about the quality of business skills in the industry focused largely on the issue of mergers. But it was frequently handicapped by a lack of persuasive empirical evidence as to whether the average productivity of coalmining would have been substantially improved by a restructuring of the industry into much larger units of production and ownership. Most of the argument on either side rested on assertion and appeals to general principle. The one systematic and empirically detailed attempt to assess the issue at the time was made by the Samuel Commission in 1925–6. It concluded that the industry *could* attain greater economies by further industrial concentration, and this conclusion was generally very influential.

The crucial statistics adduced by the Samuel Inquiry correlated the size of undertakings with labour productivity (output per manshift) and with profits per ton. And they certainly established a presumption in favour of the existence of scale economies. However, they unavoidably neglected the degree of capital investment associated with larger firms (this was an important omission, since if bigger companies invested proportionately more in machinery, the output per *man* shift and the profit per *ton*, would not have been very accurate indicators of efficiency or profitability). Moreover, the statistical differences between firms of different sizes were not always very great, and for some periods were by no means all indications of scale economies. Further, as the Samuel Commissioners themselves acknowledged, the efficiency and profits of many small firms were impressive, and of many large firms inadequate. Finally, the Commission could not take account of the general costs of restructuring the industry—costs which would necessarily have reduced the returns to the resulting more highly concentrated structure.[3]

[1] *Sunday Observer* 17 Jan. 1926, quoted in Lubin & Everett 1927, 270n.

[2] See, for example, the extreme criticism by Sir Ernest Gowers, Chairman of the Coal Mines Reorganisation Commission, in 1935: above, 348.

[3] For the Samuel Commission, and contemporary discussion of scale economies, see above, ch. 6, sect. iii.

Nevertheless, the Samuel Commission's analysis was certainly the best available, and its statistical exercise reinforced existing views that coalmining could, indeed, have attained a higher level of productivity if the mines or the firms had been bigger. Such a hypothesis outweighed the insistent assertions on the part of the owners, who argued that there was little to be gained from much more extensive reorganization; that inter-district comparisons were meaningless since natural and historical conditions varied so much between regions; and that there were fairly rigid managerial limits to the scale at which pits or firms could be run.[1] In fact the issue was clouded by the frequent failure to distinguish between the presumed advantages of larger mines and those of larger colliery undertakings.[2] In practice, of course, it was possible for economies to be attainable in either sphere, or both, although the formal distinction was extremely important in light of the possibility (exemplified in Scotland and to a lesser extent in South Wales) of relatively small-scale mines being grouped into relatively large-scale (i.e. multimine) concerns.

The more recent application of econometric techniques has also tended to confirm the existence of economies of scale (at least in terms of the size of mines, for which better data are available)—although in this instance it also indicates that mechanization was even more important than size as a determinant of varying productivity levels between mines.[3] Deficiencies in the data mean that the issue cannot be said to be definitely resolved,[4] but certainly the balance of evidence indicates that as mines and firms grew larger their efficiency also grew, and that that

[1] *Samuel Evidence* QQ 4768 ff.; 5,658 ff.; 15781 ff.

[2] Using profitability as its criterion, and excluding the South Yorkshire–North Derbyshire–Nottinghamshire field (where the largest firms were the most profitable) the *Colliery Guardian* argued that in 1935 the most effective operations were those of undertakings producing between 500,000 and 1 million tons. Above that, profit per ton decreased with size: 'these figures certainly support the view that there are limits beyond which it is impossible to secure increased efficiency by means of mergers. Those limits begin to appear when the functions of good management become strained, or out of tune, and they may vary in different cases.' (*CG* 5 June 1936, 1070–1.) Also see C. P. Markham's evidence to the Samuel Commission: *Samuel Evidence*, QQ 11200 ff.

[3] Evans and Fine, 'Economies of Scale in the British Inter-War Coal Industry' (unpublished). However, Greasley's measures suggest that mechanization was only a 'minor innovation' ('Productivity and Factor Returns'). Certainly (as the Reid Committee also pointed out) there was no simple relationship—in Britain or abroad—between increasing mechanization and increasing productivity.

[4] Thus, Fine and Evans use the average mine size as an index of scale, but this neglects the distribution of mines of different sizes. Further, they are not able to relate changes in the average size of mines to changes in the size of the firms owning those mines, and it may be that the latter explains much of the improvement in the efficiency.

increase was in part attributable to the increase in the scale of their operations, which facilitated a spreading of overheads, specialization of skills and services, the more economical application of resources, etc.

However, as the authors of this modern analysis appreciate, the fact that productivity rose as mines grew larger, does not mean that owners were necessarily 'irrational' in not proceeding faster with larger-scale operations. For one thing, just as there were undoubtedly administrative limits to the efficiency of really giant combinations, so there appear to have been organizational and marginal limits to the rapid and efficient growth of mergers. In other words, it was one thing to envisage an alternative and more productive system of larger units (whether mines or firms); but quite another to attain it speedily and without disproportionate cost.[1] At a more general level, too, there were sound economic and business reasons why coalowners should have been reluctant to pursue vigorous policies of business growth. But before examining these, it is necessary to specify more exactly how the economies of scale might have been attained.

The discussion of the coal industry's structure had commenced on the basis of an orthodox definition of the economies of scale. In fact, however, by the late 1920s the issue was beginning to shift away from the possibility of increasing productivity by organizing *larger* mines or firms, to the need to reduce unit costs by concentrating production so as to make more effective use of the best *existing* capacity or reduce cost by *eliminating* capacity. Between 1913 and 1927, capacity had grown by 10 per cent, but demand had fallen by a similar percentage, and the industry was clearly too large in relation to its market.[2] The problem of excess capacity continued into the 1930s, reinforced by the operation of the market quotas deployed in the selling scheme of the 1930 Act. Firms like Powell Duffryn (which, in the ten years after 1928, reduced the number of mines from 86 to 49 while maintaining its output of coal)[3] began to reduce capacity. But the process was painfully slow, and in the main there was relatively little of this form of reorganization. In the mid-1930s large and otherwise effective groups like the Wearmouth

---

[1] Above, 266–7.

[2] Jones 1929, 158; Clay 1929, 178. *Industrial Transference Board Report*, Cmd. 3156. 1928. In its review of the coal trade in 1928 the *Colliery Guardian* (4 Jan. 1929, 50) argued that the industry was capable of producing 300 million tons annually, but 'to do this over 75 million tons must be exported, and we may search in vain for an outlet'.

[3] POWE 25/195. A similar policy was pursued in such large Scottish concerns as the Fife Coal Co. and Bairds & Dalmellington.

Coal Co., Powell Duffryn, and Yorkshire Amalgamated Collieries were still operating well below their capacity.[1]

In fact, coalowners were not much attracted by systematic amalgamation—whether as a device to enlarge the scale of production or as a means of concentrating production through 'private rationalization'. Improvements in productivity could rarely be attained by relatively *costless* mergers. Unless amalgamations were designed simply to close down mines (in which case it still occasioned high costs to the purchaser, with poor prospects of a commensurate return), they were merely one aspect of an elaborate, and potentially exceedingly expensive, process of reorganization and re-equipping which was necessary if unit costs were to be reduced and corporate unifications were to be a success. This was especially so with respect to expansion or the increased use of capacity (i.e. positive 'economies of scale').

Mines could not be enlarged simply by exchanging or buying shares: that needed capital investment and effort, the reorganization of underground layouts and haulage systems, the levelling of roadways, and the intensification and administrative pursuit of mechanization. By the same token, formal changes in corporate entities made little direct contribution to efficiency. Indeed, by confusing lines of managerial authority or multiplying the number of directors, they might even reduce it. Productivity was a function of extensive, prolonged, and costly effort. At the level of individual corporate grouping which actually pursued it through mergers and increased scale of operations, such lessons of experience were clear. At the level of the industry as a whole, however, it was not until the 1940s that there was widespread appreciation of the financial and administrative implications of the fact that large-scale operations had to be integrated with the massive overhaul of techniques and internal organizations.[2]

It was easy, then, to *envisage* a restructured and better integrated industry, consisting of larger, better capitalized mines and companies using up-to-date machinery. But this did not necessarily mean that such a system, even if the money and will had been available to introduce it in

[1] Ivor Thomas, 'The Coal Mines Reorganisation Commission', in Robson 1937, 218–19. Thomas reported an estimate that in 1935 full-capacity operation would have reduced costs by 1 s. per ton (about 8% of the prevailing pithead price).

[2] The classic statement of this case occurred in the Reid Committee's *Report* (*Report of the Technical Advisory Committee on Coal Mining, March 14 1945*: Cmd. 6610. 1945). But it was also fully acknowledged by the coalowners in 1944–5, and is implied in the MAGB's own 'Foot Plan' for postwar reorganization (below, ch. 13, sect. iv–v). Earlier commentators seem to have underestimated the extent of new investment needed.

a wholesale fashion, could have produced results sufficiently remunerative to justify the necessary expenditures. And even if they could, it did not follow that the sole obstacle to their introduction was entrepreneurial conservatism or irrationality.

Changes of the sort generally envisaged by the industry's critics, might, in practice, have been impeded at various levels other than that of business lethargy. First, nature and history had combined to endow Britain in the 1920s with a coal industry which was widely scattered, produced a variety of products for a variety of markets, and was dominated by relatively old mines. (In 1925 about half the work-force was employed in mines more than 40 years old.)[1] These mines had been developed (in terms of the size of shafts and roadways, underground layout, haulage systems, and the like) in ways appropriate to a smaller scale of operations and a different technology from that envisaged by enthusiasts for 'progressive' change. In retrospect, it is this fact that makes any comparison of the British industry with the quite differently placed firms of, say, the Ruhr, extraordinarily simplistic. No British district, let alone the industry as a whole, illustrated the same degree of homogeneity of product (in the German case, the production of coal for coking) or the same inherited commitment to large pits, as did the Ruhr.

More generally, however, genuine transformations of industrial structures in British coalmining (as distinct from mere corporate juggling) would have necessitated very extensive capital expenditure programmes—first, to acquire smaller or less efficient mines and firms; second, to concentrate, streamline, and modernize production. As a result, the question of why the British coalowners did not reorganize their industry is, or should be, less concerned with psychological inclinations or 'the entrepreneurial spirit' than with the incentives and inhibitions to undertake a large administrative effort and very substantial investment in the pursuit of results which were bound to seem uncertain.

One area of obvious difficulty lay in the distinctive 'institutional' context within which British coalowners found themselves operating. This can be considered from four viewpoints: the pattern of control of collieries, the pattern of mineral ownership, the pattern of industrial relations and wage systems, and the pattern of government policy.

First, the industry was dominated by enterprises far more akin to private than to public, managerial institutions. There were, of course, instances of 'modern' and non-insular corporations (especially where

[1] *CYB* 1947, 512.

the colliery enterprise was closely integrated with metallurgical production).[1] Nevertheless even large-scale colliery businesses were
frequently run by private companies in the close possession of a small
group or even a single family. Thus, Lambton, Hetton, & Joicey in
Durham, and the Butterley Company in the Midlands, both had Boards
of Directors drawn entirely from one family, and there were other
giants where the family influence was very strong, even if not completely dominant.[2] Smaller companies were even more likely to be
closely owned. As a result, coalmining was among the most 'private' of
business enterprises. Indeed, most colliery undertakings, including
some of the biggest, illustrated some of the common features of private
partnerships and family businesses: a limited number of directors and
partners with a lack of technical and professional expertise among them;
a jealous guarding of information about operations and financial results;
an unwillingness to cooperate with other businesses or to delegate
authority; an extreme sensitivity on the issue of managerial control; and
a caution in the expenditure of money on long-run investments.

These characteristics were clearly the basis of the coalowners'
collective reputation for technical conservatism and lack of enterprise.
The insular and small-scale character of management (even of large
undertakings) encouraged that sense of owning a piece of private
property which made mergers with other firms psychologically as well
as financially difficult. Further, it placed durable obstacles in the way of
cooperation with other colliery enterprises in schemes which (if sufficient support had been forthcoming) would have redounded to some
general benefit. In terms of policy *within* colliery undertakings, the
nature of business control could only encourage that unyielding opposition to the sharing of managerial responsibilities or even of information
with the work-force, which undermined the schemes for consultation
offered as solutions to the problem of industrial relations in peacetime
or of production in wartime. Certainly, the fragmentation of entrepreneurial interest made it impossible for the owners willingly to accept the

---

[1] Examples of large composite firms were: Powell Duffryn, the Ebbw Vale group, and Dorman
Long. Examples of integrated, specialist coal producers were: Manchester Collieries, Amalgamated Anthracite, and Doncaster Amalgamated Collieries.

[2] Lambton, Hetton, & Joicey employed some 24,000 men in 1925 and was among the three or
four largest producers of coal in the country (its 22 mines had an output of about 4 m. tons). The
Butterley Company employed 10,000 men in 1925. Among other examples were: Pease & Partners
of Durham, a unified coal, coke, and iron and steel firm which in 1931 had a Board of nine, which
included five members of the Pease family; the Ashington Coal Company of Northumberland (in
1914, five members of its seven-man Board were drawn from two families); and the West Yorkshire undertaking, Henry Briggs, Son & Co.

idea of nation-wide wage negotiations, and generally helped exacerbate industrial relations.

The forms and organization of enterprise were also, it would seem, related to important areas of investment policy. For example, structural insularity must have encouraged caution concerning expenditure on fixed capital or the reorganization of production. As family and/or private businesses, most collieries had only limited access to the capital market. It may be assumed that most were dependent for funds on their existing shareholders or on their banks. In such circumstances, it would be very difficult to raise new money, even if the risks of new investment were not great (a situation which rarely obtained after the First World War).

As a result, investment would have to be financed from the pockets of the Board or those of a limited number of large shareholders. Even in good years Boards would be inclined to prefer techniques (e.g. longwall advancing rather than longwall retreating[1]) which promised speedy returns to essentially private investment. Even in the halcyon days before 1914 'as soon as a mine was sunk, the cry was for output. Whatever planning was done was, for the most part, done on a short-term basis.'[2] How much more serious, then, must have been the effect of private caution on decisions about investment and technical change *between* the Wars. Although detailed evidence is scarce, it may be concluded that this situation was a severely limiting factor for the overhaul and modernization of the industry. More than this, it had reverberations within individual firms, and especially in terms of the relationships between Boards and colliery managers.

More than almost any other industry, coalmining exemplified a potentially sharp disjunction between its business and its technical functions. The law on industrial safety demanded that the arrangements and oversight of the productive process should be the direct responsibility of an individual (the colliery manager) who had to be a technically qualified (and certificated) engineer. Hence critical decisions concerning both costs and safety were in the hands of a professional engineer in each mine. On the other hand, business policy, resources, investment decisions, and profits (if any) were within the purview of Boards which need not be, and frequently were not, particularly well qualified in a technical sense. Nor was it always the case that the interests of owner-directors and salaried managers were identical or even consistent. Of course, in various private firms, members of the governing family

---

[1] Above, 379.   [2] *Reid Report*, 3.

occasionally secured the qualifications which enabled them to assume a managerial role; and increasingly in the 1930s successful mining engineers (i.e. colliery managers) were to be found on the Boards of Companies and had extensive shareholdings (C. C. Reid at the Fife Coal Company, H. E. Mitton at Butterley, Austin Kirkup at Lambton, Hetton, & Joicey).

Nevertheless, there was always a latent, and frequently an actual, tension between colliery managers who wished to plough resources into development and directors who were reluctant to find more money or give up available profits. In the words of one trade-union critic in 1919 many colliery shareholders 'are afraid of the first cost of the new plant and cannot trust the management to secure a sufficient return for the outlay'.[1] This clash between the psychology of the engineer and that of the economizing businessman came to the surface with far-reaching political consequences with the Reid Report—asserting the unhindered industrial ambitions of the engineering fraternity—in 1944-5. But it was undoubtedly present to some degree throughout the troubled interwar years.

As with the question of industrial concentration, it is easy to exaggerate the extent to which such organizational conservatism persisted throughout this period. For, just as there were important examples of large-scale grouping, in the 1930s, so large firms in the van of the industry pursued policies of vigorous corporate reform—which integrated the technical and professional, on the one hand, and the business, on the other. With central services, rationalized internal structures, planning departments, and professional hierarchies, firms like the Fife Coal Company, Bairds & Dalmellington, Powell Duffryn, Manchester Collieries, Ashington Coal Company, and Doncaster Amalgamated

---

[1] One confusing aspect of the coalmining industry's economics was that the concept of 'investment' and even the difference between capital and revenue accounts, were very vague. A new shaft or new machinery clearly counted as capital investment. But in practice the labour processes and supplies needed to extend and maintain roadways (which comprised the bulk of 'investment') *also* comprised a large part of recurrent production costs. The underground development of a mine was both labour-intensive and comparable to the day-to-day exploitation of its coal seams. ('Mining differs from manufacturing industry in that the underground producing plant is built and torn down concurrently with production': *TIME* CIII (1943-4), 186.) The obscurity of the distinction between capital and revenue accounts had odd results. Thus, a colliery manager might easily circumvent his Board by 'investing' resources without authority—employing an 'élite' corps of miners to produce coal when mining conditions were difficult and it was necessary to exert considerable efforts to maintain production; but using them for development work (e.g. opening up new faces) when coal-getting conditions were easier, so that production could be maintained with fewer face-workers. In both circumstances their wages would be charged to revenue (i.e. the cost of mining to provide current output).

Collieries could hope to harness resources to long-run business needs, even if their ambitions were not always satisfied.[1] Yet the fact was that such 'modernity' was not universally characteristic of the coal industry, and that when these issues came to be closely scrutinized in the mid-1940s the deficiencies of colliery undertakings were more manifest than their success, and were connected with a regrettable narrowness of outlook.

The second possible 'institutional' obstacle to progressive industrial reform derived from the legal arrangements for mining royalties. The coal that was mined was the private property of the owners of the surface land. Unless the colliery company had managed to purchase extensive tracts of mineral rights, it would have to deal with a multiplicity of landlords. Indeed, the royalty system was even more fragmented than the industrial structure.[2] The diffusion and inconsistency of the individual interests of individual royalty owners, the frequent need for colliery firms to deal with a number of them (the Samuel Commission estimated that on average each mine had to secure leases from five mineral owners),[3] and the simultaneous existence of contracts of varying duration and severity, must have inhibited 'rational' coordination and the merging of productive operations in coalmining. Certainly, that was partly the basis of attempts to reform the law in relation to the property rights of royalty owners. And, in combination with resentment at the burden of royalties during the depression, it led some leading owners to toy with the idea of nationalization.[4]

[1] Useful, if not entirely objective sources of information on this topic are the submissions made for the purposes of valuation after nationalization. See, for example, POWE 28/239 (Manchester Collieries, Powell Duffryn); POWE 35/195, 246, 247 (Powell Duffryn, Butterley, Manchester Collieries); POWE 37/4, 30 (Ashington, Bairds & Dalmellington). There were also earlier examples of such corporate sophistication. See the evidence of C. P. Markham (to the Samuel Commission in 1925) concerning Doncaster collieries in general and the Staveley group in particular: *Samuel Evidence* QQ 9989–10474, 11198–11590.

[2] There were applications with respect to over 30,000 'units of compensation' under the Coal (Registration of Ownership) Act of 1937: see *Coal Act 1938. Reports of the Coal Commission for the years 1938 and 1939 (PP* 1939–40 V), 4.

[3] *Samuel Report*, 77. The Report pointed out that 'the planning of the mines is influenced continually by surface boundaries and surface rights. But surface boundaries have no relevance at all, and surface rights only a minor relevance to the proper organization of the industry underground.'

[4] The inhibiting effects of the fragmentation of royalty ownership and/or the specification of property law were considered by the Coal Conservation Committee (Cd. 9084. 1918) and the Acquisition and Valuation of Land (Scott) Committee (Cmd. 156. 1919). In 1923 the Mines (Working Facilities and Support) Act established machinery by which, in certain cases, those wishing to work minerals but confronted by mineral or land owners who unreasonably withheld permission or cooperation, could secure necessary rights (to work minerals, adjust boundaries, let down the surface, use surface land, etc.). For the owners' accommodation to the idea of the public ownership of royalties, see above, 346.

Both the Samuel Commission and the Reid Committee suggested that the state ownership (and therefore the unified control) of mineral on the continent facilitated the improvement and larger size of industrial structures on the continent. On the other hand, given the other reasons for withholding investment, it seems doubtful whether the royalty system prevented amalgamations (and slowed down mechanization) simply because mine-owners feared that any improvement in productivity would be appropriated by the royalty owners.[1] But the royalty system clearly helped explain the original fragmentation of the industry, presented numerous practical obstacles in structural change,[2] and in 1933 was offered by the MAGB as the reason why the efforts of the Coal Mines Reorganisation Commission to secure widespread mergers were doomed.[3] Certainly, it was this apparent link between the mechanics of structural change and the functions of royalty ownership and management which ultimately persuaded the Conservative-dominated National Government to combine measures to nationalize royalties and enforce merger schemes in one piece of legislation, and allocate the function to a single administrative authority.

A third possible 'institutional' determinant of the ease or difficulty with which technical and organizational changes could be introduced lay in the industrial relationships and wage-determination procedures of the industry. Trade-union policy, the attitudes of the work-force, and the level and systems of wages certainly influenced the course of legislation and public policy towards organization. In addition, they could obviously affect the costs of innovation, as well as the allocation of its benefits. Through their effects on the profitability of existing (non-innovative) operations, they could even influence attitudes to investment and change, since the particular circumstances which resulted in an increase in labour costs could also reduce the benefits of the labour-saving technological changes which, in other circumstances, might have been a successful response to high labour costs.[4]

Certainly, the course of wages and coal prices after 1920 squeezed

---

[1] Fine 1978.

[2] In 1934, an official investigation of conditions in Durham and Tyneside argued that 'no reorganisation . . . appears possible unless unification of the ownership of royalties has first been accomplished.' *Ministry of Labour. Report of Investigations into the Industrial Conditions in Certain Depressed Areas* (Cmd. 4278. 1934: *PP* 1933–4 XIII), 81–2.

[3] COAL 12/14.

[4] There was much contemporary discussion of whether the attitudes and aspirations of the work-force retarded mechanization or reduced its returns. But virtually all the evidence on either side was anecdotal rather than systematic.

proceeds and profits. Miners' wages were relatively 'sticky'—under-pinned by the provisions of the national wages agreements of 1921 and 1924 and by the relatively successful use of social wage arguments by the miners from 1919. Hence, even though there were sharp nominal wage reductions in 1921, and less severe decreases in 1926–7, there was at least a 'floor' to the wage cuts. More important, in the 1920s in most districts coal prices tumbled by significantly more than miners' wage rates—albeit by the 1930s market forces together with the measures to maintain prices had a beneficial effect on prices and proceeds, and had either arrested or reversed the tendency for 'own product' wage rates (i.e. wage rates deflated by the price of coal) to rise.

A more general indication of the effects of the wage agreements is provided by aggregate measures of earnings and net proceeds. Since, under the national wage agreements (and the district agreements which replaced them from 1926/7) wages were a prior charge on proceeds, miners' earnings could absorb the great bulk of proceeds in a bad year. In the loss-making years 1927 and 1928, for example, wage costs were equivalent to over 70 per cent of proceeds, and total costs, of course, *exceeded* proceeds. In such a context, and assuming that the costs of any large-scale innovation would have been inflated by forces similar to those which maintained wage rates, coalowners might have very limited degrees of freedom when it came to investment in new organization or techniques.

A related aspect of the framework within which coalowners were obliged to take investment decisions was that of government inter-vention. Quite apart from the no doubt exaggerated complaints by coalowners that political 'interference' was retarding investment and innovation,[1] the state's desire to minimize industrial disruption and, especially from 1929–30, to stabilize and protect the industry, involved an element of subsidy (either of a direct pecuniary sort, as in 1921 and 1926, or through cartel arrangements in 1930s) which undoubtedly bolstered the position of the less efficient firms. This had the result of keeping them in production, making it more expensive to absorb or eliminate them, and reducing the incentive to structural and technical change.

Given the force of such 'institutional' considerations, it is tempting to

---

[1] In general, this does not appear well substantiated, but there may have been some validity in the claim during the hectic controversy over nationalization in 1919–20. Then, even repre-sentatives of the miners' union agreed that uncertainty in the industry was leading to a neglect of investment.

attribute to them much or most of the British coal industry's relative slowness to reform its structures and techniques in the interwar period. But such a conclusion would be facile. For the very considerations—the limited scope for expansion, the apparently low yields on investment—which appeared to determine the entrepreneurial behaviour of coal-owners in the face of institutional arrangements, operated with even more force and generality in relation to the competitive position and economic structure of the industry itself. The most potent obstacle to enterprising reorganization, industrial concentration, and large-scale investments was the market situation of the coalmining *business*.

For most of the interwar period the prospects for abundant profit-making in the coal industry were poor: the demand for coal was inelastic yet the supply was competitive and the investment costs of innovation high. Above all, the market was constantly vulnerable to disruption and 'over-production' through the tenacity of small and medium-sized firms, apparently able to operate for long periods at a loss or respond very quickly with increased output to any sign of greater demand. Moreover, the proliferation of enterprises made the coordination of production and marketing, or individual attempts at amalgamation, very difficult. Hence, in addition to the most important factor of all—the disincentive to undertake substantial investments of a risky kind—the contrast at the level of the individual firm between the definite costs and the problematic benefits of amalgamation made the attainment of larger-scale structures through decentralized decisions a very uncertain exercise. This was especially so when the merger process was advocated as a means of closing down less efficient seams or mines or companies. Precisely because smaller and/or less efficient pits and firms had an apparent motive to retain their independence, the cost of acquiring them might be a significant obstacle to their elimination. And, since the benefits of their acquisition (and presumed closure) were diffused throughout the industry rather than concentrated in the hands of the new parent company, the rationality of the procedure as far as business-men were concerned was doubtful.

To spend money in order to acquire pits so as to close them was hardly a 'rational' business policy if the benefit of closing them (a reduc-tion in national supply) could not be retained in the hands of those who had borne the cost. In principle, the resolution of this tension should have been some form of *collective* action to ensure industry-wide action. But the two forms which such action might take (government funding or legislative compulsion) were precluded by the ideology and politics, as well as by the vested interest of the time. Although occasionally canvassed, any realistic level of state subsidy to encourage extensive industrial reorganization was inconceivable.

On the other hand, the legislation which aimed at the enforcement of mergers (1930 and 1938) was handicapped by the inadequacy of the law and the lack of industrial cooperation or public resources—and even more by the social costs, measured in the inevitable intensification of the unemployment problem, which would have been generated by rationalization in the 1930s.[1] As a result, structural change on an individual basis was not very common, and was frequently associated with abnormal circumstances: booming profits (as in 1918–20), complete bankruptcy of the firms to be taken over (as happened in Lancashire with the creation of Manchester Collieries), or some degree of regional distinctiveness which enabled the businessmen involved to act collectively. But, in the context of the problem of over-capacity of the industry as a whole, such developments were rare.

Indeed, this disadvantage of the fragmented structure of coalmining was a handicap even in the matter of coordinated selling, where the economic advantages were more widely acknowledged and where, after 1926, there was a large majority of coalowners in favour of collective action.[2] Yet even there compulsion rather than private action was necessary to overcome the disruptive action of a minority of companies. How much more difficult, then, was the attainment of industrial reorganization where the economic benefits were even more doubtful (and where the economic pressures on the less efficient were reduced by the legislation for selling schemes). Certainly, a reduction in the number of producing units would have increased average productivity. But equally certainly, that end could not have been achieved by private action alone.

The crucial problem of the coalmining industry for most of the 1920s and 1930s was that it was simply too big and its structure prevented any easy course of amelioration by concentration. In light of this, it seems very unlikely that the industry's plight can, after all, be blamed on the 'obstinate and senseless individualism of 150 chairmen'.[3] On the other

---

[1] The economic case for amalgamations, argued The Times (7 Feb. 1936, 15e–f) was 'unanswerable', but there was also a social problem: production would cease in the less efficient mines 'and then the present intermittent unemployment, relieved by the payment of benefit, will become permanent unemployment with benefit'. For the persistent fears of the concentration of unemployment (as distinct from its continued 'dispersal') if a merger movement were encouraged or enforced, see above, 341–3.   [2] Above, ch. 5, sect. v.

[3] Sir William Firth, quoted in CG 5 June 1936, 1070. The statement was made in the context of the fact that less than 150 companies produced 75% of the national output.

side, however, collective or 'social' action was also precluded. This was partly a matter of political philosophy: no government was prepared to take and enforce the powers that would have been necessary to coerce a reluctant industrial community. But it was also a matter of practical politics and social necessity. The state did not have access to the requisite resources; and, above all, it is doubtful if the social costs of effective amalgamation and rationalization (more concentrated unemployment, further devastation of coalmining communities) could have been borne. In the end, just as economic disincentives prevented entrepreneurial action, so social sensitivity and political inertia precluded government intervention.[1]

The historical debate about entrepreneurship in the coal industry has possibly been too much influenced by an understandable dislike of the coalowners' political and industrial-relations postures. Certainly, the owners' arguments may have been vapid and their public stance obstinately reactionary; compared with other industries they may have neglected to explore the possibility of collective action. But, given the curious structure of their industry and the survival power of apparently less efficient firms, it is hard to see how they could reasonably have been expected to be any more vigorous, enterprising, and reckless of resources and risks than any other category of businessmen.

iv. Association and ideology

The competitive weakness of the coal industry, the privacy with which business was conducted, and the continued fragmentation of its structure reinforce the impression that as far as their business affairs were concerned the coalowners' outlook in the 1920s and 1930s was highly individualistic. The one major exception to this (the gradual cartelization of marketing) was only made possible by legislation and sustained government pressure. On the other hand, the public and political reputation of the owners was one of determined and successfully maintained unity. This contrast between individualism and solidarity is, however, far from paradoxical. The independence—of regions and enterprises—so highly valued by the owners could, they felt, only be ensured and protected by unified action to preserve the framework of

---

[1] The Reid Committee pointed out that when, in the early 1920s, German industrialists appreciated the need for a contraction in coalmining, they 'resolved to abandon the policy of short-time working then being followed, and to proceed with a ruthless concentration of productive effort irrespective of the social consequences to which it would give rise': *Reid Report*, 16.

political and industrial arrangements within which it operated. As a result, even such a notorious divergence of interest as that between 'export' and 'inland' fields, could be subsumed as the owners managed to act together with effective solidarity on critical issues of economic policy and political argument. The result was a substantial conservatism. Given the variety of interests and investments, radical changes in attitude or direction were very difficult to achieve, and any determined attempt to secure them threatened the harmony and unity of the industry's owners.

The central institution of the industry's business cohesion was the Mining Association of Great Britain—a general body which was shared and limited in its policies by its constituents. The latter were the various district coalowners' associations, which provided an essential forum for discussion and policy formulation attuned to the presumed distinctive needs of the regions.[1] The district associations had evolved in the nineteenth century when, even more than in the twentieth, the different districts were, for most purposes, the equivalents of different industries. By 1912 there were 23 constituent associations (including the Scottish shale oil producers) in the MAGB, and in 1926 the number had risen to 26, including some which represented only a handful of firms (e.g. in Bristol, Cumberland, Flintshire, the Forest of Dean, Kent, Somerset, and Leicester). In the main, these local groups were sensitive to the problems of geology, marketing, working conditions, and labour supply which characterized their own areas. They were therefore jealous of their autonomy with respect to wage-setting as well as other issues relating to working conditions and practices. Even when there were potentially serious differences of interest, the need for unity persuaded district associations to sink their differences—as happened in Scotland (where the four separate associations succeeded in presenting a united

---

[1] The large number of very small firms (which in any case produced a minuscule proportion of the industry's output) were normally not represented, and never influential, at district meetings. The records of the Monmouthshire & South Wales Coal Owners, for example, indicate that in early and mid-1920s a 'normal' meeting might be attended by about 50 members; for important meetings (e.g. to discuss the national wage negotiations in Aug. 1925) attendance might rise to over 100. (MSWCOA Minutes, *passim*.) However, the *List of Mines* for 1924 indicates that there were no less than 335 colliery firms in the district, albeit only 153 employed 100 or more miners, and the 89 which employed 500 or more accounted for 92% of the labour force and, presumably, a similar proportion of the output. In his *Historical Review of Coalmining* (1926), W. A. Lee, the Secretary of the MAGB, estimated that owners representing 94% of the national output were members. Ranked in terms of size in 1924, 467 collieries accounted for this proportion of the industry's output—leaving 944 tiny undertakings employing about 6% and presumably not being represented in the MAGB.

front as the Scottish Coal Owners' Association) and for much of the time in West Yorkshire, where the owners (operating older and on the whole less productive mines) were persuaded to align themselves on many issues with the more competitive South Yorkshire enterprises.[1]

The issues which united the leading coalowners in the various districts were numerous. But their most important peacetime role—at least until they came to administer the selling and quota systems of the 1930s[2]—related to labour policy. For the district provided the basic framework within which wages, hours, working arrangements, and the quality of industrial relations and consultation were determined. And a good deal of the MAGB's political effort in the period was devoted to protecting the autonomy of the districts in these regards, even though it agreed to the *national* determination of guiding principles for wages and hours after 1921 and to accept a national wages increase in 1935–6. As with the provision of mutual financial support in relation to local stoppages and compensation claims, local negotiations over wages, hours, and conditions were traditional functions which were intensified and politicized in the changing circumstances of the twentieth century. In addition, however, the district associations came under increasing pressure to strengthen their representative voice and extend their local influence to meet the new needs of the industry.

They were, therefore, much more frequently called on to take up positions as the representative constituencies behind national discussions of industrial policy; and, at another level, to adopt more elaborate, and institutionalized, policies towards the collective support of propaganda and public relations, research, education, and welfare. As with the MAGB in the national forum, these pressures began to transform the associations' structures during and immediately after the First World War. For example, between 1914 and 1922 the Monmouthshire & South Wales Coal Owners' Association established nine new committees or departments and had come to need representation on seven national committees. Staff numbers in South Wales grew from 16 in 1914 to 102 in January 1921, although by 1922, as the Coal Control was abandoned, they had fallen to 43.[3]

---

[1] Above, 163.

[2] During the First World War the district associations also provided the basis for the committees which controlled the allocation of coal supplies. Above, ch. 2, sect. ii.

[3] MSWCOA MG15 (26 June 1922). The new district committees were for Joint Standing Disputes, Master Hauliers, Officials, Firemen, Welfare, General Traders, Commercial Information and Statistical, and Special Capital Indemnity. At the national level, the South Wales Secretary, and other members, attended the Central Council for Economic Information and six committees

Public criticism of the owners almost invariably implied that they were unanimous as well as obstinate in their view on the industry. In practice, however, they had dissidents and disagreements. Locally, this was reflected in occasional sharp divisions on strategy and policy within district associations—disagreements which could be based on differing perceptions of the industry's general needs, but were perhaps most often rooted in the contrasting economic interests of different groups. Such cleavages of interest were exposed by economic weakness and were therefore exacerbated by the prolonged economic trauma of 1926, when within some districts there were strong divergences of opinion on the terms of settlement; and also after 1927 when there were differences of opinion on the advantages of the proposed selling schemes. Yet the advantages of solidarity and unanimity invariably outweighed those of particularist interests. Given the successful maintenance of local independence on the most important issues of all—actual wage determination—the loyalty of district associations to their central grouping was never seriously in doubt.

This last point was important. The collective strength of the coal-owners was undoubtedly rooted in their local associations. But after 1913 the industry was obliged to pursue its aims or defend its interests within the national arena. The districts were determined to maintain their freedom of action in relation to business affairs, but came to appreciate that that could only be done by and through the Mining Association of Great Britain, or a settled framework which could be established only by national negotiation.

The MAGB had been established in 1854 as a loose federation of district associations and individual coalowners. Its prime purpose had been to oversee the passage and application of legislation impinging on the owners' affairs—safety regulations, taxation, workmen's compensation, etc. And with rare exceptions (for example the discussions surrounding the minimum-wage and maximum-hours legislation just before the First World War), the national body was precluded from any serious involvement with wages, employment conditions, industrial relations, prices, or business matters generally. But all this was changed after 1913 under the pressure of wartime shortages and postwar dislocation.

The centralized role forced on the MAGB by wartime needs continued

of the MAGB (Executive Council, Central Committee, Propaganda, Statistical, Exports, National Wages Board). The South Wales Statistical and Information Department was felt to be especially important. It employed 17 of the Association's 43 staff—i.e. more than the entire prewar staff.

into the postwar years since government controls of the industry lasted until April 1921, and the coal industry (including its wage levels and business performance) never ceased to be a contentious issue in national politics. But the MAGB's new role was particularly intensified by the events of 1919: the sustained assault on the ownership and organization of the industry, the adverse publicity attending the Sankey Inquiry, and the pressure for large changes in wages, hours, welfare, ownership, and control. As a result, the MAGB was obliged to reform its public activities, its procedures, and its constitution.[1]

Throughout the spring and summer of 1919 the Mining Association mustered its forces and devised new committees to contain the public and political attacks which had been stimulated by the miners' claim. The owners' responses and political representations were coordinated and an intensive publicity campaign was mounted. In November, the MAGB's members were reminded by their President, Evan Williams, that in the five years after 1914 it had been 'forced by the Government to deal collectively with the men on questions relating to conditions of labour in the districts'. He advised his members that some central organization was absolutely necessary to deal with all questions arising in the industry which were of common interest. As a result, the MAGB's constitution was radically amended and its staff and structure greatly strengthened. Full-time officials were appointed for the first time; and under the new constitution (adopted in April 1920) membership was to be confined to district associations: provision was made for a full-time staff (W. A. Lee had already been appointed as Assistant Secretary) and a variety of elected officers; and the committee structure was elaborated and extended. The four critical standing committees were to be a Central Committee, a Parliamentary Committee, a Financial Committee, and a Propaganda and Statistical Committee.[2]

In effect, the MAGB's new committee structure made formal the innovations—a more powerful watchdog central committee and a continuous propaganda group—that had been devised to meet the challenge and humiliation of the Sankey Inquiry. Now, however, they were accepted as representing the permanent character of the new situation. This was also reflected in the way in which the new system was operated: the Presidency became, in effect, a full-time and permanent office. The formidable Evan Williams, having completed the 'normal'

---

[1] Above, ch. 4, sect. v. The impact of 1919–20 on the coalowners' associations and attitudes is considered in Supple 1984.

[2] For the new constitution see *MAGB* 1921, 140.

two years of office in 1921, during which time he had imposed his personality on the MAGB and successfully fought off the most dangerous challenges to the owners, was re-elected—as he was to be until his retirement in 1944.[1]

Within this greater cohesion and closing of ranks, the MAGB still maintained the right of district associations to determine wages and working conditions for their own localities. And that became a vital point of principle in subsequent political arguments. Indeed, it was frequently criticized for a purposeful ambiguity—obstructing reforms where it could but employing what the *Manchester Guardian* called 'its famous vanishing trick' when asked to assume some responsibility for wage negotiations on behalf of the districts.[2] But the fact remained that the reforms of 1919–20 embodied a far-reaching change in the economic representation and political role of the industry.[3]

The owners' efforts to ensure favourable publicity and parliamentary support were particularly vigorous at moments of critical or legislation decision—1921, 1926, 1929–30, 1936–8. However, it is difficult to detect any very great success in terms of the swaying of public sympathy in the owners' direction. Their most powerful weapon in that regard remained the intermittent demonstration of the unyielding posture of the miners' union (just as the miners' most enduring argument remained the statements and actions of the owners). On the other hand, the effective *political* influence of the owners was considerable: they had privileged access to government Ministers and officials, had a large fund of official sympathy (although frequently capable of draining it to the point of exhaustion), and could muster effective parliamentary support. In spite of their almost consistently bad publicity, the MAGB was successful in watering down the legislation of 1920, 1929–30, and—more strikingly—of 1936–8.

In general, then, the Mining Association successfully defended its members' interests. This is not to say that the unity of the owners was unruffled. There were, for example, mavericks like C. P. Markham of the Staveley Coal and Iron Company and its associated undertakings in South Yorkshire and Derbyshire, who refused to join the district associations and proceeded on his own individualistic and hugely profitable

---

[1] Above, ch. 4, sect. v.

[2] Quoted in *CG* 29 Dec. 1933, 1216.

[3] Similar changes were taking place in other industries and, indeed, in industry as a whole. The Federation of British Industry was established in 1917 and the Confederation of Employers' Organisations two years later. The miners' union also took steps (in 1918) to strengthen their central offices and ensure that their President and Secretary became full-time officials.

way.[1] Markham, however, was a rare instance. Most commonly, dissent among the owners came from within the ranks of the MAGB—from those traditionalists who resented the Association's willingness to negotiate with the government on business matters,[2] and from more accommodating members who occasionally felt that the Association's official line was too unyielding. This happened with regard to industrial reorganization in the mid-1920s or to the national discussion of wages and industrial affairs in general.[3] These, however, were isolated and unimportant examples. The commitment to collective decision-making ensured that the threat of individual rebellion or even public disagreement was innocuous.

A more serious possibility of cleavage arose from the incentives to district associations (as distinct from individual members) to take up positions in opposition to the national consensus. This was a problem where owners in a particular coalfield sensed that their economic interests might be threatened by conformity to a national 'line' or settlement. Thus, the West Yorkshire Coal Owners' Association was reluctant to have its wage levels determined by ascertainments which involved its financial results being joined with the much more productive South Yorkshire field (where proceeds were higher, so that indicated wage

---

[1] See Markham's evidence to the Samuel Commission: QQ 9989–10474. Markham (who was much opposed to the MFGB and argued that 'The whole of the miners to-day have got into the hands of the Bolshevists') claimed that he was opposed to combines, and acknowledged that it was to his advantage to stay out of the district associations since he thereby could keep his highly productive pits out of the ascertainments and pay wages based on less productive pits which had been brought into the ascertainment. When the subsidy of 1925–6 was being paid, however, he had agreed to supply information in order to qualify for payment: 'I take anything that is going . . . It is money for nothing.' (QQ 10240 ff.) Markham, although a reasonably good employer, was paternalistic and peculiarly reactionary. In 1920 he had allowed himself to express the following sentiments to the General Meeting of the Staveley Company: 'Apparently the one idea of Labour is to ruin the country. They talk about their Soviets and Bolsheviks. They little know that the heads of these two movements are the Jews, and that the Jews are responsible, in a great measure, for the trouble we are getting in this country at the present time.' (British Steel Regional Archives, Irthlingborough: Staveley Records, Box 75, Minutes of General Meeting, No. 4, 117, 28 Sept. 1920.)

[2] There was particularly strong disagreement during the discussions of the financial arrangements under the Coal Control and after the Sankey award. Above, 84–5.

[3] W. A. Archer, a leading member of the West Yorkshire association felt that the MAGB was too inflexible in its discussions of the industry's financial arrangement in 1919 (WYCOA 17 Nov. 1919); and criticized the official policy on negotiations in 1926 (above, 250 n.). Sir Alfred Mond (admittedly, a somewhat peripheral member of the MAGB) pressed strongly, and in direct opposition to the owners' collective view, for the reform of the industry's structure in 1925–6 (above, 258). After the passage of the 1930 Act there were also complaints at the MAGB's refusal to participate in the National Industrial Board and at the lack of information provided to the ordinary membership: MAGB 1931, 15–16.

shares would be greater). It was, however, persuaded to participate (and mollified by transitional financial arrangements) in the Midland District for purposes of the 1921 National Wages Agreement.[1] Again, the Durham owners were opposed to the Coal Mines Bill of 1929–30, since as an export area they were much more suspicious of selling schemes.[2] yet even in relation to this sort of problem, the national association—i.e. majority opinion within the coalowners' groups—maintained a unitary policy on all essential issues.

Such relative harmony was facilitated not simply by an appreciation of its strategic desirability, but also by patterns of membership and representation. Thus, the national leadership (represented by men like Sir Evan Williams, or Sir Adam Nimmo and Wallace Thorneycroft of Scotland or Lord Gainford and Reginald Guthrie of Durham, or W. Benton Jones of Yorkshire) was, in effect, the local leadership too. There was little dissonance between official representatives and district membership. Moreover, the MAGB 'worked' by fairly full, and certainly continuous consultation between London and the localities. As a result the MAGB was able not merely to orchestrate the responses of its district membership to government suggestion (as happened in relation to the Sankey proposal for nationalization in 1919 or Churchill's unsuccessful attempt to initiate national negotiations in 1926),[3] But to secure a united stand on issues where the districts were divided in their initial views (as happened with the response to the Samuel Report).[4] Against such a background, it is hardly surprising that the coalowners' associations, locally and nationally, illustrated at least as potent an industrial solidarity as did the miners' union.

Although at any one time their views might appear unyielding and monolithic, the coalowners' attitudes were not completely unchanged by the events of the interwar years. On one vital matter—the acceptance and administration of production quotas and marketing controls—the MAGB and district associations transcended their original inhibitions about collective action to curb competition. And in a variety of other areas—national negotiations and consultations, holidays with pay and pensions—the traditionally inflexible attitudes of the owners were

---

[1] *MAGB* 1921, 81. Even so, West Yorkshire took a persistently more accommodating line on industrial relations at the national level. See WYCOA, 17 July 1925, 13 Mar. 1926, 18 May 1926, 23 Sept. 1929, 17 Dec. 1929, 3 Dec. 1930.

[2] DCOA, 24 Feb. 1930.

[3] Above, 134 and 248–9.

[4] Above, 240.

gradually adjusted in response to economic reality and public and political pressure. Nevertheless, on most issues and for most of the period,
their public posture appeared to justify their unenviable reputation as
one of the most insular and dogmatic of interest groups. Whether, in
reality, their selfishness and determination in pursuit of their own
economic interests exceeded that of other groups, or were merely
exceptionally provoking to those anxious to assuage political crises and
economic problems, is a matter not easily resolved.

At bottom, the national and district owners' associations were
concerned to maintain, and if possible enlarge, their members' business
strength and freedom of economic action. Initially, this meant discharg-
ing the industry from the national framework devised during the First
World War and extended in the unstable years immediately afterwards.
But the owners' pursuit of the *status quo ante bellum* was not merely a
matter of securing the abandonment of formal government control.
(Indeed, although they were entirely in favour of a return to private
enterprise, when it came to the point the owners were as vehement as
the miners in their protests at the speed and circumstances surrounding
the government decision to end control of 1921.)[1] It was also consistent
with their strongly held view that the industry's wage levels, working
arrangements, and finances could not be treated on a uniform (i.e.
national) basis, but had to be attuned to the circumstances of the individual coalfields. At another level, however, the owners were propound-
ing a distinct economic ideology: a principled opposition to most forms
of government intervention and to all proposals for worker participation in management functions; an assumption that the economic
performance of the industry was almost entirely attributable to its
labour costs, and that these were a function of wage rates and the length
of the working day; a persuasion that the only reasonable criterion for
the determination of wages was the economic capacity of the industry
to pay them.

That ideology was exemplified with greatest determination (and
success) in the 1920s. The owners were, admittedly, aided by the miners'
own unwillingness to compromise on a national wages pool in 1921 or
on the principle of wage reduction or an increased working day in 1926.
Yet the basic framework of wage agreements from 1921—the stipulation
of standard and minimum wage rates with a prior claim on revenues—in
effect introduced the concept of a social wage, established the condi-

[1] Above, 156. The rest of this chapter is largely based on the detailed story of the owners' attitudes and responses to events in the 1920s and 1930s. See above, ch. 4 and 6.

tions for a compression of profit, and frustrated any ambitions the owners might have entertained for limitless reductions in wages. These points were to be acknowledged after the wage cuts of 1926-7, when the owners recognized that it was socially undesirable, and perhaps economically irrelevant, to attempt to reduce miners' pay even more. Until then, however, the owners persisted in their politically risky behaviour. In the 1926 stoppage, for example, they provoked even Baldwin by their reiteration of fundamentalist *laissez-faire* doctrines, outraged government Ministers by the peremptory tone of arguments, and alienated public and politicians alike by their constant refusal to compromise. Even so, the owners did not have to pay the price of their unpopular obstinacy: the legal maximum of the working day underground was increased to eight hours; the miners' own refusal to compromise deflected criticism; and at the end of the stoppage the work-force had to return to the mines on the owners' terms.

Yet the fact that the MAGB combined a distasteful public presence with the achievement of its aims is not in itself evidence that the proposals for alternative industrial strategies, which they rejected so dogmatically, were viable. In fact, most disinterested proposals involved either an unrealistically high public subsidy or the transfer of the costs of employment to the owners. In reality, the industry's immediate problems related to its costs and capacity. The owners were most probably right in believing that competitiveness would depend on lowering costs, and that the immediate scope for cost reductions by structural reform was limited. Their principal failing was to ignore the psychological benefits of improved industrial relations (although they were beginning to see the light by the mid-1930s) and the potential of the 'structural' case. By neglecting the quality of their relationship with workers, they contributed to that grimly sullen atmosphere which impeded productivity growth. And by utterly refusing to pursue reorganization they ensured that in 1925-6 the miners would continue to insist on the inviolability of wages and hours which the industry simply could not sustain.

In one important respect, however, changing circumstances undermined the MAGB's position. As we have seen, by 1927 it became

---

[1] For the examples of the haranguing of government Ministers by owners' representatives, see the record of meetings with the President of the Board of Trade in 1919 (*MAGB* 1919, 90A) and the letter from the MAGB's President Sir Evan Williams to the Secretary for Mines George Lane-Fox of 29 Aug. 1926: Baldwin Papers 18/245-7. The owners' objection to national negotiations were principally based on their presumed economic disadvantages for the poorer districts but also because 'they made trade disputes into political demonstrations' (MSWCOA 10 Sept. 1926).

apparent that the salvation of the industry did not lie in wage cuts. The lower wages and longer hours which followed the 1926 stoppage did not prevent the coal industry from plunging even further into economic disarray. As a result, the owners were at last persuaded to entertain different views about the industry. Admittedly, the process was hesitant: the MAGB continued to reject national discussions with labour[1] or cooperation with government intervention; and their public statements now emphasized the need to reduce social security payments, rates, taxes, and freight charges, with the traditionalist claim that 'the fabric of the coal industry is sound, and there is little within the power of the Coal Owners that they have failed to do in order to meet the unprecedented strain which has been imposed upon it from without'.[2] Nevertheless, by 1927–8 the owners had at least abandoned their provoking wages cuts, and majority opinion began to come round to the idea of marketing controls and selling schemes which might diminish competition, share available markets, and sustain prices.

In the event, although the voluntary schemes that were almost universally adopted in 1928 could not survive the lack of unanimous support, the new broad commitment to marketing cooperation remained. It was sufficiently strong to abate the opposition to the government-backed selling schemes introduced with Part I of the Coal Mines Act of 1930 and amended by continuous government intervention in the following years. Slowly, the owners, working through their district and central associations, came to acknowledge the advantages to them of 'regulated' competition and to offer only token resistance to state action. And slowly, too, they resigned themselves to the new international environment by participating in negotiations for trade agreements and (even more radically for them) discussing with the coal industries of other countries the possibility of international regulation of competition.

It is, however, significant that there was no comparable amendment of attitude towards industrial rationalization and reform or towards government intervention in the structure of coal production. In fact, the owners' rejection of the case in favour of mergers, and their related opposition to Part II of the 1930 Act and the efforts of the Coal Mines

---

[1] The owners disagreed with the proposals emanating from the Mond–Turner talks in 1928 but were circumspectly unwilling to denounce them publicly: MSWCOA, 4 Dec. 1928.

[2] W. A. Lee, 'How to Save the Coal Industry', 1 Nov. 1927: typescript in SRO CB6/26, 3. Also see: Evans Williams to MSWCOA, 1 Nov. 1927; W. A. Lee 'Commonsense About Coal', 27 Oct. 1927.

Reorganisation Commission, were almost as inimical to their public reputation in the 1930s as their attitude to wages and hours had been in the 1920s.

Initially, the owners had been vigorously hostile to the point of foolishness in their spoiling tactics with regard to the CMRC,[1] and they were unrealistically reactionary in their expectations of the National Government in 1931—recommending the abolition not merely of the 'irritating and mischievous' CMRC, but also of the Mines Department, the Fuel Research Board, and the welfare levy.[2] Their subsequent tactics were altogether more muted. Indeed, influential men among their leadership were increasingly sensitive to the political risks they were running. In 1933, for example, Sir Adam Nimmo reminded the MAGB that the times had changed decisively; that no matter how much they might deplore government intervention, it had become inevitable, irrespective of the political complexion of the administration; and that the 'psychology of the times' demanded that the industry satisfy the country not merely that it was capable of individual success, but that it could be collectively self-supporting.[3] Such warnings became more frequent as the stabilization of the selling schemes appeared to give the owners some protection of prices and profits, and to impose some obligations on them to improve productivity and to lower costs.[4]

On the other hand, neither these symptoms nor the even more vehement criticisms of the owners' destructive reaction during the renewed controversy over legislation in 1936–8, deflected them from a determined opposition to enforced industrial amalgamation. Such adamant consistency was politically unwise, but was not entirely surprising. The owners were genuinely persuaded that there were limited economic advantages and considerable risks in a broad programme of amalgamation—which would have involved very large expenditure and investments. In any case, the politics of slump, and the fear of exacerbating the problem of unemployment, meant that the government was reluctant to enforce the existing law, and slow to strengthen it when its deficiencies were exposed. When the law was at

---

[1] They also declined to nominate representatives to the newly formed National Industrial Board for coal, thus rendering it powerless and functionless. Significantly, the West Yorkshire Coal Owners' Association was willing to cooperate, but withdrew its agreement when it appeared that other districts would remain aloof.

[2] These proposals originated in the Monmouthshire & South Wales Coal Owners' Association. See LCOA, 29 Sept. 1931. For the proposals, see *MAGB* 1932, 28–9.

[3] *MAGB* 1933, 10–11.

[4] See A. K. McCosh in SCOA, 31 Dec. 1935; and Oswald Peake MP in WYCOA, 28 Jan. 1938.

long last amended, with the Coal Act of 1938, the owners had succeeded in diluting the amendment and dragging their heels when it
was applied.

To the owners, clearly, the question of government intervention to
compel them to restructure the industry was a fundamental sticking
point on grounds of practical disadvantage as well as ideological
principle: 'the theory that industry can be coerced into prosperity by
restrictive action from outside is unsound', they had informed the
Minister of Labour in 1926.[1] However, in respects other than the
compulsory reorganization of production, their responses to the events
of the 1930s were politically more alert and ideologically much less dogmatic than had been the case in the previous decade. This applied in
particular to the national discussion of wages, on which their resistance
had been so firm in the 1920s. Thus, following the reduction of the maximum underground working day to $7\frac{1}{2}$ hours in 1930, they acquiesced in
national discussions and gave what were in effect national guarantees
concerning the wage rates to be paid. In the words of an advocate of
collective discussion within the MAGB, Sir Evan Williams and the
MAGB had been 'driven by the urgency and the importance of the question to depart from the orthodoxy of your previous creed'.[2]

Of course, such a willingness to trim embodied a pragmatic flexibility
rather than a sweeping conversion. But it *was* a sign of the times. Even
more potent examples occurred in the mid- and late 1930s when, we
may assume, the MAGB came to recognize both the political case for
accommodation in the face of a public opinion favourably inclined to
the miners, and the practical advantages of a more, rather than a less,
contented work-force. In 1935, therefore, when the miners put forward
a *national* wages claim and threatened to call a national strike, it was the
MAGB which took the initiative in approaching large customers so as to
revise their contracts in order to pay for a national award; and then
proceeded not merely to contemplate a levy to enable the export areas
to pay higher wages (a device analogous to the hated national 'pool' that
had bedevilled the negotiations of 1921), but to join the miners on a
Joint Standing Consultative Committee.

In large part, all this reflected a sense that on these issues their traditional stand would secure no public or political support.[3] But it also
flowed from a new realization that the miners were by no means mono-

---

[1] Quoted in Lubin and Everett 1927, 186.
[2] *MAGB* 1931, 10.
[3] MSWCOA, 16 Dec. 1935.

lithically 'extremist' in their attitudes, but might be weaned away from their more radical representatives. Hence, by 1935–7 there were strong signs of a more 'progressive' policy on the part of district coalowners' associations in relation to such matters as pensions and holidays with pay, the principles of which were widely accepted.[1]

As with interest groups in general, then, enlightenment among the coalowners was most often the outcome of a new interpretation of self-interest. Perhaps more than most groups, they had to be forced every step of the way. Certainly, their interwar record—given the political sensitivity of the industry and the economic and social vulnerability of the miners—was neither a good nor a proud one. And occasionally even their strongest supporters had to warn them of the practical dangers of extreme views ruthlessly held. On the eve of the Sankey débâcle, for example, the *Colliery Guardian* went so far as to criticize the owners for being unwilling to contemplate organizational charges: 'there can be no hesitation in saying, that we cannot go back to the older order of things, and it is only too true that there would be no bloody revolutions but for obstinate reactions'.[2]

In the long run, of course, it seemed as if such warnings were justified by events. Handicapped by their unenviable prewar reputation for 'obstinate reactions' (in business as well as labour affairs), showing to no better advantage in the crises of the Second World War, the owners were very badly placed to resist the campaign to nationalize the industry in 1945–6. And yet, on the other side, it could be said that in the long run, nationalization, or some equivalent form of public control, was made inevitable at least as much by the miners' attitudes and actions as by the owners' ineptness and reaction.[3] For their part, the owners might well have come to the cynical conclusion that their firm refusal to accept arrangements—whether for national wage-determination or large-scale reorganization of the industry—had been successful for a sufficiently long period to justify the determination with which they fought their campaigns. Certainly, from their own viewpoint as an interest group and during the two decades after the First World War, they were on balance better served by the principles they espoused than they might have been by the alternatives pressed upon them by the miners' union and the public critics of the industry.

[1] See in particular, the minutes of the MWSCOA and SCOA. A desire to help the 'moderates' among the miners was frequently given as a reason for supporting such departures, and was also offered in Scotland as a reason for accepting a regular half-day Saturday (SCOA, 11 oct. 1937).

[2] *CG* 28 Feb. 1919, 487.

[3] See Supple 1986.

A more important question, to which the answer is somewhat less obvious, is whether the alternative policies and structures would have been so much more advantageous in the national interest or to the miners, that on general social criteria they should have been forced on the industry. Certainly, there were critical moments—notably in 1919 and 1926—when large concessions by the owners on points of principle might have resolved the immediate tension and diminished the risk of serious social strife. But it remains extremely difficult to see how the alternative proposals (and the reallocation of huge resources to coal-mining) could have redounded to the long-run health of the industry, at least as long as it remained as large as it did. After all, joint control or nationalization, as proposed in 1919, were very much unknown arrangements and likely to expose the industry to serious risks of disruption and loss. Moreover, the owners' fears that the miners might use joint control to maximize the short-run advantages of the existing work-force were hardly imaginary.

The point is that all proposals—nationalization, a national wages and profits pool, higher wages in the 1920s, reconstruction in the 1930s, higher 'social wages', reorganization, rationalization—involved private and/or public costs. With the exception of an occasional subsidy to avoid or lessen industrial strife in 1921 and 1925–6, the state was unwilling to provide resources for industrial experiment. That left only the owners—already burdened with a stagnant industry. In essence, the owners were blamed for opposing policies that were felt to be desirable primarily as ways of attaining social peace or public benefits. Yet the costs would have to be borne privately. To the owners, therefore, the resistance to extensive change was based not merely on practicality and principle, but on the grounds of cost and risk. No doubt, their way of arguing their case, its political stupidity and lack of flexibility, meant that they brought their isolation on themselves. But the fact remains that in the last resort the industry was expected to bear the full costs of a social experiment. The subsequent history of coalmining under public ownership is not reassuring as to the ability of the industry to transform itself without the use of huge resources from the public at large or serious social strains to those within it.

CHAPTER 10

'A Disturbing Spirit from the Underworld'
The Coalminer between the Wars

Although this study is not primarily concerned with the social history of miners, some understanding of pit work and communities is an obvious element in any approach to the political economy of coal-mining in the twentieth century. The fact is that in spite of the political prominence of the mining industry between the Wars, there was wide-spread ignorance about the work and life of miners. Even to his own family, a mineworker could appear like 'a disturbing spirit from the underworld'.[1] To the rest of society his daily life was a matter of mystique and ignorance. Moreover, in the nature of the controversies which occasionally excited the attention of outsiders, public knowledge of the industry tended to be superficial or distorted—to simplify, to focus on extremes rather than patterns, to be preoccupied with formal institutions rather than the everyday realities which shaped the work and communities of the mining population, to concentrate on the spectacular or the sentimental rather than the enduring or the under-lying. As a result, contemporaries and historians have tended to rely on evidence which obscures the subtleties and regional variety of everyday life, social patterns, and attitudes in mining communities.[2]

In these respects, as with so many others, this study, too, has found it impossible to escape from the limitations of the available evidence, just as it has found it an unwieldy process to acknowledge as constantly as necessary the enormous range of regional and local experience within the industry and over time. But although it would be foolhardy to

---

[1] Scott-James 1924, 126.

[2] Two assessments of these aspects of mining life at a point in time relatively near the 1930s are: Dennis, Henriques, and Slaughter 1956; and Benny 1946. But even these were written in different circumstances from those of the 1920s and 1930s. Contemporary attempts to pursue these topics were on the whole confined to the social surveys and personal testaments stimulated by the economic plight of mining communities. See, for example, Demant 1930; Jennings 1934; Newsom 1936; 'Portrait of a Mining Town', *Fact*, No. 8 (15 Nov. 1937); Tomlinson 1937; Coombes 1939. Interesting and significant as such writings were, they naturally tended to concentrate on a narrow range of social relationships and realities.

attempt to redress the balance in one chapter, it is necessary to consider, however superficially, the content and environment of life in the industry: the work and welfare, the communities and environment, the health and self-awareness of the mining population.

i. Work

The most distinctive feature of the coalminer's working life was its abnormal location underground in conditions of isolation, discomfort, and danger. Mining was like no other occupation; and its everyday characteristics were inaccessible to those who had never been down a pit. At one level, work which involved both creating and then being constrained by a unique environment—a 'space with no outside ... a total enclosure that directs all questions back upon the questioner'[1]—established strong, unifying, and private preoccupations among miners. At another, the unique style, effort, and location of work entailed extraordinary discomforts and dangers. In public debate it was obviously the physical hazard of pit work which was most intensely appreciated by the miners and their representatives—and used to elicit sympathy for their economic arguments. As the President of the Miners' Federation of Great Britain put it in his evidence to the Buckmaster Court of Inquiry on wages in 1924:

You know the terrible dangers in our industry, the large numbers of men and boys killed and maimed every year. In 1923, 212,256 men received injuries disabling them for more than seven days, and in addition 1,297 were fatally injured. These figures mean that: Every working day more than five persons were killed. Every five hours the clock round a life was lost. Every 215,000 tons of coal raised was stained with the crimson of one man's blood. Every working day 850 men and boys were injured. ... Try and visualise this great army of bruised and broken humanity.... Marshall them in one huge procession, four men in a rank, each 1½ yards apart, and you get a procession of injured men stretching a distance of 45 miles. Every 15 yards of that tragic march you would have an ambulance conveying a man who was seriously injured, and every 61 yards a hearse. This is part of the miners' wages; part of the price he pays in the struggle with natural forces, that the people may have coal, and that he and his family may have bread. This part of his wages never gets into a balance sheet; is never seen in a quotation; is never allowed for, or even thought of, by the consumer.[2]

---

[1] Leed 1979, 145.
[2] *Buckmaster Proceedings*, 10.

Herbert Smith's formulation was sensational, but the situation it reflected was real enough. In the mid-1920s it was calculated that for every 100 men working for 20 years, the probabilities were that two would be killed, nine would suffer a major fracture or serious injury, 16 would incur a serious disease, and each would incur an accident, involving an absence from work for more than seven days, at least once every eight years.[1] Mining was 'the most dangerous of all the major industries'; with roughly 5 per cent of the working population, it experienced about 25 per cent of all industrial accidents.[2] Of all the principal occupations, only shipping had a higher mortality rate from accidents, while taking account of all moderate to serious injuries, coalmining was far and away the most hazardous: in the period 1919–24 there were some 164 non-fatal accidents per 1,000 employees in the mines, as against 30 in factories, 31 on the railways, and 74 on the docks.[3]

Against this background, it was the more worrying that, after a distinct improvement in the safety record of the industry in the late nineteenth century, there was little or no amelioration in the interwar period. (See Table 10.1.) Indeed, the incidence of accidental *deaths* actually increased. The Coal Mines Act of 1911 had propounded an elaborate system of safety regulations which undoubtedly improved conditions and arrangements in the industry. Nevertheless, when the Royal Commission on Safety in the Mines of 1935–8 came to report a quarter of a century later, it pointed out that there had been no significant change in the general level of accidents for the past 15 years, and that during the three years of its own inquiry 850 miners had died and 135,000 injuries had necessitated an absence from work of three or more days. 'These are grave figures', it asserted, 'which cry out for reduction.'[4]

Exactly why the advances in techniques, awareness, and provision should have failed to reduce deaths and accidents in the mines after the First World War was not very clear. There was, of course, the possibility—occasionally emphasized by the miners' union—that the hazards of reorganization and mechanization (involving less individual work, unfamiliar and more dangerous machinery, greater noise and dust) outweighed the advances. And the Royal Commission on Safety itself drew attention to organizational considerations which, together with the

---

[1] *Samuel Report*, 192.

[2] *RCSM Report*, 5; Bryan 1951, 842.

[3] *Samuel Appendices*, Appendix 18, 241–2.

[4] *RSCM Report*, 5. The recommendations of the Royal Commission were either instituted by general regulations or enacted after the War.

Table 10.1. *Average annual death and injury rates per 100,000 manshifts worked, British coalmining, 1922-1936*

	Killed	Injured[a]
1922–6	0.40	65.1
1927–31	0.43	69.3
1932–6	0.44	65.6

[a] Compensatable injuries: disabled more than three days (more than seven days before 1924).

Source: RCSM Report, 65.

working of thinner or more dangerous seams, made accidents more likely in the absence of countervailing reforms and regulations. These included changes in firm size and structure which blurred managerial responsibilities, the rapid advance of faces, and the changes in supervisory tasks.

On the other side, however, it was also possible that the accident statistics themselves were affected by factors not directly related to safety—in the case of minor accidents, the relative attraction of compensation depending on the level and regularity of wages and employment and the rates of compensation; in the case of more serious incidents, the average age of employees (which increased during the interwar period and even more during the Second World War). The Samuel Commission did, indeed, suggest the possibility of a tendency for minor accidents (leading to compensation payments) to move inversely with earnings.[1]

Whatever the explanation of changing trends in accident rates, however, the fact remained that mining was extremely uncomfortable, exhausting, and dangerous work. For miners, although many other aspects of their work could be the occasion of industrial and political action, its physical risks were a constant point of focus for resentment at neglect by others. In coalmining, they felt, there was 'a definite community of misfortune'.[2] To the rest of society, however, although the dangers of mining obviously touched sensitive nerves, it did so only intermittently. That the miners' working life was extraordinarily hazardous

[1] Samuel Report, 191; Samuel Appendices, Tables 20–3; MFP, Report of HM Inspector of Mines for the Years 1939–45 (1948), 7. Over the course of the Second World War, serious injury and death rates tended downwards, but the total injury rate jumped very sharply.

[2] Dataller 1925, 158–9.

was a widely recognized fact, but it tended to be acknowledged only in relation to the severe accidents that occasionally occurred—such as that at the Senghenydd Pit in Glamorgan (when 439 men were killed in October 1913) or at the Gresford Pit in Denbighshire (265 killed in September 1934) or at the Markham No. 1 Pit in Derbyshire (79 killed in May 1938)—or when the threat of political instability transformed the economic and social circumstances of mining into matters of public discussion and anxiety, so that there was dramatic scope for the comparison of miners' pay and the circumstances of their labour.

It was, however, the latter—the uniquely unfavourable and uncomfortable character of the underground working environment—rather than the immediate dangers of mining which helped shape the economic, social, and psychological significance of work for miners. In large part, this was a question of intensity of effort. Even when reduced, the length of the shift was onerous given the nature of the work.[1] And its fatiguing nature was made the worse because of the need to travel to and from the pit, often over long distances and on foot, and most commonly (on the return journey) in a filthy and wet, as well as an exhausted, condition. But it was the work at the mine, and particularly at the coal-face, which proved the most stressful part of a miner's life.

Coalmining before mechanization was the most exhausting of jobs for a variety of reasons. Hand-hewing had in the main to be carried out by a hewer lying on his side on an uncomfortable surface in a cramped and claustrophobic space; haulage systems were dependent on muscle power to supplement animal or mechanical energy; there was a constant need to use shovel and pick in the construction and maintenance of roadways as well as in the transfer of coal between face and tub or conveyor; perpetual manual labour was involved in supporting roofs and moving equipment and supplies. Moreover, the expenditure of effort was undertaken in darkness, and in choking and filthy conditions, frequently exacerbated by penetrating dampness and/or scorching heat. And the fatigue of all this was only aggravated by the common need (given the rarity of mechanical transport or horse haulage for face-workers) to travel

[1] The maximum hours for underground workers, which were specified by law from 1908, are usually defined as eight (per day) until 1919, seven between 1919 and 1926, eight between 1926 and 1930, and 7½ from 1930. However, some districts worked shorter shifts (for example, a maximum of 7½ hours in the Midlands in 1926–30 and the customary short shifts for face-workers in the North-East). On the other side, the legislation allowed a shift length to be equivalent to the maximum plus one 'winding time' (the time needed to lower or raise an entire shift of men). This naturally varied between pits and districts. District averages for a single winding time in the main fields in 1925 were estimated to range between 30 and 43 minutes. *Samuel Report*, 267–70.

between pit shaft and coalface on foot, often crouching, for an *average* of over 30 minutes in each direction.

Even when undercutting and conveying were mechanized, coal-mining still involved a huge expenditure of effort, and remained physically among the most demanding of occupations. The effect on a newcomer could be devastating:

after I had recovered from my alarm and most of the dust had passed [after a fall of undercut coal] I did my best to throw the coal into the tram. I soon found that a different kind of strength was needed than the one I had developed. My legs became cramped, my arms ached, and the back of my hands had the skin rubbed off by pressing my knee against them to force the shovel under the coal. The dust compelled me to cough and sneeze, while it collected inside my eyes and made them burn and feel sore. My skin was smarting because of the dust and flying bits of coal. The end of that eight hours was very soon my fondest wish. . . . How glad I was to drag my aching body towards that circle of daylight! I had sore knees and was wet from the waist down. The back of my right hand was raw and my back felt the same. My eyes were half closed because of the dust and my head was aching where I had hit it against the top, but I had been eight hours in a strange world.[1]

Later, even when experienced, the same man found that working an eighteen-inch seam meant weeks of 'agony and misery':

All the coal had to be blown out with powder, and the seam was so thin that I had to bore five holes before I had enough coal to fill one tram. It was quite a contract to bore even one hole. I had to lie flat and force the drill inwards with the pressure of my stomach, while my hands knocked against the top and then the bottom when I turned the handle. I had to move about by drawing myself on my elbows as would a man swimming. Fourteen inches was the length of a post to support the roof and while I was squirming about I was hitting my head or shoulders against stones and posts that I could not see because the ventilation was not good enough to clear the powder smoke. . . . There were days when I hoped that an accident would happen to me so that I would be crippled enough not to have to work there again.[2]

There can, then, be no doubt as to the significance of the nature of individual effort in the 'culture' of mining work. To the outsider, the skilled miner's efforts could appear astonishingly 'full-blooded, unrelenting and unflagging', but it was like no other physical work.[3] Both in its intrinsic effect on the miner and because it constantly reminded him of the contrast between his own working life and that of others, it

---

[1] Coombes 1939, 35, 39.   [2] Ibid., 193.   [3] Benny 1946, 39–40.

was a vital shaping force in the psychology and politics of the miners as a group. Yet the expenditure of effort and the apparently routine tasks were themselves part of highly articulated and complex structures. It was, indeed, the organization and interrelationships of the work process itself which provided the critical determinant of the miners' life and outlook.

The varied manual tasks and interlocking skills involved in the winning of coal have already been described.[1] These naturally had important organizational implications for coalmining. Unlike factory work, for example, much of it (at least until full mechanization) had necessarily to be carried on by individuals or small groups working for most of the time without direct supervision. Indeed, this was the case even with longwall working before the advent of substantial machines. It is true that supervisors (mostly deputies, but also undermanagers and overmen)[2] had an intermittently important role to play, either because of their statutory obligations in relation to safety (shot-firing, testing for gas) or because they were needed to coordinate labour where there was a high degree of specialization of task, or because they were traditionally expected to carry out specific tasks (setting timber props in the North-East, for example).

More than this, the extensive use of piece-rate payment for essential irregular tasks like timbering or 'ripping', or where there was great scope for disagreement as to the task done (e.g. the weight of coal produced or its freedom from dirt), produced constant dissension and enormous potential for ill will between worker and managerial authority. Yet the fact remained that coalmining was among the most individualistic of occupations as far as direct and continuous supervision was concerned, which helps explain the fact that so much underground management devolved into a matter of financial incentives or brutal intimidation.

This 'individualism' was, nevertheless, itself tempered by the fact that the semi-autonomous work was organized around small groups. For within, and at times between, those groups there could be a most sensitive interdependence—partly in order to ensure mutual safety, partly as a means of cohesion in the face of managerial authority, and partly to guarantee the continuity of individual effort and production on which the wages of many depended. The labour process of a coal-mine was to a large extent controlled by individual workers, but both

[1] Above, ch. 1, sect. iii.   [2] Below, 439–42.

natural and organizational imperatives obliged them to coalesce and cooperate as well as compete.

It was consistent with this work pattern that the other dominant characteristic of underground work was an extraordinarily elaborate division of labour and the most complicated payment systems in modern industry.[1] To take two extremes of specialization, in the North-East hewing, timbering, 'filling', 'putting' (getting the coal to the main roadway), 'driving' tubs to the shaft, development, repair work to roads, haulage maintenance, etc. were all in the hands of specialists; in South Wales, however, there was much less division of labour at the face, and a hewer and his helper would cut and get the coal, timber the roof, convey the coal to the main roadways, and repair local roads—and be paid not at a single tonnage rate, but at a different rate for each kind of job, with the result that Welsh 'price lists' were incredibly complex.

In large part, no doubt, the articulated division of labour in coal-mining was the outcome of varying geological and technical circumstances; but there can be little doubt that its perpetuation was also based on the weight of local tradition and the independence of mind of those involved. The result was a fierce commitment to established methods and procedures, and a militant conservatism of outlook in which skills (and even, on occasion, traditional discomforts)[2] were jealously protected and demarcation lines closely respected. Structural or economic changes which disturbed the balance of aptitudes or rewards could, equally, be disruptive in ways which transcended the disputes and resentments of more conventional wage- and task-bargaining.

Very clearly, then, mining work was a bizarre mixture of autonomy and discipline, individualism and group cohesiveness, rare skills and brute strength, hierarchy and equality. Underpinning the entire system was the constant sense that both the environment of work and the work itself were unique, giving miners a special position and a mutuality which could not be penetrated, let alone fully grasped, by others. The coalminer occupied his own world, whose physical characteristics and institutional structures he both made and sustained. And his resulting aspirations for comprehensive group autonomy were the more strengthened by the intermittent threats of those with some claim to hierarchical authority or superior control of resources. In such a situa-

---

[1] For the payments system in coalmining, see Rowe 1923, 57 ff. I am also indebted to Dr Quentin Outram for an opportunity to consult his unpublished manuscript on 'Working Methods and Payment Systems in British Coal Mining, 1900–1940'.

[2] For the varying attitudes to the introduction of pithead baths, see below, 475.

tion periods of committed application and even tranquillity could easily give way to exasperation, discontent, and anger; while physical stress and physical danger compounded the complexity and sensitivity of life underground and reinforced beyond all prospect of erosion the sense of group loyalty and unflinching solidarity which distinguished the miners from all other industrial groups.

This solidarity was by no means inconsistent with material inequality. Pay as well as prospects varied widely between different groups of workers. And wage systems frequently reinforced the cooperative group spirit even when they embodied varying levels of remuneration.[1] Thus, a group of hewers and rippers could receive one piece rate, while dividing the proceeds in different ratios. In other circumstances, rough equality could obtain, as when individuals on different shifts shared work places and tasks. The best-known version of this comradely device was the Durham system whereby partnerships of 'marrows', working the same stall or section of longwall, but on different shifts, shared their earnings, which had the incidental advantage of expediting work between shifts. Other versions of 'mutual sharing' existed elsewhere.[2]

On the other hand, a much less cooperative payments system was that of the 'butty'. In its classic form this involved one man subcontracting to deliver coal, on a piece-rate basis, to a specific point in the mine, and then employing others to fulfil the tasks. The 'big butty', under which the whole or a very large part of a mine would be contracted, had died out by the late nineteenth century. But important vestiges of the 'little butty', under which a relatively small section of a face or part of the haulage system was subcontracted, lasted in some mines until the 1930s. Analogous, but potentially less intimidating or divisive, payments systems were exemplified where groups of colliers jointly hired assistants at day rates, or (as was very common in South Wales, Lancashire, and parts of Scotland) individual coal-getters paid their assistants out of their own piece wages. Of course, much of this admixture of individual and group piece-rate payment related to work at the coalface. Elsewhere underground, and where the main haulage operated or unskilled and routine tasks were to be performed, day-rate labour was employed under closer supervision.

---

[1] For a discussion of wage-payment systems, see above, ch. 1, sect. iv.

[2] This was also related to the arrangements known as 'cavilling' in the North-East, where work places were regularly allocated and reallocated to hewers by the drawing of lots, to ensure equality of treatment as far as geological variations were concerned. Cavilling was also occasionally used to allocate work after a stoppage or to decide on the order of redundancy.

Much of all this was slow to change, and its fixity gave a special character to the work and life of miners. On the other hand, structural adaptation *did* take place in the industry, and its consequences and implications helped shape and reshape the culture of work in the period.

As far as the organization of work was concerned, and allowing for the great variety of methods and systems, the interwar years were characterized by two related developments: the extension of longwall working and the growth of mechanized mining.[1] By the 1940s almost three-quarters of British coal production was obtained from longwall faces, although alternative systems (in particular room and pillar, or some variant of it) were still widely used in the western area of the South Wales field and in parts of the North-East. As for mechanization, between the early 1920s and 1938, the percentage of coal cut mechanically rose from 14 to 61, and of coal conveyed from less than 10 to 57. Both developments implied a considerable change in the context and organization of work, although neither did much to alleviate the labour intensity of the process of mining (wage costs remained overwhelmingly important). Moreover, although both resulted in a national convergence of techniques and organization, regional and local variety naturally persisted.

The most important results of the introduction of longwall faces flowed from the disappearance of the individual 'stall'. It is true that even in longwall mining hewers and associated workmen were identified with particular lengths of the face. But the fact of its spatial continuity and the need to ensure that work at each point kept pace with all others, naturally meant that there was an intensified need to coordinate and supervise individuals and individual groups in the workforce. Skills and effort, and even different shifts, became increasingly interdependent. The nature of underground work began to change.

At the same time, mechanized mining or, rather, mining with the aid of machines (for physical effort remained very important in the handling and manhandling of machinery, maintaining roads and roofs, loading coal on to conveyors, etc.) had even more important consequences for the organization and attitudes of labour. In the 'pre-machine' age the experienced hewer, the aristocrat of the labour force, had been central to the work-force, earning relatively large wages, and occupying a critically influential place in the hierarchy of labour and trade unions. More generally, the underground work-force at the face was based on small, well-integrated teams, generally working with a

[1] Above, ch. 1, sect. iii.

high degree of autonomy. That autonomy applied whether the hewer was a man of varied skills and responsibilities (as in South Wales) or a specialist supported by other specialist workers (as in Northumberland and Durham).

Against all this, the introduction of 'machine mining' in the 1920s and 1930s—and particularly the introduction of cutters and conveyors on longwall faces—diminished the need for the traditional skills of the hewer (primarily because undercutting was now done mechanically);[1] substantially extended the size of mining teams; reduced the autonomy with which the senior face-workers and their immediate colleagues could operate; and further increased the need for supervision and the interdependence of work tasks not merely within the larger groups but also between different groups and different shifts. The scale and intensity of machine-cutting and the use of conveyors imposed a new diurnal rhythm on mining at the seam. Typically, although not universally, cutting would occupy one shift, loading (filling or getting) a second shift, and a third shift would be needed to move the conveyors to the new line of the face, clean up, rip new roads, retimber and pack new roofs.[2]

Machine mining therefore involved far more than the introduction of machinery for specific operations. Now, the coordination and interdependence of the separate shifts became of crucial importance, for neglect at one stage could disrupt all the others: a failure to fill all the coal cut would impede the movement of the conveyor pans or belts; a failure to move the conveyors would disrupt the next cutting shift; above all, a failure to complete the cutting shift could 'cause the dislocation of the whole cycle and a serious loss of output'.[3] Clearly, in addition to the disruption of conventional skills and the derogation of the hewer's traditional status, the new mining systems involved the loss of individual determination of work tasks, much closer individual supervision, and the heightened pressure which came from the interdependence of the system as a whole. Machine mining therefore implied a

---

[1] See H. T. Foster, 'The Trend of Coal Mining Practice', *CG* 27 Apr. 1945, 515: 'the value of the trained and skilful miners largely ceased to be appreciated, fillers using shovels took their place.'

[2] See *Reid Report*, 58: 'The removal of the web of coal taken by a coalcutter . . . exposes a span of roof equal to the depth of the cut, and requires a row of props to be sent between the conveyor and the coalface. Thus, the conveyor must be dismantled before it can be passed through these props for reassembly in its new track, and this operation generally requires a separate shift for its completion. Until the conveyor has been advanced, the roof supports over the old track must remain, and the packs cannot be extended.'

[3] *Reid Report*, 48.

necessary reorganization of the labour force and the mode of working and cooperation—a fundamental realignment of workplace arrangements and responsibilities.[1] As was pointed out at the time, 'Effective utilisation of coal face machinery is incompatible with [the organization, transport, and methods] appropriate . . . to hand working.' Machine mining involved a 'rigid adherence to a prearranged timetable' and a much greater attention to effective control of the total labour process—to organization, supervision, and control. 'Each man', it could be argued at one extreme, had to be 'a cog in the machine and no more.'[2]

Looking back from the mid-1930s, the Royal Commission on Safety in Coal Mines described the transformation in work processes that had taken place since 1911:

Broadly speaking the main changes are the result of concentration and mechanization coupled with the working of thinner or more difficult or more dangerous seams . . . the required output of coal is now obtained from fewer mines and from fewer and shorter faces in individual mines. The faces advance more rapidly and the mechanized system of work involves the maintenance of a steady cycle of operations, spread over three or more successive shifts. On the afternoon and night shifts the numbers employed and the relative importance of the operations have therefore become much more nearly equal to those on the day shifts than before, and this affects the character of the supervision required.[3]

To put the matter in an oversimplified way, before the introduction of machinery the face-worker was able to carry out his tasks with relatively little external interference. By and large, close supervision was not needed since face-workers tended to be paid on a piece-rate basis and inefficiency therefore principally affected the inefficient. In this situation underground officials (mostly deputies) acted more like auxiliaries than supervisors in relation to face-workers (although deputies did have an important supervisory role for haulage and non-face underground miners). After the advent of mechanized, longwall mining, however, face-work had to be overseen and coordinated. Poor or uncoordinated work might affect the operation of a large part of

[1] Subsequent appraisals of the new system of mining are to be found in Trist and Bamforth 1951, 3–38; Goldthorpe 1959, 213–30. An interesting contemporary insight is provided by Goodrich 1920. For enthusiastic contemporary descriptions of 'intensive mining' see Mavor 1924, 1510–11; Barraclough 1927–8, 177–98.

[2] The quotations in the text are from Mavor 1924, 1510; Moonie 1936–7, 247; and Greenwell 1933, 302. For other contemporary emphases of the importance of control and supervision, see Bulman 1921, 1659; and Clive 1929–30, 311.

[3] *RCSM Report*, 45.

the mine, and some degree of teamwork was essential. Supervisory staff became more important. And the inevitable result was a loss of some autonomy by individual workers at the coalface.

That loss has been the subject of social analyses which have tended to the conclusion that disaffection, alienation, resentment at the closer supervision, and a degree of 'anomie' became more marked features of working lives in the pits and of industrial relations in the mining industry.[1] And even at the time there were many observers who argued that the face-workers' skills were being destroyed and that the craftsman miner was being reduced to 'an automatic coal-heaver', whose daily work was increasingly characterized by rush and pressure.[2]

However, although mechanization obviously did transform the miner's traditional tasks, the transformation must not be exaggerated. Thus, while the disturbance of inherited skills and tasks is almost invariably interpreted as a degradation of independence and role, too much can be made of the 'independence' and even of the 'skill' of the old-fashioned hand miner. Many men before mechanization, although they had substantial personal investments in physical abilities, training, and experience relevant to the tortuous and hazardous circumstances of conventional mining, were in fact undertaking fairly straightforward manual tasks. More than this, even before mechanization, division of labour at the face, with an attendant lack of individual autonomy and a need for supervisory coordination, was quite well advanced in some regions. Nor was the speeding up which some critics associated with the introduction of machines and integrated shift-working an entire novelty in mines which had never known a powered machine.[3]

On the other side, too, machine mining was by no means lacking in its own distinctive skills. Operating coal cutters, moving and assembling conveyor belts, maintaining machinery, participating in the team effort of the new systems—all could involve specialist aptitudes and a high degree of proficiency and training (although the latter was frequently neglected). As a result, it could be argued that mechanization had not so much reduced as changed the skill necessary for the coalminer.[4]

Equally important, the actual extent of the change in occupational structures can easily be exaggerated. As late as 1951 about one-third of

---

[1] See references in 436 n., above.

[2] Mitchell 1933, 143. Also see the oral evidence on attitudes collected by Evans 1976; and Coombes 1939, 149.

[3] Coombes 1939, 85–6; *RCSM Evidence*, Q 15482.

[4] Coombes 1939, 111–12; Jones 1925, 22; Rowe 1923, 69–70; Manley 1948, 14.

the mining work-force in the principal coal-producing counties were still categorized in the Census as hewers and getters by hand, while those described as working with coal-cutting machinery accounted for a very small proportion of the total labour force, varying between 2.4 and 5.4 per cent.[1] The explicit and politicized 'culture' of underground work may well have been most affected by machinery, but a majority of underground workers, and certainly a large majority of men at the face, continued to undertake broadly similar tasks, albeit more attuned to the pace of the machine, even if the most skilled of tasks (the undercutting of the coal) was a dying art.

However, when all qualifications have been accepted, it remains the case that intensive machine mining did alter the character of pit work. Strength rather than dexterity or experience was becoming 'paramount'. At the face in particular the 'complete collier' of the past was being replaced by 'mechanics and the like semi-specialised . . . craftsmen' and 'a substantial proportion' of workmen who were 'primarily manual labourers'.[2] Old aptitudes were downgraded or rendered redundant. The hewer's underground superiority was being eroded. Elsewhere in the pit, skills might remain essentially the same, but the pressures could change dramatically. Thus, a putter working with a shovel to connect a face conveyor with the main haulage system could describe his life as 'hell': 'one machine was vomiting more than I could clean up, while the other had a larger mouth than I could fill'.[3]

For all these reasons, then, machine mining might well prove unpopular—particularly if expectations that close bargaining might establish significantly higher earnings were disappointed, or if (as too frequently happened) management neglected to provide for effective preparation or necessary training. The result was often a degree of antipathy to the new methods, a latent 'culture of anger' and even occasional acts of sabotage.[4] It should be remembered, however, that coal-mining was a conservative occupation, and the resistance to organizational change was not confined to the issue of mechanization. In the 1920s, for example, miners in many northern collieries persisted in clinging to 'the rigid customs and traditions which had grown up under the old conditions' and thereby obstructed the introduction of

---

[1] The exception to these generalizations was Northumberland, where hand-hewers and getters accounted for 27.2%, and men working with mechanical cutters for 6.4%, of the labour force.

[2] The quotations are from Stewart 1935, 36; *RCSM Report*, 46.

[3] Quoted in Brown 1934, 86.

[4] Trist and Bamforth 1951, 23; Coombes 1944, 18–19.

longwall mining. And there was certainly very strong opposition to the introduction of extended shift-working in South Wales and Northumberland.[1]

The suspicion of mechanization may have been pronounced, but in the event there was very little effective opposition to the introduction of new techniques. And although apprehension on this score may well have inhibited managers from proposing a more rapid pace of technical innovation, machinery *was* extensively introduced and work habits *were* actually changed—although the fact that labour productivity grew with such painful slowness may indicate that recalcitrant attitudes had a more subterranean effect. But as far as the actual introduction of mechanization was concerned, material incentives greatly reduced overt opposition. Of course, the existence of surplus labour naturally enhanced the bargaining position of management (in the words of one critic, years of unemployment, low pay, unsuccessful strikes, and blacklists had forced men 'to listen to the doctrine that "half a loaf is better than none", no matter how much their natures rebel[led] against it').[2] But at a more general level, and as happened so frequently with the issue of structural reform, bread-and-butter questions of pay and hours took precedence in the minds of the rank and file of miners.

One obvious result of the developments in work organization and systems was the increased significance of underground supervisory staff. Deputies, examiners, and firemen (the terms reflected regional differences in nomenclature rather than roles) loomed larger in the lives of manual workers in the pits. Between 1913 and 1924 the proportion of the underground work-force who were deputies, examiners, or firemen rose from 2.8 to 3.1 per cent (although this figure was to fall in the 1920s as a whole), while the proportion of *all* officials in the underground work-force rose from 3.5 to 4 per cent. At the same time, since in many regions deputies were largely confined to safety work, the oversight of production was often given to 'overmen'—'officers of economy', appointed to oversee work and encourage effective production within groups of 'districts' (each supervised by an individual deputy). Nationally, the proportion of *all* officials to the underground work-force rose from 3.5 to 3.9 per cent in the period 1913–24.[3]

[1] Pedelty 1925, 1381. *Samuel Evidence*, 953.

[2] Coombes 1939, 117.

[3] The quoted phrase was used by an official of the General Federation of Colliery Firemen's, Examiners' and Deputies' Associations of Great Britain in *RCSM Evidence* Q 15511. For overmen, also see QQ 23880, 23892; *RCSM Report*, 16–18 and 67–72; and Jones 1925, 51–2. The actual number of overmen was small—less than 5,000 in 1924. For this, and other figures on the

However, the numerical significance of underground officials varied from district to district even before mechanization. This was partly a reflection of differing managerial attitudes to safety, but it was also a function of important differences in organization. In the North-East, for example, greater coordination was needed simply because hewers were more specialized and timber-setting and non-hewing work around the stall was carried on by others. As a result the North-East had a much lower proportion of hewers and getters (about 40 per cent according to the Census of 1921, as against more than 60 per cent in South Wales and 57 or 58 per cent in the Midlands) and a higher proportion of supervisory personnel (about 5 per cent as against 3 per cent or less in South Wales).[1] In the nation as a whole face-workers accounted for 53.9 per cent of the underground work-force in 1913 and 50.4 per cent in 1924; hauliers (between face and shaft) rose from 20.9 to 22.6 per cent; and miners making and repairing roads rose from 18 to 19.3 per cent.

In practice, most subordinate supervision was carried on by deputies. The Coal Mines Act of 1911 had laid down the statutory duties of deputies (inspection of the mine with respect to gas, ventilation, the state of roofs and sides, and general safety) and minimum, if rather low, standards of technical competence. Admittedly, the duty of deputies was not confined to safety. It included 'measuring up' (assessing the amount of work done by miners in order to qualify for payment) and in the North-East the 1911 Act specifically allowed deputies to undertake more direct productive tasks, such as the setting of timber. Nevertheless, the general expectation was that deputies were essentially safety officers. Yet even under the system of hand-getting there was obviously a sensitive relationship between safety and production, so that deputies were frequently under pressure from both miners and management (it was for this reason that their union pressed for them to become state employees). And as mechanization proceeded, while the nature of the safety problem changed, there was a definite need for more elaborate supervision which was partly met by the appointment of overmen, but

composition of the work-force in 1913 and 1924, see *Samuel Appendices*, Appendix 18, Table 13. For the growth of subordinate officials, also see *RCSM Report*, 51.

[1] However, at the 1921 Census the proportion of supervisory personnel in Derbyshire and Nottinghamshire was just over 5%. In 1907 supervisory personnel accounted for 4.6% of the *underground* labour force in Northumberland and 5.0% in Durham. The figures for Scotland, South Wales, and Yorkshire were about 4.0, 2.7, and 2.6%. See *First Report of the Departmental Committee Appointed to Inquire into the Probable Economic Effects of a Limit of Eight Hours to the Working Day of Coal Miners* (1907), II, Table I, 40–126.

principally resulted in pressure on deputies to concern themselves more and more with questions of discipline and organization.[1]

The law which largely confined deputies to safety functions was therefore, in the words of the Permanent Secretary at the Department of Mines in 1936, increasingly 'honoured in the breach'.[2] For the fact was, that (in the absence of a new managerial hierarchy) the remoteness and small number of more senior officials inevitably meant that deputies were the only feasible representatives of managerial authority at the coalface—a situation which came into greater prominence as machine mining was extended.

From this viewpoint there was an interesting contrast in the tenor of evidence given on behalf of deputies to the Sankey Commission in 1919 and to the Royal Commission on Safety in 1938. In the former case, their representative complained that they were placed in an impossible position because of twofold pressure, from management *and* miners, to neglect their obligation to apply safety regulations. By 1938 the problem had apparently changed. Pressure, to increase production, came largely from the side of management; and deputies, as one of their union officials put it, were 'being forced on output'.[3] Moreover, as their managerial role was enhanced, their relationship with the work-force was subject to strain and deterioration.

On the other hand, the implication (which exists in some of the literature) that mechanization and longwall working produced a very large increase in the numerical significance of deputies between the Wars is not borne out by the available statistics. Between the 1921 and 1931 Censuses, for example, while the proportion of miners who were returned as 'subordinate superintending staff' rose from 5.1 to 5.3 per cent in Nottinghamshire, it was stable at 5.1 per cent in Northumberland, and actually fell in every other major district (most strikingly in Glamorgan and Monmouthshire—from 3.3 and 3.5 to 2.7 and 3.0 per cent). Similarly, the membership of the General Federation of Firemen's, Examiners' and Deputies' Associations of Great Britain, which

[1] See the descriptions of the work of deputies in Dataller 1925, 62; Day 1975, 47; Jones 1925, 49–50; Pick 1946, 77. I am much indebted to John Goldthorpe, of Nuffield College, for access to his notes and unpublished writings on the subject of deputies in the coal industry.

[2] Evidence of Sir Andrew Faulkner to *RCSM Evidence*, 7, 33. For the problem of confusion between the safety and production functions of deputies, see the *RCSM Report*, 183–4. The Commission recommended that deputies should assume full authority for both safety and production—but within smaller 'districts' within each mine.

[3] *RCSM Evidence*, Q 15702. For the changes between 1919 and 1936 see *Sankey Evidence* I, QQ 4793, 4854, 5056–7; *RCSM Evidence* QQ 15497–8, 15539–58, 15701–2.

had risen from 12,540 in 1914 to 20,200 in 1919, fell to just under 15,000 in 1936.[1]

The changes in the organization and relationships of work obviously transformed the position of deputies, who became perceptibly more identified with management. Admittedly, their training and qualifications were generally felt to be inadequate (owners and managers were said to resist efforts to improve the standards of recruitment and competence), and they worked longer hours than other underground men and were not well paid.[2] But although their rates of pay frequently fell below the best-paid hewers, they had much greater continuity of work. As a result, their actual weekly earnings might be greater than that of face-workers. In any case, they had more security of tenure, and frequently enjoyed important fringe benefits such as annual holidays with pay, sick pay, and superior housing. To that extent, too, therefore, they were distinguished from the general run of miners from whose ranks they were recruited. And, given the relatively small numbers of deputies, as well as their peripheral influence on the outlook and relationships of the mass of mineworkers, it is the position of the latter which rightly figures most prominently in any history of work and community in the British coal industry.

ii. The material welfare of miners: income, employment, and social provision

The material welfare of the mining population obviously depended on the supply of jobs, the continuity of work and the level of wages, the social provision for the casualties of economic processes, and the quality of their housing and social environments. Of these, the miners themselves, although anxious to improve their circumstances in other directions, were much more actively concerned with the question of wages and employment, if only because the levels of income and available work fluctuated so drastically throughout these years.

---

[1] *Samuel Evidence*, 631; *RCSM Evidence*, 553. By 1951 the proportion of 'subordinate superintending staff' had shot up everywhere (in the principal counties it ranged from 5.8% in Monmouthshire to 8.3% in Northumberland). Quite apart from the further development of organizational change during the 1940s, and the influence of the National Coal Board after 1946, one possible explanation of this trend was the previous managerial reluctance, under private ownership, to increase the proportion of 'oncost' employees, such as deputies, who were not directly associated with the production of coal.

[2] Mines Department, *Report to the Secretary for Mines of the Committee Appointed by him to Inquire into the Qualifications and Recruitment of Officials of Mines* (HMSO, 1929); *RCSM Report*, 200 ff.

The ultimate determinant of earnings in the coal industry was the commercial abundance or scarcity of coal, shaping as it did both market forces and the collective bargaining power of the miners and the owners (and the government). The shortage of coal dominated the labour market until the end of 1920, by which time the miners had secured an increase in their average real incomes of about 20 per cent over the level of 1914 (and a reduction in the length of the working day of one hour in most districts).[1] Beginning with the collapse of the export market in 1920–1, however, the situation was largely reversed: the stagnation of the industry imposed an irresistible pressure on wage costs.

Admittedly, the resulting reductions in earnings (which had been initiated with extraordinary abruptness in 1921–2, when money wages fell by 50 per cent and real wages by 32 per cent)[2] were in practice somewhat mitigated by transitory recurrences of world shortages (in 1923–4, for example), by the differential market for coal from different districts, and by public sympathy with the idea of a 'social wage' and wage agreements which established minima for daily wage rates. Nevertheless, earnings declined in the course of the 1920s, and the effects of a slight improvement in money wages in 1923–4 were eradicated in the turmoil of 1926, at which time the eight-hour day was legalized, and by subsequent wage cuts. By 1929 money earnings were about 12 per cent below the level of 1924 and the miners were the only important industrial group whose income had fallen in *real* terms (by 6 or 7 per cent in 1924–9).

Indeed, as is clear from Figs. 10.1a and 10.1b, it was in the 1920s that the real incomes of miners reached their interwar nadir. For in spite of the intensified depression, and the associated decline in nominal wages, during the slump of 1929–32, minimum wage *rates* were sustained by agreements, while the reduction of annual *earnings* which inevitably accompanied the rise of unemployment and short-time working, was outpaced by the fall in the cost of living. Thus, between 1929 and 1932 average annual earnings fell by 7.5 per cent (from £118 6s. 4d. to £109 8s. 5d.), whereas the cost of living fell by about 12 per cent. Thenceforth, wages rose slightly to 1935 and more sharply afterwards, while prices only began to rise (and then relatively slowly) in the late 1930s. By 1938 annual money earnings were some 23 per cent higher than they had been in 1929, whereas living costs had fallen by about 5 per cent.

[1] For details of the level of wages, and regional variations in earnings, during the 1920s and 1930s, see Table 10.2, Fig. 10.1, and above, 196–200, 276.

[2] Above, 161–7.

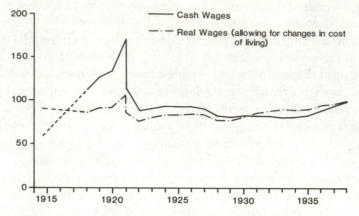

Fig. 10.1(a). Indices of average shift wages in British coalmining, 1914–1938 (1938 = 100)

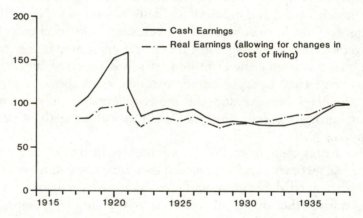

Fig. 10.1(b). Indices of average quarterly earnings in British coalmining, 1914–1938 (1938 = 100)

Sources: CYB 1939, 628–9; CYB 1948, 656–7; ARSM 1922, 121–2; Department of Employment and Productivity 1971, 166–7

There was therefore an important contrast between the 1920s and the 1930s. During the 1920s, the relatively untrammelled operation of market forces pressed on earnings in the coal industry. In the 1930s, institutional adjustments (notably the legally enforced marketing schemes) helped sustain coal prices, and therefore earnings, for those who were fortunate enough to remain at work—albeit at the apparent cost of a reduction in output. Less jobs were available in the industry, but wages were higher than they would otherwise have been. Given the existence of unemployment relief and direct assistance, it could be argued that in the 1930s 'it might . . . be in the collective interest of the miners to prefer unemployment which is subsidized to low wages which are not subsidized'.[1]

In the case of earnings, as of other variables, data on national averages exaggerate the uniformity of actual trends. In South Wales, for example, in spite of the chronically high unemployment, annual earnings for those in work in the depths of the Depression were relatively good, only declining as high unemployment persisted into the late 1930s. On the other hand, there were some districts which were moderately well protected (by geology, the character of their markets, the productivity of their pits) against the worst experience of falling wages. In South Yorkshire, Nottinghamshire, Derbyshire, and Warwickshire the rich seams provided reasonable employment and fairly good wages. The variations in average shift wages (cash payments only, excluding allowances) between different districts are exemplified in Table 10.2. Although actual earnings were, of course, a function of the number of shifts actually worked (contrast Figs. 10.1a and 10.1b), some reductions were extreme, albeit in the industry at large much of the initial wage reduction simply balanced the temporary and dramatic increases in wages (and wage costs per ton) in the artificial circumstances of 1918–20.

Nevertheless, there were many mining communities (particularly in South Wales and the North-East) where household earnings were driven down to, and even below, adequate subsistence levels in 1921–2 and for some years after 1926. This was principally a reflection of very low earning on the part of the husband, and the human misery of falling 'subsistence' wages under local wage agreements introduced quite affecting notes into the otherwise formal minutes of negotiations.[2] In addition, households in some of the most insecure areas suffered from a disproportionate dependence on male earnings. The geographical location of some mining communities, together with the social habits and past economic needs of their population, meant that women in such communities were more rarely in paid employment than was the case generally.[3] And even where female employment was more common, as was the case in the Lancashire coalfield, women's earnings also suffered in depression.

[1] Prest 1936, 331.
[2] See, for example, the Durham Coal Owners' Annual Report for 1927 (DCOA 43, 290) which summarizes negotiations in the autumn, during which the miners pleaded that it was not possible to live on less than 6s. 8½d. per shift (the owners were pressing for a reduction below this level).
[3] Below, 480.

Table 10.2. *Average cash earnings per shift of coalminers in principal districts, 1914–1946*
(shillings rounded to nearest 0.1)

	Northumberland	Durham	N. Staffordshire / Lancashire & Cheshire	Yorkshire / N. Derbyshire / Nottinghamshire / S. Derbyshire, Leicestershire, Cannock Chase / Warwickshire	S. Wales & Monmouthshire	Scotland	Great Britain
1914 (June)	6.2	6.2	6.0	6.6	6.8	6.8	6.5
1920 (Jan.–Mar.)	14.8	14.6	13.5	15.0	16.4	15.9	15.1
1921 (Jan.–Mar.)	19.0	18.8	17.2	18.5	21.5	19.3	19.2
1921 (Oct.–Dec.)	11.0	12.0	11.8	15.6	11.0	11.9	12.7
1922	8.6	9.1	9.2	11.6	9.6	9.6	9.9
1923	9.9	9.9	9.9	10.8	10.0	10.8	10.1
1924	9.9	10.2	10.2	10.7	10.5	10.9	10.6
1925	9.3	10.0	10.0	11.2	10.7	10.3	10.5
1926 (Jan.–Apr.)	9.6	9.9	9.9	10.9 (11.9)	10.7	10.3	10.4
1927	8.6	9.2	9.2	11.1 (10.8; 10.5)	10.1	9.6	10.1

Year											
1928	7.5	8.1	8.1		10.0	10.4	10.1	9.8	9.5	9.2	9.3
1929	7.4	8.0	8.0		10.1	10.3	10.1	9.7	9.5	9.2	9.2
1930	7.7	8.1	8.1		10.1	10.4	10.1	9.8	9.5	9.2	9.3
1931	7.7	8.1	8.1		10.1	10.4	10.1	9.7	9.0	9.1	9.2
1932	7.6	8.1	8.1		10.2	10.4	10.1	9.7	8.9	8.8	9.2
1933	7.7	8.0	8.0		10.1	10.4	10.1	9.6	8.9	8.8	9.1
1934	7.8	8.0	8.0		10.2	10.4	10.2	9.7	9.0	8.8	9.1
1935	7.9	8.0	8.0		10.3	10.5	10.3	9.8	9.3	8.8	9.3
1936	8.5	8.6	8.6		11.3	11.4	11.3	11.0	9.7	9.5	10.0
1937	9.0	9.1	9.1		11.9	12.7	12.0	11.5	10.2	10.3	10.7
1938	9.8	9.7	10.8	11.5	12.5	12.1	14.4		10.9	10.9	11.2
1939	10.2	9.8	11.3	12.2	12.8	12.3	15.0		11.2	11.0	11.6
1940	11.7	11.2	12.8	13.4	14.2	13.9	16.5		12.3	12.6	13.0
1941	13.3	12.9	14.8	15.4	16.0	15.8	18.8		14.1	14.5	14.9
1942	15.9	15.4	17.4	17.9	18.4	18.5	21.6		16.7	15.0	17.4
1943	17.6	17.1	19.0	19.7	20.0	20.7	23.4		18.2	18.3	19.1
1944	21.3	20.3	21.4	22.2	22.2	23.7	25.9		20.4	20.6	21.7
1945	23.2	20.2	22.7	24.1	23.8	25.1	27.5		20.5	21.7	23.1
1946	24.3	23.1	23.6	25.1	24.7	26.2	28.2		22.0	22.3	24.0

Source: CYB 1939, 628–9; *CYB* 1948, 654.

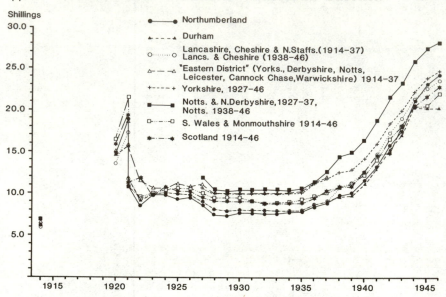

Fig. 10.2. Average cash earnings per shift in principal districts, 1914–1946

For many mining families, therefore, the reduction in their real incomes (day-labourers with dependent children and working in the export districts were especially vulnerable) greatly outweighed the fact that the *average* real incomes of miners in employment held up fairly well in the quarter-century after 1914. Nor was it much compensation for the unemployed and low paid that by the late 1930s there was to be serious discussion of holidays with pay and pensions. *Their* experience for much of the interwar period was of extreme material deprivation.

In spite of this last point, the unenviable reputation of the mining community for poverty between the Wars was not centrally based on low earnings. As has been seen, in the 1930s the economic pressures of declining markets and a huge excess capacity were reflected in the protection of prices and the reduced the supply of jobs even more than in the incomes of those actually in regular work. Between 1928 and 1936 the proportion of coalminers wholly or partly unemployed never fell below about 24 per cent, and in five years exceeded 30 per cent. (More than half the unemployment figure in each year was accounted for by those 'wholly' unemployed.) The incidence of 'full-time' unemployment was about one-third higher than in industry generally, and of *total* unemployment (i.e. those wholly and temporarily out of work) almost twice that of manufacturing industry.

Again, the averages are misleading—as is shown in Table 10.3 and Fig. 10.3. In the Midlands employment held up reasonably well; and in Scotland, in spite of its relative dependence on exports, unemployment was significantly below the levels of Wales and the North-East for much of the late 1920s, while throughout the interwar period Scottish miners (largely because they worked more shifts and longer hours) earned *relatively* high wages.

In other areas, however, the effects of unemployment were even more devastating: prolonged unemployment rates of 60 and 70 per cent were not unknown in areas of South Wales and south-west Durham, and in some communities in the latter district, 90 per cent of miners were out of work for long periods. In the South Wales coalfield, between June 1923 and June 1930, there was a fall of 40 per cent in available employment in the pits, ranging from a 19.4 per cent in the anthracite district of Amman to 49.6 per cent in the densely populated Rhondda and a horrifying 71.2 per cent in Merthyr Vale. By May 1934 unemployment rates in most of the valleys still exceeded 45 per cent (and in communities such as Blaina, Brynmawr, and Dowlais they exceeded 70 per cent).[1] In the last resort, it was worklessness which drove down the average living standard of mining communities and generated the depressed areas which loomed so large in the social controversies of the 1930s.[2]

As their economic problems grew, and especially from the mid-1920s, such communities became more dependent on the collective provision of relief. The social response to poverty in the depressed areas naturally embraced a certain amount of local self-help and, as the severity of the problem became manifest, intense philanthropic efforts on the part of people in other parts of the country. Thus, elaborate arrangements were made to collect private resources for the relief of coalmining areas during the stoppage of 1926 and even more generally in the miserable winter of 1928–9, when the Lord Mayors' Distress Fund was launched.[3] In addition to the Lord Mayors' Fund, the MFGB itself donated money to miners, as did the Save the Children Fund; and more fortunate communities also helped (Worthing 'adopted' Brynmawr and sent 20 tons of clothes, 3,000 toys, and £90 at Christmas 1929).[4] Existing philanthropic and charitable bodies also devoted their energies and resources to the

[1] For the fall in employment, see Thomas 1931, 225. For unemployment rates in May 1934, see *Reports of Investigations into the Industrial Conditions in Certain Depressed Areas* (Cmd. 4728. 1934), 145–6.

[2] Below, 463–73.

[3] Above, 262.

[4] Demant 1930, 23.

Table 10.3. *Unemployment among British coalminers in selected districts, 1927–1938*
(Mean annual % wholly (temporarily) out of work)

	1927	1928	1929	1930	1931	1932
Northumberland	14.9 (2.9)	16.0 (0.5)	11.6 (0.5)	13.3 (5.9)	19.1 (6.0)	21.2 (6.1)
Durham	20.0 (4.3)	19.2 (3.1)	13.0 (0.8)	16.4 (2.2)	25.4 (4.7)	30.3 (4.9)
Lancashire & Cheshire	6.7 (11.5)	10.5 (14.9)	11.0 (11.8)	14.1 (12.1)	17.3 (11.8)	19.5 (16.1)
Yorkshire	3.8 (8.1)	8.4 (10.0)	8.3 (5.5)	9.1 (9.8)	12.0 (19.5)	15.1 (22.4)
Derbyshire	2.9 (13.9)	5.8 (10.4)	5.1 (6.9)	6.2 (9.3)	7.9 (12.9)	10.4 (14.7)
Nottinghamshire & Leicestershire	2.1 (7.2)	5.8 (7.0)	5.0 (5.5)	5.1 (8.0)	8.7 (12.2)	12.5 (15.9)
Warwickshire	3.2 (1.0)	8.3 (1.0)	7.1 (1.0)	5.3 (2.6)	6.3 (1.6)	8.9 (2.6)
Wales & Monmouthshire	16.0 (10.5)	22.0 (8.6)	17.5 (3.1)	17.6 (8.2)	22.2 (9.6)	26.6 (14.2)
Scotland	12.7 (2.5)	17.2 (1.4)	13.7 (1.5)	16.4 (3.5)	23.4 (4.2)	26.1 (4.5)
Great Britain	10.7 (7.4)	14.4 (7.5)	11.8 (4.2)	13.3 (7.1)	18.1 (9.9)	21.3 (12.7)

	1933	1934	1935	1936	1937	1938
Northumberland	20.6 (2.9)	16.9 (1.1)	15.4 (1.1)	12.6 (0.7)	8.7 (0.3)	7.0 (3.3)
Durham	29.5 (5.0)	28.6 (2.8)	21.8 (3.9)	17.3 (1.7)	10.4 (0.6)	9.4 (4.2)
Lancashire & Cheshire	19.3 (15.2)	19.3 (9.8)	18.7 (5.4)	17.3 (5.0)	14.4 (4.5)	12.8 (4.8)
Yorkshire	17.1 (21.2)	14.8 (18.8)	13.9 (17.8)	11.0 (14.1)	7.3 (9.9)	6.1 (8.4)
Derbyshire	13.1 (8.5)	10.9 (9.2)	10.0 (4.6)	7.9 (4.8)	5.3 (3.0)	4.1 (7.5)
Nottinghamshire & Leicestershire	16.3 (13.2)	14.3 (8.0)	13.1 (4.0)	10.2 (3.6)	7.5 (3.5)	5.9 (11.7)
Warwickshire	9.5 (2.1)	7.5 (1.3)	6.4 (2.0)	5.7 (0.7)	4.3 (0.7)	5.4 (0.6)
Wales & Monmouthshire	27.8 (10.5)	27.2 (9.6)	27.5 (5.4)	25.6 (6.6)	17.7 (2.2)	14.8 (5.9)
Scotland	25.8 (3.6)	22.5 (2.7)	20.7 (2.6)	17.4 (2.5)	13.1 (1.8)	11.8 (4.0)
Great Britain	22.1 (10.8)	19.5 (8.6)	18.6 (6.6)	16.1 (5.7)	11.3 (3.4)	9.7 (5.8)

'Temporarily' unemployed included miners who expected to return on short time or for part of a week.

Source: CYB, various years.

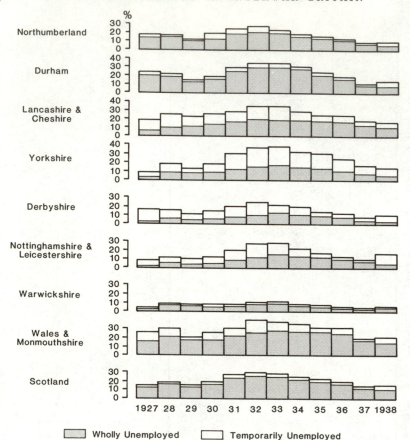

Fig. 10.3. Unemployment among British coalminers in selected districts, 1927–1938

social problems of the industry (the Society of Friends, for example, formed their own Coal Fields Distress Committee for the collection and distribution of relief and in the 1930s developed community work schemes). Yet all such efforts, even when supplemented by Treasury donations (as happened in 1928), were entirely inadequate. Rather, in company with other victims of economic stagnation, mining families, when they became dependent on the help of others, had to rely on two principal sources of organized relief: the unemployment insurance scheme and the Poor Law.

When the national insurance scheme had been introduced before the First World War, it was limited in coverage (coalminers were not initially included), took account only of the wage-earner (ignoring the existence of dependants), had assumed only moderate rates of unemployment, and provided for the payment of benefits to individuals for a limited period only. Consequently, the families of insured workers and the unemployed themselves after a strictly limited period would have to resort to Poor Law Unions (the parishes in Scotland) for the relief of 'residual' poverty.

At the end of the First World War, however, when the scheme's coverage was greatly extended, and on a more systematic basis from 1921 onwards, it was appreciated that the needs of the unemployed and their families, especially in a period of chronic depression, were more extensive than could be effectively, or humanely, met by the locally financed Poor Law system.[1] Consequently, not only were dependants' benefits introduced, but the strict insurance element in the scheme itself was abandoned and from 1918 a variety of 'doles', or 'uncovenanted', 'extended', and 'transitional' payments were devised to provide some support to the unemployed beyond the period of their strict (actuarially determined) entitlement. Even then, until 1937 the rules precluded permanent support, and therefore forced some categories of unemployed families on to the Poor Law, or (from 1931) Public Assistance Committees, after they had exhausted their extended entitlements.

Compared with unemployment insurance in other countries in the interwar years, the levels of benefits in Britain were not ungenerous. By contemporary standards of public expenditure, huge amounts were devoted to the relief of the unemployed and their dependants.[2] But even though such payments might be adequate for the most basic of needs, they represented a distinct degree of poverty, and hovered on the margin of subsistence. Nor was there much comfort in the fact that a large mining family might be no worse off on the dole than if the father were in employment at minimum rates of pay.[3] Both situations could entail much material deprivation. In the late 1920s, for example, the weekly insurance entitlement of an unemployed miner with a wife and two children was 28 shillings; it was reduced slightly in 1931 and then increased to some 30 shillings in 1934. By contrast, the lowest shift earnings varied between 6 and 8 shillings depending on the job and the

[1] For the history of unemployment insurance and poor relief in the period, see Gilbert 1970.

[2] Above, 325.

[3] For the inadequacy of unemployment and relief payment rates, see Webster 1985, 208–13. For the comparability of these rates and some wages see reports of 4 and 15 Dec. 1928 and 16 Apr. 1929 in MH 79/304; *The Times* 4 Mar. 1938.

region (unskilled workers or even skilled men in the North-East were worst off). The miner in this category who was fortunate enough to secure five days' work in a week would be hardly better off than when unemployed. Moreover, the national average wage for all miners (including the most skilled and those in relatively prosperous districts) was only about 9 or 10 shillings per shift.

Most observers agreed that such wages were inadequate for large families with no other sources of income. Certainly, the long-term unemployed were in dire straits. And even though it might occasionally be possible to arrange working schedules which enabled a community to combine the receipt of unemployment benefit and wages,[1] on the whole the regulations of the national insurance scheme tended to work to the disadvantage rather than the advantage of those without work. In the early 1920s, for example, claimants had to accept various discontinuities in entitlement which imposed a heavy burden on poor law authorities; until 1930 the condition that applicants should demonstrate that they were 'genuinely seeking work' was particularly onerous for miners living in isolated pit villages (it was the situation in coalmining that moved the Labour Government to relax this requirement in 1930); and when the payment of transitional benefits was given over to local authority Public Assistance Committees in 1931, they applied household means tests which were inconsistent as between areas and generally harsh.

The structure and limited duration of the unemployment insurance scheme, and the basis of the financing of relief in general, placed local authorities in areas of exceptionally heavy unemployment (most of which tended to be coalmining districts) at a particular disadvantage,

---

[1] The unemployment insurance regulations allowed insured people to count as 'continuous' unemployment periods of three days without work which fell within six continuous days but were divided by less than a few weeks. Official witnesses before the Samuel Commission (*Samuel Evidence* QQ 628, 1256) had implied that pits working a three-day week might so arrange their short time as to allow miners to sign on as unemployed for the intervening days. However, *The Times* pointed out (29 Mar. 1928, 17f) that miners on short time might be worse off than the fully unemployed since they could not receive unemployment benefit for the days without work unless the pit was closed for six continuous days. Further, a contemporary official claimed that in South Wales & Monmouthshire there was 'no evidence that the intermittent working has had any widespread connection with arrangements under which benefit could be secured'. (Cited in Thomas 1931, 222.) On the other hand, the South Wales coalfield did have an abnormally high rate of workers 'temporarily unemployed'. In the winter of 1927–8, for example, when its rate of 'wholly' unemployed was about 20% (the highest in the country, except for Durham which was 1 or 2% higher), the proportion temporarily out of work was about 12%, as against Durham's 1.5%. (Of the important fields, only Derbyshire, with just over 10% on short time, came anywhere near Glamorgan and Monmouthshire.) See *Labour Gazette*, various issues; *The Times* 29 Mar. 1928, 14f.

since their ability to raise monies to relieve the poor was impaired by the very problem of local poverty. As a result, many Poor Law Unions went deeply into debt. Indeed, in spite of the Ministry of Health's tendency to attribute high poor-relief expenditure to maladministration (and occasionally to deny a direct connection with high unemployment), the relationship between worklessness, poverty, and high expenditures was obvious.

In 1921–8 over half the Poor Law Unions with rates of 19 shillings or more were located in the South Wales or North-East coalfields.[1] By May 1927, when the problems of mining communities had been made worse by the 1926 stoppage,[2] almost half the 80 Unions with an above-average level of pauperism were in coalmining districts (nearly all in South Wales, Northumberland, and Durham)—and almost half of all mining Unions were in this situation. In these circumstances, the Minister of Health (Neville Chamberlain) was constrained to admit that

the continuing high figures for instance in Bedwellty, which has been administered by nominees of the Minister for the past three months, indicate the real difficulty of dealing with a population which is surplus to the openings for employment in the areas, as well as the gradualness of improvements which are to be obtained after an area has been demoralised by the policy of the Guardians.[3]

In 1935–6 (by which time poor relief was administered by county councils) the costs of relief, expressed in terms of the local rates, in Glamorgan, Monmouth, and Durham were at least four times the level of those in the more prosperous counties of the South-East.[4]

It was, then, particularly disheartening that the very districts which were most in need of abundant poor-relief expenditure and welfare services were, by virtue of their depressed character, obliged to carry an excessive financial burden. At the worst periods (in 1921–2 and 1927–8 for example) a majority of urban districts in South Wales, Durham, Northumberland, and the North Riding of Yorkshire had to impose cripplingly high poundage rates.[5] Admittedly, the reorganization of the

[1] Sykes 1939, 128, 298. For the problems of Poor Law Unions in the 1920s, see above, 260.

[2] Above, 250–1.

[3] Memorandum by Minister of Health: 'Cabinet Committee of Civil Research. Pauperism in the Coal Mining Areas', June 1927 (SRO GD 193/661/1–4). The Bedwellty Union (which had borrowed £1 million in 1926) and the Chester-le-Street Union had both been taken over by the Ministry because of excessive 'generosity' with their relief payments.

[4] Titmuss 1938, 212.

[5] Sykes 1939, 117. For the burden of the cost of welfare services on the finances of depressed local authorities, see Webster 1984, 228.

relief system in 1929 (when its administration was given over to county councils and a system of block grants from central government was introduced) alleviated some of the worst features of the situation. But to the poor and needy, whose dependence was so much emphasized by the Poor Law and public-assistance systems, these changes made little difference. Only with reform and the integration of extended unemployment benefits and public assistance, from the mid-1930s, was there some enhancement of their dignity. And even then it was significant that the coalfield population played a large part in the public demonstrations and political turmoil which, early in 1935, obliged the government to adapt its proposals for reform by agreeing to more generous benefit scales.[1]

The historical significance of the 'pauperism' and the lack of personal dignity which accompanied the increase of unemployment in the interwar years is, from one viewpoint, a clear-cut matter. Nevertheless, it is also necessary to recognize that Britain's system of social provision for the poor and workless was far in advance of that of most other nations at the time. Although it came nowhere near winning the battle against poverty, it *did* cushion the mass of the poor against the worst extremes of deprivation and hunger.

When the government initiated investigations into the depressed areas in 1934, the investigator for Durham and Tyneside argued that the absence of medical evidence of any general increase in ill health resulting from unemployment could be attributed to the provision of local health services and 'the relief afforded from public funds', amounting to annual expenditures of £7.5 million in transitional payments and public assistance (a per capita rate which was twice the national average). And yet even his somewhat suspect conclusion—that 'a tolerable standard of subsistence' was being generally maintained—was acknowledged to be unsatisfactory: 'It is a most depressing fact that the results of this immense annual expenditure should amount at best to no more than the stabilisation of a state of affairs presenting so many undesirable features.' Unemployment was having a disastrous effect on morale, on attitudes to work, and on psychological health. It was also at the very least a threat to physical well-being as well as a potent cause of social despondency.[2] That conclusion may stand as the most generous possible

[1] The restructuring of the system of unemployment benefits and poor relief, and the political unrest which accompanied it, are dealt with in Gilbert 1970, 182 ff.; Stevenson & Cook 1977, 183–4, 272–3; and Francis & Smith 1980, ch. 8.

[2] *Reports of Investigations into the Industrial Conditions in Certain Depressed Areas* (Cmd. 4728. 1934), 75–6. Health in the depressed coalfields is discussed below, sect. iv.

observation on the consequences of worklessness in mining areas between the Wars.

iii. The material welfare of miners: housing

Few aspects of the coalmining industry were more startling or shocking to outsiders than the squalid, overcrowded, and unhealthy conditions in which many mining families lived. Houses in some coalmining districts, in the words of Sir John Sankey and the businessmen on his Commission in 1919, were 'a reproach to our civilisation. No judicial language is sufficiently strong or sufficiently severe to apply to their condemnation.'[1] Indeed, the public exposure of atrocious conditions under which many miners lived made an important contribution to their propaganda victory during the Sankey hearings. Poor housing in many mining communities was an important element in the material poverty of miners' families throughout the interwar years.

The economics of miners' housing, as with so much of the industry, was distinctive. In particular, the fact that miners had to live near the pits and that pits were often developed fairly rapidly and away from existing areas of intensive settlement, meant that a high proportion of miners' houses were constructed by the colliery companies themselves. By the mid-1920s they owned between one-quarter and one-third of the housing in the principal coalmining communities. However, the pattern was far from uniform: about 40 per cent of all colliery-owned housing was in Northumberland and Durham, where virtually all of it was provided rent-free.

Hence, although the issue of colliery-owned housing was politically sensitive, it was relatively unimportant in all large districts other than the North-East.[2] Most miners rented their housing, but in South Wales there was a strong tradition of home-ownership, facilitated by building

---

[1] *Coal Industry Commission Act, 1919. Interim Report By the Honourable Mr. Justice Sankey... 20th March 1919* (Cmd. 84. 1919. Reprinted in *PP* 1919 XI), 7. The housing of Scottish miners was notoriously awful. See *Sankey Evidence* QQ 5243 ff.; and *Report of the Royal Commission on the Housing of the Industrial Population of Scotland*, 1917, in *PP* 1917–18 XIV, Ch. xiv and xxxv.

[2] In 1925 miners rented some 25,000 colliery-owned houses in Scotland (where two-thirds of the work-force lived in privately owned accommodation), 20,000 in South Yorkshire, 15,000 in South Wales and Monmouth, and just over 5,000 in each of Lancashire & Cheshire, Nottinghamshire, and Derbyshire. Unless otherwise indicated, the evidence for the number and distribution of houses comes from the *Samuel Report*, 199–201 and *Samuel Appendices*, Appendix 18, Table 37 and Appendix 35. In 1913 collieries accounting for 75% of the country's coal output owned about 135,000 houses. By 1925 the same enterprises owned some 160,000 houses.

clubs and societies, and by loans from some colliery companies.[1] In a handful of districts, as will be seen, the exceptional expansion of the interwar decades obliged colliery companies to take a prominent part in house-building. But taking the industry as a whole, the depressed state of trade and the cost of such 'unproductive' investment led coalowners to disengage themselves from the housing market in these years. Between 1925 and 1946, the net number of colliery-owned houses fell from 171,000 to 141,000 and in Durham alone it fell from 50,319 to 29,371. (By the end of the Second World War only about half of the colliery-owned housing in South Wales was occupied by active miners.)[2]

Of course, once the mining community became accustomed to paying low rents, or no rents at all, it became difficult to finance an improvement in the housing stock. But the causes of unsatisfactory houses were more complex than the attitude of the consumers. Thus, the quality of the housing stock inherited from the nineteenth century was frequently inadequate not simply because of its age, but also because the life of many pits, and therefore of the surrounding settlements, was uncertain. Hence, one reason for the 'exceptionally low standard of housing' in Scottish mining areas was the lack of incentive to long-run investment: royalty leases were traditionally for shorter periods in Scotland than in the principal English and Welsh fields (31 as against 50 or 60 years).[3]

In some districts the poor physical quality of the housing was compounded by severe overcrowding. The Scottish and North-East English coalfields were notorious in this respect. Using the Census criterion of five rooms or less occupied by more than two persons per room, the figure for England and Wales in 1921 was 7.5 per cent of the population, as against 22.2 per cent in Durham, 24.2 per cent in Northumberland, 33.7 per cent in Scotland (where, however, the average size of rooms was bigger), and 46.7 per cent in Scottish mining communities.[4] A Ministry of Health survey of overcrowding some 15 years later showed a very similar pattern, with the intensity of residence

---

[1] Of the houses associated with 163 companies in South Wales in 1925, 14,939 were owned or leased by the collieries and 12,335 by the miners. *Samuel Evidence* Q 25497; POWE 16/514.

[2] *Samuel Appendices*, Appendix 18, Table 37; *National Coal Board, Annual Report, 1947*, 141; *Ministry of Fuel and Power, Durham Coalfield. Regional Survey Report (Northern 'B' Coalfield)* (1945), Appendix VI; *Ministry of Fuel and Power, South Wales Coalfield. Regional Survey Report* (1946), Part V and Appendix VIIC.

[3] *Samuel Report*, 199.

[4] *Samuel Appendices*, App. 35. The figures for the Lanarkshire and Fife mining districts were 54.6% and 42.5% respectively. The data for Nottinghamshire, Glamorganshire, and Monmouthshire were approximately the same as for the country at large.

in Durham and Northumberland being more than three times the relevant national average.[1]

As was pointed out by the Samuel Commission, however, other than in Scotland, the coalmining industry did not appear to have any very *special* problem, since coalmining communities in England and Wales experienced a similar degree of overcrowding to industrial places in general, and to the counties in which they were located. But this is a misleading formulation. First, because the average figures were themselves influenced by the preponderance of the mining industry within major counties. Second, because the nature of the miners' work—its extremely exhausting character, the filthy, hot, and frequently damp conditions in which most miners laboured—and the shortage of pithead bathing facilities established special housing needs (too often not satisfied) for miners' families.[2] Third, because the *quality* of miners' housing could be exceptionally bad. And finally, because the presumed necessities of mining settlements led to a neglect of good site planning and geographical overcrowding. This last point was well exemplifed in the narrow valleys of South Wales, where a high proportion of houses were relatively new (half were less than 40 years old in 1921) and few were insanitary, but where the ground was congested with badly placed terraces, many were deprived of sun and air.[3]

As with the industry's operations generally, it would be a mistake to imagine that the worst features of its housing situation persisted with no alleviation or improvement during the two interwar decades. When, at the end of the Second World War, there were regional surveys of the principal coalfields, special attention was paid to housing needs. In both Scotland and Durham—the main blackspots of 1917–19—although serious problems and deficiencies remained, the investigators reported significant improvements in the condition and overcrowding of miners' housing. At another level, the accommodation for mining families associated with the modern collieries in Sherwood Forest was said to be exemplary: 12,000 employees lived in villages (Harworth, New Ollerton, and around the Bolsover pits) which were 'models of their kind'.[4]

Part of this improvement was no doubt due to the run-down of the

---

[1] Ministry of Health, *Report on the Overcrowding Survey in England and Wales, 1936* (1936).

[2] See R. A. Scott-James's Appendix on housing in Liberal Party 1924, 126.

[3] *Report of the South Wales Regional Survey Committee, 1921*, cited in POWE 16/514.

[4] *Scottish Home Department, Scottish Coalfields. The Report of the Scottish Coalfields Committee* (1944), 114–15; *Ministry of Fuel and Power, Durham Coalfield. Regional Survey Report (Northern 'B' Coalfield)* (1945), 31; *Ministry of Fuel and Power, North Midland Coalfield. Regional Survey Report* (1945), 22.

industry in the 1920s and 1930s, since a smaller industry could make better use of existing housing capacity. This was only effective in so far as miners left their depressed communities. But this *did* happen, and had important implications in the overcrowded North-East. In the Crook Urban District of south-west Durham, for example, where unemployment was particularly severe, the proportion of the population living more than two to a room dropped from 25.5 in 1921 to 12.5 in 1931 (in Stanley Urban District the figures were 32 and 16).[1] The loss of population from the mining areas of South Wales must also have alleviated housing problems, although there was less overcrowding in the Valleys. There were, however, two much more positive reasons for the amelioration of the mining industry's housing problem: government aid and the initiative of colliery companies in the newly developing coalfields.

Legislation in 1919, 1923, and 1924 offered encouragement and subsidies to house-building by local authorities, non-profit-making associations, and private contractors. By October 1929 in the country as a whole such subsidies had been used in the construction of some 650,000 houses (390,000 by private enterprise).[2] In the coalfields, the public provision of financial incentives liberated housing markets from their twin dependence on the private capital of reluctant coalowners and short-run considerations dictated by the character of the industry in older areas. Even so, the economic circumstances of the industry restrained any spectacular developments, and in the relatively depressed districts private and colliery house-ownership diminished in importance. Between 1919 and 1925 some 60 or 70 per cent of the new housing in the principal coalmining districts of Scotland, Durham, and Glamorgan was built by local authorities.[3]

The other very significant development was the growth of colliery housing around the new, long-term mines of the 1920s. As the Samuel Commission pointed out.

where modern collieries are established, to work seams that will last a long time, and under leases running for a lengthy period, the proprietors are often ready to spend very large sums of capital in the erection of good housing accommodation. They not only have the satisfaction of rendering a public service, but are enabled to draw to their undertaking the best class of workers.[4]

---

[1] Owen 1937, 343. For migration from the coalfields, see below, 489–91.
[2] *Ministry of Health, Report of the Committee of Inquiry into the Anti-T.B. Service in Wales and Monmouthshire* (1938), 124–7.
[3] POWE 16/514 (Scotland) and 16/37 (Durham and Glamorgan).
[4] *Samuel Report*, 199–200.

In sharp contrast to the situation in South Wales and the North-East, colliery companies began to play a vital role in those districts (South Yorkshire, the East Midlands, Kent) where large new pits had to be developed. This role was virtually forced on the coalowners if only because their need for rapid and guaranteed provision of housing for newcomers (who would be very low down on local official waiting lists) could not be satisfied by local authorities—especially those which lacked relevant experience. As a result, the companies had to take the lead.

This happened to a certain extent even in Scotland, where new pits were sunk in the early 1920s, and in one or two South Wales villages; but its most dramatic occurrence was based upon the great new colliery developments in South Yorkshire, Nottinghamshire, and North Derbyshire, which between them accounted for half the national total of colliery-built housing in 1919–25. In the immediate postwar years this involved very large investments for a few companies: housing accounted for just over 40 per cent of the Staveley Iron and Coal Company's total investment (£7.3 million) in four new pits. Indeed, such corporate giants as the Staveley, Butterley, and Bolsover Companies were, in effect, engaging in urban development—building houses, main drainage and sewers, spurring the creation of schools and churches and social buildings—as part of an integrated programme of industrial expansion.[1]

Much of this effort was canalized through the Industrial Housing Association, a 'public utility society' formed by 24 colliery companies from the South Yorkshire and East Midlands field. The IHA could borrow at favourable rates from the Public Works Loan Board and secured subsidies under the 1923 housing legislation (the subsidies were £6 per house per year for 20 years and were passed on to mitigate rents charged to tenants). The housing stock thus created was abundant and of high quality. In the seven years 1922–8 the Association built 12,000 houses at a cost of £6 million, and its three- and four-bedroom houses were well heated, supplied with bathrooms, electricity, modern sanitation and water supplies, gardens, and other amenities. Similar developments, albeit on a somewhat smaller scale, took place in the new Kent coalfield, where, in 1945, some 70 per cent of the work-force of almost 6,000 lived in post-1919 housing directly or indirectly provided by colliery companies and also constructed to a high quality.[2]

[1] *Samuel Appendices*, Appendix 18, Table 37 and Appendix 31; Waller 1983, ch. 4; White 1955, 269–90; Mottram and Coote 1950, 116–24; Heap 1977, 3–4.

[2] For the history of the Industrial Housing Association see Walters 1927. Neither the Butterley

The peculiarities of the coalmining industry, its geography as well as the uneven pace of its growth, explain the distinctive role that employers played in the provision of houses for wage-earners. For much of its history, and well into the twentieth century, it appeared important to locate accommodation for mining families fairly close to the mines. The need to ensure a large labour force in isolated areas, the fear that long-distance 'commuting' would encourage absenteeism, the desire to exercise some degree of control and to isolate workmen from alternative employment—all undoubtedly played a part in the owners' decisions to develop their own housing. Yet the importance of this range of arguments should not be misunderstood. A concentrated work-force might have its disadvantages in terms of miner 'solidarity' and 'militancy'; the owners soon came to resent the fact that their role in housing opened them to criticism for its poor quality; and, above all, they were obviously reluctant to sink so much capital in housing when scarce funds 'could with advantage to all concerned be reserved for direct development of their undertakings'.[1]

However, in the new fields such investment was unavoidable. And in the event, the companies appeared to have carried out their task with a widely commended regard for the decencies of life. Unfortunately, neither that fact nor the broad improvement in the average quality of mining houses in the interwar years could get anywhere near eradicating the unsanitary, overcrowded, uncomfortable, and decrepit housing in which so many mining families in the older districts lived. Nor could the owners escape all blame for the living conditions of their work-force. It was little wonder that, when persistent unemployment threw the issue of derelict communities into sharp relief in the early 1930s, the social surveys which resulted found that poor housing conditions were an integral part of their dereliction.

iv. The social health of mining communities

Mining communities lay at the heart of the social problem of the depressed areas in interwar Britain. As a result, they were also central to the contemporary concern that the effects of sustained depression on

nor Bolsover colliery companies were members of the IHA, which was dominated by the Staveley and Sheepbridge companies and by Yorkshire collieries associated with them. For housing in Kent, see *Ministry of Fuel and Power, Kent Coalfield. Regional Survey Report* (1945), 33.

[1] Ibid. For the owners' resentment of criticism, see MAGB, *What Mr Lloyd George Was Not Told* (1924), 24–5.

the health and well-being of the working poulation might be similar to its effects on the coal regions, which were 'without parallel in the modern history of this country'.[1] There developed a fear that the slump might usher in an unprecedentedly sustained deterioration in the physical well-being of whole social classes, or of large groups within them. Admittedly, the most extreme version of that fear was not explicitly and generally shared by those in government, but it was an anxiety which was frequently close to the surface of the rather helpless official discussion of the depressed areas in the years 1928–36.

Ever since the Sankey hearings of 1919 there had been intermittent public apprehension about the material welfare of mining communities; but in the initial postwar years this had been largely abated—first by the buoyancy of wages (until 1921), and then by the temporary prosperity of 1923–4.[2] In any case, the threat to health from individual poverty, like the decay of whole villages and districts, was not manifest until some years of sustained economic pressure had been experienced. And by that time (i.e. the late 1920s) the social effects of mass unemployment were compounded by the sad inheritance of the stoppages of 1921 and 1926, which had consumed private resources and left many miners deep in debt to cooperative societies, private shopkeepers, landlords, friends, and Poor Law Unions (in 1926 the Guardians of the Tynemouth Union had lent nearly £200,000 by way of relief, mostly to miners, and in Northumberland as a whole the outstanding debt in 1930 was still £228,314).[3]

It was, therefore, only in the late 1920s that general and profound anxiety was expressed about the relationship between worklessness and personal and family well-being in the coalfields. That anxiety was based principally on the experience of South Wales and the North-East. The patterns of publicity and national concern no doubt overlooked equivalent distress in other severely depressed areas—more particularly in Scotland, where 140,000 miners were employed in 1924, and in Lancashire, Cheshire, Cumberland, and Westmoreland (114,000 miners). But it seems likely that the extent and intensity of depression and social dislocation were at their most extreme in the districts that received most

---

[1] *Ministry of Health, Report on Investigation in the Coalfield of South Wales and Monmouth* (Cmd. 3272. 1929), 10. For similar sentiments, see *The Times* 28 Mar. 1928, 17f.

[2] Above, 172.

[3] POWE 20/80 'Coal Trade Dispute 1926: Loans to Miners by Public Assistance Board: Question of Repayment, 1943'. During the Second World War the Ministry of Health agreed to condone the *de facto* cancellation of the outstanding debt by turning a blind eye to the County Councils' inactivity in its recovery. Also see Webster 1985, 214.

public and official attention. And since, in any case, South Wales and the North-East coalfields between them accounted for about 40 per cent of the industry's 1924 labour force (some 480,000 men out of a total of 1.19 million), their unhappy record can be taken as more than simply a symbol of the problems of coalmining communities during the Depression.

Although the Cabinet established a committee to study the problem of unemployment in coal in 1927, and the Minister of Health anxiously drew its attention to 'pauperism' and 'surplus population' in some of the leading coalmining districts, matters only really came to a head in 1928, when the failure of the industry to recover after the miseries of 1926 had begun to take its social toll.

In the spring of that year *The Times* published a dramatic and influential series of articles ('A Stricken Coalfield') exposing what its correspondent called the 'social disaster' in South Wales, where there were over 100,000 registered unemployed and where many miners had already been out of work for two or three years. The poverty of the unemployed and of the low paid, together with the handicap of debts incurred in 1926, meant that boots and clothing and household goods could not be replaced when they wore out, and that in many cases the payment of rent and the purchase of food were both precarious.[1] The conclusion of the second article, given the newspaper's standing, could hardly be ignored, nor dismissed as merely sensational:

We merely wish to record the plain fact that men, women and children are living in parts of these valleys in a state of destitution, pitiably under-nourished, and under-clothed, and housed in surroundings which lack nearly all the amenities of our more populous industrial areas.

And on 2 April *The Times*'s correspondent went even further, drawing attention to family men who had exhausted their unemployment benefit entitlement, receiving relief of a mere 16s. weekly, when even subsistence wages for a full week's work would be some three times that figure: 'to-day men and women are starving; not starving outright but gradually wasting away through lack of nourishment.'

Of course, these were extreme examples (relief payments, although

---

[1] 'A Stricken Coalfield. Stagnation in South Wales', *The Times* 28 Mar. 1928, 17f; also see 29 Mar., 2 Apr., and 3 Apr. 1928. *The Times*'s correspondent also touched on the parallel problems of the North-East coalfield. For the Cabinet Committee on Unemployment in the Coal Fields, see CAB 27/358. The Minister of Health's memorandum (24 June 1927) is in CAB 27/358 and also in SRO GD 193/661/1-4. The Committee assumed that there were some 200,000 'surplus' miners. For the Government's concern, see above, 262.

small, were rarely that low). Nevertheless, the situation was quite obviously dangerous. In July the President of the Board of Education expressed concern about the nutritional status of schoolchildren in South Wales and Durham, and extended the provision of free school meals. More generally, in the course of that year the Ministry of Health initiated urgent inquiries into poverty, distress, and health in the South Wales and North-East coalfields.

While its investigators found no statistical evidence of serious ill health, the position was hardly reassuring. The Ministry's officials themselves drew attention to a chronic surplus of mining labour; a very low level of effective income which was frequently only barely sufficient to pay for food (in many households food consumption was said to be 'below what would theoretically be regarded as the minimum necessary to support health'); enfeeblement of mothers, whose efforts to ensure food for their children and husbands left them under-nourished; widespread listlessness and apathy, and a tendency to delayed recovery from illness; an unusual incidence of rickets (in South Wales); and considerable cause for anxiety about the long-run consequences of the Depression for the health of the mining population.[1]

The Report on South Wales was published as a White Paper in February 1929. And, even though the published version went out of its way to deny that there was any unusual increase in mortality or tuberculosis, it acknowledged the increase in rickets (which indicated dietary deficiencies), the unwholesome diet, the lack of clothing and footwear and rent, the widespread 'langour' and 'anaemia' among women, and the official apprehension about the likelihood of long-run damage to children from the shortages of good food. Poverty led inexorably to a deterioration in the quality of food consumption. In South Wales, for example (although there is reason to believe that the position was worst there), the daily diet was dominated by white bread, butter or margarine, potatoes, sugar and jam, small quantities of tea, and bacon. Meat, fresh milk and vegetables, wholemeal bread, and fruit all became scarce. The calorie intake might be maintained (although even that was not certain), but the nutrient value fell. In the words of *The Times*, ten years later, people in such circumstances were 'neither hungry nor healthy'.[2]

---

[1] For the President of the Board of Education, see CAB 24/196 (19 July 1928). For the Ministry of Health inquiries, see HLG 30/47 (Feb. 1928), and the more elaborate local inquiries, conducted by the Ministry's Chief General Inspector and its Medical Officer, and reported in Dec. 1928 and Apr. 1929: CAB 27/381; HLG 30/47, 63; MH 79/304. The quotation is from a report of 4 Dec. 1928 in MH 79/304.

[See p. 466 for n. 2]

The anxious inquiries of 1928 (which, it will be remembered, led the government to take the minor but still unusual step of making a matching public contribution to a private relief fund—the Lord Mayors' Fund for Mining Areas) reflected merely the first flush of the social 'discovery' of the 'distressed areas'. Bad as the economic situation appeared in 1928, it was to deteriorate in the following years: after a slight recovery in 1929, the coal trade slid deeper into depression from 1930, and even when the more solid national revival began in 1934, its geographic unevenness and the depths of the preceding depression meant that the worst-hit regions continued in a state of profound social distress.

In the south-west Durham coalfield in 1934, for example, there were 42,000 male workers, of whom almost two-thirds were mineworkers and over 70% were permanently unemployed (in some mining villages the unemployment rate exceeded 90 per cent). As has been seen, even at this relatively late date in large areas of the South Wales coalfield the unemployment rate exceeded 45 per cent and in some important communities 70 per cent.[1] Of course, even within the regions with the worst records the situation varied from district to district, in large part because the depression was not uniform, but also because the provision of local relief also varied according to the policies and resources of the Poor Law authority.[2]

Regional variety was exemplified in the personal response to depression as well as in its incidence and the point was occasionally made that the ability to withstand a shortage of resources (whether based on housekeeping aptitudes, psychological resilience, or geography) varied from district to district. Thus, in 1929 the mining population of Durham and Northumberland was said to be 'making a better stand against adverse circumstances than that of South Wales' through the housewife's better food management (a lesser reliance on white bread, margarine, and tea, and a greater consumption of vegetables, suet, home-baked

[2] *Report on Investigation in the Coalfield of South Wales and Monmouth* (Cmd. 3272. 1929), 6. *The Times* 13 Mar. 1936, 13b. Cf. Harry and Phillips 1937, 88–92.

[1] Sharp 1935, Introduction; *Reports of Investigations into the Industrial Conditions in Certain Depressed Areas* (Cmd. 4728. 1934), 145–6.

[2] Most of the Welsh Poor Law Unions appeared, not entirely properly, to have denied outdoor relief to able-bodied unemployed men, whereas only one or two Durham unions pursued this harsh policy. In the Sedgefield Union the majority of miners were working a five-day week and, although a large proportion of the local population were in receipt of relief payments, the Guardians had adopted a policy of using relief to supplement unemployment benefit to the level of their own (higher) scale! For the generally low levels of unemployment and public-assistance benefits, see Webster 1985, 208–13.

bread, and milk, helped in part by the greater proximity of local farms and produce). And almost ten years later, in a comparative survey, although both Crook (in County Durham) and the Rhondda were said to exemplify 'much better housekeeping' than other (non-mining) depressed areas, Crook was still said to possess more social vitality and 'more determination not to give way to unemployment and not to sub-sist on self-pity than there was in Wales'.[1]

In spite of such contrasts in adversity and response, for a huge number of families in some of the country's major coalfields, these were merely minor variations around an abysmally low level of personal and family welfare. The initial reaction of contemporary observers has been noted; is it possible to assess, with any accuracy, the consequences of 10 or 15 years of chronic unemployment and poverty on so many com-munities in some of the country's major coalfields?

There is, in fact, little scope for controversy about the immediate effects of persistent economic depression, prolonged bouts of unem-ployment, and very low relief payments: a large proportion of coal-mining families—perhaps the great majority in areas such as south-west Durham or various of the Welsh valleys—experienced extremes of social misery and material deprivation in the late 1920s and the early 1930s. Contemporary impressions of the depressed mining communities were strikingly similar: the mass of residents were inadequately supplied with clothing, footwear, household furniture, and personal possessions generally; good food was in short supply, the average diet was un-balanced and inadequate, and people were often very hungry; house-wives with young children neglected themselves in favour of their families, and were therefore particularly fatigued and vulnerable to ill-ness; the thousands of long-term unemployed were listless and depressed, and experienced, in the words of a study of Brynmawr, 'an abiding sense of waste of life'. When the government sent investigators to the depressed coalfields in 1934, the report on Durham made the pessimistic point that

Prolonged unemployment is destroying the confidence and self-respect of a large part of the population, their fitness for work is being steadily lost and the

---

[1] A. B. Lowry and J. Pearse, 'Report on Investigation in the Coalfields of Durham and Northum-berland', 16 Apr. 1929: HLG 30/63; Pilgrim Trust 1938, 74, 114. The greater social resilience in Durham appeared the more surprising in that Crook miners were poorer and had a higher unem-ployment rate than those of South Wales (75% of Crook miners had been out of work for five years or more, compared with 'only' 45% in the Rhonnda). The 'vitality' was said to be exemplified in a greater attention to allotments, poultry-keeping, keep-fit classes, and the maintenance of hobbies, and in a greater readiness to encourage their children to migrate in search of a better life.

anxiety of living always upon a bare minimum without any margin of resources or any hope of improvement is slowly sapping their nervous strength and their powers of resistance.[1]

There was, then, a widespread apprehension about the psychological and physical health of the population in the depressed coalmining communities. Yet there is surprisingly little quantitative evidence of any long-run deterioration in the health of the population through the years of the slump.

In particular, the national, and most regional, figures of infant and maternal mortality—the two indices which might most obviously reflect a chronic deterioration in nutrition and health—show either no deterioration or no general correlation with deteriorating economic conditions. Indeed, in the case of infant mortality between four weeks and one year throughout the period, and of maternal mortality from the mid-1930s, there was a distinct improvement. These findings apply to most individual depressed areas (although maternal mortality in South Wales was an exception) as well as to the nation as a whole. More generally, both contemporary official analyses and the most detailed of modern studies fail to observe any systematic connection between trends in regional mass unemployment and movements in regional vital statistics.[2]

Admittedly, miners themselves did not share in the general improvement in adult male mortality. Thus, between 1921–3 and 1930–2, death rates among miners rose at ages 16–20 and did not improve at ages 20–55. But against this must be set the fact that mortality among miners

---

[1] Jennings 1934, 141; *Reports of Investigations into the Industrial Conditions in Certain Depressed Areas* (Cmd. 4728. 1934), 75–6. For other examples of contemporary surveys of deteriorating circumstances in the coalfields see: Demant 1930; Sharp 1935; Newsom 1936; 'Portrait of a Mining Town', *Fact*, 15 Nov. 1937; Pilgrim Trust 1938; and Goodfellow 1940.

[2] See Winter 1979, 439–62; and 1983, 232–56. Also see *Report on Investigations in the Coalfield of South Wales and Monmouthshire* (Cmd. 3272. 1929), 4: 'On the criterion of infant mortality, therefore, there are no figures showing that the health of this region is suffering or need give rise to anxiety.' Cf. *Annual Report of the Chief Medical Officer of the Ministry of Health, 1932*, 16–41. (E.g. 41 'we cannot escape the conclusion that there is, at present, no available medical evidence of any general increase in physical impairment, in sickness or in mortality, as the result of economic depression or unemployment'.) Also *Annual Report of the Chief Medical Officer of the Ministry of Health for the Year 1933*, 206–21. However, it should be noted that these opinions, and the evidence adduced to support them, have been severely criticized by Dr Charles Webster (1982, 110–29). As far as maternal mortality was concerned, surveys showed no relationship with unemployment in the period 1927–34, other than in Wales (in the period 1924/8–1929/33). See *Report of an Investigation into Maternal Mortality* (Cmd. 5422. 1937), 81; *Report on Maternal Mortality in Wales* (Cmd. 5423. 1937), 114–15. The latter *Report* pointed to 'inadequate dietary and wrong feeding' as possible causes of Wales's high maternal mortality.

above the age of 55 *did* improve significantly, which led the Registrar General to suggest that the poor mortality record of younger miners in the 1920s 'may have resulted in part from selective migration of healthy young men away from coal mining into other industries'. This hypothesis was supported by figures on the decline in the younger age group as a proportion of the work-force,[1] as well as by the uneven distribution between age groups of migrants from the depressed mining areas: over 50 per cent of the large flow of workers who left South Wales and the North-East were between 15 and 29.[2]

Most commentators on the depressed areas (including public servants) acknowledged that the *quality* of nutritional intake was undesirably low. Yet, as was the case with mortality data, surviving information about malnutrition or disease (although in these respects the evidence is of a much more subjective and unreliable kind) fails to confirm the case for general deterioration. Certainly, official assessments of trends in malnutrition (perhaps the most subjective condition of all) and ill health were more reassuring than not, although there were many contemporary critics who questioned the reliability of the statistical evidence offered, and offered their own gloomy evidence concerning the presumed decline in the bodily well-being of the population in the depressed areas.[3]

Most statistical evidence therefore appears to contradict the common-sense observations of contemporaries—that the unemployed and newly poor were often at the margin of subsistence and were growing significantly less healthy. Admittedly, the principal exception was an important one: maternal mortality *did* increase in South Wales from the mid-1920s to the early 1930s (especially in the depressed coal-producing areas) and prolonged depression, working through the nutrition and health of mothers, was assumed to have influenced this trend.[4] Yet the curious fact remains that such an experience was an exception to the

---

[1] Registrar General, *Decennial Supplement. England and Wales. 1931 Part IIA*, 80 ff. In the 1920s there was an increase in the *relative*—although not the absolute—death rate from respiratory diseases (other than TB) among miners, and by 1930-2 the death rate from this cause was about 20% higher among miners than among the population at large.

[2] Titmuss 1938, 286.

[3] The official view was summarized in the *Annual Reports* of the Chief Medical Officer of the Ministry of Health for 1932 and 1933 (e.g. at 219 of the latter: 'The evidence is that *malnutrition* is not a prominent feature, nor that it is widespread or increasing'). The contrary view was represented in McNally 1935 and M'Gonigle and Kirby 1936.

[4] *Report on Maternal Mortality in Wales* (Cmd. 5423. 1937), 114-15. In 1929 the *Report on Investigations in the Coalfield of South Wales and Monmouthshire* had warned of the threat to the health of mothers from the poverty of diet.

rule. More general, among systematic official surveys, was the view articulated by the Ministry of Health in response to publicity attending a letter to *The Times* from a Durham doctor:

While we have found in the area under review [*Durham and Sunderland*] a considerable incidence of subnormal nutrition and some incidence of malnutrition, our investigation shows little evidence of any increase of disease and none of increased mortality. The physical condition of the individuals passed under review is good. Realising the long continued economic stress to which this population has been subjected and with knowledge of the home conditions of many, we have often been surprised at the high standard of health and courage which has been maintained.[1]

There have, of course, been efforts to argue the contrary case—that prolonged unemployment increased malnutrition and illness.[2] And there is abundant impressionistic evidence about health, and quantitative information about the slow development and inadequate coverage of welfare services. Nevertheless, there is no persuasive statistical demonstration of serious long-run deterioration in the health of the population of the depressed areas in general or the mining areas in particular. On the other hand, there *was* a widely shared and intense dissatisfaction with the state of things, and even those who were unable to detect epidemiological evidence for ill health, expressed anxiety with greater or lesser restraint. Indeed, one of the anomalous features of the controversy is that the very sources impugned by modern 'pessimists'— the Ministry of Health officials who are supposed to have distorted their statistical arguments for political purposes—were fertile in the provision of anecdotal and impressionistic ammunition for pessimism.[3]

If, as seems likely, there is an unresolvable ambiguity about the *changes* in the health of the coalmining districts during the depressed years of the late 1920s and the 1930s, there is greater certainty about their poor standing compared to other regions. Indeed, a good deal of

[1] *Report of an Inquiry into the Effects of Existing Economic Circumstances on the Health of the Community in the County Borough of Sunderland and Certain Districts of County Durham* (Cmd. 4886. 1935), 43. The Appendix of the *Report* reproduced Dr Walker's original letter, claiming extreme and widespread ill health (mental as well as physical) attributable to the sustained depression.

[2] In addition to the contemporary literature cited in this chapter, see Webster 1982. A more general appraisal of the deficiencies of welfare benefits and health services is ibid., 1985. Also see Lewis 1980.

[3] In addition to the investigations of 1928 and 1929 (above, 465 n.), see the *Annual Report of the Chief Medical Officer of the Ministry of Health, 1932*, 39–40: 'There is inevitably a great and undetermined mass of deprivation, hardship, social ill and anxiety which unemployment inflicts, directly on large sections of the population and indirectly on the whole community . . .'.

the confusion of the controversy concerning the consequences of mass unemployment derived from the fact that the areas with the highest unemployment were also among those with the worst *relative* experience in terms of infant (and to some extent adult) mortality and, on the whole, morbidity.

The amelioration in public health which took place was widely shared, but some of the grossest regional disparities remained. In the 1930s, for example, infant mortality in the North-East, while falling, was by far the highest in England and Wales (one-third to one-quarter above the national average) while South Wales was in the next highest category, with ten per cent and more above the national average. (The South-East, by contrast, had rates between 11 and 19 per cent below the average.)[1] Although infant mortality figures for smaller places have greater variance, there was a similar tendency for the falling mortality rates of individual coalmining communities to be associated with continuing inequalities. Table 10.4 exemplifies this for communities with some of the highest concentrations of coalmining population in the 1920s.

Such contrasts had, of course, much to do with social class distribution. But variations in health and mortality were also related to occupation (which was not always consistently related to class). This is an important aspect of the experience of mining communities, for in spite of their relatively high standing in the official classification of social groups (Class III for hewers, Class IV for partly skilled) miners had one of the worst infant mortality records in British society. From 1911 to 1939 mortality between the ages of four weeks and one year in miners' families was four times that of professional workers, ten per cent and more above that of building labourers, and between one-third and one-half higher (in this respect it deteriorated from 1911 to 1921 and from 1930-2 to 1939) than the national average.[2]

There were, no doubt, various aspects of the society and life-style of many mining communities which helped explain this sad record. For one thing, the birth rate in mining families was relatively very high, and infants born into large families were generally at greater risk than those born into smaller ones. Further, the quality of medical attention was

[1] Winter 1979, 447. Infant mortality in Scotland was consistently much higher than in England and Wales.

[2] Morris and Heady 1955, 554. Also see Winter 1983, 246; Webster 1982, *passim*; and Logan 1954. In common with all occupational groups, infant mortality in miners' families improved substantially in these years: Morris and Heady 1955, 554.

Table 10.4. *Infant mortality (deaths under one year per 1,000 live births),*
selected districts, 1923-1932

	1923-5	1930-2	% decline
England and Wales	73	64	12.3
Durham (Administrative County	94	80	14.9
Annfield Plain UD	99	79	20.2
Hetton UD	98	72	26.5
Stanley UD	99	95	4.0
Auckland RD	87	68	21.8
Chester-le-Street RD	103	80	14.6
Northumberland (Administrative County)	80	69	13.7
Ashington UD	102	83	18.6
Bedlington UD	92	75	18.5
Nottinghamshire (Administrative County)	80	69	13.7
Hucknall UD	93	55	40.9
Glamorgan (County Boroughs)	81	74	8.6
Glamorgan (Administrative County)	78	72	7.7
Merthyr Tydfil County Borough	89	90	+1.1
Aberdare UD	86	71	7.4
Maesteg UD	76	74	2.6
Rhondda UD	87	79	9.2
Monmouth (Administrative County)	77	68	11.7
Abertillery UD	80	68	15.0
Bedwellty UD	84	78	7.1
Nantyglo UD	86	70	18.6

Source: *Registrar General's Statistical Review of England and Wales, 1921-38.*

relatively poor in mining areas, which were in any case more isolated than most, and the 'management' of childbirth was seriously deficient, especially in South Wales. Cultural conservatism and social isolation may also have reduced the quality of household care, and conceivably miners' wives, more than most, exemplified that 'combination of courage, prudery and ignorance' which a classic survey found to be the characteristic attitude to health of working-class wives.[1] But these could

[1] Rice 1939, 2nd edn. 1981, 198.

not have been determining considerations, and there was no escaping the fact that mining families lived in an unhealthy social environment.

Pre-eminent among the components of that environment was the poverty of miners' housing. In 1919 Sidney Webb had asked rhetorically 'Why do twice as many babies die in a miner's cottage as in a middle-class home?' The dirt and discomfort of the home, and the hard work imposed on miners' wives, were the reasons he adduced.[1] In this respect, it was significant that the *adult* as well as infant mortality rates among miners exceeded those of most other occupations. That this was not simply a matter of low incomes or the result of poor working conditions was suggested by two facts. First, before the late 1920s, mineworkers' incomes were (by working-class standards) by no means low or irregular. Second, the mortality of miners' *wives* was comparably high.[2] Hence, over the long run, whatever may be said about the real incomes of miners' families or about the apparent amelioration in the measurable elements of their health, those who lived in mining communities continued to be disadvantaged.

In the bitter years from the mid-1920s, the story of their depression, although perhaps very occasionally exaggerated in the telling, was in effect a national scandal of misery and waste.

v. Miners' Welfare: the social provision of amenities

In spite of the severe economic pressures on the mining population and mining communities, there was one respect in which public action between the Wars placed the miners at a relative advantage compared with most other workers. This was through the creation of a Miners' Welfare Fund, financed by levies on coal output and coal royalties, and devoted to the enhancement of social, recreational, and educational facilities for mineworkers and their families. The creation of the Fund was, indeed, a powerful indication of that continuous linking of work and community which distinguished coalmining from most other industries, for it was quite specifically directed to the provision of amenities in mining villages as well as at the pits themselves.

The Miners' Welfare Fund was the only really enduring outcome of the wave of public and political sympathy following the exposure of the shocking living and working conditions in mining communities in 1919.

---

[1] *Sankey Report* II, 479.

[2] For adult mortality among miners and their wives, see Logan 1954; Registrar-General, *Decennial Supplement. England and Wales. 1931. Part IIA*, 85.

It was part of the package of measures promised by the Prime Minister when he rejected the idea of nationalization in August of that year, and although the government's immediate proposals for industrial reorganization were spurned by the miners, the plans for social welfare were incorporated in the Mining Industry Act of 1920.[1]

The Welfare Fund was financed by a levy of 1 d. per ton of coal output and was to be applied to 'purposes connected with the social well-being, recreation and conditions of living' of coalminers and with mining education and research. (Help with housing was, however, specifically excluded from the scheme.)[2] In the first five years the overwhelming bulk of grants was devoted to recreational and health facilities. 'Recreation' (which included boys' clubs and seaside holidays as well as sports facilities and social clubs for the mining population in general) absorbed some 64 per cent of the grants; and 'health' (primarily convalescent homes, but also hospitals, nursing and ambulance services), accounted for some 31 per cent. In the late 1920s, after the scheme had been extended for a further five years, the proportion spent on health increased, as convalescent homes (individually much more expensive than other projects) became more popular.[3]

In 1926 the Samuel Commission pointed out that whereas in Britain only 2 per cent of miners had access to pithead baths, their installation was compulsory on the continent and in Germany they had been in use for 25 years. As a result of the Commission's firm recommendation, the scheme was substantially enlarged by imposing on the Miners' Welfare Committee the duty of providing pithead accommodation for bathing and for the drying of clothes. This was to be financed by a new (and permanent) levy of five per cent on coal royalties.

The public stimulus of pithead baths reflected a critical, if belated, recognition of an aspect of coalminers' working lives which distinguished them—entirely to their disadvantage—from any other industrial group of comparable size. For the inability to clean themselves and to change their work clothes before leaving this most dirty and uncomfortable of occupations had two serious consequences.

---

[1] The history of the Miners' Welfare Fund may be traced in Watkins 1934, 275–314; *Report of the Departmental Committee of Inquiry (1931) on the Miners' Welfare Fund* (Cmd. 4236. 1932) in *PP* 1932–3 XV; memorandum by Secretary for Mines, 21 July 1938, in CAB 24/278; *Miners' Welfare in War-Time: Report Of The Miners' Welfare Commission For 6½ Years to June 30th 1946* (Ashtead, Surrey, 1947).

[2] The output levy and the welfare scheme were renewed for five years in 1926 and 1931; in 1934 the levy was reduced to ½d. per ton, but its life was extended for 16 years.

[3] Watkins 1934, 282.

First, it affected the personal well-being of individual workers (and, it should be added, the perception, amounting to revulsion, with which they were viewed by other members of society). Second, it marred the comfort and health of their homes, which were dominated by the need to deal with the filth and contamination consequent upon the cleaning of dirty bodies and clothing. This, in turn, imposed burdens on miners' wives or mothers or landladies, on whom fell the endless tasks of preparing hot water and baths and cleaning and drying clothes, normally in houses deprived of adequate facilities, and not infrequently more than once a day for menfolk on different shifts.

The need for pithead baths had been acknowledged before the First World War by legislation which provided for their construction by colliery companies if a majority of the work-force agreed to pay up to half the cost. But the limits set to the schemes (they were not to be entertained if the weekly cost exceeded 3 d. per man) effectively nullified the legislation. By 1920, therefore, only 10 collieries had bathing facilities (including 407 shower cubicles and catering for a mere 5,300 miners). The legislation of 1926 ensured that between 1928, when the construction programme actually began, and 1930 127 schemes were initiated, with ultimate provision for 150,396 men (and 196 women— there still being a few thousand female pithead workers, principally in Scotland and Lancashire).[1] Yet the pace was obviously very slow, and further impeded by the slump. There were, too, inhibitions on the part of miners faced with such a change in habits as bathing in public and away from the customary environment of their own homes. Initially, the engrained conservatism of miners confronted with a technical or organizational change was an important obstacle, but it was for the most part soon overcome by the experience of the obvious advantages of workplace bathing.[2]

The real problem was obviously not the customs and outlook of coal-miners but the size of what came to be known as the 'Bath Fund'.

[1] Ibid., 297.

[2] See Mitchell 1932, 328: 'The question of the installation of pit-head baths lately provided a striking example of the reluctance of the miner to move with the times. Pit-head baths are undoubtedly the greatest boon of recent years to the miner.... But in the majority of cases where they were proposed, the miners turned the proposals down almost to a man. ... Finally, in conjunction with the Trustees of the Miners' Welfare Scheme, some of the colliery companies carried on with the provision of pit-head baths on their own responsibility. In every case, so far, the baths 'caught on' immensely, after the first few days' stagnation, and are now used by practically every workman in the mines concerned.' Mitchell (and the owners who frequently claimed that miners resisted the introduction and use of pithead baths) no doubt exaggerated the opposition. But reluctance there certainly was.

Hence, in 1934, although the output levy was reduced to $\frac{1}{2}d.$ per ton, the pithead baths programme was strengthened. The output levy was to be used to augment the royalties levy to bring the annual yield of the Bath Fund up to £375,000, which, it was calculated, would enable the baths programme to be completed within 18 years—at least as far as large-scale collieries with a reasonably long expectation of life were concerned. Yet even this was soon judged to be too slow, and too inadequate in coverage.[1]

In 1936, as the industry began to recover from the worst of the slump, the Miners' Welfare Committee accelerated its construction programme to an annual level of £625,000, which, it was estimated, 'would break the back of the programme' within eight years. This was tantamount to mortgaging as-yet uncertain revenues, and in 1937 therefore the Committee secured the formal approval of the Secretary for Mines. The next year the Secretary persuaded the Cabinet of the political and social desirability, as well as the economic feasibility, of augmented financial assistance.

It was an indication of the newly prevalent political climate that the Conservative Secretary for Mines (Harry Crookshank) swept aside the owners' proposals for the extra funds to be borrowed on the security of the Welfare Fund, as well as their objections to an increased levy. Almost anxiously sensitive to the arguments of the MFGB, which threatened to press for an increase in the ordinary welfare levy if moves were made to borrow the money needed for the baths programme, Crookshank successfully urged his colleagues to extend the construction programme. Provision was to be made for all mines as well as for the renewal of existing bath-houses and legislation was introduced to increase the output levy to 1$d.$ for five years—which would enable the baths programme to be completed by 1944.[2]

In fact, of course, the outbreak and disruptions of the Second World War greatly impeded the construction of new baths (only 41 were built in 1940–5). Nevertheless, by 1945 the Mines' Welfare Commission (as it was then called) had built 348 baths. Together with 16 which had been built by colliery companies (10 of them with the aid of welfare grants) there was now accommodation for 439,107 men and 1,105 women, or

---

[1] It was estimated that some 100,000 men would be without bath accommodation because of the restrictions on the size or longevity of eligible collieries: Memorandum from Secretary for Mines, 21 July 1938: CAB 24/278.

[2] See the memorandum by the Secretary for Mines dated 21 July 1938 and approved by the Cabinet on 28 July 1938: CAB 24/278 and CAB 23/94/36.

about 63 per cent of the work-force. By the end of the Second World War in an old coalfield like Durham the antiquated pithead gear could be seen as the product of 90 years of 'hand-to-mouth industrialism' and only the 'clean, bright, new grace of the pithead bath-and-canteen building', a product of the welfare scheme, 'belonged to this age'.[1]

Two general points are worth noting about the Miners' Welfare Fund. First, in spite of suspicion and hostility on the part of a minority of miners preternaturally alert to the presumed dangers of an ameliorative capitalism,[2] the administrative arrangements for the allocation and oversight of grants quite successfully enlisted the active cooperation of the miners themselves in what amounted to a form of joint control of welfare provision. Both the Miners' Federation and the Mining Association were represented on the central Miners' Welfare Committee. Even more pertinent, however, was the equal representation of miners and coalowners on the local and district committees which were principally responsible for proposing and managing schemes. It was, in effect, a decentralized and democratic arrangement (a substantial proportion of the Fund had to be used in the specific districts from which its parts were derived).

Secondly, the Welfare Fund, although its extent was obviously limited, made a remarkable difference to the fabric of mining communities, and to the social and educational amenities and working conditions of miners. This is not to deny that there remained many communities which suffered from gross social deprivation, and by the Second World War there were clearly many miners, and miners' wives, who still had to tolerate the consequences of inadequate pit facilities and squalid domestic disruption. Nevertheless, and allowing for the economic vicissitudes of the industry in the 1920s and 1930s, there were very considerable improvements in the environmental welfare, the health and recreational facilities, and the educational outlets for mining families. To one informed observer in 1934, the achievement was intrinsically very impressive, and provided a marked contrast with the situation in the American coal industry.[3]

Obviously, the extent of such welfare provision could not eradicate the waste, poverty, and decay which were the direct consequences of the prolonged depression in major coalfields for most of the interwar years. Nevertheless, it was not the least of the ironies of that peculiar industry that so much was done at one level at a time when depression was eating away at its economic heart. Even accepting the huge scale of coalmining,

[1] Benny 1946, 42.   [2] Watkins 1934, 275.   [3] Watkins 1934, 275–6.

it was no little achievement that total expenditure on welfare projects exceeded £23 million in 1921–45. About 40 per cent of these grants were expended on pithead baths. Of the rest (i.e. from the output levy) just over 50 per cent went to 'recreation' projects, and about one-third to 'health' projects (about 75 per cent of the latter was spent on convalescent homes).[1]

vi. Mining communities, militancy and change

In coalmining, more than in any other important industry, there was an intimate and decisive relationship between work and community. In most mining districts life *down* the pit and life *around* the pit were indissolubly linked. This was most obviously the case in the older coalfields, where even quite large villages had evolved around the pits over generations, and where mining families had developed their own institutions. But it was also exemplified in the new villages of South Yorkshire or the Nottinghamshire Dukeries, where colliery companies set about the simultaneous development of mines and associated communities in the 1920s.[2]

Obviously, such communities varied widely in the degree of their social 'articulation': in the complexity of their social and cultural and educational institutions. Nevertheless, the intricacies of the relationship between work-place and society produced, in all mining areas, a diffused and almost compulsive concern with the pit and its affairs in the everyday life of chapel and church, public house and miners' institute, sports club and local council. Generally, but especially where the social evolution of mining villages had fostered cultural and political commitment, these links were reflected in a widespread and active participation of

---

[1] *Miners' Welfare in War-Time. Report of the Miners' Welfare Commission for 6½ Years to June 30th 1936* (Surrey, 1947), 74–5. Owing to the lags between commitment and expenditure in construction programmes, the actual grants for pithead baths rose in the war years:

Grants for miners' welfare

	District and general funds	Bath fund
1921–39	£12,970,432	£5,684,688
1921–45	£14,575,229	£8,655,476

[2] Waller 1983.

miners in the institutions of local government, education, and social service. Normally, such webs of identification and commitment made for a degree of political stability. Under stress, however, they could become focuses of militancy and social radicalism.[1]

In many mining communities, particularly the well-established ones, the symbiosis between work and private or social life also reinforced their distinctive homogeneity of social structure and attitude. That relative homogeneity or solidarity was based upon the nature of work and geography. On the one hand, the exotically unique environment and organization of mining work and the shared intensity of experience underground were powerful psychological and political binding agents. And the reflection above ground of the great uniformities of social existence underground, together with the communality of mining work, income, and everyday life, further combined to reduce the normal boundaries between the experience of employment and of 'ordinary' social existence. On the other hand, and providing an irresistible context in which these social and psychological factors operated, the linking of work and community was forged and continuously shaped by the economic geography of coalmining—its exceptional degree of concentration and specialization, and the relatively undifferentiated nature of its economic concerns and social relationships.

Unlike most other industrial workers, the majority of miners lived in communities which could be defined, almost in their entirety, in terms of a single occupation. Thus, in 1921, although the 1,140,000 men working in the industry accounted for 'only' 8 per cent of the adult male labour force, some 50 per cent of all miners in England and Wales (the Scottish data do not lend themselves to such detailed analysis) lived in census districts where *more than half* the adult male labour force was employed in the coal industry. (At the other extreme, only about one in ten of all miners lived in places where *less* than 40 per cent of the labour force was employed in the mines.)

Such concentrations could dominate very large areas: in the administrative counties (i.e. excluding county boroughs) of Glamorgan and Monmouthshire some 50 per cent, in Durham 46 per cent, and in Derbyshire, Nottinghamshire, and Northumberland about one-third of all adult male workers were coalminers. In somewhat smaller (but still significant) areas—the districts, towns, and villages which comprised census districts—the concentrations were even more spectacular. In

[1] See Jevons 1915, ch. XXI (especially the sections on South Wales); Francis & Smith 1980; Macintyre 1980.

South Wales, for example, about 150,000 miners lived in 19 places where 60% or more of the male labour force worked in or around the pit. If we count towns and villages with 3,000 or more miners, then in such Welsh Urban Districts as Nantyglo, Maesteg, Ogmore, Rhondda, and Mynyddislwyn the proportion of miners was some 75%; Durham had similar concentrations in places like Easington, Stanley, Hetton, and Annfield Plain; and Ashington and Bedlington in Northumberland and Featherstone in Yorkshire had between 70 and 76% of their adult male labour force working in or around the mines.

These were mining towns and villages with a vengeance. For all their inhabitants, life as well as work meant coal. Nor, as has already been suggested, were such high concentrations much alleviated by female participation in the labour force more generally. Indeed, with a few exceptions, the very isolation of accessible seams—and therefore of pits and pit villages—from other industries and centres of population reduced the opportunity for alternative paid work, while the social habits and economic needs of miners tended to keep wives and to some extent daughters at home. Thus, according to the 1921 Census, whereas 26 per cent of the female population worked, the percentage in Durham, Glamorgan, and Monmouthshire was only about 14. Similar contrasts in the 'female participation ratios' existed between other counties and coalmining communities within them. Put another way, in 1921 almost half of all miners lived in communities where between 53 and 78 per cent of adult males were employed in the mines, and in virtually all of these places the female proportion of the labour force was under half the national average.[1]

The implications of the peculiar composition and work of the labour force in mining communities are superficially paradoxical. On the one hand, their social structure and outlook frequently exemplified an exceptional homogeneity; on the other, within these 'homogeneous' societies, there was a sharp division of function and experience between the two sexes. More than this, the social stresses which accompanied rapid economic change also served to fragment the apparent homogeneity of mining communities.

The social homogeneity of most settled mining communities has always struck observers. In spite of the occupational gradations of

[1] Calculated from 1921 Census. Of the principal coalmining counties, only in Nottinghamshire and Lancashire did female employment in the main mining towns approximate to the national average. Nationally, over 300,000 miners lived in places where 12% or less of the labour force was female.

mining tasks and the élite role of hewers, the shared position (as wage-earners with a circumscribed autonomy) and work circumstances of the overwhelming mass of miners, reinforced as it was by the social pressures of such specialized communities on life-styles and culture, meant that mining villages and towns were virtually single-class societies. More than this, the economic circumstances of all their inhabitants—incomes and housing, prospects and commitments—were a matter of general knowledge. Social display and 'The pretensions of urban living were impossible. ... No family could assume higher standards than its income warranted without incurring ridicule.'[1] There was, correspondingly, much less variety of consumption patterns, social relations, cultural pursuits, and social and political attitudes than in towns with a more variegated occupational distribution.

It was, of course, the social convergence and solidarity which was thereby encouraged which helped make mining communities such formidable adversaries in pursuit or defence of their own interests. And it was made the more vivid by the relative absence of a local middle or upper class drawn from the same industry.[2] In such communities, then, as one social scientist discovered during the Second World War, vigorous aspirations and the 'demands on life' were communal rather than individual in character and personal ambition was frequently tamed to the union office, the committee table, the pulpit, and the craft of the pit.[3]

If the social patina of mining communities often appeared smooth and undifferentiated in the context of collective political and cultural attitudes, within those communities there nevertheless existed a distinction of role and social position of the sexes which ensured a powerful demarcation of life circumstances. The detailed economic and social history of women in mining communities is still to be written, although sociologists have described the male-dominated character of such communities—the exclusivity of male society outside the home, the control and division of wage-packets, the completely home- and family-centred life of wives and the restriction of their pattern of social relations, and the strict sexual division of labour within the family.[4]

[1] Benny 1946, 23–4.

[2] The uniformity of social structure in coalmining communities, especially as companies replaced locally owned enterprises, has been frequently noted, and often used to explain part of the gulf between miners and management and owners. See *The Times* 28 Mar. 1928, 17f and 20 Mar. 1934, 16a. Given their roles and the fact that they were directly recruited from working miners, deputies could not be considered the equivalent of a local middle class.

[3] Benny 1946, 23–4, 122.

[See p. 482 for n. 4]

The social constriction of wives and mothers in mining families was exposed and, if anything, aggravated in the 1920s and 1930s by the economic disruption of the depressed areas, for the shortage of resources was obviously experienced most keenly in *their* area of prime responsibility—household management. Of course, even in periods of comparative prosperity the housewife's lot—isolated in the home, ministering to the needs of a large family, and perhaps attending to the washing and feeding of lodgers and sons as well as husbands, all in inadequate housing—was far from enviable. Thus it was that some of the most affecting evidence given to the Sankey Inquiry came from miners' wives. But prolonged depression, low income, and unemployment made their situation far worse in the following two decades.

It might well have been that the new dependence on unemployment benefits or public relief gave miners' wives a greater chance of controlling *all* the household income. But the income was low and the price was high: 'the women are earning their new status by a stupendous effort of self-sacrifice'.[1] And that punishing self-sacrifice by the female household manager, neglecting her own diet and health in the interests of her children and husband, was noted by virtually all visitors to the coalfields. Indeed, in many areas malnutrition as well as ill health seemed more in evidence in mothers than in children. As one survey put it, in large families 'the wives bear the brunt of unemployment'.[2]

This last judgement was, of course, a relative one. Where the economic rationale of a mining community was destroyed—and the extreme specialization of such communities made such a destruction a more likely occurrence—the consequences were universally felt. The very pervasiveness of that experience raises an important issue. For, even accepting the notorious fact that the individual psychological response to long-term unemployment was frequently a hopeless listlessness and passivity, the relative absence of violent reaction to widespread poverty and worklessness was quite remarkable.

The well-known relative tranquillity of British society as a whole during the interwar depression implies a good deal about social relations

[4] For example, Benny 1946, 13–21, 24; Dennis, Henriques, and Slaughter 1956, ch. V. Benny worked in the Durham coalfield in the latter stages of the Second World War. Dennis and his collaborators conducted their field research in the early 1950s. They also managed to secure some anecdotal evidence of the tensions of husband–wife relationships in the stressful 1930s. See ibid., 192–3.

[1] *The Times* 21 Mar. 1934, 16a. However, for the difficulty that a miner's wife might still have in diverting 'dole' money from the bookmaker, see Dennis, Henriques, and Slaughter 1956, 193.

[2] Jennings 1934, 123.

and cohesiveness, as well as about the extent to which relief and welfare systems, primitive as they were by more modern standards, alleviated the worst consequences of the slump. Nevertheless, this seeming moderation in the face of the most provoking personal and social circumstances remains surprising in the case of most coalmining communities.[1] For, even without the apparent spur of mass unemployment, the coalminer's social, and therefore industrial, relations were rarely passive, let alone tranquil or harmonious. It is, therefore, necessary to distinguish between the normal 'militancy' of miners and the circumstances of the late 1920s and 1930s.

Obviously, mining communities and districts varied very much in terms of the characteristics and attitudes of their industrial relations. Some, like South Wales or South Yorkshire in the twentieth century, have had a well-earned reputation for industrial militancy; others (Durham and Northumberland in one context, the Nottinghamshire field in another) were far more 'moderate' in their relationships with coalowners and in their political postures generally.[2] More than this, political and industrial militancy were by no means always well correlated.[3] Yet, taking the industry as a whole, the 'militancy' of the miners—in their day-to-day social dealings as well as their formalized, union-based industrial relations—was far more obvious than in the case of any other large occupational group. Politically, too, although important regional variations in voting patterns persisted, there was a striking increase in the support for Labour Party candidates in mining communities during the 1920s: by 1929 two-thirds of their inhabitants voted Labour.[4] The assertiveness of the miners' social and industrial attitudes was derived in part from their situation and in part from their historical experience.

As has already been emphasized, the miner's employment and society were exceptional. His work and work situation were gruelling, dangerous, and calculated to excite his suspicion and antagonism towards

[1] There were, of course, exceptional incidents and areas. Thus, Francis & Smith 1980, examine a large number of examples of social and industrial militancy. But the general mood and pattern of behaviour of mining communities was much more quiescent than might have been deduced from their economic and social experiences.

[2] For contrasts in mood and militancy between the South Wales and North-East coalfields in 1917, see *Commission of Enquiry into Industrial Unrest. No. 1 Division . . . North-Eastern Area* (Cmd. 8662. 1917) and *No. 7 Division . . . Wales, including Monmouthshire* (Cmd. 8668. 1917). Also Garside 1971 and Francis & Smith 1980. Cf. Griffin 1962.

[3] Rossiter 1980, 183–4. I am most grateful to Dr Rossiter for his kindness in allowing me to consult his thesis. Also see Gregory 1968, 183.

[4] Rossiter 1980, 198.

those who employed, or were placed in direct authority over, him. He lived in communities which were isolated and characterized by a monolithic class structure which could enforce as well as reinforce 'militant' social and industrial attitudes; the very inward-looking nature of his daily social and cultural preoccupations helped perpetuate both his suspicion of the rest of the society and a formidable mutual loyalty and solidarity in the face of adversity which was such a marked feature of miners' lives and miners' disputes.

These ecological and environmental considerations were, of course, tempered by the distinctive social and cultural experiences of different areas—by the role of religion, by the size and working methods of the colliery companies, by the patterns of employment available for women, by the control of local institutions. As a consequence, there were extremely important contrasts between the outlook of miners in different districts (as well as in the same district over time). But taking the mining community as a whole, the outcome of its extremes of circumstances and social response was a relative militancy of attitude and action which was reflected in the miners' enduring role in the left-wing labour movement, in the frequency of strike action within the industry, in the assertive quality and content of negotiations at the pit or between unions and owners or government, and in the fierceness which often characterized their attitudes towards other interest groups.

Such militancy was not merely related to the 'normal' circumstances of mining work and life. Its explanation, and the explanation of a particularly bitter tone that began to overlay it from the mid-1920s, could not be divorced from the economic vicissitudes and secular changes which overtook the industry after 1913.

During and after the First World War there were brief, but intense, phases when the shortage of coal and mining labour gave the work-force and its union the upper hand in its adversarial dealings with owners and government. Yet the consequent gains—the relative advances in wages and the reduction of hours—also established expectations which magnified the miners' sense of disappointment and betrayal when hours were increased to their former level (in 1926) and wages were reduced (in 1921 and, after a temporary increase, again in 1926 and the bitter years that followed).

More than this, the sense of betrayal was heightened by the memory of the transitory public sympathy for the miners in 1919, and of how near they had come to forcing the industry into public ownership. The deeply charged disputes of 1921 and 1926, and the dramatic sequences of disputatious negotiations which preceded them, were, of course, prolonged demonstrations of the powerful emotions that the mining communities and their representatives could muster in defence of their actions. At the end of the disastrous stoppage of 1921 their attitudes could be characterized, albeit patronizingly, as follows:

Whatever is thoughtful and foresighted and faithful in the miners' movement cries out, 'We want education and art and culture and a finer way of living. We don't know very exactly what it's all like, and we suppose it's too late for us as individuals, and we all drink too much beer, and bet too much, and all that, but we want what we don't understand, and perhaps shouldn't recognise, for our children's children. And, meanwhile, if you lay a finger on that usual quarter of an hour Saturday that's always been customary at our pit, we stop the whole coalfield till we starve. For that we do understand.[1]

Attitudes like this, strengthened by the prospect of further wage reductions and a lengthening work day in 1926, proved a puzzle and a sore trial to men like Stanley Baldwin.[2] Yet the occasions on which the miners were obliged to fight, and perhaps even more their unyielding choice of grounds during both sets of negotiations and stoppages, doomed them to defeat.

In the extent of that defeat, especially after 1926, lay the seeds of the paradoxical combination of passivity and bitterness in following years: bitterness at the circumstances which had overtaken them and passivity because of the feebleness of their union and, perhaps even more, the exhaustion of their personal and material resources and the enormity of the economic problems with which they were faced. In fact, there was a good deal of union pressure and action (at least after 1928), but much of the industrial unrest was based not on any ambition to secure new privileges but on the MFGB's persistent efforts to recoup some of the lost ground of 1926, by reducing the length of the underground day and defeating the 'non-political' unions which had been founded in Nottinghamshire and South Wales. As a result, while the number of strikes per 10,000 workers in coal was as great after 1929 as in 1919–21 (and much greater in 1933–9 than it had been before), the man-days, and even more the proportionate number of miners, involved were very much less after 1926 (and even after 1932) than they had been in the years between 1918 and 1926.[3]

---

[1] Frank Betts, writing in the *Nation & Atheneum* 30 July 1921, quoted in Everett and Lubin 1927, 220–1.   [2] Above, 246.

[3] Strike statistics are considered in Knowles 1954, 162–3. For union activity generally, see Arnot 1953 and 1961; Francis & Smith 1980; Garside 1971; Williams 1962.

Much of this was reflected in the figures of the membership of the Miners' Federation of Great Britain—which was equivalent to between 75 and 80 per cent of the industry's wage-earners in the postwar years, dropped sharply after the disastrous 1926 strike (it was just over 56 per cent in 1929), and then rose again in the 1930s until it once more reached 75 per cent in 1938.[1]

This is not to say that industrial relations within the mining industry were completely transformed by the slump and the post-1926 weakness of the MFGB. Indeed, there was at least one occasion (1935) when a complete stoppage was apparently only averted by the concession of a wage claim. Moreover, there were occasional extensive regional disputes (for example, in 1930 over the issue of the 'spreadover' when underground hours were reduced), and throughout the slump as well as the subsequent recovery the incidence of coal strikes remained exceptionally high.[2]

Nevertheless, given the extent of the depression, it might have been imagined that some form of militant action and protest might have been forthcoming—as some observers anticipated.[3] Certainly, the mood of the mining communities was far from tolerant of the situation in which they were placed.

Indeed, virtually all the social surveys of derelict mining communities were alerted to the depth of local bitterness—directed not merely towards managers and owners, but also towards the larger society which failed to rescue them; and not merely towards their current desperate position, but towards the historical circumstances which

[1] Arnot 1953, 545, and 1961, 434. These figures should be treated with some caution. They do not include membership of other unions than the MFGB; and they compare the MFGB's membership with data on the average number of wage-earners, which appear to have excluded the wholly unemployed, who might nevertheless still belong to the union. Of the various major districts, the stagnation of the industry in the late 1920s appears to have hit South Wales the hardest. The membership of the South Wales Miners' Federation, which was over 197,000 in 1920 and some 148,000 in 1924, had collapsed to 74,500 in 1930, and rose to 123,700 in 1939. The Durham Miners' Association membership held up much better (151,000 in 1920, 133,000 in 1930) but the Lancashire MFGB suffered and never recovered (99,000 in 1920, 47,000 in 1930, and 42,500 in 1939), while the Yorkshire Miners' Association fell from 160,000 in 1920 to 99,000 in 1930, but recovered to some 136,000 in 1939. (Area data from FS 12/7, 10, 137, 140.) Also see *Reports of the Chief Registrar of Friendly Societies*.

[2] Knowles 1954, 162–3, 203–6.

[3] Writing about south-west Durham in 1935, Thomas Sharp argued that the local miner was normally quiet, 'fundamentally decent, quietly independent, a good citizen', but that the last few years had robbed him of his patience. His independence and antipathy to revolution, Sharp warned, might be 'the very reasons why he has been left to rot, conveniently forgotten like an inhabitant of a lost continent. But it would be unsafe to bank on these facts.' Sharp 1935, 43.

meant that 'the miner's fate is still to be ignored and forgotten for long periods between occasional bursts of sentimentality'.[1] The miners' keen, even anguished, sense of historical continuity was itself a function of the insular intensity of life and work in mining communities, as well as of their economic and political experiences.

Thus it was that the collective memory of the British coalminer came to be shaped by the experience of the lost victories of 1915–19, of the long periods of social neglect which followed brief bursts of public attention and sympathy, by what they judged to be the political trickery which prevented them from capitalizing on the Sankey Inquiry, and above all by the swingeing defeats of 1921 and 1926 and the extent to which the owners appeared to have taken advantage of their weakness. These festering recollections, magnified and mythologized by time, enhanced and compounded by the experience of depression after 1926, became part of the folklore of mining communities. Indeed, such historical memories were powerful elements in the political and industrial posture of the miners when, after 1939, they once more were able to exercise the power of scarcity. The story of war and nationalization is perhaps incomprehensible without them.[2]

The negotiations and confrontations of 1919–21 and 1925–6 were characterized by the bruising clash of committed adversaries. But in the later 1920s and early 1930s, in spite of the continued hostility towards owners and governments, and the regrouping of its forces by the MFGB and the occasional assertion of regional power, the generality of miners were clearly demoralized by their experience and recollections. Bitterness there was, but it was the bitterness of acquiescence. The miners' past political failure (attributed by them to malignant outside forces, even if frequently of their own making), the loss of younger generations who left to seek jobs elsewhere, the rise in real wages of those in employment, and the personal effects of long-run unemployment on those without jobs—all combined to neutralize mining communities as a general militant force in society. Where mass unemployment persisted miners could see 'little before them now but the prospect of 30 years of working life during which they will be either poor and insecure in the pits, or poorer out of them'. In the words of another survey of a derelict South Wales community, 'without grounds for the belief in the possibility of success, the community will remain paralysed and apathetic in its emergency . . . the need of self-preservation will not be a sufficient rallying cry.[3]

[1] Ibid., 41; Jennings 1934, 220–1.   [2] Below, Part F.

[See p. 488 for n. 3]

The social and political picture which individual mining communities presented to the world was, on the whole, a monolithic one. They were thought of as slow to change, uniform in their population, and stable in their characteristics. Yet it is as well to remember that they, like other sorts of communities, *were* subject to change and mutation. That much was, of course, clear from their economic experiences and the uneven course of their responses to it in the 1920s and 1930s. However, it is also necessary to emphasize that the very isolation of mining communities meant that their demographic composition, particularly in periods of expansion, was subject to more volatile change than most other types of settlement. Necessary additions to the labour force could rarely be recruited from within an existing mining community. Any increase in the work-force therefore had a greater proportional effect on the population of the community as a whole. By the same token, when the industry shrank, there were fewer local opportunities of alternative employment, so that the process of occupational change was the more painful.

The degree of flux in the coalmining population had been most apparent in the great days of expansion in the late nineteenth and early twentieth centuries, with the substantial recruitment of new workers and large-scale population flows into the booming 'frontier' mining villages of Britain. By 1911 some 25 per cent of the total Rhondda Valley's population of 153,000 had been born outside Wales, and 40 per cent outside Glamorgan. And this story was repeated even in the otherwise depressed interwar years, as the new fields of Nottinghamshire and Kent recruited labour for *their* dramatic expansion.[1]

Although different in kind, the social dislocation which accompanied rapid expansion might be just as dramatic as that which followed pit closures. Much of this new labour force was of course drawn from other coalfields. And there were two aspects of the flow of labour which throw a quite different light on the conventional picture of community stability in mining. First, and in spite of the unfavourable conditions in their districts of origin, many migrants did not stay long: the turnover in many of the new pits was very high (some 50 per cent in Kent and the Dukeries, for example). This was the result of family homesickness, unaccustomed work conditions, local hostility, unsettled conditions.[2]

[3] 'Portrait of a Mining Town'; Jennings 1934, 221.

[1] Lewis 1959, 238; Waller 1983, ch. 2; Johnson 1972; Harkell 1978. Also see the figures for immigration to the Kent coalfield in Thomas 1937, 336.

[2] See Waller 1983, 29 ff.; Harkell 1978, 109–11; *Samuel Evidence* QQ 11523 ff.

This mutability merely reinforced the second consideration—which was that the very speed and extent of the growth of these new, and therefore raw, communities made for a degree of social upheaval. New communities, without the advantages of a settled population or established institutions, inhabited by migrants from different regions and with the peculiar age-distribution of such immigrant communities, were vulnerable to instability, fragmentation, and disturbance.

Nor was it only in the relatively unimportant new coalfields that such demographic and social flux was exemplified. Internal migration had always characterized the industry, and its labour force seemed perennially on the move. In 1924, for example, some 28 per cent of all miners had been recruited in the course of the year, and of the 214,541 recruited for underground work, 175,72 had merely changed jobs within the industry.[1]

In terms of employment in the coalmines, the vicissitudes of different districts within the industry naturally affected the regional balance of the mining population. The resulting geographical shifts in the labour force are exemplified in Table 1.5. However, as far as mining communities were concerned, the most important demographic changes of the interwar years occurred in the depressed areas through the loss of population to other occupations and regions as hundreds of thousands of mostly young and active men and women migrated to more prosperous districts in the Midlands and the South-East, and, in so doing, radically altered the age composition of the coalfields which they left.[2] This mass movement was not entirely consistent with the miners' reputation for geographic and occupational immobility—a reputation earned by their fierce social loyalty and the dense cultural attraction of establishing mining communities. That miners *did* find it difficult to move to other industries or different sorts of communities was fairly obvious. The problem of persuading them to move between coalfields or even pits within a field was a worrying aspect of the labour crises in both World Wars.[3] And there was even more puzzled comment on the fact that in the early 1920s the prosperous pits of South Yorkshire and Nottinghamshire were having to recruit 'new' labour from other occupations even though there was already severe unemployment in the older fields. But the incentive for those in the beleaguered export

---

[1] *Samuel Appendices*, Appendix 18, Table 14. Of the new miners 17,669 were recruited from other industries and 20,100 were new entrants (i.e. juveniles).

[2] Below, 492.

[3] Above, 52 and below, 557.

districts to migrate increased enormously as their industry moved into chronic stagnation in the course of the 1920s.

The industrial and political instability of the early years of the decade might have produced the immobility of confusion, but even this was changing by 1928, when the Industrial Transference Board drew sympathetic attention to it. As the Board put it in its Report, if the miner

betrays a reluctance to regard movement from his home as a feasible alternative to chronic unemployment this trait must not be regarded as unnatural. Of recent years, his political and economic environment has revealed tendencies so conflicting as to baffle even a detached and unaffected observer. Amid all the vacillations of policy which have characterized the history of the mining industry during the past decade, it is scarcely a matter for wonder that the unemployed miner should need some real stimulus before he can be expected to uproot his home and seek a better fate in other areas.[1]

In fact, once the hopelessness of the plight of many communities was borne in upon their inhabitants, the outward movement of population became a stream. The force of that stream depended on the relative prosperity of the potential receiving areas as well as on the degree of unemployment in the supplying areas. There was, for example, a good deal of movement even *within* the generally depressed South Wales coalfield as miners left the moribund valleys of Merthyr Vale, Aberdare, Rhondda, and Port Talbot to take up work in the anthracite pits of the western part of the field, and even in the steam-coal-producing Rhymney Valley, which was less depressed than its neighbours and benefited from postwar developments by the Tredegar Coal and Iron Company.[2]

On a larger canvas, the extent of inter-regional migration also depended on the phase of the trade cycle in the Midlands and the South-East (it rose in 1929–30 and 1935–7), but its cumulative extent was considerable, and once again it was most marked from the two areas which had been most affected by the collapse of Britain's coal exports: South Wales and the Northumberland–Durham coalfield. Between them, they were estimated to have lost some 444,000 people in 1921–31 and 194,000 in 1931–6.

For South Wales the 1921–31 outflow was equivalent to 12 per cent of its 1921 population, and in Rhondda Urban District alone the migration

---

[1] *Industrial Transference Board Report* (Cmd. 3156. 1928), 11.

[2] Thomas 1931, 216–26. Between mid-year 1923 and 1930 the number of miners employed in Merthyr Vale had fallen by 71%, while the demand for mining labour in the Rhondda Valley fell by nearly 50%—displacing 31,000 workers.

(47,000 people) was equivalent to 28 per cent of the 1921 population.[1] Altogether, just over 40 per cent of *all* migrants to the South-East came from the North-East and Wales.[2] Economic forces were very powerful in all this, although the government's transference scheme (itself the outcome of the coal industry's crisis) provided an extra incentive: just over 240,000 workers from all industries and various regions, received official help in their migration in 1928–37. And although many of these sooner or later returned to their home regions ('wastage' amounted to some 35 per cent of the juveniles and 27 per cent of the adults), the total numbers were increased by the migration of dependent members of the transferees' families.[3]

While not all men who left the industry moved away from their homes, an indirect measure of the effect on the size of communities is the fall in the number of insured workers (aged 16–64) in the coal industry. Between July 1923 and July 1937, for the country as a whole, the proportionate decline was 27 per cent, but for Glamorgan and Monmouthshire (where there had been 234,000 miners in 1923) the decrease was 36.4 per cent; in Lancashire the decrease was 37.5 per cent; and in mid-Scotland 32 per cent. In the North-East, thanks partly to Northumberland's slower rate of decline, but principally to the large 'weighting' of South Wales and Scotland in the national total, the fall was at the national average; but in the West Riding, Nottinghamshire, and Derbyshire it was a mere 17.3 per cent.[4]

Such profound realignments of population were bound to have broad social as well as economic effects, particularly on the communities which lost population. Above all, perhaps, since it was the relatively young—and within that category, no doubt, the most vigorous, enterprising, and skilled—who were most mobile, there were far-reaching consequences for the age composition and social vigour of the mining communities which supplied so many migrants.[5] In the 1920s, for example, over 50 per cent of those who left South Wales and Durham were between 15 and 29 years old, and in 1931 (it was

[1] Titmuss 1938, 279–80; Owen 1937, 333. For the general characteristics of migration in the period, see Makower, Marschak, and Robinson 1939, 70–97; and 1940, 39–62. The natural rates of population growth in 1921–31 were 5.6% in the South-East, 8.6% in South Wales, and 9.7% in the North-East. These fell sharply in the 1930s.

[2] Thomas 1934, 224. Also see ibid., 1937, 323–6; and 1938, 410–34.

[3] Titmuss 1938, 282.

[4] *Royal Commission on the Distribution of the Industrial Population, Minutes of Evidence*, evidence of Humbert Wolfe, 3 Feb. 1938, 294 ff.

[5] For the possible effect on average mortality, see above, 469.

subsequently estimated) that age group in South Wales was smaller by
17.8 per cent, and in the Rhondda Urban District alone by 33.7 per cent,
than it would have been had there been no migration loss.[1]

The effects of all this on the total population were mitigated by the
relatively high birth rates in mining communities and the North-East
and South Wales generally: in 1921–31 the rate of natural increase in
these two areas exceeded the national average by about 50 per cent,
although the gap narrowed as all birth rates fell in the early 1930s. Hence
in the 15 years 1921–36 South Wales experienced an outflow equivalent
to 17 per cent of its 1921 population, but its net population fell by only
6 per cent, and the figures for Durham were 12 and one per cent.[2] Yet
the decrease in the size of relatively youthful population in the early
1930s was irretrievable and the manifold social and psychological consequences of an older, and more dependent, population were necessarily
experienced. This was part of the process of bitterly difficult change (the
diminution of numbers in the industry and the consequent laying to
waste of individual communities was another) which must moderate
any view of inherently stable mining communities. The listless and
apathetic mood of the depressed areas no doubt reflected in part the
absence of some at least of the most energetic and resolute young men
and women.

These demographic consequences of the migration associated with
the interwar depression also coincided with a fall in birth rates in coalmining communities. At the same time the bad reputation of mining as a
job was itself instrumental in reducing the flow of young men into the
industry. And in 1937 it was said that parents looked on transference as
the lesser of two evils for their boys—'the greater being pit work even if
that is available'.[3] But this fact, which became a problem during the man-

---

[1] Singer, 'Transference and the Age Structure of the Population in the Special Areas' (*Pilgrim
Trust Unemployment Inquiry, Interim Paper No. III*), 8, 15; Titmuss 1938, 284. Figures for older age
groups were:

	England & Wales	Rhondda
30–9	+5.6	−11.0
60–9	+29.1	+45.9
TOTAL	+5.45	−13.14

Source: Titmuss 1938, 286.

[2] Ibid.; Owen 1937, 340.
[3] 'Portrait of a Mining Town', *Fact*, 15 Nov. 1937, 71.

power shortage of the 1940s, was clearly aggravated by the decline in fertility.

Inexorably, the mining labour grew older: in 1925, miners under 16 accounted for 4.7 per cent and those under 20 for 16.8 per cent of all miners; by 1938 these figures had fallen to 3.5 and 14.1 per cent respectively.[1]

This combination of low fertility, migration, and an aversion to mining work generated critical problems during the Second World War. In 1942–3 in particular, it was noted that the industry was seriously short of juvenile recruits, and this was attributed partly to the unattractiveness of mining in prewar years and to the sheer reduction of numbers. It was pointed out that birth rates had fallen disproportionately in coalmining districts: the number of live births surviving to one year in a large sample of mining communities (Doncaster, Wigan, Clowne, Consett, Ashington, Hucknall, Rhymney, and Rhondda) fell by 19 per cent in the years 1923–7, thus reducing the proportion of young men in the industry during the 1940s.[2]

These figures also suggest much broader themes. For the effect of the interwar depression on the age-composition of the mining labour force was merely one aspect of the manifold reverberations—physical and political, social and psychological—of the experiences of those two troubled decades in the communities clustered around Britain's coalmines. And those experiences were felt the more keenly by virtue of the distinctive characteristics of those communities and the working lives of their inhabitants. Hence it was that the social and psychological, as well as the demographic, consequences were to endure into the quite different circumstances of the Second World War, justifying in manifold unexpected ways the forebodings, voiced in the depths of the slump, that 'we cannot know what present conditions may engender or what seeds of "a harvest all of tears" are being sown'.[3]

---

[1] *CYB* 1948, 553.

[2] Mines Department, memorandum by JHW and RSG, 12 Feb. 1942, reprinted in *MFGB* 1942, Annual Conference, 20–2 July 1942, Report of Executive Committee.

[3] *Annual Report of the Chief Medical Officer of the Ministry of Health, 1932*, 40.

PART F

THE ROAD TO NATIONALIZATION

CHAPTER 11

From Surplus to Scarcity, 1939–1942

> Unless we get the coal we cannot get the arms.
> Unless we get the arms we cannot win the War.
>
> Hugh Dalton (President of the Board of
> Trade), in the House of Commons,
> 17 March 1942

The experience of 1914–18 and the growing inevitability of hostilities in the 1930s meant that the coal industry and the government on its behalf were better prepared for the Second than they had been for the First World War.[1] Even so, the wartime story of coalmining was neither happy nor, in organizational terms, particularly successful. After 1940 a crisis of coal supply never seemed far away, the industry's productivity record was poor, oversight and control were hesitant and generally ineffective, and the various interests concerned signally failed to sink their differences in order to work towards a common goal. At the same time, however, not only was an actual crisis avoided, but the issues and problems exposed by the War led quite directly to the far-reaching controversies of 1944–5, and to the apparent resolution of those controversies in the act of nationalization in 1945–6. As a result, the experience of the war years must be seen not as an aberration, but as an integral part of the continuing history, and abrasive adjustment, of the coalmining industry in the twentieth century as a whole.

Although the unsatisfactory course of coalmining's wartime development was never decisively arrested, the official reaction to its problems, and the associated attempts to restructure the industry, did fall into two more or less distinct phases. This chapter is concerned with the first of these—the period up to the summer of 1942, when the initial pattern of indirect oversight gave way (after considerable hesitation) to an altogether more determined attempt at control and reform.

[1] As with all histories of the coalmining industry which deal with the Second World War, this one is greatly indebted to W. H. B. Court's classic study of *Coal* (1951) in the official History of the Second World War. Unless otherwise indicated, this is the source for the principal factual statements in this chapter.

i. The perception of war

Preliminary discussion of the shape and oversight of the coalmining industry during a prospective war had begun in 1936 and a control scheme was instituted at the outset of hostilities. Broadly speaking, the assumption was that the industry's management and finances could be left more or less untouched, and that the government's (i.e. the Mines Department's) role would be the exercise of a decentralized and indirect system of oversight at three levels: Coal Supplies Officers in the 17 principal coal-producing districts (who would monitor output and general allocation); Divisional Coal Officers in each of 12 civil-defence regions (who had regard to consumers' needs and facilitated supplies and the meeting of priorities);[1] and Coal Export Officers in each of the five main coal-shipping districts, together with one in London, who would control overseas sales by the issue of certificates to general licence-holders.

The essentially indirect nature of this control mechanism was exemplified in the fact that the Chairmen of the District Boards of colliery owners (administering the selling schemes under the 1930 legislation) automatically became the Coal Supplies Officers and were paid and advised by those Boards. Indeed, the coalowners' Central Council had argued that they and their Boards, rather than any government agency, should directly administer the industry in wartime, but this was rejected by the government.[2]

The relative innocuousness of this system of 'regulation' was undoubtedly influenced by the political sensitivity of the issues involved and the retrospective distaste with which many politicians and civil servants viewed the experience of 1917–21. What they apparently feared was a repetition of the process by which the state's control of the industry's prices had led inexorably to extensive participation in its financial affairs and management, to a constantly perturbing involvement in its wage settlements and industrial relations, and to an uncomfortably 'exposed' position *vis-à-vis* the miners' demand for nationalization.[3]

[1] Local and detailed problems (and retail rationing if it was introduced) were to be in the hands of Local Fuel Overseers.

[2] The operation of the control of supplies to the domestic market is described in detail in Ministry of Fuel and Power, *Funding of Departmental Experience: Coal Control, 1939-1958* (31 July 1959, in POWE 9/3). In 1940 the coal distributive trade and the government established a House Coal Distribution Scheme, involving the appointment of a hierarchy of House Coal Officers in regions and districts. In the autumn of 1941 Fuel and Power Controllers were appointed in each of the Civil Defence Regions, to administer and coordinate affairs in the event of severe air raids or invasion.   [3] This is Court's argument (1951, 37–8).

On the other side, as so frequently happened in the state's dealings with coalmining, politicians and civil servants were also very sensitive to the morale (and cooperation) of interests within the industry. Thus it was that in the first two years of the War especially the government went a long way with the owners. In 1941, for example, the Secretary for Mines, David Grenfell (himself a Labour politician and ex-miner), prevaricated when Sir Ernest Gowers, in his role as Chairman of the Coal Commission, wished to gather statistical information from colliery companies which might be construed as a threat to reactivate the operations of the Commission. In November 1941 Gowers was instructed by the President of the Board of Trade not to proceed with the matter since 'he was particularly anxious not to have the Coal Owners upset'.[1]

Whatever the reasons, however, the relatively unambitious oversight of the industry was made the easier by the calculations of anticipated wartime demand and supply, which implied that there need be no very severe problems of production. Moderately generous estimates (which, following the precedent of the First World War, included a large allowance, of 44 million tons, for exports to Allies and neutrals) suggested a wartime demand of between 260 and 270 million tons. On the other side, the industry's 1939 work-force was assumed to be able to produce some 243 million tons, and the industry's capacity (with additional workers) to be about 285 tons.

Given the implicitly sanguine assumptions about increased labour supply, it might indeed seem that no very stringent arrangements need be made for the official control of the industry's actual operations, although some oversight of its continuity and (above all) of the allocation and perhaps *de facto* 'rationing' of its output was called for. In the event, the selective control of consumption (e.g. in order to limit civilian use so as to free supplies for France) and the ensuring of strategic supplies (e.g. by substituting rail for coastal transport in the supply of public utilities in the South, and especially London) involved more specific and elaborate plans than did the oversight of the industry's actual production.[2]

ii. The experience of reality

The ingenuous expectations with which the government and the Mines Department entered the War were doomed to disappointment. Although

[1] POWE 22/127 (28 Mar., 17 Aug., 19 Sept., 29 Oct., 4 and 5 Nov. 1941).
[2] Court 1951, 32–6.

the prewar estimates of both demand and supply proved to be exaggerated, it was the mistaken estimate of production which was the more serious. Admittedly, it took almost two years for the threat of a shortage of output to manifest itself, and another year before that threat produced a fundamental realignment of the control mechanisms. Even so, long before the summer of 1942 problems of production and (above all) distribution meant that the decentralized and almost informal administrative system which had been installed in 1939 had to be extensively supplemented. The details and implications of those changes will be dealt with in the next section. First, it is necessary to trace the unpredicted, and unpredictable, events which necessitated them.

Superficially, the first twelve months of the War appeared to make very little difference to the operations of the coalmining industry. Average weekly output in 1939 (about 4.4 m. tons) was a little above, and that of 1940 (4.3 m.) a little below, the level of 1938. To this extent, of course, the outcome was disappointing, since it failed to embody that substantial increase on which war plans had been based. At the same time, however, it seemed to reflect the deceptive calm of the first few months of the War itself. And even when, in 1940 (after the Fall of France and the change of government), the pace of war and war-orientated production intensified, British needs were not yet sufficient to expose very severe production problems in the mining industry. Meanwhile, even the anticipated pressure from export demand had not materialized (it was to do so as shipping became available and overseas demand increased in the spring of 1940). As a result, and in anticipation of the transport system's ability to maintain healthy stocks, the planned limits on domestic consumers' fuel purchases were raised to prewar levels in October and November 1939, although the house coal allowance subsequently had to be cut back quite severely.

The first serious coal crisis of the War derived from the problem of transport rather than production. The scarcity of coastal shipping led to temporary pit closures in Durham and Northumberland in the early months of hostilities.[1] Soon the same problem threw an onerous burden on the 'normal' rail carriage of coal, and particularly to the public utilities and large industrial consumers of the South.

Unfortunately, the resulting difficulties were critically aggravated by atrocious weather (involving complete stoppages as well as prolonged delays) in January 1940. The result was dislocation in the supply of coal,

[1] Ironically, the North-East had also suffered at the outbreak of the First World War. Above, 46.

the running-down of stocks to dangerous levels, and extremely serious local shortages throughout the country. It therefore became necessary to adopt very strict measures, including the immediate requisitioning of coal (thirty train- and two ship-loads were so requisitioned) for important users, the enforcement of economy in use, the giving of overriding priority to the carriage of coal (together with perishable foodstuffs and Army supplies) on the hard-pressed railways, and the allocation of more rolling stock and shipping.

The crisis which had emerged in the first winter of the War was resolved by May 1940, in that shortages were no longer apparent. But the experience had demonstrated an unexpectedly important consideration: the critical role of stocks of coal and the need to anticipate the problems of future winters by accumulating stocks during the summer. This need was the more difficult to serve given the fact that the wartime demand for coal was now intensifying to the point at which the 'normal' seasonal element was much less important. The non-civilian consumption of coal in a total war was going to be more or less continuous, and the task of building up stocks during the traditionally low-demand summer season, correspondingly more difficult. From the spring of 1940, then, the primary basis of the industry's planning was to be the annual 'budget' for coal and the determination to 'cover' against both normal and unexpected winter demands by the accumulation of adequate stocks. This was pursued by means of a complex programme, initially for the year to April 1941, which urged domestic consumers and industrial firms as well as public utilities to build up their stocks, and allocated Treasury funds to the creation of government coal dumps.

In many respects, the coal industry's initial problems of distribution and allocation in the Second World War were similar to those which had dogged the industry during 1914–15.[1] Shortages of transport and difficulties in matching specific needs and supplies generated unexpected frictions. At the same time, the question of the export of coal was as central to the industry's activities as it had been in the First World War. Prewar plans had anticipated the supply of just over 40 million tons of export coal, partly to serve Britain's strategic needs with neutral customers and partly to supply France (which was of course denied its supplies from Germany and Poland). Both purposes, as in the First World War, were judged to be vital to the war effort. Until the spring of 1940, however, there was no great pressure on the export front—principally owing to the shortage of shipping to carry coal. From

[1] Above, ch. 2, sect. i–ii.

about March, however, the problem of exports, to France in particular, was growing dangerously acute.[1] (That problem was only partly an immediately strategic matter: coal was an integral component of the somewhat bizarre export drive of 1940, which was designed to serve financial and political, rather than directly military, needs.)

In fact, throughout the spring of 1940, primarily as a result of France's ambitious plans for war production, the French demand for British coal mounted. And in May the War Cabinet agreed to a critical increase in sales, basing its hazardous commitment on a reduction of stocks at British public utilities and on a hoped-for expansion of production. As a result, France's urgent needs were responsible for much of the pressure on Britain's coal-producing capacity in the late spring of 1940. And in the course of the production drive the work-force on collieries' books (which had been about 748,000 at the outset of War and some 760,000 in the winter of 1939–40) rose to 767,500.[2] But even as the effort and commitments mounted, military events rendered them nugatory. Early in May German armies swept into the Low Countries; later that month the Pas-de-Calais was invaded; between 26 May and 4 June the British Expeditionary Force was evacuated from the beaches of Dunkirk, and on 17 June, after more devastating victories for the Germans, France sued for peace and withdrew from the War.

With France's capitulation, coal shipments were hurriedly recalled or diverted. Even more important, however, the course of the War, and the Axis Powers' effective domination of continental Europe, had effected a complete transformation of the position of the coal industry (and one which contrasted with its experience in the First World War). On the one hand, official estimates, which a few weeks earlier had implied the need for a 10 per cent increase in production, now suggested that home demand and the limited need for export would be some 10 per cent *less* than current production. On the other hand, the shrinking of export markets, aggravated by shortages of shipping to serve South America, destroyed the immediate economic basis of large numbers of pits. In the late 1930s total coal exports (excluding foreign bunkers and coke and manufactured fuels) had averaged just over 3 million tons monthly; and in the winter of 1939–40 that figure was about 2.9 million. But for the

[1] France's apparent annual need for 20 m. tons of British coal exceeded her annual imports (from Britain) of some 17 m. tons during 1915–17, and greatly exceeded British shipments (just over 7 m. tons) immediately before the Second World War: Court 1951, 71.

[2] For the production drive, see below, 507. Statistics of the work-force are available, on a weekly basis, in LAB 8/1473, Appendix II.

twelve months to 30 June 1941 it was to be less than 700,000 tons. By 1942 annual exports had dropped to less than 10 per cent of their pre-war level (of about 36 million tons), where they stayed for the rest of the War.

Initially, the French collapse had severely embarrassed South Wales (which was particularly dependent on the French market). Welsh production was dislocated as the ports became choked with loaded tonnage and the dock-sides with loaded wagons, and over 40 pits were idle by early July. The problems of Welsh pits continued for some time, but over the following five or six months there was some success in seeking alternative domestic markets. The really serious consequences of the drastic fall in exports came in Durham, where shortages of specialist consumers and crippling problems with coastal shipping greatly reduced the demand for coking, gas, and steam coals. (Northumberland's production was maintained by demand from Lancashire's growing industries.) Widespread unemployment in such a serious war, and so soon after the stagnation of the interwar years, had uncomfortable repercussions for labour supply and labour attitudes.

Looked at more generally, however, the industry presented a somewhat different picture: its output was well maintained until the autumn of 1940, when German bombing began to impede distribution, and the impediments to distribution began to limit production. In fact, for some months after the Fall of France it was possible to push ahead vigorously with the coal-stocking programme, the need for which had been the principal lesson of the transport problems of January–March 1940. Consumers were urged (successfully) to increase their reserves, and in July the Treasury augmented the funds available for government coal dumps. The latter were now planned to hold 5 million (as against the original 1 million) tons, although only a very small beginning was made before air raids in September altered the situation.

Those air raids introduced yet another disruptive element into the coal industry's operations. In spite of the large accumulation of stocks (which for the country as a whole were some 9 million tons more, and for London some 1.5 million tons more, than in autumn 1939), consumption levels depended on a fairly steady current supply—and it was that which was destroyed by bombing during the autumn and winter of 1940–1.[1]

The damage to shipping and rail facilities quickly impaired distribution, and generated congestion around London. As a result, the War

[1] The details of the resulting disruptions and administrative adaptations are described in Court 1951, 90 ff.

Cabinet was obliged to appoint a high-powered ministerial committee (the Lord President's Coal Committee), which, together with a subordinate committee structure for executive and local problems, tackled the allocation and distribution of coal supplies to southern England through the winter of 1940–1.

The solutions of these winter months (improved statistical information and programming, compulsory allocation, the creation of exceptional train 'convoys', the establishment of new storage sites, the enforced speeding-up of the movement of coal) were *ad hoc* and successful: 'a model of what scientific administration of short notice ought to be'.[1] But they treated superficial rather than fundamental problems and the achievement had been precarious. The need to devise longer-term arrangements would, however, necessarily involve controversial matters.

For example, they might entail the enforcement of full train-loads for the carriage of coal; and this was opposed, by colliery companies, merchants, and the railways, partly on administrative grounds and partly because they interfered with established marketing relationships. Further, they implied the restriction of the number of grades of coal available and the pooling of orders and resources in the wholesaling and retailing of coal (representatives of the 6,000 merchant depots and the 20,000 merchants objected to that departure from traditional individualism).

In fact, official efforts to rationalize household coal distribution had already been frustrated by members of the coal trade in the summer of 1940. Early in 1941, after the chastening experience of the previous winter, the issue was once more raised by the Mines Department. By that time, however, a new problem was looming, and one which might be even more serious than the question of distribution—the likely deficiency in the *production* of coal. Steadily in the spring and summer of 1941, the problem of pit output came to dominate the industry and the government's perception of it.

The problem of production was the outcome of various influences. Chief among the proximate causes was the decline in the work-force after the Fall of France had reduced the immediate demand for labour. As pits came to a standstill and men were drawn off into the forces and other, more prosperous, or better-paying, industries the numbers employed fell by over 10 per cent, from 767,500 in mid-June 1940 to about 690,500 in the spring of 1941. More than this, there was a reduc-

[1] Court 1951, 99.

tion in the proportion of miners working at the face (to mid-1941); and (from the autumn of 1941) a fall in output per manshift at the face. As early as March 1941 it was deduced that the estimated requirements of the next six months (112.6 million tons), which included necessary stocking for the coming winter, would exceed current output levels by about 13 per cent.

In spite of increasingly anxious efforts to encourage production and augment the supply of labour, this situation hardly improved. Indeed, in the event, and unlike virtually every other strategic industry, the output of coal fell throughout the War. In 1941, for example, the average weekly output was barely 4.1 million tons, compared with over 4.6 million in 1939. More generally, the annual output data for the early years of the War (Table 11.1) demonstrate the rapid decline which ultimately (in 1942) led to drastic adaptation.

Table 11.1. *Annual output of deep-mined coal in Britain, 1939-1942* (000 tons)

1939	231,338
1940	224,299
1941	206,344
1942	203,633

Source: Ministry of Fuel and Power. Statistical Digest, 1945 (Cmd. 6920. 1945).

As has already been noted, although the transport problems of the first and second winters of the War had impeded the flow of coal to consumers, until the spring of 1941 there was relatively little thought that difficulties with coal *production* might pose a threat to the war effort (especially in the light of the apparent worrying surplus in the summer of 1940). There was, then, a concomitantly greater shock to public opinion when the President of the Board of Trade (Oliver Lyttleton) pointed out in May 1941 that 'To-day our [*coal*] problem is no longer one of transport; it is one of production.'[1] What had happened was that, as the war effort mounted, home demand for coal had risen inexorably from its somewhat depressed prewar state. Between them the critical gas and electricity industries increased their consumption from 34 million tons in 1938 to 40 million tons in 1941 (the figure was to

[1] *Hansard* 28 May 1941, col. 1878. Also see Court 1951, 109.

be 43 million in 1942). Total inland consumption rose from 178.5 million tons to 193.8 million (195.6 million in 1942).[1]

Given the decline in production, and in spite of the reduction in export demand, this increase in inland consumption was sufficient to threaten essential supplies. The implications of these developments for the industry's resources and economics, and their consequences in terms of government intervention, must now be considered.

iii. Industrial problems and government intervention, 1939–1942

The first wartime crisis of coal (the dislocation of transport as a result of bad weather from January 1940) had led to a vigorous policy of official requisition and allocation. However, this essentially *ad hoc* programme was managed by interdepartmental cooperation and through the coordination of the Mines Department, rather than by the creation of new administrative machinery. The next major threat to supplies (the disruption of traffic caused by German bombing from September 1940) was altogether more serious and provoked a correspondingly more drastic solution, emanating from the War Cabinet. In the winter and spring of 1940–1 administrative control of coal distribution was given to a senior ministerial Committee under the Chairmanship of the Lord President of the Council, Sir John Anderson. Beyond this immediate crisis, however, the involvement of the Lord President's administrative apparatus which had already been given considerable authority in relation to the civilian side of the war effort, marked an important—if still largely symbolic—change in the political economy of coal in wartime.

In fact, that change had been indirectly anticipated in the spring of 1940 with the creation of the Coal Production Council. The Coal Production Council was, in essence, a means of informed consultation and administrative exhortation within the industry, reflecting (if not quite compensating for) a deficiency in the original plans for coal. It came into being because the circumstances of war, when the central authorities had an effective monopoly of information, made it impossible to rely on the decentralized mode of operations characteristic of the peacetime industry.

In a devolved industry, the members and substructures of the industry were of necessity ignorant of national aims and needs, and of the information on which the planning and direction of effort could be

[1] *MFP. Statistical Digest From 1938* (Cmd. 6538. 1943–4), 40.

based. The Coal Production Council was created to repair that deficiency at the beginning of April 1940, when the need for a substantial production drive (to serve export as well as domestic needs) had become apparent. Primarily consultative in character, the Coal Production Council was analogous to the Coal Controller's Advisory Board in 1917–18, and also consisted of representatives of owners and miners.[1] For most of 1940 and 1941 it was chaired by the energetic and effective President of the Board of Trade, Sir Andrew Duncan (who had been Coal Controller in 1919–21). Its efforts were supported by a network of district and pit production committees, although many of these were to become inactive when the Fall of France and the collapse of the export trade generated unemployment and an apparent surplus of coal within a few weeks of their creation.

Initially, in the spring of 1940, the Coal Production Council was urgently concerned to increase manpower and output. From August 1939 about 65,000 men had left the industry, and although replaced by almost that number, the loss had involved some of the fittest miners available (half those leaving had joined the Forces). In the late spring of 1940 it was estimated that the industry needed an extra 40,000 miners and the Secretary for Mines broadcast an appeal for the return of ex-miners to the pits.[2] Meanwhile, the Coal Production Council urged that recruitment to the Services and the outflow of miners to other industries should be stopped and that experienced miners should be recalled from Civil and Home Defence units.

However, this campaign (which secured only a partial response) was soon overtaken by the difficulties consequent on the apparent surplus of coal from late June 1940. From that time, and into the early months of 1941, the immediate problem of the coal industry was unemployment rather than manpower shortages.

Later in the War, when the country was imminently short of coal and the industry desperately short of manpower, there was some controversy about the unemployment of 1940 and the associated movement of miners out of the industry into the Forces or other civilian work. In October 1943, for example, David Grenfell (who was Secretary for Mines until he lost his post when the Ministry of Fuel and Power was

---

[1] Above, 81. The records of the Lord President's Coal Committee are in POWE 16/54, 55, 56, 68.

[2] LAB 8/1473/1. This file, together with Court 1951, Chapter VII provide the principal source for the following paragraphs. In the late spring of 1940 there was a shortage of skilled and experienced underground workers in the mines even though there were also some 34,000 registered wholly unemployed miners: LAB 8/1473/1.

created in June 1942) criticized the Minister of Labour and National Service, Ernest Bevin, for having deprived the industry of manpower by encouraging the movement of some 60,000 men out of the industry (mostly into the Forces) between June 1940 and March 1941. In reply, Bevin and subsequently his officials argued that it had been politically impossible to allow the high level of unemployment to continue, and that in June 1940 the Secretary of Mines himself had requested a relaxation of the restrictions on miners leaving the industry on the grounds that there was persistent unemployment.[1]

In any event, the loss of trained miners in 1940 proved to be a fearsome handicap to the industry in its later wartime history. Yet the strategic situation of the country and the political problems of the industry placed large and perhaps insuperable obstacles in the way of any policy which might have maintained the work-force intact. After Dunkirk, it would have been extremely difficult to prevent the recruitment of unemployed miners into the Forces or munitions and munitions-related industries. And this problem was aggravated by the attitudes of the miners themselves—disturbed by the disruption of coal production and distribution in the winter of 1940–1, suspicious of any period of unemployment, especially in wartime, and resentful of any official attempt to keep them in an industry and in districts where the demand for labour and wages were still relatively low.

Admittedly, there was one possible solution for this short-run problem: the transfer of unemployed miners from the export districts (principally Durham and South Wales) to those coal-producing regions where the market for coal and the demand for labour were still buoyant. Yet compulsion was politically impossible, and the attempt to encourage the transfer of labour through District Production Committees by voluntary means was an utter failure.[2] The extraordinary specificity of working conditions and organization in pits, and of coal-mining communities, proved too great a handicap. The varying depths, size of seams, heat, wetness, working methods, and levels of pay in

---

[1] *Hansard* 13 Oct. 1943, cols. 940 ff. and LAB 8/1473/4. Also see *Hansard* 26 June 1943, cols. 1179–80.

[2] By Nov. 1940 the Coal Production Council, observing that unemployed Durham miners declined to transfer to other pits within the county, let alone to other districts, concluded that voluntary transfer 'had no hope of success': POWE 16/54 (20 Nov. 1940). Between 2 Sept. 1940 and 17 Mar. 1941 1,440 unemployed Durham miners were placed in coalmining and 15,359 in other industries; between 1 July 1940 and 10 Mar. 1941 the comparable figures for unemployed miners from South Wales were 2,819 and 21,000: LAB 8/1473/5–6. Many of those placed returned to their homes after a short time.

collieries, together with problems of local housing, generated a crippling opposition on the part of miners, even in the context of wartime needs—just as they had limited inter-coalfield migration during depression.

There now seemed no alternative to the de-reservation of mining occupations so as to allow more miners to volunteer for, or be recruited into, the Armed Forces. The Mines Department and the Coal Production Council urged that this de-reservation should be applied only to unemployed miners (of whom there were by then about 35,000, including some 12,000 of military age)[1] but the Ministry of Labour and National Service balked at the implied discriminations (between unemployed and employed miners and between mining and other occupations). In the autumn of 1940, therefore, the age of reservation for miners was raised, thus allowing unemployed miners to be called up and individuals in work to volunteer (which many did). As far as those in employment were concerned, district tribunals (with joint owner–miner representation) were established to decide on the release of miners in the pits for call-up. Again, this situation (the use of MFGB representatives on appeal boards and the protection of miners against call-up) was reminiscent of that in the First World War.[2] In fact, with the exception of 81 men in Northumberland, all district tribunals found themselves unable to recommend the release of any working miner for active service.

From attempting to deal with a threatening shortage of output in the spring of 1940, the official administrative structure concerned with coal-mining seemed in danger of presiding over a glut of production in the autumn and winter of 1940–1. And it was hardly surprising, therefore, that between 20 November 1940 and 12 March 1941 the Coal Production Council, apparently deprived of a function, only met once. But that phase, too, passed; and in the spring of 1941 the industry decisively entered into the state of threatened shortage which was to characterize it throughout the rest of the War. Meanwhile, its labour force had shrunk from over 767,000 at the end of June 1940 to barely 700,000 at the opening of the new year in 1941, and a low of 689,651 in the week ending 17 May 1941.

These manpower losses were caused by a drift of men into the Forces

---

[1] The figure in the text is taken from Court 1951, 136. The number of wholly and temporarily unemployed miners fell from some 77,000 in Sept. 1939 to 32,000 in June 1940 before rising to 89,000 in Nov. 1940. Eleven months later they had fallen to barely 5,000. See LAB 8/1473/Appendix III.

[2] Above, 93.

and other industries as well as by 'natural wastage',[1] and their consequences were made much more serious by the years of falling peacetime recruitment which produced a significantly older and therefore less effective age-distribution in the mining work-force. 'The mining industry', said the President of the Board of Trade, 'is repugnant to young men in the mining areas.'[2] The effects of these losses of skilled and vigorous manpower were to be felt throughout the War.

As has been seen, the new problem of the coal industry—a potentially crippling deficiency in production—was first adequately detected and widely publicized in the spring of 1941. By that time, however, the industry was handicapped not simply by the reduction in its labour force just mentioned, but also by the psychological consequences of the surpluses and unemployment which followed so closely on the production drive of the spring and early summer of 1940.

This last point is worth emphasizing because so many of the endemic problems in the coalmining industry during the War related to its labour supply and, within that aggregate, to the attitudes of miners to the industry, to their work, and to the war effort.

Initially, as had happened during the First World War, and by means very reminiscent of those adopted then, production policy largely relied upon exhortation and consultation. Thus, a national conference of owners, miners, and government representatives was held on 27 March 1941.[3] In spite of differences within the meeting, the conference agreed that the production programme must be fulfilled and that the structure of district and pit production committees should pursue it. Subsequently, each district production committee was given a target and requested to comment on it and consider its subdivision between pit production committees. This, however, turned out to be a feeble weapon of administration, in large part because the system of pit committees had fallen into decrepitude after the débâcle of the summer of 1940. And as output lagged more and more behind the national programme (the official target was 4.5 million tons of saleable output

---

[1] LAB 8/1473/Appendix II. In the two years after June 1939 some 80,000 men left the coalmines and colliery offices for the Armed Forces (a proportion which was much less than that during the First World War). No more miners were called up after July 1941.

[2] *Hansard* 7 May 1942, col. 1463. Between 1931 and 1941 the average age of miners rose from 34.6 to 37.1, the proportion of miners aged 21–9 fell from 29.8 to 18.5%, and the proportion over 40 rose from 33.5 to 40.6%. See *MFGB* 1942, MFGB submission to the (Greene) Board of Investigation into Wages and Machinery of the Coal Mining Industry, June 1942; also Court 1951, 119.

[3] POWE 16/54. Compare the great coalmining conference of July 1915, above, 60. That of Mar. 1941 was less spectacular.

weekly, but actual production in April and May 1941 averaged just below 4 million tons) the need for more extreme measures became apparent.

The first instalment of these more extreme measures came on 15 May 1941, when the Essential Work Order was applied to the coal industry. This ultimately provided that a miner could not leave, or be dismissed from, his employment without the permission of the National Service Officer; that all miners should be paid a guaranteed wage; and that persistent absenteeism might be dealt with by the National Service Officer. (However, coal and shipbuilding were the only industries subject to Essential Work Orders where the workers were permitted to move between workplaces *within* the industry.) In effect, a government official was given ultimate authority over the recruitment, possible dismissal, and discipline of the labour force. But the origins and consequences of the measure were far from simple. Indeed, the background to, and consequences of, the Essential Work (Coalmining Industry) Order are excellent illustrations of the labour difficulties experienced by the industry during much of the War.

As has already been indicated, the proximate cause of the decline in coal output in 1940-1 included the reduction in the number of workers and a fall in the proportion of workers at the face. And the principal purpose of the Essential Work Order was, of course, to stanch the outflow of men from the industry. At the time there was also a good deal of discussion of absenteeism as a cause of production problems. Yet at this stage of the War the issue of absenteeism was hardly straightforward: it was certainly increasing, but then so was the average number of shifts actually worked. This apparent paradox arose because continuous operations and wartime agreements (to prolong summer-time work in the Midlands household coal-pits, lengthen the normal working week, increase overtime shifts, etc.) increased the number of 'possible' shifts proportionately more than the number of shifts actually worked (and 'absenteeism' was a measure of the relationship between the two). This is illustrated in Table 11.2.

This increase in the average number of shifts actually worked in the first two full years of the War probably rules out absenteeism as a central and *diffused* cause of production deficiencies at that time (although later in the War the story was more obviously different). However, the real problem of absenteeism concerned a minority of young and potentially energetic face-workers.

Given the interdependent nature of much underground work, it was

Table 11.2. *Average weekly shifts per wage-earner in British coalmining, 1938-1942* (adjusted for holidays)

	Shifts 'possible'	Shifts worked	% 'absenteeism'
1938	5.53	5.18	6.43
1939	5.78	5.39	6.94
1940	5.89	5.40	8.27
1941	6.12	5.57	9.03
1942 (1st qtr.)	6.16	5.47	11.23

Source: Court, *Coal*, 113.

conceivable, although not easy to demonstrate at the national level, that the persistent absence of even a small number of crucial workers could have serious deleterious consequences for output even if most under-ground and face-workers turned up regularly.[1] Nevertheless, this was hardly a powerfully determining reason, and even though the propor-tionate significance of face-work and overall output per manshift both declined, the labour productivity of face-workers held up fairly well.[2]

The essence of the problem therefore seems to have been the decline in the proportionate importance of shifts worked at the face. And the principal reason for that decline was the fall in the total numbers in the industry. Since the maintenance and safety of pit operations demanded a minimum labour force irrespective of the amount of coal cut, as total numbers fell so there was an increase in the proportion of workers else-where than at the face.

On the other hand, this judgement is derived from an observation of *national* figures. As always with the coal industry, such averages conceal

[1] The Mines Department statistician (Harold Wilson) who first drew attention to the increase in the number of shifts worked and the decline in the proportion of face-workers, also pointed out that the small minority of persistent absentees had a direct effect on output. Thus, in one large Midlands colliery if the 8% who worked 4 or less shifts weekly had attained an average of 5.5 shifts (as over 50% of their workmates did) total output would have risen by 4%. He was also worried at the effect on continuity of production, and the loss of whole shifts, occasioned by the absence of key face-workers. See 'Statistics relating to output (Further Notes by the Statistics Branch)', Feb. or Mar. 1942: Cherwell Papers, H.11. In Oct. 1941 the President of the Board of Trade wrote an exhortatory letter to 41 large colliery companies, urging them to maintain a high level of output—only to be greeted by a flood of angry responses, complaining about the harmful effect of rising absenteeism on output: POWE 16/555.

[2] The proportion of all manshifts which were worked at the face fell from 38% in 1938 and 1939 to 37% in 1940 and 36% in 1941. In the four years 1938–41, overall output per manshift fell from 1.12 to 1.06 tons; manshift at the face was 2.95, 2.97, 2.93, and 2.94 tons. Court 1951, 114.

great regional variety. There were in fact large districts (in particular South Wales, Durham, Yorkshire, and Scotland) where output per manshift at the face *did* decline fairly steadily from 1938 into the early war years, and where, therefore, absenteeism was a likely reason for declining productivity.[1] Consequently, even before the winter of 1941–2 (by which time even the national average of output per manshift at the face was falling) the question of labour effort, and possibly absenteeism, which could be so disruptive of the work of those in attendance, was a relevant consideration in the performance of the industry as a whole.

This aspect of the war effort is perhaps best discussed in the context of the mounting crisis of 1942.[2] But here it is worth reminding ourselves that this issue, too, was complicated. For it involved the deterioration of morale consequent upon the fluctuations and unemployment of 1940–1 (which is perhaps one reason for the poor record of the export fields); resentment at high wages paid in other industries; the weakening effects of the ageing and more continuous work of the employed labour force during two years of War; and possible deficiencies in diet—all this in addition to the familiar and deeply rooted frictions, suspicions, and hostilities which characterized the industry's industrial relations for most of the interwar period. As in the First World War, their own attitudes as well as the objective circumstances of wartime work, made it difficult for miners to respond to the needs of the nation at war as wholeheartedly as the public at large might have wished.

However, at the time of the application of the Essential Work Order to coalmining in the spring of 1941, few of these considerations had reached a significant intensity (that was to occur in the autumn and winter of 1941–2). There was, rather, a broad anxiety about the loss of manpower from the industry, and the Order was addressed to the central issue of maintaining the industry's labour force. At the same time, since miners were now *obliged* to stay working at the same pit, the state offered the partial compensation of some guaranteed earnings; and since the management was denied the ultimate disciplinary weapon of dismissal, the state had to assume the disciplinary function, too.

As in its origins, so in its application, the Essential Work (Coalmining Industry) Order reflected many of the distinctive characteristics of the coal industry. Thus, as soon as the idea of applying an Essential Work Order to the industry was raised, the miners' union pressed for a wage increase as a quid pro quo and the resulting 'attendance bonus' (1s. per shift for adults and 6d. for boys) was rapidly awarded as a means of

---

[1] Court 1951, 120–1.   [2] Below, sect. v.

obtaining the 'full cooperation of the miners with the least possible delay'. The bonus gave rise to problems of interpretation almost immediately and, in any case, signally failed to produce an improvement in attendance. Rather, in addition to a price increase, it led to dissension and friction within the industry, as miners challenged the management's assessment of complete attendance in specific instances. Relaxations of the conditions on which the bonus was to be paid were soon granted. And by September, after the intervention of the President of the Board of Trade, all conditions were withdrawn: the bonus was converted into a 'straight advance', a simple flat-rate augmentation of wages.[1] Again, therefore, there were distinct echoes of the troubled history of industrial relations during the First World War.

A more direct problem with the Order was that it did not succeed in retaining all the labour force. Old age or medical certification of unfitness were now the only means of leaving the industry, yet it appears beyond doubt that many fit men succeeded in securing medical certificates and finding their way into more congenial and better paid jobs.[2]

At a more general level, the Essential Work Order, while not the underlying cause of fundamental changes in the position of the industry, nevertheless stimulated critical variations in attitude and action. The fact that miners were henceforth kept in the mines by the law, together with their resentment at the relative level of their wages,[3] helped produce the simmering unrest which overflowed in a rash of strikes in the early months of 1942. Further, as far as discipline was concerned, the effect of labour scarcity was reinforced by the provisions of the Essential Work Order: management was deprived not merely of its autonomy with regard to disciplinary dismissals (a prewar situation which no doubt led to manifest injustice), but also of a good deal of the authority which was an essential prerequisite of stable work routines and effective production processes. The resulting frictions and frustrations were to prove a serious handicap for industrial management in coal.

There was, then, a growing divergence between the motives and expectations of the work-force and the needs and planning of the war effort. The industry was threatening to disappoint and frustrate essential wartime planning, for as the war effort mounted and the problems of

---

[1] *Third Report of the Select Committee on National Expenditure of the Session 1941-2* (*PP* 1941-2 III), 5-6; POWE 16/54 (26 Mar., 30 May, 8 Aug., 26 Aug. 1941).

[2] CAB 71/2 (22 May 1941); CAB 66/25 (28 May 1942).

[3] *Hansard* 28 May 1941, cols. 1892-934. Similar refrains, at an even greater pitch of intensity, were heard a year later.

labour supply and productivity remained unsolved, the possibility of a critical, even disastrous, gap between supply and needs loomed ever larger. Nor were matters much helped by the drive to retain and augment the industry's manpower. In addition to the Essential Work Order in May–June 1941 and the cessation of recruitment into the Forces in July, the Minister of Labour on 23 June appealed for former miners to return to the industry voluntarily and a registration scheme was introduced. But these efforts yielded very few men, for there was a 'stubborn, if quiet, resistance' to transfer.[1] Real or feigned unfitness, the reluctance of coalowners to accept employees without their own approval, and the opposition of other Production Departments, reduced the numbers who could be retrieved. By September 1941, only 22,000, and a month later only a further 4,000, former miners had been placed. Meanwhile, natural wastage had reduced the *net* increase in the labour force to 16,000.[2]

The build-up of labour was, therefore, painfully slow. It certainly failed to approach the target of 720,000 which was assumed to be appropriate to the industry's needs. From a nadir of just under 690,000 in early May 1941, the number of miners rose to 700,000 at the end of August and 708,000 just after Christmas; it dropped again early in 1942, regained the figure of 708,000 in early May, and resumed its halting progress to reach 713,000 in December 1942.[3] By the autumn of 1941 it was becoming increasingly clear that the industry's manpower problems could not be solved by a readjustment of the civilian working population. A partial solution might be the recall of miners from the Field Force (the President of the Board of Trade was canvassing this in October 1941).[4] But even that drastic measure had limited potential.

The conclusion was plain: if the industry's problems could not be solved by an increase in the work-force, they would have to be tackled by some combination of a reduction in demand,[5] a reallocation of the industry's labour to augment the proportion working at the face, and a general increase in labour productivity through changes in methods

---

[1] Minister of Labour and National Service to President of Board of Trade, 15 Oct. 1941: CAB 71/5.

[2] LAB 8/1473/7–8 and Appendices II and V. In July and Aug. 1941, over the protests of the owners' representatives, the Ministry of Labour appointed Labour Supply Officers in an attempt to improve efficiency and economy in the supply and use of labour: LAB 8/1473/9.

[3] LAB 8/1473/Appendix II.

[4] Correspondence between Minister of Labour and National Service and President of Board of Trade, Oct. 1941: CAB 71/5.

[5] For the efforts to control consumption, see Court 1951, ch. VIII.

and organization. The last was a long-term, difficult, but ultimately more important, line of policy. It was, in fact, the context for the far-reaching discussions and dramatic policy changes which occurred in the spring and summer of 1942. However, before these are considered, it will be useful to describe the adaptations of the industry's finances to the problems of the first two years of War.

iv. The economics of coalmining, 1939–1941

The point has already been made that the government wished to avoid the assumption of any direct responsibility for the industry's wartime finances, for that issue had provoked particularly thorny problems from 1917. Indeed, there was even a reluctance to institute direct price control (which in the First World War had preceded industrial and financial control by more than 18 months), since under the prevailing system of wage- and profit-determination in 1939, that could easily have led to some responsibility for the industry's wages, profits, and finances generally.

On the other hand, and from the very outset of hostilities, the state had a clear interest in restraining the price of coal—both as a means of diminishing inflation and protecting coal-using industries and as a protection against resentment on the part of the miners. As a result, the government secured a pledge to fix maximum pithead prices by the Central Council of Colliery Owners (who exercised their authority through the national and district sellings schemes); and fixed wholesale and retail margins by statutory order. The implication was that the peacetime organization of distribution as well as production was to continue.

However, the inequalities of costs and the precariousness of price coordination within the industry were soon exposed by the abandonment of the prewar cartel arrangements and the changes in the trade patterns induced by wartime conditions. Some consumers were faced with higher or different quality (and therefore more expensive) coal than they had been accustomed to buy; producers were confronted by different markets. As the demand for coal in certain areas increased, and as transport problems obliged the government to replace consumer choice with a degree of enforced diversion of supplies, these difficulties mounted, and had to be met by *ad hoc* surcharges and subsidies (for example, to supply Lancashire with coal from the North-East).[1]

[1] Court 1951, 182–9.

Much of the burden of the reallocation of supplies because of wartime conditions fell on the consumers of coal. But in some circumstances collieries began to suffer, since they were now obliged to sell coal in different (and lower-priced) markets. Since the government was naturally unwilling to allow collieries to go out of production and was presumably also reluctant to condone reductions in profits and wages (as would have happened through the operation of the district ascertainment system if proceeds fell), compromise arrangements were introduced. From July 1941 collieries were allowed to charge the prices which would have obtained in the absence of the enforced diversion of supplies. And ultimately a new scheme for district-wide price averaging was introduced by local coalowners (in the Midland field in 1942 and in Scotland in 1944) with the agreement of the government.[1]

In addition to these adjustments there was an altogether more serious range of problems involved in the uneven pressures on costs and prices. Specifically, the government's problem was how to use the price system to ensure labour harmony and also to protect collieries against cost increases (which occurred unequally) without allowing unjustified increases in prices, thus avoiding the errors of price administration of the First World War.[2]

In the autumn of 1939, for example, a wage award of 8d. per shift was negotiated to meet the rising cost of living, and to cover this enhancement of costs there was a price increase of 1s. per ton (1s. 4d. in South Wales). Yet such a uniform application of price increases implied an unrealistic attribution of average costs to all districts and pits. It therefore imposed considerable burdens on the less profitable districts. Consequently, in 1940, *differential* price increases were permitted, although these had the effect of imposing further strains on the redistribution of supplies which consumers were obliged to accept. (In later years a further difficulty was overcome by allowing differentiation according to the quality as well as the district of the coal.)[3]

In the autumn of 1940, the problem of unprofitable pits was tackled (albeit imperfectly) by the War Emergency Assistance Scheme, which was administered by the Central Council of Colliery Owners within the

---

[1] The government was able to exercise much greater constraint on the retail trade and coal merchants supplying domestic needs. In particular, apart from an increase of 1s. per ton in Dec. 1939, no increase in margins was allowed throughout the War.

[2] Above, 91–2.

[3] Three price increases—of 1s., 8d., and 1s. 9d. per ton—were allowed in Oct. 1939 and May and Oct. 1940 (at the last date South Wales and Durham were allowed an increase of 2s. 9d.). See CAB 65/1, 6, 9.

terms of the 1930 Act. This Scheme provided for a levy on coal to form a fund to compensate those collieries which, by reason of the War, produced less than their prewar share of output. In January 1941, and under pressure from the owners (following another rise in wages), the Mines Department allowed an increase in production costs to be covered by a more than equal rise in prices, part of which went to constitute the compensation fund. Even so, some collieries received grants when they had no financial need, and other needy pits were left with insufficient compensation. In June 1941 prices were again increased (by 10d. per ton) to cover the cost of the output bonus secured by the miners when the Essential Work Order was applied to the industry. On the other hand, the owners failed to persuade the government to allow an increase in prices to pay for the guaranteed wages which were more directly associated with the Order.

Quite early on in these proceedings the Mines Department, although still reluctant to propound a firm policy, had been drawn into matters which it had originally wished to avoid—in particular, the consideration of average proceeds and profits. In the early stages of the War, prices had been levelled up both generally and in relation to the former lower prices of export and summer sales. By early 1940 the average profit balance was 2s. per ton, against a prewar amount of 1s. 6d. This henceforth became a rough target for the Mines Department in its negotiations with the owners over price increases. In the spring of 1941 (when the owners accepted the Essential Work Order without a price increase) the President of the Board of Trade agreed to consider the question of prices if net balances fell below 1s. 6d., while the industry agreed to institute a scheme to help 'necessitous undertakings' by an extension of the War Emergency (Supplementary Assistance) Scheme.

In May 1941, therefore, just as the Essential Work Order marked an important stage in the official control of the industry's manpower, so the associated financial settlement between officials and coalowners carried the government one more step down the road to a greater intervention in the industry's finances. The completion of that reluctant journey came in June 1942 as irresistible pressure on wages and costs mounted. With the creation of the Coal Charges Account in that month, the administration of levies and allocations was transferred from the owners to the new Ministry of Fuel and Power. Further, as in the First World War, the industry's prices were adjusted to cover its costs, proceeds and profits were pooled, and high-cost districts were helped by a transfer of funds from the more profitable areas. As in 1941, how-

ever, this adjustment of financial arrangements did not occur in isolation from the more general problems of the industry. For the mounting
threat of a coal crisis in 1941–2 led, in the spring and summer of the
latter year, to one of the War's great discontinuities in the government's
control of civilian industry.

v. The climacteric of coal, 1941–1942

The spring of 1942 was to witness the definitive wartime crisis of the
coal industry and its management. The industry's urgent problems and
the resulting official initiatives, muffled as they were by political inhibitions and unwieldy compromises, nevertheless resulted in a decisive
government intervention—'decisive' in terms not simply of the short-
term expedients of war but also of the long-run future of the industry
and of the political economy of coal. Never again would it be dis-
entangled from the direct oversight of the state.

Even in 1941, the threat to the continuity of coal supplies (for
example, among public utility undertakings and in the cotton industry)
had led to more rigorous control and direction in distribution.[1] At the
same time, it became clear that some restriction of consumption by
small-scale industrial and domestic consumers (who had been fairly
generously treated since late in 1939) was desirable. The Mines Department therefore launched a publicity campaign to secure voluntary
economy and imposed a rough and ready restriction of one ton per
month on deliveries to domestic consumers. Even more significantly, it
began to consider a possible rationing scheme.

After a brief respite in the late autumn of 1941, when the possibility of
the disruption of coal transport led to a slackening of the recruitment
drive,[2] problems of supply and manpower began to reappear in a
dangerously intense form at the beginning of 1942. No longer was the
issue one of regional imbalance or a marginal shortage of manpower.
The emerging coal crisis was a matter of *national* demand and supply.
As the war economy got into high gear, and after the coldest February
for 57 years,[3] it became all too clear that no feasible increase in
recruitment could solve the problem of lagging production. If the risk (it
was never a certainty) of a coal crisis was to be avoided, more elaborate
and more radical steps would have to be taken to contain consumption
and increase output.

The position within the coal industry in the spring of 1942 was

[1] Court 1951, 149–54.   [2] LAB 8/1473/9.   [3] *Hansard* 17 Mar. 1942, col. 1436.

seriously worrying on various scores. First, although the number of shifts worked, and within that the proportion of face-shifts, were both very high, the output per manshift at the face had fallen to the lowest point since the outbreak of war (2.86 tons as against 2.97 tons in 1939). And it was this which, in the words of the Lord President of the Council was 'a new and disturbing factor'.[1] Second, natural wastage in the industry was high and recruitment was low, so that manpower was still growing too slowly, even while the reduction in productivity increased the need for it. Third, and in part related to these other factors, discontent among miners (resulting from relatively low pay, especially compared with munitions workers, more demanding conditions and the pressure for production, and resentment at the continuance of private enterprise) was beginning to mount to some sort of flashpoint, which threatened not merely regular attendance and continuous effort, but the very stability of the industry.

In late February 1942, just as the problems of the industry began to manifest themselves, a senior member of the Labour Party, Hugh Dalton, became President of the Board of Trade. By inclination and ideology Dalton was prepared to augment the established policy of his Department with more adventurous, *dirigiste*, and even extreme proposals. Alarmed by what he had learned about some of the officials in the Mines Department, Dalton took steps to reorganize its personnel.[2] And within a month of taking office he had helped initiate discussions in the Lord President's Committee which transferred consideration of the coal industry's problems to an entirely new plane.

The starting-points for this consideration were the possibility of fuel rationing and the exigencies of the manpower shortage and its implication for the armed services. Fuel rationing—which was designed to save about 8 million tons annually[3]—was vigorously supported by Dalton

---

[1] *Hansard* 10 June 1942, col. 1082.

[2] Initially, Dalton relied on a report from Hugh Gaitskell, his personal assistant, who commended the work of such temporary civil servants as John Fulton and Harold Wilson ('extraordinarily able ... one of the most brilliant younger people about'), and praised a few of the permanent officials, but was scathing about the Permanent Secretary, whom he judged to be 'very much in the hands of the Coal Traders' and to have 'successfully obstructed fuel rationing'. Dalton secured the removal of the Permanent Secretary, although he was unable to remove the Secretary for Mines, David Grenfell, for whom he had little respect. See Dalton Papers 7/4/1–6 and *Dalton Diary*, 396–9 (3–5 Mar. 1942). Grenfell ceased to be Secretary for Mines when the Ministry of Fuel and Power was created in June 1942.

[3] 'Rationing' differed from the previous restrictions on coal supplies in at least three respects: it applied to fuel generally (restriction on coal allowed those who were capable of so doing to secure their fuel needs by the purchase of gas and electricity); it was based upon a definite alloca-

and was to be approved in principle by the Lord President's Committee.[1] It was, however, to excite crippling political, ideological, and practical opposition. At the same time Dalton and his advisers at the Mines Department appreciated that rationing would be an inadequate guarantee of future strategic supplies. They had, indeed, already begun to consider the advantages of establishing some National Authority to oversee the industry and the vital need to augment its labour force. And on 20 March the President of the Board of Trade urged the Lord President's Committee to recommend the release of ex-miners from the Field Force (the Committee had already accepted the idea of their release from the ranks of non-combatants).

This, of course, was an extreme proposal and, like rationing, it could only be considered in the context of the performance, and therefore structure, of the industry as a whole. As a consequence, the Lord President's Committee (noting that 'of all industries, coalmining had been the least ready to accept the changes necessary to preserve its efficiency under war conditions') asked Dalton to prepare a memorandum on the organization and efficiency of coal production. Until this question had been resolved, the owners were informed, there could be no consideration of their requests that prices be increased.[2]

Dalton worked quickly, influenced by his officials and by the opinion of men like Sir Ernest Gowers whose experience as Chairman of the Coal Mines Reorganisation Commission and then the Coal Commission had led him to a distrust of the owners and to an inclination towards a 'public corporation' solution. (Gowers, however, felt that it would be ill-advised to pursue it during the War—a view which was shared by Lord Hyndley, who had become the Department's Permanent Secretary.)

Dalton's memorandum was completed on 31 March and discussed by the Lord President's Committee on 3 April. In the short run, he felt that there was no substitute for the release of men from the Army ('We want more coal this summer'). In the longer run, however, it was advisable to improve juvenile recruitment and it was of the greatest importance to improve efficiency. For this, only 'bold action' in relation to the organization of coalmining would suffice, since the industry was notoriously

---

tion rather than a limit to market purchases; and it was related to some measure of need rather than a reference to a possibly outdated prewar level of consumption.

[1] *Dalton Diary*, 384 ff.; CAB 71/6 (9 Mar. and 17 Apr. 1942).

[2] *Dalton Diary*, 397–400 (19 Mar. 1942); CAB 71/6 (20 Mar. 1942); CAB 71/2 (27 Apr. and 8 May 1942).

inefficient, fragmented, and variable in the quality of its management. He therefore recommended that the government should requisition it (in return for a 'rent') for the duration of the War, and should manage it through a system of Regional Controllers under a National Authority (on public corporation lines). In return for this, and an output bonus, he hoped that the miners would be much more cooperative in dealing with absenteeism and mobility.

Clearly, the political implication of many of Dalton's proposals demanded that they be considered by even higher authorities, and the Lord President's Committee therefore referred to the War Cabinet the two most sensitive questions: the recall of ex-miners from the Field Force and the enforced reorganization of the industry. (It also established a departmental committee under Sir John Forster to consider the problems of juvenile recruitment.)[1]

When the War Cabinet came to consider these matters (on 10 April) it was naturally cautious. The Prime Minister was concerned at the implications for the Army's morale of any release of Field Force personnel, and although he was alone in arguing this case, the War Cabinet was forced to decide not to pursue this line of action. On the other hand, there was no doubt that *some* action was called for: whereas supply and consumption were roughly in balance in 1941–2, the prospective needs of consumers in 1942–3 were judged to be greater, and the likely output of the existing work-force smaller, than in the previous year. There was, therefore, an urgent need for an extra 15,000 face-workers, but any feasible policy of recalling ex-miners would still leave a serious shortfall. More than this, a long-run problem would remain: the Army and the munitions industries could not be 'raided' twice; manpower losses and low productivity could well persist; and it seemed very likely that output would fall to potentially disastrous levels by 1943 unless more fundamental reforms were effected. The War Cabinet therefore established an extremely powerful Committee of Ministers to work out detailed proposals

for securing such practical control over the working of the mines as is necessary to increase the war-time efficiency of the industry and put it in a position, at the end of hostilities, to compete for the early recovery of our export markets.[2]

---

[1] CAB 71/8 (31 Mar. 1942); CAB 71/6 (3 Apr. 1942).
[2] CAB 66/23 (6 Apr. 1942); *Dalton Diary*, 409 (10 Apr. 1942); CAB 65/26 (10 Apr. 1942). The War Cabinet's Committee's records are in CAB 87/92.

As far as the public were concerned (thanks to a premature announcement by Dalton and the sustained opposition of many Conservative MPs), the most controversial aspect of all this was the plan to introduce comprehensive fuel rationing. A detailed scheme was prepared by the ubiquitous Sir William Beveridge—'the Government's Jeeves'.[1] Controversy was generated not only because rationing would have affected nearly everyone in the country, but because latent hostility to government control of industry now merged with the conviction of some that a fuel rationing scheme was impracticable and with a wide-ranging prejudice against its possible application.

That prejudice was partly personal and class based, and partly ideological. It was fostered by those who imagined that they would be inconvenienced by it (the basis of Beveridge's plan—allocation according to the number of rooms—would have imposed relatively severe limitations in middle- and upper-class consumption), by those who felt that it would involve excessive bureaucracy, and by those who were deeply suspicious of Dalton and the Labour Party. As he himself put it, the groups who were 'working like tigers against fuel rationing' were also apprehensive about the introduction of nationalization 'by a side wind'.[2]

In spite of support from both *The Times* and *The Economist* (the latter journal was scathing in its attack on the government for 'irresponsible foolishness' and 'surrender' when it abandoned the scheme), and of the *Colliery Guardian*'s opinion that fuel rationing was 'inescapable', the opposition triumphed. A social survey by Mass-Observation found that the 70 per cent of those polled who had been in favour of rationing in March had turned into an opposition of 68 per cent within a few weeks. Even after Beveridge had reported and Dalton had been reassuring, those against a scheme were still twice as numerous as those in favour. Public opinion had swung, and thereby defeated the proposal.[3] Fuel

---

[1] *The Economist* 21 Mar. 1942, 389. Dalton informed the Commons of the prospect of a comprehensive scheme for fuel rationing on 17 Mar. 1942—a premature piece of publicity, which principally served to help mobilize opposition. The President of the Board of Trade found Beveridge 'full of egoism and petulance . . . a most tiresome man': *Dalton Diary*, 427 (8 May 1942).

[2] Ibid., 416–17, 423–4 (27 Apr. and 6 May 1942). For the opposition to rationing, see Dalton 1957, 392–9. On the other hand, Dalton was also aware that there were those on the Labour benches who disliked the proposal in case it proved a *substitute* for nationalization.

[3] *Dalton Diary*, 413–15 (21–2 Apr. 1942); *The Times* 29 Apr. 2, 7, 14, 28 May; *The Economist* CXLII, 388, 564, 596, 694, 819 (21 Mar., 25 Apr., 2 May, 16 May, and 13 June 1942); *CG* 15 May 1942; Mass-Observation Archives (University of Sussex), Files 1242, 1243, 1274, 1301, and 1447; *Hansard* 10 June 1942, cols. 1084–5. Dalton was grieved by the publication of a cartoon by the normally 'progressive' Low, showing Dalton and Beveridge arriving with a huge meter at the door of a dumbfounded housewife: Dalton 1957, 399.

rationing would no doubt have been complicated and very difficult to administer successfully. But it was the political opposition to the proposal which brought about its defeat. The most obviously potent *locus* of opposition in the spring came from the 1922 Committee, which was thereby responsible for the only successful Conservative revolt against the Churchill Administration.[1]

Although rationing provoked a violent public controversy, a much more fundamental discussion was taking place within government circles about the principle of the control of the mining industry generally.[2] In practical terms, the matter was given significance by the need to maintain, and if possible raise, the industry's efficiency. And once the ministerial Committee had consulted expert opinion, it became clear that the emerging departmental consensus had struck much broader echoes: the best technical and managerial advice was not equally available to all mines; there was scope for concentrating the existing manpower on the most productive seams and pits (although there was much apprehension about the practical and political problems of obliging men to transfer); and the determined pursuit of productivity in wartime circumstances demanded some substitute for the existing combination of colliery autonomy and centralized exhortation. These arguments were lent force by the strongly held views of Sir Ernest Gowers who opposed wartime requisitioning but still advocated district controllers with extensive powers which should be 'ruthlessly' used.[3]

---

[1] *Dalton Diary*, 437. Also see Court 1951, 161: 'The rationing plan became a sort of unacknowledged test of the relative strength of parties and interests within the Coalition Government and in Parliament, behind a barrage of arguments about its administrative virtues and defects.' However, Court (1951, 161–2) also pointed to the problems entailed in fuel rationing and the risks of any rationing scheme which necessarily involved a virtual promise of supplies—which in the case of coal would have been difficult to ensure.

[2] *Dalton Diary*, 437–40, 444–7 (19 and 26 May 1942). The National Council of Labour (a grouping of representatives of the MFGB, the Parliamentary Labour Party, and the Co-operative movement) advocated the wartime requisitioning and national control of the industry (through a Joint Board representing the MFGB, the MAGB, and the government). In the discussions of spring 1942 Dalton and Bevin also advocated requisitioning, 'But we met with great resistance, some from most surprising quarters, and had to fall back on a second-rate compromise.' (Dalton 1957, 391.)

[3] The experts were also very concerned at the extent of absenteeism and the fact that the guaranteed employment under the Essential Work Order had a deleterious effect on discipline. See the summary of the reports from the Fuel and Power Controllers and their Coal Production Technical Advisers; the evidence and report from T. E. B. Young (Managing Director of Bolsover Colliery and Adviser for North Derbyshire and Nottinghamshire); and Gowers's evidence: CAB 87/92 (21 and 28 Apr., 11 and 12 May 1942). Early in April Dalton had noted that Young had created 'general consternation' at a meeting of owners by asserting that the transfer of 1,100 men between two equidistant pits would increase output by 400,000 tons. (*The Fateful Years*, 391;

As usual in the coalmining industry, however, technical considerations were by no means paramount. Quite apart from the ideological overtones of state control, there was the more prosaic 'political' issue of the miners' attitudes to be taken into account. For, just as had happened at critical moments in the First World War, the growing discontent of the pitmen was nearing the point of disaffection, and it became necessary to contemplate means of enlisting their cooperation—or at least fending off their wrath.

Throughout 1941 the insecurity and ill feelings that had been bred by unemployment in the months after the Fall of France were exacerbated by a number of factors: the Essential Work Order, which seemed to tie men to the industry; the lagging of their wages behind those of most other heavy industries (which led to notorious complaints about the higher earnings not only of other men with less hard or skilled jobs, but also of their wives and daughters); fatigue after months of continuous hard work; resentment at the apparently inferior treatment in the way of subsidized transport, improved food rations, and workplace canteens (in June 1942 the MFGB claimed that canteens serving hot food existed at only 59 of the country's hundreds of pits).[1]

By early 1942, the result of all this was a major crisis of industrial relations in the coalfields. The most startling instance came at Betteshanger Pit in the Kent field, where a pay dispute led to a 'go-slow' in November 1941 and a 19-day strike, without due notice, by nearly 2,000 men in January 1942. Three officials of the Kent Miners' Association were thereupon imprisoned and summonses served on hundreds of others. The situation was impossible and the miners adamant ('I'll be eating the bloody table legs before I go back to bloody pit at 7/- a shift,' said one; 'What are we fighting for, to help Russia win the war, or keep the bloody owners rich?' asked another). In the end, the colliery company and the authorities only managed to extricate themselves by backing down and securing the release of the imprisoned men through

Dalton Diaries, MSS at London School of Economics, 2 Apr. 1942.) The coalowners were anxious to avoid such discussions partly because they were averse to any further government intervention, and perhaps because they were apprehensive about the reaction of the men. The Earl of Crawford (Regional Fuel and Power Controller in the North-West) argued that 'the game is not worth the candle. The proposal would raise a political storm.' (CAB 87/92 (4 May 1942).)

[1] For descriptions of the miners' grievances and suspicions, see the *Report of the Select Committee on National Expenditure* presented to the Commons on 19 Feb. 1942 (*PP* 1941–2 III); the MFGB's submission to the Board of Investigation into Wages and Machinery of the Coal Mining Industry, June 1942 (in *MFGB* 1942); and the Debates in the House of Commons on 28 May 1941 and 7 May 1942.

intervention with the Home Secretary. In fact the figures of disputes for the first three months of 1942 show only a mild worsening since the early years of the War (a weekly average of just over 9,000 man-days lost through disputes, as against 10,600 in 1939, 8,400 in 1940 and 6,475 in 1941). Yet a grave crisis appeared to be brewing as miners compared their wages and conditions unfavourably with those of the munitions industries.

By May, the situation appeared to be getting out of hand: miners' leaders, even relatively 'militant' ones like Arthur Horner (who talked of the 'boiling cauldron' of the coalfields), were shouted down at meetings when they ventured to discuss matters other than wages; in Durham Sam Watson, the President of the local union, complained that the coalfield was 'seething with unrest by reason of these injustices' and that his officials were losing their authority; while Dalton, when told that 12,000 men were on strike in Bolsover, concluded that if the wave of unrest had reached the moderate East Midlands field 'things must be pretty bad elsewhere'. In the second week of May the man-days lost had risen to 75,235, a week later they were 88,008—eight times the prewar average. Nationally, as at Betteshanger, there was a strong undercurrent of resentment at inadequate wages and at the presumption that the industry was being exhorted to increase productivity and output in a situation in which the owners would be the principal beneficiaries.[1]

Obviously, none of this was lost on politicians. (In May, in an attempt to persuade the War Cabinet Committee to follow his recommendations for reform, Dalton referred to the 'ugly turn' in the coalfields and the fact that miners in Durham, where his constituency was located, were 'beyond the pale of reason'.)[2] And its effect was perhaps exaggerated by the fact that, as the War in the Far East and North Africa appeared to be going disastrously wrong, the public and political unity that had characterized 1940 and 1941 was beginning to crumble amid discontent, frustration, and political dissension. (In March and April the government lost by-elections to Independent candidates.)

Certainly, Dalton appreciated (as his predecessor had appreciated in 1916, on the eve of an equivalently drastic move towards extended

[1] *Dalton Diary*, 435, 442 (15 and 21 May 1942). Horner was reported in *CG* 29 May 1942, 513. For Durham, see DCOA, 11 May 1942. Data on days lost through disputes were presented to the Greene Board of Investigation in June, as an indication of the 'volcanic' condition of the industry: POWE 20/62. A fascinating insight into the atmosphere and psychological attitudes of discontented pit communities can be gained from the reports on the Betteshanger strike in the Mass-Observation Archive (University of Sussex): Box 147.

[2] CAB 87/92 (24 May 1942).

control[1]) that the miners' cooperation might have to be purchased by organizational change as well as wage adjustments. And that was one of his main arguments in advocating not simply the operational control of the collieries but their requisition, to 'win the active good will of the miners' and to 'give them the assurance for which they often ask, that, if they work harder, this shall not increase the owners' profits'.[2]

A policy discussion which had commenced with the unpalatable (to some) possibility of consumer rationing led inexorably to a much larger issue of industrial organization. In April *The Economist* had argued that coal might have to be permanently 'socialised', and a report by Mass-Observation emphasized the link between the controversy about rationing and a more fundamental public consideration of 'the organisation and efficiency of the mining industry', as well as the fact that this led to greater public sympathy for nationalization. Meanwhile, the *Colliery Guardian* drew attention to the irony that the 'recalcitrancy' of the 1922 Committee might have 'thrown the Government straight into the arms of the Labour Party to the extent of adopting the latter's Control Board'.[3]

There was, indeed, a degree of self-consciousness about this process: on 12 May Dalton reported 'a bathroom brainwave!... If we are to have a row on coal, let us have a row on the thing as *a whole*, including organisation'. He therefore successfully pushed the idea—first with his Labour colleagues and then with the War Cabinet—that the question of rationing should be postponed until the broader issues of organization and production were settled.[4] As a result, for the direct participants the nature and extent of the discussions of industrial control in May 1942 soon overshadowed the issue of rationing.

vi. The advent of dual control

As matters turned out, Dalton and his political sympathizers, as well as those members of the industry who sensed the need for fairly drastic reorganization, secured many of the reforms they sought. On the other

---

[1] Above, 75-6.

[2] Memorandum to Lord President's Committee, 31 Mar. 1942: CAB 71/8. Dalton favoured paying the industry a flat-rate 'rent' for its property, to be divided between the different enterprises. Also see his memorandum to the War Cabinet Committee: CAB 87/92 (24 May 1942), and *Dalton Diary*, 442 (21 May 1942).

[3] *The Economist* 18 Apr. 1942, 526; Mass-Observation Archive (University of Sussex), File 1301; *CG* 15 May 1942.

[4] Dalton 1957, 399; *Dalton Diary*, 432-5 (12 May 1942).

hand, political compromise ensured that there was no 'requisitioning', that operational control of mining was still largely decentralized, and that the proposal for rationing was shelved.[1]

The need for radical change was not officially acknowledged until it was demonstrated that even the reduction of the projected shortfall of coal by adjusting estimates of needs, stocks, and contingencies *still* left a strong likelihood of a genuine crisis. In the event, the crisis remained a possibility rather than a reality, and there was no serious shortage of coal at any time. Indeed, Lord Cherwell, the Prime Minister's personal adviser, argued that Dalton exaggerated the prospective deficit and neglected the margin of production.[2] Yet even though, as Cherwell rightly argued, the country had come through the first three years of war with improved stocks and no shortages, the need to be certain of supplies for such an important raw material was perfectly understandable.

In its Report to the War Cabinet, which was accepted in all essentials, the ministerial Committee on the coal industry emphasized two vital objectives: the conservation of mining labour and an increase in output. With regard to the former, the Committee pointed out that new recruits just replaced miners lost to the industry through retirement, serious injury, or death. Beyond that, there was a net annual wastage of 25,000 which consisted in the main of middle-aged men with medical certificates. Having drawn attention to the deliberations of the Forster Committee on juvenile recruitment, the Committee urged the necessity of reassuring the mining population that the future of the industry was secure; of satisfying their aspirations with respect to pay; and of providing an improved mines medical service which would simultaneously prevent the abuse of the medical certification, which allowed fit miners

---

[1] The MFGB argued strongly that only public ownership could ensure adequate performance within the industry, because only public ownership could guarantee management in the interests of the industry as a whole, while reassuring the miner that the fruits of his industry would not be appropriated by others. The National Council of Labour, and various highly placed Labour Ministers also favoured nationalization—if only for the duration of the War (a compromise proposal also accepted by the MFGB). On the other hand, the owners were well aware that a 'temporary' wartime experiment could well become permanent (*CG* 5 June 1942, 537 and 12 June 1942, 563). Nationalization was obviously a profoundly controversial issue and it was never possible for its advocates to demonstrate that it had any straightforward relationship with the question of productivity. The contribution of the owners to the discussion was not particularly constructive. They drew the line at national wage bargaining and concentrated most of their arguments concerning production on the need to release more men from the forces.

[2] PREM 4/9/5 (27 May 1942).

[3] CAB 66/25 (28 May 1942).

THE NEW AUSTERITY

Old King Cole
Was an angry old soul,
  And an angry old soul was he:

He didn't approve
Of the Beveridge bowl
  And he called it fiddle-de-dee.

13. 'The New Austerity' (*Punch*, 20 May 1942)

to leave the industry, and allow for more adequate rehabilitation of injured or ill pitmen.

The Committee's more radical organizational proposals were based on the assumption that output could be increased by making the best technical advice generally available, by stimulating mechanization (only 60 per cent of British coal was mechanically cut and conveyed and there was no mechanical loading in British mines), by reducing absenteeism, and by concentrating work on the most productive mines and seams.[1] The Report acknowledged that some of these steps (the concentration of output in particular) would be very difficult to take. But it emphasized above all that widespread changes in individual mines *were* urgently needed, and that the requisite authoritative initiatives could not come from the centre.

The conclusions were, therefore, plain: not only would the industry have to be organized on the basis of national service, but a systematic (and official) *regional* organization for operational control was called for. Out of this argument there grew the compromise proposal for what became known as 'dual control'. Financial ownership was to remain with the colliery companies and their managers were to remain responsible for the day-to-day operation of the mines; but overall industrial responsibility was to lie with Regional Controllers, sensitive to the distinctive problems of the different areas, advised by technical experts (on engineering, labour, etc.) and answerable to a national authority, which ultimately emerged as a new Ministry of Fuel and Power. Hence, although ownership and routine administration would remain in private hands, the Regional Controller was given absolute authority over the relevant manager on all but safety matters.[2]

The financial consequences of official direction (which might lead to losses in some collieries and exceptional profits in others) would be

---

[1] A Mines Department survey of pits accounting for 44 per cent of capacity had estimated that a transfer of 17,800 men an average distance of 4 miles would raise the relevant output by 6 per cent.

[2] The Committee's Report envisaged that overall responsibility for the industry would remain with the Secretary for Mines, advised by a Controller-General of Production (himself served by Directors of Production, Labour, Services, and Finance), and in consultation with a non-executive National Coal Board. This last body was established but was never influential. When the policy was adopted, however, central direction was placed in the hands of a new Ministry of Fuel and Power, under a more senior Minister (Gwilym Lloyd George). This idea had been floating around at earlier stages of the official discussion, and on 26 May Dalton noted in his *Diary* (445) that Churchill was 'quite firm' as to the need to create a Ministry. Disappointment with the Mines Department and a sense of the need to coordinate fuel policy generally led to a widespread feeling that 'a separate and strong Ministry' was needed: *The Economist* 23 May 1942, 711.

adjusted by a remodelling of the existing systems of levies and compensations, based on the total resources of the industry and recently brought within the government's purview. In light of the miners' argument (in part based on the experience during and after the First World War) that insecurity about the industry's future was a disturbing feature, the new arrangements also stipulated that control would last until Parliament had taken an explicit decision on the industry's future.

The Committee's deliberations, and the War Cabinet's acceptance of their conclusions, were acknowledgements of the critical importance of coal, of the mounting dissatisfaction with the performance of the industry, and of the importance of morale and attitudes among the miners. It was, therefore, with great relief that Dalton recorded that the MFGB's representatives, the National Council of Labour, and the National Executive Committee of the Labour Party had accepted the compromise of dual control rather than continuing to press for nationalization.[1] One possible reason for this was the fact that by early June it was clear that the union was about to achieve its main aims with respect to the level and determination of wages.

In conjunction with the proposals for industrial reform, the government agreed that wages in the industry could no longer be determined semi-privately. They would have to be discussed on a national basis and by a national body. The proposals for industrial control were therefore associated with a commitment to official intervention in the industry's pay—a commitment which not merely reassured the miners that their contemporaneous campaign for a substantial increase would be successful, but accepted the principle of a national wage system for which they had struggled since 1921.

By the summer of 1942, then, the gathering storm over productivity, pay, and organization in the coalmining industry had produced a number of fundamental changes in the system of control, the government's role in the industry, and the prospect for wages. Following the War Cabinet's approval of its Committee's proposals, a White Paper

---

[1] Dalton contrasted the expeditious proceedings of these bodies with the three meetings needed to persuade the Parliamentary Labour Party of the advantages of compromise. See Dalton 1957, 402; and *Dalton Diary*, 452–7 (3–12 June 1942). Dalton persuaded the miners that dual control was as much as they could accept, although Shinwell continued to resist the idea and press for full nationalization. The miners' leaders, Dalton wrote, 'have learned the lesson that their traditional policy of "all or nowt" always ends in nowt. This time they have gone to the other extreme and followed the advice once given by the Rev. W. Hodgson: "Keep nibbling at the cheese, boys."' *Dalton Diary*, 457 (12 June 1942.)

was published on 3 June (Cmd. 6364) and on the same day the new financial system was introduced by the creation of the Coal Charges Account. The White paper relegated the proposal for rationing to an annexe, where it was in effect forgotten. On 10 and 11 June the new arrangements were debated in the Commons, and the new Ministry was announced. They were approved in their entirety (in the Commons a proposal for nationalization was defeated by 329 votes to 8), and the Ministry of Fuel and Power was established, with Gwilym Lloyd George at its head.

Dual control under a new Ministry was a compromise in more than one respect. In introducing the proposals, the Lord President said that requisition of the industry had been rejected as 'troubled waters', while some Labour MPs predicted that dual control would prove inadequate to its tasks. Nevertheless, it was (for different reasons) given a grudging welcome by the miners and the owners and the House of Commons. And Dalton and Cripps adopted an almost apologetic tone in introducing the White Paper. The plan for the coal industry, argued *The Economist*, with some reason, was 'like a game in which there are prizes for everyone—and at bottom no one is really satisfied'. Typically, the tentative reorganization of the industry was less an act of considered judgement than a political bargain.[1] In the Commons, in spite of the near-unanimous outcome, there were many reservations about the efficacy of the scheme, the influence of the owners, and the likely problems of pit managers 'trying to serve two masters'.[2]

Nevertheless, the importance of the new policy can only be understood in the context of the lamentable wartime history of the coal-mining industry. Throughout the first 30 months of the War the government had lacked any clear policy towards the mines, initially imagining that the supply of coal would be ample in all conceivable circumstances, and subsequently compounding its lack of foresight with a posture of 'vacillation and indecision'. Dalton himself, praised by *The Economist* for his more purposeful approach, confessed that 'That is all we can say; we have just scraped through.'[3]

---

[1] *The Economist* 13 June 1942, 819; and 22 Aug. 1942, 231. Aneurin Bevan attacked the proposals as 'economic Fascism', a state-operated private industry, and argued that the debate was conducted in a 'tepid atmosphere because all the various interests had been squared beforehand' (*Hansard* 11 June 1942, cols. 1294ff.).

[2] *Hansard* 10 and 11 June 1942. The quotation is from Clement Davies's speech (col. 1107).

[3] *The Times* 12 June 1942, 5c; *The Economist* 21 Mar. 1942, 388; *Hansard* 17 Mar. 1942, cols. 1436ff. For a feeble defence of government policy by the Secretary for Mines in May 1941 and a subsequent criticism of it, see *Hansard* 28 May 1941, cols. 1946ff. and the *Report of the Select*

Yet the failings of government went deeper than simple neglect. They were also connected with the peculiar political strengths of the industry's interest groups. As the Lord President's Committee had pointed out, of all major industries, coalmining had made the least adaptation to wartime conditions.[1] If the miners were the only significant group of wage-earners who were working no harder and producing no more than they had done before the War, it was equally true of the owners, in *The Economist*'s words, 'that no other industry of equal importance has abandoned so little of its peacetime methods'. But the ultimate blame for this was placed on the government, whose 'timidity ... has amounted almost to cowardice. ... It has retreated at every growl from either side; and it is inconceivable that it could have done less than it has.' As a result, production and distribution were still 'substantially the same as in peacetime' and the fact that the industry and each pit 'is still manifestly run for the profit of the owners reacts directly upon the attitude of the men, who use it to excuse the fact that they continue to seek their self interest by their familiar methods.'[2]

Part of the problem was no doubt the junior status of the Mines Department and its Secretary, which made it difficult to formulate policy independently of other Ministries or of the industry's interest groups—with sometimes humiliating results.[3] But in the main the government's ineptness and quiescence throughout 1940 and 1941 must be attributed to the political power of the groups involved in the industry and the fear that strong intervention would provoke a disastrously non-cooperative reaction, whether from miners or owners.

The miners gained more than the owners from their suspicious stance. For dual control, although based in part on the expectation or hope that the MFGB would prove 'cooperative' with regard to industrial policy, was to be a more stringent test of the owners' effectiveness and commitment. In so far as it proved inadequate for the country's economic and strategic needs, the new system could only really be pressed further in the direction of central control. And as the *Colliery Guardian* perceptively commented after Parliament had accepted the White Paper in mid-June 1942, if dual control failed, scapegoats would be sought, and the owners would be 'the most likely

Committee on National Expenditure presented to the House of Commons on 19 Feb. 1942 (*PP* 1941-2 III).

[1] Above, 521.   [2] *The Economist* 11 Apr. 1942, 489-90.
[3] See the *Colliery Guardian*'s valedictory comments on the Mines Department and its subservience to the 'Commissars' of other Departments: 12 June 1942, 564.

candidates for castigation'; the government was not averse to outright requisition and the owners must therefore 'mind their step'.[1]

Perhaps the most obvious indication of the changing balance of power in the industry was, however, the settlement of the wages question in June 1942. In introducing the new system of industrial control the White Paper argued that it was vital to keep the question of control separate from that of wages. Nevertheless, it reaffirmed the assurance to the miners that there would be a new system for settling wages on a national basis and by a national body. And two days after the publication of the White Paper an independent board of inquiry, chaired by Lord Greene, the Master of the Rolls, was established to adjust exist-ing levels of pay and to examine the whole question of longer-run machinery for the determination of wages and conditions in the industry.

Although both issues were part of the coal crisis of the spring of 1942, the possibility of a substantial increase in pay was the more urgent (and in any case the question of new wages machinery took longer to settle). The disaffection over pay in the mines had become a serious threat to production, and therefore the war effort, fairly early on. The Greene Board confirmed that between 1938 and early 1942 weekly earnings in coal had increased by significantly less than those in other major industries, and that miners came 59th in a list of wages in 97 industries or industry groups.[2] Moreover, the inherited system of wage-determination, which related pay to net proceeds after non-wage costs had been subtracted from gross proceeds, worked to the dis-advantage of the miners at a time when output and prices were fairly stable but industrial costs (especially stores and timber) were rising. In the circumstances, both sides of the industry agreed that they were at an impasse.[3]

The miners' anger and resentment, which produced what one of their MPs referred to as 'open insurrection against responsible authority' in almost every coalfield,[4] led directly to a very large national wage claim: an increase of 4s. (about 23 per cent) per shift for adults, 2s. for boys, and a national minimum of £4 5s. per week. (Actual cash earnings in the first

[1] CG 19 June 1942, 587.
[2] POWE 20/62. Average weekly earnings for male workers in coalmining in early 1942 were £4 3s. 7d. which was 49 per cent above 1938. These were significantly less than the corresponding figures for vehicle manufacture, engineering, shipbuilding, and metals and metal fabrication. The average for all industries was £4 13s. 1d. (+50 per cent).
[3] See transcripts of the Greene Board's hearings in POWE 20/62.
[4] Ness Edwards in Hansard 10 June 1942, cols. 1181–2.

quarter of 1942 were 17*s.* per shift and £4 11*s.* 1*d.* per week for adults.) The owners countered this claim with the argument that any increase should be in the form of bonuses for attendance and output. But there was general sympathy for the miners' position,[1] and the extraordinary speed and relative generosity with which the Greene Board worked indicated the political significance of its task.

Its first sitting was on 9 June and nine days later it recommended a flat-rate increase for adults of 2*s.* 6*d.* per shift and a national minimum of £4 3*s.* for adult underground and £3 18*s.* for adult surface workers. (Younger men—under 18 underground, under 21 on the surface—got graduated additions.) The Board also recommended that an output bonus be devised. The award, which cost £23.5 million annually, was accepted immediately and the miners' unrest was speedily dissipated.[2]

The Greene award was the first major adjustment in a series of changes which, by the end of the War, had transformed the position of miners in the 'league table' of wages. Average weekly cash earnings rose from £4 in 1941 to £5 in 1943 (they were to be £6 by the second quarter of 1944). Contrary to the advice of the owners, the Greene award was unconditional. (The subsequent introduction of an output bonus, designed to encourage productivity, was to prove unsuccessful in practice.)[3] More generally, the changes in administration and wage systems which characterized the reforms of the summer of 1942 were in many respects adaptations to the self-perceived needs and political pressures of the coal industry's interest groups. From the viewpoint of the war effort these changes were undoubtedly vitiated by the compromises which resulted from the government's painful tardiness in coming to grips with the industry's problems. More than this, their likely consequences for coal output remained problematic and uncertain. Nevertheless, considering the earlier sorry history of coal policy, the reforms of June 1942 embodied a fundamental departure for the coal industry and its relationships with the government. They certainly overshadowed an event, provided for by the 1938 legislation, which would, in earlier years, have struck louder chords—the state's assumption of mineral ownership on 3 July 1942.

[1] *The Times* 28 May 1942, 5b; *The Economist* 13 June 1842, 821. *The Times* also argued (4 June 1942, 5b) that the wages issue was urgent, since 'without the cooperation and whole-hearted support of the miners production will not rise.'

[2] It was decided to pay for the award by an increase in coal prices of 3*s.* per ton, counterbalanced by a decrease in some other items in the cost-of-living index: CAB 71/6 (18 June 1942), CAB 71/7 (3 July 1942).

[3] Below, 570.

It may well have been the case that the new arrangements for the dual control of coalmining could not, in themselves, transform the industry and its productivity. But they provided a set of expectations, and a degree of government commitment and intervention, which would lead, inescapably, to even more direct concern and intervention, and therefore to more purposeful and elaborate policies as the industry's problems persisted.

CHAPTER 12

Getting through the War, 1942–1945

The experience of the last years of the War was to make it clear that the introduction of dual control, a new Ministry, and major wage concessions in the summer of 1942 had done little to solve the coal industry's endemic problems of output and productivity. On the other side, as the Minister, Major Gwilym Lloyd George, was to point out in the course of a somewhat chastened review of his Ministry's first year, it is extremely likely that 'without Government control the position would deteriorate disastrously'. This was, of course, little comfort. *The Economist*'s subsequent verdict that in 1942 the Conservatives in the Cabinet, from Churchill downwards, had 'fobbed the country off with the usual soft soap' may well have been justified.[1]

Nevertheless, the political and therefore practical consequence of any attempt to force through a more radical policy would not have been easy to predict. In any case, the reforms of June 1942 were not simply a means of preventing an accelerated decline in output and a crippling crisis of fuel supply. First, they helped produce a universal system of 'programming' to match supply and demand in the finest detail. Second, and of much greater significance, they established a context which led inexorably to deeper reappraisals of the structure, technology, and labour relations of the industry.

After 1942 the fundamental and *long-run* characteristics of the industry were thrown into sharp relief, and the ground was prepared for its decisive postwar transformation. However, the general achievement of coalmining in wartime must be considered first. It will then be possible, in the second and third sections, to discuss the Ministry of Fuel and Power's attempts to control the industry and encourage structural and technical change. The fourth and fifth sections will appraise the concomitant policy towards labour and the outcome for the miners. The final section will examine the *business* performance of coalmining during the War—leaving until the next chapter the questions of fundamental

---

[1] Memorandum by the Minister of Fuel and Power, 17 June 1943: CAB 71/13: *The Economist* 28 Oct. 1944, 561.

reorganization which were posed by the wartime experience, and ultimately answered, by quite disparate groups, in such a radical fashion.

i. Demand and supply

As has already been suggested, the crisis of coal supplies which threatened to undermine the war effort in the years after 1940 never actually occurred. This was less because the official coal policy was wholly successful, than because the extreme circumstances quite properly envisaged as *possibilities* did not in fact materialize.

The fact that there never was an *actual* coal crisis led some observers to argue that the anxieties and proposals of the responsible officials were exaggerated, and that the 'coal scare' was spurious. This view was current in the Prime Minister's private office, where the Ministry of Fuel and Power's reputation was not high. (The Prime Minister's personal adviser, Lord Cherwell, had a penchant for statistical calculation and dogmatism which was amply catered for by the Mines Department's abundant data.)[1] Moreover, the coalmining industry suffered from excessive exposure: its productivity record might not have been exceptionally bad, 'but unfortunately for the miners there are very good statistics about coal'.[2]

Nevertheless, coal *was* exceptional in being crucial to so many aspects of the war and civilian economy; and the prospect of disaster seemed real enough to those directly involved. To this extent, the performance of the industry was patently inadequate to the circumstances of national crisis. Table 12.1 summarizes the principal data, and makes clear the fall in labour productivity. Given the trends in supply and demand in 1944-5, a prolongation of the War might well have brought on the disasters that successive Ministers had feared since early 1941.

The most immediate problem was the inexorable fall in the output of coal. And it obviously raises the question of how the economy managed

---

[1] PREM 4/9/5; and Cherwell Papers—e.g. Cherwell to Churchill, 27 May 1942 (F156/59) 7 Oct. 1943 (F185/32b), 2 Aug. 1944 (F201/109), 12 Dec. 1944 (F204/37). Characteristically, Cherwell also wrote an unsolicited memorandum to the Minister of Fuel and Power, pouring scorn on his publicity about the economy to be gained from eradicating dripping taps. He calculated that Lloyd George's plea to stop cold taps dripping would, if universally successful, save the nation 330 tons of coal! Cherwell to Lloyd George, 16 Sept. 1942 (H.12). Cherwell and MacDougall were invariably critical about the administrative and intellectual competence of the Mines Department and the new Ministry. See e.g. MacDougall to Cherwell, 5 Oct. 1943 (H.14).

[2] MacDougall to Cherwell, 5 Oct. 1943: Cherwell Papers, H.13.

Table 12.1. *British coal output and productivity, 1938–1945*

	1938	1939	1940	1941	1942	1943	1944	1945
No. of mines producing coal	1,860	1,856	1,769	1,737	1,738	1,690	1,634	1,570
Average no. of wage-earners[a] on colliery books (000)	781.7	766.3	749.2	697.6	709.3	707.8	710.2	708.9
Saleable coal produced (mines) (m. tons)	227.0	231.3	224.3	206.3	203.6	194.5	184.1	174.7
Opencast coal production (m. tons)	—	—	—	—	1.3	4.4	8.6	8.1
Output per manshift (tons) at face	3.00	3.00	2.97	2.99	2.91	{ 2.86[b] / 2.75 }	2.70	2.70
underground	1.49	1.49	1.45	1.44	1.40	{ 1.38 / 1.03 }	1.34	1.33
overall	1.14	1.14	1.10	1.07	1.05	{ 1.03 / 1.00 }	1.00	1.00
% of face shifts to total	38.03	37.85	37.04	35.96	35.94	{ 35.94[b] / 37.48 }	37.19	36.96
Shifts possible	5.30	5.53	5.75	5.91	5.96	{ 5.96[c] / 5.85 }	5.74	5.65
Shifts worked	4.96	5.15	5.27	5.37	5.34	{ 5.24[c] / 5.12 }	4.96	4.73
% of absenteeism (all workers)	6.4	6.9	8.3	9.0	10.4	{ 12.1[c] / 12.4 }	13.6	16.3

[a] These figures are bigger (by 10–12%) than statistics, available from 1943, of numbers 'effectively employed'—i.e. those who worked for at least one shift in a given week.
[b] OMS statistics were based on a different definition of 'face workers' from 1943.
[c] New basis for statistics.

Source: Ministry of Fuel and Power Statistical Digest, 1946 and 1947 (Cmd. 7548, 1948), Tables 2, 3, 10, 11.

in the later years of the War. The short answer to this is that the official control of consumption and the rationalization of allocation were much more effective than government policy towards production.[1]

We have already seen how, in the early years of the War, the original use of peacetime channels of distribution had given way to a system of programming—i.e. the monitoring and prediction of consumption and the planned allocation of fixed amounts of coal from specific collieries to specific consumer units. By the summer of 1942 this had been applied to public utilities and the Lancashire cotton industry, and (in the case of household coal) to Army units and to twelve civil-defence regions. From 1942, under the aegis of the Ministry of Fuel and Power, the inter-district coordinating committees were formalized and the programming of household coal was extended to the depot level, although opposition from coal merchants, including cooperative societies, helped prevent any experiment with the pooling of orders and supplies, or with the rationalization of household distribution.

By the summer of 1943, it was clear that the system had enormous potential and the Ministry secured Cabinet permission to extend it universally. As a result, by March 1944 every consuming unit using 100 tons or more of coal or coke annually was making regular statistical returns and its weekly needs (as to quality and size as well as tonnage) were being matched to the output of a particular colliery.

On the other hand, the idea of rationing household coal, over which the government had hesitated in June 1942, was finally abandoned in September. Quite apart from the possibility of another political row, it came to be appreciated that rationing (the regular supply of more or less guaranteed amounts of coal to all consumers) was vulnerable to dislocation and breakdown, which would present crippling problems of administration and public morale. Instead, household, as well as industrial, consumption was restricted by two more flexible means: economy drives and the physical limitation of supplies as shortages threatened. And in this respect, the system of programming proved the ideal basis of enforced reductions of supply on the highly selective basis necessary. Cuts could be made expeditiously, smoothly, and with great accuracy.

A systematic economy campaign was pursued from September 1942, organized by a Fuel Economy Publicity Committee directed by Commander Stephen King-Hall. The 'Battle for Fuel' made intensive use of

---

[1] For the distribution and consumption of coal in 1942–5, see Court 1951, 215–18 and ch. XIX and XX. The control and programming of supplies are also described in various internal official histories: POWE 9/3 and 17/53.

broadcasts, including a series of apparently influential radio communiqués or 'fuel flashes'. Mass-Observation's research found that radio communiqués were generally thought to be more concise and comprehensible than those published in newspapers. But neither its research, nor the later work of the official wartime historian, could assess with any accuracy the effectiveness of the economy campaigns.[1] However, helped by exceptionally mild weather in the winter of 1942–3, and the restriction of supplies, they were a factor in reducing domestic consumption by more than four million tons in the 'coal year' 1942–3.

Similar methods—programming restrictions and an economy drive (through a Fuel Efficiency Committee)—were applied to industrial consumers. In this case, a substantial effort was devoted to 'degrading': facilitating the use of poorer grades of coal in industrial uses which had formerly depended on high-grade or specialized coals. Altogether, in the year to April 1943 there was a saving of more than 11 million tons over the original estimate of national needs. In the next 'coal year', while programming reached a peak of effectiveness, further restrictions on domestic and industrial consumption had to be imposed, and in the case of households after December 1943 they were quite severe. Nevertheless, with a certain amount of hardship, some fortuitous savings and economies, and a drawing-down of stocks to the bare safety minimum (about 12 million tons), the War's penultimate winter passed without crisis.[2]

As far as policy was concerned, therefore, it was the masterly control of consumption, and an ability to impose flexible if arbitrary cuts, which made the principal difference between danger and disaster after 1941. On the other side, as we shall see, the obstacles to any increase in the output of deep-mined coal proved insuperable. There was, however, one respect in which industrial policy could increase output while circumventing the problems of the conventional mining industry. That was in the encouragement of opencast mining, which was one of the genuine, if less than complete, successes of wartime policy.

Surface mining, which was analogous to large-scale civil engineering,

---

[1] Mass-Observation Archives, Files 1527, 1447; Court 1951, 216.

[2] In 1943 there was some consideration of whether there should be some restriction on the free or privileged coal supplied to miners, former miners, and dependants (those receiving it secured an average of 9.1 tons, or three times the national average household consumption). There were, however, administrative and practical problems and the political timing—as frequently happened in such cases—was judged unpropitious since labour relations were deteriorating towards the end of the year. Court 1951, 359–60. In May 1942 the miners had reacted vigorously to the possibility that rationing plans might affect the miners' generous allowances of coal: Dalton 1957, 396.

was obviously a different proposition from deep mining: it was potentially costly, involved legal difficulties, and entailed the deployment of
unusual machinery. Yet these constraints were more than counterbalanced by the much higher indirect costs of, and obstacles to, a
comparable increase in conventional output at a time of labour scarcity
in the pits, and by the strategic value of even a marginal increase in
supplies.[1] Technical unpreparedness and the limitations of British
machines (which were too small to deal with many sites with a deep
overburden) were ultimately compensated for by vigorous action, and
the use of American advice and machinery. Even so, it was some time
before the necessary official initiatives were taken.

Much of the credit for the innovation lay with a coalowner Member
of Parliament, Major Braithwaite of Buckrose, who had pressed the case
for surface mining on the Secretary for Mines in the spring of 1941, only
to find that procrastination and ignorance (the Mines Department had
no plans of coal near the surface and no ideas for its exploitation) wasted
the prime operating time of the summer of 1941. The first efforts were
made late in that year and by the spring of 1942 two sites were in
operation, each producing about 1,000 tons daily.[2] Special powers were
needed to cut through the obstacles of property rights and interest
groups, and these were granted early in 1942. The management of opencast mining was in the hands of the Mines Department and then the
Ministry of Fuel and Power, until January 1943, when administrative
responsibility was transferred to the Ministry of Works (a more logical
arrangement in view of the comparability with civil engineering). Actual
production was undertaken by private firms working under contract,
the initial purchase and distribution of the coal remaining in the hands
of the Ministry of Fuel and Power.

In the event, the critical bottleneck in the opencast programme
proved to be the supply and quality of available earth-moving machines
(many of them second-hand) from the United States. But progress was
commendable. Total opencast output rose from 1.3 million tons in 1942
to 4.4 million in 1943 and 8.6 million (some 4.5 per cent of total coal
output) in 1944. By the end of this last year almost 200 sites had been
worked out and 140 (employing some 10,000 men) were producing coal.

---

[1] For the advantages of opencast mining, see POWE 16/102 (17 Feb., 11 and 12 Apr. 1944).

[2] *Hansard* 17 Mar. 1942, cols. 1407 ff. Braithwaite also spoke about opencast mining in the
Commons debate on 23 June 1943 (cols. 1210 ff.). By that time his own firm (Sir Lindsay Parkin-
son & Co.) had produced 600,000 tons from scratch in the previous 12 months, and he proudly
indicated that 2 m. tons had been produced nationally in opencast sites, even though the available
machines were only about one-quarter the number he had hoped for.

Table 12.2. *Availability and consumption of coal in Britain, 1934-1945*
('Coal Year': 1 May–30 April) (m. tons)

	1939/40	1940/1	1941/2	1942/3	1943/4	1944/5
Mined coal	228.4	212.8	206.1	201.6	188.9	182.5
Colliery stocks	−3.8	+0.6	−0.6	−0.2	−0.2	−0.2
Opencast	—	—	—	1.8	4.1	7.8
Total available	232.2	212.2	206.7	203.6	193.2	190.5
Consumption:						
Gasworks	18.8	18.4	20.0	19.9	20.8	20.9
Electricity	16.8	18.8	21.6	21.7	23.6	24.0
Waterworks	0.4	0.4	0.4	0.4	0.4	0.4
Railways	13.0	13.6	14.2	14.7	15.2	15.1
Coke ovens	21.7	21.6	21.8	21.6	20.0	20.2
Collieries	12.1	12.2	12.2	11.9	11.4	11.0
Iron & steel	} 43.7	} 14.4	11.5	11.3	11.1	10.0
Engineering			4.5	5.4	4.6	4.5
Other industry		31.3	30.5	28.4	27.7	26.5
House coal	43.7	45.5	42.7	38.1	35.3	33.6
Anthracite etc. (domestic)	1.7	1.9	2.1	2.1	2.1	2.2
Miners' coal	4.7	4.7	4.8	4.7	4.5	4.7
Other	8.2	7.8	9.2	9.2	9.6	11.5
Total GB	184.8	190.6	195.5	189.4	186.3	184.6
Shipment to N. Ireland	2.3	2.5	2.5	2.5	2.7	2.4
Overseas shipments and bunkers	45.1	16.1	8.2	7.3	8.7	6.0

Source: Court, *Coal*, 388.

Over 60 per cent of production came from the North-East and North Midlands fields, although all principal districts contributed to the total. It was a creditable and significant achievement, even though, by American standards, the intensity and efficiency of the work, even with American machines, could have been improved.[1]

[1] *Ministry of Fuel and Power. Statistical Digest, 1945* (Cmd. 6920. 1946), 54–7. Also see *Sixth Report from the Select Committee on National Expenditure, Session 1943-1944 . . . Opencast Coal Production* (22 June 1944); Ministry of Works, *Report of the United Kingdom Opencast Coal Mission to the United States of America, December 1944* (1945); 'Production and Use of Opencast Coal', *CG* 14 Jan. 1944,

Over the war years as a whole the changes in consumption levels achieved by the control of distribution were remarkable: between 1940 and 1944 industry's consumption of coal, including that of coke ovens, fell by about 5.6 million tons (some nine per cent) whereas domestic household consumption was cut by almost 11 million tons (23 per cent). On the other hand, public utility supply grew by 9 million tons (25 per cent) and that of railways by 1.8 million tons (about 13 per cent).[1] Even with the new rate of opencast extraction (nearly 10 million tons), such adjustments and savings were insufficient to fend off a serious aggravation of the problem of supply as the War drew to a close. Restrictions on consumption, programming of distribution, efficiency measures, the reduction of stocks, and the diverting of scarce American shipping to send a million tons of coal to Europe were all devices with little remaining potential. By 1944 even the Prime Minister's private office, normally given to breezy dismissals of pessimistic forecasts, expressed the gravest concern about coal shortages in 'Stage II' (i.e. after the end of the War in Europe), and persuaded Churchill to exercise personal control of commitments to relief shipments to Europe. In the end, good fortune as well as good management ensured that peace came before crisis. But it was a close-run thing, and the industry itself was clearly in a very poor condition at the end of hostilities.[2]

ii. Industrial policy and the structure of control

The White Paper of June 1942 was an emergency measure, rather than a carefully considered, long-run plan. It established a wartime system of dual control which, it was hoped, would reverse the decline in the industry's output and productivity. Colliery companies were left in private hands and under private management, and the government abjured any direct financial responsibility. On the other hand, the Ministry of Fuel and Power became responsible for general oversight and encouragement, with residual powers to oblige colliery managers to

35–7; Appleyard & Curry 1946; and 'Report of C.P.R.B. Coal (Technical and Economic) Mission to U.K. June and July 1944', FO 371/24983, 13 ff. This last report by American engineers made detailed criticisms of inadequate preliminary prospecting work, of the utilization of some machinery, of the duration of the work day (the American team recommended a 20-hour day), and of the strategic waste of using men and machines to restore land (especially golf courses, parks, and pasture) in the wartime emergency.

[1] *Ministry of Fuel and Power. Statistical Digest. 1944* (Cmd. 6639. 1945), 14. The other important category of change was in exports and bunkers, which fell by 21.3 m. tons, or about 70%.

[2] Court 1951, 387–91.

accept its directives. Within the context of the systematic oversight of the industry, the best possible technical advice would be made available to all pits on a regional basis; mechanization and the concentration of output in the most productive collieries would be encouraged; and renewed efforts would be made to ensure that the supply and effort of labour was adequate to the needs of the industry, especially by the reduction of avoidable absenteeism. Finally, it was also envisaged that the Ministry would not be directly concerned with wage issues.

In the event, the degree of control actually exercised by the new Ministry proved inadequate, in terms both of its ability to exercise direct authority and of the obstacles to change inherent in the industry itself. This unsatisfactory situation ultimately drew officials into much larger questions concerning the postwar future of coalmining, and in any case continued to give rise to controversy throughout the War.[1] Nevertheless, the efforts and achievements in each of these areas are worth some discussion.

The central organization of the new Ministry was a compromise between the needs of industrial management and technical advice and those of a conventional government department. And this was reflected in the appointment of a Controller-General as well as a Permanent Secretary.[2] As envisaged in the War Cabinet Committee's original report, the central control authority had four sections, each under a Director: Production, Labour, Services, and Finance. The various Directors, rather than the innocuous National Coal Board, became the true advisers of the Minister. At the same time, the effective authority of the Ministry was designed to be exercised in the coalfields, where eight Regional Controllers were appointed, each assisted by Directors for Production, Labour, and Services. In a more than normally bizarre example of political logic, and in deference to the coalowners' desire not to have industrial competitors in positions of authority over potential rivals, only two of the Controllers had had direct experience of the industry!

The Ministry of Fuel and Power inherited a somewhat inferior bureaucracy: the prewar Mines Department 'was an unexciting one and did not secure the best permanent civil servants'.[3] From the outset,

---

[1] Below, ch. 13, sect. iii.

[2] The first Controller-General was Lord Hyndley, a leading coal merchant and Managing Director of Powell Duffryn, who had been the government's Commercial Adviser on coal since 1918, and worked in the Mines Department (becoming its Permanent Secretary in the spring of 1942).

[3] MacDougall to Cherwell, 5 Oct. 1943: Cherwell Papers, H14.

however, the crucial problem of the Ministry's organization, and one which related directly to its central task, was the weakness and shortage of personnel on the production side. It was symptomatic of the fragility of the Ministry's links with the technical and organizational aspects of the industry that the central Production Directorate lacked a firm organization until 1944. Its original Director (T. E. B. Young, the Managing Director of the Bolsover Colliery Company, whose report had greatly influenced the War Cabinet Committee in the spring of 1942)[1] was only in post for a few months, and it was not until October 1943 that a replacement was found (C. C. Reid—General Manager of the Fife Coal Company and subsequently Chairman of the Technical Advisory Committee in 1944).

There were similar and even more serious problems in the regional organizations, which lacked technical staff generally and good production engineers to act as Directors in particular. By the summer of 1943 there was a vacancy in the North Midlands and an impending vacancy in another region. Neither could be filled at all easily. From the outset, then, the Ministry was hampered by a shortage of the very resource—technical expertise—which it had been established to deploy. The problem was twofold: the unattractiveness of employment at relatively low civil service rates of pay and the reluctance of colliery companies to release their senior production staff (the central and regional vacancies in 1943 were caused by the recall of the men concerned).[2] More than this, those production engineers who were appointed found serious cause for complaint that their influence as well as autonomy were diminished by unclear demarcation of roles between Production and Labour Directorates, and by the interference of Labour Directors (e.g. in matters of mechanization) and of non-experts generally.[3]

With all its weaknesses, this new organization became responsible for government policy towards an industry whose record of production and productivity deteriorated rapidly and depressingly. Between the last years of peace and 1941 there had been only insignificant changes in productivity or the absenteeism of face-workers (the proximate cause of the decline in output was the fall in the industry's labour force, and the associated decline in the proportion of face-workers). On the other

---

[1] Above, 524 n.

[2] CAB 71/13 (17 June 1943). The Scottish owners were particularly bad in this respect.

[3] POWE 16/522 (10 Dec. 1942). The leading mining engineers were unanimous that the real obstacle to technical progress lay in the fact that 'everyone was frightened of labour and this was the root of the trouble'.

hand, between 1941 and 1944 output per manshift at the face fell by 6 or 7 per cent and the already considerable level of absenteeism at the face rose by about 40 per cent. These reductions were equivalent to losses in production of 14 million and 8.75 million tons respectively.[1] Why, then, were the individual policy initiatives envisaged in the changes of June 1942 so inadequate? In what ways did their inadequacies lead to pressure for organizational change?

The two most obvious (in the sense of potentially *visible*) changes envisaged in 1942 were the concentration of work in the most productive seams and pits, and the extension of mechanization. The former policy was an outright failure; the latter achieved a barely discernible effect on output.

Concentration of production appeared to promise much. Before the White Paper of 1942 it was assumed that a reallocation of manpower could increase output by about 6 per cent, and in February 1943 the Ministry of Fuel and Power estimated that an annual increase of between 8.5 and 12 million tons might be attained in this way. However, much of this increase would have had to come from a reallocation of effort, and therefore of labour, between pits and even regions—for the estimates were in large part based on the huge variations in the output per manshift between units and areas of production. But the fact that productivity in the Midlands and South Yorkshire was between 75 and 100 per cent greater than in South Wales and Lanarkshire did not lead as inexorably as some civil servants imagined to the conclusion that miners should be moved between the respective districts.[2]

Concentration policy had to face the lack of cooperation and even outright hostility of both miners and owners, each consulting their own interests (the miners, as ever, reluctant to move workplace let alone home; the owners concerned at the disturbance to asset values as well as the dislocation of industrial relations). The difficulty of securing cooperation in labour transfer had been great enough when the relevant miners were unemployed (in the 1930s or 1940). During wartime full

---

[1] The OMS (face) figures were 3.00, 2.99, and 2.81 tons in 1939, 1941, and 1944 (2.79 in the first quarter of 1945). Between 1941 and 1944 absenteeism at the face rose from 12.8 to 15.9% (18.2% in the first quarter of 1945) and overall absenteeism from 9.0 to 13.3% (15.8% in early 1945). Data in Mining Association of Great Britain, 'Notes on the Proceedings of the Joint Sub-Committee on Production', 17 Aug. 1945 (COAL 11/101). This document recalculated OMS and absenteeism data on a comparable basis, the definition of 'face' having been altered in 1943. Also see *Ministry of Fuel and Power. Statistical Digest. 1944* (Cmd. 6639. 1945), 8.

[2] POWE 22/150 (11 Feb. 1943). The enormous differences in OMS—between pits within the same coalfield as well as between fields—are set out in great statistical detail in a memorandum by Harold Wilson: POWE 22/150 (8 May 1943).

employment, the administrative, personal, and political problems proved insuperable.[1] In the summer of 1942, for example, an attempt to relocate 25 South Wales miners in the North-West and 6 in the North Midlands met with such a storm of protests from South Wales branches of the miners', railwaymen's, and teachers' unions, from churches and cooperative societies, that the Regional Controller withdrew his proposal in humiliation.[2] Confronted by such opposition, and by the lack of cooperation by owners (sometimes even in regard to the more hopeful possibility of concentrating output *within* pits), the Ministry admitted defeat. In any case, it had never established an appropriately purposeful and well-prepared administrative mechanism for the task. Having painfully initiated schemes which might attain an annual increase in output of 1 million tons, the programme was abandoned by the autumn of 1943.[3]

The encouragement of increasing mechanization presented slightly fewer human problems, although it too was a halting and imperfect process. Between 1939 and 1941 the number of cutting machines and conveyors in use actually fell. Perhaps more seriously, in spite of the increase in the number of machines after 1941, the amount of coal mechanically cut and conveyed *continued* to fall throughout the war years, although the even more rapid decline in unmechanized production meant that the proportionate significance of mechanized output grew in every year in 1939–44 (from 61 to 72 per cent of coal cut and from 58 to 69 per cent of coal conveyed).[4]

In the case of machinery, as in the case of labour supply, the problems of the opening years of the War were compounded by the consequences of the Fall of France in June 1940. In particular, there was a wholesale conversion of industrial capacity from the production of mining machinery to the production of munitions—and even when, in 1941, reconversion and an increase in capacity were initiated (to a large extent with government subsidies), shortages of skilled labour meant

[1] For the problems of facilitating mobility during the interwar depression, see above, 261, 326–7.

[2] LAB 8/1473/6.

[3] POWE 22/150. Individual collieries might still find it in their interest to reorganize work within a pit. Thus, in the North Derbyshire Bolsover Colliery in 1943, a reorganization of work to reduce haulage costs took precedence over an experiment with a new cutter-loader machine face. Derbyshire Records Office, N5/box 314/S8/2.

[4] *Ministry of Fuel and Power. Statistical Digest. 1944* (Cmd. 6639. 1945), 10–11. In the three years 1939, 1941, and 1944 the numbers of cutting machines were 7,754, 7,146, and 8,218; the numbers of conveyors and power-loaders were 9,036, 8,986, and 10,940. For the initial decline in the use of machinery, see Wilson to Clegg, 10 Apr. 1943: POWE 16/522.

that there was only a very small increase in machine output.[1] The disappointing results of mechanization in terms of enhanced productivity were a much greater blow, for technical change was the principal hope of circumventing the chronic shortage of pit labour.

Yet the problem was that (as ever) effective mechanization was more than a matter of simply lowering machines into position in an unchanged mine with unaltered relationships. The training and adaptation of labour, the rearrangement of work processes and shift patterns, the working-out of new payment systems, the restructuring of the various interdependent parts of the mining process—all demanded more elaborate, and more sensitive, changes than were easily secured under wartime pressures. More generally, too, the problems were aggravated by the Ministry's position. In September 1943, for example, the Minister complained that delays following the introduction of new machinery had been due to disputes and that 'His inability to force decisions in this matter was a source of great weakness.'[2]

In spite of these problems, which related to the efficacy and overall effect of machinery, there *were* important changes in the technology of mechanization as a result of the War. These proceeded in two directions: the improvement of existing British machinery; and the import or imitation of American machinery.

Up to the Second World War 'mechanization' in British mines had been almost exclusively directed to the undercutting and conveying of coal on longwall faces. In spite of numerous efforts to design an adequate power-loader, machine-cut coal was still blasted down with explosives and loaded by hand on to conveyors. The most significant prewar experiment was probably the Mining Engineering Company's 'Meco–Moore' cutter-loader, which was designed to cut in one direction and then, after the coal had been blasted down, load it by moving back along the face. But it was very little used, and in extensive trials (for example, at the Butterley Company's Ollerton and Lowmoor pits in 1936–8) it was a dismal failure, miners and managers being 'all pleased to see the back of it'.[3]

By May 1942, however, under the pressure of wartime manpower shortages, the Mines Department—working through a Committee on Power Loading in Coal Mines—had financed the construction of three

---

[1] See memoranda on the supply position of machinery, dated 1 Feb. and 9 July 1943, in POWE 16/522.

[2] CAB 71/11 (29 Sept. 1943).

[3] Derbyshire Records Office, N5/box 314/S8/2.

prototypes of an improved cutter-loader and was anticipating its continuous production (small-scale specialized loading machinery was already in production). Out of the wartime emergency there developed the first genuine cutter-loader (the 'AB Meco–Moore', which performed the two operations simultaneously, and therefore dispensed with blasting) and improved loaders (the 'Huwood' and the 'Shelton'). The new Ministry placed orders for such new machinery, which was 'designed to suit British longwall conditions'.[1] Nevertheless, progress remained painfully slow. In May 1942 AB Meco–Moore machines were installed in only four colliery companies (Bolsover, Doncaster Amalgamated Collieries, Amalgamated Denaby, and Barber-Walker) and even by 1945 the AB Meco–Moore was responsible for loading only 0.25 per cent of the coal cut in Britain, and *all* power-loading machinery for a mere 2.0 per cent.[2]

Profound as were the difficulties of extending the use of techniques with which many British mines, workmen, and managers, were already moderately familiar, the problems became almost crippling when there were attempts to introduce the relatively exotic new techniques—American machine mining and particularly American power loading—on which so many hopes for a radical transformation were pinned. American machines (primarily the mobile 'Joy' loader, but also the 'Duckbill') were primarily designed for room and pillar working, which involved cutting into seams on a 'grid' basis and leaving pillars of coal standing to support the roof.[3] They were therefore not obviously suited to longwall methods, although some 'Joy'-type machinery had been used for the driving of headings in British mines for some time.[4] Over the long run, the American system, since it involved leaving uncut pillars of coal, was more wasteful of the mineral. But it was a *quicker*, and extremely efficient, way of extracting coal.

In this case, therefore, mechanization would have to go hand in hand with reorganization. Indeed, American engineers were adamant that the use of their machinery presupposed a switch from longwall to room and pillar mining, although British engineers did not always agree, and it was

---

[1] Gullick to Hyndley, 17 Dec. 1942, and 'Coal Face Machinery. Supply Position at 31 Jan. 1943': POWE 16/522 (13 May 1943). At that time 30 Huwood and Shelton machines had been installed, and British-made machinery on the 'American' system was being applied at four other pits.

[2] Hibberd 1955, 789–80; CAB 87/92 (22 May 1942). Data on the proportion of coal cut are in Anderson & Thorpe 1967, 783. The AB Meco–Moore was so called because it was the joint product of the Anderson Boyes and the Mining Engineering Companies.

[3] Above, ch. 1, sect. iii.   [4] CAB 87/92 (22 May 1942).

in any case feasible to use American loading equipment to expedite the cutting of new roadways and headings.[1] Quite apart from these complexities, as was pointed out by the American expert seconded to the Ministry of Fuel and Power, 'American' mechanization would necessitate collateral adaptations (simplified wages systems, the abolition of piece rates, coherent organization of teams of miners, detailed new training programmes), the introduction of which was likely to prove extremely difficult in British circumstances.[2] Finally, bureaucratic and manufacturing delays, together with shortages of specialized items, led to severe disappointment with the speed with which American machinery was delivered and commissioned.

The original initiative in the matter of American power-loading equipment, as was the case with opencast mining, was a private one. In 1941 BA Collieries approached the Mines Department, and it was this move which ultimately led to an order for American machinery (mostly Joy loaders). This was in May 1942, by which time the Mines Department, and the Ministry after it, encouraged a flurry of visits by engineers to and from the United States. In August 1942 a programme of government aid to mechanization (mostly through the provision of machinery on hire, with some elements of subsidy) was initiated. American machinery was to be acquired through lend-lease. An American mining engineer (H. R. Wheeler) was retained as a consultant and, as a result, a second requisition was made in December. At that time, although an increase in an output of 4 million tons was hoped for, the deliveries were still some months away (by mid-July 1943 only nine small Joy loaders, very much like the equivalent British machines, had been delivered, and delays and dissatisfaction were building up).[3] Poor preparation and a lack of training on the part of managers as well as men, meant that 'the industry could not digest it' and two years were lost.[4]

Ultimately, more systematic efforts were made to adapt to the new systems: a training school was established at Sheffield, 20 mine managers were sent to the United States to learn techniques, the extensive exchange of information and experience took place. Yet the frictions and obstacles proved too great for the new technology to have any very speedy effect. When an American team investigated the situation in

---

[1] Material on the rival merits of the two systems or of combinations of them is in POWE 16/522.

[2] Wheeler to Gullick, 28 Jan. 1943: POWE 16/522.

[3] POWE 16/522 (17 Dec. 1942, 19 July 1943).

[4] *Hansard* 29 May 1945, col. 101.

British coalmining in the summer of 1944, the slow absorption rate for American machinery was one of its leading criticisms of the industry: altogether, 228 machines had been delivered, yet the number actually working was only 84, and fully half of the 144 machines delivered up to the end of March 1944 were *still* not working by the summer. No wonder that the Ministry's comments on the report (which was in fact suppressed) were so defensive.[1] Up to the spring of 1945 £8 million of capital assistance had been authorized for 'British' as well as 'American' schemes—but only £2.522 million had been committed (including a mere £769,000 on American equipment) and not all of that had been spent.[2]

The failure of the two specific policies of concentration and mechanization reflected a number of obstacles to effective industrial control: the inability to secure the cooperation of the work-force or the employers (in 1944 the American investigating team expressed the disheartened view that 'many coal owners and the majority of miners do not fully realize the military necessity for increased production of coal');[3] the interlocking character of technologies and organizational structures, which made it difficult to introduce rapid change in any one part of the system of production; the shortages of skilled personnel; the neglect of large-scale industrial reform; bureaucratic unwieldiness. Above all, however, there were two aspects of the Ministry of Fuel and Power's role which had to be repeatedly addressed: its lack of realistic authority within the system of 'dual control'; and the *malaise* and even disaffection of the men engaged in coalmining. These will be discussed in the following two sections.

iii. The tensions of dual control

The drawbacks of dual control, which had been predicted when it was imposed on the industry,[4] were inherent in the ambiguous position of colliery managers, who were subject to the authority of Regional

---

[1] 'Report of C.P.R.B. Coal (Technical and Economic) Mission to U.K., June and July 1944', and attached comments: FO 371/24983.

[2] *Ministry of Fuel and Power. Financial Position of Coalmining Industry. Coal Charges Account* (Cmd. 6617. 1945), 25. Of the total of £2.522 million some £1.5 million was committed to American methods of working (including, however, £740,000 of British plant), and the rest to 'normal British' methods (£366,000), 'British' power loading and mechanical stowing (£122,000), and the increase of manufacturing capacity, servicing, and allied work (£525,000).

[3] FO 371/24983/9.

[4] Above, 532.

Controllers as regards production policy, 'but are the employees of private interests'. This was the claim of the Minister of Fuel and Power in a progress report on the first year of the White Paper scheme. He also drew attention to a variety of problems relating to the supply and productivity of the labour force, to the difficulty of recruiting adequate and well-qualified, senior technical personnel (he advocated rates of pay outside civil-service scales), and to the obstacles to the enforcement of industrial discipline. But he appeared most concerned about the contradictions of dual control, and the possible clash between 'the public and the private interests'.[1]

Lloyd George's conclusion was forthright: if production were to be increased, 'a much fuller measure of control, including financial control', was needed. More than this, given the owners' interests (which might continue to clash with that of wartime policy) and the miners' insecurity about the future, even full-blown control 'would not be fully effective if it were known to be only for the duration of the War'. By implication, the Minister was favouring some form of permanent nationalization. Yet this touched some very raw nerves. If the possibility of rationing had involved enormously disruptive political controversy in the spring of 1942, the possibility of nationalization a year later would have created even more turmoil. Indeed, Lloyd George acknowledged this quite explicitly, and his offer to soldier on with the existing system (which could do little more than satisfy the existing requirements) was accepted.

Even so, it was not long before Lloyd George was obliged to return to the same theme. In September 1943 he drew attention to the enfeebling character of dual control ('aggravated by the fact that both sides of the industry were now showing a tendency to pay too much regard to their position after the war'). And the next month he again complained about the government's complete lack of operational control over the mines:

This was due very largely to the dual position of the colliery managements who, though subject to direction in operational matters by the Regional Controllers of his Ministry, remained the servants of the coal owners and were thus bound to have regard to their own future and the owners' interests.

His recommendation was now entirely unambiguous: the 'temporary elimination of the coal owner'—for example, by the 'renting by the Government of the pits for the duration of the war', thus 'making the managements directly responsible in every respect to the State'. These

[1] CAB 71/13 (17 June 1943).

recommendations, together with the proposal for a concomitant inquiry into the postwar reorganization of the industry, were forwarded to the War Cabinet.[1] By this time the urgent sense of organizational crisis had become public property: the issue had to be tackled in Parliament as well as within the Administration.

Lloyd George himself was well aware of the contentious nature of his proposals and in order to avoid controversy was still prepared to administer a system well short of nationalization, even though permanent control was his preferred solution. And in the event that was the outcome. For public ownership, and even some commitment about the long-term future of the industry, were still much too controversial for the Coalition Government to deal with (even though a departmental committee was to go a long way towards its advocacy).[2] Cherwell warned Churchill that nationalization, or even the rumour that it was being considered 'might have serious industrial and political consequences', including strikes 'to force the issue' if the possibility were even raised.[3] Nor was it possible to demonstrate that nationalization was essential to prevent a crisis of coal supply.

As a result, the Ministerial Committee which was established on 8 October 1943 (and which, significantly, included Lord Cherwell, who had always been sceptical of the claims that there was an imminent crisis of coal supply)[4] resisted the idea of public ownership. Politically, however, the crisis was not resolved until the Prime Minister had been obliged to make a Commons statement (one of his very rare appearances on an economic issue in wartime). This came on 13 October, after much dissatisfaction had been expressed, from Conservative as well as Labour benches, about the existing control as well as about a somewhat anodyne statement from the Minister of Fuel and Power. Churchill's performance was masterly, and effectively eliminated the question of nationalization for the rest of the War. In a famous phrase, he asserted the Coalition's basic rule in such matters: 'Everything for the war, whether controversial or not, and nothing controversial that is bona fide not needed for this war.' In effect, as long as the Coalition Government lasted, the question of full-scale government control of coalmining ceased to be a political issue.

[1] CAB 71/11 (29 Sept. and 6 Oct. 1943); CAB 71/14 (4 Oct. 1943). Lloyd George pointed out that the managers' 'duty to the regional control is to produce the maximum quantity of coal now. Their duty to those by whom they are paid may lead them in another direction.' Of dual control more generally, he said: 'It has failed to win the confidence of any party within the industry. The men point to dual control as illogical; the managements feel themselves to be open to attack from all sides and are smarting under a grievance through their inability to reply adequately; the owners, without being openly defiant, are sceptical of the merits of control.'   [2] Below, 613–14.
[3] Cherwell to Churchill, 7 Oct. 1943: Cherwell Papers, F.185/32b.   [4] Above, 538.

Even if coal was not to be nationalized, however, the serious draw-backs of dual control still demanded some action. As a result, the Minister of Fuel and Power and the War Cabinet Committee (which remained in existence until February 1944) continued their delibera-tions. Those deliberations had to be extended to consider a variety of urgent issues (wage levels, bonus payments, safety, discipline, food rations) which were being pressed by the miners on the government.[1] But the central problem remained that of industrial control and the apparent disadvantages of fragmentation. This meant that some way had to be found of coalescing the diverse interests of different collieries. (The Minister of Fuel and Power even toyed with the idea of resuscitating the Coal Commission's role as an initiator of commercial amalgamations under Part II of the 1938 Act.)[2] The resulting structural adjustment of control was to prove hardly more satisfactory than the system it replaced, but the measures did at least address themselves to the points at issue.

On the one hand, in order to strengthen official policy at one of its weakest links, collieries were to be combined into groups of about 2–4 million tons' capacity, for the purposes of making the best use of technical advice. On the other hand, that advice was to be the responsib-ility of newly appointed Group Production Directors, who were to be attracted by rates of pay commensurate with industrial, rather than civil-service, scales. They were to be paid from the Coal Charges Account—i.e. from the industry's own proceeds. The idea of such groups, emanating from the Ministry of Fuel and Power, was discussed with the owners and miners in the extensive consultations of October–November 1943, proposed to the Ministerial Committee in November, and put into practice before the Committee reported in February 1944.[3] The salient importance of the technical side was underscored by the decision not to appoint Group Labour Directors, who might have weak-ened the position of Production Directors, even though both the owners and the miners favoured such appointments.[4]

The circumstances in which these plans were drawn up did not augur very well for their success. To some informed observers the new group-ing policy was 'a political farce doomed to failure', and more generally

[1] See below, 563, 568 n. Papers relating to the Committee are in CAB 87/93.

[2] POWE 22/127 (Dec. 1943).

[3] POWE 10/394 (Nov. and Dec. 1943); POWE 20/83 (Oct.–Dec. 1943); CAB 87/93; CAB 66/47/3 (16 Feb. 1944). The Minister's memorandum to the War Cabinet Committee is in CAB 87/93 (Nov. 1943).

[4] POWE 16/70 (23 Dec. 1943; 4, 11, and 12 Jan. 1944).

the policy coincided with intensive and tense consultations about wages, bonuses, discipline, and the conditions of the work-force, which were to result in severe labour troubles in the spring of 1944. In any case, neither the owners nor the miners were enthusiastic about grouping and the government could still not rely on the wartime cooperation of either interest.[1] As the problem presented itself, however, it was primarily a difficulty of labour supply and labour effort. Time and again, and with increasing intensity as the passage of the War exposed the inadequacies of other areas of policy, the centrality of the labour question was demonstrated.

iv. Labour supply and labour problems

The White Paper of June 1942 had been an acknowledgement that it was not going to be possible to attain the sort of increase in the industry's work-force which would be necessary to solve Britain's wartime coal problem. However, the resulting diversion of attention to productivity did not permit any neglect of the labour factor of production. For, quite apart from the obvious fact that productivity was itself related to the morale and quality of the industry's workers, it was still necessary to sustain the supply and recruitment of miners, both to counter the continuing decline in output per manshift and to ensure that the actual number of wage-earners was not excessively low.

At the time of the creation of the new Ministry of Fuel and Power the industry's labour force was about 709,000.[2] It rose slowly to about 714,000 in January 1943, thanks largely to schemes for the recall of ex-miners from the Forces and industry, but then began to fall again, reaching a low point of just over 701,000 in November 1943. There was then a slow increase to 713,000 a year later, and 717,000 at the end of the war in Europe (April 1945). Even at its highest, then, the work-force fell well below the target of some 720,000 whch had been considered essential in 1940-1, and a good deal of effort was devoted to its enlargement.

Once controls had been imposed on the recruitment of miners into

[1] The quotation is from Sir Ernest Gowers, addressing the Durham Coal Owners' Association: DCOA, 17 Dec. 1943. The Report of the War Cabinet Committee which produced the scheme was unwarrantably reassuring on this point. It did, however, draw attention to the fact that the Minister of Labour and National Service (Bevin) remained quite unconvinced that there was sufficient goodwill on the part of the owners to make the grouping scheme work. And the majority was in any case obliged to report that the Scottish owners were declining to release their best men for appointment as Group Production Directors. See CAB 66/47/3 (16 Feb. 1944).

[2] Figures on the number of wage-earners throughout the War are in LAB 8/1473/Appendix II.

the Forces or other industries,[1] changes in the size of the work-force were determined by the interaction between the rate at which miners left the industry through death, normal retirement, or disability, and the rate of recruitment of juveniles, new adult workers, or former miners. But the number of ex-miners in other industries was very limited after the recruitment drive of 1941, and the mining population continued to age, compared with prewar days: between 1937 and 1944 the proportion of miners aged 20-30 fell from 26.3 to 20.0 per cent.[2] This not only reduced the effectiveness of the work-force, but produced an annual loss through death and retirement which could not be offset by the reduced rate of juvenile recruitment, itself rooted in the low birth rates of the late 1920s, the psychological antipathy to coalmining employment generated by the interwar experience, and the competing claims of other occupations in wartime.

History was once again catching up with the industry. According to Mines Department statisticians, the industry was losing 38,000 men annually, compared with juvenile recruitment of about 10,000. (In 1924 juvenile recruits had totalled 30,000.) Even if juvenile recruitment were increased to 18,000, so as to maintain the under-21 strength of the industry, a further '20,000 adult workers need to be drafted into the industry each year to maintain its strength'.[3]

The outcome of such calculations was to concentrate attention on the problem of adult labour, since no feasible increase in the employment of boys could solve the industry's manpower problem, although the Interdepartmental (Forster) Committee, appointed in the spring of 1942, made some practical proposals for enhancing the attractiveness of juvenile training, welfare, and wages.[4] As far as adult workmen were concerned, the problem was the speed at which miners, still of working age, were leaving the industry. And it was this consideration which led to the decision, in spring 1942, to establish a Mines Medical Service. Extensive improvements in treatment and rehabilitation resulted, while there was a tightening of discharge procedures. In 1945 only just over 9,000 of the 38,000 applicants for release were approved.[5]

[1] Above, 511.

[2] 'Total Mining Man-Power and Wastage Estimates', 12 Feb. 1942, reproduced in *MFGB* 1942, 543-50 (Report of the Executive Committee to the Annual Conference). For interwar birth rates in mining districts, see above, 492.

[4] *First Report of the Committee on the Recruitment of Juveniles in the Coal Mining Industry, July 20, 1942* (Ministry of Labour, 1942). Minimum wages for juveniles were ultimately fixed by the National Reference Tribunal in the autumn of 1943.

[5] Court 1951, 302.

Even more intense attention was paid to the attraction, and ultimately enforced recruitment, of ex-miners and young men with no previous experience of mining. An important, if once-for-all, contribution was achieved by the decision to release ex-miners serving with non-combatant branches of the Forces, and the trawling of war industries for available former miners. As a result, adult recruitment in the 'coal year' April 1942–March 1943 just about offset the gap (of 21,000) between those leaving the industry and juvenile recruits.[1]

For obvious reasons, such an effort could not be repeated. And the government therefore turned to other devices. In September 1942, for example, men under 25 registering for military service were given the option of underground work in the mines; but by the end of June 1943 less than 3,000 'optants' had joined the work-force.[2] Another, and even more troublesome, scheme was the power to direct surface mine-workers underground when they reached the age of 18.[3] But the renewed erosion of the industry's manpower in 1943 ultimately led to a more extreme experiment.

In November, after a much publicized but unsuccessful campaign to attract more volunteers, the War Cabinet agreed, with manifest reluctance, to compulsory recruitment into the mines. A proportion of men aged 18–25, on becoming available for call-up, were to be chosen by ballot for pit work. The first ballot (20 per cent of those called up at the time) was on 14 December. Those so recruited became popularly and indelibly known as 'Bevin Boys', after the Minister of Labour and National Service, who had naturally played a central role in the new policy. As with so much that concerned mining, the 'Bevin Boy' scheme was never very popular (in March 1944, widespread strikes among Tyneside engineering apprentices, demanding unconditional exemption, spread to Clydeside and Yorkshire), but by the end of the European War, when it was discontinued, it had provided a further 21,800 men for the mines.[4]

The 'Bevin Boy' scheme was an interesting, if not particularly significant, social experiment. Those who were recruited into the mines found themselves in a strange and not always friendly environment, and their

[1] CAB 71/12 (17 May 1943). LAB 8/1473, 6 ff. Between 27 Mar. 1942 and 1 May 1943 just under 12,000 ex-miners were released from the Forces and somewhat more than that number from other industries.

[2] In July 1943 age restrictions were lifted. By Oct. 1945 the number of optants had risen to 23,500. LAB 8/1473, 14.

[3] LAB 8/1473, 14; CAB 71/11 (21 May 1943).

[4] LAB 8/1473, 14.

varying experiences gave rise to a fascinating literary genre.[1] On the wider scene, however, the scheme was controversial not merely because of the adverse reaction of many recruits and established miners, but because of doubts about its actual contribution to output. It was, however, part of a multi-level attack on the problem of the industry's labour supply. And although manpower policy in coalmining may not have been as spectacularly successful as it was in other, less insular and exotic industries, it made a distinct contribution. Certainly, in the absence of such ingenious efforts to secure more recruits and to take the politically difficult step of compulsory recruitment, the industry's labour force would have shrunk even nearer to disaster levels.

Nevertheless, as events showed, the critical problem was not to be manpower supply. Indeed, as the MFGB itself pointed out in November 1943, the targets for coal production could not be reached simply by increasing the supply of new labour. The numbers involved were quite unrealistic, and in any case unwilling recruits might not be much help. Instead, the union drew attention to the importance of increasing the productivity of men already in work and of attracting ex-miners back to the pits. The union, of course, had an obvious interest in the argument that the critical determinants of labour productivity were pay, conditions, industrial control, and the future of private ownership. Nevertheless, it was clearly on the right lines in asserting that the morale of the miners, their productivity, and their efforts were the central problems. The decline in output per manshift demonstrated that all too clearly.[2]

As happened in the First World War, the sensitive position of the mining community, and its actual and potential resentments, meant that it was treated with far greater circumspection than any other major group of workers. This naturally encouraged miners to make effective sectional use of their new-found political leverage, while its irony was not lost on some of their spokesmen (during the First World War, said one miners' MP in May 1941, nothing but good was said of pitmen and then, with industrial strife in peacetime, 'Instead of being the salt of the earth, we were the scum of the earth').[3] But whatever the decencies involved, the Second, like the First, World War was perennially characterized by anxieties about the commitment

---

[1] See Agnew 1947; Day 1975. Mass-Observation collected contemporaneous material from Bevin Boys: Mass-Observation Archives (University of Sussex), Files 1532, 1538, 2133.

[2] The MFGB's arguments are in CAB 87/93 (16 Nov. 1943). Also see *MFGB* 1943, Executive Committee, 7 Oct. 1943.

[3] *Hansard* 28 May 1941, col. 1925.

of miners, appeals to their patriotism, and reminders of their indispensable role in war.

This sensitivity to miners' opinions and claims was most significant in the negotiations and discussions concerning wages and bonuses, the Essential Work Order, and declining output. It also softened the official attitude towards the repayment of debts incurred in the 1926 stoppage.[1] Occasionally, it surfaced in mass public events, reminiscent of the set pieces of the First World War. The major example occurred in the autumn of 1942, when the Lord President's Committee was persuaded that the release of ex-miners from active service was a chimera: 'the only real solution of the coal problem [is] a greater effort by the miners resulting in an increase in output per man-shift'. It therefore decided to enlist the emotional and rhetorical authority of the Prime Minister, busy as he was, to counter the widespread 'indifference' among miners and to bring home to them the seriousness of the situation.[2]

On 31 October 1942, at Westminster Central Hall, flanked by leading members of the Coalition Government and the industry, Churchill addressed a meeting of more than 3,000 delegates of miners, managers, and owners (the press were excluded, principally to enhance the directness of the appeal and partly because there was some anxiety about interruptions from the floor). It was an occasion remarkably similar to that at the London Opera House in July 1915, when the Minister of Fuel's father had used *his* emotional powers on a comparable gathering from the industry.[3] Poignantly, Jan Smuts was present on both occasions. Churchill's own contribution was very well received and culminated in a peroration which was to be extensively publicized:

We must carry our work to its final conclusion. We shall not fail, and then some day, when children ask: 'What did you do to win this inheritance for us, and to make our name so respected among men?' one will say: 'I was a fighter pilot;' another will say: 'I was in the Submarine Service;' another: 'I marched with the Eighth Army;' a fourth will say: 'None of you could have lived without the convoys and the Merchant Seamen;' and you in your turn will say, with equal pride and with equal right: 'We cut the coal.'

But, if the appeals were similar to those of the First World War, so were the responses. In spite of the warmth with which they were received by

---

[1] Above, 463 n.
[2] PREM 4/9/2. Earlier discussion of a possible meeting between the Prime Minister and miners' delegates came to nothing because of premature publicity by the union and doubts about the response of the audience. Material relating to the Lord President's Committee's discussions is in CAB 71/9 (17 Sept. 1942) and CAB 71/7 (18 and 25 Sept. 1942).   [3] Above, 60.

their immediate auditors, exhortations did not appear to have very much effect in terms of arresting the decline in productivity. Indeed, as the War progressed, the lack of cooperation and apparent *malaise* among the miners seemed, if anything, to increase—and the efforts of trade union leaders became nugatory.

In the summer of 1944 a team of American engineers and economists, in a report on British coalmining which was too critical to be made public, expressed astonishment at the atrocious state of industrial relations, the poor morale of the work-force, and the lack of any sense of urgency about the war effort on the part of the miners (or owners or managers).[1]

More prosaically, but equally significantly, the Americans drew attention to an aspect of the miners' response to wartime conditions which was also strikingly similar to that of the First World War: an adamant refusal to amend working hours or shift-end practices so as to increase labour effort. The Americans expressed surprise that the average length of shift at the face was still only between $5\frac{1}{2}$ and $6\frac{1}{2}$ hours, and contrasted the situation with that in the USA, where the work-force was only very slightly younger, and where in November 1943 the average work-load had been lengthened to a 6-day, 54-hour week (45 to 48 hours at the face), and where voluntary absenteeism was significantly less than in Britain.

No doubt, as had happened in 1914-18, the miners had the strongest possible feelings about defending the limitations on their hours of work, as well as those other restrictive practices and customs which they brought with them from a less hazardous time of peace. These attitudes were frequently defended on the grounds that as long as the industry was in private hands the miners would not give up customs and practices which they saw as 'the main bulwarks against undue exploitation by the owners'.[2] But there is equally little doubt that such emotions were part of a determined self-protection which too frequently manifested itself to most of the rest of the community as selfishness.

---

[1] FO 371/24983/5: 'Industry-wide morale is low. There is a definite lack of confidence by the individual miner in his own leader, the coal owners and the Government. There is mutual distrust between labor and management. Coal owners seldom exhibit anything but antagonism to the Ministry of Fuel and Power. We believe that there does not exist in the minds of coal owners, management, labor leaders and the individual miners an adequate willingness to subordinate all considerations to the Military necessity of increasing production.'

[2] Letter from Sam Watson of the Durham Miners' Association to *The Economist* 9 Dec. 1944, 772.

THE BATTLE FRONT

"Down, lads, and at 'em!"

14. 'The Battle Front' (*Punch*, 15 September 1943)

Certainly, the miners' representatives used every opportunity to enhance their members' material position and mitigate any new demands on their efforts. Thus, in November 1943, confronted with a looming crisis of supply, they rejected the Minister of Fuel and Power's proposals that, where relevant (in parts of Scotland for example), a twelve-day should be substituted for an eleven-day fortnight; that as far as possible coalfaces should be cleared each day (the failure to do this— i.e. the strict insistence on the restrictions of the working day—was a serious handicap to efficient shift work, and often resulted in substantial output losses); and that in certain circumstances, miners might work one Sunday in four.

For their part, the miners appeared to be concerned solely with ensuring the security, and augmenting the present and future material rewards, of their work—on the ostensible grounds that only such rewards would elicit greater effort.[1] There were, however, other reasons for the miners' bargaining stance. The possibility of individual and group benefit was enormous, and a work-force which had experienced the pressures of the 1930s was naturally influenced by the fear that their present superior position might quickly crumble in a postwar slump and that, without new-built defences, their material position would once again be desperately vulnerable.[2] A similar confusion of motives, at an even more serious level, meant that wartime circumstances yielded an irresistible opportunity to increase individual as well as group autonomy.

In the coalmines, the rank and file were fully aware of their newfound industrial strength. Protected by the Essential Work Order as well as by effective political power, recalcitrant miners could successfully challenge the feeble disciplinary sanctions which remained with mine managers, or indulge their own conception of a reasonable working week. It was, for example, possible for some miners so to restrict their efforts as to ensure that other miners had no work available, but were yet paid the wage guaranteed by the Essential Work Order.[3] More

[1] CAB 87/93 (16 Nov. 1943). The Federation's counter-proposals included government control of the industry, the postwar continuation of the guaranteed weekly wage, the provision of pithead baths, canteens, and increased personal food rations, comprehensive workmen's compensation, an increase in the minimum wage to £6, national holidays with pay, improved bonus arrangements, etc.   [2] Below, 572–3.

[3] Regional Controller (Northern A Region) to Controller-General, 27 Oct. 1944: POWE 16/78. It was also possible for managers to abuse the system by sending men home even when work was available or likely to become available within a short time—thereby reducing production costs by securing wage payments from central funds. There was some anxiety that this practice was extensively used to secure hidden subsidies for long-run development work. *Hansard* 17 Feb. 1944, cols. 346–7; POWE 16/81; Court 1951, 349–50.

generally, it only needed a minority of uncooperative men, resistant to authority at work or persistently absent without good cause, to disrupt production for the many. And the authorities' reluctance to appear provocative by using their legal powers in the case of wilful absenteeism could render the legal framework, in one General Manager's phrase, 'a farce'.[1]

In September 1943, when the Durham Coal Owners' Association produced a report on the reasons for the decline in output, they drew attention to the miners' 'war weariness', the lack of outlets for expenditure, and other psychological factors. But their principal emphasis was on the problem of discipline: persistent absenteeism and the ease with which doctors' notes could be obtained; the high and virtually unconditional minimum wage which had 'done away with all incentive' and led to a demand for lighter jobs; and the exploitation of the security of employment and guaranteed wage brought about by the Essential Work Order. This latter, the owners argued, had led to the abrogation of agreements, lack of effort at the end of shifts, and severe delays and absenteeism in bad weather—all of which amounted to 'a complete breakdown in discipline'. By the last month of the War an Inspector of Mines blamed falling output largely on the uses to which the work-force put its new-found autonomy: 'The mines to-day are operated under the virtual control of the miners themselves', the problem was not so much *dual* control 'but . . . the multi-willed control exerted by thousands of individual miners, each of whom has the power to temper his efforts to suit his own convenience'.[2]

None of this is to claim that greater effort or more conscientious attendance would have been easy solutions to the problem of productivity. In any case, it is as well to remember that, to many miners, deeply hostile to owners and managers, industrial discipline appeared to be enforced 'by a system of organised and authorised bullying in an atmo-

---

[1] For examples of widespread complaints about indiscipline and managerial powerlessness, see A. D. Butterley (Desford Coal Co.) to R. Foot, 1 Feb. 1945: COAL 11/103 (during 1944 some 23,000 shifts had been lost through voluntary absenteeism at the Desford Pit, yet only one man had been prosecuted); POWE 16/73 ('Report on meeting between Minister and National Association of Colliery Managers', 9 Dec. 1943); Mass-Observation, 'Mining town—1942' in Mass-Observation Archive University of Sussex), File 1498P (p. 15 of Appendix, dated Sept. 1943). On the other hand, it was argued, occasionally by the *owners'* representatives, that any increase in managerial authority might impede output by provoking resentment and unrest among the miners: POWE 16/73 (D. R. Serpell to Lt.-Col. G. Alfred-Lewis, 27 Jan. 1944); CAB 66/47 (Report by the [War Cabinet] Committee on the Organisation of the Coal Industry, 16 Feb. 1944).

[2] DCOA, vol. 62, 13 Sept. 1943; Harold Storey, letter to *The Economist* 3 Feb. 1945, 148.

sphere of noise, dust, heat, sweat and blasphemy'.[1] Many decent and objective observers appreciated the historical forces which helped shape industrial relations in the industry, and were often sympathetic to the miners' view that 'its whole future is involved in its past', even to the point of accepting that industrial reform must precede a major adjustment of outlook. In September 1942, for example, the Minister of Fuel and Power drew sympathetic attention to the miners' fatigue after three years of war, and urged that there be a broader appreciation of the effect of the experiences of the last 30 years on the wartime attitudes.[2]

Nor was the issue of miners' attitudes and efforts simply one of pathological industrial relations. Mining was a particularly onerous occupation. The work-force was unaccustomed to expending continuous effort over a long period, and was in any case growing distinctly older. In such circumstances, cumulative fatigue could obviously play an important part in the flagging of application and attendance. And beyond this, the diminution of extreme effort was only to be expected from 1943, as the fortunes of war changed and victory looked assured.

Yet, when all these considerations are taken into account, the fact remains that the coalmining industry had a particularly bad wartime record of industrial effort and personal commitment and productivity. Thus it was that on 15 August 1942 the Executive Committee of the MFGB itself appealed to all miners, expressing the gravest anxiety about falling productivity, increasing absenteeism, unnecessary stoppages, and a lack of concern for the national situation: 'To live and work in a period of war the same as you did in times of peace is acting in a way to lose the war.'[3] In almost every respect the situation grew worse thereafter.

To many observers, the principal failing of miners in the last three years of the War lay in persistent absenteeism, if only because that was more easily measurable than effort. Certainly, the statistics indicate a serious and growing problem. As Table 12.1 shows, in 1943–5 the average number of shifts worked fell fairly sharply, and faster than the number of manshifts possible. Average absenteeism therefore mounted from 9.0 per cent in 1941 and 10.4 per cent in 1942, to over 12 per cent in 1943 and 13.6 per cent in 1944. In 1945 it reached 16.3 per cent. Of course, not all of this was 'voluntary', but absence from work by

---

[1] Cocks, MP in *Hansard* 12 Oct. 1943, cols. 794 ff.

[2] The first quotation is from a speech by a miners' MP in *Hansard* 12 Oct. 1943, col. 780. The Minister of Fuel and Power's comments are in 'Miners and the Present Coal Situation', 17 Sept. 1942: CAB 71/9.

[3] PREM 4/9/2; *MFGB* 1942, 131.

apparent choice grew from 4.7 per cent in the first quarter of 1944 to 6.3 per cent a year later.

Within all this, and most critically from the viewpoint of overall output, absenteeism among face-workers was very high: it reached 18.6 per cent (7.4 per cent voluntary) in the first quarter of 1945.[1] The response from owners and managers was naturally very critical, and their representatives were occasionally intemperate (even before the problem intensified, the *Colliery Guardian* allowed itself to refer to 'wrongheaded young men . . . deaf to bribes and entreaties . . . cynical children of the scrapheap').[2] But even the miners' friends were frequently on the verge of exasperation about the problem.

Throughout the latter years of the War a number of explanations of the phenomenon of rising absenteeism were advanced but with inconclusive results. Prolonged work and the fatigue of an ageing labour force (a common explanation on the part of the miners themselves) were not entirely relevant, since the most serious incidence occurred among the younger, and fitter, rather than among the older, miners. In South Wales, for example, the level of absenteeism among face-workers under 31 was about twice that among those over 40.[3] Another reason often adduced (and again by the miners themselves) was nutritional deficiency: inadequate diet in relation to the nature of their work. But there is little evidence that miners *did* suffer in this regard, and in any case there was a determined move to provide canteens serving hot meals at the pit.[4]

In fact, the problem of absenteeism dogged the Ministry of Fuel and Power throughout these years. The possibility of disciplining persistent offenders was inherent in legislation and regulations, but was rarely applied systematically for fear of the resulting aggravation of industrial relations. Initially, it had been assumed that absenteeism would be checked by the principal wartime innovation in labour policy—the Pit Production Committees. These had been created in 1940, fallen largely into disuse after the Fall of France, and were revived in 1941–2. Unfortunately, they were initially identified with the *disciplining* of absentees, and thereby earned a very low reputation in the eyes of the miners and their trade-union representatives. From August 1942 however, action

---

[1] *Ministry of Fuel and Power. Statistical Digest, 1944* (Cmd. 6639. 1945).

[2] *CG* 9 Oct. 1942, 440.

[3] MSWCOA, No. 1020: *Memorandum re Declining Standard of Production* (26 June 1945), 15. Also see COAL 11/103 (1 Feb. 1945). On the other hand, absenteeism was particularly high among 'Bevin Boys': COAL 11/101 (30 Jan. 1945).

[4] Below, 568.

with respect to individual absentees was handed over to the local National Service Officer, and the Pit Production Committees were freed for the potentially more useful task of 'discussing and advising on all questions of production and increasing output'.

In the event, relatively few of the 1,100 Committees were successful. The ingrained presumptions of miners and management too frequently prevented a meeting of minds. Suspicion or apathy on one part, resentment of interference with managerial prerogatives on the other, created insurmountable barriers to fruitful cooperation. There were, of course, exceptions; and there was some diffused psychological gain from the Committees' deliberations. But they appear to have had a negligible effect on production and productivity. Rather, their significance lies in the fact that they represent the failure of policy designed to reform labour attitudes and behaviour.[1]

v. Welfare and community

Much of the labour 'policy' so far discussed was negative in the sense of involving either exhortations or restrictions, compulsion, and at least the possibility of discipline. In practice, however, government labour policy in coalmining was much more positive than negative, and much more favourable than inimical to the miners' interests.

In the early years of the War this new climate was exemplified in the rapid settlement of wage claims and in the terms by which the Essential Work Order was applied to the industry.[2] But it was also, and fairly dramatically, seen in the cooperation of district owners and government with the mining union's drive for a closed shop. As early as 1940, for example, the MFGB mounted a campaign for the introduction of a closed shop, and the Mining Association proved amenable to the request that individual owners in the different districts should support the pressure in favour of 100 per cent unionization. In some areas (South Yorkshire and Durham, for example) the owners readily agreed to cooperate in persuading non-unionists to join a union. Elsewhere (West Yorkshire and Scotland) there was more resistance. In 1940–1, however, this was largely overcome by pressure from the Secretary for Mines, whose apprehension that the owners' independent prosecution of Scottish absentees would 'only lead to ill-feeling' was accompanied by a determined and successful effort to enlist their influence in securing complete unionization. By February 1942 the chastened Scottish owners

[1] Court 1951, 317–23.   [2] Above, 513–14.

even agreed to withhold payment of the attendance bonus to non-unionists.[1]

However, the substance of the miners' achievement during the War went far beyond the enhanced political status of their union. The scarcity of labour and the need to maintain industrial harmony combined to produce a decisive improvement in the material circumstances of miners and mining communities.

First, the need to attract and retain efficient workers led to a new concern with welfare arrangements in the industry, although by no means as extensively as the miners themselves urged.[2] Thus, although the building programme for pithead baths virtually stopped, the provision of canteens, especially canteens serving hot meals, was greatly expanded. For, quite apart from problems of the labour market, the physically demanding nature of coalmining justified special care for the miners' food consumption. (Government policy precluded differential personal rationing, other than an extra allocation of cheese for miners.)

These developments principally resulted from coordinating the work and subsidies of the Miners' Welfare Commission. Between 1940 and 1945 the number of canteens rose from 250 (all of which served light refreshments only) to 912 (including 566 which provided full, hot meals). Even so, the miners' use of canteens was disappointing and uneven (the average, for all meals, varied from 11.2 meals per miner per week in South Derbyshire to 3.4 in South Yorkshire, and, for full meals, from over 3 per person per week in the North-East to less than 1 in Scotland).[3] And until the end of the War the miners' representatives were arguing in favour of extra rations (which could be eaten at home), rather than workplace arrangements which, especially for the family man at the end of a shift and in a hurry to get home, were personally very inconvenient.

Other services were also improved. It will be remembered that the 1942 White Paper had also stipulated reforms in the medical services available to miners, in the oversight of certification for those wishing to leave the industry, and in rehabilitation after accidents. All these were

[1] WYCOA, Mar.–June 1940; SCOA (Coal Owners' Side of Conciliation Board), Sept. 1940–Dec. 1941 and 9 Feb. 1942.

[2] In a submission to the Ministry of Fuel and Power in Oct. 1943 the MFGB argued that increased coal production depended not only on government control of the industry, guarantees of postwar conditions (wages, hours, baths, and canteens at all collieries), and substantial improvements in wages, but on increased rates of compensation for accidents, augmented food rations, help with transport to and from work, and the provision of holidays with pay. See POWE 20/83 (7 Oct. 1943).

[3] *Miners' Welfare in War-Time. Report of the Miners' Welfare Commission for 6½ Years to June 30th 1946* (1947), 20–31. Miners' Welfare Fund's grants to wartime canteens exceeded £2,500,000.

put in hand—the first two under the direction of the Mines Medical
Service and the last under the control of the Miners' Welfare Commission, which subsidized hospital work and itself ran seven rehabilitation
centres.[1]

Significant as all this may have been, the most important area of
material improvement as far as miners were concerned was, of course, in
their pay, and in the structure of pay negotiations. Indeed, by an unacknowledged irony, whereas in 1942 and 1943 the MFGB had blamed
inadequate effort on low pay, by 1944 and 1945 one of the reasons
adduced for low productivity was the shortage of consumer goods on
which to spend greatly increased incomes.[2] That improvement began
with the Greene Board's award in June 1942, which produced both a
large increase in current wages and a recognized minimum for weekly
earnings. In addition, the Board recommended the institution of an output bonus, and in the course of 1942-3 devised a national negotiating
and conciliation scheme.

Boosted by the Greene Award, miners' wage rates and earnings rose
dramatically. By March 1943 the former were 58 per cent above the level
of August 1939 (compared with a weighted average of 34 per cent for 18
leading occupations). *Earnings*, and particularly face-workers' earnings,
measured from August 1938 to January 1943, had risen by considerably
more: by some 80 per cent for all adult males in the industry, as against
65 per cent for all industries.[3] The Greene Award therefore began the
decisive transformation of miners' pay. In the spring of 1944, as a consequence of the Porter Award and its aftermath, that transformation
was completed.[4] In 1944 average weekly cash earnings in the industry
were more than 9 per cent above those of 1943, and almost twice what
they had been in 1938. Using another measure, between 1939 and 1944,
when the official cost of living had risen by just under 30 per cent and
average (national) wage rates by less than 50 per cent, wage rates in coal-mining increased by about 90 per cent.

These increases in nominal and real earnings effected a virtual revolution in the relative position of miners in the wages league. In 1938, they
had been very nearly the lowest paid among workers in major
industries. By 1944 juvenile miners had become the best paid young

---

[1] *Miners' Welfare in War-Time*, 48-9; Court 1951, 299-302.

[2] Cherwell to Churchill, 7 Mar. 1944: Cherwell Papers, F.192/62; POWE 16/80/3 (5 oct. 1944);
POWE 20/72 (24 May 1945); COAL 11/101 (13 Aug. 1945).

[3] Cherwell Papers, H.14 (8 Oct. 1943).

[4] Below, 572-6.

workers in the country, and adults in the industry had risen (from 81st in 1938 and 23rd after the Greene Award) to very near the top of the list, being exceeded only by a handful of trades in munitions industries, which in any case worked large amounts of overtime.[1] Given their successful resistance to the working of *any* overtime, the miners had indeed done best of all out of wartime labour scarcities and sensitivities. Some of this gain was, on any criterion, a necessary incentive to effort and a belated recognition of the peculiar problems of work in the industry. Much, however, seemed to be the price of industrial harmony extracted by a determined work-force many of whose members were 'more pit-conscious than ... war-conscious'.[2]

The question of an output bonus was to give endless trouble (the ineffectiveness of the attendance bonus of 1941 had already been mentioned). To the consternation of those who wished to see the bonus used as a direct incentive to individual effort, the Greene Board was dissuaded, by the opposition of owners as well as miners, from recommending that it be applied on a pit basis. Instead, standard outputs and the sliding scale of extra payments for exceeding those implicit targets, were based on district tonnages. Yet the result was to sever the relationship between effort and reward, and to produce a large number of anomalies (high-productivity pits failing to earn bonuses because they were in low-productivity areas, and vice versa).

The scheme proved an almost unmitigated failure: in the first seven months of 1943 all but two or three districts failed to earn bonus payments, and productivity generally continued to fall. In the autumn of 1943, therefore, the Greene Board decided to review the bonus system. Discussion and controversy continued for some time, with the Ministry preferring a purely pit bonus, on the grounds not that it would produce more coal but that 'any refusal at this stage to accept the idea of a pit bonus scheme would lead to serious unrest in the Industry and would therefore reduce output even further'.[3] In fact, however, the whole question of bonuses became absorbed in the bigger issue of wage levels, and was abandoned in the spring of 1944, when the Porter Award and subsequent adjustments gave a very large fillip to miners' wages.[4]

The national conciliation machinery which ultimately emerged from

[1] POWE 16/178 (5 Oct. 1944); *Hansard* 12 Oct. 1944, col. 768; Court 1951, 327–8.

[2] The phrase is from a generally sympathetic article ('What is Wrong in the Coalfields?') in the *Daily Telegraph* 4 July 1943, 4d–g.

[3] Tribe to Hyndley and Minister, 10 Sept. 1943: POWE 20/76.

[4] The course of events is summarized in Court 1951, 225–8. Contemporary sources are in POWE 20/69; POWE 20/75–6.

the Greene Board's deliberations in the spring of 1943 had been envisaged in the Lord President's and the War Cabinet's discussions of a year earlier. It was a recognition of the new-found bargaining strength of the miners, of the general deterioration in the nation's industrial relations after the relatively quiescent mood of the first years of war, and of the inappropriateness of the inherited system of wage-determination in coal, which took little or no account of the situation of the industry *as a whole*.[1] In March 1943, the Greene Board proposed a National Board consisting of a Joint National Negotiating Committee (with equal numbers of owners' and miners' representatives) and a National Reference Tribunal (with three members with no connection with the industry) to settle disputes referred to it.[2] This was accepted, and 22 years after the great controversy of 1921 the miners had at last achieved their long-desired aim of a national wages system.

The National Reference Tribunal, chaired by Lord Porter, was to play an important, but ultimately disruptive, role in the coal industry's affairs in 1943–4. In September it adjudicated on the MFGB's claim for a national wage scale for youths in the industry—a sensitive issue ever since the anxieties about recruitment to coalmining had surfaced early in 1942. The resulting weekly scales (rising from 32s. at age 14 to 63s. at $20\frac{1}{2}$ for underground work, and from 27s. 6d. to 55s. for surface work) were a severe disappointment to the union, and helped generate an undercurrent of dissatisfaction which did considerable damage in the following spring. In November the Tribunal further reinforced the MFGB's position by determining that payments for overtime and week-end work were national and not local questions. And in December it was instrumental in granting a concession which had long been sought by the MFGB: annual holidays with pay (set at six days in the first instance) throughout the industry. However, the Porter Tribunal's most significant task lay in the determination of a large wage increase which was awarded in January 1944, and which produced the severest crisis of industrial relations of the War.

---

[1] Between 1926 and 1940, wage settlements were conducted within individual districts and on the basis of each district's 'proceeds'. In 1940, by the terms of a national agreement in the Joint Standing Consultative Committee which had been set up after the dispute of 1935–6, wartime wages were to be settled nationally by uniform increases based on changes in the cost of living. In 1942, however, and again in 1943–4, there was mounting pressure within the industry for wage increases well beyond the cost of living, and in the context of the industry as a whole.

[2] See *Third Report of the Board of Investigation into Wages and Machinery for Determining Wages and Conditions of Employment in the Coal-Mining Industry* (1943) and Lord Greene's broadcast description in POWE 20/67 (2 Apr. 1943).

The Porter Award of 1944 followed some months of controversy about control and the industry's disappointing performance, during which (as has been seen) the Prime Minister's rhetorical powers had to be enlisted to calm critics and fend off a renewed campaign for nationalization. Meanwhile, the patent failure of the output bonus scheme engendered troubling discussions of possible alternative incentives within the industry; and, manpower shortages having failed to respond to public appeals, the War Cabinet turned reluctantly to the device of compulsory recruitment. Finally, a ministerial committee entered on yet another prolonged examination of the future organization of the industry, which led to an overhaul of the Ministry of Fuel's pattern of control.[1]

The prevailing undercurrent in all these developments was the attitude and spirit of the miners. Indeed, in the course of the Commons Debate of 12–13 October more than one miners' MP made the crucial point that 'The initiative has passed from us to the men.' The miners, they argued, would not forget their interwar experiences, or their defeats in 1921 and 1926. They knew that they held the whip hand in the wartime labour shortages and would therefore not be fobbed off in their pursuit of high and secure wages.[2] Although much of the pressure from the miners' representatives appeared to be directed towards postwar industrial and labour policy in coalmining, in the winter of 1943–4 the principal demands of the miners at grass roots were concentrated on the level and security of their wages. As Ernest Bevin put it in a letter to the Minister of Fuel:

I doubt very much if the bulk of the miners are worrying about controls. It is more or less a peg on which to hang further demands. What the miner is concerned about, in my view, is the removal of uncertainty so far as his wages and conditions are concerned and this particularly applies to exporting districts.[3]

After the experience of the interwar years, and with no guarantee that the postwar world would be more favourable to their situation, the miners understandably, if provocatively, became preoccupied with enlarging and securing their earnings. 'To-day', claimed the *Colliery Guardian* in March 1944, 'the miners' leaders, instead of trying to

---

[1] Above, 555, 558.
[2] *Hansard* 12 Oct. 1943, col. 837; 13 Oct. 1943, col. 966.
[3] Quoted in Bullock 1967, 261. For the discussions of autumn 1943, see Court 1951, 251–3; POWE 20/83; CAB 87/93.

discover how much more coal can be gotten, are devising means of stabilising their gains and privileges after the War.'[1] But this was to underestimate the strength of feeling among the rank and file in the coalfields. There, lack of discipline was becoming endemic, and local miners' leaders were ready to confess that they were hardly able to retain control of their members. By late 1943 in Durham, for example, Sam Watson the President of the Miners' Association argued that the numerous 'unconstitutional stoppages' were caused by the fact that 'the miners thought the war was nearly over and they were concerned as to what their wages would be then', and that the industry's arrangements for the settlement of disputes were slow and unwieldy. Claiming that 'we are now sitting upon a volcano', he urged that colliery managers be given more authority and that the district seek the support of the Mining Association or financial aid from the government.[2]

To the discomfiture of the government, the MFGB attempted to raise the question of wages with the Minister of Fuel and Power (rather than with the National Negotiating Committee and Reference Tribunal). They did so, they claimed, because a government guarantee as to price increases would be necessary to meet their now very substantial, and necessarily inflationary, demands (which included an increase of almost 45 per cent in the level of minimum wages). At this stage (November 1943), the Minister managed to deflect the pressure for direct negotiations or any guarantee, but was still obliged to discuss the issue with the owners and the miners.[3] Meanwhile, and a vital if unspoken accompaniment to these complicated discussions, unrest in the coalfields was once again mounting to a dangerous level.

It was in this context that the National Reference Tribunal considered the MFGB's claim (for new minimum wages, for revised rates for juveniles, and for large increases in piece rates in order to preserve existing differentials). On 22 January 1944 the Tribunal published its verdict—which was to achieve unenviable notoriety as the Porter Award.[4] Although clearly not persuaded by the miners' arguments, the Tribunal went part of the way with their demands: minimum wages for adults were to be raised (to £5 per week for underground workers), and there was a large increase in the minimum wages for juvenile workers.

[1] *CG* 10 Mar. 1944, 302. For the wartime mood in mining communities, see below, 578.
[2] DCOA, 9 Nov. 1943.
[3] CAB 87/93 (18 Nov. 1943). The Ministry also gave evidence to the National Reference Tribunal when it came to consider the claim.
[4] The Porter Award and its destabilizing consequences are dealt with in Court 1951, 253–69; CAB 65/41–2; CAB 71/15–16; POWE 16/70–1.

On the other hand, the piece-rate claim was denied, although the Tribunal acknowledged that a thorough overhaul of the industry's wages structure was necessary.

The Porter Award was unsatisfactory on two important counts. First, it was fairly clear that, in granting any concession to what they felt was an inadequately presented and unjustified claim, the Tribunal was acting on political grounds (fearful as they must have been of the consequences of rejecting the claim entirely in the existing atmosphere). Second, they were too insensitive to the effects of the substantial increase in minimum wages on the differentials which were so vital to miners. For in the low-paid coalfields the increases had the effect of closing gaps in earnings which had long been justified by contrasts in work and responsibilities.

These apparent anomalies immediately became a source of determined activity and negotiation within the industry, with the owners not unsympathetic to the complaints of the better-paid miners on piece rates. Within a matter of days the Joint National Negotiating Committee had agreed that (although they would have to be fixed within the various districts) increases in piece rates *were* necessary, in order to keep traditionally higher-paid miners better off than the lower-paid day-rate men. Admittedly, the re-establishment of differentials by a substantial increase in piece rates would be an unrealistic aim without a corresponding increase in coal prices. Yet in spite of the government's determined refusal in early February to guarantee this way of financing changes, local negotiations went ahead with almost unseemly haste.[1]

The situation had all the makings of a serious industrial crisis, and that was exactly what occurred in the early spring of 1944. Already, during negotiations about bonus schemes in September 1943, the miners' sense of grievance was said to have been so serious that 'it would be difficult ... to worsen the present industrial relations in the industry'.[2] In February and March the difficult became easy: widespread strike action followed the announcement by the Ministry of Fuel and Power that it would not guarantee the funds necessary to meet district agreements concerning differentials. Extensive stoppages in South Wales and in Yorkshire in particular led to sharp cuts in electricity and

---

[1] The government accepted the obligation to cover the £5 million cost of the Porter Award from the Coal Charges Account. The cost of reinstating differentials was estimated to lie between £5 and £15 million. The Porter Award for overtime and weekend payments had also been £5 million. See POWE 16/70 (13 Apr. 1944).

[2] F. N. Tribe to Minister, 24 Sept. 1943: POWE 20/75.

gas supplies to less essential industries, to a worrying threat to the crucial preparations for the invasion of France, and to a continued deterioration in the public's feelings toward the miners. Puzzlement and anger were also exemplified in the Army: Tony Crosland, then fighting in Italy, noted in his Diary for 10 March 1944, after a particularly fierce and bloody battle, that his platoon was

first-class—cheerful, blinding and swearing, making attempt after attempt to recover the bodies from under House 2. And the morning after, we heard that 70,000 miners are on strike over the £5 minimum wage: these lads are not very sympathetic.[1]

It was symptomatic of the prevailing atmosphere that the Minister of Fuel and Power was furious with the owners for having raised the miners' hopes by agreeing to district negotiations to maintain relativities. And he was hardly mollified by the claim of the MAGB's President, the redoubtable Sir Evan Williams, that there would have been a strike if negotiations had *not* begun.[2] More critically, given the occasion and the character of the crisis, it proved impossible for the government to maintain its line that wages were a matter for the National Reference Tribunal rather than the state, or to insist that the money would not be found to cover the costs of post-Porter Award adjustments.

By early March 1944, the Minister of Fuel and Power had persuaded the War Cabinet that the government was obliged to intervene in the determination of a new wages structure. The two aims of the new policy, he argued, should be to establish a closer link between pay and productivity, and 'to give the mine workers a greater sense of security for the future'.[3] With Cabinet approval, then, Lloyd George took complete charge of wage negotiations, and resolved the crisis by extensive compromise with the miners' position.

As far as piece-rate workers were concerned, 4s. 6d. of the wartime flat-rate additions to shift wages (i.e. all but 2s. 8d. of all wartime increases) were merged into their pay by 'appropriate' percentage

---

[1] Quoted in Crosland 1982, 29.

[2] POWE 16/71 (16 Feb. 1944). Lloyd George protested vigorously at the burden on the consumer (£74 million) of past decisions about coal: 'the time has come to stop this because the situation is going to be such that when the war comes to an end the position of this industry will be almost the same as after the last war.'

[3] CAB 65/41 (7 Mar. 1944). Early in 1944 the idea of an attendance bonus had been revived (to give an incentive to miners to work more than four or five shifts weekly). But it had been dropped amid scepticism as to its likely effects.

increases in tonnage or yardage rates. The effect was to re-establish a large part of the differential between piece-rate and day-rate earnings and (at least ostensibly) to provide a more immediate incentive to increase output. Long-run security was offered in the form of an officially inspired agreement that the wages agreement would last at least until December 1947, at which point either side might give six months' notice of its termination. The new wages agreement was signed on 20 April 1944.

The national wages agreement of 1944 had important implications at various levels. For example, even though, as with every other wartime measure, it failed to spur the miners into a more sustained productive effort (the longer-run trends in output per manshift and attendance continued to decline), it was the culmination of the wartime elevation of miners' earnings and a decisive resolution of the abrasive issue of wages. (By the same token, it was seen as a public-relations opportunity: within a fortnight the Minister of Fuel and Power reported that unofficial stoppages had ceased and output had risen so that 'The moment seems propitious, therefore, for the removal of coalmining from the limelight'.)[1]

The cost of all this, being borne by the Coal Charges Account, entailed an increase in the price of coal (by 4s. a ton in August 1944, coming on top of 3s. on 1 February for pre-Porter costs). And it was this which brought the implications of miners' wage increases home to a patient public and which sharpened ministerial disappointment when effort and productivity in the pits failed to respond. In October 1944, for example, Ministers were briefed to warn the miners that the fact that (in spite of their progress from 81st to about 10th in the league table of industrial wages) unauthorized disputes, high absenteeism, and low productivity still persisted, meant that they were 'cutting their own throats'. They were losing public sympathy, and 'In the last resort it is the degree of public sympathy which tips the balance as between high wages and the high cost of coal.'[2]

An even more significant consequence of the 1944 wages settlement, and an obvious implication of the fact that it had to be paid for from the Coal Charges Account, was that the government could no longer avoid

[1] CAB 71/16 (3 May 1944). Lloyd George had decided to publish output statistics on a quarterly rather than a monthly basis—itself a partial confession of failure, since monthly statistics had been designed as a spur to effort.

[2] POWE 16/78 (5 Oct. 1944). Notes on the actual meeting on the same day are in POWE 16/80.

a direct involvement in the industry. Quite apart from the state's direct negotiating role, the need to adjust prices to pay the new wages meant that the government had been manœuvred into a position which it had long fought to avoid, and which was uncomfortably reminiscent of the problems at the end of the First World War. It had to take more direct responsibility for the industry and its finances.

The issue, however, was much broader than that precisely because the industrial-relations problems of the industry had presented themselves as necessitating a *long-run* guarantee (by the state) of the wages settlement. Again, as happened a generation earlier, it was now necessarily committed to continuous control and intervention for years beyond the end of hostilities. And it was indicative of the novel situation that the 1944 wages agreement abandoned the procedure for wage determination which had been created in 1921, and which had both related wage levels to the profitability of the industry and allowed them to be determined within the various districts. The system of ascertainments, with all its subtleties and its causes of dissatisfaction, disappeared.[1]

As far as the miners were concerned, the War also brought other sorts of benefit. Thus, in addition to facilitating the enforcement of the closed shop,[2] it made possible the movement towards the *national* organization of their union which was a logical consequence of the national wage arrangements following the Greene Inquiry of 1942. Having accepted the principle of a more unified structure in 1942, the MFGB entered on a long period of internal discussion. The new constitution was approved by a special conference in August 1944 and in November a national ballot accepted the idea by a majority of ten to one.

The National Union of Mineworkers (still a federal organization, but a much more coherent one) came into existence on 1 January 1945. By that time, although the miners still entertained a number of ambitions— relating to the length of the working week, the extension of paid holidays, retirement, disability compensation, and the like—which would have to wait for the end of hostilities, they had developed a renewed authority which enabled them to look forward with some confidence to the realization of their aims.

The wages agreement of 1944 played a symbolic as well as a substantive role as far as the miners' well-being and sense of industrial and political autonomy were concerned. Within a few years their social and

---

[1] Wages still varied from district to district: the 1944 agreement established new basis rates.
[2] Above, 567.

economic position had taken a giant step away from the miseries, disappointments, and hopelessness of the 1930s. The immediate effect on
mining communities was startling: unemployment disappeared, food
and purchasing power became relatively abundant, a sense of defeat was
lifted.

On the other hand, as a fascinating wartime survey of the South
Wales mining villages of Blaina and Nantyglo showed, the response to
prosperity was by no means always positive or optimistic. First, it could
lead to a sharper questioning of the prewar economic and business
system than had been exemplified at the time; second, there was a
diffuse fear 'that the system will return after the war, that there will then
be extensive economic depression. This fear conditions a very large part
of the work effort and the whole morale of Blaina . . .'. In the words of
one respondent, the majority had 'the feeling that they'll just be scrap',
and were without confidence in the possibility of change; an 'advanced
section' argued that 'they won't be hoodwinked again as they were in
the 1918 election; and another (smaller) minority of socialists asked "can
we win sufficient power to *force* a change?" '[1]

With this background and these attitudes, it was most unlikely that
the mining communities would find it in themselves to support the war
effort in a spirit of unconditional self-sacrifice. The old grievances and
resentments still existed; indeed, now they had a much greater chance of
being deployed. The material hardships and personal degradations of
the prewar depressed areas produced, even in the buoyant years of wartime prosperity, 'a living dread of black times again . . .'.[2]

Meanwhile, however, the War still had a year to run, and during that
time the wages agreement had no positive effect on production and
productivity. To that extent, the persistent scepticism of the owners
about the effects of unconditional higher pay was borne out. By the
winter of 1944–5 output per manshift had fallen to its lowest levels, and
even erstwhile optimists were deeply anxious about the possibility of a

[1] 'Mining Town—1942' in Mass-Observation Archives (University of Sussex), File 1498. A brief
summary is in File 1196, and Appendices are derived from a follow-up in 1943. The quotations in
the text are from File 1196, 1–2 and File 1498, 69. The initial survey was conducted by Mass-
Observation in the spring of 1942, and part of its sociological interest lies in the explicit comparison with a similar survey conducted in 1937, and published in *Fact*. For 15 years after the
closing of seven collieries in 1921 over 70% of the male population was unemployed. (It was of
Blaina that Edward VIII had said 'something will and something shall be done.') By 1942 the 1,176
registered unemployed at the Blaina labour exchange had fallen to six, although a good deal of the
take-up of labour, which now for the first time included many women, was in local munitions
work. The range of social, political, and economic phenomena surveyed was very great.

[2] Blaina housewife, quoted in Mass-Observation Archive (University of Sussex), File 1498, 208.

genuine coal crisis as the War moved into its final stages and planning for the supply of liberated Europe had to begin.[1]

By October 1944 an atmosphere of widespread despondency surrounded the industry. The Ministry of Fuel and Power noted that in the four months since the wages agreement weekly output per man had fallen by 5 cwt and absenteeism had risen by 25 per cent.[2] Separate meetings were arranged between government representatives and the two sides to the industry. At these meetings the owners largely concentrated on the problems of voluntary absenteeism, slackness, and indiscipline and urged that the payment of the Porter minimum wage be made conditional on good attendance and effort. The miners' leaders acknowledged some of the problems (including the rise in absenteeism and the diminution in effort) but were equally unable to proffer realistic solutions.[3] Nor did very much useful analysis or policy prescription follow from the referral of these issues to a joint committee of owners and miners, which considered the fall in output at meetings between December 1944 and August 1945.[4]

These prolonged discussions may have achieved very little, but they made it abundantly clear that, as the War drew to an end, the problems that had dogged labour productivity since 1941 were now compounded by the psychological reverberations of years of War and the imminence of peace. Throughout the work-force there was a sense that effort and sacrifice were no longer needed, satisfaction with the high wages that could be earned for less than full effort and attendance, frustration at the lack of outlets for unprecedented purchasing power, fatigue and cynicism, preoccupation with the future and with the possibility of institutionalizing the new-found strengths of the labour force.

In spite of the urgency with which the immediate questions of output and productivity pressed upon the government and those involved in the industry, the main underlying thrust of the industry's problems was towards the long term and the structural, towards organizational change and technical reform. The wartime shifts in government policy were, in a sense, minor instalments of these more profound changes. The exigencies of war and the need to secure the cooperation of those in the industry, had led not merely to an extension of official control of mining

[1] Above, 544. Also see 'Coal Position in the Second Stage', POWE 26/437.

[2] POWE 16/78 (5 Oct. 1944).

[3] Ibid. (12 Oct 1944) and 16/80 (5 Oct. 1944). The MFGB also complained about poor management practices, lack of consumer goods, etc.

[4] COAL 11/101. As a means of securing the MFGB's participation, the owners withdrew their recommendation that conditions should be attached to the payment of minimum wages.

and great improvements in the position of miners, but to official guarantees of wage levels and stability in the immediate postwar years.There was, in addition, another sphere of labour policy in which wartime labour difficulties and industrial-relations problems prepared the ground for important long-run institutional reform. This was the appreciation of the need for training and the potentialities of personnel management in coalmining.

As early as 1942, influenced by the discussion surrounding the problem of juvenile recruitment, various district joint committees of owners and miners (for example, in South Derbyshire, South Wales, and Durham) had agreed on the necessity for more systematic schemes to provide training centres and day-release possibilities for new entrants to the industry.[1] Some of these—the Durham proposals in particular—included plans for the better training and remuneration of managers, and in 1944 the Mining Association listed the recruitment and training of personnel (potential officials as well as piece-rate and datal workmen) among the foundations of a desirable new policy for the industry.[2]

The question of personnel management gave rise to even more profound considerations and changes. As has already been seen, the character of control from 1942 had given a vital role to Labour Directors, which had to be defended against the complaints of the production side. More than that, the difficulty of securing labour cooperation at a time of labour scarcity inevitably led to an increasing concern with the improvement of personnel management in an industry hitherto notorious for its bad industrial relations. As early as March 1943, Sir Evan Williams (whose attitude towards labour and industrial relations in the interwar years was hardly progressive) was warning his fellow owners in South Wales that a much broader approach was now needed:

the industry could not revert to the old state whereby 'we are the masters and they are the men'. That outlook was outmoded and unless there was a joint approach to these problems there could be no hope for the industry.[3]

Later in the same year there was extensive official discussion of the desirability of appointing personnel managers at collieries and within districts. 'A tired labour force', concluded one memorandum ('The Coal Industry—the disease and the remedy'),

---

[1] SDCOA, 4 June 1942; MSWCOA, 14 Dec. 1942, 22 Mar. 1943; DCOA, 25 Nov. 1943.
[2] 'Interim Memorandum on Certain Aspects of the Future Policy of the Coal Industry', 13 Apr. 1944, in MSWCOA 1018.   [3] MSWCOA, 22 Mar. 1943.

can neither be driven nor bribed into working harder, but it can be induced to do so by an appeal for cooperation to their intelligence. This is quite definitely the job of a trained expert and not of a tired and overworked Colliery Manager.

A similar theme was implied in the report of the War Cabinet Committee on the Organisation of the Coal Industry (February 1944). Heavily influenced by the Minister of Labour and National Service, Ernest Bevin, it recalled that the 1942 reorganization presupposed that 'there were certain labour interests—e.g. welfare and training—which should be the responsibility of officers of comparable status to that of Production Directors', and urged that there was a genuine and important need to retain them and protect their authority.[1] And, to judge from the various district associations, within the industry itself there was increasing concern at the ineffectiveness of traditional management attitudes and policies towards the labour force, and an enhanced awareness of the possible advantages of specialist managers in the field.

As with the more far-reaching discussion of public ownership, the wartime consideration of reform of personnel practices came to little before the end of the War. It was, nevertheless, symptomatic of the fact that the industry would never be the same again. And in both cases, although other factors were obviously at work, it was the posture of the work-force and the leverage that the threat of wartime crisis placed in their hands which produced the most dramatic changes in official attitudes and postwar policy. The roots of nationalization were to be found in the wartime experience in its historical context, and to that extent it was an indirect monument to the posture of disaffected miners as well as to the technical deficiencies of coalmining. The lesson which the War once more brought home was that the problem of production was in the last resort a problem of labour.

vi. The business of coalmining

The fact that the central issue of wartime policy turned on the supply and organization of the labour force did not conceal the more general issue of the adequacy with which the colliery companies met the demands of war. And this, in turn, was clearly related to a whole range of problems concerning the consequences of the War for the *business* of coal production.

---

[1] POWE 22/169 (4 June 1943); CAB 66/47 (16 Feb. 1944). Also see Bevin's memorandum (1 Feb. 1944) in CAB 87/92 and the discussion following the Reid Report in 1945 (POWE 22/187).

If performance were to be judged by public and political opinion, there would be little doubt about that of colliery companies in the early 1940s. The reputation of the coalowners had not been particularly high in the 1930s. During the Second World War it deteriorated even further. For, in spite of the intermittent obloquy that the miners attracted by virtue of the growth of absenteeism and their occasional disruption of the war effort for sectional ends, the owners, or at least the inherited structures of private ownership, were widely thought to be the real villains of the piece. The poor performance of the industry over the long run was generally believed to be the result of a failure of entrepreneurship and an unwillingness or inability to change traditional industrial structures, techniques, or attitudes to labour. The wartime experience only served to reinforce such views, and the industry's problems continued to be blamed, in large part, on deficiencies in the attitudes, policies, and cooperativeness of owners and managers.

Such a view was in many respects one-sided: it neglected the relatively low level of labour productivity (even allowing for the degree of mechanization) in 1939 and the deterioration in attendance and output per manshift during the early 1940s. 'If the Industry at the beginning of the War had been in the highest possible state of efficiency', claimed one senior mining engineer-manager in February 1945, 'the coal position during the War would have been comparably just as bad as it had been, if Labour had behaved as it has.'[1] Nevertheless, the deficiencies of industrial organization, technology, and policies seemed more profoundly enduring, as well as politically easier targets, than the attitudes of the labour force. And this was reinforced by the persistent problems encountered by the government when it attempted to reform the industry, or even to secure the cooperation of senior production engineers.

The exasperation with the performance of colliery companies, which shaped the reactions of politicians, civil servants, other businessmen, and the public at large, was even shared by many mining engineers and a few owners. As a result, by 1944-5 self-criticism and the acknowledgement of past deficiencies within the industry added force to public scepticism about the efficacy of the prevailing system of private ownership and management in coalmining. They also served to reinforce the conventional wisdom which held that, on its management and business side, the industry had performed atrociously in the early 1940s.

[1] H. Watson Smith (Managing Director, Hardwick Colliery Co.) to C. C. Reid, 6 Feb. 1945: POWE 22/178.

In fact, it is extremely difficult to determine how far the industry's poor showing during the War can be primarily attributed to its organization or it managers and owners. It is true, if only tautologically, that better organization or better management would have resulted in more production and greater productivity. But it is also true that the cooperation and effort of the labour force were increasingly lacking as the War proceeded. As far as management innovation was concerned, whatever the inadequacies of business policy during the 1930s, wartime shortages—of labour, equipment, and capital—effectively blocked any widespread progressive change after 1939. More critically, perhaps, the complexity and artificiality of the wartime environment make it exceedingly difficult to disentangle the entrepreneurial or managerial reasons for lagging performance. And by the same token, the degree of government intervention and resulting distortion of market forces make it almost impossible to assess the success or otherwise of business operations in coalmining during the War.

State intervention came to play a crucial role in the allocation of output to markets and consumers and in the determination of prices, profits, and the burden of rising costs. It therefore had the most far-reaching effect on the business side of the industry as a whole, both as regards the overall financial outcome and its geographical and institutional pattern. Superficially, the state managed to go through the War without assuming direct responsibility for wages or finances generally. Notionally, the industry's finances were self-contained: increases in costs were to be met by adjustments of prices and of the allocation of proceeds. Nevertheless, whatever the ideological theory, under the intensifying pressure of war the *practical* consequences of government industrial policy were hardly distinguishable from full-blown financial control, while inflexibilities in the system of control meant that some form of temporary subsidy became unavoidable.

In the early years of the War a good deal of this financial intervention was informal. The industry agreed not to increase prices without the approval of the Mines Department, and at the suggestion of the Mines Department the Central Council of Colliery Owners instituted a War Emergency Assistance Scheme, whereby a levy on output was used to compensate firms whose production had been impaired by wartime conditions. In 1941 the Assistance Scheme was extended to help collieries which might otherwise have gone out of business, a new levy was instituted to cover the cost of the guaranteed wages paid under the Essential Work Order, and the Board of Trade acknowledged that the industry would have a case for a price increase whenever the average national credit balance fell below 1s. 6d. per ton.[1]

By the summer of 1942, however, this system was coming under severe pressure. First, the automatic payment of subsidies on the basis of output ignored the differing profit potential of the recipient firms. As a result, the new Ministry took responsibility for the various levies (which were combined in a single charge) and for their allocation, through the Coal Charges Account, although the Central Council of the industry continued to administer the scheme on behalf of the government. Second, the large flat-rate addition to wages which followed the Greene Board's recommendations in June had very unequal effects on the tonnage costs of different enterprises (depending on their levels of output per manshift), and rather than attempt to cover these by differential price increases, firms were compensated for costs actually incurred, from an industry-wide levy. Third, from December 1942, a system of 'price allowances', devised for districts where costs had outpaced prices, was applied nationally. As district costs of production rose unevenly (in large part because production fell, and average tonnage costs therefore rose, at differing rates), it was decided to meet these costs not by allowing varying price increases on a district basis, but by increasing the *national* levy and price, pooling the proceeds in the Coal Charges Account, and paying 'price allowances' to the weaker districts. It was, in effect, a return to the system of pooling for which the miners had fought so bitterly, and unavailingly, in 1921.[2]

The accountancy involved in all this was delicate and complex, particularly because it was combined with an effective guarantee of district profits. The system of financial control assumed that the industry would attain average credit balances within a pre-set range. For the industry as a whole this was to be an average national credit balance per ton between 1s. 6d. and 2s.—with a standard of 1s. 9d. Within this, and apart from the standard of 6d. for Cumberland, the datum for district balances varied from 1s. 3d. (Durham and South Wales) to 2s. 9d. (Warwickshire). Using the TS (i.e. 'Terms of Settlement') accounting conventions of the 1921 wages agreement to measure net proceeds in each district, payments were to be made from the Coal Charges Account to cover any shortfall below the minimum balance. (It was still possible for individual collieries within a district to fall below the minimum or even lose

---

[1] *Ministry of Fuel and Power. Financial Position of Coalmining Industry. Coal Charges Account* (Cmd. 6617. 1945).

[2] Above, ch. 4, sect. vii.

money, although in the latter case they might be kept in business by grants through the emergency scheme for 'necessitous undertakings'.)

In terms of the industry as a whole, because the procedure of price allowances operated with a lag (price allowances were fixed in relation to levels of costs which were subsequently exceeded as production continued to decline), even after the application of levies and recoveries the standard of 1s. 9d. per ton was never reached, and in 1942 and 1943 the credit balances averaged 4d. and 2d. less than the 'target' minimum, and the deficiencies had to be made up from the Coal Charges Account. Overall, in the period between 3 June 1942 and 31 December 1944 the Coal Charges Account was itself in deficit by almost £26 million, which had to be met by the Treasury, although it was implicitly assumed that in the long run the Account would generate sufficient income to repay this.

Within the Account (i.e. in terms of charges and payments intended to balance the finances of the industry), Durham and South Wales were the largest and most consistent recipients of payments (they recovered 1s. 6d. and 3s. 3d. per ton in 1943 and 3s. 9d. and 7s. 11d. in 1944), and the various Midland fields were consistent contributors. Of the total expenditure of £168 million in 1942-4, wages (mostly wage increases, but also £3 million of guaranteed wage payments) accounted for £86 million, and price allowances for £63 million. Other important categories of expenditure met from the levies were the emergency assistance to individual necessitous undertakings (£6 million) and the maintenance of minimum credit balances (£4.73 million).[1]

Clearly, the operations of the Coal Charges Account were of fearsome complexity, and their true implications for the business profitability of coalmining during the War are perhaps commensurately obscured. Nevertheless, their overall consequences were clear: given the official control of price levels and the allocation of supplies, the Coal Charges Account helped sustain the industry's general level of profitability and (of perhaps much greater importance) ensured the intra-industry reallocation of aggregate profits in ways which defended the position of the less productive districts and even collieries.

Of course, prices increased during the war years—on average by 18s. per ton. But from June 1942 such increases were more or less matched by the Coal Charges levies which enabled the greater proceeds to be redistributed within the industry according to the varying incidence of

---

[1] *Coal Charges Account*, 12-13.

rising costs. More significantly, the financial consequences of wartime operations were determined by the uneven movement of costs and the unpredictable outcome of the payments under the Coal Charges Account. The Account was designed to avoid a government subsidy to the industry as a whole. But it operated (quite apart from the Treasury advances to cover actual deficits) in a way which allowed weaker districts, within a system of controlled prices, to be subsidized by more productive districts. In addition, particularly vulnerable collieries ('necessitous undertakings') received more explicit grant-aid, and the outcome of the system also involved official advances towards working expenses and even capital investment in new techniques.

Such a system (unwieldy and unpredictable as its workings may have been) did at least provide some sort of 'floor' for the profitability of coal-mining (at least in terms of the activities of entire districts), while the fact that the Account operated on a district basis helped retain some incentive for competitive activity and the attainment of productivity increases by individual enterprises. The situation was described by the historian of coal in wartime:

The development of the scheme on a district basis left some financial incentive to the colliery management to do its best. For although the guarantee of district profits through the price allowance scheme meant that any increase in costs by a particular colliery would reduce the district balance and so increase the price allowance to all collieries in the district, this increased allowance would clearly be but a small fraction of the increased costs of the individual colliery. It was unlikely that the collieries in a particular district would make a concerted attempt to secure repayment from the Account for costs improperly incurred, although this possibility did occur when districts began negotiating increased wages after the Porter Award in 1944.[1]

The wartime financial system therefore created a powerful stabilizing influence for the financial business of the industry. In addition, there was some scope for abuse. This arose particularly with illicit claims for wage subsidies under the arrangements for guaranteed wages and with the use of official funds (ostensibly allocated to increase the output of necessitous undertakings) to finance long-run development work designed to increase postwar production and productivity.[2] Even if these two factors were unimportant (accurate measurement is impossible, although the entire allocation involved in the two types of payment accounted for less than £10 million of the £167 million passing

[1] Court 1951, 351.   [2] Above, 563 and Court 1951, 349–50.

through the Account in 1942–4), the finances of collieries as a result of the War were fairly healthy. Price increases meant that overall credit balances, even after the imposition of levies, compared favourably with prewar levels (in 1940–4 they averaged just over 1 s. 6 d. per ton, compared with 3 d. in 1930–4 and 10.5 d. in 1934–8).[1] And the financial results of individual companies also reflect a relatively prosperous picture: by 1943–4 the share prices of virtually all the leading colliery undertakings had risen by between 20 and 50 per cent of their 1939 levels.[2]

The financial outcome of coalmining business in wartime clearly owed much to the trends and vagaries of public policy. In any case, however, the most important underlying consideration as far as business activity was concerned was not the industry's profit-and-loss account but the extent to which business policy was adequate to the war effort and anticipated the likely future of the industry.

In this respect, even taking account of the efforts to improve mechanized techniques under wartime pressures, it was obvious that there was very little enhancement, and much deterioration, in the efficiency of coalmining enterprises during the War. Whatever the role of the quantitative and qualitative deterioration in the industry's labour supply or the unavoidable depreciation of the industry's capital stock owing to wartime shortages, the early 1940s saw relatively few signs of managerial enterprise or purposeful preparation for a more efficient future.

The miserable productive records of the industry reflected adversely on *all* those concerned with it. Yet the fact remains that neither the structures of wartime financial control nor the experience of the recent past encouraged very much managerial initiative at the level of organization or techniques. It was no doubt possible to envisage a postwar world in which coal would be in relatively short supply, where the likelihood of political intervention was remote, and where large investment funds would be readily available. Such a vision would have justified a far more energetic and wide-ranging policy of innovation and development. But at the level of realistic expectation and action for large numbers of firms, it was sadly the case that there was little in the twentieth-century history of the British coalmining industry which offered encouraging signs of success for such strategies of commitment and investment.

[1] JRP to Paymaster-General, 20 Mar. 1945: Cherwell Papers, H.18.

[2] For share prices, see *The Iron and Coal Trades Review*, *passim*. The principal exceptions were in Lancashire, where both the Wigan Coal Company and Manchester Associated Collieries experienced a decline in the market value of their equity. The share values of 1943–4 only rarely recovered the relatively high values of 1937. Exceptions here were largely confined to the Midlands field, where the Butterley and Bolsover Companies out-performed the market.

The perennial glut in the market for coal, the likely private and social costs of any action to streamline the industry, the looming risks of individual effort, the practical and legal obstacles to collective action, the ingrained experience of industrial protectionism, the apprehensions concerning state intervention and public ownership—all combined to dampen enthusiasm for risk-taking. Wartime structural changes, even in response to the government's attempt to encourage 'concentration', had done little to amend the fragmentation which had handicapped co-operative action to close excess capacity and justify intensive reorganization in the prewar years. The same restraining influence of the structural experiments of the 1930s were still powerfully felt. Indeed, given the position in 1939, it could hardly be expected that the wartime experience would produce a much more enterprising spirit.

Of course, the industry was not entirely devoid of initiative and ambitious plans. There were collieries which made substantial efforts to maintain productivity during the war years and which attempted to build on an established reputation. The Butterley Company, for example, working mines in Derbyshire and Nottinghamshire, continued to develop its organization and mechanization programmes, and raised productivity levels.[1] More generally, and particularly in the last year or so of the War, various large and progressive colliery undertakings extended their horizons, anticipated a postwar need for greatly enhanced productivity and development, and drew up elaborate plans for intensive restructuring, occasionally based on systematic assessments of American or German best practice.[2] And at a higher level of generality, various district associations were keen to improve training programmes, introduce improved personnel-relations practices, and reorder managerial structures. Beyond that, some engineers and owners concluded that extensive structural and technical change was feasible as well as desirable, albeit only on the basis of an unprecedented collective and even minatory effort within the industry.[3]

Yet these movements had relatively little industry-wide effect, and

[1] POWE 35/246.
[2] See, for example, the reports by representatives of Doncaster Amalgamated Collieries, and the detailed arguments and proposals for 'a very ambitious, but entirely necessary, scheme of reorganisation' in 'Technical Reorganisation of Doncaster Amalgamated Collieries, Ltd., February 1945 (Revised to May 1945)', in Sheffield City Archives, NCB 1189 and 1411A. Also the reports on American mining to BA Collieries Company, in 1944-5 in Nottinghamshire Record Office: NCB 2/4-5.
[3] Below, 615-24. For training, see MSWCOA 1018, draft report (13 Apr. 1944); SDCOA, 4 June and 14 Dec. 1942, 22 Mar. 1943; WYCOA, 22 Mar. 1945; DCOA, 25 Nov. 1943.

even outstandingly successful colliery undertakings could be severely handicapped by wartime circumstances. The Ashington Coal Company, for example, for long a progressive and exceptionally profitable undertaking, whose training, safety, and health programmes were much respected by the miners and their union, ran into severe difficulties from 1941. These were attributable in part to the higher costs of its more elaborate treatment of its output (which could not be recouped by differential pricing), but principally to the fact that the Company was singled out by the district work-force who pursued a 'go-slow' on tactical grounds, on the assumption that if they could secure improved wages and conditions from Ashington—an industry leader—'it would be relatively easy to bring the other companies into line'.

The company resisted the claims, but the resulting labour troubles, together with the Ministry of Fuel and Power's direction to 'restore the output on a "regardless of cost" basis', greatly handicapped its operations and results in the last years of the War. In the late 1930s Ashington Coal had been earning about 2s. 9d. per ton, or twice as much as the North-East average; by 1941–5 its credit balances were well below the district's, standing at 9d. per ton in 1942–3 and 3d. per ton in 1944–5. The collapse of its profits meant that from September 1944 the Company suffered the humiliation of qualifying for grants under the War Emergency Assistance Scheme because its credit balances fell so far below a district standard which it had been primarily responsible for setting through the profitabilty of its prewar operations. (In spite of all this, the Ashington Company continued to develop its mining methods during the War and in 1944 decided on an extensive reconstruction and reorganization, to be financed entirely from corporate reserves.)[1]

Ashington was, perhaps, an extreme example. But it demonstrates the complexity of the forces shaping the industry's performance in these years. And the fact remains that even in the absence of such handicaps, the response of most colliery undertakings to the circumstances of the early 1940s was hardly encouraging. Nor was this any more surprising than their behaviour in the 1930s. The costs of individual initiative and change remained very high, the obstacles to collective change very great. The uncertainties of the future were hardly reduced by the War, and (as will be seen in the next chapter) even the indisputable threats of enforced reorganization in 1944–5 failed to muster a sufficiently determined cooperative action to fend off political criticism, or political action. In the last resort, institutional arrangements (the industry's

[1] COAL 37/94.

structures, the wartime system of finance, the inherited pattern of defensive controls, the politicized context of its operations) provided no 'rational' incentive to any more vigorous action and business change.

Yet if the constituent elements of the industry came through the War with little concrete indication of a readiness to change, the wartime experience was redolent with indications of new horizons and more radical thinking inside as well as outside the ranks of owners and managers. The experience of the 1930s had suggested, and that of the early 1940s reinforced, the argument that collective action was desirable, but probably unobtainable on a voluntary basis. Problems of adjusting supply and demand, of providing adequate investment funds, of concentrating output, and of reorganizing the industry and reinvigorating its technology—all necessitated cooperative action and, in the view of increasing numbers of people, public intervention. Above all, the War led to a broader and deeper perception of the symbiotic relationship between the problems of labour relations in the industry and the need for its economic transformation. To a large extent this was as much a political as a commercial development. And since it was also an integral part of a much longer-run theme, it is perhaps best considered in a broader context. For, extreme and unusual as was the experience of the industry during the Second World War, it was, in essence, a reinforcement of trends which had been manifesting themselves with increasing insistence for a generation.

CHAPTER 13

The Roots of Social Control, 1916–1945

There was not much real opposition to our nationalisation policy. It was realised on all sides that the problem of the Coal Industry had been shockingly mishandled in the past and that if men were to be got to work in the pits a new start was necessary.

C. R. Attlee, *As It Happened* (1954), 165

In 1945, as the War in Europe drew to a close, it was becoming increasingly obvious that some form of systematic public direction of the coal industry was inevitable. Recent events and experiences precluded any other approach to the industry's problems. Yet this was the intensification of a long historical process. Ever since the First World War some form of collective or state action had been canvassed as a means of stabilizing the industry. A degree of stability, especially as regards marketing, appeared to have been reached by the late 1930s, but the industry's continuing weaknesses were humiliatingly exposed by the events of the Second World War. And it was the latter, therefore, which was the occasion of a renewed—and definitive—debate about the advantages and disadvantages of more stringent social control. In particular, the experience of War brought the issue of nationalization to the forefront of the debate, and provided a momentum towards public ownership which was perhaps only marginally increased by the victory of the Labour Party in the General Election of July 1945.

This chapter is concerned with the long-run as well as the proximate causes of nationalization in the 1940s. The first section discusses the nature of government authority. The second and third sections consider the orgins of public ownership in the experience of the interwar years, and the resulting changes in the official view of the industry—which was reinforced by the wartime experience. Finally, the various responses of interest groups within coalmining, and the inevitability of public ownership will be appraised.

i. The instruments of government

Until the 1940s or 1950s coalmining was perhaps the most important industry in Britain. It was also the industry which was most persistently in the forefront of public and political consciousness. Yet, as earlier chapters suggested, it was neither its social magnitude nor its economic significance which directly provided the basis for the national sensitivity to its affairs. To most of the non-mining population, and in the absence of some immediate crisis, coalminers might be as socially 'invisible' as they were physically out of sight within their own communities. The fact was that coalminers and coalowners shared with almost all other occupations and social groups the characteristic that the public or political perception of their existence was a function of their impact— through actual or threatened crisis, political pressure or economic scarcity, or the playing-out of some social drama—on the lives of others. Coal, however, was the most crisis-prone of all industries, and it was obviously for this reason that it loomed so large in the consciousness of the rest of British society, and elicited such persistent waves of government intervention.

Given the authority of Cabinets, that intervention was only very partially and indirectly mediated through the Houses of Parliament, although there were rare occasions (as with the formulation of Part II of the Coal Mines Bill of 1929–30) when the uncertain balance of parliamentary parties enabled blocs of MPs to exercise an unusually direct and positive role. More commonly, the balance of political forces *within* parliamentary parties (especially in an area as politically sensitive as coalmining) established constraints on government authority. In the summer of 1919, for example, the restlessness of the Conservative party (successfully stirred by the newly effective propaganda machinery of the coalowners) appears to have inhibited Lloyd George's Administration in its discussions of nationalization—even though it is extremely unlikely that the Cabinet, even if left to itself, would have pursued the course of public ownership. Similarly, pressure from backbench MPs postponed and enfeebled legislation in the mid-1930s as the government struggled to nationalize royalties and apply a more determined policy of compulsory amalgamation.[1]

In fact, of course, the Houses of Parliament were important less because of their collective political authority than because they provided an arena for the interest groups which loomed so large in

[1] Above, ch. 8, sect. iii.

public discussion of the industry's affairs. The backbench contribution to parliamentary debates on the coal industry was overwhelmingly dominated by spokesmen for the MFGB and the coalowners. (The royalty owners were principally represented in the House of Lords, but had fewer opportunities of making an impact on public debate.) The direct representation of the coalowners is difficult to estimate since there were no formal links corresponding to the MFGB's sponsorship of MPs. However, the number of Members of the Commons, let alone of the Lords, who had coalowning interests and were prepared to speak out was considerable.

The MFGB-sponsored MPs were easier to identify. In the Parliament of 1918–22, for example, they amounted to some 25 out of a Labour Party total of 57. And in 1924, when Labour formed its first minority Government, the MFGB sponsored 43 (or 22 per cent) of the Party's total of 191 members.[1] Such representatives (most of them former miners), introduced a formidable voice into the proceedings of the Commons. No other industry was as well represented or as capable of making a sustained impact on the parliamentary timetable and atmosphere. There were even occasions, particularly in 1919 but also later in the 1920s, when a Commons Debate took on the appearance of a negotiating session, with government and miners' representatives exchanging offers and counter-offers across the floor of the House.

This industrial 'presence' continued throughout the period of private ownership, so that debates during and immediately after the Second World War were also continuously dominated by sectional spokesmen within the Commons. Nevertheless, for much of the time the effective influence of the MPs who were also sponsored by the MFGB or had coalowning interests was, in the last resort, limited. In so far as parliamentary opinion was swayed by the arguments of the industry, the origins of that influence came from the great extra-parliamentary institutions: the miners' union or the owners' association.

Policy towards the coal industry was not, of course, determined in an ideological vacuum or on terms of absolute objectivity as between the interest groups involved. The miners frequently had good cause to complain that the power of the state was used to frustrate their ambitions and advocacies and that Cabinets, especially in the decade after the First World War, were prejudiced in favour of the owners' view of the economics of the industry. Indeed, for their part, the owners themselves

---

[1] Butler 1986, 55. After the débâcle of the 1931 election, the miners accounted for 26 out of Labour's 46 MPs.

tended to make the same assumptions—often with reason, but occasion-ally (and especially in the period immediately after the fall of the Labour Government in 1931) to their disappointment. Yet the miners' theory that their aims were frustrated because most governments were their ideological enemies was frequently misplaced. Rather, what worked to their disadvantage was that official opinion was rarely able to ignore the economic realities of the industry. In the circumstances of interwar society, it had to cover its costs, and that need had an inescapable implication for wages and the total demand for labour.

Prejudice against the miners undoubtedly existed, but it was greatly mitigated by the experience of the late 1920s and the 1930s, which also served to engender significant official resentment and hostility towards the owners. By the late 1930s and 1940s the owners had to deal with resentment, scepticism, and even hostility when making their case to governments. When a greater measure of state economic intervention became politically legitimate, politicians were no longer excessively inhibited by ideological preference or class bias in favour of the increas-ingly isolated coalowners.

In the circumstances of the interwar years, no government could act on ideological principle alone. Just as the potential scarcity of coal had become an overriding consideration during the First World War, so with stagnation and mass unemployment in the 1920s and 1930s, the need to stabilize the industry, explore ways of controlling capacity, 'disperse' the workless, and avoid the extremes of crisis eroded the ideo-logical principles which might otherwise have kept industry and government at arm's length.

An understanding of this process must take account of the fact that the official response to the problems of the coal industry was not simply a matter for politicians. The development of government regulation and oversight was inevitably associated with a departmental 'presence' and with the accretion of knowledge, influence, and power by civil servants, whose attitudes and experience were the principal determinants of the shape of policy.

The coalmining industry had been subject to bureaucratic scrutiny since the nineteenth century; but this had been primarily confined to the Home Office's oversight of safety legislation. Quite early in the First World War, however, the government was obliged to take a much more continuous interest in the production of and trade in coal, and this resulted in the creation of a Coal Mines Department, under a Coal Controller, in the Board of Trade. From February 1917, this Department carried proximate responsibility for the controls imposed on the industry and for the elaborate negotiations with owners and miners that were incidental to the state's responsibilities for exports, distribution, and finance.[1]

Admittedly, the Coal Control was only a transient institution. Yet when the War ended, and whatever the hopes of the owners or the predilections of politicians, there could be no return to the degree of *laissez-faire* which had existed in 1913. This was appreciated even after the controversies and struggles of 1919 had been resolved by an official rejection of public ownership or industrial regrouping, and quite apart from the temporary necessities of financial control. By 1919–20 the government, which was in any case dissatisfied with the 'unqualified limpets' of the temporary civil service, accepted that it would be necessary to establish a new and permanent department for the coal industry.[2]

In the event, the putative 'Ministry of Mines' was nowhere near as influential an instrument of government as some might have envisaged. The official aversion to any systematic intrusion of the state into industrial affairs was amply reinforced by the owners' determined and successful attempt to dilute the original proposal. The 'Ministry' was downgraded to a Department of the Board of Trade, and its political head was demoted in terms of status and salary. Yet for all these limitations, a core and focus for government intervention had been established, which survived renewed assaults from the coalowners.

From one viewpoint, the Secretary for Mines occupied an influential and potentially authoritative position—if only because his Department had unique access, within government, to information, expertise, and advice. Its advocacy was therefore more likely to be influenced by knowledge and experience rather than ideology or inclination.[3] On the other hand, when the pressure of events raised the need for governments to take a stand or devise a major policy, the Mines Secretary tended to defer to other, more senior, Ministers. Yet the Mines Department remained a natural focus of official activity, even if (as happened in 1926) more senior politicians than its chief took over the formulation of policy and the pursuit of action. More than this, by the 1930s the Mines

[1] Above, ch. 3.
[2] Geddes to Lloyd George, 28 Sept. 1919: Lloyd George Papers (HLRO), F/17/5/51; CAB 23/11/17 (7 May 1919).
[3] The organization of the Mines Department in 1932 is described in POWE 10/79. It consisted of four divisions: Trade and Establishment, Fuel Treatment and Finance, Health and Safety, and Production and Labour.

Department had become an *independent* source of policy initiatives and political pressures. Thus, Alfred Ernest Brown (who headed the Department between 1932 and 1935) was particularly active in pressing for a more 'forward' coal policy on the part of the National Government (especially in relation to marketing schemes under the 1930 Act), and his successor, Captain Harry F. C. Crookshank (1935–9), pursued not only the reform of the official selling schemes, but the nationalization of royalties and the drastic revision of the law concerning mergers with some vigour.[1]

In spite of these initiatives, however, the authority of the Department's personnel varied markedly in this period. The Secretary for Mines was overshadowed by the President of the Board of Trade and was not normally a person of any very great political weight. More than this, the Department's relatively low-key position meant that it rarely attracted administrative high-flyers. It occasionally came in for severe criticism on the grounds of inefficiency, as happened in 1925–6, when Churchill was particularly scathing about 'grossly defective' departmental estimates of the outcome of the subsidy arrangements.[2] And in 1942 a systematic review of its staff by a future Minister of Fuel and Power (Hugh Gaitskell) did not give the impression that it was well supplied with able administrators. The incoming President of the Board of Trade (Hugh Dalton) in assessing the abilities of a temporary civil servant in the Department commented that 'in the kingdom of the blind the one-eyed man is king, and so it is in the Mines Department'.[3]

In spite of the poor reputation of the Mines Department, it did produce a critically significant administrator—Sir Ernest Gowers—whose influence permeated most of the interwar discussions of the industry, and endured into an altogether more considerable role in the early 1940s.

---

[1] The following men held the post of Secretary for Mines between its creation in 1920 and its suppression in 1942 (when the Ministry of Fuel and Power took over the Department's responsibilities): W. C. Bridgeman (Aug. 1920 to Oct. 1921); G. R. Lane-Fox (Oct. 1921 to Jan. 1924); E. Shinwell (Jan. to Nov. 1924); G. R. Lane-Fox (Nov. 1924 to Jan. 1928); H. Douglas-King (Jan. 1928 to June 1929); E. Shinwell (June 1929 to Aug. 1931); I. Foot (Aug. 1931 to Oct. 1932); A. E. Brown (Oct. 1932 to June 1935); H. F. C. Crookshank (June 1935 to Apr. 1939); G. W. Lloyd (Apr. 1939 to May 1940); D. R. Grenfell (May 1940 to June 1942). At least three of these kept unpublished diaries (while Shinwell published memoirs and an autobiography). Bridgeman's is in the possession of Viscount Bridgeman of Leigh Manor, Minsterbury, Salop; Lane-Fox's is in the possession of George Lane Fox of Bramham Park, Wetherby; and Crookshank's is in the Bodleian Library at Oxford. For a discussion of the role of the Mines Department in the formulation of policy, see Kirby 1979.

[2] WSC V, 656–7.   [3] Dalton Papers 7/4; *Dalton Diary*, 40.

Gowers was Permanent Secretary at the Mines Department from 1920 to 1927, and was extensively relied on by Cabinet Ministers for advice and initiatives in the crisis discussions of 1925-6. After an interlude as Chairman of the Board of Inland Revenue, he was recalled as Chairman of the Coal Mines Reorganisation Commission in 1930, and throughout the 1930s his attempts to stimulate amalgamations dominated the industrial side of the government's policy. From that position he made cogent and innovative contributions to official discussion of legislation concerning marketing controls and royalty nationalization. In 1938 he became Chairman of the CMRC's successor, the Coal Commission, and during the War, when he assumed the post of Regional Commissioner for London, he continued to play a powerful role in the departmental discussion of coal policy.

Gowers was an interventionist by experience rather than by inclination. As early as 1927 he appreciated that the industry's excessive capacity would not be eliminated, nor its disorderly markets stabilized, without a measure of coordination and cooperation.[1] Thenceforth, he was a consistent advocate of 'orderly' control and reduction of output—a posture which occasioned the most painful frustration when, in the 1930s, the owners failed to cooperate in any way with the Coal Mines Reorganisation Commission. By the 1940s Gowers had lost all political as well as economic confidence in the coalowners, and became perhaps the most influential advocate of a public-corporation solution for the industry's problems. (Dalton described him as 'a most able man, with a clear brain, a sense of irony, and . . . a very low opinion, based on long experience, of most coal owners.')[2] His political pressure and advice were felt throughout the War, and his testimony was to play an important part in the consideration of public ownership and compensation in 1945-6.

The tendency to interventionism among the civil servants at the Mines Department was accentuated by the experience of the Second World War and the advent of temporary civil servants, such as John Fulton and Harold Wilson, who were even less inhibited than their colleagues in the career civil service. As a result, the Department in its new embodiment as a Ministry of Fuel and Power, became an influential source of knowledge and initiative in relation to industrial reform. The administrators' predilection for direct public control of the industry, their scathing scepticism about the owners' belated attempts at self-regulation in 1945, and their contributions to the determination of the

[1] Baldwin Papers, 17/15 (17 June 1927).   [2] *Dalton Diary*, 405.

form of public ownership and the discussion of compensation, emphasized their powerful role in the ultimate evolution of public policy towards coalmining.[1]

ii. The interwar experience: politics and economics[2]

Compared with the urgings of the industry's critics, the changes that occurred in coalmining in the generation after the outbreak of the Great War hardly amounted to a sweeping transformation. Permanent government control, nationalization, extensive regrouping of the units of production, the formation of an export cartel, joint management or at least continuous consultation—all such proposals were ignored or rejected as possible solutions for the industry's ills. And it was the resulting apparent structural immobility which (together with its presumed technical conservatism) shaped the interwar industry's unenviable reputation. Before considering the restricted scope of structural change, however, it is as well to emphasize that from another perspective (and particularly considering the relatively short space of time involved) the extent of the institutional change that *did* take place was considerable.

The most important area of change concerned the autonomy of individual entrepreneurs and the associated role of public or collective intervention in the determination of wages and the organization of marketing. In 1913 the industry had been decentralized and fragmented: small-scale units of production operating independently, an individualistic industry coordinated by the price mechanism and the competitive market. By 1939, however, although there had been relatively little change in industrial organization, those involved in coalmining had become accustomed to a quite different context for their economic activities.

The industry had been subject to a large measure of direct government control and unified financial manipulation for four years (1917–21) and a Mines Department had been in existence for almost 20 years. Mineral royalties were taken into public ownership in 1938 (although the Act did not take effect until 1942). Legislative obligation and administrative pressure had produced a national system for coordinating and unifying sales and prices, and the government was seriously

---

[1] Below, 613–15, 623, 657.
[2] For the detailed evolution of public policy towards the coal industry in the interwar decades, see above, ch. 4, 6, and 8.

contemplating a system of export subsidies. An official levy on production had been introduced and was being spent on improvements to community and pithead welfare services. For some years after 1926 labour recruitment had been officially restricted. A government commission charged with the encouragement and if necessary the enforcement of industrial mergers, had been in existence for a decade, and although ineffectual for most of that time, it had helped the climate of public and official opinion and in 1938 had been reformed and strengthened. Government subsidies had been used, however grudgingly, to temper the blasts of industrial crises in the years after the First World War. The coalmining districts had figured most prominently in the embryonic evolution of a labour and regional policy for the 'distressed areas'. Above all, few people any longer questioned that the coalmining industry in general, and its labour relations and labour force in particular, were legitimate objects of continuing public concern.

Judged by any realistic criteria, all this had taken place fairly quickly. In terms of the relationship between the state and industry, and of the associated reform of industrial structures and market systems, the coalmining industry was a notable example of the possibility of new economic arrangements that were so extensively, if often vaguely, discussed in the 1930s. '[N]o other industry', reflected a wartime civil servant in 1943, 'had so nearly brought a revolution in the structure of industry as a whole as the coalmining industry did in the period between the two wars.'[1] Admittedly, from the viewpoint of a modern mixed economy little progress had been made. But the troubled history of coalmining, and the reactions of the state to it, had by 1939 at least pushed it some way down the road to new forms of social awareness and control, and in large areas of activity had replaced individualistic and competitive forces with collective decision-making *within* the industry.

In 1937, considering the economy as a whole, a student of the 'new pattern of industrial organization' argued that the 'growing confidence in the merits of concerted action among producers' derived from 'spontaneous' developments rather than government circumscription.[2] But the distinction is somewhat artificial: the scope for minorities to disrupt or undercut 'controlled' markets or agreed prices meant that businessmen were rarely able to enforce collective agreements without government help; and government attempts at industrial reform were always dependent on business cooperation for their success. As a result,

[1] J. S. Fulton, 'Organisation of the Coal Mining Industry' (spring 1943), POWE 26/420.
[2] Lucas 1937, 1–2.

structural change in the staple industries was most often associated with legislative authority and the harnessing of state power. This was certainly the case with the reform of coal's marketing structures, just as the unwillingness of the owners to cooperate with the Coal Mines Reorganisation Commission completely frustrated that body's attempts to bring about amalgamations of production units.

Even so, it is important not to be misled by the phrase 'public policy', with its implications of coherence and purposefulness. For neither in the economy as a whole, nor even within a single industry, is it possible to trace any very striking firmness or continuity on the part of the state. Rather, government policy reflected *ad hoc* reactions to specific pressures and crises (or the threat of crises), imperfect compromises between conflicting interests, and piecemeal efforts to stabilize institutions and welfare. On the other hand, however, in so far as state action embodied a series of means to attain general ends, the potential consistency of those ends (the avoidance of economic breakdown, the maintenance of entrepreneurial morale, the diffusion rather than concentration of unemployment) introduced a potential if unwitting consistency into 'policy' itelf.

Consideration of that policy must start with the experience of the First World War, which offered a persuasive model to the advocates of central coordination and public control. They made intensive use of it in the debates about the coal industry's future structure in the spring and summer of 1919.[1] On the other hand, very few men of influence realistically envisaged that the principal economic characteristics of wartime intervention—the central control of financial arrangements, wage bargaining, marketing, transport, and prices, together with the pooling of proceeds so as to establish national wage levels—could endure beyond the extreme conditions that had given rise to them.

Whatever the future of the formal coal control, however, wartime experience and postwar dislocations meant that there was no real possibility of disengaging the government completely or permanently from the institutional arrangements and economics of the coal industry. Nor was the extent to which the postwar role of collective or state control departed from the 1913 model predetermined. In 1919, for example, the owners' association itself had briefly contemplated a radical restructuring of the industry's selling organization and labour relations; there was considerable public pressure (including pressure from the owners' own trade journal) for structural reform; and the

---

[1] Above, ch. 4, sect. ii–iv; Money 1920.

bargaining strength of the miners had obliged the government to contemplate (however half-heartedly) nationalization of the mines and (more seriously) the enforced restructuring of the industry and profit limitation. Nothing came of these moves, even though the social pressures of 1919 *had* led to government intervention to increase wages, reduce hours, establish a welfare fund, and promise the nationalization of royalties.

In fact, the government would never again be able to ignore, although it might neglect, the affairs of the industry. The creation of a Mines Department in 1920 was a formal recognition of the new situation, and its existence, together with the other legal and administrative consequences of the 1920–1 settlement, provided a base on which further government preoccupations and interventions were to be built. More than this, the Sankey Inquiry in 1919 and the attendant publicity had led to a widespread acceptance of the miners' argument that there should be a social element in the determination of their wages, which would take account not merely of the economics of the industry but of broad principles of decency, need, and merits. The creation of the Miners' Welfare Fund was a partial recognition of the argument. But its principal embodiment was in the discussion of money wages.

There were, of course, years between the Wars when the miners felt that the principle of a social wage was being viciously ignored, and there was to be intense controversy concerning its appropriate level. But the fact remains that even when the miners were defeated in the stoppage of 1921, the settlement ensured that wages should have overriding priority in the allocation of the industry's proceeds, while in all important wage negotiations (even those of 1926) public opinion and government influence were available to press for some 'decent' minimum for miners' earnings. By the late 1920s the inability (moral as much as economic and political) to cut wages further had become a determining feature of the industry, and it was the pressure to lower hours (in 1929–30) or to raise wages (in 1935–6) which led to the government imposition of marketing controls to increase unit profitability—even if that were at the expense of sales and employment.

In spite of all this, the initial result of the events of 1919–21 was a reduction in the immediate influence of the state on the structure of the coal industry. As far as the government was concerned, there appeared to be no validity in the arguments of 1919 (put forward by 'technocrats' such as Sir Richard Redmayne, as well as by more radical commentators) that there were important economic gains to be had from the creation of much larger collieries, and that some enforced industrial restructuring was acceptable. In the 1920s, in the face of the need to increase competitiveness, the government's residual policy was to disengage itself from any systematic industrial intervention. For a decade after the War, in coalmining as in other industries, the institutional world of 1913 was still envisaged as an attainable as well as worthwhile ideal.

Nevertheless, the postwar decade was not all of a piece. Doubts about the efficacy of market mechanisms, competition, and existing entrepreneurial resources in the coal industry were not new, but by the mid-1920s they were being expressed with a mounting urgency, and much more generally. They were part, too, of the larger discussion, then beginning, of industrial rationalization, and some of the same personnel were involved in both the general and the particular debate. The arguments in favour of intervention had received an extensive airing in front of the Samuel Commission (1925-6), which was established in a vain attempt to resolve the industrial-relations crisis which was associated with the slump. And the Commission's Report, although unambitious, was moderately firm in its sketch of a positive if still limited programme: the nationalization of royalties; legislation to encourage mergers where owners or potential owners needed coercive powers to secure the co-operation of a minority; cooperative selling agencies; the reform of labour relations; and the continuance (and strengthening) of a national wages agreement.

In 1926 the Baldwin government, more concerned with the immediate industrial-relations crisis, took only some of these proposals seriously. Above all, to the Prime Minister, determined 'to wean this great industry from the breast of the State', and persuaded that major structural reform might be a chimera, major intervention still seemed inadvisable.[1]

Yet the fact remains that, whatever its reservations about the possibility of fruitful relations between the state and the coal industry, the events of 1926 and after pushed the government further down the road away from *laissez-faire*. It had become a party to the dispute and to the negotiations which marked its sorry course. In the event, prejudice against the miners' principal demand (that there be no reduction in wages or increase in hours), the tortuous character of negotiations, and the principled bias in favour of the owners' view of competitive reality, meant that state intervention remained relatively limited: a reluctant participation in the wages settlement; legislation to increase the

[1] Above, 246.

maximum underground working shift to eight hours; an official inquiry (which came to nothing) into selling agencies; and a law which was designed to facilitate mergers where most existing owners were broadly agreed on their desirability, to raise funds for pithead baths by a new levy on output, and to restrict new recruits to the industry's labour force.[1]

Nevertheless, a start had been made and (of equal importance) the experience of the coal industry in 1925–6, and the anxious debate about its economics, had begun to influence much broader areas of public and political opinion. The Samuel Report in particular had persuaded many outsiders that there was still a good deal of scope for organizational change in the industry, and that its management and owners were lacking in enterprise. Reorganization—mergers enforced by varying degrees of government intervention—became a commonplace of public discussion of the industry.

By the late 1920s all this was being discussed with increased intensity because the wage cuts of 1926–7 did not provide a viable basis for business strategy. The reasons for this were relevant to larger themes in the history of coalmining.

First, even after wage reductions, British coal (especially in export markets) was not able to pay its way at anywhere near capacity output. Even drastically lower levels of pay were not commensurate with profitable sales given overall productivity and average prices. The owners acknowledged this in 1927–8. The need to cast around for alternative policies was reinforced by a second fact: the miners' success in popularizing the idea of a 'social wage'. They had successfully urged their case during and immediately after the Great War. And in spite of reverses as a result of their defeat in the stoppages of 1921 and 1926, they did ultimately succeed in establishing a widespread sense that there was a lower limit to what they might decently be paid. This mitigated the fall in earnings after their defeat in 1926, and was explicitly acknowledged by the owners the next year. Politics, culture, and compassion had combined to protect the pay of working miners against the more extreme pressures of the market—albeit at the possible cost of an increase in the number of unemployed.

The third reason for the relative stickiness of wages in coalmining was inherent in the second: the conflicts which accompanied attempts to reduce wages (or increase hours) in mining were more severe and prolonged than in any other industry. The consequent threats to social

---

[1] Above, 244–5.

and economic stability inevitably meant that the public interest became involved in coal disputes, and equally inevitably drew the government into attempts to resolve or even anticipate and deflect them. Quite apart from the wartime examples, the influence of government was exercised in 1919–21, 1925–6, 1929–30, and 1935–6.

Such a situation also had a collateral consequence, for in spite of a frequent official distaste for any government commitment to industrial intervention, once government had become involved in an industrial dispute it was almost impossible to avoid postulating some official view of the industry's affairs. Any attempt to resolve crises such as characterized the coalmining industry necessarily implied an involvement in measures to shape and perhaps reform the industry. Once again, market forces engendered institutional, political, and administrative responses.

By the late 1920s, when miners' wages could not be cut any further and the competitive position of British coal continued to deteriorate, it proved necessary to explore two divergent policies: market control (which might sustain proceeds) and industrial restructuring (which might lower costs). And it was widely appreciated that each of these would have to be supported by state intervention if it was to be adopted on any scale.

As far as market controls were concerned, the desperate plight of the industry in 1927–8 finally overcame the individualism of the industry's leaders. Even the export districts (historically the strongholds of competition) began to formulate schemes to regulate output and prices. After having decried the need for selling associations as recently as 1926, influential owners now adopted a defensive policy, designed to share existing demand and restrain price competition. Yet in spite of the fact that in each of the principal coalfields a large majority of owners agreed to participate in district marketing associations, the voluntary schemes could not endure in the face of inter-district competition and a minority of owners who took advantage of the resulting favourable environment for 'rogue' behaviour. Market control was only possible if all, or virtually all, collieries participated, and the only way of ensuring this was to make membership compulsory. Once again, therefore, the state was recruited on the side of collective decision-making—albeit the proximate reason for government compulsion (embodied in Part I of the Coal Mines Act of 1930) was the minority Labour Government's commitment to reducing hours of work underground with no diminution in pay, which necessitated some protection to the industry's proceeds.[1]

[1] Above, 332–5.

In the event, this aspect of the 1930 Coal Mines Act was found to have severe limitations, which were disconcertingly exposed by the severe depression which affected the coal industry in 1930–3. The original marketing controls did not achieve their objectives. There was excessive inter-district competition, and prices and stability were once more eroded. In the face of such developments there was no longer any pretence that market competition encouraged efficiency; rather, it seemed to bring the threat of industrial and social strife.[1] The conjoint threat of industrial collapse and a labour crisis was, as usual, a powerful stimulus to public intervention. This occurred in 1933–4; while later, in 1935–6, it was the need to fend off a national strike during a mild recovery, which once more brought governmental authority into play— this time to oblige the owners to accept fully coordinated and centralized marketing schemes, as a way of augmenting the industry's proceeds and thereby being able to pay higher wages.

By 1936, therefore, largely under the auspices of the state, coal sales had been placed under district committees and were regulated by quotas, rules against inter-district competition, and monopolistic selling agencies. This transformation of marketing and market structures reflected a newly urgent emphasis on social and industrial stability, and on helping the industry to pay more to those in work, rather than maximizing employment or encouraging productivity. It was defensive crisis-management, a welfare rather than a purely economic policy.

The coal industry's marketing schemes were perhaps the most dramatic example of industrial 'cartelization' in the 1930s. Yet they alleviated one of the industry's problems (chronic over-capacity and industrial demoralization) only at the expense of neglecting or compounding others. In particular, they did little to encourage productive efficiency, and probably inhibited it by protecting inefficient firms or by facilitating the maintenance of surplus capacity. Industrial reorganization—the second alternative to wage cuts—was not pursued. Why was this so? Why, given the intense public pressure in favour of restructuring, did it have such negligible results?

The answers to this question have already been implied in the analysis of interwar economic history.[2] Compared with the control of marketing, the reorganization of the productive side of the coalmining industry was an altogether more complex matter. Reorganization, or rationalization as it came to be known, meant overcoming a host of reluctant private interests; it was initially dependent on problematic theories

[1] Above, 338–41.   [2] Above, ch. 7, sect. iv–v; ch. 8, sect. iii.

about the existence of large, unattained economies of scale; and ultimately, since it implied making the best use of existing capacity, it would have led to the closing down of mines and colliery undertakings and the exacerbation of the problem of unemployment. As a result, it at first ran into ideological obstacles and then (in the 1930s) appeared to pose a choice between social welfare and economic efficiency. Contemporary governments found it impossible to choose the latter.

This is not to deny that the generality of industry's businessmen and managers lacked some of the drive and enterprise which might have cushioned decline and salvaged some of the output, employment, and profit which were lost in the interwar years. But it *is* to acknowledge that the industry's structure and the markets that it faced made it very difficult to transcend the restrictions imposed by circumstances on individual decision-making.[1] Doubts about the existence of abundant scale economies were certainly justified as far as economies of *production* were concerned: the basic unit of production was the mine, and while many well-informed men in the industry denied that larger mines were necessarily more productive than smaller ones, it was in any case clear that the merger of colliery firms would very rarely allow the merging and transformation of the actual pits involved. Further, against the frequently adduced argument that the industry was short of managerial resources (so that larger-scale colliery undertakings were needed in order to spread scarce skills over a large proportion of the industry's output) had to be set the potential disadvantages of managerial limits in the case of large, or rapidly growing, enterprises.[2] The more general issue was summarized by the *Iron and Coal Trades Review* in 1931: 'We do not think it has been proved ... that the largest mine has always the lowest cost. Still less is it proved that the costs of the low-cost mine, be it large or small, will be further reduced by combining it with a high-cost mine.'[3]

In any case, as has been seen, the debate about 'rationalization' took a new turn in the late 1920s and 1930s, when it had come to mean the concentration of production to *eliminate* capacity. Mergers and the growth of firms were now favoured as means of concentrating production in the most efficient units.

This pressure towards rationalization was a general response to shrinking markets for Britain's staple industries. But it involved peculiar

---

[1] Above, 401–4.
[2] For the managerial problems of large-scale and rapid growth, see Hannah 1974.
[3] 4 Dec. 1931, quoted in Lucas 1937, 96.

problems for coalmining. On the one hand, the industry was fragmented into an abnormally large number of units of production. Co-ordinated action to reduce capacity was therefore particularly difficult. On the other hand, the economics of coalmining—the nature of capital investment and the willingness of banks to continue to lend money to firms in difficulties in the hope of recouping earlier losses—meant that unsuccessful collieries could hang on with extraordinary tenacity, operating at an overall loss but covering, or nearly covering, prime costs. And this excess capacity made it almost impossible for potentially efficient firms to operate at the levels of output which would have realized the maximum benefit from their efficiency.

Herein lay the paradox of private and collective choice. It would have been in the interest of the majority of those in the industry if its capacity had been reduced by closing less efficient pits and enterprises. But it was in few firms' private interest to act *individually* to pursue this end. The cost of acquiring and then closing marginal collieries could well have exceeded the benefit (less competition, higher utilization of existing capacity) to the individual firm. This inability to 'capture' the benefits of individual action meant that restructuring could be brought about in only one of two ways. Either market forces would have to operate until individual firms were pushed into complete bankruptcy; or it would be necessary to find some form of collective device, to bring about a simultaneous reduction of potential output.

Institutional obstacles prevented the attainment of either route to rationalization. This was, perhaps, predictable in the case of the 'free market' solution of the industry's structural problems. The combination of the ability of marginal firms to survive and the protective effects of Part I of the 1930 Act (which guaranteed even the least efficient a modicum of sales through the quota system)[1] meant that competitive forces would only slowly and uncertainly be able to adjust capacity to demand.

Even more significantly, the absence of unanimity of attitude or determination of political purpose proved a crippling handicap to central direction or legal compulsion. And in spite of the creation of a Coal Mines Reorganisation Commission (by Part II of the Coal Mines Act of 1930), the official encouragement let alone enforcement of individual schemes of rationalization was never successfully achieved.[2]

[1] The legislation allowed colliery firms to purchase quotas, and thereby increase their utilization of capacity. Nevertheless, since a price was involved, such a move would be inhibited to the extent of the extra cost.

[2] For the unsuccessful pursuit of a merger policy, see above, ch. 8.

First, the great majority of the coalowners were hostile and unco-operative, fearing government intervention and being unpersuaded of the advantages of larger-scale enterprises. The resulting combination of influential political opposition and non-cooperation with the Reorganisation Commission (as well as with its successor, the Coal Commission) proved too much for the hesitant campaign of those who wished to reorganize the industry by sponsoring mergers. Second, ideological inhibitions outside the industry and the gross imperfections of the law made it impossible to enforce official merger schemes. Finally, the government found itself unable to accept the social costs of actually enforcing a policy of rationalization at a time of mass unemployment.[1]

Interwar governments were not noted for the vigour with which they sought policies to counter the scourge of worklessness; but they *were* sensitive to the dangers of adopting industrial policies which would certainly have deepened the miseries of the unemployed and created even more dereliction in the depressed areas on Britain's coalfields. This explained not merely the adherence to Part I of the 1930 legislation, but a good deal of the official inhibition about enforcing Part II. As long as there was a chronic surplus of coal and an over-large industry located in already depressed areas, the social costs of rationalization and structural change were considered too great to warrant a vigorous policy aimed at economic efficiency.

Yet, although public policy failed to alter the structure of production in coalmining between the Wars, the relationship between the industry and the state *was* changed by the repercussions of public policy on the organization of coal marketing and by the continuous assertion of the public interest in the industry's affairs. Moreover, by the mid-1930s, once the industry had begun to recover from the worst of the Depression, the official apprehension about the social costs of change began to abate somewhat. By then it was counterbalanced by the view that the industry's failure to reorganize itself was chronic, and that a strengthening of the 1930 legislation for mergers was essential. This policy was now associated with the nationalization of royalties which reformers had been advocating since at least 1919. And it was taken up (albeit hesitantly and with setbacks) by the Conservative Party and the National Government.[2] The Coal Act of 1938, which took three years to mature, did not remove all the formidable obstacles to compulsory amalgamations. But it represented a relationship between the industry

---

[1] Above, 341–58.   [2] Above, 349–54.

and the state, and reflected a public regard for the affairs of coalmining, which had been transformed in a mere two decades.

The interwar years had witnessed a diffuse disillusion with the efficacy of market forces and competition, especially in relation to the staple industries. As a result, governments were willing to contemplate, encourage, and even legislate for schemes designed to control output and prices, and reduce industrial capacity. In agriculture, iron and steel, cotton, and shipbuilding there was a new readiness to discuss 'self-regulation' backed by legislative authority. Frequently, but by no means invariably, powerful pressures and initiatives for such schemes came from within the relevant industry, where leading businessmen became disillusioned with the destabilizing effects of market competition. In fact, as already indicated, the combination of business eagerness and government willingness was an essential prerequisite for any action.

Industrial policy towards coalmining was characteristic of this general position. On the one hand, the pressure towards controlled marketing had no effective consequences until after influential sections of the industry had been belatedly persuaded of its possible advantages. On the other, the continued opposition of most leading coalowners to government-sponsored mergers precluded any enforcement of the legal provisions for reorganization. Nevertheless, the fact remains that the basis for a large measure of social control had been laid within a relatively short period. It remained for the urgent pressures of national crisis in the Second World War, accompanied by the transition from a superfluity to a possible chronic scarcity of coal, to bring about the last most drastic step.

iii. War, state, and public policy

Although wartime policy towards coal in the 1940s involved a system of partial control and government intervention, it stopped well short of fundamental changes in the essential structure and ownership of the industry.[1] The pragmatic and political inhibitions about radical change, even for the duration of the War, were publicly exemplified in the controversies about fuel rationing in 1942 and the nationalization of the industry in 1942 and 1943. Dual control, although embodying a far greater *potential* measure of state power than had hitherto been deployed, proved an inadequate basis for effective reorganization.

---

[1] See ch. 11 and 12.

Behind the scenes, too, there were occasions on which potentially radical departures were restrained for fear of their consequences for political harmony or practical cooperation.[1] In some respects, then, there was a deadweight of caution which prevented a fundamental realignment in the political economy of coal even under the pressure of war. In fact, however, the *official* response to the possibilities of organizational change in coalmining is a seriously misleading indication of shifts in wartime opinion. For the War, through its definitive exposure of the problems of productivity and of the role of labour attitudes within them, was a watershed in the history of the structure and social control of coalmining.

That this was the case as far as the miners' union and the Labour Party were concerned was hardly surprising. Both groupings had been committed to the public ownership of coal for many years. The War merely provided a dramatic opportunity to present their well-rehearsed arguments. Indeed, those arguments were now amply reinforced by the industry's poor wartime performance and the incessantly repeated reluctance of the miners to commit themselves to all-out effort as long as the fruits of industrial success were likely to go to the private owners.

The miners were, of course, the most consistent advocates of public ownership. More significantly, however, the Labour movement, and especially the TUC and the Labour Party, began to formulate a much more specific and detailed case in favour of coal nationalization than had been put before 1939. Hence, to the urging of the National Council of Labour (itself much influenced by the MFGB) and the political arguments in favour of requisition in the winter of 1941–2, there was added the official voice of the Labour Party and various committees—notably its Coal and Power Sub-Committee (one of 13 on postwar reconstruction) which met between October 1941 and March 1944 and recommended a 'unified industry under public ownership and control', broadly directed by a public corporation.[2]

This much was predictable, but it was not only among the already converted that belief in some more drastic experiment in social control was associated with wartime conditions. In 1942–5 Cabinet Ministers, civil servants, some owners, and an influential group of mining engineers and managers were all obliged to consider the need for wider

[1] Above, 499; below, 621.
[2] Labour Party Archives, RDR 157 and 255. Also see *Coal and Power. Report by the National Executive Committee of the Labour Party to be presented to the Annual Conference to be held in London from May 29th to June 2nd 1944* (1944).

structural innovation. The bases of this new outlook were the problems of productivity exposed by the War, and (perhaps even more emphatically) the realization that the obstacles to reorganization inherent in the miners' attitudes towards the owners could not be overcome within the traditional structural forms of the industry. Indeed, these three issues—structure, efficiency, industrial relations—were clearly intimately related. The point was put succinctly by Sir Ernest Gowers in an address to the Mining Association of Great Britain in January 1944. The industry, he argued, needed bigger, stronger, and more efficient colliery firms, and 'prompt, bold and comprehensive reforms'; until its structure was changed, nothing useful could be attained: 'In particular, there can be no security for labour without that change, and so long as this problem remains unsolved coal will remain in the forefront of politics.'[1]

The history of wartime control provides numerous examples of political or pragmatic argument in favour of direct public control—and not merely by Socialist Ministers such as Hugh Dalton at the Board of Trade. As we have seen, the Liberal Minister of Fuel and Power, Lloyd George, was also persuaded by the drawbacks of dual control and the insistence of the miners that they did not wish to work for the profit of colliery companies, to propose the requisition of coalmining, even though he failed to carry the War Cabinet with him.[2] And the frequently repeated (and accepted) assertion that long-run security and reassurance were necessary prerequisites of the miners' cooperation in the war effort, was the stock-in-trade of government discussion and policy. In fact, by 1944 an important group of junior Conservatives had accepted the case for the compulsory formation of larger industrial groupings within coalmining, for a much enlarged role for the state, and for the institutionalization of improvements in miners' circumstances and their direct participation in the industry's administration.[3]

Even more than among politicians radical questions relating to reorganization and public ownership were canvassed among civil servants. Indeed, *their* experience may be seen as a vital element in the growing acceptability of the idea of public ownership in the early 1940s. At the same time, however, the significant feature of their deliberations (as of the subsequent investigations of the industry by mining engineers)

[1] COAL 17/179 (13 Jan. 1944).
[2] See *Dalton Diary*, 379 ff.
[3] Hogg, Lancaster, and Thorneycroft 1944. Also see Thorneycroft in *Hansard* 13 July 1944, 1957–9.

was the fact that they transcended the simple questions of direct government intervention which had been posed by the threat of immediate crisis. Instead, discussions of control were derived from more searching consideration of the history of the industry's structure and productivity, of its technical needs on the one hand, and the attitudes of its labour force on the other.

The focus of much of this discussion was Sir Ernest Gowers, whose prewar experiences had proved sufficiently exasperating for him to harbour the most damning opinions concerning the conservatism and deviousness of the owners, and to conclude that only public intervention could produce the necessary industrial reforms.[1] Frustrated by the outbreak of War in his attempt to test the 1938 legislation, Gowers found much of his energy absorbed in his job as Regional Commissioner for London. Nevertheless, he was still Chairman of the Coal Commission, which continued to discuss industrial matters during the War and was, in any case, responsible for the administration of mineral royalties, which had been taken into government ownership from July 1942.

It was from this position that in 1941 he argued in favour of preparatory work which would enable the Commission, when the right time came, to press for schemes of reorganization 'before comfortable people have time to sit back with the idea that they can just go on in the old ways'. (The 'right wing' of the owners, he claimed, were already arming themselves for 'the tactics of obstruction that have served the die-hards so well in the past'.) Precluded from pursuing this course of action by political directive, Gowers nevertheless continued to argue that much larger-scale units were essential in the industry. In a memorandum of January 1942 he insisted that reorganization would ultimately have to be *forced* on the owners, and that the need to use legal compulsion to create giant enterprises meant that the industry would have to be the responsibility of a public corporation.[2]

Gowers, of course, was not alone in these views. Wartime problems created influential allies in the Mines Deartment—notably Lord Hyndley (who was to become Permanent Secretary of the Department and subsequently Controller-General at the Ministry), who advocated that the industry should ultimately be run 'on Public Corporation lines'. Two relatively junior, but still influential, wartime officials (John Fulton and Harold Wilson) also advocated eventual nationalization.[3]

[1] Above, 597 and *Dalton Diary*, 405.
[2] POWE 22/127; 'The Coal Industry after the War' (16 Jan. 1942): POWE 26/429.

[*See opposite page for n. 3*]

As subsequent events showed, there was in fact no realistic prospect of public ownership during the War. However, the reforming instincts uncovered by Dalton in the Mines Department in March 1942, found much greater scope for advocacy in the autumn and winter of 1942–3, with the creation of a secret departmental committee to consider the postwar organization of the coal industry. The committee was the product of the circumstances which had created the Ministry of Fuel and Power (it was proposed in July by the Ministry's Permanent Secretary F. N. Tribe, although the political sensitivity of the issue was such that its existence was kept secret from much of the rest of Whitehall). The committee was chaired by Gowers and its membership included Hyndley, Fulton, the Secretary of the Coal Commission (C. S. Hurst), and two businessmen. In later stages Harold Wilson participated in its discussions. It reported in June 1943.[1]

Gowers and his fellow civil servants argued that the industry should be reorganized into district amalgamations run by public-service corporations, coordinated, financially and commercially, by a national coal corporation. At the root of their argument lay the belief (largely founded on prewar experience) that the owners were incapable of reforming the industry, or of responsible behaviour if the industry were compulsorily reformed yet remained in private hands. The economies of scale in coalmining, they felt, necessitated integrated management and unified finances; but such amalgamations could not be imposed on reluctant owners without an extensive departure from private enterprise—a return to which was, in any case, politically unthinkable. More than this, postwar public control was also necessary because of 'the fundamental importance of labour in the industry, and the need to win its cooperation' and sustain its wages.

The Committee's Final Report was hardly as straightforward as this summary implies, since the businessmen-members were reluctant to commit themselves unconditionally to public ownership. A degree of stalemate resulted. Although the Report got as far as recommending large-scale, financially unified amalgamations in each district, and sketching the public corporations which might bring that about, it left open the question of whether the owners should be allowed a period of

[3] *Dalton Diary*, 405 (27 Mar. 1942); Gaitskell to Dalton, Dalton Papers, 7/4/4. Hyndley became Chairman of the National Coal Board after the War.

[1] The committee's papers are in POWE 26/420 and its Final Report in POWE 26/429. The committee's businessmen-members were John Morison (a chartered accountant) and W. H. Coates (from ICI).

grace within which they might form 'voluntary' amalgamations and so fend off public ownership. Even more feebly, the Report exposed a further division of opinion: as to whether, even if the 'last chance' option were permitted, there should be some form of government regulation of dividend policy, board membership, capitalization, and finances to prevent abuse of the resulting monopolistic enterprises or ensure unified financial development.

The outcome was hardly a decisive document. Beneath the hesitant tones, however, firm views and prejudices were to be heard. Above all, it was clear that the officials had lost confidence in private enterprise in the industry. Their description of the possible dangers of uncontrolled private amalgamations was a significant commentary on their ill opinion of the owners' behaviour over the previous two decades:

There is a risk that in times of under-capacity the amalgamated undertakings might make common cause with one another and with the miners to form a monopolistic ring with the object of exploiting the consumer. There is a risk that in times of over-capacity they might indulge in fierce and destructive competition at the expense of depressed wages and conditions for the miners instead of concentrating on increased efficiency of organization and mining techniques. There is a risk that, obsessed by the fear that further movement towards public control was inevitable, they would tend to concentrate on quick profits to the detriment of long-term planning and development. . . . There is a risk that all these dangers would be accentuated by a swollen board of directors drawn from the boards of the constituent companies, all tending to think in terms of their former divergent allegiances, and not well placed to combat parochial thinking on the part of the company's servants.[1]

[1] Gowers's influence is very marked in this passage. He had for some time been critical of the owners on such grounds as these. In Jan. 1942, for example, he had written a memorandum on 'The Coal Industry after the War' (POWE 26/420 (16 Jan. 1942)) which contained a passage already quoted, but which is worth reproducing at length: 'We can see now that the war of 1914/18 marked the end of an epoch. . . . The industry took a long time to realise the implications of this change, to recognise that laissez-faire is only tolerable in an epoch of expansion, and that when such an epoch comes to an end salvation can only be found in changing over from competition to cooperation. The miners were the first to see the truth. In the upheaval of 1925/26 they were essentially in the right, although they committed every sort of tactical mistake. Their contention was that the colliery owners would never face up to reorganisation except under the grim compulsion of immediately impending disaster, that if they were allowed to remove that spectre by the easy-going method of a reduction in wages they would forget all about reorganisation, that in their insensate competition they would reduce prices by an amount at least equivalent to the reduction in wages cost, so that the only result would be that the men would be worse off without the employers being any better off. This is exactly what did happen after the miners were beaten. . . . [Even after the owners accepted cooperation in selling in the 1930s] they still jibbed at recognising that this was not enough; it would have to be supplemented by some measure of cooperation on the productive side, more scientific than the quota system of restricting output all

Attitudes such as these had, of course, begun to take shape in the Mines Department and the Coal Commission during the 1930s. But it was the combination of the day-to-day anxieties of war and the contemplation of the discontinuities that it brought, which definitively confirmed the culture of reform, intervention, and control in the civil service. By 1944–5, the leading civil servants associated with the Ministry of Fuel and Power appeared to have set their faces firmly against any last-minute compromise on the subject of public intervention.[1]

iv. Industrial attitudes and structural change

Changes in the political and bureaucratic view of the coal industry were obviously important elements in the evolution of policy. The fact remains, however, that during the last years of the War the barriers to fundamental structural change were also lowered by developments *within* the industry. In part, the influences at work were the same as those which had shaped most radical policy proposals since the early years of the First World War: the industry's unenviable labour relationships and the degree to which the miners were prepared to cooperate with particular patterns of industrial organization. By 1944–5, however, a new element was present—the readier acceptance on the part of managers and (to a lesser but far from insignificant extent) owners of the need for extensive industrial reform.

The critical transition of opinion was undoubtedly effected by the deliberations and Report of the Technical Advisory (or Reid) Committee. In September 1944, while preparing to consult owners and miners about the potentially disastrous decline in production, the Minister decided to take a longer and less politically charged view, by appointing an expert departmental committee. The Reid Committee (it took its popular name from its Chairman, C. C. (later Sir Charles) Reid, who had been General Manager of the Fife Coal Company and was then Production Director at the Ministry) had precise yet broad terms of reference: 'To examine the present technique of coal production from coal-face to wagon, and to advise what technical changes are necessary in order to bring the Industry to a state of full technical efficiency.' Unlike all other

round, which was all they would then tolerate. . . . they laid themselves open to the charge of neglecting the troublesome expedient of reducing costs by all possible means, and relying merely on the easy expedient of fleecing the consumer.

[1] Below, 623.

departmental committees of inquiry into the efficiency and business of coalmining, the Reid Committee was exclusively technical in composition as well as objective: all its members were drawn from among mining engineers with senior managerial experience.[1]

The Reid Committee worked intensively through the winter of 1944–5 and reported in March. Its Report had an enormous influence,[2] which was clearly based not only on its timeliness but on the combination of its expert membership, the thoroughness of its appraisal, the decisiveness of its recommendations, and the fact that in spite of the standing of its members within the industry, their technical criticism of mining practice was sweeping and their judgement on private ownership adverse. The bulk of the Report was devoted to a detailed appraisal of individual techniques (mining systems, cutting, loading, conveying, ventilation, surface work, etc.). But its most influential passages derived from the Committee's damning assessment of the industry's organization and technology by comparison with its international rivals.

According to the Committee, the industry's relative backwardness was general, but was at its most extreme at the level of underground transport (of men as well as coal) where antiquated methods and the handicap of inconvenient layouts had crippling effects on labour productivity. The overall problems of the British industry were attributed to various causes: a shortage of investment funds (in part caused by uncertainty about the industry's future); private ownership of the mineral, leading to a proliferation of small and inefficient mines exploiting badly shaped leases; excessively dispersed ownership of the collieries, handicapping concentration and closures; poor underground layout (in particular, undulating and circuitous roadways) and inefficient haulage systems; inadequate training; neglect of grading and classification of coal before marketing; conservatism and short-sighted policies on the part of the owners; a lack of independence and an excessive traditionalism on the part of mining engineers; and an absence of effective cooperation between miners and employers, and particularly an opposition by the work-force to mechanization.

---

[1] The members and their company connections were: Reid (Fife Coal), H. J. Crofts (Chatterley–Whitfield Collieries), D. A. Hann (Powell Duffryn), J. Hunter (Doncaster Amalgamated Collieries), A. Kirkup (Lambton, Hetton, and Joicey Collieries), J. A. Nimmo (United Steel), and H. Watson Smith (Hardwick Colliery). In all but two cases they held or had held the senior managerial post in the relevant company. Reid, Crofts, and Nimmo were currently employed by the Ministry. The Committee's Report is: *Ministry of Fuel and Power. Coal Mining. Report of the Technical Advisory Committee* (Cmd. 6610. 1945). Its papers are in POWE 22/179.

[2] Below, 618–19.

In its concluding sections the Reid Report took up those issues relating to the labour force, the nation's coal resources, and overall structure and planning, which were implicit in any realistic assessment of the industry's technical needs. And it was in these respects that the Committee had its most resounding public and political effects. This was less because of any very specific recommendations than because of the inescapable implications of what it had to say: the problems of the industry could only be approached on a national and planned basis; technical improvement presupposed a degree of official intervention and a very extensive programme of reorganization and investment which was very unlikely to proceed from the existing pattern of ownership in the industry. In the end, the Reid Report helped persuade even those who considered the conventional advocacy of nationalization a mere dogma, that the practicalities of the situation necessitated state intervention. In *The Economist*'s words

if it can be proved that some form of public ownership is *technically* necessary for efficient production, then the opposition to it, in this pragmatic land, will melt away. And the proof is now very nearly complete. It might conceivably be possible, though only with great difficulty, to bring about the necessary amalgamations by private negotiation; but the provision of the additional capital is a task for the State alone.[1]

As with virtually all wartime commentators on the coal industry, the Reid Committee was aware of the extent to which technical progress and industrial efficiency depended on reasonably harmonious labour relations. Consequently, it made proposals for better training, high wages, and machinery to settle grievances, security of employment, and improved health and safety—all 'balanced' by the miners' presumed duty to give a full and fair day's work, accept proper discipline, abandon lightning strikes and antiquated customs, etc. It was perhaps a bland set of prescriptions, but it drew attention to a central problem, and one which was more responsible than any other for the breadth of public pressure for changes in the industry's structure.

But it was in the final substantive chapter on 'Planning for Production' that the Committee invaded the most sensitive areas of discourse. There, its detailed recommendations presupposed policies so far neglected by the majority of the industry.[2] 'The thorough reorganisation

[1] 7 Apr. 1945, 436.
[2] e.g. the Committee advocated bigger mines, the driving of roadways through strata rather than seams, double-shift working, the employment of full-time planning staff, and a uniform work pattern of eight-hour shifts and five-day weeks.

of the Industry', it argued, 'requires the examination of the problems on a coalfield basis rather than mine by mine.' Clearly, the 'reconstruction' of which it spoke was not to be confined to matters technical. And at the end of its Report, the Committee appended three pages on 'The Conditions of Success' and made its most telling point:

it is not enough simply to recommend technical changes which we believe to be fully practicable, when it is evident to us, as mining engineers, that they cannot be satisfactorily carried through by the Industry organised as it is to-day.

Because developments in one mine had inevitable consequences for others, because of the different stage of development and potential of different mines, because of the technical advantages of overriding the distinctions between different units of colliery ownership, because of the shortage of good mining engineers—nothing less than the reconstruction of the industry would suffice:

it is evident to us that it is not possible to provide for the soundest and most efficient development and working of an area unless the conflicting interests of the individual colliery companies working the area are merged together into one compact and unified command of manageable size, with full responsibility, financially and otherwise, for the development of the area.

The Reid Committee members were not prepared to stipulate the best size or sizes of the resulting units of production, but they were confident 'that geological, geographic and technical considerations should be the determining factors', and that a national Authority would be needed to ensure that the industry was reorganized into optimum units, and that the resulting units devised and executed long-run plans for development. In a sentence which, in effect, sounded the death-knell of the traditional pattern of ownership and control in the British coal-mining industry, these representatives of the leading managerial personnel in some of the leading collieries in the country rounded off their argument: 'The existence of such an Authority, endowed by Parliament with really effective powers for these purposes, is, we are satisfied, a cardinal necessity.'

The public reception of the Reid Report was almost universally favourable and its argument almost universally persuasive. Even within the industry the basic criticisms of the Report were more or less accepted as points to be taken very seriously (the *Colliery Guardian* acknowledged that it was 'one of the most important of the numerous documents relating to the British mining industry that have been issued in our time').[1] And the non-specialist response was emphatic. 'At last', wrote *The Economist*, 'there is a real report on coal', and referred to its 'full and penetrating diagnosis'. *The Times* described it as 'a document as challenging as any that has been issued on any subject throughout the war'. The *Manchester Guardian* accepted it as a definitive indication that 'The industry has to undergo a revolution in its ideas and practice— owners and engineers as well as men'. And even the Communist MP Willie Gallacher spoke of it as 'one of the most valuable reports on the mining industry we have ever had'.[2]

v. Industrial debates

The signatories of the Reid Report were not men who, by inclination or experience, would normally have favoured a large degree of government intervention in industrial affairs, let alone outright nationalization of their industry. Their radicalism was therefore the more remarkable and the more indicative of the unusual ground swell of opinion brought about by the War. In fact, the self-scrutiny implied in the Reid Committee's official deliberations was the hard edge of a debate about the industry's postwar structure which had been in progress among the coalowners for almost a year *before* the Reid Committee met.

The origins of that debate lay in the controversy about wartime control which had surfaced in the autumn of 1943,[3] when the apparent shift of public opinion obliged the Mining Association of Great Britain to consider the situation with some seriousness. Spurred by Sir Ernest Gowers (who warned the owners that unless they took a 'middle course ... the only alternative to the existing structure of the industry is nation-alization'), the MAGB's War Committee decided that the owners had to formulate a 'constructive policy' for the postwar industry.[4] In December

[1] *CG* 6 Apr. 1945, 429. Also see *ICTR* 6 Apr. 1945, 523, which accepted that the Report was 'a document that must receive the close consideration of all in authority in the industry'.

[2] *The Economist* 7 Apr. 1945, 435; *The Times* 29 Mar. 1945, 5c; *Manchester Guardian* 2 Apr. 1945, 4; *Hansard* 29 May 1945, col. 123. The *New Statesman and Nation* (7 Apr. 1945, 219–20) argued that the members of the Reid Committee were really very sceptical of private ownership's ability to carry through the necessary reconstruction, that 'in the last resort ... public ownership is the only solution', and that the miners' suspicions of private monopoly and their fear of redundancy meant that 'There would be no prospect at all of getting cooperation on such terms, and without the mineworkers' cooperation, no plan of reorganisation, however technically perfect, can ever be made to work.'

[3] Above, 553–6.

[4] The deliberations of the MAGB and the constituent district associations are recorded in the

1943, therefore, the district associations were asked to report on the best means of reducing the number of producing units in their areas; and in February 1944, persuaded that the industry had to pose an alternative to a 'public-utility solution', the central authority of the MAGB agreed on a policy of self-reform.

On the one hand, it was decided to strengthen the Association's organization—a reform which was very similar to the restructuring which had been such an effective basis for the defence against nationalization in 1919–20.[1] To this end, the Presidency was made a fixed-term post (Sir Evan Williams had been President since 1919) and a full-time Chairman was to be appointed from among 'eminent commercial men' outside the industry, with administrative and political experience. On the other hand, the district associations were formally asked to devise local schemes to obtain 'the supposed benefits of unification', and to ensure that whatever the exact form of any such scheme it should 'provide a means for reducing the number of units'.

The local discussions which followed these requests were prolonged, confused, and occasionally resentful (the Chairman of the Durham Coal Owners' Association had to deny, more than once, that there was a 'bogy man' at work in the shape of Gowers).[2] While there was a fairly widespread acknowledgement of the technical–economic need for some mergers, it was clear that the owners generally were suspicious of any scheme or general principle (even a 'voluntary' one) which might interfere with the independent decision-making powers of colliery companies. At the same time, however, it was almost universally accepted that the political climate now necessitated a more positive response to the concept of amalgamations than had characterized the industry in the 1930s. The coalmining industry, it was increasingly felt,

should have it own positive policy defined and that parliamentary support for the maintenance of private enterprise should be provided with a constructive policy in opposing the proposals of advocates of State or semi-State organization of the industry.

entries for 1943–5 in DCOA (which is the best source for 1943–4); COAL 11/106; SDCOA; LCOA; LCMA; and MSWCOA. These report Gowers's remarks, which are also reproduced in COAL 17/179 (13 Jan. 1944).

[1] Above, ch. 4, sect. v.

[2] One Durham owner 'believed Sir Ernest Gowers was trying to panic the Mining Association so as to justify his existence'. (DCOA, 29 Feb. 1944.) All this also coincided with Gowers's attempt to reactivate the Coal Commission's pursuit of mergers—which was subsequently vetoed by the Minister of Fuel and Power: below, 621. The Scottish reaction in spring 1944 is summarized in LCMA UGD/59/1/20 (7 Mar. 1944).

The political motives in all this were perfectly apparent, and at owners' meetings throughout the country it was urgently argued that the industry was 'being driven to amalgamations to avoid something worse'.[1]

On the whole, however, because of the lack of unanimity, both the district responses and the MAGB's 'proposals' were too vague to be politically useful. This was pointed out in the spring of 1944 when a number of younger members from the Midlands districts, who (in their own words) 'would have the burden of trying to run the industry in future years', presented a 'Charter for Coal' to their colleagues. They proposed that the industry be reduced to between 40 and 50 undertakings, each producing about 5 million tons annually; that the reorganization take place within two or three years, under threat of compulsion by the Coal Commission; and that there be a guaranteed weekly wage and steady employment as well as other improvements in working conditions and industrial relations.[2]

In spite of the growing threat of distasteful alternatives, nothing came of these initiatives. And, possibly in a reaction against the lack of results, in July the Coal Commission reactivated its concern with mergers and pressed the district associations of owners to specify their plans, if any. It received imprecise or prevaricating answers and by November the Minister once more obliged the Commission to suspend its activities.[3] Nevertheless, the owners must have been persuaded of the impossibility of the industry being returned to them with its prewar structures intact. ('No Government', they had been warned by Gowers, 'could face another 1921.')[4] As the MAGB's newly appointed publicity officer pointed out, the owners would have to formulate a concrete plan: 'Something done was of far greater value for propaganda than something hoped for or promised and if the Owners were to be "forward looking" they also had to be "forward going".'[5] It was, after all, for this reason that the MAGB had decided to recruit a full-time Chairman from

[1] LCOA, 21 Jan., 28 Feb., 11 July 1944. Cf. DCOA, 24 Feb. 1944; LCMA UGD/59/1/20 (7 Mar. 1944).

[2] Documents and discussion noted in DCOA, 6 Apr. 1944. These events had been partly foreshadowed in an article in *The Times* on 29 Jan. (p. 5c), which argued that the 'forward-looking and enterprising mineowners' would have to assume the leadership if the whole body of owners could not act.

[3] SDCOA, 26 June 1944; LCOA, 11 July 1944; COAL 11/106 (12 Oct. 1944); COAL 17/179 (25 Jan. 1944–12 Mar. 1945); *The Economist* 8 July 1944, 59, and 25 Nov. 1944, 712.

[4] COAL 17/179 (13 Jan. 1944). In the Commons, Peter Thorneycroft warned the owners that this might be their last chance to put their own house in order: *Hansard* 13 July 1944, col. 196.

[5] Major H. J. Gillespie in DCOA, 1 May 1944.

outside the industry and to reorganize itself, as well as to explore a reorganization of the industry.

The outcome was the appointment of Robert Foot as Chairman of the MAGB in April 1944; 'a more cordial and direct approach to unification upon a regional basis';[1] and the devising of a set of proposals (published as the 'Foot Plan' early in 1945) which represented the last, albeit still inadequate, attempt at partial compromise by the coalowners.

Robert Foot was a distinguished businessman, who had been Chairman of the Gas, Light & Coke Company before moving to the Chairmanship of the BBC's Board of Governors. Whatever the expression of objective concern for the efficiency of the industry, however, the principal purpose of his appointment to the MAGB was explicitly acknowledged in his report for 1944: 'to save this industry for private enterprise and from the dreadful fate of nationalisation or of control by a public corporation.'[2] His appointment showed a distinct, if belated, recognition on the part of the owners, of the disadvantages of their notorious insularity.

Foot prepared himself by a comprehensive tour of the various coal-producing districts. However, when it was published (in January 1945), the Foot Plan turned out to be a predictably cautious document, entirely consistent with all previous informed discussion within the industry. Its basic assumption was that if the owners were to have any hope of regaining control of coalmining, they would have to assume some *collective* responsibility for its efficiency, harmonization, and overall structure—or, in Foot's words, to guarantee to Parliament and the public that they would be 'prepared to face up to their full responsibilities as an industry'. They therefore needed to adopt a scheme 'which while keeping alive the best elements of private enterprise, would somehow bring the industry under a national policy to be controlled by the industry itself'.[3]

These were fine-sounding words, but Foot was trapped between the need to reorganize industrial control, and the owners' unyielding reluctance to compromise on their autonomy. In its first version Robert Foot's *Plan for Coal* proposed a private and independent Central Coal Board exclusively composed of representatives of colliery companies. Every colliery company employing more than 30 workers would bind itself to comply with the Board's directives, although the Plan implied that voluntary rather than compulsory amalgamation would still be the aim. This proved unsatisfactory to both the generality of owners (who

---

[1] CG 6 Apr. 1944, 428.   [2] MAGB 1944, 9.   [3] COAL 11/106 (12 Oct. 1944).

were exceedingly reluctant to abandon their private interests quite so unequivocally) and to critics of the owners (who argued that the scheme amounted to a 'gigantic private monopoly uncontrolled by the State').[1] To one very senior civil servant in the Ministry of Fuel and Power, the Foot Plan appeared 'half-baked', 'absurd and repulsive', with corporatist and fascist overtones.[2] Equally important, however, was the fact that the Plan was extremely vague as to what sort of industrial policy would be pursued and how the necessary vast changes in the industry would be financed.

Such imprecision on matters of vital concern attracted criticism from within as well as outside the industry.[3] The British Iron & Steel Federation, whose member firms were responsible for 25–30 per cent of all coal produced, condemned the Foot Plan not merely for the potentially authoritarian nature of the Central Coal Board, but because it promised no improvement in productivity or reduction in costs.[4] More generally, and with devastating logic, it could be claimed that the scheme proposed by the Chairman of the MAGB took no account of the central issues. As *The Economist* put it,

There would be no effective movement towards closer integration—for at this time of day it is simply impossible to believe that voluntary methods plus an appeal to the Coal Commission will achieve anything. There would be no drastic re-equipment—because the capital does not exist within the industry and cannot be raised on market terms. There would be no improvement in the labour position—because the men would regard the scheme as reactionary. . . . the plain truth is that the industry is past self-help . . .'[5]

This critique established the central issues in an almost irrefutable manner. And Foot's subsequent amendments to his Plan, since they

---

[1] *New Statesman & Nation* 3 Feb. 1945, 71. A similar point was made by *The Times* 23 Jan. 1945, 5b; 3 Mar. 1945, 5c. Although the balance of owners' opinion was probably favourable to the Foot Plan, as the least of the evils confronting the industry, it attracted very telling criticisms during the nation-wide discussions at district association meetings—especially on the point that the concentration of power in a London-based body contradicted the responsibilities of colliery company Directors, who would in any case have no right of appeal: LCMA UGD/59/1/20 (5 Feb. 1945).

[2] R. N. Quirk to Nott-Bower, 8 Mar. 1945: POWE 28/108.

[3] See LCMA UGD/59/1/20 (5 Feb. 1945) (the Chairman of the Lanarkshire owners complained that the Plan provided for the amalgamation of management without touching on the amalgamation of finance) and *CG* 26 Jan. 1945, 112–13 (the Plan was said to be 'loose and vague almost to the point of disingenuity').

[4] MSWCOA Box File 732, 27 Mar. 1945.

[5] *The Economist* 27 Jan. 1945, 104–5. *The Economist* concluded that the state would have to sponsor a public plan for coal. Below, 626.

hardly touched the problems of finance, detailed policy, or labour relations, did nothing to alter the widespread impression that the MAGB was making an empty gesture rather than a genuine bid for reform. Its Plan read like a feeble and apprehensive death-bed repentance. In *The Economist*'s words, 'The blunt truth is that no one, outside the ranks of the coal owners themselves, has the slightest confidence in their willingness or ability to do more than tinker with the problem.'[1] Worst of all, the amended Plan commanded only very half-hearted support within the industry. In May 1945, with the European War over, and a General Election likely, agreement on an industrial policy was still disastrously remote.

In the course of their discussions of industrial reorganization as the War came to an end, the owners had been warned by that lifelong stalwart of individualism, Sir Evan Williams, that they 'must decide whether they were to do the job themselves or allow someone else to do it for them'.[2] In the event, the self-doubt which had crept into their deliberations was sufficiently strong to erode their resistance to change, without being sufficiently purposeful to allow an effective measure of self-reform. As the War ended, the industry lay open to the flood of change which technical advocacy, political events, and the broader public consensus were preparing for it.

vi. The inevitability of nationalization

The events and discussions of 1944–5 had embodied decisive changes in public mood and political attitudes towards the coal industry.[3] These precluded any attempt to return to prewar modes of organization or structural experiment. And the impulse towards reform was reinforced by the continuing problems of production, not merely in relation to the immediate needs of a devastated Europe, but also to the long-term recovery of the British economy. As the Prime Minister's adviser pointed out, the 1930 Coal Mines Act had destroyed normal com-

---

[1] COAL 11/106 (12 Apr. 1945); *The Economist*, 21 Apr. 1945, 518.

[2] COAL 17/106 (17 May 1945).

[3] One indication of the universality of the new mood was the series of surveys of the condition, prospects, and needs of individual coalmining regions, initiated by the Ministry of Fuel and Power in 1944, but published after the War. These followed a survey of the Scottish field, which had been undertaken on behalf of the Scottish Home Department and published in 1944: *Scottish Home Department, Scottish Coalfields. The Report by the Scottish Coalfields Committee* (Edinburgh. Cmd. 6575. 1944). That for South Wales was by far the most detailed and analytical: *South Wales Coalfield... Regional Survey Report* (HMSO 1946). The various reports were reviewed in Beacham 1950.

petitive forces and 'unless we go back to free enterprise, which would presumably be rejected on all sides, the only chance of getting the cheap coal we need seems to lie in amalgamation'.[1] That much was an almost universal opinion. The only point of contention was the *means* of bringing about amalgamations and technical change.

To its varied advocates, public ownership was the most effective way of ensuring reorganization. A sense of the industry's desperate technical needs, an exasperation with the owners which had been mounting for two decades, and an apprehension about the extent to which the miners would cooperate with any private-enterprise solution to the industry's problems—all combined to establish new expectations about the political economy of coal. Indeed, in terms of perceptions such as these, the War had brought about a shift of opinion even within the ranks of those ideologically opposed to public ownership.

This was exemplified not merely in the Tory Reform Committee's *A National Policy for Coal*,[2] but also in the announcement by the Conservative Caretaker Government in May 1945, during its brief period of office before the postwar General Election, of a policy which accepted the Reid Report and proposed a central authority for the industry. The authority was to be appointed by the Ministry of Fuel and Power, and charged with encouraging amalgamations—voluntary if possible, obligatory if necessary. Although the plan did not embody a particularly persuasive programme, it was significant that the owners were quick to accept the proposals for a government-appointed central authority and to allow their own (Foot) Plan to become absorbed in the transitory schemes of the Caretaker Government.[3]

The owners, even while they were grudgingly resisting Foot's compromise proposals for a feeble central authority, could hardly challenge his conclusions that after the next Election the Labour Party would nationalize the industry and that 'no Conservative Party which was returned would dare to hand back the Industry to be organized as it was in 1939'.[4] Even those reluctant to advocate nationalization looked to the

---

[1] Cherwell Papers, Cherwell to Churchill, May 1945 (H19). This memorandum was apparently not sent.   [2] Above, 611.

[3] COAL 11/106 (14 June 1945). The Liberal Party similarly advocated a national board to supervise amalgamations: *CG* 18 Jan. 1946, 80–1. Although *The Economist* subsequently saw some merit in Lloyd George's proposals on behalf of the Caretaker Government, it was initially sweeping in its condemnation of the plan's inadequacy: 'Even if the Tory Party wins every seat in the House of Commons, a real coal policy will have to be produced before long.' *The Economist* 2 June 1945, 727. But cf. 16 June 1945, 809.

[4] SRO CB7/3/1: 'Notes of Proceedings at Meeting of the Coal Owners in the Lanarkshire Area ...' 12 Feb. 1945.

state. Indeed, this was the general case in the economy: the War had persuaded the business community that a degree of government control over industry might be necessary in the postwar world. Efficiency was to be the overriding criterion, and intervention might be a prerequisite of productivity.[1] Within the coalmining industry, there were owners who opposed nationalization but still advocated 'a national policy for coal' and 'a lead in this matter from the government'.[2]

Such a national policy was made the easier by the outcome of the War, which overcame much of the prewar fragmentation of coal-producing districts and miners' unions, which had created a potentially powerful central machinery in the form of the Ministry of Fuel and Power, and which had established a system of national conciliation and wage-determination. More specifically, from at least 1944 the industry's problems presented themselves in a way which established beyond doubt the relationship between ownership, structure, and efficiency. As a result, the general shift of opinion in favour of a large degree of public intervention and even public ownership was based on the presumed prerequisites of 'technical' measures: harmonious industrial relations, industry-wide coordination and planning, the provision of large and unprecedented capital funds.[3] This conclusion was, of course, emphasized by left-wing commentators.[4] But it was also the strong if implicit lesson of the Reid Committee, and it was adduced by *The Economist* in January 1945 on the grounds that the will to change, the necessary investment funds, and the cooperation of the miners would all be lacking:

the plain truth is that the industry is past self-help. . . . neither the owners nor the miners can put the industry on its feet, neither separately nor together. The State, the Government, the public, will have to abandon the role of neutral umpire and evolve their own plan.[5]

Similar opinions about the need for neutrality between the sectional interests were voiced by observers far more sympathetic to the miners:

[1] *Reconstruction* (Report by the Federation of British Industries, May 1942), 20. *The Challenge to Industry* (Speech by Sir Clive Baillieu, President of the Federation of British Industries, delivered at Manchester on 30 Nov. 1945. FBI 1945).

[2] Lancaster (a member of the Tory Reform Group) in *Hansard* 13 July 1944, cols. 1945 ff.

[3] See Arthur Beacham's assessment of the implications of the Reid Report: Beacham 1945.

[4] Heinemann 1944; Wilson 1945.

[5] *The Economist* 27 Jan. 1945, 104–5. In 1944 *The Economist* had pointed out that the real case for change was the failure of the existing private ownership, with a few bright exceptions, 'to make even a beginning' in the vital task of reorganization (15 July 1944, 107; 29 July 1944, 664; 19 Aug. 1944, 238).

both sides are now preparing for their final battle which, if either succeeds in imposing its own terms on the other, will spell ruin for the country. The battle will be joined on the issue of the technical rehabilitation of the industry. The prize will be a hundred million or more of public funds: the cost to the Government of bringing the mines up to the technical level of their continental competitors. To spend this money on the pits and allow the present system of ownership to continue would be infamous. The owners have proved themselves wholly incapable, as a body, of departing from their traditional practices and obsessions. But any form of nationalisation which allowed the miners themselves executive responsibility for the running of the pits would be fatal: nothing is clearer than that their very history has unfitted them for this responsibility; they are far too prone to pull off the tablecloth to get at the cake.[1]

There were, therefore, multitudinous strands in the movement towards postwar nationalization. But the common element was a sense that for 25 years the coalmining industry had suffered from 'productive anaemia', and that 'The country must realise that it simply cannot afford this sort of bungling, this reckless inaction masquerading as caution.' Instead, every effort must be made to secure 'technical rationalisation and managerial reform'.[2]

All this, of course, was an embodiment of the long-run and diffused movements which were to lead to the extension of public ownership in Britain generally. By 1945 surveys of public opinion showed that there was a substantial majority in favour of the nationalization of coal both during 1944 and immediately after the 1945 General Election, while there was reason to believe that those sceptical of public ownership in general were nevertheless willing to accept it in the case of coalmining.[3]

In Sir Ernest Gowers's words, 'the opportunity for gradualness has been lost'; the owners' plans were quite unrealistic. The industry had, at last, met the destiny predicted for it by David Lloyd George in 1919: 'It has to come. The State will have to shoulder the burden sooner or later.'[4]

---

[1] Benny 1946, 175–6.
[2] *The Economist* 28 Oct. 1944, 561.
[3] Cantril 1951, 343 and 476; 'The Journey Home', *Change*, No. 5 'A Report Prepared by Mass-Observation for the Advertising Service Guild, 1944), 103–4; *The Times* 26 June 1945, 7.
[4] Riddell 1933, I, 11 Apr. 1919.

CHAPTER 14

Nationalizing the Coal Industry, 1945–1946

As we have seen, the coal industry was the object of widespread discussion and multifarious proposals in the early months of 1945. The Reid Committee's Report, the Foot Plan, and the Caretaker Government's programme all envisaged major changes in organization and a new role for collective decision-making. But it was the Labour Party's spectacular victory in the General Election of July which resolved the question beyond any doubt.

Ever since the First World War, although there had been few attempts to formulate precise plans, the Labour Party's official programme had included the nationalization of coal. 'Dogmatic ideology' no doubt played a part in the Party's commitment to this end, but the experience of the 1930s, and even more of the early 1940s, had lent substantial pragmatic support to the principled arguments in favour of state control. Private enterprise was held to be pathologically incapable of solving the industry's technical, structural, and financial problems, while its work-force was unyieldingly opposed to anything less than a nationalized system of labour relations. More than this, Labour's huge victory in the General Election of July 1945 was based in large part on a widespread public sympathy for the sort of social and economic reform of which the public ownership of the mines was among the least controversial examples. It was hardly surprising, therefore, that the act of nationalization, which the miners had urged since the 1890s, was given the highest priority by the new government.

Given the scope and unprecedented nature of the measure, events moved very quickly. Emanuel Shinwell (who had, of course, served as Secretary for Mines in the minority Labour Governments of the 1920s) was appointed Minister of Fuel and Power on 3 August 1945. Ministerial discussions over the next few months were followed by the introduction of the Coal Industry Nationalisation Bill on 19 December 1945. The Bill received its Second Reading on 29 and 30 December, and was considered in Committee and amended in the spring and early summer of 1946. It received the Royal Assent on 12 July 1946, and the industry's assets were finally vested in the National Coal Board on 1 January 1947. The political passage of the legislation was relatively smooth and the resulting legal form (a public corporation) reflected the main trend in Labour Party thinking on public ownership over the previous 10 or 15 years. In spite of the apparent ease of this process, nationalization involved a number of important economic and political choices. But few of these gave rise to much controversy. Their historical significance lies in the fact that they set the seal on a generation of economic disruption and political conflict, and (like all political and administrative decisions) laid the basis for future problems.

i. Labour and guidelines for nationalization

In many respects the objectives and structure of the state-owned coal industry had to be decided with little reference to established guidelines. (Indeed, much of the Coal Board's organization was only determined *after* the Act had passed.) And in later years, Shinwell made a great deal of the fact that nationalization had to be discussed from scratch:

For the whole of my political life I had listened to Party speakers advocating state ownership and control of the coal mines, and I had myself spoken of it as a primary task once the Labour Party was in power. I had believed, as other members had, that in the Party archives a blue-print was ready. Now, as Minister of Fuel and Power, I found that nothing practical and tangible existed. There were some pamphlets, some memoranda produced for private circulation, and nothing else. I had to start on a clear desk.[1]

It was certainly true, of course, that few of the previous discussions and controversies within the Labour Party had produced a clear consensus on exactly how the nationalization of coal should be effected and organized. But, given the context of these considerations and the remoteness of the event, it would be surprising had they done so. There was, in fact, an element of *fausse naïveté* in Shinwell's assertion.

The two most detailed plans for the nationalization of coal before 1945 had been produced by, or on behalf of, the Miners' Federation of Great Britain as submissions to the Sankey and Samuel Commissions in 1919 and 1926 respectively.[2] Both proposals recommended direct state ownership, with the industry run by a combination of central and district control boards, and both contained administrative details and

---

[1] Shinwell 1955, 172–3. Cf. Wigg 1972, 123–4.
[2] *Sankey Evidence* II, 922–7; *Samuel Evidence* QQ 1020–5.

suggestions as to the determination of compensation to the owners. But neither had much to say about the appropriate boundaries or powers of district units, and their principal characteristic was their advocacy of 'joint control and administration'—with the miners' nominees having a large (in the 1919 plan a 50 per cent) representation on the relevant councils. However, this type of structure failed to find favour in the Labour movement. In the 1930s the Labour Party accepted the idea of public corporations (rather than state departments) as the appropriate form for nationalized industries;[1] and by 1945 TUC documents, although accepting the principle of employee representation, called for 'public control of industry rather than workers' control as such', and argued that governing bodies should be appointed primarily 'on the basis of competence and ability to run the industry efficiently in the public interest'.[2]

None of this offered very specific guidance. And the Labour Party's own wartime Coal and Power Sub-Committee (of which Shinwell was a leading member), while it naturally concluded that the industry should be run by a public corporation, was extremely vague in its plans for postwar energy policy.[3] Yet although it was hardly realistic to expect very much more from such discussions, there *was* more concrete and directed deliberation within the Labour movement than Shinwell publicly allowed. In 1944, for example, the TUC produced a 'Report on Postwar Reconstruction' which was a far from negligible guide to general policy; and, even more important, between May and August 1945 a Joint Committee of the Labour Party, the NUM, and the TUC, chaired by Shinwell himself, considered the subject of nationalization in considerable detail and produced a range of specific proposals, which (in Shinwell's own words) were designed to provide 'the first Labour Minister of Fuel and Power with a practical scheme that he can carry out.'[4]

[1] Barry 1965, ch. 13.

[2] *77th Annual Conference Report of the TUC, 1945*, 202. Shinwell himself had for long been a sceptic on the subject of workers' control: 'You must not conceal facts; taking the miners as a whole, they are more concerned about improving wages than workers' control.' (Shinwell 1931?, 6.)

[3] Labour Party Archives, RDR 255, 'A Draft Report on the Coal and Power Industries'.

[4] *76th Annual Conference Report on the TUC, 1944*, Appendix D, 'Interim Report on Postwar Reconstruction'; TUC Archives, File 603.431 ('Mining Industry—National Joint Committee'). The Report of the Joint Committee was not published but was forwarded to the new Minister (i.e. Shinwell, the Committee's own original Chairman) 'for his information and guidance'. Shinwell drew attention to the committee at the 1945 Labour Party Conference: *Report of the Forty-fourth Annual Conference of the Labour Party* (Blackpool, 1945), 138.

In the event, the resulting schemes, although they understandably avoided any elaborate discussion of industrial organization, prefigured many of the central principles of the act of nationalization. They recommended that the industry be run by a Board whose members should be appointed by the Minister, should be full-time, and 'should be persons having a wide experience and proven ability in the conduct of industry or the organisation of workpeople'. They defined the scope of the Board's acquisition, to include coalmines and directly ancillary undertakings. They proposed that compensation should be based on the reasonable 'net maintainable revenue' of the acquired firms; and that it should be paid in normal government stock rather than specific and earmarked bonds.

Nor did the Minister's desk contain merely the fruits of the Labour movement's recent discussions. He was also able to draw on an extensive range of bureaucratic experience. Quite apart from the general discussions within Whitehall, which produced reports on organizational forms, Shinwell had access to well-informed advice on coal from his own civil servants. These included men who had been concerned with the nationalization of royalties in 1938, who had been involved with all the problems of wartime control, and who had long deliberated on the deficiencies of private ownership and the variety of options available for more positive state intervention.[1]

Certainly, the Labour Government's inheritance included no massive blueprints for the public ownership of coal or the structure of a public corporation in the industry. But then, the Minister's desk was not quite as 'clear' as he subsequently liked to claim. The central principles of nationalization were almost certainly decided *before* Shinwell assumed ministerial powers. And when it was necessary to embody those principles in practical discussions and proposals, there was a wealth of experience and opinion, as well as prejudice, to call on. The Bill which took shape in 1945–6 was certainly no *ad hoc* measure cobbled together under pressure from the Cabinet and the NUM.[2]

At the same time, however, very little administrative detail *could* be settled at such an early stage in the modern history of nationalization.

[1] The Minister's Departmental Committee included Sir Hubert Houldsworth, who had been in the Mines Department since 1939 and Coal Controller since 1944; L. H. H. Lowe, Finance Director since 1942; W. G. Nott-Bower, who had joined the Mines Department in 1920; Sir Charles Reid, who had chaired the Technical Advisory Committee and was still Technical Adviser to the Ministry. In addition, Gowers was still in the wings.

[2] This is the underlying explanation in Shinwell's accounts: Shinwell 1955, 172–3; and 1963, 182.

And it was a significant indication of the impossibility of adducing articulated plans for industrial reorganization before the event, that the Coal Industry Nationalisation Bill itself hardly touched the issue of industrial structure and decision-making. Instead it, too, abjured the drawing-up of a blueprint. As the next section indicates, the legislation laid down the ways in which the industry's assets were to be taken into public ownership, created a National Coal Board, and stipulated its broad guidelines. But it was obliged to allow the actual organization and workings of the nationalized industry to be determined by those who would be directly responsible for its management.

ii. Drafting the Bill

Whatever the scope of earlier discussions, the practical problems involved in drafting a Coal Nationalisation Bill were considerable.[1] Dealing with such a large and complicated industry (about 850 firms and 1,650 collieries, quite apart from ancillary enterprises) was itself a matter of formidable complexity.[2] In addition, in spite of the enthusiasm or quiescence about public ownership within the industry, there had to be extensive consultation with those involved. Nor was this all, for the Minister was also pressed for time: within a few days of his appointment at the beginning of August 1945, Shinwell learned that the Cabinet had scheduled a Coal Nationalisation Bill to be introduced before the Christmas Recess. Indeed, the proposed timetable meant that the Coal Bill had to be formulated before the government had finally created the machinery to oversee its general nationalization programme.[3]

It was, therefore, for reasons of speed as well as convenience that the Minister's Departmental Committee on Coal Nationalization, at its second meeting, on 27 August, decided that the proposed measure would have to involve a large element of delegated legislation.[4] The Bill would be 'framed along the simplest possible lines, with many questions

---

[1] The administrative and political processes of nationalization are described with great thoroughness in Chester 1975.

[2] In the event, however, many small enterprises were not brought into public ownership. The final figure was about 1,000 pits and 400 colliery firms. See National Coal Board, *Annual Report for the Year ending 31st December 1946*, 28–9.

[3] There was a preliminary meeting of the relevant Ministers early in November, followed by the creation of a Committee of Officials and (on 1 Jan. 1946) of Ministers. See Chester 1975, 40 ff.

[4] POWE 28/20 (29 Aug. 1945). The Departmental Committee was normally attended by Shinwell, Sir D. Fergusson, Sir H. Houldworth, Sir S. Low, Sir C. Reid, and a number of more junior, but still influential, officials, including Innes, Lowe, Nott-Bower, and de Peyer. Its Minutes and Papers are in POWE 28/20.

to be left over to the discretion' of the National Coal Board. This decision was crucial, as well as perhaps the only realistic strategy. Because of it, Shinwell was able to meet his deadline, and the Bill was presented to the Commons on 19 December.

The Minister's task was the further simplified because virtually all the substantive official discussion was carried on by his own Departmental Committee, with the Lord President's Committee and the Cabinet (which naturally considered formal proposals and drafts) rarely contributing much of significance to policy.[1] Within the Ministry's Committee, too, consensus reigned: official drafting could begin after merely four meetings, and the only serious internal disagreement (on the possibility of having part-time Board members drawn from business backgrounds) was immediately resolved by a ruling from Shinwell that the Board should contain only full-time and fully committed people.[2]

A further reason for the Bill's relatively untroubled passage was the readiness of the owners to accommodate themselves to government policy. This was in striking contrast to their political campaigns and blusterings in response to the legislative proposals of 1919 or the 1930s,[3] although it was hardly surprising in view of their poor standing in the eyes of the public and politicians in 1945. The MAGB decided to offer their full cooperation within days of the King's Speech, and in subsequent consultations with the Minister on 5 September, both sides were emphatically conciliatory.

The owners' representatives went out of their way to place 'our experience and knowledge of the Industry and its problems at your disposal' during the interim period and under the future nationalized regime. For his part, Shinwell welcomed the promise of cooperation and was equally conciliatory, attempting as far as possible to deal fairly with the owners, and also undertaking to reimburse colliery companies for all legitimate capital expenditures undertaken after 1 August and before Vesting Day. At the same time, however, the Minister made it clear that there would be no genuine consultations, other than on the questions of compensation and the arrangements for the transitional period.[4] Of

---

[1] CAB 71/19 (35th, 42nd, and 44th meetings of the Lord President's Committee) and CAB 128/2 (Cabinet consideration in CM 62 (45) 6). In spite of the relative ease with which the Bill was formulated and accepted, because of the inherent legal problems and the frequent changes of detail, the drafting process proved extremely time-consuming. The Bill presented to the Commons was the twelfth printed version (Chester, 1975, 47 and 99).

[2] POWE 28/20 (1st, 2nd, and 4th Meeting: 27 and 29 Aug. and 11 Sept. 1945).

[3] Above, 133–4, 352.

[4] On 11 Sept. the Permanent Secretary to the Ministry of Fuel and Power wrote to the MAGB

course, this is not to deny that important disagreements occurred. But they never threatened to cripple procedures, and can be considered in the context of the principal problems tackled as the Bill was drafted and proceeded through Parliament.

During the Second Reading of the Coal Nationalisation Bill, Shinwell emphasized the practical advantages of simplicity: 'It will not create a rigid organisation, either nationally or regionally, which would tie the hands of the proposed National Coal Board.' Given this decision, the Bill was concerned with only a limited number of large-scale issues. These primarily involved the specification of the property to be transferred; the terms of compensation, including the manner in which it would be paid; the transitional arrangements; the constitution, functions, and duties of the public bodies; the financial arrangements for borrowing; and a group of miscellaneous questions, including the safeguarding of the interests of employees and consumers. Some of these were relatively uncontroversial and provoked little discussion even within ministerial circles in the weeks leading up to the presentation of the Bill to Parliament.

The industry was to be managed and developed by a National Coal Board, charged with furthering the public interest, advancing the welfare of the work-force, and paying its way, taking an average of good and bad years. However, the Minister was empowered to give directions as to these activities where they impinged on the public interest. The Board was to consist of nine full-time members, drawn from people with experience in commerce, industry, or the organization of workers, but not representing any particular interest group nor chosen on the basis of any formal consultation. And the Minister was required to establish two Consumer Councils (for industrial and domestic supplies respectively). So much gave rise to a working consensus in the summer and autumn of 1945. In other areas, however, more substantive discussions and negotiations were necessary. The two most important of these concerned the assets to be expropriated and the basis and form of compensation.

The definition of exactly what was to be brought into public ownership presented a problem because the 'coal industry' did not exactly coincide with a given number of firms or a given range of assets. Firms

promising full compensation for capital outlays after 1 Aug., with a corresponding threat of reductions where maintenance was neglected. For transcripts of the first meeting with Shinwell and his officials and Fergusson's letter, see MSWCOA Box File 732. The MAGB opening statement is reproduced in Lee 1954, 247–50.

producing coal also produced many other things (iron and steel, coke, patent fuel, gas, bricks, shipping services), frequently in direct connection with their coalmining activities, and owned a wide variety of non-commercial (as well as productive) assets, including hospitals, baths, canteens, and a huge housing stock.[1] It was for this reason that 'the nationalization of coalmining' meant the state acquisition of assets and property, rather than corporate enterprises, and that erstwhile colliery companies continued in independent existence.

The distribution side of the coal trade was excluded at an early stage, on the grounds that it would make the Bill much more cumbersome and was unnecessary since the NCB, once in being, could exercise almost complete influence over the wholesale and retail trades.[2] On the producing side, the core property was relatively easily identified as unworked coal (which was transferred from the Coal Commission) and the coalmines and selling agencies included in the TS (Terms of Settlement) returns used for wage-determination.[3] There were, however, very extensive ancillary or subsidiary assets associated with the industry (coke ovens, by-product plants, assets more or less directly associated with the production and marketing of coal or the working of mines). The final compensation payments reflected their relative importance: they accounted for £90.6 million, as against £164.7 million for the industry's TS assets, £80.9 million for the unworked coal, and £34.6 million for stocks of products and stores.[4] In the controversial matter of what was to be brought into public ownership, the Minister's view prevailed over that of the owners and the British Coking Industry Association, which was anxious to retain assets 'leading away' from coalmining, and coke ovens in particular.

The final Act provided for the compulsory acquisition of all assets judged essential to the efficiency of coalmining—not merely coal reserves and collieries, but also such ancillary assets as colliery transport and social facilities, and colliery manufactured-fuel plants and coke ovens (except coal carbonization and by-product activities primarily

[1] The question of defining the industry's assets and deciding the principles on which they should be dealt with is discussed in detail in Chester 1975, 91-104.

[2] Shinwell to Lord President's Committee, 2 Oct. 1945: CAB 71/19.

[3] Although the distinction between TS assets and ancillary assets was important in the discussions leading up to the Act, and the TS assets and returns were taken into account in the compensation arrangements, the relevant sections of the Coal Mines Nationalisation Act did not, in fact, use the term. Nor did the final categorization of assets, each subject to different treatment, coincide with the TS definitions.

[4] Chester 1975, 257.

related to iron- and steel-works operated by the concern). Assets less intimately associated (such as housing or wharves) could be transferred at the option of the Board or the owners, where the Board found it advantageous or the owners felt that the value had been significantly reduced by the loss of their principal activities. Thirdly, there was a category of asset, including manufactured-fuel plants and transport assets not owned by collieries, which could be transferred at the option of either party, subject to arbitration in cases where the option was contested. Brickworks, which had originally been in the second category, were transferred into the third after Parliamentary criticism that the possibility of compulsion might enable the Coal Board to insist on the acquisition of major brickworks simply because the company owned a small coalmine.

Of the assets ultimately specified (usually with no objection) by the National Coal Board for acquisition, the most important were colliery stores, wharves, all colliery housing, land, and brickworks managed as part of collieries. As a result, in addition to the 1,000 mines acquired on Vesting Day (many small pits were not taken over), the Board found itself the owner of 55 coking plants (producing 40 per cent of the nation's 'hard' coke), 20 manufactured-fuel plants, 83 brickworks, 29 building estates and 150,000 houses, and almost 2,000 farms. It produced a significant proportion of the country's output of tar, benzole, sulphate of ammonia, and town gas. Nationalization had created not merely a huge but a complex composite business, replacing specialist colliery companies or the colliery-related assets of composite firms which stayed in business in areas outside coal production.

The second main issue—the criteria and form of compensation for the expropriated property—was potentially the most contentious of all. As far as the criteria were concerned, however, the disagreement concerned the statistical bases of the calculations. There was relatively little opposition, either from within the left wing of the Labour Party or from the coalowners, to the broad principles enunciated at the outset: the initial valuation would be global (i.e. of the industry as a whole, rather than of individual firms) and 'fair' in the sense of reflecting the price that might be arranged between a willing buyer and a willing seller, taking full account of the past history, present circumstances, and future prospects of the industry.

Given these stipulations, it was quickly acknowledged that the best method of determining the amount would be to capitalize the industry's 'reasonable net maintainable revenue' (by deciding on a number of years' purchase by which annual average profits would be multiplied).[1] This formula had been accepted by the Labour Party as the determinant of compensation for nationalized enterprises from the early 1930s. It had the advantage of apparent fairness and of relating purchase price to earning power in an obvious and efficient way; but, in addition, it was exceedingly attractive in the case of the coal industry (where it had already been used to value coal royalties when they were nationalized in 1938) since global profit and loss figures had been collected ever since the 1921 Terms of Settlement wages agreement. The availability of such data was also an important consideration in the Ministry's decision to aim at a *global* valuation.[2]

This, therefore, was the starting-point for compensation: the 'TS assets' of the industry (i.e. those involved in the direct production of coal and utilized in the wage agreements to determine proceeds) would be valued as a multiple of 'net maintainable revenue'. On the other side, there was no equivalent basis for valuing the very extensive ancillary or subsidiary assets that were due to be nationalized, and it was decided that these would have to be valued independently and directly. In addition, since the government's global compensation was only part of the necessary process, it was further decided that the subdivision of global proceeds between the various districts, and within the districts to the numerous individual firms, would have to be a matter for specially constituted Valuation Boards.[3]

The official stance on the question of the *form* in which expropriated owners were to be paid was decided with equal expedition. Cash payments were out of the question, if only because of the likely disruption of money and equity markets. An alternative possibility might have been the issue of 'Coal Board Stock', but in the case of the mining industry this seemed politically inadvisable: it would be interpreted, particularly by the miners, as re-creating the coalowning class in a new guise. With the agreement of the Treasury, therefore, and 'for reasons

---

[1] For a fuller description of this method of valuation, see below, 651 n.

[2] See the first meeting of the official Committee on the Socialisation of Industry (CAB 134/693: 29 Nov. 1945): 'In the case of the Coal Industry, however, the reason why a global valuation had been decided upon was the practical one that all the data in the shape of statistical returns in the whole industry were readily available.' For the evolution of official thinking on the subject of compensation see the discussion during the first meeting, and the papers relating to the 4th and 5th meetings, of the Ministry's Departmental Committee (POWE 28/20) and the memorandum from Shinwell to the first meeting of the Cabinet's Committee on the Socialisation of Industry on 9 Nov. 1945 (CAB 134/693). The possible bases of compensation and the emergence of Labour Party policy are discussed in Chester 1975, 217-25.

[3] Below, 652-3.

largely arising out of the psychology of the miners', the compensation was to be paid in government stock.[1] More than this, it was stipulated that the compensation stock could only become transferable on the open market *after* it had been distributed by the colliery company to its shareholders or creditors. In other words, an expropriated company could not pay out cash—a point on which considerable, but unavailing, criticism was to be generated, not all of it from the coalowners.[2]

The Mining Association greeted certain aspects of these proposals with consternation.[3] They were incensed by the Minister's refusal to contemplate a cash payment, which they thought was sanctioned by precedent as well as by the imperatives of natural justice. But their protestations were brushed aside: there was to be no question of a cash compensation.

Shinwell was on less secure ground with respect to the basis of compensation for the industry's coalmining (as distinct from its ancillary) assets. The owners, while not opposed to the principle of using net maintainable revenue as the basis of valuation, were naturally very concerned about the choice of the two vital statistical variables: the number of years' purchase (in essence the choice of a presumed rate of return on capital) and the actual base years to be used in the calculation of average profits. The variability of interest rates and of the industry's own performance over the previous 20 or 25 years meant that the outcome might be very unfavourable indeed. For example, depending on the period selected, the relevant estimate of average net maintainable revenue over a number of years in the past (derived from TS assets) might lie anywhere betwen £8.1 and £13.3 million. Considering only individual years, prewar results had fluctuated between a loss of £10 million in 1928 and a profit of over £27 million in 1923.

On 2 October the MAGB extracted a Ministry estimate that a fair value might lie between £115 and £160 million. This came as a shock to many leading owners (although in South Derbyshire, for example, the local association was strongly of the opinion that if the industry was

[1] CAB 134/693 (meeting of Ministers to consider Socialisation of Industries, 9 Nov. 1945, 3). Also see Chester 1975, 225–36 and report of a meeting between Shinwell and the Chancellor of the Exchequer on 9 Oct. 1945: POWE 28/23.

[2] Chester 1975, 242. *Hansard* Standing Committee C, Jan.–Apr. 1946, cols. 1537–55. *The Economist* considered this a 'monstrous provision . . . an astonishing piece of tyranny': 22 Dec. 1945, 900.

[3] For the discussions between the government and the MAGB, see POWE 28/23. Also see the MAGB's Valuation Advisory Committee's memorandum on 'Compensation on Transfer of the Coal Industry to Public Ownership' (26 Sept. 1945) in the same file, and Chester 1975, 96.

offered as much as £150 million 'it would be wiser to accept this than to go to arbitration as was contemplated by the Mining Association').[1] The national association therefore protested vigorously that this rough estimate ignored changes in the value of money, the prewar trends in profits, and the industry's real worth. As a result, Sir Donald Fergusson, Shinwell's Permanent Secretary, anticipated a political impasse. He thought that a net maintainable revenue of £11 million at 14 years' purchase was 'about right' but acknowledged that the owners, who were hoping for about £200 million compensation, would regard the outcome (£154 million) as 'a mean and unfair figure', while the £11 million would be considered as too generous within the Commons.[2]

The political implications as well as practical difficulties of the problem were sufficiently great for Shinwell to accept a compromise on this issue. At the outset, it appears that he was opposed to arbitration and rather assumed that the figure for the global compensation sum would be settled by the government and included in the Bill. He 'thought it better, in relation to his own supporters in Parliament, that there should not be any agreement with the Mining Association as to the global figure'.[3] But this procedure was soon judged to be politically hazardous. It had therefore been decided to refer the question of the number of years' purchase to an independent tribunal; now, after the meetings with the Mining Association, it was confirmed that the estimate of the net maintainable revenue would also be determined by arbitration, although the Tribunal would be told to ignore the artificial finances of the industry during the War. Pressure was placed on the Mining Association to accept arbitration under the threat of costly delay in the legislation, for which they would be blamed.[4] But it was a compromise which gave little away and contained a good deal of political astuteness.

In referring the issue of compensation to a Tribunal, Shinwell avoided parliamentary embarrassment and placated his own left wing and the NUM-sponsored MPs by dissociating himself from any suspicion of agreement on compensation with the despised owners. On the other

[1] SDCOA N9/B30 (15 Oct. 1945).

[2] Fergusson to Shinwell, 5 Oct. 1945: POWE 28/234.

[3] POWE 28/20 (Third Meeting of Departmental Committee, 3 Sept. 1945).

[4] POWE 28/23 ('Meeting between the Chancellor of the Exchequer and the Minister of Fuel and Power', 9 Oct. 1945) and POWE 28/234 (Meeting of Ministers concerning outstanding issues relating to compensation). For the official attitude to arbitration, also see POWE 28/20 (NCM 4 and 5–2 and 31 Aug. 1945), POWE 28/234 (Fergusson to Shinwell, 5 Oct. 1945 and Shinwell to Cripps, 10 Oct. 1945); CAB 134/693 (Shinwell memorandum, dated 31 Oct. 1945, to meeting of Ministers, 9 Nov. 1945); and Chester 1975, 244–7.

side, he could not be accused of imposing a mean settlement on the industry and, indeed, was able to pursue what he genuinely considered a generous policy towards an industry whose future under private enterprise was far from secure.[1] As late as the end of October, Shinwell still appeared to be contemplating including the global sum in the Bill. However, early in November the Lord President's Committee wisely overruled the Minister. He was advised to proceed with the Bill *before* the Tribunal was established.[2] Finally, all attempts by the MAGB to have a say in the choice of the proposed Tribunal's actual membership were brushed aside. The government selected the two judges and the accountant who formed this critically important body, and it was established in February 1946 (its Chairman was Lord Greene, who had already played a very busy role on the boards which had determined the compensation value of the industry's royalties in the late 1930s and in the beginnings of a new wages policy in 1942).

In contrast to the owners' sharply expressed anxieties about the form and content of compensation, there was surprisingly little comment from the side of the National Union of Mineworkers or other unions on the issue of worker participation.

Before the Bill was presented to Parliament, Shinwell met the TUC's Fuel and Power Committee, which pressed him on two issues which had long been discussed in relation to public ownership: the representation of employees on the Board and the lack of any formalized consultative machinery. To these questions the Minister gave answers which were to remain unchanged during the following months. Statutory provision, he argued, was unnecessary. Any Labour Government would be bound to consult the unions on at least certain aspects of its appointments policy, and any nationalized industry, given its responsibilities, could not avoid seeking the views of the work-force. If necessary, a subsequent regulation could be issued to this effect. In any

---

[1] When Shinwell had submitted a memorandum to the meeting of Ministers convened to discuss nationalization (CAB 134/693: Memorandum dated 31 Oct., meeting held on 9 Nov.) he made the following significant point: 'I should like to conclude by advocating a fairly generous treatment in this the first industry to be nationalised. It is possible, of course, that even generous treatment may not allay the opposition of some of the dispossessed coal owners, but where generosity will not impose a serious burden on the future costs of the industry and where it will allay apprehension and promote co-operation its practice is desirable. Even with very generous compensation nationalisation will inevitably yield some capital savings. . . . The dissipation of part of these savings by a more generous scale of compensation is of negligible importance in this industry where capital costs are responsible for less than 10 per cent of total costs.'

[2] Shinwell to meeting of Ministers on 9 Nov. 1945: in CAB 134/693, and the Minutes of the Lord President's Committee in CAB 71/19 (9 Nov. 1945).

case, it was quite unnecessary to include such arrangements in the proposed legislation, and TUC fears were unfounded.[1] The TUC appeared to be satisfied with these answers, and the Bill went ahead.

In January 1946, as the Bill went into Committee, the NUM returned to some of these issues, pressing the Minister for clarification. Once again, and with equal firmness, Shinwell insisted that there was no need for any formal provision: the necessity for consultation was implied in the Bill and any more explicit statement 'would suggest that the National Union of Mineworkers were not strong enough to protect their own interests'.

On the more sensitive issue of representation on the Board, he was even more adamant. The principle that Board members should be entirely independent of any sectional allegiance had been established at the outset of the Ministry's internal discussions.[2] Although both the NUM in its prewar proposals for nationalization and the Labour Party's own wartime Coal and Power Sub-Committee had advocated worker participation, the official view within the Labour party was quite different. Ever since the late 1920s, and flowing from the acceptance of the idea of public corporations managed by experts as the best vehicle for public ownership, the idea of worker control, or any very extensive formal trade-union representation on management boards, had been rejected. Indeed, Shinwell himself had been joint author of a 1928 Report which argued that the question of coal nationalization should be regarded 'as purely and simply a business one'.[3] There could be no concession to worker participation, let alone control: 'persons appointed would be representative of the interests of the nation and not of any particular interest. He would not bind himself in any way to formal consultations with any person or association in regard to the appointments.'[4] Such a viewpoint, emphasized by the phrasing of the Bill, produced, among some observers, gratification that the mines were being transferred, as *The Times* put it, 'to the community and not to the miners'.[5]

Those mining trade unionists who in 1912, 1919, and 1926 had urged a large measure of worker participation, and some who had looked for punitive expropriation of the owners, would no doubt have been

[1] POWE 28/6 (4 Dec. 1945).

[2] POWE 28/20 (29 Aug., 11 Sept., and 29 Oct. 1945).

[3] Ostergaard 1954, 210-11.

[4] POWE 28/66 ('Answers given by Minister of Fuel and Power to points on which information was sought by the NUM ... 14th January 1946').

[5] 21 Dec. 1945, cited in POWE 28/34 ('Press Comments on the Bill').

severely disappointed at the way in which their dreams of nationalization were realized. But the formulation of a policy and procedure for public ownership in 1945 followed logically on the technical reconsideration of the problems of coalmining during wartime. It was, moreover, entirely consistent with the majority view within the Labour Party and the trade-union movement generally. Of course, by comparison with the heated prewar debates or even the political anxieties of wartime, the projection of the Coal Industry Nationalisation Bill was an almost bland event. But that reflected the way in which times, and moods, had changed rather than any abrupt and opportunistic undermining of pristine socialist ideals. By the same token, once presented, the Bill was enacted in an atmosphere of moderation and calm acceptance, even on the left—closing an unsatisfactory era rather than embodying some fearful radical experiment.

iii. The Final Act

Considering its significance and complexity, the Coal Industry Nationalisation Bill had a relatively smooth passage through Parliament. But this was hardly surprising. On the one hand, history had prepared public opinion for the public ownership of coal. Even the grudging *Colliery Guardian* was forced to acknowledge that 'for years the affairs of the coal industry have been drifting towards a lee shore and that it was inevitable that the rickety boat of nationalisation would sooner or later be sent to the rescue'.[1] On the other hand, a good deal of potential criticism had been defused by the deliberations of the summer and autumn of 1945 and perhaps even more by the postponement of such sensitive decisions as the amount of compensation, the internal organization of the National Coal Board, or the regional structure of the industry.

Press reaction to the Bill was rarely very unfavourable, and most critical comments concerned specific points, such as the embargo on corporate sales of compensation stock or the extent of the Minister's implied powers or the lack of effective consumer protection. Considered in general, however, even those who might have been entirely sceptical found important aspects of the proposed legislation praiseworthy or, in the *Daily Telegraph*'s words, 'better than might have been feared'. *The* (normally acerbic) *Economist* was almost enthusiastic:

[1] 28 Dec. 1945, 792.

The decision to nationalise the mines once having been taken (and it is a decision from which only a small minority will dissent), the Bill is on the right lines. In nearly every matter where a decision has been taken and is recorded in the Bill, it is the right decision. With the one outstanding exception [the embargo on the transfer of compensation stock] (which is the Chancellor of the Exchequer's responsibility rather than that of the Minister of Fuel and Power), it is a good beginning.[1]

For its part, the *Colliery Guardian*, which was, predictably, the most hostile of the leading journals, voiced 'technical' or practical complaints, rather than root-and-branch condemnation: the Bill was thought to be too vague, the procedure for determining compensation unsatisfactory, the appropriation of ancillary assets too extensive. But for the *Colliery Guardian*, as for the other principal trade journal, the *Iron and Coal Trades Review*, the inevitability of public ownership and the lack of specificity in the Bill helped disarm any violent criticism.[2] In public discussion, therefore, critical response was muted—an apt reflection, on the right of the political spectrum, of the new mood which had been induced by the experience of the early 1940s, and, on the left, of the euphoria of Labour's Election victory.[3]

The same relative lack of drama or severe contention characterized the formal consultations with the owners and miners during the period between the introduction of the Bill and its enactment. The MAGB discussions produced more specific assurances by the government and a degree of satisfaction on various procedural points (e.g. the finances of the interim period before Vesting Day). But the owners had no effect on the main contours of the legislation as it applied to the assets to be nationalized or the method and type of compensation, although with the help of Parliamentary allies, they did secure a minor amendment to the restrictions on the transferability of the compensation stock.[4]

[1] *Daily Telegraph* 21 Dec. 1945; *The Economist* 22 Dec. 1945, 900. Also see *The Times* 2 Jan. 1946, 5.

[2] *CG* 14 Dec. 145, 736-7; 28 Dec. 1945, 790-2; 15 Feb. 1946, 223-5. Also see *ICTR* 28 Dec. 1945 (cited in POWE 28/34): 'It [*the Bill*] is drawn in such wide terms that it may just as easily be made a benevolent measure, fair to everyone concerned, as it may become a narrow and bigoted instrument designed to meet a political desire and nothing else.'

[3] For low-key criticism from the left, see 'The Tories and the Coal Bill', *New Statesman and Nation* 26 Jan. 1946, 58. There was a surprising absence of any detailed discussion of the legislation in the more popular socialist journals.

[4] There were ten meetings between the Ministry and the Mining Association after the presentation of the Bill. The records are in POWE 28/23 and 28/69. Also see Chester 1975, 72-4. For the Federation of British Industries' response, see the Press Release and letter to the Ministry of Fuel and Power in POWE 28/33.

There was, of course, a much closer potential relationship between the Labour Government and trade unionists. Quite apart from the intimacy of pre-election policy-making, there was an overlap of personnel: of the 393 Labour MPs, 120 were sponsored by unions, and 34 (of whom 10 had ministerial posts) by the NUM. Even so, there was relatively little official consultation about public ownership once Labour assumed power. Nor, surprisingly, was there a formal meeting with the National Union of Mineworkers before the publication of the nationalization Bill.

In fact, the first formal discussions took place with the TUC in January 1946. The Coal Industry Nationalisation Bill was considered at length at the initial meeting of the Fuel and Power Advisory Committee, which had been established by the TUC at the request of the Minister. The TUC representatives expressed their full agreement with the main principles of the legislation, but raised various points of detail concerning the absence of worker representation or formal provision for consultation. On the former question, Shinwell gave an assurance that he would appoint two trade unionists to the Board, after hearing advice from the TUC and the NUM (Walter Citrine and Ebby Edwards, the General Secretary of the NUM, were subsequently appointed). On the latter, he put forward his now-familiar case that formal consultative procedures would be superfluous. In both cases he avoided any commitment to the general principles advocated by his interlocutors.

The Minister had similar success with the miners, who were at this time preoccupied with questions of pay and conditions raised in the 'Miners' Charter'.[2] But it is none the less remarkable that they appear to have neglected many aspects of an enormously important measure for which they had argued for so long.[3] However, in spite of the fact that the government initially yielded little ground on the issue of consultation, trade-union pressure ultimately helped secure an amendment to the Bill, while the informal commitment to appoint two trade unionists was perhaps as far as the TUC or the NUM wished to push the question at that time.[4] It was in any case consistent with the miners' assumptions and strategies that they should have imagined that the replacement of private owners by a public corporation (in which their own General

[1] TUC, *78th Annual Conference. Report, 1946*, 208–12.
[2] Below, 684–7.
[3] For the meeting between the Minister and the NUM on 14 Jan. 1946 see POWE 28/66.
[4] *National Union of Mineworkers. Annual Conference, 1946. Report of Executive Committee, May 1946*, 10–11.

Secretary was to take charge of labour relations) would be a sufficiently major step after decades of frustration.

Within Parliament, as with formal consultations, Opposition criticism did not dispute the principle of nationalization.[1] The Conservatives did make a great deal of the apparent wide powers conceded to the Board and the Minister, of the restrictions on cash pay-outs, and of the Bill's lack of specificity about the shape and management of the industry and the amount of compensation (Harold Macmillan referred to it as 'a mere buck-passing Bill').[2] But these attacks were not pressed home with any decisiveness, and it was plain that the government was determined to make no concessions on the issues of compensation or the extent of the nationalization proposals. The Opposition was on more fertile ground in its criticisms of the Bill's alleged deficiencies in the area of consumer protection and the neglect of any substantive proposals on labour relations. And in these areas the government reacted with more flexibility.[3] The Bill was amended (albeit not very radically) so as to give the Minister specific powers to issue directives to the NCB if either of the Consumer Councils so recommended. More significantly, there were changes in the proposed legislation as it affected labour relations and consultative procedures.

In introducing the Second Reading, as in consultation with the NUM, the Minister had argued somewhat disingenuously, that he had 'not provided for statutory consultations with the workers employed in the industry' because 'Such consultation is certain, and statutory provision is superfluous.'[4] But in the course of parliamentary consideration of the Bill Shinwell came under sustained and varied pressure to introduce explicit legislation. This pressure came from the Conservative Opposition, from many of the government's supporters, and from the NUM. However, the most telling intervention came from the Minister of Labour George Isaacs, who in January 1946 successfully urged the inclusion of a statutory obligation on the NCB to establish joint negotiating machinery for wages and conditions and a procedure to settle disputes.[5]

[1] The Second Reading of the Bill took place on 29 and 30 Dec. It was in Committee between 12 Feb. and 10 Apr. 1946, and the Report Stage in the Commons was on 13 to 15 May. After further consideration in the two Houses the amended Bill returned to the Lords in early July, and was signed on 12 July.

[2] *Hansard* Standing Committee C, Jan.–Apr. 1946, col. 1271.

[3] Many relatively minor details were also changed. Altogether, about 250 amendments were ultimately discussed.

[4] *Hansard* 29 Jan. 1946, col. 712.

[5] POWE 28/67 (15 and 26 Jan. 1946); CAB 134/687 (29 Mar. 1946). In March, Harry Crookshank (Secretary for Mines in the 1930s) and Harold Macmillan wrote to the *Daily Telegraph*

The Bill was correspondingly amended in Committee, and the final version directed the Board to consult its employees about its operations and to discuss with the industry's unions the joint machinery needed to secure such consultation and to settle terms and conditions of employment.

With these changes, which did nothing to amend the basic principles of the scheme of nationalization drawn up in the summer of 1945, the Coal Industry Nationalisation Bill passed into law. It represented a culmination of a trend towards social control which had been operating, with intermittent strength, ever since the First World War. But because of its character, it left a wide range of questions to be determined by subsequent events. Among the most important of these were the amount of the compensation to be paid to coalowners, the organization of the industry below the level of the National Coal Board, and the position of the miners within the structure of decision-making and negotiation. There was, therefore, a sense in which matters always considered vital in discussions of reorganization and public control were postponed and placed outside the direct influence of the government—although it has to be acknowledged that the manner of the postponement was tantamount to a set of economic and political decisions.

In the first case, the fact that the government decided to approach the question of compensation in a spirit of 'fairness' and 'generosity', and referred the decision as to the amount to an independent tribunal, ensured that the owners were not treated in any punitive way. Given the pattern of the British political system and the need for the new Administration to retain a degree of political consensus, that was perhaps inevitable. Yet it certainly went against the grain of many radical commentaries on the owners' past failings. The process by which the final sum was ultimately determined will be discussed below,[1] but the amount, although not as much as the owners' more sanguine claims, was hardly negligible. The Tribunal estimated that the fixed (i.e. TS) assets were worth £164,660,000. Direct estimates of subsidiary (ancillary) assets by Valuation Boards produced a total of £90,562,000. Stocks were judged to be worth £34,631,000.[2]

---

claiming credit for the resulting amendment to the Bill, and Shinwell contemplated writing to refute this and to accept that the Minister of Labour had been the prime influence. He was dissuaded from doing so on political grounds: POWE 28/67.

[1] Below, 649–65.

[2] Chester 1975, 257. Minor elements in the compensation calculations amounted to a further £4,513,000 and the reimbursement for capital outlays after 1 Aug. 1945 was £16,774,000. The total

The nationalization of the coalmining industry was a critical precedent in the Labour Government's economic programme, and it is therefore not surprising that the government should be intent on sustaining morale and cooperation among industrialists generally, as well as avoiding political perturbations. It was also no doubt the case that the amount of compensation appeared to most advocates of public ownership an unimportant consideration when set against the final achievement of nationalization. Admittedly, the provisions for payment in government stock and the bar to its corporate sale took a good deal of political determination. But, considered as a whole and in its historical context, the act of coal nationalization probably treated the owners with more generosity than they might have expected from most previous discussions of such a structural change—and the decision to refer the valuation of the industry to a non-governmental agency ensured that this would be the case.[1]

The question of the organization of the industry raised more 'objective' issues. It was, indeed, very difficult to contest Shinwell's argument that regional and district structures could only be definitively determined by those who would have the ultimate responsibility for running the corporation (i.e. the National Coal Board itself). This was both a valid administrative observation and a politically necessary assumption if the Coal Industry Nationalisation Bill was to be formulated and passed within a reasonable time.[2] Yet the implications of the Bill for industrial organization pointed towards a degree of centralization which was bound to give rise to subsequent controversy.[3]

Throughout the discussions and debates Shinwell insisted that there was no alternative to *financial* centralization. This was because the variations in costs between districts and the distorting effects of recent policies (especially the wartime wage awards) would have made regional financial autonomy, with respect to pricing or sales policies for example, impossible to sustain. But the fact remained that the (central) National Coal Board was the *only* body with a statutory existence and definition. When, therefore, the time came to impose a regional and district structure on coalmining, it was hardly to be expected that the national

for the coalmining *industry* was, therefore, £311,140,000. In addition, the NCB took over the coal resources from the Coal Commission (£80,888,000).

[1] The owners were not excessively unhappy about the outcome: Foot to Fergusson, 7 June 1946: POWE 28/69.

[2] For the somewhat diffident discussion at the Committee stage of the possibility of stipulating a regional and administrative structure for the NCB, see *Hansard* 20 Feb. 1946, cols. 1149–60.

[3] Below, 675–6. For the question of organization, see Chester 1975, 389–91.

Board (which determined the type of intermediate boards and their membership) would be too daring in its departure from a centralized model.[1]

The third area in which an explicit decision was postponed—the precise relationship between the work-force and the corporation—offered an even clearer example of the extent to which the *absence* of positive provision nevertheless amounted to a policy commitment. Theories of worker control had long since disappeared from the centre of Labour's official thinking. More than this, the nationalization measure was based on the assumption of an 'open' management structure, with no particular role for worker representation. Even when the Minister agreed to amend the Bill to impose upon the NCB the duty of consulting its employees, he added 'that in his opinion the most effective way in which the experience of the workers could be harnessed to the management of the industry was to provide the broadest possible ladder whereby the really able individual worker could rise to managerial responsibility'.[2]

All this was in most respects a logical consequence of the circumstances of 1945–6 and the decision to nationalize the industry through a public corporation pledged to restructuring and efficiency. It was significant, for example, that the Minister's brief for the Second Reading had pointed out that nationalization was inevitable and was supported by a large majority in the country, and that its principal justifications were pragmatic: to secure adequate finance for industrial reorganization, the full cooperation of all personnel, the optimum use of the best mining engineers, and low-cost coal.[3] Such 'technocratic' views left little room for experiment with social forms. But given the circumstances of the time and the basis of most recent arguments in favour of state ownership, it is not easy to see what other decision about the role of the work-force could have been arrived at—even by a Labour Government.

That the consequences for the miners within the industry's structure were so remote from the expectations of earlier advocates of nationalization was hardly relevant in the circumstances of 1945–6. Indeed, by that time neither the TUC, which publicly approved the Bill,[4] nor the NUM raised very much protest. And from even further left in the trade

[1] Below, 676.
[2] CAB 134/687 (Sixth Meeting of Committee of Ministers on the Socialisation of Industries, 29 Mar. 1946).
[3] POWE 28/34.
[4] TUC, *What the TUC is Doing* (Apr. 1946), 20.

union movement, confronted with what was thought to be a new era, criticism was rare.[1] The existence of a Labour Government, reforming and sympathetic, obviously made all the difference to many socialist commentators. Even the staunch Guild Socialist G. D. H. Cole acknowledged that it would be necessary to get the industry back on its feet and develop a new spirit of public responsibility before a more 'representative' Board or any measure of self-government could be introduced into the nationalized coal industry.[2] As the TUC noted, its Interim Report on Reconstruction (which had advocated a measure of worker representation) 'was drafted and approved at a time when it was not known whether or not the transfer of industries to public ownership would take place under a majority Labour Government'.[3] In the event, it did so—and the majority was huge.

As a result, in the flush of victory, and confronted with the problems of postwar Britain, only a few left-wing critics of the government were anxious about the ideological moderation of the nationalization of coalmining or the emergence of 'State capitalism'.[4] To the overwhelming majority of the advocates of public ownership, it had been so much desired and so long coming, that the fact was infinitely more important than the form.

iv. Compensation

The nationalization of coalmining, considered as a political act and a transfer of legal ownership, appeared to resolve a problem which had infected the industry's economic relationships and performance for decades. It removed what had been presented as the grievance of the work-force, and although other grievances and material aspirations prevented any very far-reaching transformation of attitudes, the miners had at least achieved their principal long-run goal. Their victory, however, was not reflected in a commensurate defeat for the owners, except in the sense that they were obliged to exchange one set of assets for another.

In 1945, as we have seen, the owners had proved surprisingly accommodating to the idea of nationalization—offering almost immediate

[1] Horner 1946, 41–6.
[2] Cole 1946, 313–14.
[3] TUC Archives, 603.4 (4 Jan. 1946).
[4] See G. Cooper, 'The Team Spirit' in *New Statesman and Nation* 18 May 1946, 355: 'A cynic might summarise the nationalisation measures briefly: "for private enterprise read State capitalism".' Cf. Harold Macmillan's verdict ('It was pure State capitalism') in Macmillan 1959, 73.

cooperation to the Minister of Fuel and Power. Such acquiescence was no doubt based on an awareness of political reality: a change of heart on the part of the Labour Government was inconceivable. But it was also possibly influenced by a sense that if the troublesome and hazardous ownership of coalmines could be abandoned in return for a good measure of compensation (a likelihood which would be the greater if the owners proved cooperative with the new Administration), they would not after all have struck a particularly bad bargain. Such emotions had been anticipated in 1919.[1]

From September 1945, then, the terms of compensation rather than the possibility of expropriation, were the contentious issue as far as the owners were concerned. And even on this question, they could be reasonably confident that they would be treated with a measure of generosity. Since at least the early 1930s the Labour Party and the TUC had accepted that public ownership would not involve confiscation, and that 'fair compensation' would be paid for nationalized property.[2] Moreover, as we have seen, at the outset of its nationalization programme the new Labour Government felt it to be politically and practically expedient to be as generous as possible towards the dispossessed owners. The Mining Association therefore received a promise of fair compensation in the opening weeks of the new Administration.

What was to be the basis of that compensation? Although there were those who toyed with the idea of paying for nationalized property with reference to its stock-market valuation, the consensus within the government, and a view shared by the industry, was that the principal basis of payment should be that accepted by the Labour Party before coming to power, and already used in the 1930s (at the creation of the London Passenger Transport Board in 1931 and to acquire coal royalties under the Coal Act of 1938): the annual 'net maintainable revenue' (i.e. profits) of the property should be estimated on the basis of past earnings adjusted to existing and reasonable circumstances (e.g. excluding abnormal or monopolistic determinants of profits) and taking account of the probability of their continuing. This annual revenue was, in essence, an assessment of probable future profits in a more or less competitive situation, *and assuming that the property had not been nationalized*. The revenue figure would then be translated into a notional capital value by being multiplied by an appropriate number of years' purchase—a

---

[1] Above, 134–5.

[2] For a discussion of Labour attitudes to the terms of compensation for nationalized property, see Chester 1975, ch. III.

number which itself reflected an appropriate rate of return on the capital derived from an estimate of the reliability or riskiness of the revenue.[1] The resulting value would be the figure used for compensation purposes.

Straightforward as these principles might appear, the position of the coal industry, in this as in so many other ways, proved exceedingly complicated, and gave rise to a characteristically complicated procedure.

First, the estimate of the prospective net maintainable revenue in an industry with coal's record was itself an extremely subjective matter which could generate endless disputation. Secondly, the method was only really appropriate to part of the industry's assets. This was because the only unambiguous basis for a historical view of revenues were the 'TS' (Terms of Settlement) 'ascertainments' of output and tonnage profits agreed between miners and owners under the various district wage agreements since 1921. However, these figures related to a strictly defined range of business activities (and therefore of assets) which were central to coalmining proper, whereas the Coal Industry Nationalisation Act would provide for the acquisition of a much wider range of 'ancillary' assets (coal wagons, coke ovens, brickworks, houses, land, etc.). As a result, since an adequate statistical series of net revenue existed only for the former category, it was only the 'coal industry assets' which were obligatorily to be valued in terms of their net maintainable revenue multiplied by a number of years' purchase. The other properties—'subsidiary assets' as they were known—might have to be valued on other bases and probably in more direct ways. Nor would it have been possible to assess the worth of colliery companies in their entirety, since many of the leading coal producers were also 'composite' companies, undertaking business activities which would be outside the scope of nationalization. Finally, the

---

[1] Thus, suppose the net maintainable revenue of an industry was estimated at £10 million. If it was assumed that this was an extremely secure profit, perhaps analogous to the guaranteed yield on government securities paying, say, 4%, then the appropriate number of years' purchase would be 25 (i.e. a capital sum of [£10 million × 25] would yield an annual revenue of £10 million). If, on the other hand, the net maintainable revenue was assumed to be analogous to the return on average industrial investment, and that return was found to be 8%, then the appropriate number of years' purchase would be 12.5 (since a capital sum of [£10 million × 12.5] would, at 8%, yield an income of £10 million). Obviously, the greater the risks of a business the higher the yield but the lower the number of years' purchase—and vice versa. It was therefore in the interests of the owners to argue that their profits were secure (as well as large), not only because this implied a large net maintainable revenue (in the future) but also because it increased the number of years' purchase that would be applied to the revenue figure to derive a capital value for compensation purposes.

resulting unwieldiness was compounded by the size and fragmentation of the industry. And this necessitated a multi-tiered, and very pro-longed, procedure.[1]

At the heart of the process of valuation was a global estimate (by an independent Coal Industry Nationalisation Compensation Tribunal under the chairmanship of Lord Greene) of the 'coal-industry value' of the assets to be brought into public ownership. The resulting total sum was then allocated, by a Central Valuation Board, between the various districts (although the principles to be used for the diversion were not formally laid down).[2] Meanwhile, the Minister of Fuel and Power pre-scribed District Valuation Boards (he designated eight Boards to oversee valuations in 21 coalmining districts), and it was these Boards which had the most complex task of all—the valuation of 'compensation units'. The concept of a compensation unit also derived from the complexity of the coal industry, since it was a way of meeting the fact that companies which produced coal might have only part of their assets nationalized and often operated in more than one district.

It was the Minister of Fuel and Power's responsibility to propose compensation units consisting of assets belonging to one company and attributable to one coal district.[3] He was also required to stipulate which of a compensation unit's assets were pertinent to the coal industry valuation. It was the District Valuation Boards' task to assess the market value of each compensation unit, and to decide the distribution of that worth between coal industry and subsidiary assets. It could then distribute, with respect to the compensation units, the district's share of

---

[1] The procedures which determined the valuation and compensation of the coal industry are described in POWE 9/2 (*Ministry of Power. Funding of Departmental Experience. Compensation arrangements in Nationalising the Coal, Electricity and Gas Industries*. By R. L. M. James (3 June 1959)); Chester 1975, ch. III; Mozoomdar 1953, ch. 6.

[2] Although TS figures for output and tonnage profits were available for individual districts, it was not possible simply to scale down the global coal industry value in some proportion to the recorded output and profits of individual districts. This was because such data for the various districts were likely to be affected by quite different considerations in the course of time and in the future. Thus, the relative prospects of the Nottinghamshire and Lancashire fields in 1946 were not precisely predictable from their relative output and profit performance in the 1930s. If the net maintainable revenue method were to be used for the allocation of the global sum between districts (and it was not precluded by the legislation), it could only have been done by separate discussions and calculations for each district. In the event, the Central Valuation Board did not divulge the basis on which it finally allocated the global sum between districts.

[3] All nationalized assets had to be in compensation units—i.e. the total of compensation units was the total of the industry to be nationalized. Each compensation unit would belong to one company (which also, of course, might own non-coal assets outside the scope of the Act). How-ever, it was not necessarily the case that all of a company's relevant assets in one district would be in one compensation unit. It might be decided to divide its assets between more than one unit.

the global sum for coal industry value in proportion to the units' notional coal industry value, while awarding the units' owners the full assessed values of their subsidiary assets (which were not restricted by any figure equivalent to the global sum attributable to the coal industry assets).

The administrative detail involved in all this was extraordinary: the central government staff employed on stipulating compensation units was about 100, and the documentation listing each unit's assets averaged 100 foolscap sheets and in one case reached 250,000. More than this, since the procedure provided for lengthy appeals and *ad hoc* arbitrations, while many of those involved had little incentive to expedite matters, the whole process was prolonged to the point of scandal. This problem did not apply to Lord Greene's National Tribunal, since its rules were straightforward and its main data readily available. Hence, it met in February and was able to report in August 1946.

The much more complex task of allocating the resulting global sum between districts (and considering claims and counter-claims) took much longer: it was not completed until February 1949. Yet even this applied only to the coal industry values for the industry and for the districts. The actual compensation to be paid to companies could only be determined after all *subsidiary* values (for every compensation unit) had been decided and after every unit's coal industry value had been determined.[1] It was in fact not until early 1952, a full five years after Vesting Day, that there was a sufficient supply of information about compensation units for District Valuation Boards to begin their work in earnest; and although partial payments were made in the interim, the final valuations were not completed until December 1956—a decade after nationalization had taken effect. The cost of the exercise to the taxpayer had been £6.5 million.[2]

Once the principles and procedures for compensation had been established, the central government's direct role in valuing the industry's assets was confined to providing evidence to the Tribunal which was to determine the global sum for property relevant to coal industry purposes. It so happened that this award turned out to be less than 60 per cent of the total compensation eventually paid to colliery companies.[3] Nevertheless, the consideration of this category of asset is

---

[1] This was because the share of each unit in the global (coal industry) sum allocated to its district was determined by its proportion of the total of assessed coal industry values for *all* units.

[2] POWE 9/2.

[3] Below, 660.

of considerable significance, for it was the last important occasion for a large-scale review of the private industry's twentieth-century history and of the multiple influences which bore upon its performance and profitability.

The Terms of Reference for the determination of compensation stipulated that the Tribunal should base its ascertainment of a fair compensation for coal industry assets on an estimate of the sum that a willing buyer might pay a willing seller in the open market, basing his decision on the net annual maintainable revenue (in the absence of public ownership) and a number of years' purchase.[1] There was to be no allowance for the fact that the acquisition was compulsory or that there might be an increase in value by virtue of there being a single owner. The Tribunal was provided with agreed figures of prewar profits, and was steered away from taking account of the abnormal wartime years. Of necessity, then, the Tribunal was expected to undertake a task in which history (past performance and experience) and counterfactual analysis (how well the industry might have done in the postwar world had it remained in private hands) both figured prominently.

The owners' claim, presented through the MAGB, was generous to the point of grandioseness. They argued that the causes of low profits before 1936 (excess capacity, lack of market discipline and selling organization, the slump and export dependence) had been largely eliminated. In addition, they drew attention to the rising trend of production and profits in the late 1930s, to the growth of industrial self-discipline, full employment, and a widespread appreciation of the advantages of technical modernization and reorganization. The industry's future prospects under private enterprise, they asserted, would have been made the more rosy by full-employment policies, the owners' determination to restructure the industry, and the labour force's appreciation of the rationality of the Foot Plan. They therefore argued that they could easily have produced and sold 240 million tons of coal annually, with every expectation of earning a net profit of 1s. 9d. per ton even while holding down prices. This increase in unit profits on a larger output would have been achieved by a dramatic improvement in productivity.

Translated into future financial prospects, the figures (according to the MAGB) would mean a global revenue of £21 million—of which £11 million would have been certain, and of such low risk as to be capitalized at $16\frac{2}{3}$ years' purchase (implying an equivalent rate of return of only 6 per cent). The remaining future income of £10 million would

[1] *Coal Industry Nationalisation. 1945* Cmd. 6716.

have had a present value of £6 million, and might be thought to be twice as risky as the certain income, and therefore should attract 8⅓ years' purchase (reflecting a return of 12 per cent because of the greater risk). Taken together, these figures implied a current net maintainable revenue of £17 million and a coal industry value of some £233 million.[1]

Within the Ministry of Fuel and Power, these assertions met with incredulity and scorn. The officials' first view was that the coal industry's prospective revenue would have been only about £11.3 million (i.e. the prewar level for 1935–9 less permitted deductions), although this was revised to £11 million in the official submission to the Greene Tribunal.[2] Looking to the stock-market valuation of companies and their dividends, the civil servants felt that this revenue should be capitalized at between 12 and 14 years' purchase—giving a capital sum of between £132 and £154 million, from which would have to be deducted the agreed figure of £25 million for working capital. The government's estimate of the industry's compensation value (between about £107 and £129 million) was, therefore, roughly half of the owners' valuation.[3]

Of course, given that it was in the government's interest to moderate the sum paid in compensation, it was only to be expected that the Ministry of Fuel and Power and its representatives and consultants should mount a multi-pronged argument designed to demonstrate the unsatisfactory record and poor prospects of the coalmining industry under private enterprise.[4] Yet the strength of their arguments, the

[1] POWE 28/236 ('Coal Industry Nationalisation Arbitration. Case for the Mining Association of Great Britain').

[2] The revised figure was apparently based on a more exact calculation of permissible deductions from the prewar figures. The Ministry assumed that changes in the value of money between the late 1930s and 1946 (which might have led to a scaling-up of the figures for nominal profits to take account of inflation) had been counterbalanced by a deterioration in the circumstances of private enterprise in the industry (which reduced the real value of profits).

[3] POWE 28/236 ('Coal Industry Nationalisation Compensation Tribunal. Case on behalf of His Majesty's Government'); POWE 28/235 ('Notes on the MAGB Case' and 'Coal Industry Compensation Tribunal. Outline of Government Arguments'). The Ministry's original, internal estimate of compensation value had been between £135.6 and £158.2 million, less £25 million of working capital.

[4] Material relating to internal discussions within the Ministry and formal proofs of evidence (by the owners as well as government representatives) to the Greene Tribunal are in POWE 28/108, 235–40. Sir Ernest Gowers, Sir Charles Reid, John Armstrong (the Ministry's Labour Adviser), Sir Henry Clay (the economist), and a number of prominent civil servants, accountants, and engineers participated in the preliminary discussions and gave evidence to the Greene Tribunal. POWE 28/236 contains the formal submission (in summary) of the government's case; POWE 28/329 contains the MAGB's general case. Each was supplemented by detailed submissions relating to particular aspects of the industry. Transcripts of the Greene hearings are in POWE 28/44.

scepticism about the owners' record, and even the occasional note of
acerbic contempt, were hardly inappropriate in light of the MAGB's
assertions, which were thought to be 'fantastic'. Looking back to the
prewar record, the Ministry pointed out that the level of profits had
fluctuated wildly, and included years of large losses. It was, however,
prepared to accept the aggregate profit levels of 1935–9 as a baseline,
even though they also marked a peak, with annual output at 213 million
tons, and annual profits of 1 s. 1 d. per ton and £11.63 million in total.[1]

The officials were entirely unwilling to go beyond these levels. They
argued that on every score the owners could not have been expected to
do better than that in the postwar world, and that a prospective
purchaser could not have been optimistic about profits. The purchase
would be speculative because of the industry's unstable history and the
'long canvassed possibility of its nationalisation'; the markets for coal
were likely to be very difficult as competition, fuel economies, and coal-
substitutes (oil, atomic power) continued to develop;[2] labour supply, in
light of the industry's bad reputation among prospective employees,
would have continued to be a severe restriction on output; the industry's notorious labour relations, in the absence of public ownership,
would have undermined the owners' efforts to raise productivity; labour
shortages, trade-union power, and political sensitivities would have
imposed higher wage costs while simultaneously limiting the owners'
ability to sustain prices, with a consequent profits squeeze.

The strength of these arguments was very considerable, for the
owners' case involved an assumption which was exceedingly difficult
to accept: that there had been an abrupt transformation of the power-

---

[1] The annual average figures were:

Years	Tonnage commercially disposable (m.)	Profit per ton (d.)	Balance (£ m.)
1922–39	211	7.75	6.90
1930–9	208	8.50	7.36
1933–9	209	10.75	9.26
1935–9	213	13.00	11.63

Source: POWE 28/235 ('Coal Industry Compensation Tribunal. Outline of
Government Arguments').

[2] POWE 28/240 (Proof of evidence of Sir Harold Hartley); POWE 28/235 ('The Internal
demand for Coal in the United Kingdom in the Period between the two Wars. By Mr J. N. R.
Stone').

ful and deeply rooted economic and political trends which had determined the industry's market, labour relations, and prices since the First World War.

But the most telling points in the Ministry's case concerned the owners' claims that the growth of output and productivity would have been attained by a massive programme of industrial reorganization, consolidation, and technical innovation. For it was almost ridiculously easy to mount the most devastating critique of such claims. Within the Ministry, for example, sharp words were uttered concerning the owners' 'lamentable record in the matter of reorganization throughout the period between the Wars' and on their 'stubborn opposition' which had 'completely stultified' the work of the Coal Mines Reorganisation Commission in the 1930s.

Hardly surprising, Sir Ernest Gowers (who chaired the departmental committee which assembled the government's case) produced a swingeing attack on the owners' record and potential for change. He dismissed the Foot Plan (which, by 1946, had turned out to be a vulnerable hostage to fortune) as entirely inadequate to postwar needs. It was, he argued, the very antithesis of what was needed—which was rapid, comprehensive, and assured reorganization. Under continued private ownership, the industry would have lacked the essential prerequisites of structural and technical change: substantial support from the owners and the presence of compulsory devices to discipline recalcitrant minorities and share the burdens of reorganization.[1]

These arguments were also lent considerable force by Sir Charles Reid's evidence. For although Reid was not as openly condemnatory of the owners' record as Gowers, he was able to demonstrate that the Report which bore his name contrasted very markedly with the owners' own pre-nationalization plans (the mechanism to encourage amalgamations in the Foot Plan, he told the Tribunal, was 'useless'). He confirmed the conclusions of the Reid Report, to the effect that the industry needed a strong central authority, large-scale efforts, the cooperation of labour, and a lengthy and complicated programme of modernization and reorganization extending over 10 or 20 years—all of which were inconsistent with the insubstantial assertions concerning

---

[1] The internal discussions, from which the direct quotations in the text are taken, and which led to the formulation of Gowers's evidence, are in POWE 28/235 ('Coal Industry Compensation Tribunal. Outline of the Government Arguments'). Gowers's Proof of Evidence is in POWE 28/108, and a transcript of his appearance before the Tribunal is in POWE 28/44, Part 4 (20th Day).

the ease and speed of reform put forward by the MAGB in its submission to the Tribunal.[1] As the government's summary submission put it, the industry's structure under private enterprise was 'inimical to its overall efficiency', and private enterprise was unlikely to be able to secure the reorganization necessary to overcome that most severe of handicaps.[2]

Clearly, the owners were at a double disadvantage in their arguments to the Compensation Tribunal. Not only did they have a poor historical record with respect to the very issues (harmonious labour relations, industrial reorganizaton) which were central to their case for future prosperity, but the plans they had formulated as the War drew to a close, and which might be assumed to reflect their aspirations unencumbered by the need to make a case for high compensation, were patently inadequate to the objectives they now wished to embrace before a Compensation Tribunal. And it was obvious from the tone of members of the Tribunal as they questioned the MAGB representatives that there was, indeed, some scepticism about the authenticity of their new arguments and what Lord Greene called their sudden 'change of heart'.

The Tribunal itself appeared to share the Ministry's view that the evidence of modernization schemes undertaken by private companies was largely spurious as an indication of any substantial change in the industry as a whole. In effect, the MAGB arguments in the spring and summer of 1946 looked suspiciously like a second, and even less credible, instalment of the 'death-bed repentance' that some observers had detected in the claims that surrounded the appearance of the Foot Plan eighteen months earlier.

But if the heavy hand of history lay restrainingly on the owners' rather airy claims for a very generous level of compensation, and even though they appeared to have had the worst of the arguments before the Tribunal, the financial outcome was by no means punitive. On 1 August 1946 the Compensation Tribunal reported to the government and the MAGB that the compensation value of the coal industry assets was, in their judgement, £164,660,000.

Unfortunately, Lord Greene and his colleagues were laconic in the extreme, for they provided neither an indication of their assumptions concerning net maintainable revenue and the number of years' pur-

---

[1] POWE 28/240; POWE 28/44, Part 4 (19th Day).
[2] POWE 28/236 ('Coal Industry Nationalisation Compensation Tribunal. Case on Behalf of His Majesty's Government').

chase, nor any other explanation of how they arrived at their decision. (Within the Ministry there were various attempts to guess at the Tribunal's methods, including the possibility that there had been a simple splitting of the difference between rival claims concerning total value and the extent of working capital.)[1] Nevertheless, in light of the Tribunal's hearings, as well as of contemporary circumstances and past experience, this level of compensation does seem more on the generous than the mean side. Certainly, the share prices of leading colliery companies (particularly in South Yorkshire and the East Midlands), which had been firm since the original announcement of the government's nationalization plans, rose strongly after the Tribunal's announcement, and shares of other industries likely to be nationalized were also marked up. Representatives of both the owners and the government expressed satisfaction with the outcome of the proceedings.[2]

One reason why shares in companies in the more prosperous fields rose more than the average on 1–2 August 1946 was the expectation that when the global sum came to be divided among the various districts, those areas would benefit disproportionately, and that the district valuations of subsidiary assets would also favour the strong units. This is a reminder, of course, that the Greene Tribunal's estimate was only a first step in the process of compensation, and that the later ones would provide more scope for the direct assessment of capital worth—both to determine the district and company shares of the global figures and (of perhaps greater significance) to build up a compensation value for the subsidiary assets which were not to be subject to an upper limit.[3] As we have seen, that process was excessively tedious and prolonged. And its duration and the methods used take it outside our immediate field of interest. However, the outcomes *are* important as an indication of the grand denouement of the business side of the history of the coalmining industry under private ownership.

In round figures, the owners received £310 million for the industry, although this included about £17 million of direct repayment of expenditures on capital development undertaken in 1945–6. The final reckoning

---

[1] POWE 28/237; Chester 1975, 250.

[2] For example, the shares of the Bolsover, Butterley, Sheepbridge, Shipley, and Staveley Companies all rose by between 4 and 7% on the day. Increases in colliery shares were general. They were reported, and official and industry reactions to the Tribunal's verdict were discussed, in *Financial Times* 2 Aug. 1946, 1, and 3 Aug. 1946, 1 and 2; *Daily Mail* 3 Aug. 1946, 3; *The Times* 3 Aug. 1946, 7; *The Economist* 10 Aug. 1946, 223–4; *Daily Herald* 2 Aug. 1946, 1.

[3] Above, 652–3.

in the public accounts, listing compensation payments to colliery companies under the Coal Industry Nationalisation Act, came to a total of £309,653,176 8s. 9d. The broad composition of this total is summarized in Table 14.1.

Table 14.1. *Total compensation under the Coal Industry Nationalisation Act*

	£
Coal industry value	164,660,000
Main subsidiary value	78,059,404
Short workings, former freehold leases, etc.	2,360,988
Stocks and stores	33,606,976
Wagons	12,331,841
Superiorities	288,601
Severance payments	689,137
Capital outlay refunds	17,656,229
TOTAL	309,653,176

Using the NCB's accounts for 1954, the historian of nationalization quotes a figure of £392,028,000 for total payments: Chester, *Nationalisation*, 257. However, £80,888,000 of this represented payments for minerals, of which the overwhelming bulk embodied the take-over of the nation's coal resources from the Coal Commission. This left payments to colliery companies and others of £311,140,000. The NCB's figures were divided as follows:

	£000
Coal industry (TS) assets	164,660
Subsidiary (ancillary) assets	90,562
Stocks of products and stores	34,631
Severance payments	689
Capital outlay refunds	16,774
Disputed (irrecoverable) liabilities taken over	3,824
TOTAL	311,140

There are minor discrepancies between this account and the final reckoning in the public records, but the differences are very small.

Source: POWE 35/244.

If, therefore, we ignore the small sum on account on 'severance payments' (compensation for the increased burden of overheads in companies which remained in private business), and the self-balancing repayment of expenditures undertaken between the announcement of the nationalization plans and Vesting Day, the total direct compensation for expropriation was £291,307,804—of which £164,660,000 represented coal industry value and £126,647,804 (much more than had been originally assumed by Ministry officials) 'subsidiary value'. Of even more interest, perhaps, was the geographical breakdown of the compensation payments, indicated in Table 14.2.

Table 14.2. *Compensation payments to colliery companies in principal districts*[a]

	Coal industry value £	Subsidiary value £
Northumberland	9,547,000	7,197,680
Durham	13,005,000	26,476,508
Lancashire & Cheshire	8,086,000	5,156,649
Yorkshire	35,701,000	27,608,244
North Derbyshire	13,414,000	7,764,294
South Derbyshire	3,318,000	568,351
Nottinghamshire	17,983,000	9,309,558
Leicestershire	3,671,000	938,243
Cannock Chase	5,142,000	2,126,553
North Staffordshire	5,752,000	2,174,642
Warwickshire	7,286,000	2,560,927
South Wales & Mons.	14,231,000	19,579,644
Scotland	21,837,000	11,972,628
Other	5,693,000	3,213,883
TOTAL	164,660,000	126,647,804

[a] Excluding severance payments and capital outlay refunds.

Source: POWE 35/244.

The division of the global compensation between the various coal-mining districts was far from straightforward, since they differed in terms of their profitability as coal producers and the extent to which they undertook the sort of ancillary activities which justified compensation for subsidiary assets. Durham and South Wales, for example, had subsidiary values which were larger than their coal industry values—no doubt because they combined substantial coking and other allied plant with a relatively weak coal-trading business. In all but two of the main fields, however, the proportionate distribution of the final coal industry

Table 14.3. *Average market values (January–June 1945), yields and compensation,*[a] *selected public colliery companies (£000)*

	Market value of ordinary, preference, and debenture shares (i)	Yield % (ii)	Coal industry value (iii)	Subsidiary value (iv)	(iii) + (iv)
DURHAM					
Bearpark Coal & Coke	269.3	7.9	80.4	269.8	350.2
John Bowes & Partners	715.5	5.9	695.1	1,446.8	2,141.9
Hordern Collieries	2,011.1	8.3	1,202.5	1,799.4	3,001.9
Lambton, Hetton & Joicey Collieries	2,263.6	7.0	1,213.4	2,154.7	3,368.1
South Hetton Coal	703.9	6.0	638.5	555.9	1,194.4
Wearmouth Coal	796.5	6.8	854.0	675.0	1,529.0
YORKSHIRE					
Airedale Collieries	1,275.0	7.8	1,322.0	168.1	1,490.1
Briggs Colliery	1,207.0	4.4	1,948.0	15.3	1,963.3
Carlton Main Colliery	2,846.4	8.4	2,050.6	599.1	2,649.7
Cortonwood	299.5	8.0	290.2	247.9	538.1
Doncaster Amalgamated Collieries	5,835.0	6.9	4,888.4	1,689.6	6,578.0
Houghton Main	903.0	10.7	468.3	113.7	582.0
Lofthouse Colliery	102.7	10.9	321.6	22.1	343.7
Manvers Main	1,040.0	6.8	1,305.8	1,058.7	2,364.5
Nunnery Colliery	511.1	6.6	97.1	240.1	337.2
Wharncliffe Silkstone	202.5	7.4	132.3	121.2	253.5

North Derbyshire & Nottinghamshire					
Bolsover Colliery	8,057.7	5.8	7,737.1	551.2	8,288.3
Butterley	3,777.5	6.3	2,932.0	423.2	3,355.2
Grassmoor	434.2	6.8	119.5	369.0	488.5
New Hucknall	1,593.8	6.5	1,025.5	855.6	1,881.1
Shipley	1,535.7	6.2	1,631.8	109.1	1,740.9
North Staffordshire					
Cannock & Rougeley	2,797.7	6.7	1,287.2	206.3	1,493.5
Norton & Biddulph Collieries	1,088.2	7.3	1,123.6	99.5	1,223.1
Sneyd Collieries	865.5	7.8	472.9	134.3	607.2
Kent					
Chislet Colliery	668.0	5.1	356.0	105.0	461.0
South Wales & Monmouthshire					
Ocean & United National Collieries	5,609.2	6.3	1,739.3	425.1	2,164.4
Partridge, Jones & John Paton	2,092.5	8.2	1,030.8	371.5	1,402.3
Powell Duffryn	15,785.6	6.3	4,662.7	7,509.1	12,171.8
Scotland					
Fife Coal	3,371.7	5.7	4,219.0	803.5	5,022.5
Lothian Coal	1,876.5	7.7	1,881.1	946.2	2,827.3
Niddrie & Benhar	865.0	6.9	932.9	433.2	1,366.1

[a] Excluding payments for shortworkings, unworked minerals, severance compensation, stocks, stores, capital outlay refunds, and all other items excluded from global figures for coal industry value and subsidiary value.

Source: POWE 28/235 (market values and yields); POWE 35/244 (compensations).

valuation corresponded fairly closely with or exceeded estimates produced at an early stage by the Ministry's former Director of Finance. The exceptions, not surprisingly, were Durham and South Wales, which got significantly less.[1]

The experience of individual companies naturally varied—and for reasons which are too complex to be easily reconstituted so long after the event. Table 14.3 lists the direct compensation paid to a number of companies whose stock-market value (for early 1945) was calculated within the Ministry of Fuel and Power. From this it will be seen that there were predictably large differences in the relative importance of coal industry and subsidiary values (mostly depending on the degree of specialization in the production, rather than the processing, of coal). Looking to the total compensation, however, there were relatively few startling disparities between market valuations on the eve of the decision to nationalize and the actual compensation paid. Most colliery companies outside South Wales did better than their market values indicated—and Manvers Main in Yorkshire together with most companies in Durham and those in Scotland did very much better, often by between 50 and 100 per cent (again, no doubt, because of the relative significance of their subsidiary assets, for which no upper limit of compensation was stipulated).

Two general points can be made about these statistical comparisons.

---

[1] The following figures (in £ million) of estimated and actual valuations of coal industry assets are derived from POWE 28/235 (estimate by L. H. Lowe, 18 Mar. 1946) and POWE 35/244:

	Ministry estimate	Actual
Scotland	19.0	21.9
Northumberland	7.5	9.5
Durham	16.0	13.0
Yorkshire	31.0	35.7
Derbyshire	12.5	16.7
Nottinghamshire	15.0	18.0
Lancashire & Cheshire	8.0	8.1
South Wales & Monmouthshire	15.0	14.2
Other	26.0	27.6
TOTAL	150.0	164.7

Lowe's total estimate was derived from the stock-exchange value of 36 leading colliery companies (accounting for 50% of the industry's profits).

First, the stock market appears to have taken good account of the value of the relatively prosperous collieries of Nottinghamshire and North Derbyshire. Secondly, the sorry history of South Wales colliery companies continued right down to the act of nationalization: each of the three large companies listed in Table 14.3 secured compensation much below their stock-market value (Powell Duffryn suffered less, although still receiving only about 80 per cent of its stock-market value, in the main perhaps because of its greater dependence on subsidiary and collateral activities).

It is impossible to estimate how representative these figures were, since the companies listed were selected on a more or less arbitrary basis. For example, the Table includes only 12 of the 23 colliery companies which received compensation (coal industry value plus subsidiary value) in excess of £1.5 million.[1] Yet it is unlikely that the broad picture would be changed by more comprehensive figures. For the coal industry as a whole the 'offer' with which the MAGB had intimidated the government in 1919—nationalization at a fair price[2]—had, a generation later, been accepted.

It was, perhaps, as well for the coalowners that, as far as they were concerned, the transition to public ownership took place at the level of arbitration and commercial valuation. Given the history of adversarial politics which had characterized the industry for so long, they might have done much worse if public attitudes and the miners' resentments had been allowed more sway. As it was, however, the government's desire to avoid controversy and the application of rules of equity meant that the end of private enterprise as the dominant force in coalmining came in a much more tranquil atmosphere than had marked its dominance over the previous 40 years.

---

[1] See Appendix 14.1.
[2] Above, 134.

Appendix 14.1

Colliery companies whose compensation exceeded £1.5 million
not otherwise listed in Table 14.3

Company	Coal industry value £000	Subsidiary value £000
NORTHUMBERLAND		
Ashington Coal	2,601.7	1,605.6
Bedlington Coal	1,026.8	102.0
LANCASHIRE		
Manchester Collieries	3,346.2	714.8
YORKSHIRE		
Amalgamated Denaby Collieries	3,368.4	2,352.8
Barber Walker (but also see Nottinghamshire)	1,197.4	276.4
Earl Fitzwilliam's Collieries	2,112.8	1.3
NORTH DERBYSHIRE		
Hardwick Industries	1,574.7	163.0
Sheepbridge Coal & Iron	1,321.6	433.3
Staveley Coal & Iron	1,019.8	654.8
NOTTINGHAMSHIRE		
Barber Walker (but also see Yorkshire)	1,530.4	2,106.6
Newstead Colliery	1,627.0	280.6
SCOTLAND		
Bairds & Dalmellington	2,904.8	770.0

Source: POWE 35/244.

CHAPTER 15

A National Enterprise in Historical Perspective

After decades of controversy and anguish, the nationalization of coal-mining was achieved with little hesitation in a relatively few months of 1945–6. No doubt that was largely because all alternative courses of action had been decisively rejected by one or other influential body of opinion. Only public ownership remained as a virtually non-partisan policy. In 1946, *The Economist* pointed out that against the possibility that nationalization might have little success in dealing with the twin crises of industrial relations and technical reorganization, had to be set the fact that 'no other device seems able to achieve any at all'.[1] In an important sense, public ownership emerged as national policy *faute de mieux*, and it may be that the subsequent deficiencies of public owner-ship, particularly the lack of any systematic forethought as to the struc-ture and policy of a nationalized coal industry, flowed from that fact.

Nevertheless, it is also well to re-emphasize that the advocacy of public ownership had its positive sides, which the experience of the 1920s and 1930s, and even more of the war years, had brought into increasing prominence. On the one hand, given the fragmentation and weakness of private enterprise in the industry, direct national control was assumed by many to be the only effective way of bringing to bear the scarce financial and technical resources, and introducing the co-ordinated programmes of industrial modernization which, for at least two decades, had been urged as prerequisites of economic survival. On the other hand, and politically more telling among many who were otherwise sceptical of state intervention, nationalization was assumed to be the only way of harnessing the cooperation of the work-force to the tasks of continuous operations, let alone the improvement of productiv-ity.[2] To many observers, as well as to the miners themselves, the War had offered decisive proof that the labour force was not prepared, nor (given its new-found power) did it *need* to be prepared, to lend its

---

[1] *The Economist* 20 July 1946, 89.   [2] Above, ch. 13.

support or cooperation to industrial development as long as the system of private enterprise continued.

Whether nationalization ultimately effected a transformation of industrial relations and the extent to which it was able to solve the problems of structure, technology, and productivity which had plagued the coalmining industry after 1913, cannot be discussed here. It is, however, appropriate to indicate the difficulties and policies associated with the first few months after the decision to nationalize the coal industry had been taken. For the economic problems which industry encountered at the end of the War, the initial organizational decisions of the National Coal Board, and the corporation's embryonic staffing and industrial-relations policy were all related by tangible threads to the themes which had characterized the history of the coalmining industry throughout the years since the First World War.

i. Output and manpower, 1945–1946

The end of the War found the coalmining industry in a bruised condition which could only be remedied by a prolonged period of investment and reconstruction. Nationalization and a more direct government role in the affairs of the industry were the presumed means by which that long-run reform would be tackled. They offered a possible way out not simply because of their hoped-for effects on labour relations and structural reform, but because they brought the promise of ample investment and planned reorganization. When the Coal Industry Nationalisation Act became law, for example, it was perceptively pointed out that 'Although labour relations have the limelight at present, it will be the investment policy of the Board that will tell in the long run', and that for the first time in 25 years the industry would have access to adequate capital for re-equipment and development. Correspondingly, the government's promise of £150 million of new investment funds over the next five years appeared to reinforce the potential for change.[1]

All this, however, lay in a hypothetical future. In the meantime the industry also had to encounter immediate peacetime pressures—a likely

---

[1] *The Economist* 20 July 1946, 108; 18 May 1946, 806. In May, *The Economist* argued that 'Cheap coal has gone for ever, but only increased mechanisation and reorganisation offer any sort of guarantee against ever-dearer coal, with its frightening tide of rising coal costs flowing in inflationary waves through every . . . door of industry. Coal is no longer King, but a pauper requiring costly public assistance. The fundamental argument for nationalization is that such assistance may enable the industry to gain a new efficiency.'

greater freedom of labour mobility (although miners continued to be unable to leave the industry on their own volition), a critical demand for coal (at home and abroad) to serve the needs of industrial recovery, and a heightened political exposure as the patience with which the civilian population greeted the shortages of wartime was dissipated by the false promises of peace. In the event, the circumstances of coal production in the first eighteen months of the Labour Government were not profoundly different from those of the early 1940s: the anxiety about coal supplies never quite produced the crisis that was feared.

Of course, such a crisis, precisely of the sort which was assumed to be a potentially disastrous threat to the war effort after 1940, did finally descend on the country in the early months of 1947. But its origin lay less on the side of production (except in so far as earlier restrictions on output had prevented the accumulation of abundant local stocks) than in the field of distribution. In December 1946, drawing attention to the increase in new recruitment and output, the *New Statesman and Nation* also pointed out that the industry was under pressure because of full employment and heightened demand for coal in other sections of the economy. Nevertheless, it spoke more accurately than it knew when it warned that 'Despite everything which has been achieved in the past twelve months, an extended period of snow or fog could still cause something like a national close-down of industry.'[1] It was in fact the weather, not the flow of output, which was to disrupt supplies in the fuel crisis of 1947, and bring much of British industry to a halt.[2]

Even before this event, however, the coal industry had limped its way towards its new regime without great assurance, albeit with a modicum of success—although the balance of supply and demand remained precarious and little enough coal could be spared for the important (and potentially remunerative) supply of the exhausted European economies.

As Table 15.1 indicates, there was a modest yet distinct recovery in output in 1946, a reversal of the depressing downward trend which had marked the wartime years. This took place in spite of a fall in the industry's manpower, because of a countervailing increase in productivity. The manpower problem, which had dogged the industry since 1941, was if anything aggravated by peace, which facilitated natural wastage among an ageing labour force. With the end of the War in Europe the conscription of youths into the mines, which had always been unpopular, came to an end. Admittedly, recruitment to the industry was considerable as almost 50,000 ex-miners returned to the pits (just over

[1] *New Statesman & Nation* 28 Dec. 1946.   [2] Ashworth 1986, 130–7.

Table 15.1. *British coal production and overseas shipments, 1938-1946*

	Production (m. tons)	Exports & foreign bunkers (m. tons)
1938	227.0	48.7
1939	231.3	46.5
1940	224.3	26.6
1941	206.3	9.4
1942	204.9	7.8
1943	198.9	8.0
1944	192.7	8.1
1945	182.8	8.6
1946	190.0	9.2

Source: See Table 1.1.

37,000 from the Forces and 12,000 from other industries). Altogether, with the addition of 17,600 new juvenile recruits, some 6,000 volunteers from other industries and 3,000 optants under the National Service Acts, the total addition to the mining labour force between mid-1945 and the end of 1946 was approximately 97,000. Yet there was an obvious limit to the pool of ex-miners, while existing workers began to leave the industry in large numbers. The number of workers on the colliery books, which had been 711,000 in the mid-1945 fell to 699,000 a year later and 692,000 on the eve of Vesting Day.[1]

This decline was the most worrying feature of the industry's immediate postwar history and led the government to make strenuous efforts to augment the work-force: a Director of Recruitment was appointed in January 1946, in May the Ministry of Labour publicized coalmining work among the unemployed, a campaign was initiated to draw workers from Ireland, and the government attempted to persuade the NUM—with only minimal success—to accept workers from the Polish Resettlement Corps. These efforts did relatively little to tilt the balance, and the manpower shortage helps explain the extreme sensitivity of the govern-

[1] LAB 8/1473. Between spring 1945 and spring 1946 the industry gained 55,000 entrants but lost 70,600 of its pre-existing labour force. The net wastage (15,600) compared with a net recruitment of 12,000 in 1944–5 and a wastage of 4,900 in 1943–4. See POWE 28/240: *Coal Industry Nationalisation Compensation Tribunal Proof of Evidence of A. F. Hemming*, 53.

ment to the NUM's arguments in favour of a five-day week and other substantial improvements in conditions, hours, and wage agreements.[1] Once more, the union's power was fertilized by a manpower crisis.

Apart from problems relating to the size of the work-force, there was at least some improvement in labour productivity in 1946 when compared with 1945. As far as weekly and annual output per man was concerned, this was not due to any large change in absenteeism, which (in spite of some ministerial optimism in June 1946) was only very marginally reduced below the very high levels of 1945.[2] Rather, there was progress on three other fronts: an increase in the number of shifts actually worked (out of an increasing total of *possible* shifts), a slight rise in the proportion of manshifts worked at the face, and an improvement in the 'quality' of the labour force as the number of unwilling miners ('Bevin Boys' and optants) and older men decreased, and more youthful or more skilled ex-miners entered the industry.[3] The second and third of these considerations, together possibly with a general improvement of worker morale as nationalization drew near, must have explained the belated reversal of the downward trend in the critical figure of output per manshift. This had declined from 1.14 tons in the prewar years to 1.00 tons in each of 1944 and 1945. In 1946 it rose to 1.03 tons—still only equal to the figure for 1943, but at least a change in direction.[4]

Clearly, there were few grounds for easy optimism about coal supplies for postwar reconstruction, and this was reflected in the sombre exhortations with which Vesting Day was greeted in January

[1] Below, 686. In a memorandum to the Cabinet in June 1946, Shinwell argued that adequate coal supplies would only be forthcoming if conditions were improved so that the industry were made 'substantially more attractive than at present to the existing miners, thereby securing both that the miners give regular attendance at their work and do a full day's work during each shift' and in order to 'draw recruits into the industry in much larger numbers than at present'. CAB 129/10 (17 June 1946).

[2] POWE 20/124 (8 May 1946); CAB 129/10 (17 June 1946), Annex; *Ministry of Fuel and Power. Statistical Digest for the Years 1946 and 1947* (Cmd. 7548. 1948), Table 11; *CYB* 1947, 543. Annual average absenteeism was estimated at 16.3% (7.1% 'voluntary') in 1945 and 16.0% (8.4% 'voluntary') in 1946. There was, however, a striking decrease in absenteeism in 1947, after the introduction of the five-day week on 1 May. Figures for the third quarter were 15.8% (8.8% 'voluntary') in 1946 and 10.97% (5.53% 'voluntary') in 147.

[3] Between 1945 and 1946 the average number of shifts *possible* rose from 5.65 to 5.76, and the average number *worked* rose from 4.73 to 4.84: *CYB* 1947, 543. The proportion of manshifts worked at the face rose from 36.96% in 1945 to 37.09% in 1946 (it had been 37.48% in 1943 and 37.19% in 1944). In 1947 it jumped to 37.59% (still well below prewar levels); *CYB* 1948, 573. For the change in the 'quality' of the labour force, see CAB 129/10 (17 June 1946).

[4] *Ministry of Fuel and Power. Statistical Digest for the Years 1946 and 1947* (Cmd. 7548. 1948), Table 10. In 1947 OMS reached 1.07. The figures for output per manshift at the face in 1938-9, 1944-5, and 1946 were 3.00, 2.70, and 2.76 tons.

1947. Overriding and serious problems still dogged the industry—or, at least, its core capacity. Within the national picture of coalmining there were, as usual, some bright spots. To take one example, in January 1946 BA Collieries had begun the developments of a new coal shaft at New Calverton in south-east Nottinghamshire. The pit was due for completion at the end of 1948 at a cost of about £1.5 million and was capable of producing one million tons annually. It was a further sign of the steady shift in the balance of coalmining activity and prosperity which had been proceeding ever since the early 1920s. It presaged the rise to central importance of the East Midlands field for the production and profitability of the National Coal Board.

As was pointed out at the time, the intensified exploitation of the rich Nottinghamshire coal seams would help offset the exhaustion of supplies from older districts such as Lanarkshire and Lancashire. Any plan for the development of national resources, *The Economist* perceptively argued, would necessitate the closing of uneconomic pits and the concentration of output. Anticipating future problems, as well as obliquely commenting on past deficiencies, the journal also focused attention on the consequent difficulties for displaced miners ('the least mobile section of the industrial community'), and advocated some 'cushion of relief' through the provision of alternative work by means of the Distribution of Industry Act.[1] In spite of the likely shortage of coal, postwar issues of productivity and profitability were to give rise to problems which share important features with those which had dogged the industry throughout its troubled interwar experience.

ii. The National Coal Board: policies and problems

The members of the National Coal Board were pre-appointed by the Minister of Fuel and Power on 1 March 1946. Because the Board had no legal existence until the Coal Industry Nationalisation Act became law, in July, its members could initially only operate as an organizing committee. Even so, they had to commence work immediately they were appointed, since their task was enormous. It included not only the creation of administrative, financial, and managerial systems to oversee an unprecedentedly large enterprise, but the devising of the basic industrial structure that had been purposely ignored in the enabling legislation.[2]

---

[1] *The Economist* 19 Jan. 1946, 108.
[2] For the initial work and organization of the NCB, see National Coal Board, *Annual Report for the Year ending 31st December 1946* and Nott-Bower and Walkerdine n.d. 1957?

As Shinwell had insisted from the outset, the Board's members were all full-time. He had also promised that two members would be drawn from men with strong union connections, and these were Lord Citrine (General Secretary of the TUC, who oversaw the NCB's manpower and welfare functions), and Ebby Edwards (General Secretary of the NUM, who took charge of the Board's Labour Relations Department). The first Chairman of the NCB was Lord Hyndley, who, in spite of his close connections with private enterprise (he had been Managing Director of Powell Duffryn, a Director of Guest, Keen and Nettlefold and of Stephenson Clarke), had had many years' experience as an adviser and then administrator within the Mines Department and its successor Ministry and had favoured public ownership since at least 1942.[1] The Deputy Chairman was a senior civil servant Sir Arthur Street—Permanent Under Secretary at the Air Ministry during the War and then Permanent Secretary to the Control Office for Germany and Austria.

All other Board members had explicit functional responsibilities (this was to change in the later 1940s). Thus, two of the Board members were leading mining engineers, and took joint responsibility for production. They were: the Fife Coal Company's Sir Charles Reid (whose Technical Advisory Committee was largely responsible for the impetus to public approval of nationalization in early 1945), and T. E. B. Young, who had been Managing Director of the Bolsover Company and an influential adviser to the War Cabinet at a critical stage of the War.[2] The Board members with responsibility for financial affairs and marketing were, respectively, L. H. H. Lowe (a partner in the accounting firm of Thomson McLintock and Director of Finance at the Ministry 1943–5) and J. C. Gridley (a man of extensive experience in the coal trade, including a directorship in the leading firm of Gueret and Llewellyn and Merrett). The ninth member of the Board, with responsibility for scientific and research matters, was Sir Charles Ellis, Professor of Physics at King's College, London.

Given the context of nationalization—which leaned neither towards any measure of worker control nor towards a simple continuation of traditional power at the top—the NCB's supreme governing body seemed a well-balanced and potentially influential team. By any standards its administrative achievement in the short space of ten months was spectacular. In round figures, it successfully assumed responsibility for some 1,000 collieries (run by over 400 undertakings), coking plants, brickworks, a multitude of ancillary activities, over

[1] Above, 612 n.   [2] Above, 524 n.

one million acres of land, and about 150,000 houses.[1] It shaped these enterprises, employing over 700,000 men and involving a bewildering diversity of activities and property, into an organization of a scale and complexity hitherto unknown in Britain, and probably the world. It was also obliged to devote a vast amount of energy to negotiating with representatives of the labour force even before the Corporation took responsibility for the industry.[2] And it did all this under great pressure from the government (which was itself under great pressure from the Executive Committee of the NUM) to bring forward the date at which assets would be formally vested and the NCB begin operations: in October 1946, fearing 'trouble at the pits' if the Vesting Date were postponed, the government began to urge that it be set for 1 January 1947. Shinwell acknowledged that administrative confusion and financial loss might be involved, but left no room for doubt as to the outcome by asserting that any postponement beyond 1 January 'would create difficulties and dangers of a most serious and lasting character which would outweigh any temporary advantages arising from postponement'.

Obliged 'to choose between the administrative dangers of an early vesting date and the psychological dangers of a later one', the Board reluctantly made the final commitment in mid-November—a bare six weeks before the take-over.[3] As all this implies, however, the almost breakneck speed at which the Board had to work in 1946 had administrative drawbacks. Together with the lack of directly relevant experience of some of its members, and their unavoidable preoccupation with highly detailed functional responsibilities and the ever-pressing problems of labour relations, it probably diverted their attention away from a sufficiently rigorous scrutiny of organizational policy. That was certainly the view of one of their number, Sir Charles Reid, who subsequently resigned (in 1948) and complained that

---

[1] In the spring of 1946 it was estimated that 1,650 pits (i.e. all those in the country except the collieries worked by the Freemen of the Forest of Dean), worked by about 850 undertakings, would be nationalized. Later that year, however, it was pointed out within the Ministry that it was unlikely that the Board would wish to concern itself with small collieries (employing less than 51 men), of which there were 318—each run by a separate undertaking. These, it was assumed, would be licensed for private operation. And this would leave 1,144 pits, run by 449 undertakings. On the other hand, the NCB's first Annual Report listed only 980 pits as coming under its direct management. See POWE 28/33 (20 May 1946); COAL 28/47 (30 Sept. 1946); National Coal Board, *Annual Report for the Year ending 31st December 1946*, 28–9.

[2] Below, 686.

[3] NCB, *Annual Report... 1946*, 20; NCB Minutes (COAL 21/1), 25 and 29 Oct., 1 and 19 Nov. 1946; Arnot 1979, 194 n. The first two quotations are from the Board Minutes of 1 Nov., the final quotation is from the NCB's *Annual Report* for 1946.

Most of those appointed [to the Board] had little or no experience of running any business at all, not to speak of a really large-scale enterprise. No plan, no blueprint, no instructions were ever given to the board. It was merely told to take over the industry and run it in the national interest.[1]

This is not the appropriate place in which to assess the efficacy of the administrative structures devised by the NCB in the hectic months of 1946, although it is only fair to note that the size and scope of the NCB meant that relevant precedent or experience was universally lacking, and it is hardly surprising that managerial problems and changes—as well as frequent reviews—continued to characterize the Corporation.[2] There are, nevertheless, aspects of the NCB's policies and problems in its first few months which were so intimately related to the history of the industry and the origins of nationalization that they call for some comment. These primarily concern the basic structure of the Corporation and the human resources (managerial and labour) that it had at its disposal.

During the Parliamentary consideration of the Coal Industry Nationalisation Bill there had been some anxiety about the lack of specificity or direction concerning the industry's internal structure under public ownership. However, most commentators had accepted Shinwell's argument, albeit not without misgivings, that the degree of centralization or decentralization would have to be determined by the Board itself.[3] In the event, the industry's structure was fairly heavily tilted towards central control. Of course, the sheer size of the industry necessitated extensive structural articulation: coalmining operations were divided between 48 Areas, which were envisaged as basic planning and managerial units 'of the size envisaged in the Reid Report'.[4] All but five of the Areas had outputs varying between 2 and 7.3 million tons; 31 had outputs between 3 and 5.5 million tons. They therefore approximated to the presumed optimum size of groupings (intended to be large-scale yet manageable) that had been so frequently discussed since the 1920s. Each Area would have a Manager who 'would not be responsible for policy, only for carrying out policy'[5]—a restriction on initiative which gave rise to subsequent criticism.

[1] Sir Charles Reid, 'The Problem of Coal' (the second of three articles), *The Times* 23 Nov. 1948, 5f.
[2] See C. A. Roberts, 'The Development of the Organisation', in Nott-Bower and Walkerdine 1957; Ashworth, 1986, 612–29; National Coal Board, *Report of the Advisory Committee on Organisation* (1955).
[3] Above, 647.   [4] NCB, *Annual Report*, 1946, 3.
[5] NCB Minutes (COAL 21/1), 25 oct. 1946. In addition to the Area General Manager, the Area

At the same time, however, it was obviously necessary to devise an intermediate level of oversight between such a large number of Areas and the central Board, and this was done through the creation of eight geographical Divisions (each with its own Board) under which the different Areas were grouped.[1] Nevertheless, the central board and London-based departments retained a good deal of authority over policy and appointments in the Divisions, and it was subsequently claimed that this was excessive (and irrationally employed), that central managerial direction was remote and tended to become imprecise, and that Area as well as colliery managers were denied initiative and responsibility.[2] On the eve of Vesting Day Divisional Boards were complaining at their lack of discretion and it was acknowledged that Divisional Directors in production, marketing, and finance tended to visit London for discussion and then put into effect what had been agreed without consultation with their own Boards.[3] Whatever the validity or seriousness of these claims, it is clear that the organizational challenges of a nation-wide public corporation were only imperfectly met by the structural devices of 1946.

Contrary to some expectations, managerial inadequacy was another inherited weakness of the industry which was not easily susceptible to reform by public ownership. This was not simply a question of technical competence, although the broader and more effective use of scarce engineering abilities had always been one of the arguments in favour of consolidation. It also related to problems of managerial skills and recruitment—at the higher levels as well as in individual collieries. That such problems continued to affect the industry's productivity in the initial years of public ownership was partly a function of its interwar

officials were to be a Labour Relations Officer, a Training, Education, and Welfare Officer, a Sales manager, a Chief Accountant, and an Administrative Officer. These were to work as 'a team, with the Area General Manager as their leader', although 'the members of the Area team will each get their instructions on technical, professional and administrative matters from Divisional level'. It was decided to avoid a Board structure for the Areas since, in Lord Hyndley's words, 'It would be unfortunate if the industry should get the reputation of being Board-ridden.'

[1] NCB, *Annual Report... 1946*, 28–9. The South-Eastern Division, with four pits in Kent, had no separate Area organization.

[2] Sir Charles Reid, 'The Problem of Coal', *The Times* 22, 23, and 24 Nov. 1948; National Coal Board, *Report of the Advisory Committee on Organisation* (1955).

[3] NCB Minutes (COAL 21/1), 27 Dec. 1946.

[4] See NCB, *Report of the Advisory Committee on Organisation* (1955), 53–4: 'The Colliery Manager has been taught how to mine but not how to manage. And he is expected to do too much unaided.' The Committee argued that each large colliery needed an administrative and a personnel officer.

history, when 'an atmosphere of poverty and unrest' had deterred the recruitment of men of executive ability. But these initial handicaps were aggravated by the inability of the new National Coal Board to attract many *existing* senior managers into its service. It was claimed that the Managing Directors of most large private firms did not join the Corporation and

Thus the industry lost virtually a complete level of management at the moment when, because of the great size of the new undertaking, managerial and administrative talent was needed more than ever before. The gap has not yet [*in 1955*] been filled.[2]

This may have been partly a matter of ideological aversion, but it seems more likely to have resulted from the counter-attractions (of remuneration as well as working environment) of continuing in private enterprise at very senior levels.

Over the years the staffing of the Corporation was seen primarily as a question with administrative and technical implications. However, it also raised in some minds the more far-reaching issues of political commitment, philosophical goodwill, and interest-group control. The absence of any very large controversy, or even determined pressure from the miners' union, on the issue of worker control or managerial representation has already been noted.[3] In fact this had hardly been a very live issue after the pre-1914 campaigns and the proposals for nationalization in 1919 and (less confidently) 1926. Worker control or representation had been largely scouted by the prevailing advocates of nationalization. And among the miners it may be assumed that, confronted with the actual existence (rather than the remote prospect) of a public corporation which was an employer, it was felt that organized labour stood to gain more from an organizational 'distancing' and a concomitant continuance of bargaining and negotiation, than from the sort of active participation in management which would have entailed some direct responsibility for, and therefore acquiescence in, managerial decisions. This was probably a majority view, and was in any case

[1] NCB, *Report of the Advisory Committee on Organisation*, 23.

[2] Ibid., 23. Also see P. M. D. Roberts, 'Getting to Grips', in Nott-Bower and Walkerdine ?1957, 9. In Sept. 1946 concern was expressed at the NCB about the problem of filling the chief Area posts in the Scottish Division: 'It would not be easy to build up a team in that Division owing to the shortage of men of sufficiently large calibre. This would probably be true of some other Divisions.' NCB Minutes (COAL 21/1), 17 Sept. 1946. In these weeks the Board expressed frequent concern at the obstacles to recruitment and the problems of retaining well-qualified managers.

[3] Above, 640, 645.

consistent with the traditional preference of rank-and-file miners to concern themselves with bread and butter rather than structural matters. Even so, there was a certain amount of critical comment on the presuppositions implicit in the staffing of the NCB.

Part of this criticism came from socialist circles outside the industry, where there was a good deal of dissatisfaction with the continued role of capitalists in general and former directors of colliery and allied companies in particular. In 1948, for example, the fact that there were four such men (as against 'only' two trade unionists) out of the central Board's membership of nine, and 18 out of a total of 43 Divisional Board members, was felt to be decidedly unsatisfactory. Capitalists should not be recruited because 'nationalised industry needs true believers, and they cannot be bought for thirty pieces of silver'.[1]

In addition, there was a degree of restlessness within the industry, even though it was not manifested at the level of national negotiations. In June 1946, for example, the Edwistone (Nottinghamshire) Labour Party (undoubtedly representing miners' opinion) protested at the appointment to the central NCB of T. E. B. Young, who had supported the Conservative Party in the recent General Election. And four months later the Lady Windsor Colliery Lodge of the NUM expressed 'concern and resentment' at the large number of officials from Powell Duffryn, an undertaking considered to be peculiarly hostile to the union, who were being given posts in the Corporation. In each case Shinwell returned an emollient answer—arguing that the socialized industries needed 'higher technical personnel', that with experience of such enterprise they would abandon their past habits of mind, and that to assume that technical experts would behave in the same way under public as private enterprise was to make the same mistake as those who argued that nationalization would make no difference to the attitude of the miners to managers.[2]

In the event, however, the desperate shortage of well-qualified men and the alternative preoccupation of the union with the 'Miners' Charter' and the improvement of wages and conditions, meant that the issue of managerial staffing did not loom very large in the deliberations of 1946. By the same token, such pleas as that of three employees at Bardykes Colliery in Lanarkshire, that more miners should have seats on local boards and that each colliery should have a worker-based

---

[1] Heinemann 1948, 58–61, and quoting Ernest Davies, *National Enterprise* (1946).
[2] POWE 37/4. In December, at a union conference, the South Wales Area of the NUM also complained at the disproportionate representation of Powell Duffryn personnel in NCB appointments in their Area: Arnot 1979, 199.

production committee,[1] were not reflected in either extensive discussion or any elaborate action when the NCB came to fashion its own structure (except in so far as central and divisional Board Directors responsible for labour relations tended to be drawn from former union officials).

An altogether more serious issue concerned managerial relationships with the work-force and its place within a nationalized industry which had, in large part, been brought into public ownership with the intention of accommodating the miners to the management of the industry. Industrial relations, rather than constitutional structures, continued to be the central preoccupation of the industry. Before these are considered, however, it will be useful to appraise the long-run relationships between the miners and the movements for industrial reform.

iii. The miners' authority and industrial reorganization

The interwar, and even more the wartime, history of the coalmining industry had amply demonstrated the extent to which industrial performance was dependent on the peculiarities of work processes, the intermittent goodwill of the labour force, and the experience and attitudes of the miners. Indeed, precisely because of the labour-intensive nature of mining there was an indissoluble link between labour 'problems' on the one hand and the prospects for technical change and structural reform on the other. In the last resort the need to reassure the miners, to assuage their doubts about the industry's ownership, or to secure their commitment to work tasks, came to be the predominating criteria for would-be reformers of the industry.

Hence, as has already been emphasized, there was a direct thread linking the introduction of control in 1916, in order to bring peace to the troubled South Wales field, to Sir John Sankey's advocacy of nationalization in 1919, on the grounds that it might be the only way to avoid the continuance of industrial unrest, to the resolution of the industrial problems of 1929–30 by the passage of the Coal Mines Act, to the introduction of dual control in 1942, and to the transition to public ownership in 1945–6. In each case the demands of the miners persuaded advocates or policy-makers that structural change was a necessary prerequisite of ensuring the cooperation of the miners in continuity of production.

Obviously, this latent authority of the workers was not uniformly exercised or even available throughout the period between 1913 and

[1] POWE 37/4 (15 Apr. 1946).

1946. In 1921 and 1926, for example, they were defeated on the issue of wages, as they had been in 1919–20 on the question of nationalization. More generally, there were clearly occasions on which that authority virtually disappeared—as witness the long years of lower pay and higher hours than the work-force wanted. Yet the course of its twentieth-century history was such that the structural evolution of coalmining was ultimately heavily influenced by the large degree of autonomy with which actual or potential shortages endowed its work-force.

On the other hand, the power and situation of the mining labour force were never straightforward matters. And two implications of their political bargaining position were directly relevant to the question of public ownership. These relate to the tension, as far as the mass of the miners were concerned, between material and structural aims, and to the moral force of their position within the arena of public opinion and national politics.

The striking thing about the miners' leaders' use of their bargaining position at critical moments in the history of coal was less its existence than their inability or unwillingness to deploy it to its fullest extent in pursuit of very long-run aims. In part, this dispersing of authority could be attributed to a sense of responsibility and proportion (during the Second World War, for example, when the miners did not attempt to force national ownership at a time when their cooperation was indispensable to the war effort). And at other times they appear to have been outwitted by the owners or the government (postponing a confrontation in March 1919 or the summer of 1925, for example). In addition, however, at moments of crisis it was also clear that the reforming instinct of the miners' unions, their commitment to structural change, and their almost continuous advocacy of nationalization, did not always reflect the determination or priorities of the mass of their members.

What this meant in particular was that confronted (as was almost invariably the case) with simultaneous opportunities of pursuing improvements in their material welfare (wages, hours, conditions, 'job control') and pressing home a campaign for organizational reform and public ownership in the industry, the rank and file of miners were far more inclined to take sustained and collective action in the former than the latter cause. Thus, throughout the period with which we have been concerned, the strike weapon was almost invariably deployed for material rather than organizational ends. This happened in particular in 1919–20 (when many observers imagined that the government would have to concede the MFGB's powerful demand for public ownership of the mines, but the union campaign dissipated once wages had been increased and hours reduced) and in 1942 and the winter of 1942–3 (when the prospect of substantial wage increases overshadowed the pursuit of industrial reform).

Nor is this particularly surprising. The nature of work and social life in mining communities placed a premium on using personal resources and sacrifice in order to defend or increase immediate and tangible benefits. These naturally took precedence over the pursuit of extreme or uncertain experiments in the framework of the industry. This theme ran through commentaries on labour relations in the industry: 'There is no deep-laid plot or conspiracy', it was said in *The Economist* in 1912, on the subject of syndicalism (which, it felt, was not understood by most miners). 'The working class, like any other class, want to better themselves.' In 1919 Sidney Webb advocated compromise on the grounds that the miners were more concerned with wages than nationalization—a point reiterated a decade or so later by Emanuel Shinwell: 'You must not conceal the fact; taking the miners as a whole, they are more concerned about improving wages than workers' control.' As has already been seen, this was Ernest Bevin's opinion during the labour crises of the Second World War: 'I doubt very much if the bulk of the miners are worrying about controls. It is more or less a peg on which to hang further demands. What the miner is concerned about, in my view, is the removal of uncertainty so far as his wages and conditions are concerned.' And a similar scale of priorities seems to have affected negotiations about the future in the formative months of the new National Coal Board.[1]

Such considerations explain more than anything else the inability of the MFGB to drive home its apparent advantage in the spring of 1919 and the failure of its 'Mines for the Nation' campaign in the subsequent winter. More generally, they explain why the occasions when the union leadership got nearest to losing control of its membership tended to involve disputes about wages; and they imply that during those rare moments when a crisis of industrial relations or a shortage of coal appeared to give the miners an absolute whip hand the effective limit on power lay within the union itself—and was based on the reluctance of its members to strike in favour of industrial reform. Rather, their influence on the structural history of the industry was derived from their ultimate unwillingness (anticipated in both Wars) to cooperate in orderly and

[1] *The Economist*: quoted in Porter 1970; Webb: Cole 1952, 146 ff.; Shinwell ?1931, 6; Bevin: quoted in Bullock 1967, 261.

productive effort when they felt that the result would augment private profit and sustain private enterprise.

The miners' power had a moral as well as an economic or strategic dimension. The extraordinary character of mining work, the kaleidoscopic history of the industry, the vicissitudes in the personal lives of pitmen, the exposure of atrocious housing and dangerous working conditions through innumerable Inquiries and journalistic publicity—all helped shape a distinctive public sympathy for the industry's workforce and communities. Such sympathy had only an intermittent political effect; it needed constant renewal, and it could be eroded by the wilfulness, and occasional selfishness, which marked the miners' pursuit of their industrial aims. Nevertheless, it stands out as the single most important element in their political bargaining power.

Public knowledge and guilt about miners' lives, together with aversion to the insular and assertive owners, established a large moral bank on which the miners were frequently able to draw in their prolonged disputes with the owners and the government. Even so, of course, they experienced defeats. But their ability—even in such years of relative adversity as 1927–8, 1929–30, and 1935–6—to minimize their effects or make positive gains owed much to the intense sympathy they were able to generate. At other times—in the spring of 1919, for example, or in 1942—the political position of the miners was almost impregnable because the tide of public opinion ran so strongly in their favour.

It should, of course, be emphasized that the miners' union was able to take advantage of this situation not because they were cynical (although they were perfectly capable of using rhetoric rather than reason in their public and private negotiations), but because they, too, were influenced by history, emotion, and moral fervour.

No one who had serious dealings with the miners at any time in the twentieth century could fail to recognize the potent role in their lives and politics of individual and collective memory, of myth and cultural continuity. From minor local disputes to major national confrontations such as occurred in 1919 and 1926, from resentment at the petty injustice of minor officials to profound distrust of the whole class of coalowners, experience of the past irradiated the present. What was taken to be the betrayal by the government on the issue of the Sankey Report, or the desperate humiliation of defeat in the 1926 stoppage, continued to influence the aspirations and politics of miners long after the principal participants had lost their authority, and indeed, long after the generation which had lived through these experiences had subsided into comparative insignificance.

It was characteristic of coalmining that the influence of the past should have endured down the generations with such vivid force. The situation was described with great sympathy by Major Lloyd George, the Minister of Fuel and Power, in a submission to the War Cabinet in 1943. It had even greater generality than he imagined:

The mining community, more than all other industrial groups, is profoundly conscious of its history and traditions. Miners tend to see present events in the light of the history of their own community and of their experience as miners. . . . The last thirty years, seen through the miners' eyes, have been a period of decline and frustration. The growing mechanisation of mining has left less scope for the individual miner's pride in his vocation and in his skill as a workman. More important still, the prolonged depression and contraction in employment in the industry have left bitter memories of the catastrophic wage reductions after the last war, the long strikes of 1921 and 1926, and the growing unemployment and slackness in the industry, which was combined with more exacting conditions for those in work. These years of friction and of unsuccessful struggle have developed in the miner a deep-seated distrust of the coal owners. . . . This distrust . . . has tended to make the workmen suspicious of their own leaders. . . . Until recently they have tended to resent the spectacle of their leaders urging more production side by side with managers and owners, and the leaders' conciliatory attitude in colliery disputes.[1]

Such bedrock attitudes and memories were to last well beyond the end of private ownership. They are still with us—as is the latent public sympathy for the miners (almost irrespective of the cause) whenever they resort to strike action. In effect, the prolonged engagement with history has never been a matter for the miners alone. The experience and evolution of the entire coalmining industry in the twentieth century were fashioned by its own history. Throughout the industry, and among those who observed and attempted to influence it, the attitudes and institutions which were the outcome of one phase of development determined responses and performance in the next. More than any other industry, coalmining has been a prisoner of its past. It was, therefore, hardly surprising that the shaping of industrial relationships under public ownership could not be based on an entirely fresh beginning.

[1] 'Miners and the Present Coal Situation', 17 Sept. 1942: CAB 71/9.

iv. Industrial relations under public ownership

As far as the leaders of the labour force were concerned, the nationalization of coalmining provided an opportunity to pursue familiar aims in a more favourable environment, rather than to devise fundamental new relationships between the miners and the purposes of the industry.

At an early stage in this process the union leaders were criticized for not attempting to bridge the gulf between the generality of the workforce and the government. And it may well be that they missed an early opportunity of accommodating union tone and outlook to the new circumstances.[1] Nevertheless, there seems little reason to question the fact that, in pursuing improved wages and conditions, the NUM negotiators were conforming to their members' desires and pressures. Thus it came about that industrial relations in the industry for most of 1946 were shaped organizationally by the union's successful determination to extend the existing system of deliberation through the Joint National Negotiating Committee, and substantively by the NUM's demands for improvements in conditions, effective remuneration, and the wage system. Beyond the victories of 1944, the men's leaders obviously saw scope for even more substantial improvements. And since the miners seemed unwilling to associate the resulting discussions with any fundamental reconsideration of production, productivity, or costs in the industry, there seemed little change (except in the greater political leverage enjoyed by the miners) from private enterprise days.

That there should have been little change will come as a surprise only if an excessive weight is placed upon an almost selfless ideology. In fact, to the mass of miners, and in spite of their deeply engrained resentment of private ownership, the crucial determinants of their outlook lay in the combination of a keen sensitivity to wages and hours, the immediate material circumstances of their work, their direct economic aspirations, and a day-to-day reaction to the hierarchies and work conditions of their jobs. Very little of this was transformed by the mere act of nationalization.

These considerations were reflected in the 'Miners' Charter'—a set of demands which, in much more favourable circumstances for its signatories, paralleled the demands with which the miners had signalled the ending of War in 1918–19.[2] The Miners' Charter had been formulated in December 1945 and presented in January 1946, in response to the government's appeal for the union's help with the task of stanching

---

[1] *The Economist* 6 July 1946, 10.   [2] Above, 122–3.

and reversing the loss of manpower from the industry. As had happened before, during the War, the NUM, with an eye to the immediate interests of its own members, argued that only by a prior and substantial amelioration in the industry's conditions of work could a larger workforce and greater output be achieved. They therefore submitted a lengthy shopping list of improvements in the miner's situation. Taken together, at a time of difficulty for the industry, their proposals were disconcerting. They pressed for rapid modernization, an extension of day-wage payments, enhanced training and safety regulations, extended compensation for incapacity, the maintenance of miners' pay at the top of the wages league, a seven-hour underground day and a forty-hour surface week, a five-day week with no reduction of pay, a guaranteed weekly wage after the Essential Work Order was withdrawn, two week's (instead of one week's) paid holiday and six paid public holidays annually, pensions at 55 for miners unable to continue work, new towns and improved housing and transport, and the complete reorganization of the industry's health and welfare schemes. The NUM also requested that the government should provide a definite timetable for the introduction of these far-reaching reforms.

The government had asked for an increase in productivity and a lowering of cost—and been handed a set of expensive demands. Shinwell put a brave face on his response (which was sent in March 1946). He welcomed and agreed with the union's aspirations; reminded them that greatly improved conditions 'can only be achieved as the industry is reorganised under nationalisation and output is increased'; and remitted detailed consideration of the proposals to discussions between the union and the putative National Coal Board. But the Charter's demands could hardly have embodied the sort of practical cooperation in an immediate drive for recruitment and production that the Minister had hoped for. And within the Ministry there were feverish and despondent attempts to calculate the deleterious effects of such reforms on output and costs of production.[1]

Although the NUM was concerned to relax the restrictions on new wage bargaining imposed by the 1944 agreement, the critical issues which emerged in 1946 involved the conditions rather than the remuneration of work. Indeed, adjusting existing information for

---

[1] POWE 20/123; POWE 28/67; Arnot 1979, 125–7. Initial Ministry estimates assumed a loss of between 8 and 18 m. tons annually, an increased overall cost of £40 to £42 million (on an existing cost of £225 million), and an increase in labour cost per ton of more than 20% (from 25s. to between 30s. 10d. and 33s.).

deficiencies in the statistical sources, it seemed obvious that the wartime achievements of the miners were being maintained into the peace: their wages remained at the top of the list of major industrial occupations.[1] No doubt the miners were well aware of this, although they still pressed the Minister to provide an assurance that they would always remain the best-paid workers. However, they reserved their principal political and industrial strength for their campaign for a five-day week with no reduction of take-home pay (with which they coupled the demands for an extra week's holiday and six paid public holidays annually)—and it was this, ultimately successful, campaign which introduced the main destabilizing note into the early months of industrial relations in the nationalized industry. (There was less acrimony on the question of conciliation machinery: in the event, an extended version of the existing national system was agreed to before Vesting Day, and an agreement on a procedure for pit-level discussions was signed on Vesting Day itself.)[2]

The political element in the miners' campaign for a reduced working week was more important than the industrial. They were therefore disinclined to wait for the creation of the NCB and its negotiating machinery. Instead, throughout the spring of 1946 they maintained pressure on Shinwell (who had already initiated a special study of the feasibility of a shorter week). The Minister expressed sympathy with the union's aim, although he was constrained to point out that manpower was continuing to fall and that a crisis of coal supplies threatened in the winter of 1946–7. But Shinwell achieved very little by attempting to make serious consideration of a five-day week dependent upon the active cooperation of the miners in the task of raising productivity and output.

On 26 June 1946, before the official creation of the NCB, Shinwell was obliged to make a statement to the effect that the government offered no objection in principle to the introduction of a five-day week. (He also accepted the claim for six paid public holidays annually, although rejecting that for an extra week's paid holiday annually.)[3] The

---

[1] 'Miners' Charter. Further meeting with the NUM on 28th March' (1946) in POWE 20/123; *Ministry of Labour Gazette* LIV, Nos. 7 and 10 (July and Oct. 1946); Bowley 1947, 10.

[2] See NCB, *Annual Report . . . 1946*, 13–14 and papers in COAL 26/24 and COAL 26/83. Nationally, the machinery continued the Joint National Negotiating Committee (consisting on the union's insistence, of its full Executive Committee and all members of the NCB) and the (independent) National Reference Tribunal. In addition the NCB created a National Consultative Council (with representatives of the Board, the NUM, the National Association of Colliery Managers, and the Deputies Federation).

[3] Shinwell to Lawther, 8 May 1946: POWE 20/124; *Hansard* 26 June 1946, col. 1329. In the course of discussion in a joint NUM–Ministry Committee the NUM had declined to accept most

announcement was coupled with a reiteration of the need to establish conditions which would protect output. But the fact was that such an early, and open-handed, statement about the working week effectively undermined the National Coal Board's negotiating position even before it came into existence. More seriously, it indicated that the government would continue to be drawn into the affairs and disputes of the industry, and that political pressures could continue to outweigh economic considerations.

Such lessons were not lost on the informed public. To *The Economist* the hopes that nationalization would keep coal out of politics, enable decisions to be taken on their technical merits, and persuade the miners to work more wholeheartedly were already 'beginning to look fly-blown'.[1] In such a context, the government's accession to the demand for a five-day week just as a crisis of supply loomed, seemed like 'Appeasement in the Mines'. And the aggressiveness of NUM statements, together with the rejection of the proposal to use foreign labour to sustain output, were causes for gloom, not unmixed with an attempt to grasp the psychological undertones:

It is clear that the first years of nationalisation and full employment will still be haunted by the ghost of the unemployment and hunger marches of the Twenties and Thirties. It is also clear that mining is going to stay in politics; the officially proclaimed independent status of the National Coal Board is beginning to look distinctly tenuous. . . . The Government has inherited much of the suspicion and ill will against the existing owners. The average miner, on his side, can scarcely be expected to forget the ingrained outlook of a lifetime. In any case the Government and the miner have no direct contact. [*The union hierarchy has failed to provide a bridge.*] Trained to act as the spearhead of miners' demand against the management, union officials have been far too slow to adapt themselves to the need for a more constructive type of leadership.[2]

Such pessimism, and the realization that it would 'take some time to wean them [*miners*] from the idea that a nationalised industry is one run

of the conditions and safeguards proposed. Instead, it accepted solely a bonus arrangement to protect earnings (bonuses would only be paid to those miners working the maximum number of shifts available in a working week) which, it estimated, would within six months more than compensate for the initial loss of production. The Committee's Chairman (Sir Donald Fergusson, the Ministry's Permanent Secretary) reported the details in a dispirited fashion and, in light of the government statement, discontinued the Committee's meetings. 'Report Submitted to the Minister of Fuel and Power by the Chairman of the Joint Committee on the 5-Day Week': POWE 20/124.

[1] *The Economist* 1 June 1946, 963–4.
[2] Ibid. 6 July 1946, 10.

exclusively in the interests of the workers', was only in part tempered by the acknowledgement that nationalization seemed the only feasible policy.[1]

It followed from all this that in 1946 the National Coal Board, pre-occupied as its members were with the hectic task of creating a new enterprise larger than any other the world had known, was also obliged to devote an enormous amount of its energy to negotiating with the NUM on issues which were of the greatest economic sensitivity—well before it could have any firm idea of the leeway which the new Corporation would provide for the concessions demanded of it. Indeed, within a week of its formal creation the Board was confronted by the NUM with the Minister's explicit and emphatic commitment to a five-day week, and with a demand for the abrogation of the Clause in the 1944 wages agreement which provided that there should be no application for any change in wages until the expiry of the agreement in 1948. Most of the latter demand was granted by November. The Union was already begin-ning to advance from the very favourable bridgehead attained as a result of the industrial strife of 1944.[2]

Meanwhile, the impossibility of the Board's bargaining position on a five-day week and payment for statutory holidays became increasingly obvious. As regards the latter, with the political support of the Minister the union was able to secure unconditional payment for Christmas and New Year, sweeping aside the Board's attempt to impose the arrange-ment which applied to the August Bank Holiday—that the men should have worked during the preceding week.[3] And the outcome of the 'negotiations' on a five-day week was even more humiliating—if only because it involved major economic and managerial issues which were central to the Board's independence and responsibility. Wriggle as the Board members would, they could find no way of circumventing the

---

[1] *The Economist* 20 July 1946, 89.

[2] COAL 26/83: 17 and 23 July and 2 Oct. 1946; COAL 26/24, letter of 8 Nov. 1946. On 8 Nov. the Board, having already acknowledged that it was prepared to discuss national issues irre-spective of the terms of the 1944 agreement, was also constrained to agree to lift the restrictions on the discussion of wages issues at the pit level six months after an agreement on local con-sultative machinery had been reached. Such an agreement was signed on 1 Jan. 1947, so that the union was free to make wage claims at pit level from 1 July 1947.

[3] COAL 21/1 (5, 19, 22, and 26 Nov. 1946); COAL 26/24 (21 Nov. 1946). The NUM was able to produce a letter from Shinwell indicating that the August condition had been 'without prejudice' to other holidays. The Board's capitulation met with dissent on the part of the Directors responsible for production (Sir Charles Reid and T. E. B. Young), who argued that the lack of any condition would give 60,000 miners the possibility of receiving holiday pay without the need to put in an appearance, and that the result would be the serious erosion of managerial morale.

commitment entered into by the government before they assumed office. Armed with this fact, the NUM was able to insist that an announcement as to timing be made before Vesting Day. More than this, they were simply not prepared to discuss in any detailed way the implications of the reduction of the length of the working week for output, productivity, or costs:

The NUM would not have anything to do with costs ... they were not prepared to continue with a six day week.... whatever the terms and whatever the costs involved, they were insisting that they should have the Five Day Week. ... [The miners' representatives] were determined to enforce their demands.... They were relying entirely on the Minister.[1]

It became a point of considerable political importance that the NUM should be able to announce the prospect of a five-day week beginning on 1 May 1947. Finally, pushed by a desperate Minister, denied the opportunity of assessing the consequences and costs of the move, and with the damage to their self-esteem only slightly limited by the wording of the agreement, the Board members were obliged to accede to the union's demands. On 20 December—11 days before Vesting Day and within a few weeks of the fuel crisis of 1947—a Press Statement was issued, promising the introduction of a five-day week no later than 1 May.[2] A week later The Economist reported that the President of the NUM had cheerfully agreed that no other miners in the world had better and brighter prospects: 'Such bonhomie is scarcely surprising when so far the union has won hands down in every rubber.'[3]

The advent of public ownership did little to resolve the tensions inherent in the industry's industrial relationships. Admittedly, the extreme—even violent—resentments which had characterized prewar attitudes were greatly mitigated by the disappearance of private ownership. But it was perhaps too late for a really fundamental alteration of

---

[1] Minutes of NCB (COAL 21/1), 3 Dec. 1946.

[2] Ibid., 15 and 19 Nov., 3, 6, 10, 13, and 17 Dec. 1946; COAL 26/24 (2 and 17 Dec. 1946). Some questions relating to the form and calculation of bonuses and overtime still had to be settled—if necessary by arbitration. (In the event of arbitration, the five-day week was to be introduced within one month of the judgement.) The wording of the agreement retained a slight shred of the Board's self-respect by retaining the 'condition' originally agreed to by the NUM in June (that the bonus should not be paid to miners who worked less than a full week) and by reiterating the union's promise to use its best endeavours to maintain output. Although a number of Board members wished to oblige the government to take full responsibility for the five-day policy, it was finally decided to retain some superficial authority with the Board, by making it an NCB decision, although it was assumed that there would ultimately have to be a government subsidy to meet the resulting increase in costs.

[3] The Economist 28 Dec. 1946, 1039.

KING COAL AND THE MAGIC WAND

"Back, Demon Frost. Though you may do your worst,
I am his fairy guardian from Jan. First."

15. 'King Coal and the Magic Wand' (*Punch*, 1 January 1947)

outlook. The miners were still reluctant to reconcile themselves to acquiescence or relax their traditional suspicions and ambitions.

The problem of industrial relations survived Vesting Day, and shaped the atmosphere as well as the structure of the public corporation. Adversarial politics were not immediately eliminated—in October 1947, to the manifest distress of the Board, there were widespread unofficial strikes in Scotland and the threat of similar action in South Wales. Just as nationalization had failed to resolve the problem of manpower supply, so it achieved a less than complete victory in the struggle for worker cooperation. Without such cooperation, however, it would be difficult for the strategies on which public ownership had been based—subsidized investment, the concentration of managerial skills, and the coordination of a national policy for coal—to secure an adequate transformation of the industry. In the event, and even before Vesting Day, the obstacles to internal harmony proved incredibly more formidable than had ever been imagined in the 27 years since public ownership had first been advocated as a way of removing them.

v. Coal and twentieth-century Britain

As we have seen, the history of coalmining in the twentieth century endowed the industry with peculiar moral force in the minds of the rest of society. In this respect, although public opinion was not infrequently exasperated by their obstinacy or outraged by their single-minded defence of sectional interests, the position of the miners and the social state of their communities played an emblematic role in Britain's social and political history—representing the economic pressures and social costs of change in the structure and performance of the economy. The darker side of British social history between the Wars—the emergence of depressed areas, the prolongation of mass unemployment, reductions in living standards, enforced mobility, the destruction of staple industries—found its most dramatic and most widely perceived embodiment in Britain's stagnating coalfields. The public's perception was not always accurate: some important mining areas experienced relative prosperity and many miners who stayed in employment enjoyed rising real wages. But the picture was sufficiently representative, the adjustments sufficiently painful, to allow the social history of coalmining to stand as a symbol of the human costs of economic adaptation and negligent social policy in twentieth-century Britain.

For much of the period, however, and certainly as far as concerned policy-makers (within and outside the industry) it was the economic not the social experience of coalmining which seemed to call for positive response. And in this respect, too, the history of the industry cannot be divorced from the evolution of the larger society.

Coal provided perhaps the most important example of the transmutation of the British economy, and of the pressures on British enterprise, as the new century eroded the bases of nineteenth-century prosperity. The deceleration of the demand for its products, the growth of international competition, the exposure of its disproportionate dependence on booming overseas markets—all placed a premium on a mobility of the factors of production and an adaptability of structures and techniques which were too limited to provide much effective economic protection.

Like other staple industries, coalmining turned out to have few resources with which to encounter adversity. In particular, its inherited corporate structure and labour relations handicapped the industrial reorganization and technical innovations which might have cushioned the blows of changing markets. It has been one of the conclusions of this study that the apparent failure of those involved in coalmining to adapt the industry more successfully is not to be attributed to irrationality or abnormal psychology. Rather, the context of decision-making in coal created a disjunction between private and social costs and benefits. This was most marked among the owners, who lacked individual incentive to expend resources on private (and therefore limited) investment and innovation, and whose private interests militated against collective action. At the same time, their consequent short time-horizons found a parallel in the reluctance of employed miners as a group to forgo improvement or stability in their material standards, or to accept industrial change in the setting of private ownership without ample compensation—even if this resulted in a long-run threat to employment levels in the industry. And all such problems were compounded by the prevailing sourness of industrial relations in coalmining, which was itself in large part the result of earlier deficiencies of structure and outlook.

Looked at more generally, the problems of coal (antiquated technology, immobile factors of production, fragmented decision-making, shortage of investment funds, uncoordinated production, confrontation between interest groups) seemed characteristic of the staple industries of 'Outer Britain'. Little wonder, therefore, that the coalmining industry should have become the principal object of the state's hesitant involvement in the 1920s and 1930s in matters of labour relations, marketing organization, and industrial structures; or that it should have occasioned a mounting tempo of public intervention in the 1940s.

During the period with which this book has been concerned, the positive results of that intervention were limited. But their outcome is not to be measured in terms of industrial change alone. In effect, the depression of coalmining in the context of the interwar economy provided a critical bridge between an era of private enterprise and the emergence of a mixed economy. And the larger symbolic role of the industry in the twentieth century therefore lies in its stimulus to the transfer and centralization of decision-making in business and industrial policy.

It may also be the case that the evolution of policy towards the coal industry exemplifies a defensive, sentimental, and ultimately conservative strain in modern British economic history. At least until nationalization, the purpose of most interventions was to solve crises and stabilize the industry, rather than to streamline production and increase efficiency. As we have seen, this was largely because the intervention occurred at a time of deep depression around the coalfields, such that the prevailing fear was of the exacerbation of the problem of worklessness. Whatever the omissions of public policy in terms of a positive attack on the problems of unemployment and derelict areas, governments were cautious in pursuing policies which would have aggravated these problems, even in the short run. But, as was exemplified during the Wars, intervention could also be defensive of existing interests and viewpoints at a time when there was an urgent need for change and expansion. The process by which policy came to be centralized, and the nature of the pressures which induced political intervention, almost inevitably worked with the grain of the industry's interest groups. And when it came to the point, the costs—social or political or both—of 'progressive' change were judged to be too high for ruthless action.

On the other hand, the apparent need for ruthlessness had diminished by the mid-1940s. By then, the prerequisites of industrial advance (investment, restructuring, technical change) coincided with a shortage of coal, so that unemployment and overt social costs were no longer obstacles to reform. By that time, too, the presumed lessons of the three decades after 1913 had been driven home. The industry's continuing record of bad industrial relations, the shortage of available risk capital, and the assumption that productivity could only be enhanced by a concerted and large-scale effort of reconstruction, all pointed towards a major role for government and a diminution in the autonomy of individual owners.

Nationalization, which brings this particular story to an end, therefore appeared to be a logical response to the problems which had dogged the industry for 30 years, as well as an ideological reflex. On it there rested many hopes: of more harmonious relationships between miner and employer and manager, of effective management and increased productivity, of major investment programmes. Many of these hopes were to be realized, some frustrated. With nationalization and postwar economic developments there came new problems as well as new opportunities. And these remind us of the hazards of simplistic historical comparisons. Forty and more years later, however, it is apparent that, with public ownership, coalmining had still not divested itself of its own history—nor of its significance for our understanding of Britain's economic and social destiny.

Given the nature of the industry and its history, it is appropriate that this study should end by considering the miners at the moment of nationalization. Once achieved, public ownership seemed to have enhanced the miners' bargaining position, without securing the 'psychological' advantages that had been predicted for it ever since 1919. But those advantages were always somewhat problematic, precisely because they related solely to the pattern of *ownership*. For whereas the miners had undoubtedly resented and spurned the system of private enterprise, the ultimate ownership of the industry was by no means the only determinant of their attitudes to work and reward. Industrial relations in coal were shaped by the nature and organization of labour within mines, by the authority relationships which administered the production of coal, by the systems of pay, and the web of human relationships and aspirations. It was, perhaps, inconceivable that all these could be altered by a piece of legislation concerning the ownership of assets. Such a transformation would have to rely on much more complex changes, and could only be attained after years of application and effort by all concerned. Meanwhile, the routines of daily life—of work and pay—were hardly at all amended. In the short run, once the political gratification of public ownership had been savoured, the miner would recognize little new in his circumstances. This point had been perceptively made by Gwilym Lloyd George in the Debate on the Second Reading of the Nationalisation Bill:

On the date when the State takes over the mines, what will the effect on him [*the miner*] be? He will go to the same pit and get the same lamp from the same man; he will go into the same cage, will probably be lowered by the same man, and when he gets to the bottom, he will, if he is in certain parts of the country, see the same expression on the face of the pony. He will see the same manager, the same deputy, the old roadway, the same coalface, and, on the Friday, he will probably be paid by the same man.[1]

The achievement of public ownership in coalmining was, therefore, an ambiguous event as far as many miners were concerned, and given the industry's manifest problems, it was initiated at a time of sober doubt as well as optimism for those responsible for the management of the industry. These moods were reflected in the uncertain ceremonials which accompanied the formal transfer of the industry, and which provide a fitting end to this book.

Vesting Day—1 January 1947—fell on a Wednesday. In South Wales, dawn meetings, undemonstrative but well attended, marked the occasion before a new shift went underground.[2] In many other coalfields, however, local ceremonies were postponed until the subsequent weekend in order to avoid interference with the continuity of production—although in the North-West all miners took the statutory New Year's Day holiday, and throughout Yorkshire there was a 50 per cent rate of absenteeism.[3] The pithead ceremonies, when they did take place, were universally accompanied by serious appeals for application and productivity, cooperation, forgiveness, and dedication. In Durham, large crowds attended at the principal collieries. But the weather was not always favourable: in Ayrshire a bitterly cold day reduced the numbers and the duration of the ceremonies; and at the Wigan Junction Colliery in Lancashire, where only a few men braved 'the cold, snow-threatening morning', it was reported that 'the hour, the season, and the programme much more betokened an armistice day ceremony . . .'.[4]

The actual transition to public ownership was, after all, an unspectacular event. But that may have been an apt symbol of the transition, for it occurred at a difficult and unpropitious time for British coalmining. There was, indeed, widespread appreciation of the fact that the problems which had dogged the industry for so long, which had sapped its vitality and recuperative powers, and which had been aggravated by decades of neglect, were not, and could not be, solved simply by the

[1] *Hansard* 30 Jan. 1946, col. 879.
[2] *Western Mail & South Wales News*, 2 Jan. 1947, 3.
[3] *The Times* 2 Jan. 1947, 4a–b.
[4] *Durham Chronicle* 10 Jan. 1947, 1; the *Ayrshire Post* 10 Jan. 1947, 6; *Manchester Guardian* 6 Jan. 1947, 3a.

hoisting of the NCB flag, or the erecting of notices throughout the coal-fields announcing that 'This colliery is now owned and managed by the National Coal Board on behalf of the people.' For all the lack of heroics, for all the suspicions which endured, and irrespective of ideological differences and commitments, the hundreds of thousands of men and women whose lives were still bound up in this most poignant of industries must have appreciated that, for coalmining and the coalminer, as for the pit manager and his superiors, the burden of History could not be laid down in 1946.

Bibliography

The following lists of manuscript and printed sources refer only to material used and cited in this study. A much more comprehensive listing is contained in *Bibliography of the British Coal Industry* (1981), compiled by John Benson, Robert G. Neville, and Charles H. Thompson. Where no place of publication is given, the relevant book was published in London.

A. Manuscript Sources

Bank of England Archives
  Securities Management Trust Papers (SMT)
Bodleian Library, Oxford University
  Asquith Papers
  Milner Papers
Bramham Park, Wetherby
  Lane-Fox Diary
British Library of Political and Economic Science, London
  Dalton Papers
British Steel East Midland Region Records Centre, Irthlingborough
  Stanton and Staveley Papers
Brotherton Library, University of Leeds
  Henry Briggs Son & Co. Papers
  West Yorkshire Coal Owners' Association
Cambridge University Library
  Baldwin Papers
Derbyshire Record Office, Derby and Matlock
  Bolsover Colliery Company Papers
  Butterley Company Papers
  South Derbyshire Coal Owners' Association
Durham Record Office
  Durham Coal Owners' Association Papers
  Wearmouth Coal Company Papers
University of Glasgow Archives
  Lanarkshire Coal Masters' Association Papers
  Scottish Coal Owners' Association Papers

Labour Party Archives, London
   RDR
Lancashire Record Office
   Lancashire and Cheshire Coal Association
   Lancashire Coal Owners' Association Papers
   Manchester Collieries Company Papers
Leeds City Archives Department
   Henry Briggs Son & Co. Papers
Leicestershire Record Office
   Leicestershire Coal Owners' Association Records
Leigh Manor, Minsterbury
   Bridgeman Diary
House of Lords Record Office
   Lloyd George Papers
National Library of Wales, Aberystwyth
   Monmouthshire & South Wales Coal Owners' Association Papers
University of Newcastle upon Tyne
   Runciman Papers
Northumberland Record Office, Newcastle upon Tyne
   Ashington Coal Company Papers
   Northumberland Coal Owners' Association
   Northumberland and Durham Coal Owners' Association
Nuffield College, Oxford
   Cherwell Papers
   Gainford Papers
Public Record Office, Kew
   Board of Trade Records (BT 189)
   Cabinet Records (CAB 21, 23, 24, 27, 30, 37, 42, 65, 66, 71, 87, 128, 134)
   Coal Records (COAL 11, 12, 17, 21, 26, 37)
   Department of Scientific and Industrial Research Records (DSIR 8)
   Foreign Office, General Correspondence (FO)
   Registrar of Friendly Societies Records (FS 12)
   Ministry of Housing and Local Government Records (HLG 30)
   Ministry of Labour Records (LAB 2, 8)
   Ministry of Health Records (MH 79)
   Ministry of Munitions Records (MUN 4)
   Ministry of Fuel and Power Records (POWE 9, 10, 16, 17, 20, 21, 22, 26, 28, 35, 37, 42)
   Prime Ministers Records (PREM 1, 4)
Scottish Record Office, Edinburgh
   Coal companies and owners papers: CB3, 6, 7
   Steel-Maitland Papers (GD 193)
Sheffield Central Library

Doncaster Amalgamated Collieries Papers
South Yorkshire Coal Owners' Association
University of Sussex
Mass-Observation Archives

B. Parliamentary and British Government Publications

(Where a date is given other than within brackets, it refers to the date of the sessional parliamentary papers and is followed by a number indicating the Command number or the order in which the relevant paper was presented, and a roman number indicating the relevant volume in that Session's series.)

Final Report of the Royal Commission Appointed to Inquire into the Subject of the Coal Resources of the United Kingdom, 1905 Cd. 2353 XVI.

Reports, Minutes of Evidence and Appendices of the Departmental Committee Appointed to Inquire into the Probable Economic Effects of a Limit of 8 Hours to the Working Day of Coal Miners, 1907 Cd. 3426, 3427, 3428, 3505, 3506 XIV–XV.

Metalliferous Mines & Quarries, Second Report, 1914 Cd. 7476 XLII.

Report of the Departmental Committee Appointed to Inquire into the Conditions Prevailing in the Coal Mining Industry Due to the War, 1914–16 Cd. 7939, 8009, 8147 XXVII–XXVIII; 1916 Cd. 8345 VI.

Report of the Departmental Committee Appointed by the Board of Trade to Inquire into the Causes of the Present Rise in the Retail Price of Coal sold for Domestic Use, 1914–16 Cd. 7866, 7923 XXIX.

List of Coal Merchants in the London District who have Accepted an Arrangement for a Limitation of Profits, 1914–16 Cd. 8070 LXI.

Report of the Royal Commission on the Housing of the Industrial Population of Scotland, Rural and Urban, 1917–18 Cd. 8731 XIV.

Commission of Inquiry into Industrial Unrest, 1917–18 Cd. 8668 XV.

Report of the Committee Appointed to Enquire into the Actual Increase since June 1914 in the Cost of Living to the Working Classes, 1918 Cd. 8980 VII.

Reports of the Coal Conservation Committee Sub-Committee of the Ministry of Reconstruction on Electric Power in Great Britain, 1917–18 Cd. 8880 XVII; 1918 Cd. 9084 VII.

Report of the Departmental Committee Appointed by the President of the Board of Trade to Consider the Position of the Coal Trade after the War, 1918 Cd. 9093 XIII.

Metalliferous Mines and Quarries, General Report for 1918.

Reports of the Royal Commission on the Coal Industry (Sankey), 1919 Cmd. 84, 85, 86, 210, 359 XI; Cmd. 210, 360, XII; Cmd. 361 XIII.

Report (Third) of the Acquisition and Valuation of Land Committee of the Ministry of Reconstruction, on the Acquisition for Public Purposes of Rights and Powers in Connection with Mines and Minerals, 1919 Cmd. 156 XXIX.

Statement Showing the Basis upon which the Increase in the Cost of Coal to the Consumer by Six Shillings a ton is Calculated, 1919 Cmd. 252 XLV.

Report by Messrs. Tongue & Co., Chartered Accountants, on the Coal Industry; being an Analysis and Examination of the Board of Trade Statement as to the Basis of the Six Shilling a Ton Increase, as set forth in Cmd. 252 of 1919, in which the Late Controller of Coal Mines Extracted the Deficiency Likely to arise in the Year's Working, 16th July 1919 to 15th July 1920, 1920 Cmd. 555 XIII.

Accounts of Receipts and Payments by the Board of Trade and the Commissioners of Inland Revenue respectively, under the Coal Mines Control Agreement (Confirmation) Act, 1918, for the period 1st April, 1917, to 31st March, 1919, 1920 XXVII.

Proposed Terms of Settlement of the Dispute in the Coal Mining Industry, 1921 Cmd. 1387 XXXI.

Correspondence Between the Mining Association and the Mines Department Regarding the Operation of Part II of the Mining Industry Act, Together with a Report of Proceedings at a Meeting Between the Secretary for Mines and a Deputation from the Association, 1921 Cmd. 1551 XXXI.

Mines Department. Retail Prices and Qualities of Household Coal. Report of a Conference Between the Secretary for Mines and Representatives of the Co-operative Societies, 1924 Cmd. 2185 XI.

Mines Department. Retail Prices and Qualities of Household Coal. Correspondence Between the Mines Department and the Coal Merchants' Federation of Great Britain, together with the Report of a Conference Between the Secretary for Mines and the Federation of Great Britain, 1924 Cmd. 2117 XIX.

Report by a Court of Inquiry Concerning the Wages Position in the Coal Mining Industry (Buckmaster), 1924 Cmd. 2129 XI; *Minutes of Proceedings* (Ministry of Labour, 1924; copy in Library of British Coal).

Industrial Courts Act, 1919. Report by a Court of Inquiry Concerning the Coal Mining Industry Dispute, 1925, 1924–5 Cmd. 2478 XIII.

Report of the Departmental Committee on Co-operative Selling in the Coal Mining Industry, 1926 Cmd. 2770 XIII.

Report of the Royal Commission on the Coal Industry (1925) (Samuel), 1926 Cmd. 2600 XIV; *Minutes of Evidence and Appendices* (Mines Department, 1926).

Eighteenth Abstract of Labour Statistics, 1926 Cmd. 2740 XXIX.

Committee on Industry and Trade (Balfour). Factors in Industrial and Commercial Efficiency (1927).

Final Report of the Committee on Industry and Trade (Balfour), 1928–9 Cmd. 3282 VII.

First Report by the Board of Trade under Section 12 on the Working of Part I of the Mining Industry Act, 1928–9 Cmd. 3214 VIII.

Report on Investigations in the Coalfield of South Wales and Monmouthshire on the Social Conditions of the Miners' Families, 1928–9 Cmd. 3272 VIII.

Industrial Transference Board Report: 1928–9 Cmd. 3156 X.

Report to the Secretary for Mines of the Committee Appointed by him to Inquire into the Qualifications and Recruitment of Officials of Mines (Mines Department, 1929).

Report of the British Coal Delegation to Sweden, Norway, and Denmark, 1930–1 Cmd. 3702 XV.

Twentieth Abstract of Labour Statistics, 1930–1 Cmd. 3831 XXXII.

Report of the Departmental Committee of Inquiry (1931) on the Miners' Welfare Fund, 1932–3 Cmd. 4236 XV.

Final Report of the Unemployment Grants Committee, 20th December 1920 to 31st August 1932, 1932–3 Cmd. 4354 XV.

Coal Mines Reorganisation Commission. Report to the Secretary for Mines. December 1933, 1933–4 Cmd. 4468 XIV.

Twenty-First Abstract of Labour Statistics, 1933–4 Cmd. 4625 XXVI.

Reports of Investigations into the Industrial Conditions in Certain Depressed Areas, 1933–4 Cmd. 4728 XIII.

Report of an Inquiry into the Effects of Existing Economic Circumstances on the Health of the Community in the County Borough of Sunderland and Certain Districts of County Durham, 1934–5 Cmd. 4886 IX.

First Report of the Commissioner for Special Areas (England and Wales), 1934–5 Cmd. 4957 X.

Report of the Coal Mines Reorganisation Commission to the Secretary for Mines. 13 January 1936, 1935–6 Cmd. 5069 XIV.

Ministry of Health. Report on the Overcrowding Survey in England and Wales, 1936 (1936).

Report of an Investigation into Maternal Mortality, 1936–7 Cmd. 5422 XI.

Report on Maternal Mortality in Wales, 1936–7 Cmd. 5423 XI.

Twenty-Second Abstract of Labour Statistics, 1922 to 1936, 1936–7 Cmd. 5556 XXVI.

Committee of Imperial Defence. Sub-Committee on Oil from Coal, 1937–8 Cmd. 5665 XII.

Report of the Royal Commission on Safety in Coal Mines, 1938–9 Cmd. 5890 XIII; *Minutes of Evidence* (Mines Department, 1936–8).

Report of the Departmental Committee on the Distribution of Coal Coke and Manufactured Fuel (Sir Walter Monckton) (Mines Department, 1938).

Ministry of Health. Report of the Committee of Inquiry into the Anti-TB Service in Wales and Monmouthshire (1938).

Reports of the Coal Commission for the Years 1938 and 1939, 1939–40 (122) V.

Third Report of the Select Committee on National Expenditure, Session 1941–2, on Coal Production, 1941–2 (54) III.

First Report of the Committee on the Recruitment of Juveniles in the Coal Mining Industry, July 20th, 1942 (Sir John Foster) (Ministry of Labour, 1942).

Third Report of the Board of Investigation into Wages and Machinery for

Determining Wages and Conditions of Employment in the Coal-Mining Industry (1943).

Ministry of Fuel and Power. Statistical Digest from 1938, 1943–4 Cmd. 6538 VIII.

Sixth Report from the Select Committee on National Expenditure, Session 1943–1944, on Opencast Coal Production, (22 June 1944), 1943–4 (88) II.

Scottish Home Department. Report by the Scottish Coalfields Committee, 1944–5 Cmd. 6575 IV.

Ministry of Fuel and Power. Coal Mining. Report of the Technical Advisory Committee. March 14, 1945 (Charles C. Reid), 1944–5 Cmd. 6610 IV.

Ministry of Fuel and Power. Financial Position of the Coal Mining Industry, Coal Charges Account, 1944–5 Cmd. 6617 X.

Ministry of Fuel and Power. Statistical Digest. 1944–5, Cmd. 6639 1945 X.

Ministry of Works. Report of the United Kingdom Opencast Coal Mission to the United States of America, December 1944 (1945).

Report of the Coal Commission for the Year Ended Mar. 31 1945, 1945–6 (14) XIII.

Ministry of Fuel and Power. Statistical Digest, 1945, 1945–6 Cmd. 6920 XXI.

Ministry of Fuel and Power, Durham Coalfield. Regional Survey Report (Northern 'B' Coalfield) (1945).

Ministry of Fuel and Power, Kent Coalfield, Regional Survey Report (1945).

Ministry of Fuel and Power, North Midland Coalfield. Regional Survey Report (1945).

Report of the Coal Commission for the Year 1945–6, 1945–6 (14) XIII.

Ministry of Fuel and Power, South Wales Coalfield. Regional Survey Report (1946).

Miners' Welfare in War-Time: Report of the Miners' Welfare Commission for 6½ Years to June 30th 1946 (Ashtead, Surrey, 1947).

National Coal Board. Annual Report and Statement of Accounts for the Year ending 31st December 1946, 1947–8 (174) X.

National Coal Board. Annual Report and Statement of Accounts for 1946–7, 1947–8 (175) X.

Ministry of Fuel and Power. Statistical Digest for the Years 1946 and 1947, 1948–9 Cmd. 7548 XXIX.

National Coal Board, Report of the Advisory Committee on Organisation (1955).

Department of Employment and Productivity, British Labour Statistics: Historical Abstract, 1886–1968 (HMSO 1971).

Hansard, *Parliamentary Debates, House of Commons*, Fifth Series.

History of the Ministry of Munitions.

Mines Department, *Annual Report of the Secretary for Mines, 1922– .*

Mines Department, *List of Mines in Great Britain and the Isle of Man* (annual).

Ministry of Labour Gazette.

Public Health Reports. Annual Reports of the Chief Medical Officer of the Ministry of Health.

C. Journals, Non-Governmental Annuals, and Newspapers

Colliery Guardian and Journal of the Coal and Iron Trades
Colliery Year Book and Coal Trades Directory
Daily Herald
Daily Telegraph
The Economist
Iron and Coal Trades Review
Manchester Guardian
Miners' Federation of Great Britain, Annual Reports
Mining Association of Great Britain, Annual Reports
New Statesman and Nation
The Times
Transactions of the Institution of Mining Engineers

D. Contemporary Typescript and Limited Circulation Material

The Challenge to Industry (Speech by Sir Clive Baillieu, President of the Federation of British Industries, delivered at Manchester on 30 November 1945. FBI 1945).

Coal and Power. Report by the National Executive Committee of the Labour Party to be presented to the Annual Conference to be held in London from May 29th to June 2nd 1944 (1944).

Deputation of the Coal Owners' Association to the Prime Minister, 14 November 1919 (British Coal Headquarters Library).

Interim Report of the Central Joint Committees for the Administration of the Lord Mayors' Fund for Relief of Distressed Mining Areas, July 1929 (copy in MH 79/304).

Miners' Federation of Great Britain. Coal Mining Organisation . . . 2 September 1915. Conference . . . on Matters arising out of the Report of the Coal Mining Committee (copy in Northumberland Record Office, NRO 759/28).

Mining Association of Great Britain. Miners' Federation of Great Britain, *Minutes of Proceedings of a Joint Sub-Committee appointed to investigate the Economic Position of the Coal Industry* (3 volumes, 18 March to 23 June 1925; copy in British Coal Library).

Mining Association of Great Britain, *What Mr Lloyd George Was Not Told* (1924).

Monmouthshire and South Wales Coal Owners' Association, *Survey of the Position of the South Wales Coal Trade* (26 January 1939; copy in MSWCOA Box File 729).

Peat, Marwick, Mitchell & Co., *Statistical Summaries of the Costs of Production. Proceeds and Profits of the Coal Mining Industry during the years 1930 to 1945* (copy in British Coal Library).

Proceedings of the National Coal Board for the Coal Industry (1921–3; copy in British Coal Library).

A Suggested Scheme of Reconstruction for the Coal Mining Industry (1919; copy in Scottish Record Office CB6/2).

TUC, *What the TUC is Doing* (April 1946).

Unification of Coal Royalties. In the Matter of a Reference between the Mineral owners Joint Committee and His Majesty's Government. . . 12th April–27th April 1937 (1937; copy in British Coal Library).

E. Books, Articles, and Theses

AGNEW, DEREK, *Bevin Boy* (1947).

ALDCROFT, DEREK H. & BUXTON, N. K. (eds.), *British Industry between the Wars: Instability and industrial development, 1919–1939* (1979).

ANDERSON, F. S. & THORPE, R. H., 'A Century of Coal-face Machinery', *The Mining Engineer*, No. 83 (August 1967).

APPLEYARD, K. C. & CURRY, G., 'Opencast Coal Production in Wartime', *Journal of the Institute of Civil Engineers* (1946).

ARMITAGE, SUSAN, *The Politics of Decontrol in Industry* (1969).

ARNOT, R. P., *The Miners: Years of Struggle from 1910 Onwards* (1953).

ARNOT, R. P., *The Miners in Crisis and War, from 1930 Onwards* (1961).

ARNOT, R. P., *South Wales Miners Glowyr de Cymru: A History of the South Wales Miners Federation (1914–1926)* (Cardiff, 1975).

ARNOT, R. P., *The Miners: One Union, One Industry* (1979).

ASHWORTH, WILLIAM, with the assistance of Mark Pegg, *The History of the British Coal industry*, Vol. 5: *1946–1982, The Nationalized Industry* (Oxford, 1986).

ASKWITH, GEORGE, *Industrial Problems and Disputes* (1920).

ASTERIS, MICHAEL, 'Britain and the European Coal Trade, 1913–1939' (M.Soc.Sc. Dissertation, University of Birmingham, 1971).

BAMFORTH, K. W.—see TRIST.

BARNES, J. & MIDDLEMAS, K., *Baldwin* (1969).

BARRACLOUGH, L. J., 'Some General Considerations of Machine-Mining Practice', *TIME* 74 (1927–8).

BARRY, E. E., *Nationalisation in British Politics* (1965).

BEACHAM, ARTHUR, 'Efficiency and Organization of the British Coal Industry', *Economic Journal*, LV (1945).

BEACHAM, ARTHUR, 'The Present Position of the Coal Industry in Britain', *Economic Journal*, LX (1950).

BEER, S. H., *Modern British Politics: A Study of Parties and Pressure Groups* (1954).

BEER, S. H., *British Politics in the Collectivist Age* (1965).

BENNY, MARK, *Charity Main: A Coalfield Chronicle* (1946).

LORD BEVERIDGE, *Power and Influence: An Autobiography* (1953).

BOWLEY, A. L., 'Wages, Earnings and Hours of Work, 1914–1947, United Kingdom', *London and Cambridge Economic Service Special Memorandum No. 50* (May 1947).

BREACH, R. W. & HARTWELL, R. M., *British Economy and Society, 1870–1970* (1972).

BRIGGS, ASA & SAVILLE, JOHN (eds.), *Essays in Labour History 1918–1938* (1977).

BRITAIN'S INDUSTRIAL FUTURE, BEING THE REPORT OF THE LIBERAL INDUSTRIAL INQUIRY (1928).

BROWN, A. BARRATT, *The Machine and the Worker* (1934).

BRYAN, ANDREW M., 'Safety in Mines', *Journal of the Royal Society of Arts*, XCIX (1951).

BULLOCK, ALAN, *The Life and Times of Ernest Bevin*, II: *Minister of Labour, 1940–1945* (1967).

BULMAN, H. F., 'The Limitations of Coal Cutters', *CG* 16 December 1921.

BULMAN, H. F. & REDMAYNE, R. A. S., *Colliery Working and Management* (various editions).

BUTLER, DAVID & GARETH, *British Political Facts* (1986).

BUXTON, N. K., 'Entrepreneurial Efficiency in the British Coal Industry between the Wars', *Economic History Review*, n.s. XXIII (1970).

BUXTON, N. K., 'Entrepreneurial Efficiency in the British Coal Industry between the Wars: Reconfirmed', *Economic History Review*, n.s. XXV (1972).

BUXTON, N. K., *The Economic Development of the British Coal Industry* (1978).

CANTRIL, H. (ed.), *Public Opinion, 1935–1946* (Princeton, 1951).

CARPENTER, L. P., 'Corporatism in Britain, 1930–45', *Journal of Contemporary History*, XI (1976).

CHESTER, D. N., *The Nationalisation of British Industry, 1945–51* (1975).

CHURCH, ROY, with the assistance of Alan Hall & John Kanefsky, *The History of the British Coal Industry*: Vol. 3: *1830–1913, Victorian Pre-eminence* (Oxford, 1986).

CLAY, HENRY, *The Postwar Unemployment Problem* (1929).

CLAY, HENRY, *Lord Norman* (1957).

CLIVE, R., 'Abstract of the "Report of an Investigation of the Underground Conveying and Loading of Coal by Mechanical Means" ', *TIME* 78 (1929–30).

COLE, G. D. H., *Labour In the Coal-Mining Industry, 1914–21* (Oxford, 1923).

COLE, G. D. H., 'The National Coal Board', *Political Quarterly*, XVII (October–December 1946).

COLE, M. I. (ed.), *Beatrice Webb's Diaries, 1912–1924* (1952).

COOK, CHRIS—see STEVENSON.

COOMBES, B. L., *These Poor Hands: The Autobiography of a Miner Working in South Wales* (1939).

COOMBES, B. L., *These Clouded Hills* (1944).

COOTE, C. & MOTTRAM, R. H., *Through Five Generations. The History of the Butterley Company* (1950).

COURT, W. H. B., *Coal* (1951).

CROSLAND, SUSAN, *Tony Crosland* (1982).

CURRY, G.—see APPLEYARD.

DALEY, MARY E., 'Government Policy and the Depressed Areas in the Interwar Years' (Oxford University D.Phil. Thesis, 1978).

DALTON, HUGH, *The Fateful Years: Memoirs, 1931–1945* (1957).

DALTON, HUGH, *The Second World War Diary of Hugh Dalton, 1940–1945* (1986), edited by Ben Pimlott.

DARMSTADTER, J., *Energy in the World Economy* (Baltimore, 1971).

DATALLER, ROGER (pseud.), *From a Pitman's Notebook* (1925).

DAVISON, JACK, *Northumberland Miners, 1919–1939* (Newcastle, 1973).

DAY, D., *The Bevin Boy* (Kineton, Warwick, 1975).

DEMANT, V. A., *The Miners' Distress and the Coal Problem* (1930).

DENNIS, NORMAN, HENRIQUES, FERNANDO, and SLAUGHTER, CLIFFORD, *Coal is our Life: An Analysis of a Yorkshire Mining Community* (1956).

DIGEST OF EVIDENCE GIVEN BEFORE THE ROYAL COMMISSION ON COAL SUPPLIES (1901–1905) (1905).

EVANS, G. EWART, *From the Mouths of Men* (1976).

EVANS, TREVOR & FINE, BEN, 'The Diffusion of Mechanical Cutting in the British Inter-War Coal Industry' (unpublished).

EVANS, TREVOR & FINE, BEN, 'Economies of Scale in the British Inter-War Coal Industry' (unpublished).

EVERETT, H. & LUBIN, I., *The British Coal Dilemma* (1927).

FEINSTEIN, C. H., *Statistical Tables of National Income, Expenditure and Output of the U.K., 1855–1965* (Cambridge, 1976).

FINE, BEN, 'Royalties and the Inter-War British Coal Industry' (Birbeck College Discussion Paper, No. 62, 1978).

FINE, BEN—see T. EVANS.

FOSTER, H. T., 'The Trend of Coal Mining Practice', *CG* 27 April 1945.

FOX, W. R., *Coal Combines in Yorkshire* (1935a).

FOX, W. R., *Who's Who in Anthracite?* (1935b).

FRANCIS, HYWEL & SMITH, DAVID, *The Fed: A History of the South Wales Miners in the Twentieth Century* (1980).

GARSIDE, W. R., 'The North-Eastern Coalfield and the Export Trade, 1919–39', *Durham University Journal*, 62 (1968).

GARSIDE, W. R., *The Durham Miners, 1919–1960* (1971).

GILBERT, B. B., *British Social Policy, 1914–1939* (1970).

GILBERT, MARTIN, *Winston S. Churchill*, Vol. V, Companion Part I (1979).

GLEASON, ARTHUR, *Inside the British Isles* (1917).

GLYNN, S. & HOWELLS, P. G. A., 'Unemployment in the 1930s: The "Keynesian Solution" Reconsidered', *Australian Economic History Review* (1980).

GOLDTHORPE, J. H., 'Technical Organisation as a Factor in Supervisor–Worker Conflict', *British Journal of Sociology*, X (1959).

GOLLIN, A. M., *Proconsul in Politics: A Study of Lord Milner in Opposition and in Power* (1964).

GOODFELLOW, D. M., *Tyneside: The Social Facts* (Newcastle, 1940).

GOODRICH, CARTER L., *The Frontiers of Control: A Study in British workshop politics* (1920).

GREASLEY, DAVID, 'The Diffusion of Technology: The Case of Machine Coal Cutting in Great Britain, 1900–1938' (University of London Ph.D., 1979).

GREASLEY, DAVID, 'The Diffusion of Machine Cutting in the British Coal Industry, 1902–1938', *Explorations in Economic History*, 19 (1982).

GREASLEY, DAVID, 'Productivity and Factor Returns at the Coal Face in Great Britain, 1900–38' (unpublished).

GREENWELL, H., 'The Employers' Point of View', *The Human Factor*, VII, 9 (Sept. 1933).

GREGORY, R. G., *The Miners and British Politics, 1906–1914* (Oxford, 1968).

GRIFFIN, A. R., *The Miners of Nottinghamshire, 1914–44: A History of the Nottinghamshire Miners' Union* (1962).

GRIFFIN, A. R., *Coal Mining* (1971a).

GRIFFIN, A. R., *Mining in the East Midlands, 1550–1947* (1971b).

GRIFFIN, A. R., 'The Non-Political Trade Union Movement' in Asa Briggs and John Saville (eds.), *Essays in Labour History, 1918–1939* (1977).

HANNAH, LESLIE, 'Managerial innovation and the rise of the large-scale company in interwar Britain', *Economic History Review*, n.s. XXVII (1974).

HANNAH, LESLIE, *The Rise of the Corporate Economy* (1976).

HANNAH, LESLIE, *Electricity Before Nationalisation: A Study of the Development of the Electricity Supply Industry in Britain to 1948* (1979).

HARE, A. E. C., *The Anthracite Coal Industry of the Swansea District* (Swansea, 1940).

HARKELL, GINA, 'The Migration of Mining Families to the Kent Coalfield between the Wars', *Oral History*, 6(1) (1978).

HARRISON, ROYDEN, 'The War Emergency Workers' National Committee, 1914–20', in Asa Briggs and John Saville (eds.), *Essays in Labour History, 1886–1923* (1971).

HARRY, E. W. & PHILLIPS, J. R. E., 'Household Budgets in the Rhondda Valley', *Western Journal of Agriculture*, XIII (January 1937).

HART, P. E., *Studies in Profit, Business Savings and Investment in the United Kingdom, 1920–1962* (1965), I.

HARTWELL, R. M.—see BREACH.

HEADY, J. A. & MORRIS, J. N., 'Social and Biological Factors in Infant Mortality', *Lancet*, CCLXVIII (12 February 1955).

HEAP, C., *Mines and Miners of Doncaster* (1977, Doncaster Museums and Arts Services Publication).

HEINEMANN, MARGOT, *Britain's Coal: A Study of the Mining Crisis* (1944).

HEINEMANN, MARGOT, *Coal Must Come First* (1948).

HENDERSON, H. D., *The Inter-war Years and Other Papers* (Oxford, 1955).

HENRIQUES, FERNANDO—see DENNIS.

HIBBERD, G., 'A Century of Mechanical Coal-cutting', *ICTR* 8 April 1955.

HOGG, QUINTIN, LANCASTER, C. G., and THORNEYCROFT, PETER, *Forward–By the Right! A National Policy for Coal* (Issued by the Tory Reform Committee, 1944).

HORNER, A., 'Nationalisation of the Coal Industry', *Labour Monthly*, XXVIII, 2 (February 1946).

HOWELLS, P. G. A.—see GLYNN.

HOWSON, S., 'Slump and Unemployment' in R. C. Floud & D. N. McCloskey (eds.), *The Economic History of Britain Since 1700* (1981), II.

HOWSON, S. & WINCH, D. N., *The Economic Advisory Council, 1930–1939* (Cambridge, 1977).

INTERNATIONAL LABOUR OFFICE, *The World Coal-Mining Industry* (Geneva, 1938), I.

JENNINGS, HILDA, *Brynmawr: A Study of a Distressed Area* (1934).

JEVONS, H. STANLEY, *The British Coal Trade* (1915).

JOHNSON, P. B., *Land Fit for Heroes: The Planning of British Reconstruction, 1916–1919* (Chicago, 1968).

JOHNSON, W., 'The Development of the Kent Coalfield, 1890–1946' (Ph.D., University of Kent at Canterbury, 1972).

JONES, J. H., 'Organized Marketing in the Coal Industry', *Economic Journal*, XXXIX (June 1929).

JONES, J. H. *et al.*, *The Coal-Mining Industry: An International Study in Planning* (1939).

JONES, T. J. PARRY, *The Other Story of Coal* (1925).

JONES, THOMAS, *Whitehall Diary* (Oxford, 1971), edited by Keith Middlemas.

'THE JOURNEY HOME' (A Report Prepared by Mass-Observation for the Advertising Service Guild), *Change*, No. 5 (1944).

KAHN, A. E., *Great Britain in the World Economy* (New York, 1946).

KEYNES, JOHN MAYNARD, *The Collected Writings of John Maynard Keynes* (1971–), edited by Donald Moggridge.

KIRBY, J. & M'GONIGLE, G. C. M., *Poverty and Public Health* (1936).

KIRBY, M. W., 'The British Coal-Mining Industry in the Interwar Years: A study in industrial concentration' (Sheffield University Ph.D. Thesis, 1971).

KIRBY, M. W., 'Entrepreneurial Efficiency in the British Coal Industry between the Wars: A Comment', *Economic History Review*, n.s. XXV (1972).

KIRBY, M. W., 'The Control of Competition in the British Coal-Mining Industry in the Thirties', *Economic History Review*, n.s. XXVI (1973).

KIRBY, M. W., *The British Coalmining Industry, 1870–1946: A Political and Economic History* (1977).

KIRBY, M. W., 'The Politics of State Coercion in Inter-war Britain: The Mines Department of the Board of Trade, 1920–1942', *Historical Journal*, XXII (1979).

KNOWLES, K. G. J. C., *Strikes: A Study in Industrial Conflict* (Oxford, 1954).

LABOUR RESEARCH DEPARTMENT'S publications: *South Wales: A Study of the Coal, Steel and Railway Industries in Britain's Running Sore* (March 1934).

LANCASTER, C. G.—see HOGG.

LEAGUE OF NATIONS, *Memorandum on Coal* (Geneva, 1927), I.

LEAGUE OF NATIONS, *The Problem of the Coal Industry: Interim Report on its International Aspects by the Economics Committee of the League of Nations* (12 April 1929).

LEE, W. A., *Historical Review of Coalmining* (1926).

LEE, W. A., *Thirty Years in Coal, 1917–1947* (1954).

LEED, ERIC J., *No Man's Land: Combat & Identity in World War I* (Cambridge, 1979).

LEWIS, E. D., *The Rhondda Valleys* (1959).

LEWIS, JANE, *The Politics of Motherhood: Child and Maternal Welfare in England, 1900–1939* (1980).

LIBERAL PARTY, *Coal and Power: The Report of an Inquiry Presided over by the Right Hon. D. Lloyd George* (1924).

LLOYD GEORGE, DAVID, *Through Terror to Triumph* (1915).

LOGAN, W. P. D., 'Social Class Variations in Mortality', *British Journal of Preventive and Social Medicine*, Vol. 8 (3 July 1954).

LONG, PAUL BROOK, 'The Economic and Social History of the Scottish Coal Industry, 1925–1939, with Particular reference to Industrial Relations' (Ph.D. Thesis, Strathclyde University, 1978).

LOWE, RODNEY, 'The Failure of Consensus in Britain: The National Industrial Conference, 1919–1921', *Historical Journal*, XXI (1978).

LUBIN, I.—see EVERETT.

LUCAS, A. F., *Industrial Reconstruction and the Control of Competition: The British Experiments* (1937).

McCRONE, G. M., *Regional Policy in Britain* (1969).

M'GONIGLE, G. C. M.—see J. KIRBY.

MACINTYRE, STUART, *Little Moscows: Communism and Working-class Militancy in Inter-war Britain* (1980).

MACMILLAN, HAROLD, *Tides of Fortune, 1945–1955* (1969).

McNALLY, C. E., *Public Ill-Health* (1935).

MAKOWER, H., MARSCHAK, J., & ROBINSON, H. W., 'Studies in the Mobility of Labour: Analysis for Great Britain', Parts I and II, *Oxford Economic Papers*, No. 2 (May 1939), and No. 4 (September 1940).

MANCHESTER JOINT RESEARCH COUNCIL, *Aspects of Fuel and Power in British Industry* (1960).

MANLEY, E. R., *Meet the Miner* (Pontefract, 1948).

MARQUAND, DAVID, *Ramsay MacDonald* (1977).

MARSCHAK, J.—see MAKOWER.

MARWICK, A., 'Middle Opinion in the Thirties: Planning, Progress and Political Argument', *English Historical Review*, LXXIX (1964).

MAVOR, S., 'Problems of Mechanical Coal Mining', *CG* 13 June 1924.

MIDDLEMAS, K., *Politics in Industrial Society* (1979).

MIDDLEMAS, K. (1969)—see BARNES.

MIDDLETON, ROGER, *Towards the Managed Economy: Keynes, the Treasury and the fiscal policy debate of the 1930s* (1985).

MITCHELL, B. R., *Abstract of British Historical Statistics* (Cambridge, 1962).

MITCHELL, J. H., 'The Worker's Point of View. VII The Personal Element in the British Coal Industry', *The Human Factor*, VI, 9 (September 1932).

MITCHELL, J. H., 'The Mechanisation of the Miner', *The Human Factor*, VII, 4 (April 1933).

MOGGRIDGE, D. E., *British Monetary Policy, 1924–1931: The Norman Conquest of $4.86* (Cambridge, 1972).

MOND, SIR ALFRED, *Industry and Politics* (1927).

MONEY, L. G. CHIOZZA, *Nationalisation* (1920).

MOONIE, A. C., 'Machine-Mining in Northumberland and Durham', *TIME* 92 (1936–7).

MORGAN, ALFRED, 'The Coal Problem as seen by a Colliery Official', *Economic Journal*, 36 (December 1926).

MORGAN, KENNETH O., *Consensus and Disunity: The Lloyd George Coalition Government, 1918–1922* (Oxford, 1979).

MORRIS, H. L., *The Plight of the Bituminous Coal Mines* (Philadelphia, 1934).

MORRIS, J. N.—see HEADY.

MOSLEY, NICHOLAS, *Rules of the Game* (1982).

MOTTRAM, R. H.—see COOTE.

MOZOOMDAR, A., 'Compensation for the Nationalisation of Industries. A study of the nationalisation measures in Great Britain, 1945–50' (Oxford University D.Phil., 1953).

NATIONAL UNION OF MINEWORKERS, *Annual Conference, 1946. Report of Executive Committee, May 1946.*

NELSON, R., 'Electricity in Coal Mines: a Retrospect and a Forecast', *Institution of Electrical Engineers' Journal*, Vol. 84, No. 510 (June 1939).

NEUMAN, A. W., *Economic Organisation of the British Coal Industry* (1934).

NEWSOM, JOHN, *Out of the Pit: A Challenge to the Comfortable* (Oxford, 1936).

NOTT-BOWER, G. & WALKERDINE, R. H. (eds.), *National Coal Board: The First Ten Years* (n.d. 1957?).

OSTERGAARD, G. N., 'Labour and the Development of the Public Corporation', *Manchester School*, No. 2 (May 1954).

OUTRAM, QUENTIN, unpublished manuscript on 'Working Methods and Payment Systems in British Coal Mining, 1900–1940'.

OWEN, A. D. K., 'The Social Consequences of Industrial Transference', *Sociological Review*, XXIX (1937).

PAULL, C. A., 'Mechanisation in the British and American Bituminous Coal Mines, 1890–1939' (University of London M.Phil., 1968).

PAYNE, P. L., *Colvilles and the Scottish Steel Industry* (Oxford, 1979).

PEDELTY, J. FAIRLEY, 'The Human Element in Percussive Coal Cutting', *CG* 5 June 1925.

PHILLIPS, G. A., *The General Strike: The Politics of Industrial Conflict* (1976).

PHILLIPS, J. R. E.—see HARRY.

PICK, J. B., *Under the Crust* (1946).

PIGOU, A. C., *Aspects of British Economic History, 1918–25* (1947).

PILGRIM TRUST, *Men Without Work* (Cambridge, 1938).

POLITICAL & ECONOMIC PLANNING, *Report on the British Coal Industry* (1936).

POLLARD, S. (ed.), *The Gold Standard and Employment Policies between the Wars* (1970).

POPE, P. C. (ed.), *Coal: Production, Distribution, Utilisation* (1949).

PORTER, J. H., 'Wage Bargaining Under Conciliation Agreements, 1860–1914', *Economic History Review*, n.s. XXIII (1970).

'PORTRAIT OF A MINING TOWN', *Fact*, No. 8 (15 November 1937).

PREST, W. R., 'The British Coal Mines Act of 1930: Another Interpretation', *Quarterly Journal of Economics*, L (1936).

PREST, W. R., 'The Problem of the Lancashire Coal Industry', *Economic Journal*, 47 (1937).

READER, W. J., *Imperial Chemical Industries: A History* (Oxford, 1978).

RECONSTRUCTION (Report by the Federation of British Industries, May 1942).

REDMAYNE, R. A. S., *The British Coal-Mining Industry During the War* (1923).

REDMAYNE, R. A. S., *Men, Mines and Memories* (Oxford, 1942).

REDMAYNE, R. A. S.—see BULMAN.

REID, SIR CHARLES, 'The Problem of Coal', *The Times*, 22, 23, and 24 November 1948.

RHODES, E. C., 'Output, Labour and Machines in the Coal Mining Industry in Great Britain', *Economica*, n.s. XII (1945).

RICE, MARGERY SPRING, *Working-Class Wives: Their Health and Conditions* (Harmondsworth 1939, second edition 1981).

LORD RIDDELL, *Lord Riddell's Intimate Diary of the Peace Conference and After, 1918–23* (1933).

ROBERTS, C. A., 'The Development of the Organisation', in Nott-Bower and Walkerdine (eds.), *National Coal Board: The First Ten Years* (n.d. 1957?).

ROBERTS, P. M. D., 'Getting to Grips', in Nott-Bower and Walkerdine (eds.), *National Coal Board: The First Ten Years* (n.d. 1957?).

ROBINSON, H. W.—see MAKOWER.

ROBSON, W. A. (ed.), *Public Enterprise: Developments in Social Ownership and Control* (1937).

ROSSITER, D. J., 'The Miners' Sphere of Influence: An Attempt to Quantify Electoral Behaviour in Mining Areas Between the Wars' (Ph.D. Thesis, University of Sheffield, 1980).

ROWE, J. W. F., *Wages in the Coal Industry* (1923).

SAVILLE, JOHN—see BRIGGS.

SAYERS, R. S., *The Bank of England, 1891–1944*, I (Cambridge, 1976).

SCOTT-JAMES, R. A., 'Housing Conditions in Mining Areas', in *Coal and Power: The Report of an Inquiry Presided Over by The Right Hon. D. Lloyd George* (1924).

SHADWELL, ARTHUR, *Coal Mines and Nationalisation* (1919).

SHARP, THOMAS, *A Derelict Area: The South-West Durham Coalfield* (1935).

SHINWELL, E., *Nationalisation of the Mines. A Practical Policy* (ILP, 1931?).

SHINWELL, E., *Conflict Without Malice* (1955).

SHINWELL, E., *The Labour Story* (1963).

SINGER, H. W., 'Transference and the Age Structure of the Population in the Special Areas' (*Pilgrim Trust Unemployment Inquiry, Interim Paper No. III*, 1938).

SINGER, H. W., 'The Coal Question Reconsidered: Effects of Economy and Substitution', *Review of Economic Studies*, VIII (1940–1).

SLAUGHTER, CLIFFORD—see DENNIS.

SMART, R. C., *The Economics of the Coal Industry* (1930).

SMITH, DAVID—see FRANCIS.

STAMP, J., *Taxation During the War* (1932).

STEVENSON, JOHN & COOK, CHRIS, *The Slump: Society and Politics during the Depressions* (1977).

STEWART, W. D., *Mines, Machines and Men* (1935).

SUPPLE, BARRY, ' "No Bloody Revolutions but for Obstinate Reactions"? British Coalowners in their Context, 1919–20', in Donald Coleman and Peter Mathias (eds.); *Enterprise and History: Essays in Honour of Charles Wilson* (1984).

SUPPLE, BARRY, 'Ideology and Necessity: The Nationalisation of Coal Mining, 1916–1946', in N. McKendrick & R. B. Outhwaite (eds.), *Business Life and Public Policy: Essays in Honour of D. C. Coleman* (1986).

SYKES, JOSEPH, *A Study in English Local Authority Finances* (1939).

THOMAS, BRINLEY, 'Labour Mobility in the South Wales and Monmouthshire Coal-Mining Industry, 1926–30', *Economic Journal*, XLI (1931).

THOMAS, BRINLEY, 'The Movement of Labour into South-East England', *Economica*, n.s. 2 (May 1934).

THOMAS, BRINLEY, 'The Influx of Labour into London and the South-East, 1920–36', *Economica*, n.s. 15 (1937).

THOMAS, BRINLEY, 'The Influx of Labour into the Midlands, 1920–1937', *Economica*, n.s. 20 (November 1938).

THORNEYCROFT, PETER—see HOGG.

THORPE, R. H.—see ANDERSON.

TITMUSS, RICHARD M., *Poverty and Population: A Factual Study of Contemporary Social Waste* (1938).

TOMLINSON, G. A. W., *Coal-Miner* (1937).

TRIST, E. L. & BAMFORTH, K. W., 'Some Social and Psychological Consequences of the Longwall Method of Coal-Getting', *Human Relations*, IV (1951).

UNITED STATES DEPARTMENT OF COMMERCE, *Historical Statistics of the United States* (1960).

WALKERDINE, R. H.—see NOTT-BOWER.

WALLER, ROBERT J., *The Dukeries Transformed: The Social and Political Development of a Twentieth-Century Coalfield* (Oxford, 1983).

WALTERS, SIR J. TUDOR, *The Building of Twelve Thousand Houses* (1927).

WATKINS, H. M., *Coal and Men* (1934).

WEBSTER, CHARLES, 'Healthy or Hungry Thirties?', *History Workshop*, 13 (Spring 1982).

WEBSTER, CHARLES, 'Health, Welfare and Unemployment during the Depression', *Past & Present*, 109 (November 1985).

WHITE, P. H., 'Some Aspects of Urban Development by Colliery Companies, 1919–1939', *Manchester School of Economic and Social Studies*, XXIII, 3 (September 1955).

LORD WIGG, *George Wigg* (1972).

WILLIAMS, D. J., *Capitalist Combinations in the Coal Industry* (1924).

WILLIAMS, J. E., *The Derbyshire Miners: A Study in Industrial and Social History* (1962).

WILLIAMS, KAREL, *From Pauperism to Poverty* (1981).

WILLIAMS, W. H., *Coal Combines in Northumberland* (1937).

WILLIAMS, W. H., *Coal Combines in Lancashire and Cheshire* (1938).

WILLIAMS, W. H., *Coal Combines in Durham* (1939).

WILSON, J. HAROLD, *A New Deal for Coal* (1945).

WINCH, D. N., *Economics and Policy* (1969).

WINCH, D. N. (1977)—see HOWSON.

WINTER, J. M., 'Infant Mortality, Maternal Mortality and Public Health in Britain in the 1930s', *Journal of European Economic History*, Vol. 8, No. 2 (Fall 1979).

WINTER, J. M., 'Unemployment, Nutrition and Infant Mortality in Britain, 1920–50', in J. M. Winter (ed.), *The Working Class in Modern British History: Essays in Honour of Henry Pelling* (1983).

WINTER, J. M., *The Great War and the British People* (1986).

WOODHOUSE, M. G., 'Rank and File Movements among the Miners of South Wales, 1910–26' (unpublished Oxford University D.Phil. thesis, 1969).

WOODHOUSE, M. G., 'Mines for the Nation or Mines for the Miners: Alternative Perspectives on Industrial Democracy, 1919–21', *Llafur*, 2 (Summer 1978).

WRIGLEY, C. J., *Lloyd George and the Labour Movement* (Hassocks, Sussex, 1976).

Index